Service Delivery

Office of Government Commerce

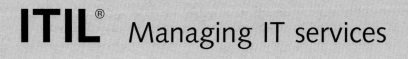

ITIL® Managing IT services

London: TSO

Published by TSO (The Stationery Office) and available from:

Online
www.tsoshop.co.uk

Mail, Telephone, Fax & E-mail
TSO
PO Box 29, Norwich NR3 1GN
Telephone orders/General enquiries: 0870 600 5522
Fax orders: 0870 600 5533
E-mail: customer.services@tso.co.uk
Textphone: 0870 240 3701

TSO Shops
123 Kingsway, London WC2B 6PQ
020 7242 6393 Fax 020 7242 6394
16 Arthur Street, Belfast BT1 4GD
028 9023 8451 Fax 028 9023 5401
71 Lothian Road, Edinburgh EH3 9AZ
0870 606 5566 Fax 0870 606 5588

TSO@Blackwell
and other Accredited Agents

For further information on OGC products, contact:

OGC Service Desk
Rosebery Court
St Andrews Business Park
Norwich NR7 0HS
Telephone +44 (0) 0845 000 4999

This document has been produced using procedures conforming to
BS 5750 Part 1: 1987; ISO 9001: 1987

First published 2001
Eleventh Impression 2006

ISBN-10 0 11 330017 4
ISBN-13 978 011 330017 4

Printed in the United Kingdom for The Stationery Office
N5449973   c60   10/06

Titles within the ITIL series include:

Service Support (Published 2000)   ISBN 0 11 330015 8
Service Desk and the Process of Incident
Management, Problem Management, Configuration
Management, Change Management and
Release Management

Planning to Implement Service Management (Published 2002)   ISBN 0 11 330877 9
ICT Infrastructure Management (Published 2002)   ISBN 0 11 330865 5
Application Management (Published 2002)   ISBN 0 11 330866 3
Security Management   ISBN 0 11 330014 X
Business Perspective: The IS View on Delivering Services to the Business   ISBN 0 11 330894 9

ITIL back catalogue – an historical repository available as PDF downloads from www.tso.co.uk/ITIL

The managers' set
The complimentary guidance set
Environmental management, strategy and computer operations set

Contents

FOREWORD

Organisations are increasingly dependent on electronic delivery of services to meet customer needs. This means a requirement for high quality IT services, matched to business needs and user requirements as they evolve.

OGC's IT Infrastructure Library (ITIL) is the most widely accepted approach to IT Service Management in the world. ITIL provides a cohesive set of best practice, drawn from the public and private sectors internationally, supported by a comprehensive qualification scheme, accredited training organisations, implementation and assessment tools.

Bob Assirati

Director IT Directorate

Office of Government Commerce

PREFACE

The ethos behind the development of the IT Infrastructure Library (ITIL) is the recognition that organisations are increasingly dependent upon IT to satisfy their corporate aims and meet their business needs. This growing dependency leads to growing needs for quality IT services – quality that is matched to business needs and user requirements as they emerge.

This is true no matter what type or size of organisation, be it national government, a multinational conglomerate, a decentralised office with either a local or centralised IT provision, an outsourced service provider, or a single office environment with one person providing IT support. In each case there is the requirement to provide an economical service that is reliable, consistent and fit for purpose.

IT Service Management is concerned with delivering and supporting IT services that are appropriate to the business requirements of the organisation. IT service providers are continually striving to improve the quality of the service, while at the same time trying to reduce the costs or, at a minimum, maintain costs at the current level. ITIL provides a comprehensive, consistent and coherent set of best practices for IT Service Management processes, promoting a quality approach to achieving business effectiveness and efficiency in the use of information systems. ITIL processes are intended to be implemented so that they underpin, but do not dictate, the business processes of an organisation.

For each of the processes described in this book, one or more roles are identified for carrying out the functions and activities required. It should be noted that organisations may allocate more than one role to an individual within the organisation (although this book indicates where specific roles should not be merged), or may allocate more than one individual to a role. The purpose of the role is to locate responsibility rather than create an organisation structure.

The best-practice processes described in this book both support and are supported by the British Standards Institution's Code of Practice for IT Service Management (PD0005), and in turn underpin the ISO quality standard ISO9000.

The authors

The guidance in this book was distilled from the experience of a range of authors working in the private sector in IT Service Management. The material was written by:

John Bartlett	Insight Consulting
David Hinley	DS Hinley Associates
Brian Johnson	Pink Elephant
David Johnston	Fox IT (Ultracomp)
Chris Keeling	Insight Consulting
Vernon Lloyd	Fox IT (Ultracomp)
Ian MacDonald	Barclays Bank PLC
John Mather	Primax Consulting Ltd
Gerry McLaughlin	Fox IT (Ultracomp)
Colin Rudd	IT Enterprise Management Services (itEMS) Ltd
David Wheeldon	CEC Europe
Rob Young	Fox IT (Ultracomp)

The project was managed and co-ordinated by Hilary Weston of Fox IT (Ultracomp).

A wide-ranging national and international Quality Assurance (QA) exercise was carried out by people proposed by OGC and itSMF. OGC and Ultracomp wish to express their particular appreciation to the following people who spent considerable time and effort (far beyond the call of duty!) on QA of the material:

Joy Attwood-Harris	F.I.GROUP PLC
Graham Barnett	DMR Consulting
David Bingham	DMR Consulting
Jeroen Born	Quint Wellington Redwood
Chris Bradbrook-Armit	The Grey Matters
Ian Bridge	F.I.GROUP PLC
Graham Briscoe	Royal & Sun Alliance
Tony Brough	Exel
Keith Bullard	UK – CMG
Michael Busch	IT Masters
Steven Cain	HM Treasury
Derek Cambray	Amdahl
Martin Carr	OGC
Duncan Carroll	Scottish Provident
Alison Cartlidge	F.I.GROUP PLC
David Cronin	Dartmouth Park Systems Ltd
Steve Daniels	Insight Consulting
Michael Davies	ProActive Services Pty Ltd, Australia
Kevin E Ellis BA MBA	Profission Group
Jenny Ellwood-Wade	Bowood Ltd (NZ)
Ivor Evans	Ivory Consulting Ltd
Karen Ferris	ProActive Services Ltd, Australia
Mary Fishleigh	itSMF Publications sub-committee
David Forster	UNICOM
Judith Fulcher	F.I.GROUP PLC
Dave Green	Fox IT (Ultracomp)
John Groom	OGC
Paul Habershon	DMR Consulting
Ken Hamilton	ManageOne
Lex Hendriks	EXIN
Marc Hodes	Interpharm
Steve Houlding	Inter Access b. v.
Lesley Hughes	Hewlett Packard
Sjoerd Hulzinga	Pink Elephant
Tony Jenkins	Parity Training Ltd
Chris Jones	CPT Global (Australia)
Colin Keeley-Huggett	IBM UK
Magda Kilby	ECsoft UK Ltd
Maggie Kneller	itSMF / Powergen UK PLC
Arry Koetsier	Inter Access b.v.
Vladimir Kufner	Hewlett Packard
Ronnie Lachniet	Quint Wellington Redwood NL
Shirley Lacy	Change IT Ltd
Cameron Law	The WM Company (A member of the Deutsche Bank group)
Aidan Lawes	itSMF International

Adrian Leach	Parity Training Ltd
Rudolf Liefers	Syntegra (Netherlands)
Peter Lijnse	Hewlett Packard (Canada)
Chris Littlewood	F.I.GROUP PLC
Martin Lucas	Fox IT (Ultracomp)
Ivor Macfarlane	ISEB / Guillemot Rock
Steve Mann	Sysop
Simon Marvell	Insight Consulting
Rob Mersel	Inter Access b.v.
Stephen Moran	The British Library
Alan O'Connor	HM Treasury
Paul Overbeek	KPMG Information Risk Management
Eric Overvoorde	EXIN
Dave Owen	Alliance & Leicester
Joel Pereira	Pink Elephant
Louk Peters	Pink Roccade IT Management
Rene Posthumus	Ultracomp B.V.
Tony Price	Fox IT (Ultracomp)
David Pultorak	Pultorak & Associates Ltd
Susan Reay	Hambleton District Council
Lloyd Robinson	CEC Europe Ltd
Kathryn Rupchock	Microsoft
Frances Scarff	OGC
Andy Smith	EDS
John Stewart	OGC
Richard Stone	Fox IT (Ultracomp)
Mark Sutton	Amdahl
Ed Tozer	Edwin E Tozer Ltd
Bridget Veitch	F.I.GROUP PLC
Jan Maarten Willems	Sx Consultants NV
John Windebank	Computacenter
Peter Youart	Morse Group Ltd

Contact information

Full details of the range of material published under the ITIL banner can be found at www.itil.co.uk.

For further information on this and other OGC products, please visit the OGC website at www.ogc.gov.uk/. Alternatively, please contact:

OGC Service Desk
Rosebery Court
St Andrews Business Park
Norwich
NR7 OHS
United Kingdom
Tel: +44 (0) 845 000 4999
Email: ServiceDesk@ogc.gsi.gov.uk

1 INTRODUCTION TO THIS BOOK

This book is one of a series issued as part of the updated IT Infrastructure Library that documents industry best practice for the support and delivery of IT services. Although this book can be read in isolation, it is recommended that it be used in conjunction with the other IT Infrastructure Library books. Service Management is a generic concept and the guidance in the new IT Infrastructure Library books is applicable generically. The guidance is also scaleable – applicable to both small and large organisations. It applies to distributed and centralised systems, whether in-house or supplied by third parties. It is neither bureaucratic nor unwieldy if implemented sensibly and in full recognition of the business needs of the organisation.

1.1 The IT Infrastructure Library

Developed in the late 1980s, the IT Infrastructure Library (ITIL) has become the world-wide *de facto* standard in Service Management. Starting as a guide for UK government, the framework has proved to be useful to organisations in all sectors through its adoption by many companies as the basis for Service Management, as well as consultancy, education and software tools support. Today, ITIL is known and used worldwide.

The reasons for its success are explained in the remainder of this Section:

1.1.1 Deleted

1.1.2 Best practice framework

The IT Infrastructure Library documents industry best practice guidance. It has proved its value from the very beginning. Initially, OGC collected information on how various organisations addressed Service Management, analysed this and filtered those issues that would prove useful to OGC and to its Customers in UK central government. Other organisations found that the guidance was generally applicable and markets outside of government were very soon created by the service industry.

Being a framework, ITIL describes the contours of organising Service Management. The models show the goals, general activities, inputs and outputs of the various processes, which can be incorporated within IT organisations. ITIL does not cast in stone every action required on a day-to-day basis because that is something which differs from organisation to organisation. Instead it focuses on best practice that can be utilised in different ways according to need.

Thanks to this framework of proven best practice, the IT Infrastructure Library can be used within organisations with existing methods and activities in Service Management. Using ITIL doesn't imply a completely new way of thinking and acting. It provides a framework in which to place existing methods and activities in a structured context, providing a strategic context that improves tactical decision-making and has an aligning influence on the tasks of Service Management. By emphasising the relationships between the processes, any lack of communication and co-operation between various IT functions can be eliminated or minimised.

ITIL provides a proven method for planning common processes, roles and activities with appropriate reference to each other and how the communication lines should exist between them.

1.1.3   De facto standard

By the mid-1990s, ITIL was recognised as the world *de facto* standard for Service Management. A major advantage of a generally recognised method is a common language. The books describe a large number of terms that, when used correctly, can help people to understand each other within IT organisations.

An important part of IT Infrastructure Library projects is getting people to speak that common language. That is why education is the essential basis of an implementation or improvement programme. Sharing a common language is a critical element to the efficiency and effectiveness of any project.

1.1.4   Quality approach

In the past, many IT organisations were internally focused and concentrated on technical issues. These days, businesses have high expectations of the quality of services and these expectations change with time. This means that for IT organisations to live up to these expectations, they need to concentrate on service quality and a more Customer oriented approach. It means doing these things at the right price. In short, it means managing IT as a business.

ITIL focuses on providing high quality services, placing particular emphasis on Customer relationships. This means that the IT organisation should provide whatever is agreed with Customers, which implies a strong relationship between the IT organisation and their Customers and partners.

Tactical processes are centred on the relationships between the IT organisation and their Customers. Service Delivery is partially concerned with setting up agreements and monitoring the targets within these agreements. Meanwhile, on the operational level, the Service Support processes can be viewed as responding to the Changes needed in, and any failures in, the services laid down in these agreements. On both levels there is a strong relationship with quality systems such as ISO 9000 and a total quality framework such as European Foundation for Quality Management (EFQM). ITIL supports these quality systems by providing defined processes and best practice for the management of IT Services, enabling a fast track towards ISO certification. Attaining a quality standard is beneficial for organisations but it has to be recognised that this alone does not guarantee delivery of good service. There needs to be on-going review of quality of processes aligned with business requirements.

Appendix D provides more information on quality management. Overall benefits include:

- improved quality service provision
- cost justifiable service quality
- services that meet business, Customer and User demands
- integrated centralised processes
- everyone knows their role and knows their responsibilities in service provision
- learning from previous experience
- demonstrable performance indicators.

Business case for using the ISO 9000 quality standards

Many companies require their suppliers to become registered to ISO 9001 and because of this, registered companies find that their market opportunities have increased. In addition, a company's compliance with ISO 9001 ensures that it has a sound Quality Assurance system.

Registered companies have had dramatic reductions in Customer complaints, significant reductions in operating costs and increased demand for their products and services.

ISO 9000 registration is rapidly becoming a 'should' for any company that does business in Europe. Many industrial companies require registration by their own suppliers. There is a growing trend toward universal acceptance of ISO 9000.

Of course this applies to other standards, for example the British Standards, and in fact most European and many other standards worldwide have been consolidated in the new ISO 9000-2000 standards.

1.1.5 *it*SMF

The *it*SMF (IT Service Management Forum) was set up to support and influence the IT Service Management industry. It has, through its large membership, been influential in promoting industry best practice and driving updates to ITIL.

1.2 Restructuring the IT Infrastructure Library

The concept of managing IT services for the improvement of business functions is not new; it predates ITIL. The idea of bringing all of the Service Management best practice together under one roof however was both radical and new. The first series of ITIL amalgamated Service Management from an IT standpoint but could have done more to capture the interest of the business. The Business Perspective series was published to bridge the gap between business and IT management and although a success, the series was published at a time when the original ITIL guidance was becoming outdated in some areas. The impact of the new series was therefore limited in the market, but a catalyst in the Service Management industry.

ITIL was originally produced in the late 1980s and consisted of ten core books covering the two main areas of Service Support and Service Delivery. These core books were further supported by 30 complementary books covering a range of issues from Cabling to Business Continuity Management. In this revision, ITIL has been restructured to make it simpler to access the information needed to manage the services. The core books have now been pulled together into two books, covering the areas of Service Support and Service Delivery, in order to eliminate duplication and enhance navigation. The material has also been updated and revised for consistency and sharpness of focus. Lastly, the material has been re-engineered to focus on the business issues of infrastructure management as well as to ensure a closer synergy with the new IS guides published by OGC.

1.3 Target audience

This book is relevant to anyone involved in the delivery or support of IT services. It is applicable to anyone involved in the management or day-to-day practice of Service Management. It is recognised that there are several ways of delivering an IT service, such as in-house, out-sourced and partnership. Even though this book is written mainly from an in-house service provider's perspective it is generally relevant to all other methods of service provision. So most of this book is applicable to those involved in out-sourced service provision or working in partnerships. Business managers should find the book helpful in understanding and establishing best practice IT services and support. Managers from supplier organisations should also find this book relevant when setting up agreements for the delivery and support of services.

1.4 Navigating the IT Infrastructure Library

Following consultation with Service Management organisations and User groups, OGC designed the diagram shown in Figure 1.1. This illustrates that the new library series will comprise five principal elements, each of which have interfaces and overlaps with each of the other four. The elements are:

- the business perspective
- managing applications
- delivery of IT services
- support of IT services
- manage the infrastructure.

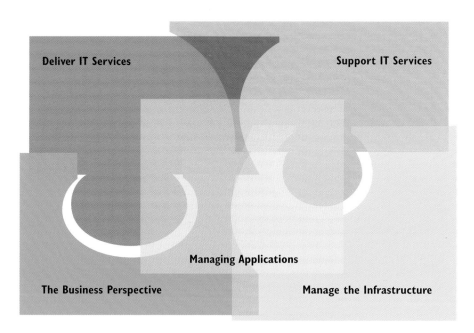

Figure 1.1 – Jigsaw diagram

The Business Perspective book will cover a range of issues concerned with understanding and improving IT service provision, as an integral part of an overall business requirement for high quality IS management. These issues include:

- Business Continuity Management
- partnerships and outsourcing
- surviving change
- transformation of business practice through radical change.

The Service Delivery book looks at what service the business requires of the provider in order to provide adequate support to the business Customers. To provide the necessary support the book covers the following topics:

- Capacity Management
- Financial Management for IT Services
- Availability Management
- Service Level Management
- IT Service Continuity Management.

The Service Support book is concerned with ensuring that the User has access to the appropriate services to support the business functions. Issues discussed in this book are:

- Service Desk
- Incident Management
- Problem Management
- Configuration Management
- Change Management
- Release Management.

The ICT Infrastructure Management book includes:

- Network Service Management
- Operations Management
- Management of Local Processors
- Computer Installation and Acceptance
- Systems Management (covered here for the first time).

Lastly, the book on Applications Management will embrace the software development lifecycle expanding the issues touched upon in Software Lifecycle Support and Testing of IT Services. Applications Management will expand on the issues of business change with emphasis on clear requirement definition and implementation of the solution to meet business needs.

The major elements of the ITIL books can be likened to overlapping jigsaw puzzle pieces (or perhaps better as tectonic plates), some of which have a precise fit, and some of which overlap or do not fit together accurately. At the highest level, there are no strict demarcation lines. Indeed, consider further the analogy of tectonic plates, sliding over and under one another, joining and separating. The earthly problem of points of instability or friction caused by the imprecise nature of the pieces has an IT Infrastructure Library equivalent. It is precisely where process domains overlap or where demarcation lines cannot be clearly drawn that many management problems arise. It is not possible to stop all the problems from occurring (just as earthquakes cannot be avoided) but it is possible to provide advice on how to prepare for and deal with them.

1.5   Why choose a jigsaw concept?

To clarify how the concepts within ITIL work together, OGC produced a set of process models to describe the makeup of ITIL – the process model for Service Delivery can be found at Appendix G. These process models have been used in practice and enhanced since first produced and now form the cornerstones of the ITIL core books. The process elements for management of services can be defined precisely. However, in practice, when analysing the processes in more detail, elements overlap. This situation illustrates the need for both consistency across the guidance, and advice on how to deal with management problems that may arise. The cause of these management problems may be the result of boundaries drawn that perhaps have more to do with the span of control than with logical grouping of related processes.

1.6   The Service Delivery book

Figure 1.2 expands the service delivery jigsaw puzzle pieces. The ITIL process elements covered in this book are also shown.

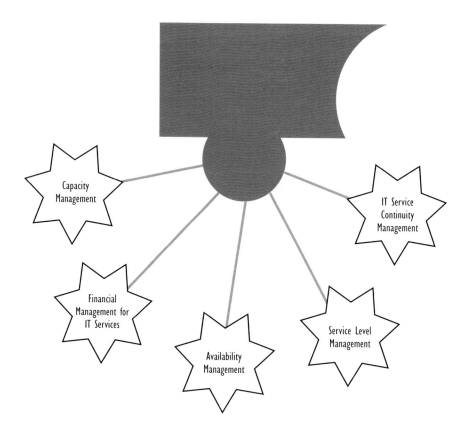

Figure 1.2 – Service Delivery; the coverage

Note that all of the Chapters relate to processes.

1.7 Service Management

All the processes described in ITIL relate to each other. Half of these processes are detailed in this book, half in the book on Service Support. To better understand how these processes inter-relate, consider this example life cycle of an Incident:

1. A User calls the *Service Desk* to report response difficulties with the on-line service.

2. The *Incident Management* process deals with Incident.

3. The *Problem Management* process investigates underlying cause and calls in *Capacity Management* to assist in this process. Service Level Management alerted that the SLA has been breached. Request For Change (RFC) raised if appropriate.

4. The *Change Management* process co-ordinates the RFC.

5. The *IT Financial Management* process assists with the business case cost justification for any upgrade.

6. The *IT Service Continuity* process gets involved in the *Change Management* process to ensure recovery is possible onto current back-up configuration.

7. The *Release Management* process controls the implementation of the Change by rolling out replacement hardware and software. Release Management updates Configuration Management with details of new Releases and versions.

8. The *Availability Management* process is involved in considering the hardware upgrade to ensure that it can meet the required availability and reliability levels.

9. The *Configuration Management* process ensures the Configuration Management Database (CMDB) information is updated throughout the process.

1.8 Customers and Users

To avoid confusion regarding roles and terminology the terms 'Customer' and 'User' are used throughout the new books to differentiate between those people (generally senior managers) who commission, pay for and own the IT Services (the Customers) and those people who use the services on a day-to-day basis (the Users). The semantics are less important than the reason for differentiation. The primary point of contact for Customers is either the Service Level Manager or the Business Relationship Manager, while the primary point of contact for Users is the Service Desk. A poorly functioning Incident Management process affects the User population immediately. A service that is poor value for money has a greater impact on the Customer.

It is therefore important to distinguish the different, but related, needs of Users and Customers in the provision of services. Certainly, their goals may be at odds and need to be balanced; for example Users may demand high availability whereas Customers look for value for money at different levels of availability. There are information flows that should be maintained and key process elements that should be defined for use by both parties.

1.9   A Standard and Code of Practice for IT Service Management

The British Standards Institute have published 'Specification for IT Service Management' (BS15000) and 'A Code of Practice for IT Service Management' (PD0005), both of which are based on the principles of ITIL; the context diagram from BS15000 is reproduced below. The diagram is not a process model but simply a pictorial description. It can be viewed in the same way as Figure 1.1, i.e. the main principles (of Service Management in this instance) are placed in a coherent context, providing guidance that enables the reader to make links between related process elements.

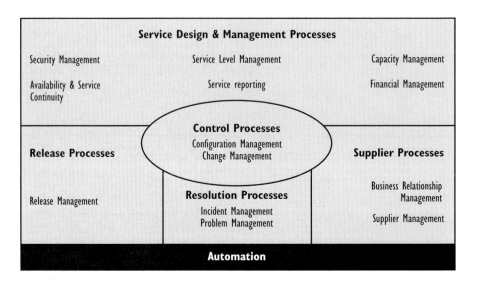

Figure 1.3 – BS15000 Service Management processes

Considering PD0005 in the context of Figure 1.3, it is obvious that the new IT Infrastructure Library models can be seen as an expansion of the BSI model, taking IT Service Management forward. The process elements are nearly the same, the principle of Change and Configuration Management as a linchpin is the same, the difference relates to the level of detail. Both BSI and OGC promote similar, if not identical, principles of best practice for IT Service Management.

1.10   Service Management: a process approach

The Chapters in this book focus on Service Delivery as a set of integrated processes. Service Delivery focuses on processes in order to achieve goals; some managerial functions are required to enact the processes, but fundamentally it is the process and its suitability for purpose that is important.

More details about process theory and practice are provided in Appendix B to this book.

1.11   Recommended reading

These OGC IS Management Guides are also related to Service Management and are recommended additional reading. They can be obtained from the publisher, your ITIL bookseller or The Stationery Office:

Strategic Management of IS
Published by Format
1 90309 1 02 0
Approx. 70 pages
October 1999
£25.00

This guide describes the context within which organisations in the public sector need to think strategically about the exploitation of IS and IT, and the impact of current sector-wide policies and initiatives. It sets out the approach which senior business managers should take to the management of information systems and their IS strategy, together with guidance on managing the required changes.

Managing change
Published by Format
1 90309 1 01 2
Approx. 80 pages
September 1999
£25.00

This guide is intended for senior managers who are responsible for managing complex IS-related change. It investigates the issues associated with business transformation, organisational and cultural change. It provides practical advice on working across organisational boundaries and breaking the 'all pain, no gain' barrier. The guidance also provides clear interfaces to Programme Management and benefits realisation.

Acquisition
Published by Format
1 90309 1 03 9
Approx. 110 pages
September 1999
£25.00

This guide focuses on business objectives and outcomes in making the right IT acquisitions. It explains the key issues relating to sourcing options and partnerships, together with procurement strategies for new ways of working and new kinds of contracts.

Managing performance
Published by Format
1 90309 1 05 5
Approx. 110 pages
October 1999
£25.00

This guide developed in collaboration with NAO, focuses on three levels of performance management: business management; contribution of IS/IT to the business; and performance of the IS/IT function. It examines the role of the EFQM Excellence Model®, balanced scorecards, bench-marking and other widely adopted techniques.

Managing services
Published by Format
1 90309 1 04 7
Approx. 100 pages
October 1999
£25.00

This guide explains the foundations for effective Service Management, appropriate contracts and good working relationships. It helps the customer of IS/IT services to understand the suppliers' perspective on Service Delivery. It provides practical advice on how to achieve better performance from service providers and continuing value for money.

2 RELATIONSHIP BETWEEN PROCESSES

This book refers to the need for Service Level Management, Financial Management for IT Services, IT Service Continuity Management, Availability Management and Capacity Management. Each component of Service Delivery is discussed separately in the book. The purpose of this Section is to show the links and the principal relationships between all the Service Management and other Infrastructure Management processes.

2.1 Service Level Management

The Service Level Management (SLM) process is responsible for ensuring Service Level Agreements (SLAs) and underpinning Operational Level Agreements (OLAs) or contracts are met, and for ensuring that any adverse impact on service quality is kept to a minimum. The process involves assessing the impact of Changes upon service quality and SLAs, both when Changes are proposed and after they have been implemented. Some of the most important targets set in the SLAs will relate to service availability and thus require Incident resolution within agreed periods.

SLM is the hinge for Service Support and Service Delivery. It cannot function in isolation as it relies on the existence and effective and efficient working of other processes. An SLA without underpinning support processes is useless, as there is no basis for agreeing its content.

2.2 Financial Management for IT Services

Financial Management is responsible for accounting for the costs (costing) and return on IT service investments (IT portfolio management), and for any aspects of recovering costs from the Customers (charging). It requires good interfaces with Capacity Management, Configuration Management (asset data) and Service Level Management to identify the true costs of service. Financial Management is likely to work closely with Business Relationship Management and the IT organisation during the negotiations of the IT organisation's budgets and individual Customer's IT spend.

2.3 Capacity Management

Capacity Management is responsible for ensuring adequate capacity is available at all times to meet the requirements of the business. It is directly related to the business requirements and is not simply about the performance of the system's components, individually or collectively. Capacity Management is involved in Incident resolution and Problem identification for those difficulties relating to capacity issues.

Capacity Management activities raise Requests for Change (RFCs) to ensure that appropriate capacity is available. These RFCs are subject to the Change Management process, and implementation may affect several CIs, including hardware, software and documentation, requiring effective Release Management.

Capacity Management should be involved in evaluating all Changes, to establish the effect on capacity and performance. This should occur both when Changes are proposed and after they are implemented. Capacity Management should pay particular attention to the cumulative effect of Changes over a period of time. The negligible effect of single Changes can often combine to cause degraded response times, file storage problems, and excess demand for processing capacity.

2.4   IT Service Continuity Management

IT Service Continuity Management is concerned with managing an organisation's ability to continue to provide a pre-determined and agreed level of IT Services to support the minimum business requirements following an interruption to the business. Effective IT Service Continuity requires a balance of risk reduction measures such as resilient systems and recovery options including back-up facilities. Configuration Management data is required to facilitate this prevention and planning. Infrastructure and business Changes need to be assessed for their potential impact on the continuity plans, and the IT and business plans should be subject to Change Management procedures. The Service Desk has an important role to play if business continuity is invoked.

2.5   Availability Management

Availability Management is concerned with the design, implementation, measurement and management of IT services to ensure the stated business requirements for availability are consistently met. Availability Management requires an understanding of the reasons why IT service failures occur and the time taken to resume service. Incident Management and Problem Management provide a key input to ensure the appropriate corrective actions are being progressed.

Availability targets specified in SLAs are monitored and reported on as part of the Availability Management process. Additionally Availability Management supports the Service Level Management process in providing measurements and reporting to support service reviews.

2.6   Configuration Management

Configuration Management is an integral part of all other Service Management processes. With current, accurate and comprehensive information about all components of the infrastructure, the management of Change, in particular, is more effective and efficient. Change Management can be integrated with Configuration Management. As a minimum it is recommended that the logging and implementation of Changes be done under the control of a comprehensive Configuration Management system and that the impact assessment of Changes is done with the aid of the Configuration Management system. All Change requests should therefore be entered in the Configuration Management Database (CMDB) and the records updated as the Change request progresses through to implementation.

The Configuration Management system identifies relationships between an item that is to be changed and any other components of the infrastructure, thus allowing the owners of these components to be involved in the impact assessment process. Whenever a Change is made to the infrastructure and/or services, associated Configuration Management records should be updated in the CMDB (see Figure 2.1). Where possible, this is best accomplished by use of integrated tools that update records automatically as changes are made.

The CMDB should be made available to the entire Service Support group so that Incidents and Problems can be resolved more easily by understanding the possible cause of the failing component. The CMDB should also be used to link the Incident and Problem records to other appropriate records such as the failing Configuration Item (CI) and the User. Release Management will be difficult and error prone without the integration of the Configuration Management process.

The Service Delivery processes also rely on the CMDB data. For example:

- Service Level Management needs to identify components that combine together to deliver the service so that underpinning agreements can be set up

- Financial Management for IT needs to know the components utilised by each business unit especially when charging is in place

- IT Service Continuity and Availability Management need to identify components to perform risk analysis and component failure impact analysis.

Figure 2.1 shows, as an example, the relationships between Configuration Management and some other Service Management processes.

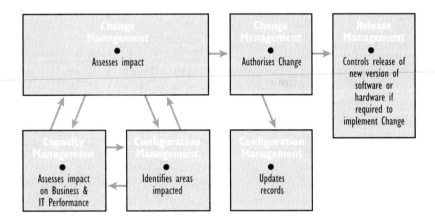

Figure 2.1 – Relationship between Change Management, Configuration Management, Capacity Management and Release Management

2.7 Change Management

The Change Management process depends on the accuracy of the configuration data to ensure the full impact of making Changes is known. There is therefore a very close relationship between Configuration Management, Release Management and Change Management.

Details of the Change process are documented in SLAs to ensure that Users know the procedure for requesting Changes and the projected target times for, and impact of the implementation of Changes.

Details of Changes need to be made known to the Service Desk. Even with comprehensive testing there is an increased likelihood of difficulties occurring following Change implementation either because the Change is not working as required or expected, or because of queries on the change in functionality.

The Change Advisory Board (CAB) is a group of people who can give expert advice to the Change Management team on the implementation of Changes. This board is likely to be made up of representatives from all areas within IT and representatives from business units.

2.8 Release Management

Changes may often result in the need for new hardware, new versions of software, and/or new documentation, created in-house or bought in, to be controlled and distributed, as part of a new 'packaged Release'. The procedures for achieving secure, managed rollout should be closely integrated with those for Change Management and Configuration Management. Release procedures may also be an integral part of Incident Management and Problem Management, as well as being closely linked to the CMDB in order to maintain up-to-date records.

2.9 Incident Management

There should be a close interface between the Incident Management process and the Problem Management and Change Management processes as well as the function of the Service Desk. If not properly controlled, Changes may introduce new Incidents. A way of tracking back is required. It is therefore recommended that the Incident records should be held on the same CMDB as the Problem, Known Error and Change records, or at least linked without the need for re-keying, to improve the interfaces and ease interrogation and reporting.

Incident priorities and escalation procedures need to be agreed as part of the Service Level Management process and documented in the SLAs.

2.10 Problem Management

The Problem Management process requires the accurate and comprehensive recording of Incidents in order to identify effectively and efficiently the cause of the Incidents and trends. Problem Management also needs to liaise closely with the Availability Management process to identify these trends and instigate remedial action.

2.11 Service Desk

The Service Desk is an important function for the different Service Management processes. It is a single point of contact between service providers and Users, on a day-to-day basis. It is also a focal point for reporting Incidents and making service requests. As such, the Service Desk has an obligation to keep Users informed of service events, actions and opportunities that are likely to impact their ability to pursue their day-to-day activities. For example, the Service Desk might act as the focal point for Change requests from Users, issuing Change schedules on behalf of Change Management, and keeping Users informed of progress on Changes. Change Management should therefore ensure that the Service Desk is kept constantly aware of Change activities.

The Service Desk is in the direct firing line of any impact on the SLAs and as such needs rapid information flows.

The Service Desk may be given delegation to implement Changes to circumvent Incidents within its sphere of authority. The scope of such Changes should be predefined and the Change Management function should be informed about all such Changes. Prior approval of Change Management is essential before Changes of specification of any CI are implemented.

2.12 ICT Infrastructure Management

ICT Infrastructure Management functions are involved in most of the processes of Service Support and Service Delivery where more technical issues are concerned.

2.13 Application Management

OGC plans to produce guidance that discusses the major processes required to manage applications throughout their lifetime. Service Management is typically concerned with a product (software/hardware) at a particular point in time to support the service requirements of the business. But it should be more than this. It delivers a maintainable service for the business – this means delivering the skills, training, and communications with the application. Applications Management considers the issues from feasibility through productive life to final demise of the application.

2.14 Security Management

The Security Management function interfaces with IT Service Management processes where security issues are involved. Such issues relate to the Confidentiality, Integrity and Availability of data, as well as the security of hardware and software components, documentation and procedures. For example, Security Management interfaces with Service Management to assess the impact of proposed Changes on security, to raise RFCs in response to security problems; to ensure confidentiality and integrity of security data and to maintain the security when software is released into the live environment.

2.15 Environmental infrastructure processes

Changes to the environment may affect the quality of service, and Changes to the infrastructure may have implications for the environmental infrastructure. It is recommended that all relevant aspects of the environmental infrastructure be brought under Configuration Management control and subjected to the Change Management procedures described in the Service Support book.

2.16 Project Management

When implementing new processes in an organisation there are benefits to running the activity as a project. Accordingly, this book refers to Service Management projects that are implemented to introduce new processes or to improve the current processes for the delivery or support of IT services.

There are a variety of structured project management methods that can be adopted. Within ITIL when we discuss project management if we need to draw on a particular method we will use PRINCE2 which is owned by OGC and widely adopted throughout UK Government bodies, the Public and Private sectors, and internationally.

3 GETTING STARTED

Chapter 10 discusses how to set about planning and implementing the project of introducing Service Management. Within this Chapter we look at how to build commitment from management so that they will provide the necessary funding and communicate support for the project.

The first thing you need to know is the benefit of using the method and how to market the message of those benefits to the organisation. These issues can form part of a business case for process implementation or improvement. An important part of the business case is likely to be concerned with articulating the problems with the current position and demonstrating the benefits of the new vision. A business case should look at the benefits, disadvantages, costs and risks of the current situation and the future vision so that management can balance all of these factors when deciding if the project should proceed. Appendix F provides some costed examples for developing a business case for introducing ITIL-based management processes into an organisation.

3.1 Service Management benefits

It is important to consider the benefits for the organisation of having a clear definition of the Service Management function. Some of the benefits that could be cited include:

- improved quality of service – more reliable business support
- IT Service Continuity procedures more focused, more confidence in the ability to follow them when required
- clearer view of current IT capability
- better information on current services (and possibly on where Changes would bring most benefits)
- greater flexibility for the business through improved understanding of IT support
- more motivated staff; improved job satisfaction through better understanding of capability and better management of expectations
- enhanced Customer satisfaction as service providers know and deliver what is expected of them
- increased flexibility and adaptability is likely to exist within the services
- system-led benefits, e.g. improvements in security, accuracy, speed, availability as required for the required level of service
- improved cycle time for Changes and greater success rate.

The importance and level of these will vary between organisations. An issue comes in defining these benefits for any organisation in a way that will be measurable later on. Following ITIL guidance can help to quantify some of these elements.

3.2   A process-led approach

Appendix B provides detailed information about using process models and definitions to complement a process-led approach to implementing IT Infrastructure Library guidance in a programme of continuous improvement.

Figure 3.1 represents a model that can be used by an organisation as the framework for process improvement.

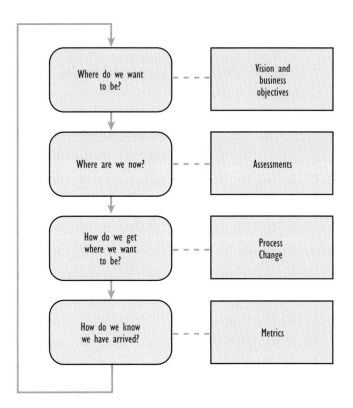

Figure 3.1 – Process improvement model

In short, if a process model of best practice is drawn up – or any practice in fact that is more effective than the current way of doing things – then that model can be compared with a description of current practice and used to define improvements. If this is done in the light of the business direction or critical success factors, it is possible to define measures of how to demonstrate improvements and achievements that are truly useful.

As a process based method, the IT Infrastructure Library is particularly suited to use in this way. Appendix B provides more information.

There are a number of different methods and notations by which processes can be defined and documented – each often associated with a specific design/modelling tool.

Taking a fairly generic view, Figure 3.2 illustrates the typical components one might find in a process definition.

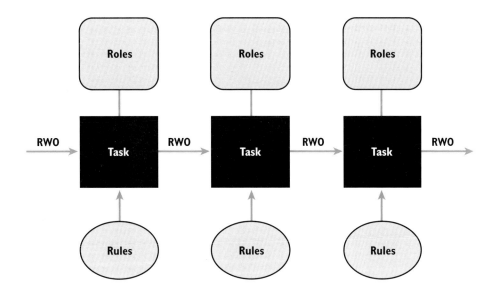

Figure 3.2 – Typical components in a process definition

Each process has a clear objective. To reach that objective the process is broken down into a series of tasks. For each task, there will be Inputs and Outputs (shown as **Real World Objects**, **RWO**, in the diagram). Whether these RWOs have a physical form, e.g. as a piece of paper, or are merely held as electronic information, is irrelevant.

Each task is executed by a **role**. This may be embodied in a human being or performed by a piece of software. If human-centric, then there are a set of competencies that an individual needs in order to perform the role.

The execution of the role is governed by a set of **rules**. These range from the simple ('All boxes on the form should be completed') to the very complex ('Credit is only allowed if a set of criteria are met according to an algorithm').

Often, a process will span various organisational boundaries. It is important, therefore, that each process has an **owner**. This is another **role**.

The process owner is responsible for the **process definition** itself, which should be treated as a Configuration Item (CI), subject to all the usual Change control rigours. The process owner is responsible for ensuring that all that are involved in the execution of the process are kept informed of any Changes that occur. The process owner may not undertake the work in person, but will be responsible for ensuring that the work is being done.

3.3 Management commitment

Management commitment is about motivating and leading by example. If management do not support the use of best practice openly and demonstrably, or if you are not fully committed to Change and innovation, then staff cannot be expected to improve themselves, Service Management processes or service to Customers. Genuine management commitment is absolutely essential to 'staying the course' when implementing Service Management in an organisation.

3.3.1   Aspects of management commitment

Modern organisations require IT/business alignment, and therefore a total quality approach to leadership is required from managers. The different aspects of management commitment can be found in commonly used Total Quality Models such as the EFQM (in Europe) or MBNQA (in North America) models.

3.3.2   Management commitment in the planning stage

Why do implementations fail?

This question has been asked many times in the past. If we examine the causes for failures at the highest level a pattern appears. Simply designing and implementing a new or updated process does not guarantee success. A number of factors could result in the process not realising its objectives. In most cases failure is caused by lack of attention to the 'Process enablers'. It is not enough for management to provide the funds for the implementation process and then sit back expecting everything to work. Management should be committed during the entire '*plan-do-check-act*' cycle, and should also address all aspects of the Service Management framework. Other common reasons for failure include:

- lack of staff commitment and understanding
- lack of training
- the staff given the responsibility for implementation are not given sufficient authority to make the required decisions
- loss of the Service Management 'champion' (the person driving the implementation)
- loss of impetus after the initial hype
- lack of initial funding and lack of quantifiable long term cost benefits
- over-focus on tactical, isolated 'solutions' rather than a strategic solution, i.e., addressing individual elements of Service Management rather than the overall picture
- overly ambitious expectations of immediate benefits or trying to do everything at once
- unrealistic implementation timetable
- no one accountable
- difficulties of changing the culture of the organisation
- tools unable to support the process, requiring tailoring of the process or of the tool
- inappropriate approach taken to implementation – not under Project Management controls
- inappropriate scoping of the process
- lack of appreciation for the hard work and discipline required to implement Service Management.

As you can see, management commitment is essential to Service Management success. But management, and indeed 'Process owners' alone cannot make Service Management successful. It takes the commitment and personal leadership of every IT professional in the organisation.

3.4 Cultural aspects

It would appear obvious that, in order to prosper, a business should have Customer satisfaction as its prime objective. Unfortunately, until recently, many IT departments have been too obsessed with technology to recognise that they have Customers at all.

In recent years pressure has been put on IT service providers to become more aware of their role in supporting the business and to be run as accountable business units. This pressure has come from many quarters:

- outsourcing
- market testing
- compulsory competitive tendering
- the Customers themselves (who are, in increasing numbers, being given their own budgets and the freedom to use them where they see fit).

The days when staff in IT departments regarded their 'Customers' as a *necessary evil* or just *difficult colleagues* have (hopefully) passed. There is a growing awareness that in order to retain the in-house IT department they have to stay close to their Customers, understand and predict their requirements and satisfy them. IT departments are now raising the priority of Customer satisfaction from being merely 'nice to have' to 'essential'.

The provision of quality IT services with high levels of availability and performance can be achieved with the correct hardware, software and underlying support processes. This level of service may satisfy, but may not lead to 'Customer Delight'! Extra effort is needed for the Customer to enjoy the experience and want to come back for more. The way in which the service is delivered is dependent on the people delivering the service. Customer delight will only be achieved if the people involved are responsive to their Customers' needs, are attentive, reliable, and courteous, delivering the service in the way they themselves would like to receive it.

We all know what a Customer is – someone who deals with a trader and habitually purchases from him. Similarly, we are all familiar with service – an act performed for the benefit or advantage of a person, institution or cause. Customer service therefore is concerned with performing acts that benefit Customers in a way that will encourage them to purchase service again and again.

3.4.1 What is culture?

It is important that all staff involved in delivering service are committed to the concept of Customer delight. This can only be achieved if the organisation's culture demands it. The prevalent culture within any organisation is a product of a variety of factors: the age and history of the organisation, its size, the technology in use, its objectives, the market as well as geography and the personalities and backgrounds of people employed.

There are many influencing factors and it is not reasonable to expect all organisations to have, or adopt, the same culture, organisational structure or systems. Despite the growing literature on the culture of organisations there is no textbook formula for organisational culture.

The term 'culture' is used in this context to refer to the values and beliefs of the organisation – the normal way of doing things. Component parts of the culture include:

- the way authority is exercised and people rewarded

- methods of communication – see Appendix E for more details
- the degrees of formality required in working hours and dress and the extent to which procedures and regulations are enforced.

An organisation's culture can be immediately recognised by an outsider by the staff's attitudes and morale; their vocabulary – the phrases and buzz words they use and the stories and legends they tell of the organisation's heroes.

3.4.2 Responsibilities

Most often, responsibility for creating and maintaining an organisation's culture rests with its leaders. The prevailing culture dictates the shape of the organisation's structure and the nature of the systems and procedures used.

In their best-selling book *In Search of Excellence*, a study of the best run American companies, Tom Peters and Robert Waterman noted:

'...Without exception, the dominance and coherence of culture proved to be an essential quality of the excellent companies. Moreover, the stronger the culture and the more it was directed toward the market place, the less need was there for policy manuals, organisation charts, or detailed procedures and rules... people ...know what they are supposed to do in most situations because the handful of guiding values is crystal clear.'

Procedures, therefore, should support the culture and not govern or influence it.

3.4.3 What is meant by 'service culture'?

In order to achieve business success the culture of every organisation should embrace the concept of service and Customer care. The idea of a service culture can be summed up in one true saying, 'People don't care how much you know until they know how much you care'. A service culture means an orientation towards helping people. The technical quality of the work is important – that's precisely why a service culture is so important. Without it, the value of technology can remain largely untapped in organisations.

The satisfaction of Customer requirements should be the number one priority – for everyone, whatever their role in the organisation. The concept of service should permeate through all layers of the organisation – from staff in the front line responsible for delivering service to those in a supporting role – either as managers or in the back room.

Service Delivery should ensure that Customer requirements are met in a way that makes them feel that they are valued and respected – they should be made to feel good at every transaction. The aim should be to exceed Customers' expectations (not in what is delivered but in the way it is delivered) and give them confidence in your ability to satisfy all their future needs.

By taking the time and effort to listen to Customers it is possible to understand the service being provided from their perspective. The key point about providing service is attention to detail; to go that little bit further to delight the Customer.

3.4.4 How is this relevant to IT service provision?

Achieving a service culture in an IT organisation should, in essence, be no different from achieving a service culture in a bread shop or a carpet wholesale business; the technology used and the product delivered may be different but the end result is the same – Customers receive service. Customers of IT services have come to expect the same levels of service at work as they receive at their local shopping mall – and they use the same criteria for choosing it.

If it is accepted that the quality of the delivery of IT service is important then it should be agreed that the way Customers are treated is an important part of Service Delivery.

3.4.5   What do Customers want?

Having recognised that IT departments are now in the business of service provision it is important to adopt a whole new way of thinking and embrace the same business concepts as those used by all service providers. There is a lot of catching up to do.

Before any business goes into production of a new product or service it should perform some market research to find out what Customers actually want and will buy.

So, what do Customers want?

- **Specification** – they want to know, up front, what they are going to get. The problem in the delivery of IT services is that Customers frequently don't know what they want – the 'IT experts' should translate their business requirements into solutions. Customers don't buy products or services, they buy services that provide solutions.

- **Conformance to specification** – once the appropriate IT solution has been found then it should conform to the specification. Customers want to know when they can receive it and should be satisfied that it will fulfil their business requirement.

- **Consistency** – they want it to be the same every time they come back for more.

- **Value for money** – the price they pay should be a fair one for the product or service they receive.

- **Communication** – they want to be told what they are getting, when, how and what to do if they have a problem with it.

Popular misconceptions about Customer care

Many people are cynical about the concept of Customer care and, in many cases, they have good reason to be. The following Paragraphs describe areas of Customer care.

'The Customer Is King posters' (and other clichéd campaign material)

Allegedly witty and amusing posters proclaiming the virtues of Customer care can be a decorative addition to an office or corridor, on their own they achieve very little. If the same slogans are used continually on posters then they become part of the wallpaper and are ignored – be prepared to change them and beware of empty slogans that can be misinterpreted. Ensure that all staff are aware of the nature, scope and intention behind any Customer care promotion otherwise the material will be greeted by cynicism if it arrives unannounced.

A by-product of ITIL/BS5750/ISO 9001/TQM

A service culture will not develop unaided. The adoption of the best practice in the delivery of IT services described in ITIL will help improve service quality. Improving the quality of procedures and obtaining quality certification will certainly focus the mind on service quality but these alone are not enough to ensure the IT department is truly Customer focused – a structured approach to cultural change is necessary.

Customer Charters and Service Level Agreements

Published guaranteed levels of service (such as SLAs) are worthless if the supplier consistently fails to meet the targets. The payment of recompense through penalty clauses is unlikely to satisfy the purchaser in the long term. These agreements tend to set targets for the tangible elements of service – Availability, response times etc. and ignore the intangible elements, which are so crucial to Customers – the way in which service is delivered.

(Another) Management initiative

If Customer service is placed high on the agenda one month and them allowed to slip back, people will think that 'the management have been on another training course and have come back with some bright ideas and this actually has nothing to do with us'. Staff should be made to realise that Customer care is not management or technology driven – instead it is Customer driven, and that it makes sound business sense to adopt a service culture.

Someone else's responsibility

Where organisations have Customer Liaison departments or Customer Service Managers, staff may be tempted to relinquish the responsibility for Customer care, thinking it is someone else's job. The concept of Customer service should permeate throughout the whole organisation.

Something new

Although the concept of satisfying Customers' requirements is only now hitting some IT departments, it is nothing new. Man has been trading ever since he came down from the trees and learned how to make a surplus. Those men and women who produced something that wasn't marketable starved to death!

3.4.6   Common excuses for conducting 'business as usual'

Most management gurus preach what is little more than 'common sense' – to treat Customers as individuals, to ask Customers what they want, listen to them and then provide what they want, to wander around amongst Customers and staff and engender a feeling of trust. It sounds easy. So why do so many organisations still fail to provide consistent Customer satisfaction? Some of the common excuses include:

- 'we are increasing our market share and expanding our product portfolio'

- 'our Customers are happy – the number of Customer complaints is down on last year and the results of our Customer satisfaction survey show that we are improving our service'

- 'we are the market leaders – we are the best'

- 'Customer service is an important issue, that is why we have a Customer service department – Customer satisfaction is their responsibility'

- 'we are highly skilled IT people – we haven't been trained to deal with Customers'

- 'we tried Customer care before – it cost us a lot of money for little if any return'

- 'we have always treated our Customers as Customers and always provided an excellent service'

- 'we are not in a competitive situation – our Customers are tied to internal services. We are not a business unit – we run the IT department'.

Some of these arguments show an element of arrogance, some complacency and some that someone else is responsible. These attitudes must be addressed otherwise there is a danger that Customers will be dissatisfied or in some cases lost.

3.4.7   How much will all this cost?

Aiming to "exceed Customers' expectations" sounds very expensive. Indeed, if a Customer is promised a visit within four hours to fix a printer and someone turns up in ten minutes with a brand-new replacement, it will certainly incur extra costs. The manpower overhead of having staff sitting around waiting for a call, the cost of having spare printers on-site etc. The Customer may very well be delighted with this level of service and expect the same service every time – and will certainly be disappointed if it takes four hours next time.

Exceeding Customer expectations does not, therefore, mean 'giving away service'. In the above example, the Customer may have been quite happy with the four hour target and a ten minute response may actually in this case have been inconvenient, having arranged to do something else for the next four hours. The Customer may have been happy with the old printer and not want anew one – particularly if it is a different model or it takes some time to configure it.

The IT supplier can delight the Customer without incurring unnecessary cost by:

- logging and understanding the technical nature of the difficulty at the first point of contact

- responding in line with the urgency as stated by the Customer

- keeping the Customer informed of what will happen, when – and keeping the promise

- carrying out the work with the minimum level of disruption in a cheerful and professional manner

- reviewing the action taken to ensure that the difficulty has been fixed and that the Customer is happy.

Getting the job done in accordance with the Customers' wishes, correctly, first time, actually saves the cost of a potential repeat visit.

Implementing a Customer care programme *will* cost money – staff time, training, changes to operating methods, promotional material etc, but the cost of doing it should be weighed against the cost of not doing it – and the risk of losing dissatisfied Customers to a competitor. It will cost a lot more to find new Customers than to retain existing ones, so any money spent keeping existing Customers happy is going to be money well spent.

3.4.8 What are the potential benefits of Customer care?

Whatever the motivations behind the move towards a service culture the end result will be increased profitability as:

- operating costs decrease as less effort is wasted giving Customers products or services they don't want

- profits margins improve as more repeat business is won – it is much cheaper to sell to an existing Customer than to court a new one

- efficiency improves as staff work more effectively as teams

- morale and staff turnover improve as staff achieve job satisfaction and job security

- service quality constantly improves, resulting in an enhanced reputation for the IT department, which will tempt new Customers and encourage existing Customers to buy more

- the IT department becomes more effective at supporting the needs of the business and becomes more responsive to changes in business direction.

3.4.9 Service Management training

It is vitally important that the concepts of the IT Infrastructure Library are well known and understood in the Service Management function. ITIL foundation and management training is now widely available leading to an internationally recognised qualification developed by the EXIN and ISEB examination boards. At the turn of the Millennium, over 10,000 people now hold qualifications in IT Service Management worldwide, and many more have received awareness and other training.

In addition it is beneficial for an organisation to receive business-related training covering the broader aspects of Infrastructure Management. Far too often IT is accused of not knowing enough about the business and its needs; ITIL the business perspective series of books should be referred to for more information.

4 SERVICE LEVEL MANAGEMENT

4.1 Introduction

4.1.1 Why Service Level Management?

Service Level Management (SLM) is essential in any organisation so that the level of IT Service needed to support the business can be determined, and monitoring can be initiated to identify whether the required service levels are being achieved – and if not, why not.

Service Level Agreements (SLA), which are managed through the SLM process, provide specific targets against which the performance of the IT organisation can be judged.

4.1.2 Goal for SLM

The goal for SLM is to maintain and improve IT Service quality, through a constant cycle of agreeing, monitoring and reporting upon IT Service achievements and instigation of actions to eradicate poor service – in line with business or cost justification. Through these methods, a better relationship between IT and its Customers can be developed.

4.1.3 Scope for SLM

SLAs should be established for all IT Services being provided. Underpinning Contracts and Operational Level Agreements (OLAs) should also be in place with those suppliers (external and internal) upon who the delivery of service is dependent.

4.1.4 Basic concept of SLM

Service Level Management is the name given to the processes of planning, co-ordinating, drafting, agreeing, monitoring and reporting on SLAs, and the on-going review of service achievements to ensure that the required and cost-justifiable service quality is maintained and gradually improved. SLAs provide the basis for managing the relationship between the provider and the Customer.

When the first ITIL SLM book was published in 1989, very few organisations had SLAs in place. Today most organisations have introduced them – though with varying degrees of success. This version includes some coverage of the common causes of failure, and guidance on how to overcome these difficulties.

What is an SLA?

A written agreement between an IT Service Provider and the IT Customer(s), defining the key service targets and responsibilities of both parties. The emphasis must be on agreement and SLAs should not be used as away of holding one side or the other to ransom. A true partnership should be developed between the IT provider and the Customer, so that a mutually beneficial agreement is reached, otherwise the SLA could quickly fall into disrepute and a culture of blame prevent any true service quality improvements from taking place.

Figure 4.1 outlines the normal Customer/Service Level Management relationship:

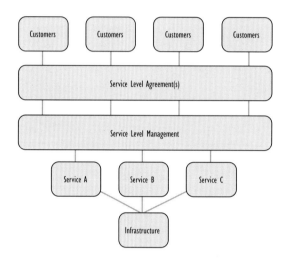

Figure 4.1 – Customer/Service Level Management Relationship

4.2   The SLM process

There is a definite SLM process that must be planned, implemented, executed and controlled. Figure 4.2 gives an overview of this:

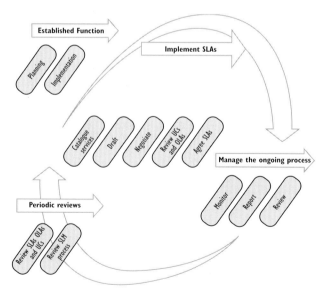

Figure 4.2 – SLM process

The steps in the process are described in detail in Sections 4.3 and 4.4.

4.2.1   Benefits of SLM

The improvements in service quality and the reduction in service disruption that can be achieved through effective SLM can ultimately lead to significant financial savings. Less time and effort is spent by IT staff in resolving fewer failures and IT Customers are able to perform their business functions without adverse impact.

Other specific benefits from SLM include:

- IT Services are designed to meet Service Level Requirements

- improved relationships with satisfied Customers

- both parties to the agreement have a clearer view of roles and responsibilities – thus avoiding potential misunderstandings or omissions

- there are specific targets to aim for and against which service quality can be measured, monitored and reported – 'if you aim at nothing, that is usually what you hit'

- IT effort is focused on those areas that the business thinks are key

- IT and Customers have a clear and consistent expectation of the level of service required (i.e. everyone understands and agrees what constitutes a 'Priority One' Incident, and everyone has a consistent understanding of what response and fix times are associated with something called 'Priority One')

- service monitoring allows weak areas to be identified, so that remedial action can be taken (if there is a justifiable business case), thus improving future service quality

- service monitoring also shows where Customer or User actions are causing the fault and so identify where working efficiency and/or training can be improved

- SLM underpins supplier management (and vice versa) – in cases where services are outsourced the SLAs are a key part of managing the relationship with the third-party in other cases service monitoring allows the performance of suppliers (internal and external) to be evaluated and managed

- SLA can be used as a basis for charging – and helps demonstrate what value Customers are receiving for their money.

The cumulative effect should lead to a gradual improvement in service quality and an overall reduction in the cost of service provision.

Anecdote

One organisation found that one of its local offices consistently showed up as having Incidents causing downtime on a regular basis every month. This was adversely affecting the national Availability figures for the entire organisation. When SLA breaches were investigated it was found that one particular set of Users were incorrectly entering commands which took the server down. This highlighted a service fragility but also a training need within that particular office, which, when addressed, dramatically increased their effectiveness and efficiency, and brought the national Availability figures back to what were more acceptable levels.

In addition SLM establishes – and keeps open – regular lines of communication between IT and its Customers. The beneficial impact of this should not be underestimated.

When a true 'partnership' develops then Problem identification and solving becomes much easier and productive. Where a 'blame' culture develops, this in itself becomes a block to service quality improvements, as both sides become protective and defensive in their dealings with each other.

4.2.2 Costs

The costs associated with implementing and executing SLM include:

- staff costs (salaries, training, recruitment costs, consultancy – if needed), both initial and ongoing
- accommodation costs
- support tools (monitoring and reporting, plus some element of integrated Service Management tools)
- hardware on which to run these tools
- marketing costs e.g. production of Service Catalogue.

This expenditure should however be seen as an investment and value-added rather than a cost.

4.2.3 Possible problems

Possible problems that might be encountered with SLM include:

- monitoring of pre-SLA achievements (particularly achieving the same perception as that held by the Customers) – *this is perhaps the most difficult problem that must be addressed first, as it impacts upon the next three*
- ensuring targets are achievable before committing to them
- verifying targets prior to agreement
- SLAs that are simply based upon desires rather than achievable targets
- inadequate focus, resources and time – often SLM is seen as something that can be done 'in the margins of time' – the ongoing resources are sometimes overlooked
- not enough seniority/authority given to Service Level Management to push through negotiations/improvements
- SLAs may not be supported by adequate contracts or underpinning agreements (see Paragraph 4.4.8)
- the responsibilities of each party are not clearly defined, creating a danger that some things fall 'between the cracks' and both parties deny responsibility for them
- being IT based rather than business aligned, especially where the business does not know its requirements
- SLAs may be too lengthy, not concise, not focused
- SLAs are not properly communicated
- for companies, SLM may be seen as an overhead rather than a Chargeable service
- many IT and business people seeing the SLM process primarily as a exercise in contract arbitration, to the exclusion of one of the primary aims of the SLM process: relationship building – as a result, the SLM process can become an exercise in 'relationship breaking'.

Why have some attempts to introduce SLM failed?

Each of the difficulties described above could have contributed to failure. If SLAs are not consistently and accurately defined, documented and monitored, and regular reviews held, then potential service improvement are not realised and SLAs may fall into disuse (or even disrepute). If this has occurred it is more difficult to resurrect them or to re-launch SLM. It is far better to recognise the potential difficulties in advance, to put the correct monitoring in place, to ensure that the function is properly resourced, and make sure that the initial attempt is successful.

In other cases, SLAs have been successfully agreed to at a management level, but the fact that they exist, and details of the agreed upon targets, have not been cascaded down to the operational level (either on the IT or Customer side, or both). In such cases the SLAs have not been actively used to drive up service quality as they should be. To avoid this difficulty it is recommended that SLAs are widely publicised and that summaries of agreed targets are held by all operational IT areas and particularly by the Service Desk. All staff should be clear on what is expected of them in order to ensure targets are met, and made aware of any penalties or consequences if targets are not met.

Anecdote

An Australian insurance company established some very basic SLAs in the late 1980s. Although very simple, they did specify the key Customer requirements and the Customer-supplier relationship was pretty good. After a few years a new IT manager was appointed who felt that the SLAs were too simplistic. They were replaced by far more complex documents including many targets that could not accurately be measured and reported. Within a fairly short time, Customers became dissatisfied with the SLA arrangements and IT grew disheartened because they could no longer show they were meeting requirements.

When the IT manager departed the decision was made to return to basics in order to regain Customer confidence in the SLA process. Key message: keep things simple and concentrate on the core customer requirements.

4.3 Planning the process

4.3.1 Initial planning activities

If SLM is not yet in place, there are a number of activities that must be planned. These include:

- appointment or nomination of Service Level Management and any necessary supporting staff – Annex 4A gives a description of the Role of a Service Level Manager
- production of a mission statement
- definition of the objectives and scope of the function
- an awareness campaign to win support for the function and to advise people how and when they might be affected
- definition of roles, tasks and responsibilities

- quantification of activities, resources, funding, quality criteria
- identification of risks
- planning of a Service Catalogue and an SLA structure
- drafting of a pilot SLA format
- identification of support tools, particularly for SLA monitoring
- setting and agreeing Incident priority levels and escalation paths, with Customers, and Internal and External providers (in conjunction with Service Desk and Problem Management).

In most cases it is appropriate for these activities to be incorporated within a formal project and managed via a recognised project management method, such as OGC's PRINCE2.

4.3.2 Plan monitoring capabilities

The importance of adequate capabilities for monitoring SLAs cannot be overstressed. Current monitoring tools and techniques must be reviewed – and action must be taken to improve these where necessary. See Paragraph 4.4.7 for further details.

4.3.3 Establish initial perception of the services

Before embarking on the introduction of SLM, it is worthwhile to attempt to evaluate the Customers' current perception of service levels, so that later the effectiveness of the SLA might be judged. This may also assist in determining the pace at which to proceed and the prioritisation of services to be addressed.

Be aware that the senior managers who are paying for the services may not be the ones who use them on a daily basis – so it is necessary to gather perceptions at all levels within the Customer community. At the same time it is also worthwhile seeking the perception of the service providers – they may not have been asked before and will have a different perspective from the Customers.

If monitoring is not yet in place, production of firm metrics may not yet be possible – but some form of Customer satisfaction survey or questionnaire may allow an overall impression to be gained. It is important to seek views both at management and at User/operational levels to gain the full perception. It is often the case that the operators of a system have a totally different perception from the Management, particularly where each is following a different agenda.

Experience has shown that face-to-face discussions or telephone surveys are more successful than questionnaires alone (both in terms of percentage returns and accuracy of information), though they are more costly and take longer to complete. A combination of the two is usually the most effective approach.

It may also be worthwhile trying to 'network' and get some ideas of reasonable expectation and targets (e.g. attend conferences, join User groups such as the itSMF).

4.3.4 Underpinning contracts and Operational Level Agreements

Plans must be made to review or implement contracts with external suppliers and OLAs with internal suppliers to ensure that underpinning services support the SLA targets. See Paragraph 4.4.8 for further details.

4.4   Implementing the process

When planning activities have been completed, the following activities must be undertaken to implement SLM.

4.4.1   Produce a Service Catalogue

Over the years, organisations' IT Infrastructures have grown and developed, and there may not be a clear picture of all the services currently being provided and the Customers of each. In order to establish an accurate picture, it is recommended that an IT Service Catalogue is produced.

Such a catalogue should list all of the services being provided, a summary of their characteristics and details of the Customers and maintainers of each. A degree of 'detective work' may be needed to compile this list and agree it with the Customers (sifting through old documentation, searching program libraries, talking with IT staff and Customers, looking at procurement records and talking with suppliers and contractors etc). If a CMDB or any sort of asset database exists, these may be a valuable source of information.

Hint

Service Desk Incident records are a good pointer to those old systems that everyone else but the User has forgotten about.

What is a service?

This question is not as easy to answer as it may first appear, and many organisations have failed to come up with a clear definition in an IT context. IT staff often confuse a 'service' as perceived by the Customer with an IT system. In many cases one 'service' can be made up of other 'services' (and so on) which are themselves made up of one or more IT systems within an overall Infrastructure including operations, networks, applications, etc. A good starting point is often to ask Customers which IT Services they use and how those services map onto their business processes. Customers often have a greater clarity of what they believe a service to be.

One possible definition may be: 'One or more IT systems which enable a business process'.

To avoid confusion, it may be a good idea to define a hierarchy of services within the Service Catalogue, by qualifying exactly what type of service is meant e.g. business service (that which is seen by the Customer), Infrastructure services, network service, application service (all invisible to the Customer – but essential to the delivery of Customer services).

When completed, the catalogue may initially consist of a matrix, table or spreadsheet. Some organisations integrate and maintain their Service Catalogue as part of their Configuration Management Database (CMDB). By defining each service as a Configuration Item (CI) and, where appropriate, relating these to form a service hierarchy, the organisation is able to relate events such as Incidents and RFCs to the services affected, thus providing the basis for service monitoring via an integrated tool (e.g. 'list or give the number of Incidents affecting this particular service'). This can work well and is recommended.

The Service Catalogue can also be used for other Service Management purposes (e.g. for performing a Business Impact Analysis (BIA) as part of IT Service Continuity Planning, or as a starting place for Workload Management, part of Capacity Management). The cost and effort of producing the catalogue is therefore easily justifiable. If done in conjunction with prioritisation of the BIA, then it is possible to ensure that the most important services are covered first. An example of a simple Service Catalogue that can be used as a starting point is given in Annex 4B.

4.4.2 Expectation Management

From the outset, it is wise to try and manage Customers' expectations. This means setting proper expectations in the first place, and putting a systematic process in place to manage expectations going forward, as satisfaction = expectation − perception. SLAs are just documents and in themselves do not materially alter the quality of service being provided (though they may affect behaviour and help engender an appropriate service culture, which can have an immediate beneficial effect, and make longer-term improvements possible). A degree of patience is therefore needed and should be built into expectations.

Where charges are being made for the services provided, this should modify Customer demands (Customers can have whatever they can cost justify − providing it fits within agreed corporate strategy − and have authorised budget for, but no more!). Where direct charges are not made, the support of senior business managers should be enlisted to ensure that excessive or unrealistic demands are not placed upon the IT provider by any individual Customer group

4.4.3 Plan the SLA structure

Using the catalogue as an aid, Service Level Management must plan the most appropriate SLA structure to ensure that all services and all Customers are covered in a manner best suited to the organisation's needs. There are a number of potential options, including:

Service based

Where an SLA covers one service, for all the Customers of that service. For example an SLA may be established for an organisation's E-mail service, covering all of the Customers of that service.

This may appear fairly straightforward. However, difficulties may arise if the specific requirements of different Customers vary for the same service, or if characteristics of the IT Infrastructure mean that different service levels are inevitable (e.g. head office staff may be connected via a high-speed LAN while local offices may have to use a lower speed leased line). In such cases, separate targets may be needed within the one agreement. Difficulties may also arise in determining who should be the signatories to such an agreement.

Customer based

An agreement with an individual Customer group, covering all the services they use. For example, agreements may be reached with an organisation's Finance Department covering, say, the Finance System, the Accounting System, the Payroll System, the Billing System, the Procurement System and any other IT systems that they use.

Customers often prefer such an agreement, as all of their requirements are covered in a single document. Only one signatory is normally required, which simplifies this issue.

Hint and tips

**A combination of either of these structures might be appropriate, providing all
services and Customers are covered, with no overlap or duplication.**

Multi-level SLAs

Some organisations have chosen to adopt a multi-level SLA structure. For example, a three-layer
structure as follows:

1. Corporate Level: covering all the generic SLM issues appropriate to every Customer
   throughout the organisation. These issues are likely to be less volatile and so updates are
   less frequently required.

2. Customer Level: covering all SLM issues relevant to the particular Customer group,
   regardless of the service being used.

3. Service Level: covering all SLM issues relevant to the specific service, in relation to this
   specific Customer group (one for each service covered by the SLA).

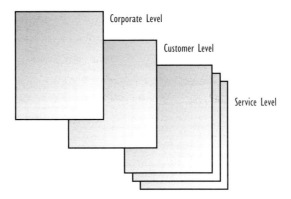

Figure 4.3 – Multi-level SLAs

As shown in Figure 4.3, such a structure allows SLAs to be kept to a manageable size, avoids
unnecessary duplication, and reduces the need for frequent updates.

Example

The UK Employment Service successfully used a three-level SLA format. They
used the titles: Framework, Standard, Specific to describe their 3 levels – but
the concept was basically the same as described above.

4.4.4   Establish Service Level Requirements and Draft SLA

It is difficult to give guidance on which of these should come first – since it is often an iterative
process. Once the SLA structure has been agreed, a first SLA must be drafted. It is advisable to involve
Customers from the outset, but rather than going along with a blank sheet to commence with, it may
be better to produce a first outline draft as a starting point for more detailed and in-depth

discussion. Be careful though not to go too far and appear to be presenting the Customer with a fait accompli.

It can be difficult to draw out requirements, as the business may not know what they want – especially if not asked before and they may need help in understanding and defining their needs. Be aware that the requirements initially expressed may not be those ultimately agreed – they are more likely to change where charging is in place. Several iterations of negotiations may be required before an affordable balance is struck between what is sought and what is achievable and affordable.

Many organisations have found it valuable to produce a pro-forma that can be used as a starting point for all SLAs. The proforma can often be developed alongside the pilot SLA. Guidance on the items to be included in an SLA is given in Section 4.6.

Hints and tips

Make roles and responsibilities a part of the SLA. Consider three perspectives, the IT provider, the IT Customer, and the actual Users.

4.4.5   Wording of SLAs

The wording of SLAs should be clear and concise and leave no room for ambiguity. There is normally no need for agreements to be couched in legal terminology, and plain language aids a common understanding. It is often helpful to have an independent person, who has not been involved with the drafting, to do a final read-through. This often throws up potential ambiguities and difficulties that can then be addressed and clarified.

It is also worth remembering that SLAs may have to cover services offered internationally. In such cases the SLA may have to be translated into several languages. Remember also that an SLA drafted in a single language may have to be reviewed for suitability in several different parts of the world (i.e. aversion drafted in Australia may have to be reviewed for suitability in the USA or the UK – and differences in terminology, style and culture must be taken into account).

4.4.6   Seek agreement

Using the draft agreement as a basis, negotiations must be held with the Customer(s), or Customer representatives to finalise the contents of the SLA and the initial service level targets, and with the service providers to ensure that these are achievable. Guidance on general negotiating techniques is included in the ITIL Business and Management Skills book.

One problem that might be encountered is identifying a suitable Customer to negotiate. Who 'owns' the service? In some cases this may be obvious, and a single Customer manager is willing to act as the signatory to the agreement. In other cases, it might take quite a bit of negotiating or cajoling to find a representative 'volunteer' (beware that volunteers often want to express their own personal view rather than represent a general consensus), or it may be necessary to get all Customers to sign (messy!).

If Customer representatives exist who are able to genuinely represent the views of the Customer community, because they frequently meet with a wide selection of them, this is ideal. Unfortunately, all too often so-called representatives are head-office based and seldom come into contact with genuine service Customers. In the worst-case, Service Level Management may have to perform his/her own programme of discussions and meetings with Customers to ensure true requirements are identified.

Anecdote

On negotiating the current and support hours for a large system an organisation found a discrepancy in the required time of usage between Head Office and the field offices Customers. Head Office (with a limited User population) wanted Service Hours covering 8am to 6pm, whereas the field (with at least 20 times the User population) stated that starting an hour earlier would be better – but all offices closed to the Public by 4pm at the latest and so wouldn't require a service much beyond this. Head Office won the 'political' argument and so the 8am to 6pm band was set. When the Service came to be used (and hence monitored) it was found that Service extensions were usually asked for by the field to cover the extra hour in the morning, and actual usage figures showed that the system had not been accessed after 5pm, except on very rare occasions. The Service Level Manager was blamed by the IT staff for having to cover a late shift, and by the customer Representative for charging for a service that was not used (i.e. staff and running costs).

Hints and tips

Care should be taken when opening discussions on service levels for the first time, as it is likely that 'current issues' (the failure that occurred yesterday!) or long-standing grievances (that old printer that we have been trying to get replaced for ages!) are likely to be aired at the outset. Important though these may be, they must not be allowed to get in the way of establishing the longer-term requirements. Be aware however that it may well be necessary to address any issues raised at the outset before gaining any credibility to progress further.

If there has been no previous experience of SLM, then it is advisable to start with a pilot SLA. A decision should be made on which services/Customers to be used for the pilot. It is helpful if the selected Customer is enthusiastic and wishes to participate – perhaps because they are anxious to see improvements in service quality. The results of the initial Customer perception survey may give pointers to a suitable pilot.

Hints and tips

Don't pick an area where large Problems exist as pilot. Try to pick an area that is likely to show some quick benefits and develop the SLM Process. Nothing breeds acceptance of a new idea quicker than success.

One difficulty sometimes encountered is that staff at different levels within the Customer community may have different objectives and perceptions. For example a senior manager may rarely use a service and may be more interested in issues such as value for money and output, whereas a junior member of staff may use the service throughout the day and may be more interested in issues such as responsiveness, usability and reliability. It is important that all of the appropriate and relevant Customer's requirements, at all levels, are identified and incorporated in SLAs.

Some organisations have formed focus groups from different levels from within the Customer community to assist in successfully ensuring that all issues have been correctly addressed. This takes additional resources, but can be well worth the effort.

The other group of people that have to be consulted during the whole of this process is the appropriate representatives from within the IT provider side (whether internal or from a third-party supplier). They need to agree that targets are realistic, achievable and affordable. If they are not, further negotiations are needed until a compromise acceptable to all parties is agreed. The views of suppliers should also be sought and any contractual implications should be taken into account during the negotiation stages.

Where no past monitored data is available, it is advisable to leave the agreement in draft format for an initial period, until monitoring can confirm that initial targets are achievable. Targets may have to be re-negotiated in some cases. When targets have been confirmed, the SLAs must be signed.

Once the pilot has been completed and any initial difficulties overcome, then move on and gradually introduce SLAs for other services/Customers. If it is decided from the outset to go for a multi-level structure, it is likely that the corporate-level issues have to be covered for all Customers at the time of the initial pilot. It is also worth trialling the corporate issues during this pilot phase.

> **Hints and tips**
>
> **Don't go for easy targets at the Corporate level; they may be easy to achieve but have no value in improving Service Quality. Also if the targets are set at a high enough level the Corporate SLA can be used as the standard that all new services should reach.**

One point to ensure is that at the end of the drafting and negotiating process, the SLA is actually signed by the appropriate managers on the Customer and IT provider sides to the agreement. This gives a firm commitment by both parties that every attempt will be made to meet the agreement by both sides. Generally speaking, the more senior the signatories are within their respective organisations, the stronger the message of commitment. Once an SLA is agreed, wide publicity needs to be used to ensure that Customers and IT providers alike are aware of its existence, and of the key targets.

It is important that the Service Desk staff are committed to the SLM process and become proactive ambassadors for SLAs, embracing the necessary service culture, as they are the first contact point for Customers' Incidents, complaints and queries. If the Service Desk Staff are not fully aware of SLAs in place and do not act upon them then Customers very quickly lose faith in SLAs.

4.4.7   Establish monitoring capabilities

Nothing should be included in an SLA unless it can be effectively monitored and measured at a commonly agreed point. The importance of this cannot be overstressed, as inclusion of items that cannot be effectively monitored almost always result in disputes and eventual loss of faith in the SLM process. A lot of organisations have discovered this the 'hard way' and as a consequence, have absorbed heavy costs both in a financial sense as well as in terms of negative impacts on their culture.

Anecdote

A global network provider agreed Availability targets for the provision of a managed network service. These Availability targets were agreed at the point where the service entered the Customer's premises. However, the global network provider could only monitor and measure Availability at the point the connection left its premises. The network links were provided by a number of different national Telecommunications service providers, with widely varying Availability levels. The result was a complete mis-match between the Availability figures produced by the network provider and the Customer, with correspondingly prolonged and heated debate and argument.

Existing monitoring capabilities should be reviewed and upgraded as necessary. Ideally this should be done ahead of, or in parallel with, the drafting of SLAs, so that monitoring can be in place to assist with the validation of proposed targets.

It is essential that monitoring matches the Customer's true perception of the service. Unfortunately this is often very difficult to achieve. For example, monitoring of individual components, such as the network or server, does not guarantee that the service will be available so far as the Customer is concerned – a desktop or application failure may mean that the service cannot be used by the Customer. Without monitoring all components in the end-to-end service (which may be very difficult and costly to achieve) a true picture cannot be gained. Similarly, Users must be aware that they should report Incidents immediately to aid diagnostics, especially if performance related.

Where multiple services are delivered to a single workstation, it is probably more effective to record only downtime against the service the User was trying to access at the time (though this needs to be agreed with the Customers). Customer perception is often that although a failure might affect more than one service all they are bothered about is the service they cannot access at the time of the reported Incident – though this is not always true, so caution is needed.

A considerable number of organisations use their Service Desk, linked to a comprehensive CMDB, to monitor the Customer's perception of Availability. This may involve making specific Changes to Incident/Problem logging screens and require stringent compliance with Incident logging procedures. All of this needs discussion and agreement with the Availability Management function. Chapter 8 gives guidance and examples of the formulae that might be used to determine service Availability levels, and the amendments that may be needed to capture the required data.

The Service Desk is also used to monitor Incident response times and resolution times, but once again the logging screen might need amendment to accommodate data capture, and call logging procedures may need tightening and must be strictly followed. If support is being provided by a third-party, this monitoring may also underpin supplier management.

It is essential to ensure that any Incident/Problem handling targets included in SLAs are the same as those included in Service Desk tools and used for escalation and monitoring purposes. Where organisations have failed to recognise this, and perhaps used defaults provided by the tool supplier, they have ended up in a situation where they are monitoring something different from that which has been agreed in the SLAs, and are therefore unable to say whether SLA targets have been met, without considerable effort to massage the data.

Some amendments may be needed to support tools, to include the necessary fields so that relevant data can be captured.

Another notoriously difficult area to monitor is transaction response times (the time between sending a screen and receiving a response). Often end-to-end response times are technically very difficult to monitor. In such cases it may be appropriate to deal with this as follows:

a. Include a statement in the SLA along the following lines 'The services covered by this SLA are designed for high-speed response and no significant delays should be encountered. If a response time delay of more than x seconds is experienced for more than y minutes this should be reported immediately to the Service Desk'.

b. Agree and include in the SLA an acceptable target for the number of such Incidents that can be tolerated in the reporting period.

c. Create an Incident category 'poor response' (or similar) and ensure that any such Incidents are logged accurately and that they are related to the appropriate service.

d. Produce regular reports of occasions where SLA transaction response time targets have been breached, and instigate investigations via Problem Management to correct the situation.

This approach not only overcomes the technical difficulties of monitoring, but also ensures that incidences of poor response are reported at the time they are occurring. This is very important as poor response is often caused by a number of interacting events, which can only be detected if they are investigated immediately (the 'smoking gun' syndrome!).

The preferred method however is to implement some form of automated client/server response time monitoring. These tools are becoming increasingly available and increasingly more cost effective to use. These tools provide the ability to measure or sample actual or very similar response times to those being experienced by a variety of Users.

Hints and tips

Some organisations have found that in reality 'poor response' is sometimes a problem of User perception. The User, having become used to a particular level of response over a period of time, starts complaining as soon as this is slower. Take the view that 'if the User thinks the system is slow – then it is'.

If the SLA includes targets for assessing and implementing Requests for Charge (RFCs), the monitoring of targets relating to Change Management should ideally be carried out using whatever Change Management tool is in use (preferably part of an integrated Service Management support tool) and Change logging screens and escalation processes should support this.

There are a number of important 'soft' issues that cannot be monitored by mechanistic or procedural means, such as Customers' overall feelings (these need not necessarily match the 'hard' monitoring). For example, even when there have been a number of reported service failures the Customers may still feel positive about things, because they may feel satisfied that appropriate actions are being taken to improve things. Of course, the opposite may apply and Customers may feel dissatisfied with some issues (e.g. the manner of some staff on the Service Desk) when few or no SLA targets have been broken.

It is therefore recommended that attempts are made to monitor Customer perception on these soft issues. Methods of doing this include:

- telephone perception surveys (perhaps at random, or using regular Customer liaison representatives)

- periodic questionnaires

- satisfaction survey handouts (left with Customers following installations, service visits etc.)

- User group meetings.

Where possible, targets should be set for these and monitored as part of the SLA (e.g. an average score of 3.5 should be achieved by the service provider on results given, based on a scoring system of 1 to 5, where 1 is poor performance and 5 is excellent). Ensure that if Users provide feedback they receive some return and demonstrate to them that their comments have been incorporated in an action plan, perhaps a Service Improvement Programme.

4.4.8   Review Underpinning Contracts and Operational Level Agreements

Most IT Service Providers are dependent to some extent on their own suppliers (both internal and/or external). They cannot commit to meeting SLA targets unless their own suppliers' performances underpin these targets. Contracts with external suppliers are mandatory, but many organisations have also identified the benefits of having simple agreements with internal support groups, usually referred to as OLAs. Figure 4.4 illustrates this.

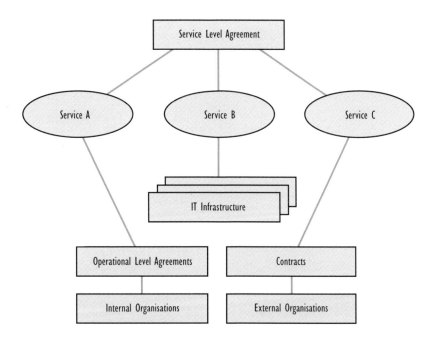

Figure 4.4 – SLA Support Structure

OLAs need not be very complicated, but should set out specific back-to-back targets for support groups that underpin the targets included in SLAs. For example, if the SLA includes overall time to respond and fix targets for Incidents (varying on the priority levels), then the OLAs should include targets for the each of the elements in the support chain (target for the Service Desk to answer calls, escalate etc, targets for Network Support to start to investigate and to resolve network related errors assigned to them). In addition, overall support hours should be stipulated for all groups that underpin the required service Availability times in the SLA. If special procedures exist for contacted staff (e.g. out of hours telephone support) these must also be documented.

It must be understood however that the Incident resolution targets included in SLAs should not normally match the same targets included in contracts or OLAs with suppliers. This is because the SLA targets must include an element for all stages in the support cycle (e.g. Detection time, Service Desk logging time, escalation time, referral time between groups etc, Service Desk review and closure time – as well as the actual time fixing the failure). The SLA target should cover all of this.

Before committing to SLAs, it is therefore important that existing contractual arrangements are investigated and where necessary, upgraded. This is likely to incur additional costs, which must either be absorbed by IT, or passed on to the Customer. In the latter case the Customer must agree to this, or the more relaxed targets in existing contracts should be agreed for inclusion in SLAs.

OLAs should be monitored against these targets and feedback given to the Managers of the support groups. This highlights potential problem areas, which may need to be addressed internally or by a further review of the SLA. Serious consideration should be given to introducing formal OLAs where they do not already exist.

4.4.9 Define Reporting and Review Procedures

The SLA reporting mechanisms, intervals and report formats must be defined and agreed with the Customers. The frequency and format of Service Review Meetings must also be agreed with the Customers. Regular intervals are recommended. Periodic reports should fit in with the reviewing cycle.

The SLAs themselves must be reviewed periodically (e.g. annually in line with financial cycle) to ensure that they are still current and indeed still relevant – does the SLA still fit the needs of the business and the capabilities of IT? All SLAs should be under strict Change Management control and any Changes should be reflected in an update to the Service Catalogue, if needed.

4.4.10 Publicise the existence of SLAs

Steps must be taken to advertise the existence of the new SLAs amongst the Service Desk and other support groups with details of when they become operational. It may be helpful to extract key targets from the SLAs into tables that can be on display in support areas – so that staff are always aware of the targets to which they are working. If support tools allow it, these targets should be included as thresholds and automatically alerted against when a target is threatened or actually breached. SLAs and the targets they contain must also be publicised amongst the User community, so that Users are aware of what they can expect from the services they use, and know at what point to start to express dissatisfaction.

4.5 The On-going process

The following ongoing activities must be undertaken to execute the process.

4.5.1   Monitoring and Reporting

Immediately the SLA is agreed, monitoring must be instigated, and service achievement reports must be produced. Operational reports must be produced frequently (daily – perhaps even more frequently), and where possible, exception reports should be produced whenever an SLA has been broken (or threatened if appropriate thresholds have been set to give an 'early warning').

Periodic reports must be produced and circulated to Customers (or their representatives) and appropriate IT managers a few days in advance of SLA reviews, so that any queries or disagreements can be resolved ahead of the review meeting. The meeting is not then diverted by such issues.

The periodic report should incorporate details of performance against all SLA targets, together with details of any trends or specific actions being undertaken to improve service quality. Annex 4C gives an example of an SLA Monitoring (SLAM) chart which can be used at the front of the report to give an 'at a glance' overview of how achievements have measured up against targets. These are most effective if colour coded (**R**ed-**A**mber-**G**reen, and sometimes referred to as RAG charts as a result). Other interim reports may be required by IT management for internal performance reviews and/or supplier or contract management. This is likely to be an evolving process – a first effort is unlikely to be the final outcome.

The resources required to produce and verify reports should not be underestimated. It can be extremely time consuming, and if reports do not reflect the Customer's own perception of service quality accurately, they can add insult to injury.

Service Level Management should identify the specific reporting needs and automate production of these reports, so far as possible. The extent, accuracy and ease with which automated reports can be produced should form part of the selection criteria for integrated support tools.

4.5.2   Service review meetings

Periodic review meetings must be held on a regular basis with Customers (or their representatives) to review the service achievement in the last period and to preview any issues for the coming period. It is normal to hold such meetings monthly, or as a minimum, quarterly.

Actions must be placed on the Customer and provider as appropriate to improve weak areas where targets are not being met. All actions must be minuted, and progress should be reviewed at the next meeting to ensure that action items are being followed up and properly implemented.

Particular attention should be focused on each breach of service levels to determine exactly what caused the loss of service and what can be done to prevent any recurrence. If it is decided that the service level was, or has become, unachievable, it may be necessary to review and re-agree different service targets. If the service break has been caused by a failure of a third-party or internal support group, it may also be necessary to review the underpinning agreement or OLA.

Hints and tips

'A spy in both camps' – Service Level Managers can be viewed with a certain amount of suspicion by both the IT Service Provider staff and the Customer representatives. This is due to the dual nature of the job where they are acting as an unofficial Customer representative when talking to IT staff, and as an IT provider rep when talking to the Customers. This is usually aggravated when having to represent the 'opposition's' point of view in any meeting etc. To avoid this the Service Level manager should be as open and helpful as possible (within the bounds of commercial propriety), when dealing with both sides. Ambassador for IT, lonely job, finds allies in other Service Level Managers (e.g.via itSMF). Never vent frustrations about colleagues with the client community – or criticise a colleague in public.

4.5.3   Service Improvement Programme

The SLM process often generates a good starting point for a Service Improvement Programme (SIP) – and the service review process may drive this.

Where an underlying difficulty has been identified which is adversely impacting upon service quality, Service Level Management must, in conjunction with Problem Management and Availability Management, instigate a SIP to identify and implement whatever actions are necessary to overcome the difficulties and restore service quality. Further guidance on this and the specific techniques that might be used can be found in Chapter 6 of the Service Support book and in Chapter 8 of this book. SIP initiatives may also focus on such issues as User training, system testing and documentation. In these cases the relevant people need to be involved and adequate feed-back given to make improvements for the future. At any time, a number of separate initiatives that form part of the SIP may be running in parallel to address difficulties with a number of services.

Some organisations have established an up-front annual budget held by SLM from which SIP initiatives can be funded. This means that action can be undertaken quickly and that SLM is demonstratively effective. This practice should be encouraged and expanded to enable SLM to be become increasingly proactive and predictive.

If an organisation is outsourcing its Service Delivery to a third party, the issue of service improvement should be discussed at the outset and covered (and budgeted for) in the contract, otherwise there is no incentive during the lifetime of the contract for the supplier to improve service targets if they are already meeting contractual obligations and additional expenditure is needed to make the improvements.

4.5.4   Maintenance of SLAs, contracts and OLAs

SLAs, underpinning contracts and OLAs must be kept up to date. They should be brought under Change Management control and reviewed periodically, at least annually, to ensure that they are still current and comprehensive, and still aligned to business needs and strategy.

These reviews should ensure that the services covered and the targets for each are still relevant – and that nothing significant has changed that invalidates the agreement in any way (this should include Infrastructure Changes, business Changes, supplier Changes etc). Where Changes are detected, the agreements must be updated under Change Management control to reflect the new situation.

4.6   SLA contents and key targets

The specific content and the initial targets to be included in SLAs must be agreed. It is difficult to be prescriptive, as each situation is unique, and content varies depending upon the type of SLA, but there are a number of common features that often occur within SLAs. These include:

Introduction

- parties to the agreement
- title and brief description of the agreement
- signatories
- dates: start, end, review
- scope of the agreement; what is covered and what is excluded
- responsibilities of both the service provider and the Customer
- a description of the services covered.

Service hours

- the hours that each service is normally required (e.g. 24x7, Monday to Friday 08:00 – 18:00)
- arrangement for requesting service extensions, including required notice periods (e.g. request must be made to the Service Desk by 12 noon for an evening extension, by 12 noon on Thursday for a week-end extension)
- special Hours (e.g. public holidays)
- service calendar.

Availability

- Availability targets within agreed hours, normally expressed as percentages – measurement period and method must be stipulated. This may be expressed for the overall service, underpinning services and critical components or all three. However, it is difficult to relate such simplistic percentage Availability figures to service quality, or to Customer business activities. It is therefore often better to try to measure service UnAvailability (see Paragraph 8.4.4) in terms of the Customer's inability to carry out its business activities. For example, 'sales are immediately affected by a failure of IT to provide an adequate POS support service'. This strong link between the IT Service and the Customer's business processes is a sign of maturity in both the SLM and the Availability Management processes.

Reliability

- usually expressed as the number of service breaks, or the Mean Time Between Failures (MTBF) or Mean Time Between System Incidents (MTBSI).

Support

- support hours (where these are not the same as Service hours)
- arrangement for requesting support extensions, including required notice periods (e.g. request must be made to the Service Desk by 12 noon for an evening extension, by 12 noon on Thursday for a week-end extension)
- special hours (e.g. public holidays)

- target time to respond, either physically or by other method (e.g. telephone contact, email), to Incidents

- target time to resolve Incidents, within each Incident priority – targets varies depending upon Incident priorities.

Throughput

- Indication of likely traffic volumes and throughput activity (e.g. the number of transactions to be processed, number of concurrent Users, amount of data to be transmitted over the network). This is important so that performance issues which have been caused by excessive throughput outside the terms of the agreement may be identified.

Transaction response times

- target times for average, or maximum workstation response times (sometimes expressed as a percentile – e.g. 95% within 2 seconds – but see recommendations in Paragraph 4.4.7).

Batch turnaround times

- times for delivery of input and the time and place for delivery of output.

Change

- targets for approving, handling and implementing RFCs, usually based upon the category or urgency/priority of the Change.

IT Service Continuity and Security

- a brief mention of IT Service Continuity Plans and how to invoke them, and coverage of any security issues, particularly any responsibilities of the Customer (e.g. back-up of freestanding PCs, password Changes)

- details of any diminished or amended service targets should a disaster situation occur (if no separate SLA exists for such a situation).

Charging

- details of the charging formula and periods (if charges are being made). If the SLA covers an outsourcing relationship, charges should be detailed in an Annex as they are often covered by commercial in confidence provisions.

Service reporting and reviewing

- the content, frequency and distribution of service reports, and the frequency of service review meetings.

Performance incentives/penalties

- Details of any agreement regarding financial incentives or penalties based upon performance against service levels. These are more likely to be included if the services are being provided by a third-party organisation. It should be noted that penalty clauses can create their own difficulties. They can prove a barrier to partnership if unfairly invoked on a technicality and can also make service provider staff unwilling to admit to mistakes for fear of penalties being imposed. This can, unless used properly, be a barrier to effective problem solving.

It should be noted that the SLA contents given above are examples only. They should not be regarded as exhaustive or mandatory, but they provide a good starting point. A Skeleton SLA is provided at Annex 4D.

4.6.1 New services

Service Level Requirements

While many organisations have to give initial priority to introducing SLAs for existing services, it is also important to establish procedures for agreeing Service Level Requirements (SLRs) for new services being developed or procured.

The SLRs should be an integral part of the service design criteria, of which the functional specification is a part. They should, from the very outset, form part of the testing/trialling criteria as the service progresses through the stages of design and development or procurement. A draft SLA should be developed alongside the service itself, and should be signed and formalised before the service is introduced into live use.

Support planning

Another area that requires attention, if new services are to be introduced in a seamless way into the live environment, is the planning and formalisation of the support arrangements. Advice should be sought from Change Management, Configuration Management and Release Management to ensure the planning is comprehensive. Specific responsibilities need to be defined and either added to existing contracts/OLAs, or new ones need to be agreed. The support arrangement and all escalation routes also need adding to the CMDB, so that Release Management, the Service Desk and other support staff are aware of them. Where appropriate, initial training and familiarisation for the Service Desk and other support groups must be instigated before live support is needed.

It should be noted that additional support resources (i.e. more staff) may be needed to support new services. There is often an expectation that an already overworked support group can magically cope with the additional effort imposed by a new service!

4.7 Key Performance Indicators and metrics for SLM efficiency and effectiveness

The following Key Performance Indicators (KPIs) and metrics can be used to judge the efficiency and effectiveness of the SLM processes and function:

- what number or percentage of services are covered by SLAs?
- are underpinning contracts and OLAs in place for all SLAs and for what percentage?
- are SLAs being monitored and are regular reports being produced?
- are review meetings being held on time and correctly minuted?
- is there documentary evidence that issues raised at reviews are being followed up and resolved (e.g. via an SIP)
- are SLAs, OLAs and underpinning contracts current and what percentage are in need of review and update?
- what number or percentage of service targets are being met and what is the number and severity of service breaches?

- are service breaches being followed up effectively?
- are service level achievements improving
- are Customer perception statistics improving?
- are IT costs decreasing for services with stable (acceptable but not improving) service level achievements?

Hints and tips

Don't fall into the trap of using percentages as the only metric. It is easy to get caught out when there is a small system with limited measurement points (i.e. a single failure on a population of 100 is only 1%, then the SLA is already breached. Always go for number of Incidents rather than a percentage on populations of less than 100 and be careful what targets are accepted. This is something some organisations have learned the hard way!

Annex 4A   Service Level Manager – Role, responsibilities and key skills

The SLM process must be 'owned' in order to be effective and achieve successfully the benefits of implementation. This is not meant to imply that this should be a single post, unless that is appropriate within the organisation. However if the role is split, care should be taken to avoid giving tasks to people with 'fire-fighting' type roles, as they will not have the time to manage the majority of the required tasks pro-actively.

The skills list given is an indication of the types of skills which would be present in an 'ideal candidate in an ideal world'. As long as most are present then a potentially good candidate for the post has been found.

Role

To implement and maintain the SLM process to the level required by the parent organisation.

Role positioning

The role must be of an appropriate level to negotiate with Customers on behalf of the organisation, and to initiate and follow through actions required to improve or maintain agreed service levels. This requires adequate seniority within the organisation and/or clearly visible management support.

Responsibilities

- creates and maintains a catalogue of existing services offered by the organisation
- formulates, agrees and maintains an appropriate SLM structure for the organisation, to include
  - SLA structure (e.g. Service based, Customer based or multi-level)
  - OLAs within the IT Provider organisation
  - Third Party Supplier/Contract Management relationships to the SLM Process
  - accommodating any existing Service Improvement Plans/Programmes within the SLM process
- negotiates, agrees and maintains the Service Level Agreements with the Customer
- negotiates, agrees and maintains the Operational Level Agreements with the IT provider
- negotiates and agrees with both the Customer and IT Provider any Service Level Requirements for any proposed new/developing services
- analyses and reviews service performance against the SLAs and OLAs
- produces regular reports on service performance and achievement to the Customer and IT provider at an appropriate level
- organises and maintains the regular Service Level review process with both the IT Customer and IT provider which covers
  - reviewing outstanding actions from previous reviews
  - current performance
  - reviewing Service Levels and targets (where necessary)
  - reviewing underpinning agreements and OLAs as necessary
  - agreeing appropriate actions to maintain/improve service levels
- initiates any actions required to maintain or improve service levels
- conducts annual (as appropriate) reviews of the entire Service Level process and negotiates, agrees and controls any amendments necessary

- acts as co-ordination point for any temporary Changes to service levels required (i.e. extra support hours required by the Customer, reduced Levels of Service over a period of maintenance required by the IT provider etc.).

Key skills

- Relationship Management skills
- a good understanding of the IT Providers services and qualifying factors in order to understand how Customer requirements will affect delivery
- an understanding of the Customer's business and how IT contributes to the delivery of that product or service
- excellent communication and negotiation skills
- patience, tolerance and resilience
- knowledge and experience of contract and/or supplier management roles
- good people management and administrative skills
- good understanding of statistical and analytical principles and processes
- good presentational skills
- reasonable numeric skills
- the ability to interact successfully with all levels of the Customer and IT Provider organisation
- reasonable technical understanding and an ability to translate technical requirements and specifications into easily understood business concepts and vice versa
- innovative in respect of service quality and ways in which it can be improved within the bounds of the organisation's limits (resource, budgetary, legal etc.)
- a good listener with the ability to apply the knowledge gained effectively
- even-handed and fair in dealings with other parties.

Annex 4B Example of a simple Service Catalogue

Service	Customer	Accounts	Sales	Marketing	Legal	Production	Retail	Warehouse	Transport	Design
Payroll System		✓								
Accounts System		✓	✓	✓	✓		✓			
Invoicing		✓	✓		✓		✓			
Customer D/Base		✓	✓	✓	✓		✓	✓	✓	
Sales D/Base		✓	✓	✓			✓	✓	✓	
Stock Control						✓		✓	✓	
Legal System					✓					
Factory Production						✓		✓		✓
Suppliers D/Base		✓	✓	✓	✓	✓	✓	✓	✓	
Ordering		✓	✓	✓	✓	✓	✓	✓	✓	
Logistics						✓	✓	✓	✓	
Postal Addresses		✓	✓	✓	✓	✓	✓	✓	✓	
CAD/CAM						✓				✓
Intranet		✓	✓	✓	✓	✓	✓	✓	✓	✓
Internet		✓	✓	✓	✓		✓			✓
Routemaster			✓					✓	✓	
Office Suite		✓	✓	✓	✓	✓	✓	✓	✓	✓
E-mail		✓	✓	✓	✓	✓	✓	✓	✓	✓

Annex 4C   Example SLAM Chart

Period / Target	1	2	3	4	5	6	7	8	9	10	11	
A										■		
B												
C								■				
D												
E				■								
F						▨						
G												
H		▨		■							▨	
I				■								
J												

□ SLA MET	■ SLA Breached	▨ SLA Threatened

Annex 4D   Skeleton Service Level Agreement

SERVICE LEVEL AGREEMENT

FOR THE

ABC SERVICE

Version 1.0
dd/mm/yy
Author: whoever

SERVICE LEVEL AGREEMENT FOR THE ABC SERVICE

This agreement is made between...

and..

The agreement covers the provIsIon and support of the ABC services which..... (brief service description).

This agreement remains valid until superseded by a revised agreement mutually endorsed by the signatories below. The agreement will be reviewed annually. Minor Changes may be recorded on the form at the end of the agreement, providing they are mutually endorsed by the two parties.

Signatories:

Name.. Position...................................... Date ....

Name.. Position...................................... Date ....

Details of previous amendments:

Service Description:

The ABC Service consists of .... (fuller description to include key business functions, deliverables and all relevant information to describe the service and its scale, impact and priority for the business).

Service Hours

A description of the hours that the Customers can expect the service to be available (e.g. 7 x 24 x 365, 08:00 to 18:00 – Monday to Friday).

Special conditions for exceptions (e.g. weekends, public holidays etc).

Procedures for requesting service extensions (who to contact – *normally the Service Desk* – and what notice periods are required).

Details of any pre-agreed maintenance or housekeeping slots, if these impact upon service hours, together with details of how any other potential outages must be negotiated and agreed – by whom and notice periods etc.

Procedures for requesting permanent Changes to services hours.

Service Availability

The target Availability levels that the IT Provider will seek to deliver within the agreed service hours (normally expressed as a percentage – e.g. 99.5%).

Agreed details of how this will be measured and reported, and over what agreed period.

Reliability

The maximum number of service breaks that can be tolerated within an agreed period (may be defined as number of breaks e.g. 4 per annum, or as a mean-time-between-failure (MTBF)).

Definition of what constitutes a 'break' and how these will be monitored and recorded.

Customer Support

Details of how to contact the Service Desk, the hours it will be available, and what to do outside these hours to obtain assistance (e.g. on-call support, third-party assistance etc). May include reference to Internet/Intranet Self Help and/or Incident logging.

Call answer targets (no of rings, missed calls etc).

Targets for Incident response times (how long will it be before someone starts to assist the Customer – may include travelling time etc). Definition is needed of 'response' – a telephone call back to the Customer? Or a site visit? – as appropriate.

Targets for Incident resolution (Fix) times.

Note. Both Incident response and resolution times will be based upon whatever Incident impact/priority codes are used – details of which must be included here.

Note. In some cases, it may be appropriate to reference out to third-party contacts of OLAs – but not as a way of diverting responsibility.

Service Performance

Details of the expected responsiveness of the IT Service (e.g. target workstation response times, details of expected service throughput on which targets are based, and any thresholds that would invalidate the targets).

Note. Workstation response is very difficult to agree and monitor. Organisations may therefore wish to include a statement to the effect:

'This service has been designed for high speed performance. Any workstation response times that exceed n seconds for a period of n minutes must be reported immediately to the Service Desk (*please see Section n.n for further details of how to handle such reports*).'

If appropriate, details of any Batch turnaround times, completion times and key deliverables.

Functionality (if appropriate)

Details of the number of errors of particular types that can be tolerated before the SLA is breached. Should include Severity Levels and the reporting period.

Change Management Procedures

Brief mention of and/or reference out to the organisation's Change Management procedures that must be followed – just to re-enforce compliance.

Details of any known Changes that will impact upon the agreement, if any.

IT Service Continuity

Brief mention of and/or reference out to the organisation's IT Service Continuity Plans, together with details of how the SLA might be affected. Details of any specific responsibilities on both sides (e.g. data back-up, off-site storage).

Security

Brief mention of and/or reference out to the organisation's Security Policy (covering issues such as password controls, security violations, unauthorised software, viruses etc). Details of any specific responsibilities on both sides (e.g. Virus Protection, Firewalls).

Printing

Details of any special conditions relating to printing or printers (e.g. print distribution details, notification of large centralised print runs or handling of any special high value stationery etc).

Charging (if applicable)

Details of any charging formulas used, or reference out to charging policy document. Details of invoicing and payment conditions etc.

Details of any financial penalties or bonuses that will be paid if service targets do not meet expectations. What will the penalties/bonuses be and how will they be calculated, agreed and collected/paid (more appropriate for third-party situations).

Service Reviews

Details of how and when the service targets will be reviewed. Details of reporting that will take place and of formal review meetings etc. Who will be involved and in what capacity.

Glossary

Explanation of any unavoidable abbreviations or terminology used, to assist Customer understanding.

Amendment Sheet

To include a record of any agreed amendments, with details of amendments, dates and signatories.

5 FINANCIAL MANAGEMENT FOR IT SERVICES

5.1 Introduction

5.1.1 Why introduce formal Financial Management for IT Services?

IT Services are usually viewed as critical to the business or organisation. The increases in User numbers, demands for new technologies and complexities of client-server systems has frequently caused IT Services costs to grow faster than other costs. As a result, organisations are often unable or unwilling to justify expenditure to improve services, or develop new ones, and IT Services may become viewed as high-cost or inflexible.

Due to the complex nature of Accounting for IT usage, it is rare that the actual running costs of the IT Services are properly identified and this often leads to dissatisfaction with the perceived 'value for money' of the services.

> 'Why can't the IT organisation provide a better level of service?'
>
> 'Why does the IT organisation budget have to be so large?'
>
> 'How much will it cost to implement and run this new system?'
>
> 'Why do we spend so much time performing redundant tasks, like reprinting large reports that are not read?'

The above are examples of the questions asked inside and outside an IT organisation, often in emotive situations, such as project over-runs or during periods of loss of critical service. The answer is often: 'We're doing the best that we can with the money that we have'; but **... is that true?**

To understand whether an IT organisation is doing the best that it can and to demonstrate this to its Customers, it has to both understand the true cost of providing a service and manage those costs professionally. To do this, it is usual to implement IT Accounting and Budgeting processes and often to implement Charging processes as well.

5.1.2 Basic concepts of Financial Management for IT Services

Financial Management is the sound stewardship of the monetary resources of the organisation. It supports the organisation in planning and executing its business objectives and requires consistent application throughout the organisation to achieve maximum efficiency and minimum conflict.

Within an IT organisation it is visible in three main processes:

- **Budgeting** is the process of predicting and controlling the spending of money within the organisation and consists of a periodic negotiation cycle to set budgets (usually annual) and the day-to-day monitoring of the current budgets

- **IT Accounting** is the set of processes that enable the IT organisation to account fully for the way its money is spent (particularly the ability to identify costs by Customer, by service, by activity). It usually involves ledgers and should be overseen by someone trained in accountancy

- **Charging** is the set of processes required to bill Customers for the services supplied to them. To achieve this requires sound IT Accounting, to a level of detail determined by the requirements of the analysis, billing and reporting processes.

The aim of Budgeting is that the actual costs match the budget (predicted costs). This budget is usually set by negotiations with the Customers who are providing the funds (although this sometimes happens at a very gross level i.e. the business leaders agree proportions of their revenue which is to be used to fund IT, based upon what IT have told them their costs are). Good Budgeting is essential to ensure that the money does not run out before the period end. Where shortfalls are likely to occur the organisation needs early warning and accurate information to enable good decisions to best manage the situation.

Organisations which need to account and charge to a very high level of accuracy, e.g. commercial IT Service providers, need to invest much more effort in developing IT Accounting and Charging systems than those who seek only a fair, simple apportionment of costs back to business units. IT Accounting can be used to determine the exact costs of resource usage down to CPU, filestore and bandwidth but it is rarely advisable to use this as the basis for charging as the costs of so doing may outweigh the benefits. It is in the interest of all parties to keep the overall cost of service low and the bureaucracy to a minimum, even at the expense of total precision.

Current leading practice is to use IT Accounting to aid investment and renewal decisions and to identify inefficiencies or poor value but to charge a fixed amount for an agreed Capacity (determined by the level of service agreed in the Service Level Agreements or SLAs). In this case, IT Finance Management works with Service Level Management (they may even be the same person) to ensure that the overall costs of running the agreed services should not exceed the predicted costs. Charging is then often a matter of billing for agreed periods at an agreed rate, for example 1/12 of each Customer's IT budget each calendar month. Additional charges are made for work above the agreed service levels (e.g. office moves, major roll-out, unplanned hardware upgrade).

A commercial organisation, such as a supplier of outsourced services, is likely to have to develop more precise methods of charging and display a greater flexibility in linking charges to costs incurred, than an in-house organisation, in order that the requirements of commercial marketing and profit-making can be supported.

This Chapter looks at methods for an IT organisation to predict and calculate the costs of service and discusses ways of estimating the proportion of costs that can be attributed to each Customer where an IT Service is shared. The simple diagram at Figure 5.1 is used as a basis for the whole Chapter.

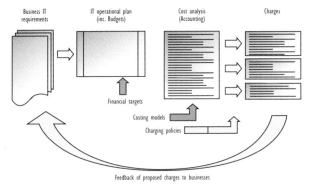

Figure 5.1 – IT Accounting, Charging and Budgeting cycle

In summary:

Budgeting enables an organisation to:

- predict the money required to run IT Services for a given period
- ensure that actual spend can be compared with predicted spend at any point
- reduce the risk of overspending
- ensure that revenues are available to cover predicted spend (where Charging is in place).

IT Accounting enables an organisation to:

- account for the money spent in providing IT Services
- calculate the cost of providing IT Services to both internal and external Customers
- perform cost-benefit or Return-on-Investment analyses
- identify the cost of Changes.

Charging enables an organisation to:

- recover the costs of the IT Services from the Customers of the service
- operate the IT organisation as a business unit if required
- influence User and Customer behaviour (note the discussion in Paragraph 5.4.2).

5.1.3 Scope of IT Financial Management

The scope of IT Financial Management includes Budgeting, IT Accounting and Charging, although the responsibility for the processes and tasks may lie with the Finance department. In many organisations the budget rules are set for all parts of the organisation and the monitoring and reporting of budgets is performed by staff who report to the Finance department rather than to the IT organisation.

For the purpose of this Chapter, it is assumed that Budgeting, IT Accounting and Charging for IT Services is the responsibility of IT Services Management. In some organisations the design and implementation may be the responsibility of a Finance department or shared with them. Even if the IT Services Management assume total responsibility for the process, it is advisable to work closely with the Finance department and with qualified accountants.

5.1.4 Goal for Financial Management for IT Services

For an in-house organisation, the goal should be:

- 'to provide cost-effective stewardship of the IT assets and resources used in providing IT Services'.

In a commercial environment, there may be a goal statement that reflects the profit-making and marketing aims of the organisation.

The aims for any IT Services organisation should include:

- 'to be able to account fully for the spend on IT Services and to attribute these costs to the services delivered to the organisation's Customers'
- 'to assist management decisions on IT investment by providing detailed business cases for Changes to IT Services'.

5.1.5 Relationship with other IT Service Management processes

Financial Management for IT Services interacts with most IT Service processes and has particular dependencies upon and responsibilities to:

- **Service Level Management** – The SLA specifies Customer expectations and IT Services obligations. The cost of meeting the Customer's requirements may have major impact on the shape and scope of the services that are eventually agreed. IT Finance Management liaises with Service Level Management about the costs of meeting current and new business demands, the Charging policies for the organisation, their effects on Customers and how the policies are likely to influence Customer and User behaviour. The more that the SLA allows individual Customers to request variations to service levels, the greater is the scope for (and potential benefits of) Charging for IT Services but also the greater the overheads of Budgeting, IT Accounting and Charging.

- **Capacity Management** – Cost information can be used to estimate the costs of the desired Capacity and Availability of the system. In planning the Capacity it may be necessary to discuss the costs with individual Customers or the organisation as a whole. Data that is collected so that costs can be determined may also be relevant to Capacity assessments, e.g. staff effort, machine usage.

- **Configuration Management** – Financial Management requires asset and cost information that may be managed by large organisation-wide systems. Configuration Management is responsible for managing the data relating to assets (Configuration Items) and their attributes (e.g. cost).

5.1.6 Impact on the organisation

Changes to Budgeting and IT Accounting or the introduction of Charging for IT Services are strategic business decisions. They may impact service levels, perceptions of value and usage of services. They also require an investment in planning and maintaining the processes. Business leaders throughout the organisation should be fully aware of the Changes likely from the implementation of Changes to any or all of the above.

It is essential that the organisation recognises the cost of introducing and maintaining Budgeting, IT Accounting or Charging as well as the benefits. The proposed benefits must be clear to both the IT organisation and to its Customers. Evaluation of these costs and benefits prior to implementing new systems is essential if the systems are to be quickly accepted by the Customers and IT Services staff.

Charges for IT Services must be simple, fair and accurate and this requires accurate, effective IT Accounting. The organisation must also be clear on its overall policies on Charging e.g. whether to break-even, to subsidise or to make profits. It is essential that the organisation is fully aware of the benefits and the pitfalls of the proposed system of Charging.

It is unlikely that IT Accounting can be introduced solely for IT Services – the whole organisation must be prepared to account in the same way for monies spent. If Charging is introduced in an organisation where no other form of inter-departmental charges are levied, anomalies may have to be addressed when, for instance, IT 'charges' Personnel for running the Personnel database but Personnel cannot charge the IT organisation for their services.

5.1.7   Benefits of Financial Management for IT Services

The term 'Customer' is used to refer to the organisation, department or division 'buying' the service. The 'User' is the person who makes day-to-day use of the service, e.g. a salesperson or Customer Service representative. Most of the benefits discussed are benefits to the organisation as a whole, or to the Customers of the IT organisation. The benefits to Users are realised through improved service, arising from efficient use of IT spend. Figure 5.2 shows how Financial Management can be seen as the brace that 'locks' IT to the business, preventing the IT organisation from drifting away from the needs of the business and preventing businesses from pursuing private deals outside the organisation.

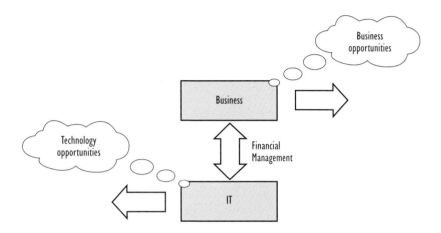

Figure 5.2 – Locking IT to the business

The benefits of Budgeting, IT Accounting and Charging for IT Services are discussed fully in the Sections on each topic. In summary they are:

- increased confidence in setting and managing budgets
- accurate cost information to support IT investment decisions
- accurate cost information for determining cost of ownership for ongoing services
- a more efficient use of IT resource throughout the organisation
- increased professionalism of staff within the IT organisation.

Budgeting

The benefits of Budgeting should be self-evident, but in summary are:

- ensuring that the business provides sufficient funds to run the IT Services it requires
- ensuring that IT Service levels can be maintained throughout the year
- providing early warning of under- or over-consumption of service (provided that some form of IT Accounting is in place).

Accounting for IT Services

The fundamental benefit of Accounting for IT Services (IT Accounting) is that it provides management information on the costs of providing IT Services that support the organisation's business needs. This information is needed to enable IT and business managers to make decisions that ensure the IT Services organisation runs in a cost-effective manner. Cost effectiveness is defined here as ensuring that there is a proper balance between the quality of service on the one hand and expenditure on the other. Any investment that increases the costs of providing IT Services should always result in enhancement to service quality or quantity.

IT Accounting helps the business to:

- base decisions about the services to be provided on assessments of cost-effectiveness, service by service

- make more business-like decisions about IT Services and investments in them

- provide information to justify IT expenditure

- plan and budget with confidence

- demonstrate under- or over-consumption of service in financial terms

- understand the costs of **not** taking advantage of opportunities for Change.

Put simply, there is no prospect of IT Service providers maximising value for money if the costs of providing the services are not accurately known. A key justification for investing in more IT resources is to support new or better business processes. IT Accounting provides the cost basis for cost-benefit analyses.

Charging

The fundamental benefit to the organisation of charging Customers is that it provides a sound business method of balancing the shape and quantity of IT Services with the needs and resources of the Customers. Customers are charged for the services they receive and because they are paying, they have a right to influence decisions on its provision. If they do not think the services represent good value for money, they may stop using them or make formal complaints but professional IT organisations invest time in discussing the balance of charges and service levels with their Customers.

Services can be improved by spending more, if there is a business justification for it. The introduction of formal Charging often provides more evidence to support this and hence more organisations choose to invest in IT. Conversely, if Customers believe that they can save themselves money (directly or indirectly, by reducing overall organisation expenditure) by changing the way in which they use the IT Services, they are able to discuss this more openly with the IT organisation.

Charging enables the IT Services Management to:

- make formal evaluations of IT Services and plan for investment based on cost recovery and business benefits

- recover IT costs in a fair manner

- influence Customer behaviour (where appropriate – see Paragraph 5.4.2).

Notional Charging, where bills are produced but no money changes hands, is sometimes introduced to ensure that Customers are aware of the costs they incur. The effectiveness of introducing Notional Charging depends on the supporting management processes: if Customers ignore the information and management takes no action, there is little point in providing the information.

The introduction of Real Charging (i.e. actual money changing hands), as opposed to Notional Charging, is not always necessary. Customers and organisations that see the calculated costs may improve service provision and decision making without transferring money within the organisation. Further, the cost of introducing Charging should be justified by better value for money for Customers but overheads and system constraints may mean that the expected savings cannot be realised. For instance, it may not be possible to provide a higher quality of service to an individual Customer even if that Customer is prepared to pay a premium for it, nor to provide less service to a Customer who expects a discount.

Real Charging is therefore desirable in principle but its introduction must actually improve effectiveness of IT spend and value for money and do so to an extent that savings outweigh the administrative costs. The level of detail available in Charging depends upon the level of detail of the IT Accounting and usage information and may require a redesign of the IT Accounting systems if detailed Charging is required.

5.1.8 Costs

The costs associated with Budgeting, IT Accounting and Charging fall into 3 broad categories:

1. the administration and organisation costs for the planning, implementation, ongoing operations and management of the process (both staff directly working in these areas and Operations or other staff involved in the data collection)

2. the extra computing resources needed to automate and facilitate IT Accounting and Charging

3. the purchase and support of tools required in carrying out the processes (some of these tools are also required for other Service Management processes).

Once costs are visible, and particularly when Real Charging is in place, the demand for some services may fall. This results in reduced revenue but is not really a cost of implementation, as it is in the organisation's interest to identify and reduce inefficient use of IT resource.

5.1.9 Possible problems

There are a number of possible problems in implementing IT Accounting and Charging:

- IT Accounting and Charging are often new disciplines in IT Services and there is limited understanding of leading practice in Cost Modelling and Charging mechanisms which could lead to over-complex or ineffective systems

- IT Accounting relies on planning information provided by other processes both within and outside of IT Services Management which may not be routinely available, delaying the project

- staff combining accountancy and IT experience are rare, so many activities may need to be shared with staff from outside IT Services who may not have this as their priority

- the IS strategies and objectives of an organisation may not be well formulated and documented and prediction of Capacity requirement not accurate

- senior business managers may not recognise the benefits of IT Accounting and Charging and may resent the administrative overheads and the limitations on workload

- the IT organisation may not be able to respond to Changes in Users' demands once costs become an influence

- the IT Accounting and Charging processes are so elaborate that the cost of the system exceeds the value of the information produced

- the monitoring tools providing resource usage information are inaccurate, irrelevant or cost too much to develop and maintain.

The guidance contained in this Chapter is intended to enable IT Finance Management to manage better the risks associated with these problems.

5.1.10 Accountancy

This Chapter assumes an IT organisation serving a single organisation or related organisations in the same country. It does not cover taxation or Accounting legislation. Guidance on IT Accounting practice should be sought from other publications or from qualified accountants.

This Chapter specifically refers to Budgeting, IT Accounting and Charging in an IT organisation. However, the principles and advice apply to all service provision (e.g. software development, in-house consultancy, procurement, direct works departments and so on) and to the supply of services in a commercial environment i.e. outsourcing and shared service centres.

5.2 Budgeting

5.2.1 Introduction

Budgeting is the process of ensuring that the correct finance is available for the provision of IT Services and that during the budget period they are not over-spent. The Budgeting process has a key influence on strategic and tactical plans. It is also the means of delegating control and monitoring performance against predefined targets. It is paramount that budgets are effectively integrated within the organisation and that managerial responsibility and accountability is matched and communicated in an efficient way.

As all spend affects profitability, it must be recognised that decisions about investment in IT Services and the integrated management IT Accounting discipline can help provide the competitive edge necessary for survival of an organisation.

All organisations have a periodic (e.g. annual) round of negotiations between the business departments and the IT organisation covering expenditure plans and agreed investment programmes which ultimately sets the budget for IT. These are closely linked to reviews with the businesses (individually or collectively) that cover:

- current projects and service levels
- a review of the last 12 months
- plans for the next 1 – 3 years.

The final budget agreed for an IT organisation may include financial disciplines imposed by the organisation, including:

- limits on capital expenditure (see the definition in Paragraph 5.3.4)
- limits on operational expenditure (see the definition in Paragraph 5.3.4)
- limits on variance at any point in time, between actual and predicted spend
- guidelines on how the budget must be used
- an agreed workload and set of services to be delivered
- limits on expenditure outside the organisation or group of organisations
- agreements on how to cope with exceptions.

Further, the business departments which provide the revenue to the organisation, from which departmental budgets are drawn, may themselves have rigid limits on the way in which they pay for services – they may not be able to fund a Change in service or service level mid-year despite IT being able to provide it.

An example, very simplified, budget is shown in Table 5.1.

Budget Item	Capital	Purchase Cost	Annual Maintenance	Spend This Year	Budget Next Year	Notes	Annualised Cost
Hardware							
UNIX Server	Yes	£80.000	£8,000	£8,000	£8,000	No changes	£34,667
NT Server	Yes	£10.000	£1,000	£1,000	£1,000	No changes	£4,333
Netware Server	Yes	£3.000	£300	£300	£300	No changes	£1,300
PCs (50)	Yes	£60.000	£6,000	£6,000	£6,000	No changes	£26,000
Routers (5)	Yes	£3,000	£300	£300	£300	No changes	£1,300
LAN Cabling	Yes	£40,000	£4,000	£4,000	£4,000	No changes	£17,333
Software							
General Ledgers	No		£20,000	£20,000	£24,000		
ORACLE	No		£7,000	£7,000	£8,400		
Marketing and Sales appl.	No		£3,000	£3,000	£3,600		
MS Windows (50-user)	No		£2,500	£2,500	£3,000	Staff increase	
No MS Office (20-user)	No		£3,000	£3,000	£3,600	from 50 to 60	
Netware	No		£3,000	£3,000	£3,600		
NT	No		£2,500	£2,500	£3,000		
Employment							
Manager	No		£50,000	£50,000	£52,000	4% pay rise	
Senior Operator	No		£30,000	£30,000	£30,000	Just joined	
Operator	No		£20,000	£20,000	£21,000	5% pay rise	
Contractor	No		£100,000			Paid by Marketing	
Accommodation							
Computer Room	No		£10,000	£10,000	£10,200	2% rise in	
Office	No		£ 10,000	£10,000	£10,200	charges	
External Service							
Wide Area connection	No		£20,000	£20,000	£20,000	Fixed price,	
DR contract	No		£10,000	£10,000	£10,000	3-year contracts	
			Total	£210,600	£222,200		

Note the annualised cost is taken as 1/3 of the purchase cost, plus the annual maintenance cost and will be used in the Cost Model in Paragraph 53.3

Table 5.1 – Example budget calculation

5.2.2   Estimating the cost of budget items

The categorisations in Table 5.1, of hardware, software etc, are arbitrary but help ensure that all of the budget items can be identified. Other categorisations can be chosen: the test is that all budget items are identified. The categorisation needs to be consistent for two reasons. The first reason is to enable an organisation to make true comparisons, year on year, both with its own expenditure trends and with the costs of other organisations. The second reason is to provide a simple basis for activity based costing, as expenditure items likely to be treated in the same manner logically, are grouped together. This may also be important if different accounting rules, e.g. depreciation (see Paragraph 5.3.5), are to be applied to different categories of costs. Cost Types in Paragraph 5.3.4 provides more detail to these categorisations.

The cost of some budget items may not be known at the time a budget is drawn up, e.g. overtime payments, contractor payments, consumables, external network charges. These have to be estimated, usually based upon a previous IT Accounting period, or on a forward prediction of the costs of the estimated workload.

Some costs may vary from the estimates, depending upon the usage. An example of this is software licences that may increase (in steps) as further Users are introduced. Other costs may need to be estimated to cover out-of-hours support, major equipment re-location.

IT Finance Management must be cautious in estimating changes in costs where they do not fully control them. For example, planning a reduction of 20% computer accommodation usage by removing old disk drives and closing one room is unlikely to result in 20% saving in costs, as the rental for the space may be fixed by the lease.

5.2.3   Estimating the cost of workload dependent budget items

Another reason for costs changing, is when the IT workload Changes. For this reason, workload estimates and forecasts should be considered when drawing up budgets. Such estimates and forecasts are also required for the preparation of Service Level Agreements and for Capacity Management.

Estimates of workload volumes are normally obtained from historical data, and forecasts are made on the basis of updated information and revised plans. A fuller approach to workload estimating can be seen in Chapter 6.

In the simplified example, Table 5.2, a calculation is performed for the cost (for budgetary purposes) of the Wide Area Network (WAN).

Factor	Current Year			Budget Year			Note
	Quantity	Unit Cost	Cost	Quantity	Unit Cost	Cost	
Users	30	–		40			
64k dial-up lines	5	£200	£1,000	10	£200	£2,000	
64k dial-up telephony			£3,000			£6,000	Demand per user doubles each year
ISDN lines	2	£1,000	£2,000	7	£1,000	£7,000	Higher proportion of customers use ISDN
Routers required	1	£500	£500	3	£500	£1,500	1 router handles up to 8 lines
Network Budget			£6,500			£ 16,500	

Table 5.2 – Estimating workload-dependent budget items

5.3   Developing the IT Accounting system

5.3.1   Scope of IT Accounting

The basic IT Accounting principles (why do it, what to do and who it affects) are common to all business processes. To a large extent, the implementation of IT Accounting is similar throughout the organisation but the detail of what to cost, and how to cost it, is dependent upon the type of service being provided.

To implement IT Accounting may require improved IT Accounting in many areas, for example in staff time and activity recording, supplier contracts, software licensing, resource metering or accommodation costs.

Other items which rely upon the information provided by IT Accounting and hence may dictate the shape of a IT Accounting model include:

- Budgeting guidelines
- Charging policies

■   investment guidelines.

IT Accounting can be very complex and if implemented at too high a level of detail, may cost more than the benefits realised. The IT Accounting systems described here should enable an organisation to:

■   track actual costs against budget

■   support the development of a sound investment strategy which recognises and evaluates the options and flexibility available from modern technology

■   provide cost targets for performance and Service Delivery

■   facilitate prioritisation of resource usage

■   make day-to-day decisions with full understanding of the cost implications and hence the minimum of risk

■   support the introduction, if required, of Charging for IT Service.

5.3.2   Business Perspective

IT Accounting and Charging are integral parts of IT Infrastructure Management responsibilities. The policies must be agreed by the organisation, i.e. at board level.

The difference between IT Accounting and Charging and the responsibility for each, has to be defined and made clear by the IT organisation. They are different but have linked sets of activities.

The most visible of the two disciplines, **Charging**, is concerned with the recovery of the cost of IT Services expenditures in a simple, fair, affordable way. **IT Accounting** is concerned with providing detailed information on where and for what reason expenditure is incurred within IT Services and is inward-looking.

The management of the IT organisation can choose to implement Accounting for IT Services (IT Accounting) with no Charging, or to charge for IT Services (either to break-even or to make profits). If IT Services have to make a book profit, the organisation may even create IT Services as a separate legal entity:

■   *Accounting Centre – simply costing inputs with maybe some element of Budgeting.* The benefit of this policy is that sound IT Accounting focuses awareness on costs and enables investment decisions to be better founded, without the overheads of billing and bookkeeping. However, it is less likely to shape Users' behaviour and does not give the IT organisation the full ability to choose how to financially manage itself, for example in funding IT investment.

■   *Recovery Centre – costing outputs (services) and simply apportioning those costs.* Organisations running as Recovery Centres are designed to account fully for all IT spend and recover it from the Customers. These accounts include both cash and non-cash costs that, in effect, identify the full economic cost of running the business. The benefits of running as a Recovery Centre (before Charging is considered) include improved cost control over service provision, recognition of true costs by Customers and consistency in approach by different organisations.

■   *Profit Centre – the full panoply of separate Accounting.* A Profit Centre is a method of managing the IT organisation in which it has sufficient autonomy to operate as a separate business entity but with business objectives set by the organisation. A Profit Centre can be created with the business objective of making a profit, breaking even or operating with a subsidy. The key characteristics are that:

- deliverables or products are clearly identified and sold into a marketplace
- each product or service carries a price tag.

The IT Services organisation must be assumed to pay for its own upkeep, probably with some financial support for capital expenditures. Choosing to operate as a Profit Centre is usually the first step along the path to a truly commercial IT Services organisation – one in which the Customers (the people who pay for the services) have some freedom of choice to go elsewhere if they are not satisfied with the quality and/or price. The Profit Centre approach provides the IT Services organisation with a certain amount of autonomy, but it also carries risks, such as the Customer becoming aware that the IT organisation is 'making a profit' from them. This can be more serious if another service provider can offer a cheaper service of similar standard (corporate loyalty disappears very quickly in this situation).

5.3.3   Building the Cost Model

To calculate the costs of IT Service provision, it is necessary to design a framework in which all known costs can be recorded and allocated to specific Customers, activities or other category. This is called a **Cost Model**. Most Cost Models are based on calculating the cost for each Customer but other models can be developed to show the cost for each service or the costs for each location. This Chapter concentrates on a Cost Model that enables the calculation of Costs-by-Customer, which is the usual start-point if a Charging system is to be introduced.

5.3.4   Cost Types

As discussed in 5.2.2 Estimating the cost of budget items, it is useful to categorise costs to ensure that they are correctly identified and managed. This categorisation should use consistent and easily understandable Cost Types. For producing a Cost Model, the suggested Cost Types are:

- ■ hardware costs
- ■ software costs
- ■ people costs
- ■ accommodation costs
- ■ External Service costs
- ■ Transfer costs

External Service costs and Transfer costs need further explanation. It is now common to buy in services from external parties (external services) that are a mixture of cost types, for example an outsourced service for providing an organisation's application development or the provision of a datacentre. It may be difficult to break down this cost (into each of the first four categories), as it is likely to contain elements that are indivisible or that the supplier will not wish to detail. It is easier and more usual to categorise this as an External Service Cost.

Transfer costs are those that represent goods and services that are sold from one part of an organisation to another (often within a multi-national or other large organisation that has a sophisticated internal accounting system). Transfer costs may be for:

- ■ hardware (an IT organisation buying PCs on behalf of a business Customer)
- ■ software (the corporate Finance Department producing control mechanisms for IT to manage their costs)

- people (the HR overhead levied by the corporate HR department)

- accommodation (a charge made by the Facilities Management department).

Transfer costs should be visible in the cost model because people may forget that internal goods and services represent a cost to the organisation and are part of the cost of providing service. Hence a false figure may be reached when assessing costs if a service is dependent upon activity from another part of the organisation but this cost is excluded from calculations. Some organisations will insist on these transfer costs being accounted for in each part of the organisation while others may only use them when modelling costs and no money will actually pass across the organisation. In this publication, it is assumed that it is not necessary to separately identify transfer costs in the Cost Model examples.

The Costs-by-Customer Cost Model requires that all major cost elements in the current or proposed IT budget are identified and then attributed to the Customers who 'cause' them. To do this, the costs first have to be identified as either Direct or Indirect:

- **Direct Costs** are those clearly attributable to a single Customer, e.g. Manufacturing systems used only by the Manufacturing division.

- **Indirect Costs** (sometimes called overheads) are those incurred on behalf of all, or a number of, Customers e.g. the network or the technical support department, which have to be apportioned to all, or a number of, Customers in a fair manner.

Any Indirect Costs, which cannot be apportioned to a set of Customers (sometimes called **Unabsorbed Overheads**), have then to be recovered from all Customers in as fair away as is possible, usually by uplifting the costs calculated so far by a set amount. This ensures that the sum of all of the costs attributed to each Customer still equals the total costs incurred by the IT organisation – in Table 5.4, this is referred to as the 'balance check'. This 'balance check' can be applied to costs divided in other ways e.g. by service or by location; always, the sum of the parts should equal the whole.

If the Cost Model is being produced for the first time the categories and Cost Elements for it need to be developed first, to a level of detail that meets the needs of IT Accounting and of any Charging to be performed. Hence an understanding of Charging policies (see Paragraph 5.4.2) is necessary when the Cost Model is drawn up.

If costs are mainly Direct, perhaps because each Customer has independent hardware and software, the method of recording and of apportioning costs can be very simple. For example, if Finance are the only Customers of the General Ledgers and the system on which it runs, all costs directly associated with the General Ledgers, including purchase, maintenance and support, can be attributed to Finance department's code in the ledgers (often called a cost-centre or charge-code).

However, if resources are shared, for instance a mainframe running applications for more than one Customer, the hardware costs may have to be classified as indirect and apportioned to each Customer, say by CPU-seconds/disk storage/print volumes/etc from workload predictions. To do this requires a model that allows these costs to be spread across a number of Customers.

In the example in Figure 5.3, it is assumed that there are 3 businesses or departments, who together are responsible for all of the IT costs. The three departments are Marketing and Sales, Manufacturing and Finance and all of the IT systems and services have been implemented on their behalf.

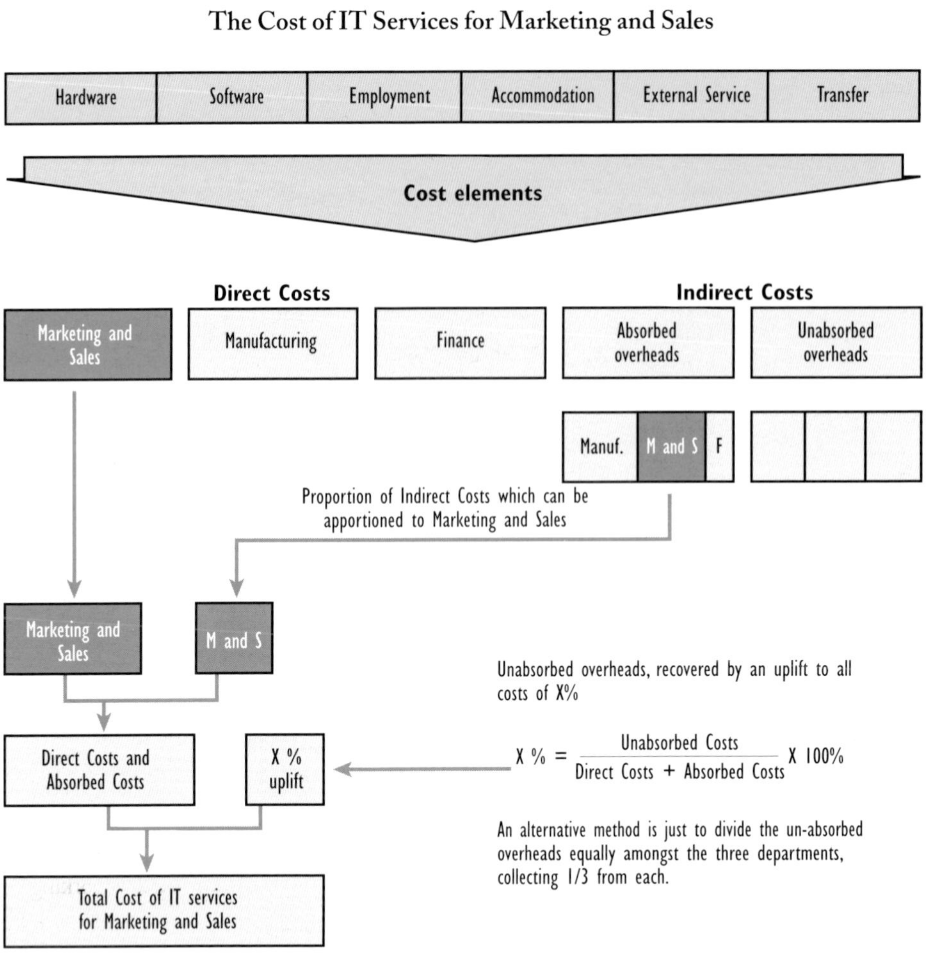

The Cost of IT Services for Marketing and Sales

Hardware	Software	Employment	Accommodation	External Service	Transfer

Cost elements

Direct Costs   **Indirect Costs**

Marketing and Sales	Manufacturing	Finance	Absorbed overheads	Unabsorbed overheads

Manuf.	M and S	F				

Proportion of Indirect Costs which can be apportioned to Marketing and Sales

Marketing and Sales		M and S

Unabsorbed overheads, recovered by an uplift to all costs of X%

Direct Costs and Absorbed Costs	X % uplift

$$X\% = \frac{\text{Unabsorbed Costs}}{\text{Direct Costs} + \text{Absorbed Costs}} \times 100\%$$

An alternative method is just to divide the un-absorbed overheads equally amongst the three departments, collecting 1/3 from each.

Total Cost of IT services for Marketing and Sales

Figure 5.3 – Cost Model of Costs-by-Customer

An example of the calculation of a Cost Model for a simple Cost-by-Customer is shown in Figure 5.3. The same principles can be applied to calculating the costs of individual application services or even parts of a service e.g. support and maintenance.

If the cost of providing some element of a service is desired, for instance producing large reports for the Marketing and Sales department, this may require measurement of resource usage to apportion indirect costs to this one activity e.g. computer time consumed, printing and operations staff and facilities. This can become very complex and would normally be treated as a separate exercise rather than as part of the standard Cost Model used for calculating Costs-by-Customer.

To be able to derive cost information and report it in the formats required by different parts of the organisation, it is necessary to ensure that all costs recorded are classified to a standard system with a level of detail that anticipates future Changes, e.g. New Cost centres, new equipment types, new project codes.

Cost Elements

If more detail is required in calculating costs, the chosen major Cost Types of hardware, software, people, accommodation and transfer can be further divided. For instance, hardware might be divided into *Office, Network, and Central Servers*. The purpose of this is to ensure that every cost identified in the IT organisation can be placed within a table of costs, by type. This enables analysis to be performed by type e.g. all *Network* costs.

The decision on whether to identify more detailed cost units often depends upon whether more detail is required to apportion charges. In general, Cost Elements are the same as budget line items where the purpose of the model is simple recovery of costs.

If a more detailed analysis of costs is required, e.g. for organisations providing shared services, then more detailed Cost Elements have to be identified. Typical Cost Elements within each major Cost Type are shown in Table 5.3.

Major type	Cost Elements
Hardware	Central processing units, LANS, disk storage, peripherals, wide area network, PCs, portables, local servers
Software	Operating systems, scheduling tools, applications, databases, personal productivity tools, monitoring tools, analysis packages
People	Payroll costs, benefit cars, re-location costs, expenses, overtime, consultancy
Accommodation	Offices, storage, secure areas, utilities
External Service	Security services, Disaster Recovery services, outsourcing services, HR overhead
Transfer	Internal charges from other cost centres within the organisation

Table 5.3 – Cost Element examples

For organisations providing services based upon central mainframes, the hardware costs may be the largest proportion but it is more common to see a rough balance amongst hardware, software and people. Increasingly, the proportion of costs attributed to networking devices and network services is becoming more significant and may be identified as a separate Cost Type.

Organisations that purchase software products, rather than developing them, find a higher proportion for costs categorised as Software. Organisations that use outsourcing services (such as offshore development or computing services) may see External Service costs as the largest proportion of costs.

Classification of Cost Elements

When each Cost Element has been identified, it should be classified, as a minimum, as either Capital Costs or Operational Costs (also known as Current Expenditure or Revenue Expenditure).

For financial purposes, costs are classified into either Capital or Operational when the financial ledgers are reported (the 'books'). This is because Capital expenditure is assumed to increase the total value of the company, while Operational expenditure does not, although in practice the value of Capital expenditure decreases over time (depreciates).

This distinction affects IT Accounting because the Cost Model needs a method of calculating the annual cost of using a capital item (e.g. mainframe) to deliver IT Service. The annual costs must make allowance for the decreasing value of capital items (assets) and make for timely renewal of capital items e.g. buildings, servers, applications. Usually, this is taken as the annual depreciation, from a method set by the Finance department (within the boundaries of the country's laws).

Capital Costs are typically those applying to the physical (substantial) assets of the organisation. Traditionally this was the accommodation and machinery necessary to produce the organisation's product. Capital Costs are the purchase or major enhancement of fixed assets, for example computer equipment, building and plant are often also referred to as 'one-off' costs. It is important to remember that it is not usually the actual cost of items purchased during the year that is included in the calculation of the cost of the services but the annualised depreciation for the year as shown in Table 5.4 (see Paragraph 5.3.6).

Operational Costs are those resulting from the day-to-day running of the IT Services organisation, e.g. staff costs, hardware maintenance and electricity, and relate to repeating payments whose effects can be measured within a short timeframe, usually less than the 12-month financial year.

The following list gives typical examples of the Cost Elements, classified into Capital expenditure and Operational expenditure (revenue) items:

Capital

- computer equipment
- building and plant software packages.

Operational

- staff costs
- maintenance of computer hardware and software
- consultancy services, rental fees for equipment
- software licence fees
- accommodation costs
- administration expenditures
- electricity, water, gas, rates
- disaster recovery
- consumables.

Organisations that measure themselves primarily on cash flow or budget adherence may have specific rules about the categorisation of costs in the accounts that differ from those who measure Return on Capital Employed (ROCE – see Paragraph 5.3.12).

The organisation's accountants explain the rules for identifying capital items and this depends upon a number of business decisions. Many organisations choose to identify major expenditure as Capital, whether there is a substantial asset or not, to reduce the impact on the current financial year of such expenditure and this is referred to as 'Capitalisation'. The most common item for this to be applied to is software, whether developed in-house or purchased.

The reason for this is that a business that is investing in a major software development, that provides service for a number of years, does not want to show all of the costs in a single year (and so, potentially, an operating loss). The board wants the value of the company and its shares to reflect the investment made but adding the cost of the item to the assets of the company without adjusting cash flow in some way would also give a false picture. The agreed method is to show Capital and Operational expenditure separately but to apply rules of depreciation, described later in this Section, to provide a balance. This system allows an organisation to spread the cost of a major purchase over a number of years although, as with all systems, many additional rules (and laws) have to be written to prevent fraud or misleading of investors.

Direct or Indirect

Some costs can be directly attributed to a single Customer or group of Customers and these are referred to as **Direct Costs**. Examples of direct costs would be a server or application used exclusively by a single cost-centre. Usually, all direct costs are attributed to the Customer incurring them but there are occasions when these might be subsidised, shared, deferred or ignored, such as for the use of a new system which is subsequently 'rolled-out' throughout the organisation.

Other costs, such as operations staff in a Data Centre cannot be easily attributed to the running of a specific Customer's service and these are referred to as **Indirect Costs** or *shared costs*.

To fully attribute all costs requires some form of division of indirect costs by a fair method of reapportioning. An example would be operations staff whose total cost could be apportioned to the businesses on the basis of the number of Users in each business. Often this apportionment is not completely accurate but the costs to the organisation of a more accurate calculation, is far too high. The system of apportioning has therefore to be affordable, clear, fair and in accordance with good IT Accounting practice.

Cost Centre

It is usually necessary to be able to apportion Direct Costs to a specific business group, department or external Customer. Most businesses allocate **Cost Centres** to units within the organisation that relate directly to the general ledger system. The number and types of Cost Centres differ from installation to installation due to size and organisational structure. Occasionally, specific projects or initiatives may be allocated a separate Cost Centre to enable costs for them to be 'ring-fenced'.

Fixed or Variable

Costs that do not vary even when resource usage varies are referred to as **Fixed Costs**. Examples of this would be a maintenance contract for a server or a corporate software licence (within agreed User limits).

Variable Costs are those that vary with some factor, such as usage or time. They are likely to be used for Cost Elements which cannot be easily predicted and which it is to the benefit of both supplier and Customer to determine the costs exactly, perhaps for variable charges to be applied. Examples of charges that might vary, because the underlying cost varies, are out-of-hours cover, major equipment re-location, and the production of additional quarterly reports.

A Cost Element such as filestore may be considered to be variable. If a Customer requires an additional 10Gb it may be possible to calculate that the cost of this is £1000 and hence the cost per Gb is £100. The danger of this approach is that there are often sharp changes in costs because they cannot be continuously scaled: the next disk drive may require another cabinet, an additional process run on the server may cause queuing problems resulting in all jobs taking longer to run.

It is sometimes necessary to view a cost as having a fixed element and a variable element, for example, using filestore at all requires disk controllers and bandwidth, causing a fixed cost. The variable cost of additional disk drives can then be calculated and added to the fixed portion. This level of detail is not usually needed in calculating the cost of a service but can be useful when evaluating competing technologies or services.

5.3.5 Depreciation

Depreciation is the measure of the wearing out, consumption or other reduction in the useful economic life of a fixed asset, whether from use, passage of time, or obsolescence through technological or market changes. Depreciation should be allocated so as to charge a fair proportion of cost or valuation of the asset to each IT Accounting period expected to benefit from its use. This point can be a delicate balance and many IT organisations face a difficulty in funding the replacement of apparently useful items that have no capital value (i.e. are fully depreciated).

An example is a PC which cannot perform at the level required but has not yet been fully depreciated. The organisation may not be willing to replace it because it still is an asset with a value. Similarly, a PC may be perfectly functioning but has been fully depreciated and now has no value in the business accounts – strictly, it is no longer a cost in providing services but it is unlikely that costs will be recalculated to take account of this.

The assessment of depreciation, and its allocation to IT Accounting periods, involves the consideration of three factors:

- the current cost (or valuation) of the asset

- the length of the asset's expected useful economic life to the business of the organisation, having due regard to the incidence of obsolescence

- the estimated residual value of the asset at the end of its useful economic life in the business of the organisation.

The useful economic life of an asset may be:

- pre-determined, as in the case of a lease

- dependent on its physical deterioration through use or passage of time

- reduced by economic or technological obsolescence.

The depreciation methods used should be the ones most appropriate having regard to the types of assets and their use in the business. The Finance department gives guidance in this. The most common methods of assessing depreciation are:

- **Straight line method** – where an equal amount is written-off the value of the asset each year. Usually a fixed percentage of purchase cost, this results in the item having zero Net Book Value after a pre-set number of years (although it may continue to be used).

- **Reducing balance method** – where a set percentage of the capital cost is written-off the Net Book Value each year. Often this is of the form 40% in the first year, 30% in the second year and 30% in the last year. The Net Book Value is the capital cost minus the depreciation written-off to date.

- **By usage** – where depreciation is written-off according to the extent of usage during a period. It is usual to estimate the total useful 'life' of a device and to calculate the proportion of this that has been 'used' during the year. For example, a laser printer may be estimated to have a useful 'life' of 5,000,000 pages. If the average usage is 1,000,000 pages in a year, it can be depreciated by 20% in that year. Again, an anomaly arises if after 5 years it is still in use.

The Finance department may require IT assets to be 'written-off' before the end of their useful life, increasing the apparent cost of services but facilitating a charging system that generates revenue for the early replacement of systems.

5.3.6   Apportioning the IT Services costs

Consider a company with three departments who require IT Services – Marketing and Sales, Manufacturing, and Finance. Each is asked to contribute towards the IT budget, based upon the services they require. Each Cost Element in the IT budget has to be identified; classifying them by type (hardware, software etc.) helps ensure that all such costs are found. It must then be decided whether these are Direct Costs or Indirect Costs and how they are allocated to Customers (in this case, other departments of the company),

In the example at Table 5.4, all the costs of providing the shared computer Infrastructure – cables, servers, routers, software, have been grouped into a single Indirect Cost Element called 'Infrastructure' for which a common apportionment method can be used; in this case, the number of Users of the Infrastructure. This simplifies the spreadsheet and enables a simple calculation of the cost of adding new Users to the network.

	Capital	Annualised Cost (see note 1)	Direct	Apportionment Method (see notes 6, 7 and 8)	Customer Marketing and Sales	Manuf-acturing	Finance
Hardware							
UNIX Server	Yes	£34,667	No	50/50 split	£17,333	£17,333	
NT Server	Yes	£4,333	Yes		£4,333		
Netware Server	Yes	£1,300	No	Infrastructure			
PCs (50)	Yes	£26,000	No	By PC	£5,200	£19,240	£1,560
Routers (S)	Yes	£1,300	No	Infrastructure			
LAN Cabling	Yes	£17,333	No	Infrastructure			
Software (see note 2)							
General Ledgers	No	£20,000	Yes				£20,000
ORACLE	No	£7,000	Yes			£7,000	
Marketing and Sales appl.	No	£3,000	Yes		£3,000		
MS Windows (50-user)	No	£2,500	No	By PC	£500	£1,850	£150
MS Office (20-user)	No	£3,000	No	Licence	£1.500	£1,050	£450
Netware	No	£3,000	No	Infrastructure			
NT	No	£2,500	No	Infrastructure			
Employment (see note 3)							
Manager	No	£50,000	No	Unabsorbed overhead			
Technical Support	No	£30.000	No	Unabsorbed overhead			
Assistant	No	£20.000	No	Unabsorbed overhead			
Contractor (see note 4)	*No*	*£100,000*	*No*				
Accommodation (see note 5)							
Computer Room	No	£10,000	No	Unabsorbed overhead			
Office	No	£10.000	No	Unabsorbed overhead			
External Service							
Wide Area connection	No	£20,000	No	Infrastructure			
DR contract	No	£10,000	No	Unabsorbed overhead			
Total Costs		**£275,933**					
Direct and apportioned costs		£100,500			£31.867	£46,473	£22,160
Absorbed costs (Infrastructure)		£45,433		20%/74%/6%	£9,087	£33,620	£2,726
Unabsorbed costs		£130,000	89.1% uplift		£36,482	£71,349	£22,169
		£275,933			**£77,436**	**£151,442**	**£47,055**

balance check for the 3 customers above: £275,933

Notes

1   For capital items, this is 1/3 of the purchase price (the agreed depreciation) plus the annual operational cost

2   The M&S application will cost £100,000 to develop (one year of contractor), and the support contract is £3,000 annually

3   Includes NI, pension and other benefits, usually adding between 30% and 50% to salary

4   Contractor is employed to develop new system for Marketing and Sales and is funded directly by them

5   Accommodation costs set by Finance department

6   Marketing has 10 PCs with all software, Operations has 37 PCs but only 7 with Microsoft Office, Finance has 3 PCs with all software

7   Infrastructure costs will be added (absorbed) based upon numbers of PCs in each department, i.e. Marketing 20%, Operations 74%, Finance 6%

8   Unabsorbed overheads are added onto each cost centre by uplifting it by 89.1 %, to ensure full recovery

Table 5.4 – Spreadsheet example at full Costs-by-Customer

Rather than trying to determine the actual usage of the Infrastructure that all departments rely upon, it is simpler to group all Infrastructure Cost Elements into one and determine a fair way of recovering those costs, e.g. by number of Users in each department.

In practice, the Cost Elements in each of the major Cost Types may be groups of items. For instance the UNIX server Cost Element may consist of a number of items e.g. central processor, UPS, filestore, peripherals but these rarely need to be identified individually unless the Cost Model has to show costs to that level.

5.3.7 Level of detail required in cost calculations

Some organisations wish to calculate the cost of delivering individual services or activities. To do this requires a more complex Cost Model, with Cost Elements apportioned by Cost Units. These Cost Units are usually things that can be easily counted, such as staff numbers, software licences or things easily measured, such as filestore usage, CPU usage, network packets sent.

A higher level of detail is required to apportion fairly Cost Elements that are Indirect, but very few apportionment methods can ever be completely accurate. For instance, if central server usage is attributed by CPU-seconds, the issues of filestore and filestore transfers arise. Then, who 'pays' for the queuing and 'paging' of virtual store? Large servers are rarely dedicated to a single function and the expense of apportioning their use to each Customer can be both divisive and prohibitive. Similarly, it is difficult to apportion the time of support staff to individual Customers without detailed timesheets, and the benefits of this level of detail may be less than the cost of obtaining it.

At all times, when performing a detailed cost analysis it is essential to ensure that the value provided by the answers is not outweighed by the costs of data collection and analysis. For most business driven Cost Models, apportionment should be firstly simple, secondly fair and thirdly accurate (if possible).

5.3.8 Variable Costs or Indirect Costs requiring apportionment

Cost Unit

Cost Units are the basic items of resource for which Customers are held accountable i.e. provide the method of apportioning Indirect Costs or calculating the actual cost of Variable Costs.

Cost Units should be chosen to enable simple, fair apportionment. As central hardware costs have become a small proportion of costs in many organisations, the use of CPU-seconds as a Cost Unit has decreased. It is used as an example here because it is one of the simplest measures, easy to measure on mainframe systems, accurate and apparently fair.

Staff hours are another easily identifiable cost unit, as is floor space. In the example at Table 5.5, PCs and software licences are both Cost Units.

Cost per Cost Unit

After the Cost Unit has been set, the cost of each Cost Unit must be determined. Following the example above of CPU-seconds, if a business's IT organisation knows the total cost of the necessary Capacity, the average unit cost of a CPU-second can be calculated and apportioned to each Customer as it is used, in the same manner that an electricity company calculates the consumption of each of its Customers in KWh. In a Cost Model using Cost Units for every Cost Element, the sum of [units consumed **x** the cost per unit] should be demonstrated to be equal to the total cost of the IT Services (see also the 'balance check' in Table 5.4).

5.3.9   Calculating the Cost-by-service

Figure 5.3 considered the Cost Model for calculating costs attributable to a Customer. To calculate the Costs-by-service, the Cost Model may require more detail, as discussed in Paragraph 5.3.7.

The basic approach is similar:

1. identify all those costs that can be directly attributed to the service being analysed, for instance any dedicated hardware, software, staff or contracts

2. decide how to apportion the Indirect Costs such as Infrastructure

3. adjust the total to allow for 'hidden costs' or 'Unabsorbed overheads' such as IT management or buildings – this must be the same uplift figure calculated for the whole model, or used from the Costs-by-Customer Cost Model, i.e. 89.1 %.

It is best to consider the model as being one layer of a set of models, one for each service, so that, if the costs for each service provided are added together, this would again give the total of the costs incurred by the IT organisation. Even if only Service A is of interest, it is important to ensure that all costs are identified and attributed to the other services, as shown in Figure 5.4.

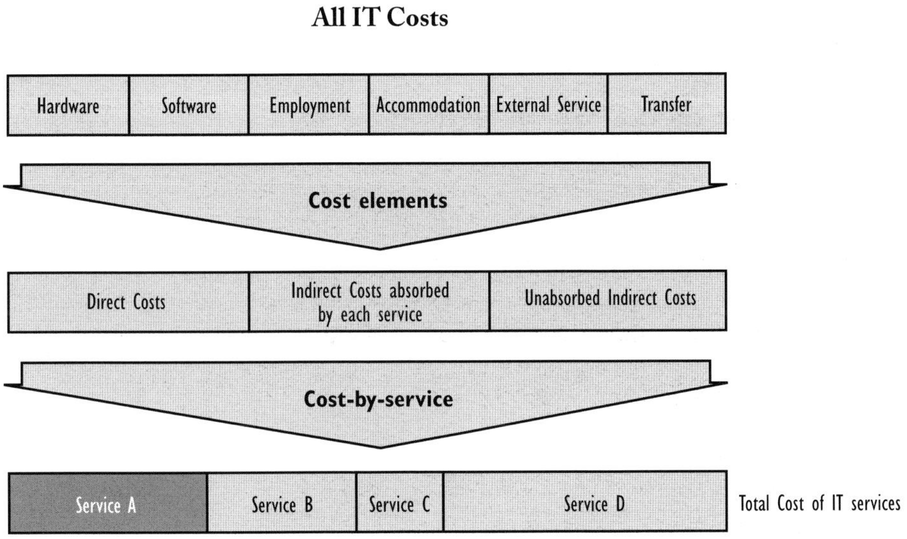

All IT Costs

Figure 5.4 – Complete view of the Cost-by-service

The original spreadsheet in Table 5.4 can be used as a start-point. It is then necessary to identify those costs that can fairly be attributed directly to the provision of this service and to apportion those Indirect Costs in a manner that reflects the proportion of them that result from the provision of this service.

It may not be possible to identify costs in every category. For example there may be no Direct Accommodation costs and no Absorbed Accommodation or Staff costs – these may all be included in the Unabsorbed Costs (see Figure 5.5), which have to be included fairly in the costs of every service.

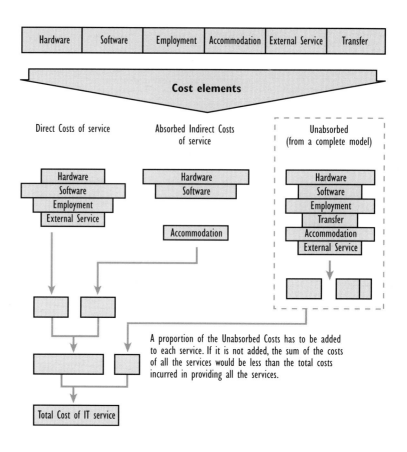

Figure 5.5 – Cost Model for a Cost-by-service

The remaining complexity is how to account for the £100,000 development costs (one year of contractor's time). Since this software is owned by the company (an asset), the Finance department value it. If its net value is less than £100,000 after development is completed, there has been some misunderstanding when the business case was made for spending £100,000. If the software is to be used for the next 5 years, it could be depreciated over that period, representing £20,000 pa costs (excluding maintenance) and this cost attributed to the cost of the service to the Marketing and Sales department.

	Capital	Annualised Cost	Direct	Cost Unit	Total Capacity or numbers	Cost per Cost Unit	Usage by M&S	Cost
Hardware								
UNIX Server	Yes	£34,667	No	Average % CPU	100%	£34,667	37%	£12,827
NT Server	Yes	£4,333	Yes	N/A				£5,000
Netware Server	Yes	£1,300	No	Infrastructure				
PCs (50)	Yes	£26,000	No	PC	50	£520	5	£2,600
Routers (5)	Yes	£1,300	No	Infrastructure				
LAN Cabling	Yes	£17,333	No	Infrastructure				
Software								
General Ledger	No	£20,000	Yes	User	5	£4,000	0	£0
ORACLE	No	£7,000	Yes	User	5	£1,400	I	£1,400
Marketing and Sales appl.	No	£3,000	Yes	N/A				£3,000
MS Windows (50-user)	No	£2,500	No	PC	50	£50	5	£250
MS Office (20-user)	No	£3,000	No	Licence	20	£150	0	£0
Netware	No	£3,000	No	Infrastructure				
NT	No	£2,500	No	Infrastructure				
Employment								
Manager	No	£50,000	No	Unabsorbed overhead				
Technical	No	£30,000	No	Unabsorbed overhead				
Support Assistant	No	£20,000	No	Unabsorbed overhead				
Contractor (see note I)								
Accommodation								
Computer Room	No	£10,000	No	Unabsorbed overhead				
Office	No	£10,000	No	Unabsorbed overhead				
External Service								
Wide Area connection	No	£20,000	No	Infrastructure				
DR contract	No	£10,000	No	Unabsorbed overhead				
Total Costs		£275,933						£25,077
Absorbed Costs								
Proportion of Infrastructure Costs (£45,433)				Employee using Infrastructure	50	£909	5	£4,543
							Total	£29,620
				89.1% uplift to recover Unabsorbed Costs (see note 2)				£26,391
								£56,011
				Application Cost (annual)				**£20,000**
				Total Annual Cost				**£76,011**

Notes

I. The contractor cost is spread over 5 years of the application, i.e. £20,000 pa

2. The uplift is the amount calculated from the overall Cost-by-Customer model, discussed previously

Table 5.5 – Calculating the cost of an individual service

When comparing the cost of internal provision of service against a bureau or packaged solution, a figure of £74,568 is reached, for comparison. The most contentious issue this brings to light is the 89.1% uplift (£26,391) that is mainly caused by the unabsorbed overheads of People and Accommodation cost. If the Customer feels that they could run the application themselves with the existing staff in their department administering it, they will argue strongly that the IT organisation is inefficient.

There is no immediate solution to this. All analyses that break costs down to the minute suffer both from not taking the whole picture into account (i.e. the provision of IT throughout the organisation is most likely to be more efficient if centralised) and from the fact that single Cost Units cannot alone be used to calculate the cost of service provision. However, the bureaucracy involved in more detailed calculation may be prohibitive.

The exercise is valid, however, providing that these issues are understood and discussed. Ultimately, strong corporate support is required for central IT systems.

Note that if the 89.1 % uplift were ignored, the costs calculated would not be a true reflection of the cost of service provision and could mislead decision-making.

5.3.10 Calculating the costs of Cost Units

When calculating how to apportion Indirect Costs or how to assess the actual cost of a Variable Cost, it is important to select a Cost Unit that is a factor that directly and fairly represents the cost incurred. For example, using the PC as a Cost Unit for calculating the apportionment of Infrastructure costs.

When calculating the cost of a Cost Unit, it may be that the precise calculation results in an amount that is dependent upon when the item is used or upon how many Customers use the resource. For instance, if processor-second is chosen as a Cost Unit for determining the apportionment of costs across a number of Users, this varies with the total usage of the server. That is, the cost per Cost Unit varies unless the server runs at full Capacity all of the time.

To prevent absurdities arising, such as attributing all the costs during overnight running of an unattended server to the sole Customer, it is usual to set fixed rates based upon the calculation of the Capacity available in a fixed period. Hence a Standard Cost for a processor-second can be derived **but this must be regularly recalculated** to prevent anomalies from creeping in.

Table 5.6 demonstrates the calculation of some simple Costs of Cost Units but even this is beyond that which would normally be performed by an in-house IT organisation.

Cost Unit	Total available in 1 month	Total cost in one month	Cost per Cost Unit	Note
CPU-seconds	792.000	£100.000	£0.126 / CPU-sec	Based upon 10 hours x 22 days i.e. excluding out-of-hours
Filestore	4,000 Gb	£ 12,000	£31Gb	Based upon allocated filestore (not actual used space) and annual cost of £36 1Gb
Tapes	10,000	£2,500	£0.25/tape	Based upon tapes allocated, £30 each with a life of 10 years, hence annual budget for new tapes is £30x 1000
Operator hours	528	£30,000	£56/hour	3 operators, working, on average, 22 days x 8 hours

Table 5.6 – Calculating the Cost of Cost Units

Table 5.7 shows the cost of a given activity that requires 10,000 CPU-seconds of processing, 100Gb of filestore, 40 tapes and 3 operators for 10 hours can then be calculated by adding the costs of each Cost Element.

Cost Unit	Quantity	Cost per Cost Unit	
CPU-secs	10,000	× £0.126	£1,260
Filestore	100	× £3	£300
Tapes	40	× £0.25	£10
Operator hours	30	× £56	£1,680
		Total	**£3,250**

Table 5.7 – Calculating Activity Costs

It is possible to simplify this further. By using only the CPU-seconds as the factor and by dividing the £3,250 by 10,000 future cost calculations can be based on £0.325 per CPU-second, ignoring the other factors. This, of course, assumes that the other items are always used in broadly the same ratios as the example above.

To ensure true costs, 'Tapes' might have to include the cost of tape decks and maintenance, Operator hours may have to include Service Desk and support staff. In current practice it is rare to perform these calculations 'from the bottom up', i.e. by first breaking down all resource usage to its component parts. Most businesses are content with choosing a fair factor that is agreed to be the measure of usage and use this.

Even after calculating these detailed costs, many installations reduce all measures of usage to two Cost Units: **processor time** and **filestore occupancy**. By taking the total costs (including accommodation, hardware, staff etc) of storage and dividing this by the storage Capacity, a cost per Cost Unit can be determined. Similarly, the cost of providing the processor time (including accommodation, staff, Disaster Recovery etc.) can be divided by the cumulative processor-seconds of processing time to arrive at a cost for each CPU-second. Costs are then allocated to Cost Centres solely on the basis of processor time and filestore occupancy.

5.3.11 Changes affecting costs

When systems change, underlying costs also change. To avoid having to recalculate costs for Cost Units too frequently, IT Finance Management may choose to anticipate Changes or to defer the inclusion of the cost in the Cost Model until stable usage has been established.

An example would be the addition of extra filestore. The purchase cost of the extra filestore can be easily determined but this may affect the calculated cost per Cost Unit of filestore. This is because some overhead costs used in calculating the cost of filestore Cost Units may not change e.g. accommodation, people cost, and some factors may increase the overall costs for filestore, such as the need for additional disk controllers or accommodation.

When performing detailed cost analysis, a cost recovery plans is needed to provide a picture of under (or over) calculation. IT Finance Management may choose to leave the cost per Cost Unit unchanged until the error is greater than, say, 5% to avoid copious recalculations.

There are a number a methods employed to reduce the effect on costs of Changes to equipment and services. They are included here for completeness as they were widely used in the past by mainframe-based organisations and computer bureaux.

Average cost

One common method involves establishing only the average cost of machine time and using this average as the sole Cost Unit. To do this, the total costs for providing the machine during a given period are divided by the total number of hours it is used and the resultant cost per hour of service time is used to calculate costs incurred by each Customer or usage.

The main advantage of the method is that all costs are attributed and a simple rate per hour of machine time is available for budgetary purposes.

The main disadvantages to a Customer, however, are:

■ the rate for machine time can vary from period to period, depending upon the number of other Users.

The main disadvantages to an IT organisation are:

■ as everything is based upon machine time only, changes in other costs, such as staff are not properly recovered

■ if usage decreases, revenues decrease immediately

■ if usage increases (and Capacity was available) an excess profit may be made.

Standard Rate

Standard Rate is calculated by estimating the costs of the resources necessary to meet an estimated Capacity, based upon the forecast workloads and service requirements of all the Customers, and dividing this by a usage factor, such as number of Customers files or system Users. The resultant rate is then fixed for an agreed period.

The advantage of this approach is that a consistent rate is used for a whole period, allowing Customers to predict costs simply.

The disadvantage is that the calculation differs from true cost if the workload changes, for instance if a Customer changes their business process or submits increased volumes of work. Providing that Charging is not directly based on this rate calculation, the impact is minimal and can be addressed when the rate is next calculated.

The current installation life of the equipment has a direct bearing on the rate. Thus, recently installed equipment tends to be lightly loaded giving a high average cost, while a machine just about to be upgraded and, therefore, heavily loaded, gives rise to a low average rate. The major flaw in this method, therefore, is that as usage increases so the cost of machine time per hour decreases. The effect is to show reducing costs when, in fact, no such decrease is actually taking place.

Standard Rate using a standard machine

The use of Standard Rate on a standard machine is a refinement of the Standard Rate described above and is an attempt to overcome the disadvantages that are produced by that method. The rate is not based on the actual forecast machine usage but rather on use of a machine at an average load. The effect is to fix the costs of machine time at what should reflect 'the market rate' – that is the rate charged by external organisations. Estimates can be made of a probable optimum configuration and the resultant additional costs and throughput potential added to the calculation.

The advantage of using this method is that a constant rate is obtained, which is not influenced by the actual equipment installed and allows Customers to match their usage to the anticipated costs. The disadvantage is that the IT organisation has to be capable of delivering service, at all times, to this

Standard Rate. It may not be able to sustain this as business environments and Customer usages change.

5.3.12 Investment appraisal

Basic principles

Sound IT Accounting methods, including the Cost Models described previously, enable businesses to determine the costs of IT Service provision. These costs can be used in Investment Appraisal, a process of determining whether the business benefit from changes to IT Service quantity and quality. Techniques of appraisal have been developed mainly in the context of decisions on capital spending, but the general principles apply to any proposal for spending or saving money that involves changes in the use of resources. Systematic appraisal entails:

- being clear about objectives
- thinking about different ways of meeting them
- estimating and presenting the costs and benefits of each potentially worthwhile option.

Used properly, appraisal leads to better decisions by policy makers and managers; it encourages both groups of people to question and justify what they do and it provides a framework for rational thought about the use of limited resources. It establishes the link between business operations and the cost of underpinning them; it enables the IT organisation to support the business in its cost/benefit analyses.

Investment Appraisal has long been recognised as an essential prerequisite to sound financial management both in the public and private sectors. The importance of Investment Appraisal has grown in recent years as an aid to decision-making in its broadest sense, as a means of identifying efficiency savings and controlling investment expenditure to maximum effectiveness.

There is often a trade-off between capital investment and running cost expenditure: i.e. between maximising effectiveness in the long-term and the risk of failing to achieve short-term goals. Capital investment decisions are essentially longer-term decisions, and thus it is more difficult to hold management responsible and accountable for such decisions. However, because the performance of a manager is often measured on the efficient and effective use of allocated resources within a budget period (of one year), there are only limited ways of holding managers responsible for investment decisions: this is why sound Investment Appraisal procedures are essential to an organisation.

The purchase of IT equipment and software is one of the most important investment decisions an organisation must make. It is therefore crucial that such decisions are properly included in the organisation's strategic planning. In all well-run businesses, there is a requirement to prepare and update a business IS Strategy, thus IT managers both at the strategic and operational levels have a central role in helping to achieve organisational aims and objectives.

From the viewpoint of the business manager, IT investment and the supply of IT Services is the same as any other planned expenditure or allocation of resource in that it is measured in terms of its contribution to the effective, efficient and economic achievement of business goals. It must enable the business to determine whether, for example, the returns would be better from a new IT system or from increased advertising.

Return on Investment

Many organisations now insist that IT projects, in line with other business projects, calculate a Return On Investment (ROI). This enables decision-making to be based on common business standards and allows comparisons between investment in IT and non-IT projects.

The factors classed as a 'Return' vary from organisation to organisation and from year to year. In concept, a return is a revenue or benefit, or the prevention of a lost benefit or revenue (opportunity cost), which is attributable to the project. If the return is divided by the expenditure required to complete the project, a figure is derived which can be compared with the returns on doing nothing (often taken as the bank base rate) or the returns from other projects or initiatives.

$$\text{ROI} = \frac{\text{average increase in profits}}{\text{Investment}} \quad \text{(average taken over an agreed number of years)}$$

The Investment figure may take into account the cost of borrowing money.

The accuracy of the estimates for ROIs is often challenged but that is the nature of estimating benefits. To improve the acceptance of these calculations, it is important to involve the business in determining the returns and how they are to be measured. It is essential that the Capital (one-off) and Operational (on-going) costs for a given project or initiative are identified and can be recorded in the manner previously shown.

Frequently, the benefits lag behind the expenditure and the Return has to be calculated over an agreed period. For some financially aggressive companies this could be 12 months. For others, it could be between 5 and 10 years. The exact expectations of the Financial Management may be dictated by board-level strategies, in turn responding to shareholder demands.

Return on Capital Employed

Shareholders and potential investors in a company look very closely at a number of 'ratios'. The actual ratios felt to be important are subject to fashion but a primary one is the ROCE.

$$\text{ROCE} = \frac{\text{Net Profit Before Tax and Interest}}{\text{Total assets less current liabilities}}$$

This ratio, of the Returns over the Capital Employed, is one frequently used by business analysts to judge the effectiveness of the organisation as a whole. Any changes to services or products would normally be expected to improve this figure and hence the ROCE calculated for a proposed project should be higher than the overall organisation ROCE.

The use of ROCE enables comparisons of different investment opportunities in a fair way and represents how effectively an organisation generates revenue from its assets (the capital employed). At its most basic, this can be compared with bank base rate that offers a ROCE that has minimal risk.

Adventurous organisations usually seek to employ their capital in furtherance of their business while organisations that are undergoing a period of stabilisation reserve the capital for future use.

5.3.13 Total Cost of Ownership

The Gartner Group pioneered a method of calculating the costs of a product or service with the title of 'Total Cost of Ownership' (TCO). This referred to assessing the lifecycle costs of an item rather than just the visible capital expenditure.

The most widely known example was that for Personal Computers. In an era where the price of a PC on a desk had fallen to $2,000, Gartner demonstrated that the 5-year cost of a PC, when taking into account purchasing overheads, upgrades, maintenance, a proportion of support staff and Service Desk costs, disposal etc. was closer to $35,000.

They argued that the cost per PC per year was thus $7,000. This is actually the same process as that described in Paragraph 5.3.9 but applied to a single product/activity rather than a Customer or service.

It remains a vivid demonstration of the difference between purchase price and ownership cost which many Customers of IT organisations still find surprising, particularly when IT budgets are discussed.

The current extension of this is to include Social costs such as recycling, environmental damage or work injury to produce Total Life Cost.

5.3.14 Budgeting, IT Accounting and Charging cycles

If the Cost Model is being developed during the IT financial year, the figures used are based upon the costs already incurred and those predicted for the remainder of the year.

If the Cost Model is being developed to enable the calculation of future IT budgets, it depends upon workload, Capacity and technology requirements from the businesses. It is likely that there will be some iteration or adjustment to both the model and the resulting costs during the budget preparation period (see Figure 5.1).

Table 5.8 shows that there are two distinct cycles associated with Budgeting, IT Accounting and Charging:

- a planning cycle (annual) where cost projections and workload forecasting form a basis for cost calculations and price setting

- an operational cycle (monthly or quarterly) where costs are monitored and checked against budgets, bills are issued and revenue collected.

	Budgeting	IT Accounting	Charging
Planning (annual)	Agree overall expenditures	Establish standard unit costs for each IT resource	Establish pricing policy Publish price list
Operational (monthly)	Take actions to manage budget exceptions or changed costs	Monitor expenditure by cost-centre	Compile and issue bills

Table 5.8 – Budgeting, IT Accounting and Charging cycles

It is important to plan the expenditure and cost recovery profiles periodically. The plans should cover each month in the financial year to facilitate monthly monitoring and cover peaks and troughs. Actual expenditures and recoveries are monitored and compared at the end of each month: the expenditures and recoveries are also compared with what was planned. It is also appropriate to plan Changes to the IT Accounting system to coincide with SLA reviews and any Change should be reflected in the SLAs.

5.3.15 Charging in Profit Centres

In a Profit Centre the objective is to recover, through Charging, an amount greater than the costs incurred. To manage this, it is usual to be able to report the profitability of individual Customers and services at various points in time. The revenues and expenditures are controlled through the Budgeting cycle and operational management of the agreed budgets. The performance of the IT organisation and its managers may be evaluated by measuring both profitability and expenditure.

This may require the overall Financial Model for the IT organisation to include profit and margin information for individual services and the Cost Model must have sufficient detail to enable these calculations.

5.4 Developing the Charging System

5.4.1 Scope of Charging

The concept of Charging for incurred internal costs is not new but is often seen as too bureaucratic and too difficult to implement fairly.

The Charging systems described should enable an organisation to:

- determine the most suitable Charging policies for their organisation
- recover fairly and accurately, the agreed costs of providing the services
- shape Customer and User behaviour to ensure optimal return on IT investment by the organisation.

Such a system controls IT Service costs and influences the proper use of IT resources, so that these scarce resources are used in the manner that best reflects business need.

To calculate the charge for providing IT Services internally, or between (or to) subsidiaries, an organisation must decide, *prior to implementation*, what it is hoping to achieve. One key factor is to analyse the motivational aspects of Charging, considering both the effects upon the provider and the Customer of the service. The objective is to optimise the behaviour of both parties in achieving the organisation's aims.

5.4.2 Charging policies

Traditional, centrally funded, IT Service organisations are under pressure from many sides. They are expected to reduce overall costs while maintaining or improving service in an increasingly complex environment. Business divisions may make unrealistic, competing and unjustifiable demands on the fixed resource available. Within the organisation, staff may feel trapped into a slave role with little opportunity to manage workload or to develop new skills.

Charging for IT Services is seen as a method of:

- forcing the business divisions to control their own Users' demands
- reducing overall costs and highlighting areas of service provision which are not cost effective
- allowing the organisation to match service to justifiable business need, through direct funding.

'Customers will only value what they have to pay for': the corollary is that once Customers have to pay, **they will demand value for their money**.

To implement charging requires a management commitment to resolving the issues that this brings to the organisation as a whole. **Unless the IT Service organisation has the support of the whole company in introducing Charging, it will fail**. It has to be *simple, fair and realistic*:

- *Simple* – 'I can see three more administrators but two less IT professionals' – the overheads of Cost Management must deliver the benefits of an improved overall cost-effectiveness without the bureaucracy commonly associated with IT Accounting for costs.

- *Fair* – 'I can obtain the services cheaper elsewhere and that's what I'll do' – the system must be fair and realistic, services which are not cost-effective need to be reviewed and hard decisions taken. Each business should pay the same money for the same service.

- *Realistic* – 'I'm saving money, even though it must be costing the company more' – anomalies in the charging system will be exploited by businesses. The charging mechanisms must be designed to achieve optimal behaviour.

The image of the IT Service organisation is likely to change; they may be seen initially as demanding money without providing the required service, as having become bureaucratic and focused on trivial accounting. To limit this risk, IT organisations considering the implementation of charging should

- publicise the programme and work with the businesses to define charging policy

- ensure that Service Level Agreements are in place and representative of actual service

- ensure that the benefits are quantifiable and demonstrable.

Four factors govern the requirements of a Charging system in the organisation. For example, full commercial Charging requires that costs can be forecast and collated in a manner that provides profitable revenues in the chosen marketplace. In a simple environment, the aims of a Charging system may be solely to make costs more visible and to cause Customers to pay more attention to them. The four factors are as follows:

1. *Level of recovery of expenditure required*   If the IT organisation opts for full recovery of all costs, then it is opting to function as an autonomous unit, financially self-sufficient. This then requires that costs can be forecast and a Charging system selected that is rational, easily understood and very accurate (although not necessarily based on business unit Charging).

2. *Desire to influence Customer and User behaviour*   Customers and Users are encouraged to make more efficient use of IT resources through levying charges that vary with usage. This can be applied to:

   - reducing the inefficient use of IT resources e.g. reprinting large reports

   - reducing the peak Capacity required e.g. running lower priority work in periods of lower demand.

   There is a conflict between the aim of simple, fixed charges referred to in Paragraph 5.1.2, and the levying of variable charges (which makes the Customer's task of Budgeting more difficult). Leading practice would be to help the Customer identify where poor process or lack of knowledge was increasing the costs of providing their service and work with them to reduce this excess cost to zero over a number of years.

3. *Ability to recovery according to usage*   Recovering costs according to usage requires that the selected Chargeable Items have a reasonable correlation with the amount of resources required to produce them, thereby promoting the perception of a fair pricing and Charging structure.

4. *Control of the internal market*   Introducing market-priced services requires an efficient and effective IT Infrastructure Management with Capacity properly managed, costs well controlled, and services delivered according to expectations.

Pitching services at market price in turn leads to being able to provide quality services consistently, and at reasonable prices, thereby establishing a professional interface with Customers. Ideally, the Charging is based on business deliverables, recognisable to the Customers e.g. business transactions, monthly reports.

5.4.3   Leading practice

Charging Customers by resource usage, particularly where they have no control over that usage, is one of the most hotly debated topics. Most organisations which seek to charge for service, particularly those who are Charging internal business divisions or departments, levy the charges as a method of forcing sound IT Service procurement discipline in both Customers and suppliers (the latter usually being the in-house IT organisation).

In this situation, the business division benefit from being able to evaluate the best options for the supply of IT Service while the in-house IT organisation benefits by the increased awareness of costs resulting in greater efforts by the Customer to reduce or remove inefficient use of IT.

The actual charges made are usually negotiated annually, with the Customer forecasting service quantity and quality requirements and the IT organisation attempting to balance the requirements from all of its Customers with a corporate strategy to provide the lowest cost core services and to support the IT-enabled directions that the businesses and the organisation need to take.

In order to prevent over-Capacity and under-Charging, or under-Capacity which results in overbudget or insufficient service to meet business needs, the majority of organisations separate the provision of core services from the more optional and variable services, such as installing, moving, adding and changing hardware and software Infrastructure components. This excludes applying 'fixes' to hardware and software, which should be seen as part of the cost of providing the agreed IT Services (defined in the Service Level Agreements).

Additional Capacity is often made available through the use of contractors or third-party service agents. The role of a modern IT organisation can often include being an 'honest broker' by assisting the Customers in the selection of the most suitable service provider and reducing costs by 'bulk-buying' on behalf of all Customers.

It is still necessary to fully understand the Cost Model for the in-house IT organisation if the core charges are to be fairly assessed and most Customers need to see this broken down by Chargeable Item in order to perform full comparisons with alternative suppliers of service. Any comparison should take into account the different environment and scope of services provided by external suppliers.

One of the greatest dangers for an IT organisation beginning to apply charges to internal divisions or departments is that, in the absence of a breakdown by element of service, the service provided appears more expensive than outsourcing or third-party suppliers. This is often due to levels of service being offered that could not be duplicated by an external organisation. It is therefore critical that the level of service being provided is discussed with Customers at the same time as proposals to introduce Charging.

5.4.4   Deciding Chargeable Items

The key decisions for Charging are the choice of what to charge for (Chargeable Items) and how much to charge for them. Chargeable Items should be understandable and controllable by the

Customer. Suitable Chargeable Items would be PCs connected to the network or number of batch enquiry jobs submitted. The Customer can then manage their budget by controlling their demand for these items.

The more closely the Chargeable Items relate to the organisation's business deliverables the better the interface to the Customers. Only a lack of information should force Charging to be directly based on resource usage; this lack of information must be overcome and it is important that in the analysis phase, steps are taken to ensure the future Availability of information.

> ### Example
>
> Airlines sell tickets for a journey; they do not issue a bill covering usage of plane, fuel, food, proportional crew costs and so on. The flight or journey is the chosen Chargeable Item.

Often, business deliverables are not suitable as Chargeable Items because they require too detailed a measurement of the resources consumed. For example a Customer may require a service to produce sales analyses but calculating the individual cost of one analysis or even of many types of analysis could add to the total costs unacceptably. In such cases, a structure may have to be established in which the service is charged for as a whole.

Another example is work performed by a statistical analysis program that on one occasion may run through very quickly and on another, consume vast amounts of resource. Although over a period of time, Charging by the business deliverable (the report) may collect the appropriate money for resources consumed, more accurate Charging for the resource-intensive runs may influence the Customer to alter the way in which the program runs enabling a more effective use of IT.

Often, business deliverables cannot be easily attributed to single processes or applications. Programs are rarely written to produce single logical business deliverables: often many Customers utilise portions of a multitude of programs, each of which contributes to the production of parts of many business deliverables. Batch systems in particular are characterised by this trait and identifying the costs of running a large suite of batch jobs may not be possible.

Where a Customer requires charges to be variable, dependent upon usage, the Chargeable Items have to be more specific to that Customer and easily attributable to that Customer. The more freedom the Customer has to define their own service, the more detailed the Charging structure required.

5.4.5   Variable costs and charges

Other costs that are known to vary, for instance computer consumables or overtime hours, have to be managed carefully. In the budget, it may be necessary to estimate the likely annual total and manage the cost by checking monthly that the usage is in proportion to the period measured.

The Customer wants an estimate of the likely charges and possible upper and lower limits, in order that they can budget. If a service depends upon staff costs and the effort required cannot be predicted accurately, the charge calculation might be in the form of:

e.g. first 1000 hours @ £60/hour, subsequent hours @ £100/hour (reflecting the need to pay contractors).

When estimating Costs-by-Customer or Costs-by-service for a new or Changed service, the potential variation from estimate could be large. For example if a major project is due to be implemented, a large variable cost may be the overtime necessary to install equipment outside normal working hours or additional processor time to re-run work.

Often, apparently variable costs do not decrease with decreasing usage, for example decreased usage of a mainframe server may not result in any decreased costs, unless licence, maintenance or hardware charges can be reduced.

Hence, IT Finance Management must be cautious in identifying a cost as variable if this figure is to be used in calculating Costs-by-Customer or Costs-by-service. At the very least, it needs to be rechecked whenever there is a Change to the system or its usage.

5.4.6   Pricing

Pricing is just one element of the marketing quartet – 'product, pricing, promotion, place'. Deciding upon the appropriate charge/price is, therefore, not merely a question of cost recovery but also of its impact upon the demand for the product. If an organisation charges for its product in an open marketplace (i.e. no constraints upon the businesses to buy the service) there must be clear understanding of whether the product (i.e. IT Service) is attractive to the marketplace.

The pricing of any product or service involves:

- the determination of a pricing objective
- understanding the true (not perceived) demand for the service
- accurate determination of Direct and Indirect Costs
- the level of control of the internal market
- understanding the services available externally if Customers have a choice
- legal, regulatory and tax issues.

Achieving an anticipated rate of return figures greatly in many managers' considerations. For the IT Service Management, selling services to internal divisions, the price to be charged is often based on what has to be charged to recover costs, with any cost above market prices explained through the benefits of internal spend, the assumed flexibility of internal organisations or the value-added aspects of working for a common organisation.

Whatever pricing decision is taken it is essential for IT Services Management to first know the actual costs of providing the service.

Examples of pricing methods include:

- cost
- cost-plus
- going rate market price
- fixed price.

Cost   The cost can be defined in several ways, for example:

- full cost (calculated as a total cost of ownership, including depreciation/planned renewal)

■ marginal cost (the cost of providing the service now, based upon the investment already made).

Cost plus There are a number of cost-plus pricing models. The basic form is:

Price = cost + x%

The mark-up (x%) can either be set by the organisation as a standard Target Return, comparable with returns on other business investments, or varied by the IT organisation to meet strategic business needs e.g. encouraging the use of strategic applications but discouraging the use of legacy applications.

Cost plus may be used for large one-off original projects where the costs cannot be easily predicted. The contract protects the supplier.

Going rate The price is comparable with other internal departments within the organisation or with similar organisations.

Market price The price is the same as that charged by external suppliers. Care should be exercised in asking external suppliers to quote prices – they may well disguise a discount to gain the business.

Fixed price The IT organisation sets a price based upon negotiation with the Customer for a set period, based upon a predicted consumption.

However the prices are determined, it is essential that they are visible to Customers so that they can tailor their budget forecasts and Service Level Requirements to match the likely costs.

5.4.7   The internal market

Tied Customers In many IT organisations, Customers are tied to using the internal IT Services. Where the IT organisation is intending to operate as an independent business unit, the stages usually followed are:

- tied, services provided 'free'
- tied, notional Charging introduced
- tied, actual charges introduced (sometimes subsidised, initially)
- untied, real Charging.

Where no direct charge is levied, Customers do not take account of the cost of producing a service and tend to treat it as free. As a consequence they may be extravagant and uneconomical in their use of IT Services.

Untied Customers In an untied situation Charging becomes particularly important because it enables Customers to choose between using the in-house IT Services organisation or outside suppliers, based on the relative quality and price of services offered.

If IT provision is to be untied (i.e. Customers can buy in from other sources), the IT providers should operate on a commercial basis with the aim of recovering full cost, including return on capital employed. When Customers are first freed from being tied to internal IT Services, it is not uncommon to find some organisations subsidising the cost of the internal IT Services, to discourage Customers from switching suppliers. In practice, subsidising IT Services should be discouraged, since prices appear to be unrealistically low.

Charging at full cost entails recovering all revenue spend costs associated with providing an IT Service (including a share of overheads), insurance premium, depreciation of fixed assets and interest on capital employed. It is important that the charge for each service provided by an IT Services organisation should, wherever possible, be charged out at full cost.

Cross-subsidisation between different Customers of the same service should be avoided whenever practicable. Where surpluses and deficits accumulated by a number of services are pooled so that they break-even in total, the effect is to subsidise the cost of one service with the income from another. Such cross-subsidies may lead to a department being criticised for taxing one group of Customers for the benefit of another group.

An IT organisation might not charge out a particular service at full cost when:

a. it is possible to distinguish between internal and external Customers and where the external Customers are the ones with the primary reason for establishing the services – in this case the external Customers could be charged a premium rate in order to make a profit but internal Customers would not be charged

b. there is excess Capacity created for specific Customers that can be used on a short-term basis by other Customers at no cost or at marginal cost.

5.4.8 Differential Charging

Setting different charges for different usage of the same or similar services enables an organisation to reward some usage patterns over others. For instance the use of Differential Charging to increase charges for batch work during peak daytime processing periods may encourage changes in Customer behaviour which reduce overall costs, often without the IT organisation being blamed for poor value of service. This can result in smoothing demand for Capacity and reducing the overall Capacity required.

However, if Customers are not tied to the IT organisation, great care has to be taken in applying differential charges that are not seen in the open market or cannot be justified on a business basis. For instance, trying to discourage the use of daytime development work on a mainframe because of the impact on the Service Levels of the production service, may cause a Customer to move their development workload, decreasing the revenues for the IT organisation without reducing their need for Capacity (i.e. revenue drops, costs stay constant).

5.4.9 Pricing flexibility

IT Finance Management in a Profit Centre may wish to set prices for an annual period to guarantee revenues. However, where new resource requirements are committed to meet the needs of particular Customers it may be necessary to build into any contract for the provision of such services a clause to permit Changes to the Capacity available during the contract period. This reduces the risk of having excess Capacity. The alternative is to be able to sell excess Capacity to other Customers, but it is rare for this to be effective, as other Customers' budgets will also have been fixed.

IT Finance Management in a Profit Centre may wish to consider the stability and duration of a Customer requirement for IT Services and seek regular updated forecasts if demand is likely to change. This may be particularly important if there are large peaks and troughs in Customer demand especially when these are not synchronised to the Availability of additional Capacity. It may be that the management should consider setting specific prices for particular times of usage; but this depends upon size, circumstance, and objectives of the Profit Centre.

5.4.10 Billing

Three objectives are key to Billing:

- the bills must be simple, clear and matched to the ability to pay (in amount, time and method)

- Chargeable Items must be understood by the Customer, with reasonable correlation to usage of resources, including hardware, software, accommodation, and people

- IT Accounting data must be available to provide details on, and justification for, bills.

Bills   Charging information is passed to Customers to make them aware of the cost of the resources used by their business. This can be done by:

- calculating and circulating to managers the full details of the cost of providing each business's IT or services (No Charging)

- as above, but including details about how much the IT organisation would charge, should a charge-back system be operated, without applying transactions to the financial ledgers (Notional Charging)

- as above, but applying transactions to the financial ledgers (Full Charging).

Often the first two options above lead ultimately to the introduction of Full Charging. Whichever approach is followed, the presentation of the information to the Customer must be simple, understandable and honest.

Notional Charging is useful when a Charging system is being introduced for the first time. Notional Charging allows the IT Services organisation to gain experience and time to correct errors in the Charging formulae or cost recovery plans and familiarises Customers with the concept of being charged for using IT resources. Notional Charging is not recommended for long-term use unless the organisation does not intend to move to a real Charging system, because the incentive to become cost conscious is lessened when money does not change hands.

Billing cycle   If Full Charging is introduced, the organisation may also expect the IT organisation to manage cash flow. If a bill is only paid annually, the organisation may have to account for the gap between revenues and expenditure in the same way that a separate company would have to manage its cash flow.

In the simplest example, an IT organisation which pays licence fees annually in advance, has monthly Operational expenditure and some Capital expenditure but does not bill its Customers until the end of the year would operate at a loss throughout the year and only break-even when all bills are paid. This is recognisable to businesses as a cash flow problem, which requires funding. For most organisations, the budgets are agreed and monitored monthly by the Finance department, which takes care of any cash flow issues for the organisation as a whole and can include those of the IT organisation.

In the simplified example in Table 5.9, the overall cost of implementing a service has to be borne within the financial year ending August 31 but the Customer only begins paying once installation is complete.

Expenditure	January	February	March	April	May	June	July	August
Software	£20,000							
Development		£10,000	£10,000	£5,000	£2,000			
Testing				£ 10,000				
Hardware			£30,000					
Installation			£5,000	£2,500				
Support				£2,000	£5,000	£4,000	£1,000	£1,000
Total	£20,000	£10,000	£45,000	£19,500	£7,000	£4,000	£1,000	£1,000
Charge					£26,875	£26,875	£26,875	£26,875
Revenue-expenditure	-£20,000	-£30,000	-£75,200	-£95,002	-£75,882	-£53,965	-£28,858	-£3,530
Cumulative cash/low	-£20,000	-£30,000	-£75,502	-£95,757	-£76,840	-£54,733	-£29,405	-£3,824
Interest @ 1%	£200	£302	£755	£958	£768	£547	£294	

Table 5.9 – The effects of interest on late billing

The result of interest applied to the cash flow is to show a £3,824 shortfall in recovery. Even if the Finance department takes responsibility for managing this, they often want to see the Cash Flow profile to aid their planning.

5.4.11   Conditions for Charging to be effective

In considering whether it is worth investing time and resources in setting up a Charging system, regard should be given as to whether Customers:

a.   have meaningful budgets in which internal IT Services charges are regarded as real costs to be set against other items in the budget – if this is not the case, many of the advantages of Charging are reduced; though it is still worthwhile doing the IT Accounting to provide cost data as management information

b.   have an element of choice in their level of usage of the services provided by the IT Service organisation, both overall and at particular times.

If demand is not sensitive to pricing, Charging is effective only as a mechanism for funding IT Service provision: alternative arrangements such as inter-departmental reviews must take place to verify and assure the cost effectiveness of IT Service provision (see also Paragraph 5.7.11).

Any considerations, however, must take into account the fact that Customers' perception of IT is constantly changing and that they increasingly expect their IT Services supplier to be a thoroughly professional organisation, whether in-house or external.

5.4.12   Case Studies

The intent of this Section is to provide the reader with a few examples of how Charging may become a real hindrance for an organisation if the initial strategy is not clearly defined or the implementation imperfect.

Case Study One: Internal money versus external money

A company has an underground parking lot. This parking lot is for the use of all employees but is over-subscribed. The company decides to introduce Cost Accounting and calculates that the

£200,000 yearly cost of the car parking facility will have to recovered by an internal charge to each department of £50/month for each car park pass issued.

The company parking lot is:

- underground, at the office
- provided as a benefit to staff
- fitted with electronic remote control to open/close the main door
- under surveillance by cameras and security guards.

A hotel nearby provides parking facilities:

- outside, 200m away
- with a hotel-operated barrier
- with no security or guarantee of safety.

Because the hotel has the space free during working hours, it need only recover costs of administration plus any profit it wishes to make. It decides to charge £30/month for business car parking. The result of this is that the internal parking lot is only used at 20% of its Capacity while the hotel parking lot is full.

Using the external hotel parking facility costs less to the department manager but more overall to the organisation, as it has to pay the costs of the building and would usually prefer to minimise external spend. They cannot reduce their overall costs, as the company parking is an integral part of the offices and grounds.

Resolution

The company agreed that it should subsidise parking to reduce the charge to £40/month while also banning managers from purchasing outside services when suitable internal services are available.

Bottom Line

Do not allow businesses to buy external services when suitable internal services are available.

Avoid higher internal prices than the market prices.

Case Study Two: Exceeding business need

One company is charging £860 a year for the provision of an Infrastructure to which Users' workstations are connected. This Infrastructure is available 24 hours a day, monitored 16 hours a day and includes a number of facilities such as office automation tools, shared printers, e-mail, external gateways (faxes, Internet, access to large servers).

Some small departments (from 5 to 20 Users) were used to very simple peer-to-peer Infrastructure that suited their needs. Moving to the new, more expensive common Infrastructure did not appear to provide any benefits and even seemed to add to overheads.

Several of these departments conducted a study and found that it would be less expensive for them to continue with their dedicated Infrastructure and just have one shared workstation connected to the common Infrastructure for e-mail purposes.

Resolution

The charges were adjusted by reducing the standard charge and adding an additional charge for those requiring the additional facilities. The standard charges were raised above true cost, under the direction of the organisation management, to encourage Customers to adopt the systems that were felt to be strategic and to wean them from outdated systems.

Bottom Line

A small, dedicated Infrastructure tailored to specific needs is always cheaper than a company wide Infrastructure.

However, several small, dedicated Infrastructures always cost much more than a global one and are also unlikely to meet strategic aims.

Case Study Three: Discouraging use of services

A company provided its Users with a dedicated, outsourced Service Desk facility. The vendor charged the company on a per-call basis, the price varying in bands, depending upon the total number of calls during the month. The charging policy was to recharge all IT spending to the business on the basis of true cost.

Once the Service Desk was in place, Customers realised that they could reduce their costs by not placing Service Desk calls. Some business managers instructed their Users not to use the Service Desk, or to route all issues through a single, local support person.

Decreasing the total number of calls decreased the calculated charges to the Customer but did not reduce overall price of the service by the same amount. It also resulted in:

- increased wasted time for Users
- reduced effectiveness of IT systems
- poor perception of the IT Services and the IT organisation
- additional work for the IT organisation to discover problems
- reduced leverage in negotiating service costs with the outsourcing vendor.

Resolution

The charging method was changed to one in which a fixed fee per User was negotiated, based upon an estimated call rate taken from previous years' volumes and business predictions. This charge was reviewed quarterly to check that call levels were within agreed thresholds.

Bottom Line

Some cost should be fixed and should not depend on actual usage.

Case Study Four: Hidden costs

In the same Service Desk context as the previous example, business managers may be tempted to set up their own Service Desk facility by appointing staff dedicated to this. It may cost less to the business department than a centralised desk and allows the business to direct the efforts of the staff toward the Incidents and Problems that concern them. However, the total cost to the organisation of allowing one or more businesses to do this is:

- the quality and level of service will obviously not be the same
- knowledge will not be shared with other departments
- studies will be undertaken on a department basis where they should have been on the company or group basis
- costs for this dedicated facility will not be monitored or at least not monitored centrally.

98

This results in an under-used central facility and an increase in hidden costs of IT as the business Service Desks are not accounted for in the IT budget and probably not fully costed by the businesses.

Resolution

The organisation forced all business units to measure effectiveness and introduce cost analysis. This demonstrated that the internal Service Desk and support services were actually costing more in total than would be the case if the central facility were correctly used.

Bottom Line

If the businesses are allowed to develop private Infrastructure or services, it may result in:

- a decreasing influence for the IT organisation

- an increasing IT cost to the organisation

- inefficient use of resources and IT

- arguments where the department and the central Service Desk are asked to resolve problems or maintain service in areas of overlapping responsibility.

5.5 Planning for IT Accounting and Charging

This Section covers the evaluation and planning activities necessary to prepare for the implementation of sound IT Accounting and Charging systems within IT organisation. It is not exhaustive and is intended to provide specific activities within a formal project framework such as PRINCE2.

The planning phase can be expected to take 3-6 months, mostly dependent on the size and complexity of the IT organisation and the Availability of data. The preparation for IT Accounting can be carried out at any time but it is recommended that any new or amended IT Accounting system be brought into use at the start of a new financial year. See also Paragraph 5.3.14.

5.5.1 The project

The first step in planning the introduction of, or Changes to, IT Accounting and Charging is to confirm the scope and requirements with agreed Terms of Reference (TOR).

The responsibility for IT Accounting and Charging in the operational environment does not need to be decided at this point although in many organisations, the person most suitable for this role would take the project management responsibility for its introduction.

The Project Board This should comprise the following:

- the director of IS in the organisation

- a senior manager in the Financial Services division

- one or more of the Customers to be billed

- IT Services Management.

The project team It is vital that the team has a fundamental appreciation of both the organisation's business and the IT Services organisation in order to understand the options available to management. Team members must understand the principles of IT Accounting and the following Sections are intended to provide the proper context and background for the work.

The board make all of their business decisions based on the recommendations of the project team's feasibility study and set appropriate budgets for the development and implementation project.

5.5.2 Feasibility study

Decisions about the scope and objectives of any implementation are based on the findings of the feasibility study, although decisions may be imposed because of management adoption of Profit Centre, or Shared Services initiatives.

The feasibility study objectives should include:

- evaluation and quantification of the likely benefits and costs of the introduction of IT Accounting and/or Charging

- recommendations on Charging policy

- outline implementation plans

- identification of the resources, staff and costs needed to introduce and run IT Accounting and Charging

- specification of the financial interfaces to the rest of the organisation

- recommendations on Customers' control of budgets: are they simply for information purposes ? can Customers spend the money externally?

- assessment of scope for customisation of billing and purchasing systems to support the IT Accounting and Charging system

- evaluation of any support tools (e.g. monitoring, IT Accounting) that are already available, or can be obtained

- identification of Charging or IT Accounting activities already being carried out within the IT organisation

- the likely business components (for example, timesheets, cheques, enquiries, pay-slips) upon which the recommended Charging system is to be based

- any risk areas that might militate against successful introduction of IT Accounting and Charging

- performance indicators for the successful implementation of IT Accounting and Charging.

The following information should be included in the TOR for the study:

- the organisation's management requirements (what IT Accounting and Charging are intended to achieve, and whether the IT organisation wish simple cost recovery or the creation of a Profit Centre)

- specification of how any new systems are expected to interface with any existing systems.

It is important for the project team to gain a clear understanding of the business of the organisation and highlight areas of doubt for a senior management decision. For example how to charge an intermediate Customer such as Personnel or Finance, who are using the systems on behalf of another business department.

When management approval has been given, a project plan must be produced for the development and implementation phase (based upon the outline plan produced by the feasibility study).

5.5.3   The project plan

Planning for the introduction of, or Changes to, IT Accounting and Charging must be carried out in an integrated fashion. The project may require discrete stages and the project plan must cover:

- analysis of costs and potential Charging policies

- design and development of IT Accounting and Charging systems

- implementation

- post-implementation and review.

The project team must:

- establish and agree the organisational and budget boundaries of IT Services

- identify the business objectives of the organisation in introducing IT Accounting to IT Services

- align the review of IT Accounting and Charging with other IT organisation planning

- determine whether Charging will be implemented, with what objectives and to what level of detail

- develop a spreadsheet to capture the projected expenditures allocated to projected usage of major resource types

- establish the Cost Units to be used and the costs for each Cost Unit

- develop a feed-back system to verify that the actual expenditure and usage are, within acceptable limits, comparable with cost and workload projections

- ensure the mechanisms for recovering under- and over-charge are in place (if it becomes necessary to correct mismatches)

- examine the cost of maintaining existing quality levels and how much the organisation loses through waste, inefficiency or poorly specified service.

The initial analysis can be carried out by developing stand-alone spreadsheets or computer applications. On-going analysis and reporting is best carried out with the assistance of a proprietary package, designed for IT organisations.

5.5.4   Designing the Cost Model and related processes

To design the Cost Model, it is necessary to determine the way in which the businesses set out their IT requirements and even to assist in setting this in place if no formal process exists. The IT organisation budget information and policies for IT Accounting and Charging are also needed. There are a series of steps that should be followed in developing the Cost Model:

Identify the planning cycle

It is important to analyse the planning cycles in the organisation so that the source, timing and content of required plans are identified.

Business divisions must produce business plans that include IT requirements (i.e. service requirements and workload forecasts) for their expected use of IT Services. These plans provide the information that enables the IT Executive to design the target Technical Architecture and produce the Operational Plan for the IT organisation. The production of these business plans is iterative and the IT organisation often develops a key role in advising on their production

A simple model of this process was discussed in Paragraph 5.1.2.

Establish current costs

Identify the IT Services that will be provided for the coming financial year, then estimating the total cost of resources needed to provide these services. Determine the Cost Units that are to be used for apportioning Indirect Costs and calculate a Cost per Cost Unit for each, as described in Paragraph 5.3.6. Use this data to produce a first estimate of the Cost-by-Customer or Cost-by-service, whichever is required.

The data necessary to identify costs is not always readily available in most IT Service organisations. It may be necessary to know, for each Customer, the proportionate use of resources that are not currently accounted for, e.g. staff, accommodation, hardware, and software. Ideally, monitoring of resource usage should be automatic, using one or more software tools but some data is likely to be collected from paper records and reports or from stand-alone systems.

If costs are not properly identified it is likely that the initial calculations will be shown to be inaccurate during the monitoring periods. This could entail a redesign of the system, at the very least, complex recalculation of the spreadsheets will be needed.

To paint a more complete picture of cost estimates, the Project Team must attempt to quantify the anticipated growth (or other change) in workloads expected in each financial year. This information might be present in the SLA, may be obtained from Capacity Management or from the User community. This workload information is necessary to establish the amount of work by business units (i.e. the business units to be charged, if Charging is to be implemented) that is to be undertaken by the IT organisation and from this, the unit costs for the future years.

Check the data and the model

To validate the Cost model, it is important to calculate and check the identified costs more than once. The model should be checked by performing a full balance check. This check should be made in more than one way, e.g. by totalling all the individual Customers' costs and proving that this equals the budget figures as shown in Figure 5.3 and also by totalling the individual service costs and proving that this comes to the same figure.

5.5.5   Performance indicators

The obvious measures of the success of the IT Accounting and Charging systems are that:

- cost recovery profiles and expenditure profiles prove to be accurate
- charges, where applied, are seen to be fair
- the IT organisation is provided with the expected income/level of profits
- IT Customers' and Users' behaviour and perceptions change.

The business objective of either break-even or profit whichever is the objective of the organisation, should therefore be met.

However, even the most accurate Cost Model may become invalid because of changes in Customer behaviour, perhaps resulting from changes in the behaviour of their clients. While accuracy in the calculations of the costs and associated charges is the objective, there are additional aspects of success that can be measured and used to determine the effectiveness of the IT Accounting system. Examples of other performance indicators that could be used include:

- plans and budgets produced on time
- specified reports produced at the required time

- the inventory schedules are kept up-to-date all costs are accounted for

- timeliness of annual audits

- meeting of monthly, quarterly and annual business objectives

- the number (and severity) of Changes required to the IT Accounting system

- accuracy of monthly, quarterly and annual profiles

- number of Changes made to the Charging algorithm (where appropriate).

5.5.6 Dependencies

The three most important project dependencies are:

- senior management must fully understand the implications and costs of the introduction of IT Accounting and Charging and fully support it

- Service Level Management must provide information on the impact on service levels of different usage patterns that may result from Charging (and also to help to ensure delivery of service in accordance with User expectations)

- IT Infrastructure Management should be set in place to ensure that IT Services provided are efficient and effective, at reasonable cost.

The most important dependency is that there is senior management commitment to the introduction of IT Accounting and/or Charging systems. Senior managers must also be prepared to specify what they require from the systems and how these systems should interface with other systems in the organisation (e.g. Capacity Management). A fully functioning system also depends on the Availability of detailed and accurate information.

Professional IT Accounting skills are required to help ensure the IT Accounting and Charging systems are well designed. Where accountants are not available, company auditors may be able to advise.

5.5.7 Organisation

IT Accounting is an integral part of the IT Services Management structure and must be permanently staffed. IT Services Management is responsible for the IT Accounting discipline and whoever performs the Finance Manager role should report directly to IT Services Management.

IT Finance Management is responsible for the day-to-day operation of the IT Accounting and Charging systems and ensuring that the planned structure is operational. The Project Management Office and other IT Services managers also have responsibilities for preparing and checking budgets and for assisting IT Finance Management in determining suitable IT Accounting methods.

It is likely that IT Finance Management needs support to carry out the work. In a small organisation the process of Service Level Management and the disciplines of IT Accounting and Charging could probably be combined so long as sufficient assistance is available to support the day-to-day activities. It is also common to share the responsibility for the IT Accounting aspects of IT Accounting and Charging with the Finance department.

Responsibility for IT Accounting and Charging for IT Services should belong to the IT organisation, since it is their task to ensure that the business objectives underpinned by IT are met; responsibility for IT Accounting of IT Services cannot be placed anywhere else.

5.5.8　Tools

Except for very small IT Services organisations, it is not practical to attempt IT Accounting without the Availability of a suitable application or software tool. Facilities required include the management of ledgers, reporting of resource usage, and the calculation of costs according to the chosen Cost Model. Tools are available to provide the data that IT Accounting and Charging require but most IT organisations use standard spreadsheets for developing budgets and Cost Models.

Frequently, the General Ledgers and Purchasing systems are already in place, and the tools for producing Cost and Charging analysis require methods of importing data from these. Service Desk and integrated Service Management processes are likely to be able to provide data to be input to cost calculation but care must be exercised that the development and implementation of such facilities does not lead to systems which are too expensive to maintain.

5.5.9　Training

Everyone involved with IT Accounting should be provided with appropriate training about IT Accounting. It is also recommended that they understand the fundamentals of Capacity Management, Change Management, Configuration Management and Service Level Management issues.

Many training organisation offer courses with titles similar to 'Financial Management for non-Finance Managers' which cover the understanding of Budgeting, annual reports and balance sheets necessary to undertake the implementation of IT Accounting for IT Services.

5.6　Implementation

The time necessary to implement IT Accounting and Charging depends heavily on the tools and information already available but can take six or more months even with good tools and information readily available. It is impossible to introduce full Charging other than at the start of a financial year, although Notional Charging can be introduced at any time, providing that the impact on behaviours has been fully anticipated (see Paragraph 5.6.3).

IT Accounting can be introduced at any time although it is usual to use a full year's data in calculating Costs per Costs Unit. Where a full year's data is not available or is inconsistent (perhaps as the result of organisational Changes) the extrapolations made should be clearly identified and appraised for risk.

5.6.1　Documentation

The operational procedures covering normal daily, weekly, monthly and yearly operation of all the aspects of IT Accounting should be documented, including the planning, cost reporting, cost recovery reporting and billing activities. In addition to the documents covering IT operational procedures, User manuals should be developed covering learning, references and User guide for IT Finance Management and staff.

It is advisable to attempt to implement a system without proper and complete documentation to help the Customers and support personnel and to complement training, particularly when the system involves accounts procedures that may be unfamiliar to staff outside the Finance department. The complexity of the support documentation varies depending on whether the Customer is the IT Accounting team, the Service Desk or a business Customer.

It is vital to cover:

- how and when IT management and Customer management will be informed of costs
- how IT Accounting data is to be collected
- how the Charging system works and what pricing structures are to be used
- how budgets are monitored between bills
- how accounts are to be settled
- who is responsible for policing the IT Accounting system and producing reports, bills, and so on
- how and when auditing takes place
- what contingency option(s) are in place
- how errors in billing will be handled
- what Change Control is applied to the IT Accounting system.

The analysis and design deliverables should be retained as detailed support documents.

5.6.2   Preparation

Set up the Cost centres and Cost Units

IT Accounting is dependent upon the analysis of cost data collected from a variety of sources. Some is collected from automatic meters (e.g. processor-seconds, Service Desk calls) other data may be from semi-automatic processes (e.g. timesheets, purchasing systems, equipment movement forms) or from manual calculation (e.g. support out-of-hours records). Coding should therefore be simple to ensure an easy fit from these different sources.

The data has to be consolidated in away that enables the total costs to be easily checked against financial ledgers and for sub-sets of cost information to be easily derived.

Frequently, the Finance department has already allocated the Cost Centres and the main tasks for Finance Management in coding Cost Units are:

- Separating capital and operational costs (in concert with Finance)
- classifying costs (using agreed Cost Types)
- identifying the Direct Costs and Indirect Costs
- agreeing a fair system of apportioning Indirect Costs (some iteration may be necessary as outline requirements for Charging become clearer and practical considerations of measurement affect intellectual requirements)
- checking the above with technical, financial and Customer staff.

Set up data recording

In parallel with implementing the system design, examine the existing data recording mechanisms for information about planning, reporting and (eventually) Charging. Information is needed about:

- workloads/schedules
- services/Customers
- costs/cost centres

■ resource inventories (hardware and software).

Workload and service data should be available from the Capacity Management database: cost information (including future acquisitions) should be available from Accounts departments or from Configuration Management. Configuration Management should also be capable of providing inventories of all resources.

The data-recording task does not end once the initial data is available. IT Accounting is based on an annual cycle and it is important to ensure that all required data is made available on time, every time. It is not possible to perform accurate cost analysis unless the required data is routinely available.

Select, install and test software tools

Many organisations use spreadsheets, both to work out the Costs per Cost Unit (and the Price) and to calculate the costs and charges to each Customer. Data is often typed into the spreadsheets which may become very complex but due to the wide range of sources of data, very few integrated packages exist other than for the specific Charging for mainframe usage.

A number of Data Mining, Data Warehouse or OLAP products can be configured to use the data embedded in other applications e.g. Time Management, Work Management or Systems Management products. Where software tools have been developed or purchased, install and test them at this stage to ensure that they function as expected.

Extend measuring

Once data collection has begun and early analyses performed, it may become necessary to extend existing monitoring systems or develop new ones. Timesheets frequently have to be automated to be used in IT Accounting and procedures need to be put in place to enforce use of them.

Usage data from the network or distributed systems may have to be collected if apportionment of costs is required at this level.

5.6.3 Awareness

Mounting a cost awareness campaign in the organisation prior to project initiation has significant benefits in reducing the resistance to new processes and in helping Customers and Users to gain a fuller understanding of how they can affect costs. Short presentations should be given about identifying costs and why costs must be controlled.

The presentation must cover plans for cost recovery and the timescale over which it is intended to recover the identified costs. If it is the policy of the organisation to profit from IT, or indeed to plough back profit into IT, then some information about how the profits are to be used is also appropriate.

Capacity and cost

Improving the level of services may increase costs because it is necessary to increase Capacity. Similarly, cutting costs may alter the Capacity, the quality and variety of services provided. It is the balance between costs and Capacity that must be maintained if services are to be provided which are matched to agreed business need.

Customer reaction

Identifying all of the costs necessary to provide IT Services and establishing a fair means of Charging for those services places IT Service provision on a business-like footing. Customers become aware that they have to pay for the cost of their IT Services and, if charged, may change the amount of service they use or the pattern of their usage.

Even without explicit charges, awareness of costs focuses attention on the effectiveness, efficiency and management capability of the IT organisation and it is important to be as open and honest as is possible about the true costs uncovered. Where costs are felt to be unacceptable, a forward path has to be negotiated between IT and the business.

Flexibility of charges

Customers may want flexible Charging, where lower use of a service results in lower charges and vice versa. While this is reasonable, there are key reasons for an IT organisation to limit flexibility in Charging:

a.   if the IT organisation cannot reduce its own costs in tandem with any reduced consumption, it risks having to subsidise Customers (e.g. if there is a fixed contract for mainframe or network Capacity)

b.   it is not usually in the overall organisation or business interest to encourage short-term or paper cost-saving, e.g. if charges are related to Service Desk calls, management may discourage the use of the Service Desk, resulting in inefficient use of the IT systems and hidden User dissatisfaction.

Current leading practice for IT organisations running a mainly in-house service is to determine the desired Capacity of each Customer and provide core services that meet, in concert with the requirements of other Customers, the bulk of the needs of the Customers. Flexibility is then reserved for the additional services that either cannot be predicted or are used differently by different Customers. Some element of flexibility may be retained using external service suppliers to assist during periods of peak demand and by setting thresholds outside of which the Service Levels are suspended, removing the need for over-Capacity.

Perceptions

The fact that charges are made is likely to cause Customers and Users to recognise that the resources are not a low-cost commodity that can be wasted. However, services that were previously perceived as good value may suddenly be perceived as poor value when charges are made. It is the responsibility of all IT Services Managers to ensure that the true cost of providing IT Services is published.

Adopting sound IT Accounting practices should establish in people's perceptions that the IT Services organisation is business-oriented and cost conscious.

Implementation resource

Staff with accountancy and practical IT experience are rare. IT Accounting and Charging may be new disciplines in IT Services meaning that expertise outside of IT Services Management must be made easily available to Finance Management.

5.6.4   Pilot the system

If the IT Accounting information is new or involves Charging Customers for the first time, it is recommended that the first year of running the system should be viewed as a pilot scheme, perhaps using Notional Charging. This enables the IT organisation to influence the demands of the Customer before Charging is fully implemented if that particular Customer is using resources at a higher rate than was first measured or estimated.

If the system is to be piloted, one approach is to begin with mission critical services and to leave less important services for later. A new or Changed system should begin at the start of the financial year, providing that there is sufficient data available to estimate costs and budgets for the first year of full operation.

If monitoring of the costs or charges identifies discrepancies or anomalies, the credibility of the IT Accounting process may be compromised. Providing that this occurs during a pilot, the Charging algorithms and/or the cost projections can be re-examined and corrected before introducing the system fully, thus maintaining credibility.

Customers should be notified at the earliest possible stage about events that are likely to cause changes to their bills. It is important that Customers are aware of any likely alterations to charges that may result from Changes to:

- the IT Infrastructure and services
- the IT organisation
- the business environment outside Customer control.

5.6.5   Monitor the system

Monitor the actual resources being consumed (regardless of whether a Charging system is to be introduced) three to six months in advance of system implementation in order to gain experience. It is essential to make sure that this data can be correlated with that from financial planning and Capacity Management.

For example, if support staff costs are now to be attributed to the Customer using the application or system requiring support, it is essential to be able to check that the total time being logged is true and reasonable before using it in any calculation of cost (and particularly of charge).

5.6.6   Plan IT Accounting and Charging Continuity

It is possible that, in the event of a major disaster, the IT Service Management Plan is to withdraw the IT Accounting and Charging systems entirely. If not, then IT Accounting and Charging must be tested as part of the Disaster Recovery testing.

The IT Service Management Plan should reflect the organisation's use of IT Accounting and Charging. Simply holding paper copies of spreadsheets and bills does not provide sufficient contingency in the event of, say, a spreadsheet corruption. The dependency of the organisation on IT Accounting and Charging varies with the type of organisation, e.g. a bureau would find it difficult to operate without some form of Charging.

IT Finance Management should determine which reports and plans are indispensable to the organisation and ensure that they can be produced in the event of a major Incident affecting the IT Accounting or Charging systems. The contingency arrangement for IT Accounting and Charging needs to be regularly reviewed.

The impact of a disaster is minimised by keeping off-site back-up of all required data and by maintaining stand by or spare equipment upon which to run the IT Accounting and Charging systems but the data sources on which they rely may not be available in the event of a disaster. Any integration that has facilitated the transfer of data from these sources to the Cost Model or Charging application may be impossible to use in the event of a disaster. See also Chapter 7.

5.7   Ongoing management and operation

This Section is concerned with the review of the IT Accounting and Charging systems and with the ongoing operation of the IT Accounting and Charging system, including dealing with variance from forecasts.

5.7.1   Ongoing operation

The day-to-day operation of the IT Accounting system includes both the production of cost and Charging data and the checking of its accuracy. Checks to be performed are broadly covered in Paragraph 5.3.14 but a more detailed schedule is provided in the rest of this Paragraph:

Daily/Weekly

- collect cost data and check accuracy and completeness

- instigate Changes, if necessary through Change Management

- attend Change Advisory Boards (CAB) as required.

Monthly

- run the cost reporting system

- check that costs are in line with predictions and explain any variances

- produce cost analyses

- produce charges per Customer and compare to budgets

- circulate a monthly balance sheet

- review cost recovery metrics against IT business targets.

Quarterly/half-yearly

- prepare for the annual budget cycle by checking quarterly, half-year or interim forecasts (inward from businesses and upward from IT)

- assess the accuracy of the Charging algorithms by balancing the actual revenue against expected revenue (similarly for actual costs against predicted)

- assess the accuracy of forecasts as a means of improving them in the future

- verify the price lists

- plan the Changes necessary for next year's staff and resources and any alterations to cost projections and cost recovery projections.

Annually

- review and audit the IT Accounting system and produce final accounts for the previous financial year

- produce annual cost analyses

- circulate a final balance sheets

- review standard Cost Units (amending only if critical to accuracy as changes make any year-on-year comparisons difficult)

- recalculate Costs per Cost Unit to check for conformance with predicted results

- review Charging policies and IT Accounting methods

- assist Customers and other IT managers to set IT budgets for new financial year

■ review the IT Accounting and Charging systems to ensure that the IT organisation's business objectives are being met

■ review the IT Service Continuity Plans and ensure that the dependency on IT Accounting or Charging systems is clear.

5.7.2 Change Management

The IT Accounting system, when running in production, is based on an annual cycle for which plans and budgets are produced. Expenditure and revenue can be compared against these plans and budgets. If fundamental Changes to the system are needed they should be aligned to this annual cycle. However, it should be noted that to be in place for the start of a financial year, they have to be apart of the budget cycle and may require planning 3 – 6 months earlier.

If Changes cannot wait to be implemented until the beginning of a new financial year, there may be severe consequences involving Customers (prices may have to go up, costs must be curtailed, demand reduced and so on). It may be possible to arrange for packages of Changes to be aligned to the Changes made to SLAs between IT Services and its Customers.

Where Changes are unavoidable, their introduction must be subject to Change Management procedures. Small-scale Changes must also be subject to Change Management. Such small-scale Changes can, however, be made through short-term special arrangements, but must be included in the IT Accounting system for the coming financial year. Agree all decisions about Changes to the system under the control of Change Management, with representatives from:

■ IT Financial Management

■ Service Level Management

■ Finance department

■ IT Services Management.

If Customers are affected, Customer management must also participate in the decision-making.

5.7.3 Reasons for changing the IT Accounting and Charging system

With a complex IT Accounting system there may be many reasons for Changes needing to be made. Examples of these are:

■ Changes to the organisation or the IT organisation

■ mathematical or base data errors in the IT Accounting or associated systems leading to incorrect forecasts, budgets or calculations

■ workloads varying from forecast, leading to recovery above or below predictions

■ Customers demanding volumes of service which would or have exceeded their budgets.

Careful monitoring of the system during the pilot phase reduces the likelihood that major Changes will become necessary and where Changes are identified, certainly lessens their impact.

5.7.4 Dealing with variances

It is recommended that any variances between calculated costs and current Customer budgets are reduced or eliminated prior to implementing Charging.

Any errors must be rectified at source to prevent recurrence; where forecasts are at variance with actuals, the appropriate expenditure plans, cost recovery plans or proposed charges, must be altered. At all times, openness with Customers, even in a commercial environment is advisable.

It is recommended that where Charging is introduced (real or notional) the charges should not be altered, even during the pilot, unless serious errors are discovered which have caused very large variance in recovery forecasts leading to severe over-charging (and of course, excessive revenue) or under-charging leading to severe losses.

Where price lists must be altered and charges raised or lowered, give advance notice to provide a warning to Customers about the impact of the impending changes on their budgets.

5.7.5 Workload variance

Explicit in the organisation's SLAs should be statements about what happens if a Customer's workload exceeds (or falls below) agreed levels. The statements should cover this eventuality where:

- spare Capacity is available
- spare Capacity is not available.

In any organisation it is likely that the importance of the business in question will directly affect the contingency action for this type of problem. In every case however, the first question to answer is 'Who pays the bill?' – the second is 'How?'

IT organisations usually have a margin of Capacity in addition to forecast. It is likely that increased Capacity will be provided, if available, and the IT Services organisation will negotiate an uplift in charges for the next IT Accounting period if the usage continues.

If spare Capacity is not available, it might be necessary to engage a bureau or even to upgrade machine Capacity. The cost will probably be met centrally, but it is very important to ensure that SLAs are not compromised and are specific on these issues.

The organisation as a whole may need to consider whether a Customer is allowed to continue to use excess resources to the detriment of other Customers (whether staff time or computing resource). Every case, however, is likely to require a management decision and mechanisms must be in place to cater for such problems.

When spare Capacity is plentiful, its ad hoc use must not set a precedent. Spare Capacity is usually earmarked for future use (indeed it is wasteful to maintain plentiful spare Capacity). Customers wishing to increase their use of resources on a long-term basis must provide a business case and obtain authorisation via the normal channels. It is vital that the SLAs made with other Customers are adhered to and not compromised to accommodate a single Customer.

5.7.6 Cost variance

Costs for Cost Units (see Paragraph 5.3.10) are the basis of the budgeted costs of IT Services. If they have been miscalculated, they affect the overall recovery of costs (i.e. Charges) and this has to be addressed by recalculation as soon as is possible (see Paragraph 5.7.4).

Where there has been some change in the expenditure required to purchase or maintain the IT Services, it may be possible to pass this on to the Customer, with their agreement, particularly if the costs are clearly attributable to a single Customer; an example of this might be increases in software or hardware maintenance.

Usually, such changes should have been predicted and it is seen as a responsibility of the IT organisation to have managed any changes in the price of the commodities they purchase to provide IT Service.

5.7.7 Revenue variance

Although the organisation may decide to run the IT Services at a profit, it is possible that monitoring reveals either too great a profit (leading to Customer dissatisfaction) or a shortfall. Where too much revenue is generated the cause must be identified and justified or corrected; unless absolutely necessary the charges must not be altered. Some of the reasons for generating excessive revenue include:

- workload has grown faster than forecast and flexible Charging has resulted in increased charges although sufficient Capacity was available without the IT organisation incurring additional costs

- Customers are being forced to buy more IT resource than they anticipated possibly because there is insufficient Capacity or inefficient service

- charges really are excessive.

Where a poor service is the difficulty, the underlying causes must be addressed. When workload growth is a problem, forecasts must be revised (otherwise trouble is being stored) and it may become necessary to make a case to procure additional Capacity.

If the IT Services are sustaining a loss, possible causes include:

- running insufficient work (perhaps forecasts of workload were too high)

- running costs are too high (perhaps because of too much overtime, because staffing is above complement or underlying costs of operation have increased)

- charges really are too low.

Once more, forecast revision may become necessary. Where running costs are the problem, the IT Services organisation will have to examine the possibility of making economies.

5.7.8 Service level issues

Demands for Changes in service levels are similar to workload Changes and should be handled through Service Level Management.

Demand for extra resource (which is incurring cost) is often due to attempts to resolve poor service or due to additional work to complete budgeted tasks where the estimates are now shown to be inaccurate. Customers usually expect IT Services to manage this without additional cost although there may be no IT budget available. The likely effect is a stretching of resource, which impacts all service levels; hence Service Level Management must be involved in any decisions to provide Chargeable service in excess of agreed budgets.

Since no IT organisation can actually 'turn off the tap', it is essential that the IT Finance Management tracks Customer budgets to be able to identify over-runs before they occur.

5.7.9 Ongoing planning

Any Changes to IT Capacity (or indeed any other IT or human resources) that were not present in the tactical plans must be reported to Finance Management for inclusion in revised cost plans, projections and so on.

Typically, workload changes as agreed at SLA reviews must also be reported. Cost implications and Charging implications must be explicit in SLAs. SLA changes are normally aligned to annual budget negotiations but IT Services Management may delegate to Service Level Management the powers to vary SLAs within agreed bounds during the year (see Chapter 4).

If there is along lead-time between planning and bringing into service (e.g. due to delaying implementation to the start of the financial year) it may become necessary to revise the cost plans, projections and so on. Cost planning should use data that is no more than 3 months old.

5.7.10 Management reporting

Regular monthly reports for each supported business are required. A monthly summary of costs and revenue should be provided to IT Services Management, together with a balance sheet. Senior IT management committees may also require a report, probably each quarter.

Although the format of management reports is largely dependent on the standards set by the organisation it is suggested that reports to Customers are kept simple but include details of:

- how much they have spent on IT during the financial year
- whether the charges made match the predicted profile
- the current Charging policies and IT Accounting methods
- how the IT organisation is investing any profits (e.g. in Infrastructure or service improvements)
- any variances, what caused them and what actions are being taken.

Reports to IT Services Management should cover:

- cost total, broken down by business
- cost analyses by service line, equipment domain or other relevant view
- revenues total, broken down by business
- costs and cost recovery against profile
- outlook on costs and cost recovery
- problems and costs associated with IT Accounting and Charging systems
- recommendations for changes
- future investments required.

Senior IT executive committee reports should contain similar information. Reports from any external efficiency and effectiveness reviews or from auditors are also of interest and these should include details of any recommendations that were followed up from previous reports.

5.7.11 Auditing the systems

The purpose of the checks during an audit or review is to demonstrate that:

- the systems are delivering the expected benefits

- the systems are efficient, effective and cost-justified
- procedures are formal and strictly followed.

The post-implementation review and subsequent periodic reviews of the IT Accounting and Charging systems should check that they are working effectively. They also check that IT Finance Management is continually reviewing the system and that all identified deficiencies are corrected at source to prevent recurrence.

Audits may be performed by internal staff or by external auditors. In both instances audits are intended to confirm that IT Finance Management and the supporting personnel are adhering to defined procedures.

Management should however operate its own controls and not rely solely on audit, whether internal or external. IT Finance Management should therefore perform their own audits and checks to reassure management that the system runs properly and is policed effectively. Independent audit should confirm this and also provide comparison with other organisations.

Budgeting

Audits should confirm that:

- budgets are provided for all activities
- budgets are monitored and reported regularly
- budget projections are reviewed at the end of the budget period
- escalation procedures exist for budget over-runs.

IT Accounting

Auditing of IT Accounting should check that:

- cost projections are accurate each month and at the year end (overall and for each business supported)
- the sum of (Cost per Cost Unit x Cost Unit) is equal to the total cost of providing IT Services
- all costs, including unexpected costs, are accounted for (Hardware, Software, People, Accommodation and Transfer)
- regular and accurate reports are produced for management (including the production of price lists)
- the IT Accounting system is understood and Customers are satisfied with the manner in which it operates
- the IT Accounting system identifies clearly and easily where IT Services' business objectives are being met (e.g. profit margins, cost recoveries and so on)
- interfaces to Configuration Management, Capacity Management and Service Level Management are working and provide the necessary workload information
- the appropriate Configuration Items are up-to-date and accurate
- Change Management and Problem Management procedures are strictly followed.

Charging

Audits should check that:

- bills are simple, clear, accurate and issued on time

- charges are considered fair

- income is collected on time

- price lists are available and any changes to the charges or price lists are implemented within target timescales

- Customers are neither under-charged nor overcharged for their IT Services (this is in terms of correctness according to price lists

- discrepancies in charges are identified quickly and resolved with the Customers

- senior managers (across the organisation and within IT Services) are satisfied with the reports produced

- cost recovery plans are on target (cost recovery provides a barometer of how well prices have been set in relation to predicted costs of IT usage)

- interfaces to Service Level Management are effective.

IT Finance Management should perform an audit or review on a quarterly basis initially and six-monthly after the project has been in successful operation for one year. Where possible, reviews should be synchronised with those for Service Level Management and Capacity Management.

An audit should also:

- check that regular reviews are carried out regularly and non-conformances followed up

- randomly select bills to test for clarity, accuracy and timeliness

- examine cost recovery projections and revenue to assess the accuracy of the system

- ensure that audit trails are provided

- ensure that revenues are collected and properly accounted for

- check that all documentation is accurate, up-to-date and complete.

Annex 5A   IT Finance Manager – Role, responsibilities and key skills

Some organisations have a dedicated IT Finance Manager. Others may share the tasks amongst the Finance department senior IT managers, especially those with responsibility for other Service Management processes (Service Level Management and Capacity Management, for example) and the head of IT.

The IT Financial Management processes must all have an 'owner', that is someone responsible for developing and reviewing them. The IT Finance Manager may be able to agree that some of these are 'owned' by the main Finance Department. However if this responsibility is split, care should be taken to avoid giving them to people with primarily administrative roles as they are unlikely to have the time or seniority required to manage the required tasks.

The skills list given is an indication of the skills that would be present in an ideal candidate for a post that takes full responsibility for all the topics discussed in this Chapter.

Role

To work, at an appropriate level, with representatives of the organisation management and the Finance Department, to develop the policies of Budgeting, IT Accounting and Charging.

To implement and maintain the IT Financial Management process, convening Budgeting, IT Accounting and Charging.

To assist in developing account plans and investment cases for the IT organisation and its Customers.

Responsibilities

Budgeting

- manage the IT organisation budget
- prepare budget forecasts and assist Customers in preparing IT elements of their budgets
- report regularly to IT managers and Customers on conformance to budgets.

IT Accounting

- select suitable tools and processes for gathering cost data
- develop suitable cost models
- agree suitable IT Accounting policies, e.g. depreciation
- assist in developing cost-benefit cases for IT investments
- advise senior management on the cost-effectiveness of IT solutions.

Charging

- identify methods of charging within the organisations charging policy
- provide justifications and comparisons for charges
- prepare regular bills for Customers
- prepare a price list of services, if required.

Other

- provide close support to Service Level Management, Capacity Management and Business relationship Management, especially during budget and IT investment planning

- recommend scope for internal audits

- assist external auditors.

Key skills

- sound numerical and financial skills

- ability to interact successfully with all levels of Customer and IT organisation management

- thorough approach to documentation and schedules

- excellent communication and negotiation skills

- good presentational skills.

Relevant knowledge or experience

- understanding of the Customers' businesses and how IT can affect the delivery of their products or services

- accountancy and company financial reporting

- contract or supplier management

- statistical and analytical principles and processes.

6 CAPACITY MANAGEMENT

6.1 Introduction

Capacity Management is responsible for ensuring that the Capacity of the IT Infrastructure matches the evolving demands of the business in the most cost-effective and timely manner. The process encompasses:

- the monitoring of performance and throughput of IT Services and the supporting Infrastructure components

- undertaking tuning activities to make the most efficient use of existing resources

- understanding the demands currently being made for IT resources and producing forecasts for future requirements

- influencing the demand for resource, perhaps in conjunction with Financial Management

- the production of a Capacity Plan which enables the IT Service provider to provide services of the quality defined in Service Level Agreements (SLAs).

As shown in Figure 6.1, Capacity Management is essentially a balancing act; balancing:

- cost against Capacity – i.e. the need to ensure that processing Capacity that is purchased is not only cost justifiable in terms of business need, but also the need to make the most efficient use of those resources, and

- supply against demand – i.e. making sure that the available supply of processing power matches the demands made on it by the business, both now and in the future; it may also be necessary to manage or influence the demand for a particular resource.

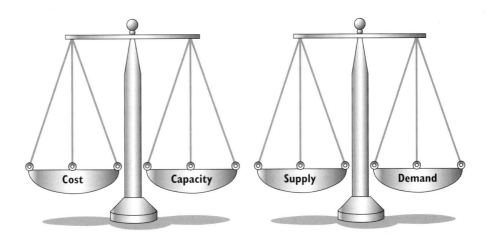

Figure 6.1 – Capacity Management – a balancing act

This Chapter provides guidance on:

- how to justify and establish a Capacity Management process

- the activities and tasks that need to be undertaken

- planning and implementing Capacity Management in an IT organisation

- the responsibilities of the Capacity Management process.

6.1.1 Why Capacity Management?

Capacity Management is often viewed as on old-fashioned, mainframe-oriented discipline. IT Services Managers in charge of distributed computing facilities have argued that Capacity Management takes more time and effort, and therefore cost, than it is worth, and that it would be better to 'pay for upgrades as required'. IT organisations with this view tend to exhibit the following symptoms:

- procurement of IT equipment is justified on an individual capital return basis, rather than the overall corporate requirement

- there are no corporate Capacity Plans

- no business Capacity forecasts are produced

- network Capacity Management is done reactively

- Capacity Management of servers is also done reactively, albeit less often

- little or no Capacity Management is performed on desk top equipment.

This insular, short-term attitude is the very antithesis of Capacity Management.

Managing the Capacity of large networks of distributed equipment is more complex than in the 'good old days' of the mainframe, and for all thriving organisations the financial investment in IT is increasing. Therefore it makes even more sense to plan for growth. While the cost of the upgrade to an individual component in a distributed environment is usually less than the upgrade to a component in a mainframe environment, there are often many more components in the distributed environment that need to be upgraded. Also there could now be economies of scale, because the cost per individual component could be reduced when many components need to be purchased. So Capacity Management should have input to the procurement process to ensure that the best deals with suppliers are negotiated.

A corporate Capacity Management process ensures that the entire organisation's Capacity requirements are catered for. The cost of upgrading all the desktop equipment in an organisation could easily exceed the cost of a mainframe upgrade. Capacity Management should have responsibility for the 'refresh policy', ensuring that desktop equipment has sufficient Capacity to run the applications that the business requires for the foreseeable future.

Capacity Management provides the necessary information on current and planned resource utilisation of individual components to enable organisations to decide, with confidence:

- which components to upgrade (i.e. more memory, faster storage devices, faster processors, greater bandwidth)

- when to upgrade – ideally this is not too early, resulting in expensive over-Capacity, nor too late, resulting in bottle-necks, inconsistent performance and ultimately Customer dissatisfaction and lost business opportunities

- how much the upgrade will cost – the forecasting and planning elements of Capacity Management feed into budgetary lifecycles, ensuring planned investment.

Many of the other Service Management processes are less effective if there is no input to them from the Capacity Management process. For example:

- can the Change Management process properly assess the effect of any Change on the available Capacity?

- when a new service is implemented, can the Service Level Management (SLM) process be assured that the Service Level Requirements (SLRs) of the service are achievable, and that the SLAs of existing services will not be impacted?

- can the Problem Management process properly diagnose the underlying cause of Incidents caused by poor performance?

- can the Service Continuity process accurately determine the Capacity requirements of the key business processes?

Capacity Management is one of the forward-looking processes, which, when properly carried out, can forecast business impacts before they happen.

KEY MESSAGE

Good Capacity Management ensures NO SURPRISES!

6.1.2   Goal for Capacity Management

Capacity Management needs to understand the business requirements (the required Service Delivery), the organisation's operation (the current Service Delivery) and the IT Infrastructure (the means of Service Delivery), and ensure that all the current and future Capacity and performance aspects of the business requirements are provided cost-effectively.

However Capacity Management is also about understanding the potential for Service Delivery. New technology needs to be understood and, if appropriate, used to deliver the services required by the business. Capacity Management needs to recognise that the rate of technological change will probably increase and that new technology should be harnessed to ensure that the IT Services continue to satisfy changing business expectations.

Hints and tips

The two laws of Capacity Management:

Moore's Law

In 1965 Gordon Moore, one of the founders of Intel, observed that each new memory chip produced contained about twice as much processing Capacity as its predecessor, and that new chips were released every 18 – 24 months. This trend has continued ever since, leading to an exponential increase in processing power.

Parkinson's Law of Data

We all know that work expands to fill the time available to complete it, but a variation on that law is that 'data expands to fill the space available for storage'.

While these two laws hold true then effective Capacity Management is even more important as supply and demand grow exponentially.

Goal Statement

The Capacity Management process's goal is 'to ensure that cost justifiable IT Capacity always exists and that it is matched to the current and future identified needs of the business'.

6.1.3   Scope of Capacity Management

The Capacity Management process should be the focal point for all IT performance and Capacity issues. Other technical domains, such as Network Support, may carry out the bulk of the relevant day-to-day duties but overall responsibility lies with the Capacity Management process. The process should encompass, for both the operational and the development environment:

- all hardware – from PCs, through file servers, up to mainframes and super-computers
- all networking equipment (LANs, WANs, bridges, routers etc.)
- all peripherals (bulk storage devices, printers etc.)
- all software – operating system and network software, in-house developments and purchased packages
- human resources, but only where a lack of human resources could result in a delay in end-to-end response time (e.g. overnight data backups not completed in time because no operators were present to load tapes) – in general human resource management is a line management responsibility, though the staffing of a Service Desk might well use identical Capacity Management techniques.

However the driving force for Capacity Management should be the business requirements of the organisation.

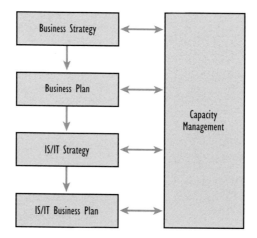

Figure 6.2 – Capacity Management and the business

Figure 6.2 shows that Capacity Management has a close, two-way relationship with the business strategy and planning processes within an organisation. On a regular basis, the long-term strategy of an organisation is encapsulated in an update of the business plans. The business plans are developed from the organisation's understanding of the external factors such as the competitive market-place, economic outlook and legislation, and its internal capability in terms of manpower, delivery capability etc.

Capacity Management needs to understand the long-term strategy of the business while providing information on the latest ideas, trends and technologies being developed by the suppliers of computing hardware and software.

The organisation's business plans dictate the specific IT/IS strategy and business plans, the contents of which Capacity Management needs to be familiar with, and to which Capacity Management needs to have had a large input. In the IT/IS specific business plans, particular technologies, hardware and software are identified, together with some indication of the timescale in which they are to be implemented.

For more information on the interface between the business plans and strategy, and how they need to be reflected in IS/IT specific business plans and strategy, see the ICT Infrastructure Management book.

Anecdote

On November 29th, 1999 an American Internet Service Provider (ISP) specialising in on-line mail order sales of children's toys issued a press release. The recent system crashes had been due to an unexpected 30% increase in Customer demand during the previous week.

'Unexpected increase' in the demand for toys just before Christmas? I'm sure the sales and marketing departments produced some forecasts. Were these communicated to the Capacity Manager?

The same day another press release from a research company reported that the US internet audience is growing significantly slower than it used to, forcing ISP marketing departments to focus more attention on attracting Customers from competitors and on improving Customer service to existing Customers.

Moral

Uncertainty in business demand always exists – even the experts can't agree.

Capacity Managements needs to take account of this uncertainty, keep abreast of marketing and business plans and provide cost-effective, timely processing Capacity.

Capacity Management is a key enabler for business success.

6.2   The Capacity Management process

Figure 6.3 shows the inputs to, the sub-processes within and the outputs from the Capacity Management process.

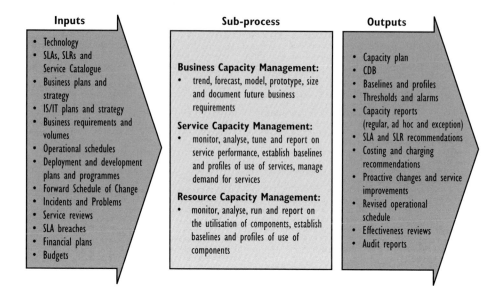

Inputs

- Technology
- SLAs, SLRs and Service Catalogue
- Business plans and strategy
- IS/IT plans and strategy
- Business requirements and volumes
- Operational schedules
- Deployment and development plans and programmes
- Forward Schedule of Change
- Incidents and Problems
- Service reviews
- SLA breaches
- Financial plans
- Budgets

Sub-process

Business Capacity Management:
- trend, forecast, model, prototype, size and document future business requirements

Service Capacity Management:
- monitor, analyse, tune and report on service performance, establish baselines and profiles of use of services, manage demand for services

Resource Capacity Management:
- monitor, analyse, run and report on the utilisation of components, establish baselines and profiles of use of components

Outputs

- Capacity plan
- CDB
- Baselines and profiles
- Thresholds and alarms
- Capacity reports (regular, ad hoc and exception)
- SLA and SLR recommendations
- Costing and charging recommendations
- Proactive changes and service improvements
- Revised operational schedule
- Effectiveness reviews
- Audit reports

Figure 6.3 – The Capacity Management process

The inputs

There are a number of sources of information that are relevant to the Capacity Management process. Some of these are as follows:

- external suppliers of new technology

- the organisation's business strategy and plans, and financial plans

- the IT strategy and plans and current budgets

- the Incident and Problem Management processes with Incidents and Problems relating to poor performance

- the SLM process with details of the contents of the SLAs and SLRs, and possibly from the monitoring of SLAs, service reviews and breaches of the SLAs

- the Change Management process with a Forward Schedule of Changes and a need to assess all Changes for their impact on the Capacity of the Infrastructure

- the IT Operations team with schedules of all the work that needs to be run and information on the dependencies between different services, and the interdependencies within a service.

The sub-processes

Capacity Management consists of a number of sub-processes, within which there are various activities. The sub-processes of Capacity Management are:

- **Business Capacity Management:** This sub-process is responsible for ensuring that the future business requirements for IT Services are considered, planned and implemented in a timely fashion. This can be achieved by using the existing data on the current resource utilisation by the various services to trend, forecast or model the future requirements.

These future requirements come from business plans outlining new services, improvements and growth in existing services, development plans etc.

■ **Service Capacity Management:** The focus of this sub-process is the management of the performance of the live, operational IT Services used by the Customers. It is responsible for ensuring that the performance of all services, as detailed in the targets in the SLAs and SLRs, is monitored and measured, and that the collected data is recorded, analysed and reported. As necessary, action is taken to ensure that the performance of the services meets the business requirements. This is performed by staff with knowledge of all the areas of technology used in the delivery of end-to-end service, and often involves seeking advice from the specialists involved in Resource Capacity Management.

■ **Resource Capacity Management:** The focus in this sub-process is the management of the individual components of the IT Infrastructure. It is responsible for ensuring that all components within the IT Infrastructure that have finite resource are monitored and measured, and that the collected data is recorded, analysed and reported. As necessary, action must be taken to manage the available resource to ensure that the IT Services that it supports meet the business requirements. In carrying out this work, the Capacity Management process is assisted by individuals with specialist knowledge in the particular areas of technology.

The activities that are carried out by the sub-processes are described in Section 6.3. Each of the subprocesses carry out many of the same activities, but each sub-process has a very different focus. Business Capacity Management is focused on the current and future business requirements, while Service Capacity Management is focused on the delivery of the existing services that support the business and Resource Capacity Management is focused on the technology that underpins all the service provision.

The outputs

The outputs of Capacity Management are used within other parts of the process, by other Service Management processes and by other parts of the organisation, as follows:

■ **Within other parts of the Capacity Management process.** For example the data monitored and collected as part of Resource and Service Capacity Management is used in Business Capacity Management to determine what hardware or software upgrades are needed, and when. The Capacity Management Database (CDB) holds the information **needed by all the sub-processes within Capacity Management.**

■ **By other Service Management processes.** For example the Capacity Management process verifies new SLRs, and assists the Financial Management process by identifying when money needs to be budgeted for hardware or software upgrades, or the purchase of new equipment.

■ **By other parts of the organisation.** For example IT Operations needs to implement any Changes that Capacity Management may recommend to the schedule of when services are run, to ensure that the most effective and efficient use is made of the available resource. The Capacity Plan needs to be acted upon by the management of the IT Service provider and the senior management of the organisation.

Capacity Management – reactive or proactive?

Some activities in the Capacity Management process are reactive, while others are proactive. The proactive activities of Capacity Management should:

- pre-empt performance Problems by taking the necessary actions before the Problems occur

- produce trends of the current resource utilisation and estimate the future resource requirement

- model the predicted Changes in IT Services, and identify the Changes that need to be made to the component parts of the IT Infrastructure to ensure that appropriate resource is available to support these services

- ensure that upgrades are budgeted, planned and implemented before SLAs are breached or performance Problems occur.

- actively seek to improve the service provision.

However there will be occasions when the Capacity Management process needs to react to specific performance Problems. For example the Service Desk may refer Incidents of poor performance to Capacity Management for resolution.

KEY MESSAGE

The more successful the proactive activities of Capacity Management, the less need there will be for the reactive activities of Capacity Management.

The remainder of this Section describes the sub-processes of Capacity Management in more detail, and Section 6.3 explains the activities that constitute these sub-processes.

6.2.1 Business Capacity Management

A prime objective of the Business Capacity Management sub-process is to ensure that the future business requirements for IT Services are considered and understood, and that sufficient Capacity to support the services is planned and implemented in an appropriate timescale.

The Capacity Management process must be responsive to changing requirements for processing Capacity. New services will be required to underpin the changing business. Existing services will require modification to provide extra functionality. Old services will become obsolete, freeing up spare Capacity.

As a result, the ability to satisfy the Customers' SLRs will be affected. It is the responsibility of Capacity Management to predict these Changes and cater for them.

These new requirements may come to the attention of Capacity Management from many different sources and for many different reasons. They may be generated by the business or may originate from the Capacity Management process itself. Such examples could be a recommendation to upgrade to take advantage of new technology, or the implementation of a tuning activity to resolve a performance Problem.

Capacity Management needs to become included in as many of the planning processes as possible particularly Change Management and Project Management.

Figure 6.4 shows how new requirements for Capacity cause the Business Capacity Management sub-process to work closely with many of the other Service Delivery and Service Support processes, for example SLM and Change Management, together with other processes such as procurement.

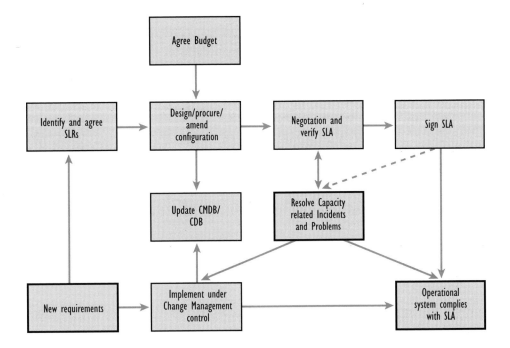

Figure 6.4 – How new requirements for Capacity drive the Business Capacity Management sub-process

Much of the work that needs to be done by the Business Capacity Management sub-process is carried out in conjunction with other processes. In Figure 6.4 the three highlighted elements are largely the responsibility of Capacity Management, and of these only 'Identify new requirements' is the focus of Business Capacity Management. 'Ensure operational service complies with SLA' and 'Resolve Capacity related Incidents and Problems' are the responsibilities of the Service Capacity Management and/or Resource Capacity Management sub-processes.

The involvement of the Business Capacity Management sub-process with the other processes is explained below.

Identify and agree Service Level Requirements

Capacity Management should assist SLM in understanding the Customers' Capacity requirements, for example in terms of required response times, expected throughput and pattern of usage, terminal population. Capacity Management should help in the negotiation process by providing possible solutions to a number of scenarios. For example, if the terminal population is less than 20 then response times can be guaranteed to be less than two seconds. If more than 20 Users connect then extra network bandwidth is needed to guarantee the required response time. Modelling or Application Sizing may be employed here, see Paragraphs 6.3.7 and 6.3.8.

Design, procure or amend configuration

Capacity Management should be involved in the design of new services and make recommendations for the procurement of hardware and software, where performance and/or Capacity are factors. In some instances Capacity Management instigates the implementation of the new requirement through Change Management, where it is also involved as a member of the CAB. In the interest of balancing cost and Capacity, the Capacity Management process obtains the costs of proposed solutions.

Update CMDB and CDB

The details of the new or amended CIs should be recorded in the CMDB under Change Management. The Change Management process must identify the anticipated throughput, which is then translated into requirements for specific resources. In addition, the Change Management process identifies the performance requirements of the planned Change, for example response times. This information should be held as CI attributes within the CMDB.

The CDB should be updated to include the technical specification of the procured or amended CIs, e.g. disk space, speed of processor, the service performance requirements and expected workloads and demands that are to be placed on the IT resources. From this information thresholds can be identified and monitored. Any threshold breaches and near misses should be addressed by some of the iterative activities of the Capacity Management sub-processes. See Paragraph 6.3.5 for a full description of the CDB.

The CMDB and CDB may be the same database, but even if not a single database, there is a data set that is common between the two databases. For example the CMDB CIs and the attributes that are relevant to the Capacity Management process are held in both the CMDB and CDB.

Verify SLA

The SLA should include details of the anticipated service throughputs and the performance requirements. Capacity Management provides SLM with targets that have the ability to be monitored and upon which the service design has been based. Confidence that the service design will meet the SLRs and provide the ability for future growth can be gained by using modelling.

Sign SLA

The results of the modelling activities provide the verification of service performance capabilities. There may be a need for SLM to renegotiate the SLA based upon these findings. Capacity Management provides support to SLM should renegotiations be necessary, by recommending potential solutions and associated cost information.

Once assured that the requirements are achievable, it is the responsibility of SLM to agree the service levels and sign the SLA.

6.2.2   Service Capacity Management

A prime objective of the Service Capacity Management sub-process is to identify and understand the IT Services, their use of resource, working patterns, peaks and troughs, and to ensure that the services can and do meet their SLA targets, i.e. to ensure that the IT Services perform as required. In this sub-process, the focus is on managing service performance, as determined by the targets contained in the SLAs or SLRs.

When the business requirements for a service have come through the Business Capacity Management sub-process as described above in Paragraph 6.2.1, and the service has become operational, then the Service Capacity Management sub-process is responsible for ensuing that it meets the agreed service targets. The monitored service provides data that can identify trends from which normal service levels can be established. By regular monitoring and comparison with these levels, exception conditions can be defined, identified and reported upon. Therefore Capacity Management informs SLM of any service breaches or near misses.

There will be occasions when Incidents and Problems are referred to Capacity Management from other Service Management processes, or it is identified that a service could fail to meet its SLA targets. On some of these occasions the cause of the potential failure may not be resolved by Resource Capacity Management. For example, when the failure is analysed it may be found that there is no lack of resource, or no individual component is over-utilised. However the design or programming of the application is inefficient, and so the service performance needs to be managed, as well as individual hardware or software resources.

The key to successful Service Capacity Management is to pre-empt difficulties, wherever possible. So this is another sub-process that has to be proactive and anticipatory rather than reactive. However there are times when it has to react to specific performance Problems. From a knowledge and understanding of the performance requirements of each of the services being run, the effects of Changes in the use of services can be estimated, and actions taken to ensure that the required service performance can be achieved.

The activities that need to be carried out as part of this sub-process are described in Section 6.3.

6.2.3   Resource Capacity Management

A prime objective of Resource Capacity Management is to identify and understand the Capacity and utilisation of each of the component parts in the IT Infrastructure. This ensures the optimum use of the current hardware and software resources in order to achieve and maintain the agreed service levels. All hardware components and many software components in the IT Infrastructure have a finite Capacity, which, when exceeded, has the potential to cause performance Problems.

This sub-process is concerned with resources such as processors, memory, disks, network bandwidth, network connections etc. So information on resource utilisation needs to be collected on an iterative basis. Monitors should be installed on the individual hardware and software components, and then configured to collect the necessary data.

As in Service Capacity Management the key to successful Resource Capacity Management is to pre-empt difficulties, wherever possible. Therefore this sub-process has to be proactive and anticipatory rather than reactive. However there are times when it has to react to specific Problems that are caused by a lack of resource, or the inefficient use of resource.

From a knowledge and understanding of the use of resource by each of the services being run, the effects of Changes in the use of services can be estimated. Then hardware or software upgrades can be budgeted and planned. Alternatively, services can be balanced across the existing resource to make most effective use of the resource currently available.

New technology

Resource Capacity Management also involves understanding new technology and how it can be used to support the business. It may be appropriate to introduce new technology to improve the provision and support of the IT Services on which the organisation is dependent. This information can be gathered by studying professional literature (magazine and press articles) and by attending:

- promotional seminars by hardware and software suppliers
- User group meetings of suppliers of potential hardware and software
- User group meetings for other IT professionals involved in Capacity Management.

Each of these fora provides sources of information relating to potential technology, hardware and software, which might be advantageous for IT to implement for the benefit of the business. However at all times Capacity Management should recognise that the introduction and use of this new technology must be cost-justified and it should be required by the business.

Resilience

The Resource Capacity Management sub-process is also responsible for identifying the resilience inherent in the IT Infrastructure or any subset of it. In conjunction with the Availability Management process, Capacity Management should use techniques such as highlighting how susceptible the current configuration is to the failure of individual components and make recommendations on any cost-effective solutions. See Chapter 8 for a full description of Component Failure Impact Analysis.

Capacity Management should be able to identify the impact on the available resources of particular failures, and the potential for running the most important services on the remaining resources.

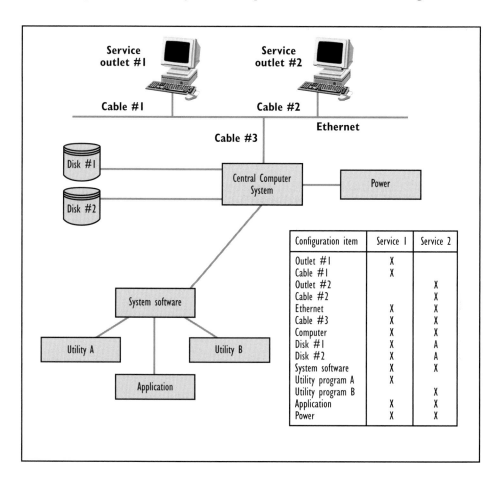

Figure 6.5 – Sample configuration and basic CFIA grid

Figure 6.5 shows a sample configuration and a basic CFIA grid that identifies the components that are critical in the provision of the services. In the above example the central computer is critical to the provision of both Service 1 and Service 2. For resilience reasons it may be decided to have a number of processors in the central computer, so that if one processor fails the computer can continue to operate with the remaining processors. This may satisfy the resilience requirement, but is there sufficient Capacity in the remaining processors to provide the two services to the levels documented in the SLAs? In the final solution the requirements of both Availability Management and Capacity Management must be addressed.

Ideally the requirements for resilience in the IT Infrastructure should be considered at the time of the application design, see Paragraph 6.3.8. However for many services, the resilience of the service is only considered after it is in live operational use.

6.3 Activities in Capacity Management

The activities described in this Section are undertaken when carrying out any of the sub-processes of Capacity Management and these activities can be done reactively or proactively.

The major difference between the sub-processes is in the data that is being monitored and collected, and the perspective from which it is analysed. For example the level of utilisation of individual components in the Infrastructure is of interest in Resource Capacity Management, while the transaction throughput rates and response times are of interest in Service Capacity Management. For Business Capacity Management, the transaction throughput rates for the on-line service need to be translated into business volumes, for example, in terms of sales invoices raised or orders taken.

A number of the activities need to be carried out iteratively and form a natural cycle as illustrated in Figure 6.6.

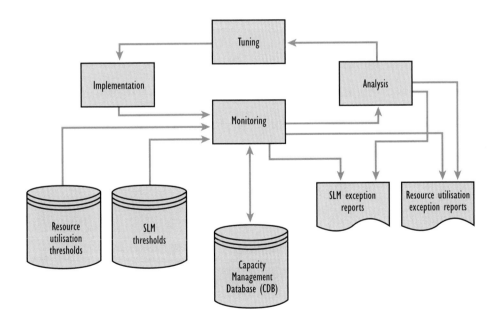

Figure 6.6 – Iterative activities in Capacity Management

Monitors should be established on all the components and for each of the services. The data should be analysed, using wherever possible, expert systems to compare usage levels against thresholds. The results of the analysis should be included in reports, and recommendations made as appropriate. Some form of control mechanism may then be put in place to act on the recommendations. This may take the form of balancing services, changing concurrency levels, and adding or removing resource. The cycle then begins again, monitoring any Changes made to ensure they have had a beneficial effect and collecting the data for the next day, week, or month.

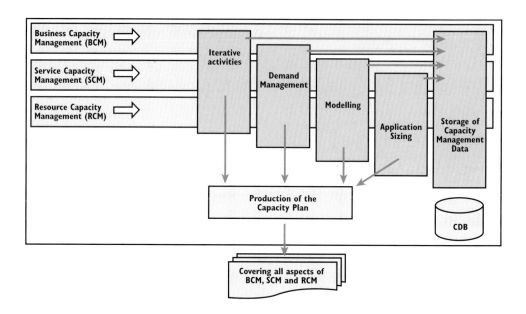

Figure 6.7 – Activities in Capacity Management

Figure 6.7 shows the iterative activities as shown in Figure 6.6, together with the other activities of Capacity Management that need to be carried out:

- on an on-going basis: Iterative activities, Demand Management and the storage of data in the CDB
- ad hoc: Modelling and Application Sizing
- regularly: The production of the Capacity Plan.

Any one of the sub-processes of Capacity Management may carry out any of the activities, with the data that is generated being stored in the CDB. This Section describes all the activities of Capacity Management in detail and shows how the various sub-processes of Capacity Management use each of them as required.

6.3.1   Monitoring

Objective

It is important that the utilisation of each resource and service is monitored on an on-going basis to ensure the optimum use of the hardware and software resources, that all agreed service levels can be achieved, and that business volumes are as expected.

Description

The monitors should be specific to particular operating systems, hardware configurations, applications, etc. Some of the monitors should be free utilities within a hardware or software product, while others form part of a larger systems management tool set and need to by purchased independently. It is important that the monitors can collect all the data required by the Capacity Management process, for a specific component or service.

Typical monitored data includes:

- CPU utilisation
- memory utilisation
- % CPU per transaction type
- IO rates (physical and buffer) and device utilisation
- queue length (maximum and average)
- file store utilisation
- transactions
- transactions per second (maximum and average)
- transaction response time
- batch duration profiles
- number of hits
- number of logons and concurrent Users
- number of network nodes in use (e.g. network devices, PCs, servers etc).

In considering the data that needs to be included, a distinction needs to be drawn between the data collected to monitor Capacity (e.g. throughput), and the data to monitor performance (e.g. response times). Data of both types is required by the Service and Resource Capacity Management subprocesses. The data should be gathered at total resource utilisation level and at a more detailed profile for the load that each service places on each particular resource. This needs to be carried out across the whole Infrastructure, host or server, the network, local server and client or workstation. Similarly the data needs to be collected for each service.

Part of the monitoring activity should be of thresholds and baselines or profiles of the normal operating levels. If these are exceeded, alarms should be raised and exception reports produced. These thresholds and baselines should have been determined from the analysis of previously recorded data, and can be set on:

- individual components, for example monitor that the utilisation of a CPU does not exceed 80% for a sustained period of one hour
- specific services, for example monitor that the response time in an on-line service does not exceed 2 seconds and that the transaction rate does not exceed 10000 transactions per hour.

All thresholds should be set below the level at which the resource is over-utilised, or below the targets in the SLAs. When the threshold is reached, there is still an opportunity to take corrective action before the SLA has been breached, or the resource has become over-utilised and there has been a period of poor performance.

> **Hints and tips**
>
> **Many monitors do not report the whole picture, and beware of the monitor that requires so much resource that a processor or memory upgrade is required to get the monitor to run.**

Often it is more difficult to get the data on the current business volumes as required by the Business Capacity Management sub-process. These statistics may need to be derived from the data available to the Service and Resource Capacity Management sub-processes.

Response time monitoring

Many SLAs have User response times as one of the targets to be measured, but equally many organisations have great difficulty in supporting this requirement. User response times of IT and network services can be monitored and measured in several ways:

- **By incorporating specific code within client and server applications software.** This can be used to provide complete 'end-to-end' service response times or intermediate timing points to break down the overall response into its constituent components. The figures obtained from these tools give the actual response times as perceived by the Users of a service.

- **By using 'Robotic scripted systems' with terminal emulation software.** These systems consist of client systems with terminal emulation software (e.g. browser or VT100 systems) and specialised scripted software for generating and measuring transactions and responses. These systems generally provide 'end-to-end' service response times and are useful for providing representative response times particularly for multi-phase transactions or complex interactions. These only give sample response times not the actual response times as perceived by the real Users of the system.

- **By using distributed agent monitoring software.** Useful information on service response times can be obtained by distributing agent systems with monitoring software at different points of a network (e.g. within different countries on the Internet). These systems can then be used to generate transactions from a number of locations and give periodic measurements of an Internet site as perceived by international Users of an Internet web site. However, again the times received are only indications of the response times and are not the real User response times.

- **By using specific passive monitoring systems tracking a representative sample number of client systems.** This method relies on the connection of specific network monitoring systems, often referred to as 'sniffers' being inserted at appropriate points within the network. These can then monitor, record and time all traffic passing a particular point within the network. Once recorded this traffic can then be analysed to give detailed information on the service response times. Once again however these can only be used to give an approximation to the actual User response times, although these are often very close to the real world situation but this depends upon the position of the monitor itself within the IT Infrastructure.

In some cases a combination of a number of systems may be used. The monitoring of response times is a complex process even if the service is an in-house service running on a private network. However if this is an external Internet service, the process is much more complex because of the sheer number of different organisations and technologies involved.

Anecdote

A private company with a major Internet web site implemented a web site monitoring service from an external supplier that would provide automatic alarms on the Availability and response time of their web site. The Availability and speed of the monitoring points were lower than those of the Internet web site being monitored. Therefore the figures produced by the service were of the Availability and response time of the monitoring service itself, rather than those of the monitored web site.

Hints and tips

When implementing external monitoring services, ensure that the service levels and performance commitments of the monitoring service are in excess of those of the service(s) being monitored.

6.3.2   Analysis

Objective

The data collected from the monitoring should be analysed to identify trends from which the normal utilisation and service level, or baseline, can be established. By regular monitoring and comparison with this baseline, exception conditions in the utilisation of individual components or service thresholds can be defined, and breaches or near misses in the SLAs can be reported upon. Also the data can be used to predict future resource usage, or to monitor actual business growth against predicted growth.

Description

Analysis of the data may identify issues such as:

- contention (data, file, memory, processor)
- inappropriate distribution of workload across available resource
- inappropriate locking strategy
- inefficiencies in the application design
- unexpected increase in transaction rates
- inefficient use of memory.

The use of each resource and service needs to be considered over the short, medium and long term, and the minimum, maximum and average utilisation for these periods recorded. Typically, the short-term pattern covers the utilisation over a 24-hour period, while the medium term may cover a one-week to four-week period, and the long term, a year-long period. Over time the trend in the use of the resource by the various IT Services will become apparent.

It is important to understand the utilisation in each of these periods, so that Changes in the use of any service can be related to predicted Changes in the level of utilisation of individual resources. The ability to identify the specific hardware or software resource on which a particular IT Service depends, is improved greatly by an accurate, up-to-date and comprehensive CMDB.

135

When the utilisation of a particular resource is considered, it is important to understand both the total level of utilisation and the utilisation by individual services of the resource.

Example

If a processor that is 75% loaded during the peak hour is being used by two different services, A and B, it is important to know how much of the total 75% is being used by each service. Assuming the system overhead on the processor is 5%, the remaining 70% load, could be split evenly between the two services. If a change in either Service A or B is estimated to double its loading on the processor, then the processor would be overloaded.

However if Service A uses 60% and Service B uses 10% of the processor, then the processor would be overloaded if Service A doubled its loading on the processor. But if Service B doubled its loading on the processor, then the processor would not necessarily be overloaded.

6.3.3   Tuning

Objective

The analysis of the monitored data may identify areas of the configuration that could be tuned to better utilise the system resource or improve the performance of the particular service.

Description

Tuning techniques that are of assistance include:

- balancing workloads – transactions may arrive at the host or server at a particular gateway, depending where the transaction was initiated; balancing the ratio of initiation points to gateways can provide tuning benefits

- balancing disk traffic – storing data on disk efficiently and strategically, e.g. striping data across many spindles may reduce data contention

- definition of an accepted locking strategy that specifies when locks are necessary and the appropriate level, e.g. database, page, file, record, and row – delaying the lock until an update is necessary may provide benefits

- efficient use of memory – may include looking to utilise more or less memory depending upon the circumstances.

Regarding the efficient use of memory, note that a process may utilise resources more efficiently if data is read into memory and manipulated there rather than a sequential read through files. Alternatively, many processes may be contending for memory resource. The excessive demands may lead to increased CPU utilisation and delays while pages are swapped in and out of memory.

Before implementing any of the recommendations arising from the tuning techniques, it may be appropriate to consider using one of the on-going, or ad hoc activities to test the validity of the recommendation. For example, 'Can Demand Management be used to avoid the need to carry out any tuning?' or 'Can the proposed Change be modelled to show its effectiveness before it is implemented?'

6.3.4   Implementation

Objective

The objective of this activity is to introduce to the live operation services any Changes that have been identified by the monitoring, analysis and tuning activities.

Description

The implementation of any Changes arising from these activities must be undertaken through a strict, formal Change Management process. The impact of system tuning changes can have major implications on the Customers of the service. The impact and risk associated with these types of changes are likely to be greater than that of other different type of changes. Implementing the tuning Changes under formal Change Management procedures results in:

- less adverse impact on the Users of the service
- increased User productivity
- increased productivity of IT personnel
- a reduction in the number of Changes that need to be backed-out, but the ability to do so more easily
- greater management and control of business critical application services.

It is important that further monitoring takes place, so that the effects of the Change can be assessed. It may be necessary to make further Changes or to regress some of the original Changes.

6.3.5   Storage of Capacity Management data

The CDB is the cornerstone of a successful Capacity Management process. Data in the CDB is stored and used by all the sub-processes of Capacity Management because it is a repository that that holds a number of different types of data viz. business, service, technical, financial and utilisation data. However the CDB is unlikely to be a single database and probably exists in several physical locations.

The information in the CDB is used to form the basis of performance and Capacity Management reports that are to be delivered to management and technical personnel. Also the data is utilised to generate future Capacity forecasts and allow the Capacity Management to plan for future Capacity requirements.

Capacity and performance data from the necessary system components should be identified or extracted and delivered to a central location where a CDB is housed. Data from components that make up the service can then be combined for analysis and provision of technical and management reporting.

The inputs to the CDB

Each of the Capacity Management sub-processes generates and uses any of the types of data stored in the CDB. For example, the technical data relating to the limiting Capacity of a component part of the IT Infrastructure is identified and stored by the Resource Capacity Management sub-process. Then this sub-process uses the data item as the threshold at which alarms are raised and exception reports are produced by the monitoring activity. The same data item can be used by the Service Capacity Management sub-process to identify the point at which SLAs are likely to be breached, while the Business Capacity Management sub-process uses the data item together with the current level of utilisation of the component in deciding whether the component needs to be upgraded.

The full range of types of data in the CBD is:

Business Data

To understand exactly what drives the Capacity and performance of an IT system it is essential to have quality business data. The future business plans of the organisation need to be considered, and the effects on the IT Services understood. The business data is used to forecast and validate how changes in business drivers affect the Capacity and performance of the system. Typically business data includes:

- number of accounts and products supported number of calls into call centres
- number and location of branches
- number of registered Users of a system
- number of PCs
- anticipated workloads
- seasonal variations of anticipated workloads
- number of web site business transactions.

Service Data

It is essential that the Capacity Management process considers at all times the effect that the IT Infrastructure has on the work of the User. To achieve this service-orientated approach to Capacity Management, service data should be stored within the Capacity Management Database. Typical service data are transaction response times that are consistent with the perceived level of service delivered to the User.

Another example of service data would be the times taken for batch jobs to be processed. In general the targets in the SLAs and SLRs provide the service data that the Capacity Management process needs to record and monitor. To ensure that the targets in the SLAs are achieved, SLM thresholds should be included, so that the monitoring activity can measure against these thresholds and raise exception reports. By setting the thresholds below or above the actual targets, action can be taken and a breach of the SLA targets avoided.

The Capacity Management process as well as the SLM process is interested in service data. This enables the IT provider to be more focused on the delivery of SLA-compliant services. T o do this the service data should be correlated with technical and business data to forecast future breaches of service targets.

Technical Data

Most of the components in the IT Infrastructure have limitations on the level to which they should be utilised. Beyond this level of utilisation the resource will be over-utilised and the performance of the services using the resource will be impaired. For example the maximum recommended level of utilisation on a CPU could be 80%, or the utilisation of a shared Ethernet LAN segment should not exceed 40%.

Also components have various physical limitations beyond which greater connectivity or use is impossible. For example the maximum number of connections through a network gateway is 100, or a particular type of disk has a physical Capacity of 15Gb.

The technical limits and constraints on the individual components can be used by the monitoring activities as the thresholds at which alarms are raised and exception reports are produced. However care must be exercised when setting thresholds, because many thresholds are dependent on the work being run on the particular component.

Financial Data

The Capacity Management process requires financial data. For example, when proposing various scenarios in the Capacity Plan, the financial cost of the upgrades to the components of the IT Infrastructure, together with information about the current IT hardware budget must be known and included in the considerations. Financial data can be obtained from a number of sources, including:

- Financial plans, which may indicate long-term plans to reduce the costs of IT Service provision

- IT budgets, which may include specific budgets for hardware and software expenditure in the next year

- external suppliers, for the cost of new hardware and software component upgrades

- the CMDB, for the purchase or rental costs of current hardware and software components.

Most of this data may be available from the Financial Management for IT Services process but Capacity Management needs to consider this information when managing the future business requirements.

Utilisation Data

Potentially there is a vast amount of utilisation data available. Ideally data is required that shows the current utilisation of all components of the IT Infrastructure, minute-by-minute, hour-by-hour, day-by-day etc. However after a period of time, for example one week, the minute-by-minute utilisation data will no longer be required. Similarly after one month, the previous month's hour-by-hour data is not required. However even one year later the average daily utilisation of each component, or service transaction throughput rate and average response times may be required.

So in the collection of the utilisation data, there need to be facilities to enable data to be consolidated or refined, so that data can be deleted as it becomes out-of-date.

The utilisation data needs to be recorded for each component and service, and examples of utilisation data are shown in Table 6.1

Technology	Example metrics available for collection		
Mainframe	CPU utilisation	Paging rates	I/Os per second
Application	No of transactions	Response times	
UNIX server	CPU utilisation	Memory utilisation	No of processes
Middleware	Average queue lengths	No of transactions serviced	
Network	Bandwidth utilisation	No of connections	Error rates
Database	Shared memory utilisation	No of queries per second	
PC Client	CPU utilisation	Memory utilisation	

Table 6.1 – Example utilisation data

Capacity Management stores data that is relevant to the IT systems, services and the Customers. There are many hardware and software tools that monitor systems and store performance data across all technology types and Infrastructure components. Some are free utilities within a hardware product, while others form part of a larger systems management tool set. It is important that any tool is chosen based on the data requirements of the Capacity Management process to be implemented.

The outputs from the CDB

The aim of a CDB is to provide the relevant Capacity and performance information to the appropriate sub-processes of Capacity Management. In addition, these reports could be used by a number of the other Service Management processes. This information is provided through various reports.

Service and Component Based Reports

For each Infrastructure component there should be a team of technical staff responsible for its control and management, and management staff who are responsible for the overall service. Reports must be produced to illustrate how the service and its constituent components are performing and how much of its maximum Capacity is being used.

Exception Reporting

Reports that show management and technical staff when the Capacity and performance of a particular component or service becomes unacceptable are also a required output from a CDB. Exceptions can be set for any component, service or measurement that is stored within a CDB. An example exception may be that CPU percentage utilisation for a particular server has breached 70 % for three consecutive hours, or that the hit rate from Users exceeded all expectations.

In particular, exception reports are of interest to the SLM process in determining whether the targets in SLAs have been breached. Also the Incident and Problem Management processes may be able to use the exception reports in the resolution of Incidents and Problems.

Capacity Forecasts

To ensure the IT Service Provider continues to provide the required service levels, the Capacity Management process must predict future growth. To do this, future component and service Capacity must be forecast. This can be done in a variety of ways depending on the technology used by the component. Changes to workloads by the development of new functionality must be considered alongside growth in workload that is driven by business growth. A simple example of a Capacity forecast is a correlation between a business driver and a component utilisation, e.g. CPU utilisation against the number of accounts supported by the company. Then this data can be correlated to find the effect that increased numbers of accounts will have on the utilisation of particular components of the configuration.

If the forecasts on future Capacity requirements identify a requirement for increased resource, this requirement needs to be input to the IT budget cycle.

6.3.6 Demand Management

Objective

The prime objective of Demand Management is to influence the demand for computing resource and the use of that resource.

Description

This activity can be carried out as a short-term requirement because there is insufficient current Capacity to support the work being run, or, as a deliberate policy of IT management, to limit the required Capacity in the long term.

Short-term Demand Management may occur when there has been a partial failure of a critical resource in the IT Infrastructure. For example, if there has been a failure of part of the memory on a processor, it may not be possible to run the full range of services. However a limited subset of the services could be run. Capacity Management should be aware of the business priority of each of the services, know the resource requirements of each service (in this case, the amount of memory required to run the service) and then be able to identify which services can be run while there is a limited amount of memory available.

Long-term Demand Management may be required when it is difficult to cost-justify an expensive upgrade. For example, many processors are heavily utilised for only a few hours each day, typically between 10:00 – 12:00 and 14:00 – 16:00. Within these periods, the processor may be over-loaded for only one or two hours. For the hours between 18:00 – 08:00 these processors are only very lightly loaded, and the resource is under-utilised. Is it possible to justify the cost of an upgrade to provide additional resource for only a few hours in 24 hours, or is possible to influence the demand and spread the requirement for resource across the 24 hours, thereby avoiding the need for the upgrade?

Demand Management needs to understand which services are utilising the resource and to what level, and needs to know the schedule of when they must be run. Then a decision can be make on whether it will be possible to influence the use of resource, and if so, which option is appropriate.

The influence on the services that are running could be exercised by:

- physical constraints – for example, it may be possible to stop some services from being available at certain times, or to limit the number of Customers who can use a particular service, for example by limiting the number of concurrent Users; the constraint could be implemented on a specific resource or component, for example by limiting the number of physical connections to a network router or switch.

- financial constraints – if Charging for IT Services is occurring, reduced rates could be offered for running work at certain times of the day, that is the times when there is current less demand for the resource.

Demand Management can be carried out as part of anyone of the sub-processes of Capacity Management. However Demand Management must be carried out sensitively, without causing damage to the business Customers or to the reputation of the IT organisation. It is necessary to understand fully the requirements of the business and the demands on the IT Services, and to ensure that the Customers are kept informed of all the actions being taken.

6.3.7   Modelling

Objectives

A prime objective of Capacity Management is to predict the behaviour of IT Services under a given volume and variety of work. Modelling is an activity that can be used to beneficial effect in any of the sub-processes of Capacity Management.

Description

The different types of modelling range from making estimates based on experience and current resource utilisation information, to pilot studies, prototypes and full scale benchmarks. The former is cheap and a reasonable approach for day-to-day small decisions, while the latter is expensive but may be advisable when implementing a large new project.

Trend Analysis

Trend analysis can be done on the resource utilisation and service performance information that has been collected by the Service and Resource Capacity Management sub-processes. The data can be held in a spreadsheet and the graphical and trending, and forecasting facilities used to show the utilisation of a particular resource over a previous period of time, and how it can be expected to change in the future.

Typically trend analysis only provides estimates of future resource utilisation information. Trend analysis is less effective in producing an accurate estimate of response times in which case either analytical or simulation modelling should be used.

Analytical Modelling

Analytical models are representations of the behaviour of computer systems using mathematical techniques, e.g. multi-class network queuing theory. Typically a model is built using a software package on a PC, by specifying within the package the components and structure of the configuration that needs to be modelled, and the utilisation of the components, e.g. CPU, memory and disks, by the various workloads or applications. When the model is run, the queuing theory is used to calculate the response times in the computer system. If the response times predicted by the model are sufficiently close to the response times recorded in real life, the model can be regarded as an accurate representation of the computer system.

The technique of analytical modelling requires less time and effort than simulation modelling, but typically it gives less accurate results. Also the model must be kept up-to-date. However if the results are within 5% accuracy for utilisation and 15 – 20% for on-line application response times, the results are usually satisfactory.

Simulation Modelling

Simulation involves the modelling of discrete events, e.g. transaction arrival rates, against a given hardware configuration. This type of modelling can be very accurate in sizing new applications or predicting the effects of Changes on existing applications, but can also be very time-consuming and therefore costly.

When simulating transaction arrival rates, have a number of staff enter a series of transactions from prepared scripts, or use software to input the same scripted transactions with a random arrival rate. Either of these approaches takes time and effort to prepare and run. However it can be cost-justified for organisations with very large systems where the cost (millions of pounds) and the associated performance implications assume great importance.

Baseline Models

The first stage in modelling is to create a baseline model that reflects accurately the performance that is being achieved. When this baseline model has been created, predictive modelling can be done, i.e. ask the 'what if?' questions that reflect planned Changes to the hardware and/or the volume/variety of workloads. If the baseline model is accurate, then the accuracy of the result of the predicted Changes can be trusted.

Effective Service and Resource Capacity Management together with modelling techniques enable Capacity Management to answer the 'What if' questions. 'What if the throughput of Service A doubles?' 'What if Service B is moved from the current processor onto a new processor – how will the response times in the two services be altered?'

6.3.8   Application sizing

Application sizing has a finite life-span. It is initiated at the Project Initiation stage for a new application or when there is a major Change of an existing application, and is completed when the application is accepted into the operational environment.

Objective

The primary objective of application sizing is to estimate the resource requirements to support a proposed application Change or new application, to ensure that it meets its required service levels. To achieve this application sizing has to be an integral part of the applications lifecycle.

Description

During the initial systems analysis and design the required service levels must be specified. This enables the application development to employ the pertinent technologies and products, in order to achieve a design that meets the desired levels of service. It is much easier and less expensive to achieve the required service levels if the application design considers the required service levels at the very beginning of the application lifecycle, rather than at some later stage.

Other considerations in application sizing are the resilience aspects that it may be necessary to build into the design of the new application. Capacity Management is able to provide advice and guidance to the Availability Management process about the resources required to provide the required level of resilience.

The sizing of the application should be refined as the development process progresses. The use of modelling can be used within the application sizing process.

The SLRs of the planned application developments should not be considered in isolation. The resources to be utilised by the application are likely to be shared with other services and potential threats to existing SLA targets must be recognised and managed.

When purchasing software packages from external suppliers it is just as important to understand the resource requirements needed to support the application. Often it can be difficult to obtain this information from the suppliers, and it may vary, depending on throughput. Therefore, it is beneficial to identify similar Customers of the product and to gain an understanding of the resource implications from them. It may be pertinent to benchmark trial the product prior to purchase.

> **KEY MESSAGE**
>
> **Quality must be built in.**
>
> **Some aspects of service quality can be improved after implementation (additional hardware can be added to improve performance, for example). Others – particularly aspects such as reliability and maintainability of applications software – rely on quality being 'built in', since to attempt to add it at a later stage is in effect redesign and redevelopment, normally at a much higher cost than the original development. Even in the hardware example quoted above it is likely to have cost more to add Capacity after service implementation rather than as part of the original project.**
>
> *from Quality Management for IT Services, ITIL*

6.3.9 Production of the Capacity Plan

Objective

The prime objective is to produce a plan that documents the current levels of resource utilisation and service performance, and after consideration of the business strategy and plans, forecasts the future requirements for resource to support the IT Services that underpin the business activities. The plan should indicate clearly any assumptions made. It should also include any recommendations quantified in terms of resource required, cost, benefits, impact etc.

Description

The production and update of a Capacity Plan should occur at pre-defined intervals. It is, essentially, an investment plan and should therefore be published annually, in line with the business or budget lifecycle, and completed before the start of negotiations on future budgets. A quarterly re-issue of the updated plan may be necessary to take into account changes in business plans, to report on the accuracy of forecasts and to make or refine recommendations.

The typical contents of a Capacity Plan are described in Annex 6B.

6.4 Costs, benefits and possible problems

6.4.1 Costs

The costs associated with establishing a Capacity Management process include:

- procurement of required hardware and software tools including:
  - monitoring tools (performance and utilisation) covering hardware, operating system and application Capacity. These tools should be capable of monitoring and collecting data from all required host, network and client environments
  - CDB for holding a historic record of all service, technical, utilisation, financial and business data
  - modelling tools for performing simulation modelling and statistical analysis
  - graphical and textual reporting tools (often web-enabled)

- project management – implementation of Capacity Management should be treated as a project

- staff costs – recruitment, training and consultancy costs associated with the set-up of the Capacity Management process

- accommodation – provision of an adequate working environment and facilities, which may be distributed.

The costs associated with maintaining a Capacity Management include:

- annual maintenance and required upgrades of all hardware and software tools

- on-going staff costs including salaries, further training and ad-hoc consultancy

- recurring accommodation costs such as leasing, rental and energy costs.

As discussed earlier Capacity Management responsibilities may be distributed either geographically or functionally within the organisation. Where this is the case, additional costs will be incurred for the central co-ordination and reporting of Capacity information.

6.4.2   Benefits

Increased efficiency and cost savings

Capacity Management leads to increased efficiency and cost savings in several areas, including:

- **Deferred expenditure** – if it is possible to defer the cost of new equipment to a later date, then the money that is currently in the budget can be spent in other ways. It may be possible to defer the expenditure permanently, so that the money need never be spent. Also, with the pace of technological change, the later a purchase is left, the more Capacity is obtained for the money.

- **Economic provision of services** – Capacity is matched to business need. Unnecessary spare Capacity is not being maintained and therefore cost savings result. Use of existing Capacity is optimised as far as possible, again resulting in cost savings through not paying for unwanted Capacity during quiet usage periods.

- **Planned buying** – is always cheaper than panic buying.

Reduced risk

Reduced risk is a major benefit of Capacity Management. Effective Capacity Management reduces the risk of performance Problems and failure in the following ways:

- for existing applications the risk is minimised through managing the resources and service performance

- the risk to new applications is reduced through application sizing – as new applications can have an adverse effect upon existing applications, the risk to those applications is also minimised

- the Capacity Management process should be included on the Change Advisory Board (CAB) to assess the impact of Changes upon existing Capacity, thus reducing the risk of Capacity Problems caused by Changes

- the number of urgent Changes to increase Capacity are reduced, and hopefully eliminated, through effective Capacity planning.

More confident forecasts

Capacity planning improves over time. By establishing normal operating baselines and monitoring usage over time, Capacity requirements for existing services become more accurate. Through application sizing and modelling for new services more accurate forecasting and greater confidence results.

Value to applications lifecycle

Throughout its lifecycle, application development is influenced by Capacity Management. Additional Capacity requirements can be identified during the early development stages and built into the Capacity Plan. This is in contrast to the more usual approach of thinking about Capacity just before go-live. There are, therefore, benefits in terms of reduced risk and more economic provision of new services.

6.4.3   Possible problems

Over expectation

Customer expectations often exceed technical capability. Therefore it is essential that Customer expectations for new applications be managed from the outset. Capacity Management needs to discuss with Customers the technical feasibility and, more importantly, the cost implications, of meeting over-ambitious requirements. The opportunity to achieve this is provided as part of the application sizing activity, where requirements and expectations should be discussed and agreed between all parties.

The improvements that can be made through regular tuning may not be significant. However if a service or application has been badly designed or implemented, a large performance gain may be possible.

Also Demand Management is often constrained by the requirement for constant on-line access to corporate information. It is not always easy or possible to re-schedule the use of services to quieter off-peak periods. For example, it would be difficult for an Internet site selling flowers to influence the demand for flowers on or around St. Valentine's Day!

Vendor influence

Where budget and sales target deadlines coincide, it is not uncommon to be offered what seems to be the deal of a lifetime i.e. 'purchase sufficient Capacity for today and tomorrow at yesterdays prices'. On face value, cost efficiencies can be realised, however, before purchasing, remember:

- the pace of change is rapid – today's special offer is often tomorrow's end-of-line product
- technological advancement – tomorrow's technology will perform faster and have more built-in Capacity than today's technology
- the overall reducing cost of technology – today's performance and Capacity will always be cheaper tomorrow and considerably cheaper in six months time.

Manufacturer's quoted performance figures are often not achievable within a production environment. Care should be taken when negotiating with vendors for additional performance. Where possible, performance figures should be verified before purchase through reference site visits and by simulation testing where appropriate.

Lack of information

Time-to-market demands are ever decreasing and as a result business planning cycles are shorter. This is not an excuse, but a statement of fact about the environment within which Capacity

Management must function. Traditionally, it has always been difficult to obtain accurate business forecasts, in order to predict increases and decreases in demand for IT Capacity.

However, even the best business planning function cannot always accurately predict demand. There have been numerous recent examples of unprecedented and unpredicted consumer demand for either the latest product or latest information. Internet sites that are suddenly popular, are good examples of consumer demand far outstripping supply and causing failed or drastically delayed delivery of information or products. The Internet is a prime example where consumers literally 'at the click of a button' are lost forever as they go elsewhere to receive a service, never again to return to a temporarily unavailable or slow site.

It is not possible to provide consistently high quality service levels, cost effectively, without timely, accurate business planning information being made available. However Capacity Management can work effectively, even with crude business estimates. Also it helps if the Capacity Management process understands the business and can talk to the Customer in their language. The business is much more likely to know how many chocolate bars it is going to sell, than the amount of CPU seconds it uses in the process. The Capacity Management process always improves over time.

Capacity Management in a distributed environment

Capacity Management is often considered only as a requirement within the host environment. The network and client environments are not included as part of the Capacity Management process.

Anecdote

A group of Network Managers were asked 'When is the first time you get involved in Capacity planning for new applications to be utilised across the network?' Unfortunately the most common answer was 'Usually during the first week of live running, when Users complain about poor performance'. Another common answer was 'During Customer acceptance testing, when the application is being tested by Users just before transition to live running'.

However when also asked 'If you had been involved from the outset, when the new applicant was just a Customer requirement, could you have provided accurate figures on spare network Capacity within the target environment?' only a handful were confident in their ability to do so.

Result

There are a number of results and lessons to be learned from the above:

- the network is not within the scope of Capacity Managements, but it should be

- huge potential for new applications to perform poorly or fail totally

- Customer perception that IT fails to deliver (again)

- potential financial costs incurred by the business due to application failure

- unpredicted and unbudgeted IT costs to resolve the performance Problems, which usually require to be addressed urgently and thus cost even more.

Level of monitoring to be implemented

Tools available today provide extremely comprehensive monitoring capabilities. It is possible to monitor most aspects of most components in the IT Infrastructure. However careful consideration should be given to the level of monitoring to be undertaken, and the decision should be based upon:

- business impact of component failure – can monitoring be justified on the basis of potential impact of failure?

- utilisation volatility – is utilisation subject to a steady growth or decline over time, or do highly volatile changes in utilisation occur?

- ability to monitor components – can monitoring and reporting be automated?

- cost of component monitoring and reporting – are costs greater than the potential use that can be made of the data collected?

Question

Should an organisation with 40,000 desktops in over 1,000 locations monitor spare Capacity and performance for every desktop?

Answer

It is very unlikely that this will prove cost effective, especially when it is realised that none of the desktops store any local data and they all run a standard application set that cannot be added to by Users. However there would be some benefit in monitoring at least a sample (if not all) of the servers located in each of the 1,000 locations used to store local data. The level of monitoring to be implemented would need to be based upon business criticality and volatility of the server based applications. The requirement is for exception report monitoring, with reports being produced only when predefined threshold have been reached or exceeded.

6.5 Planning and implementation

The introduction of a Capacity Management process needs to be planned carefully prior to implementation. Probably some of the activities, such as monitoring and tuning are already taking place. However with many different hardware and software components in the IT Infrastructure, it is unlikely that all the necessary platforms are being monitored, and it is probable that some activities in the sub-processes of Capacity Planning are not being carried out.

6.5.1 Review what exists already

It is possible that some parts of the Capacity Management process are already in place in the organisation, so it is necessary to establish details of the existing procedures and tools. These details are required to identify the gap between the current functionality and the required functionality. In particular this review should identify:

- current responsibility for any Capacity Management

- the tools already in use

- current and desired requirements by other Service Management processes, especially SLM, Availability Management and Financial Management

- current budget and cost-effectiveness

- the management commitment to the introduction of Capacity Management.

When the review has been completed, it should be possible to produce a report on:

- the assessment of the current situation re Capacity Management

- the improvements that need to be made

- the need for Capacity Management and the benefits that can be expected

- how the improvements can be implemented

- example output from the Capacity Management process

- a project plan, showing timescales, staffing levels, costs and specifying the objectives, main tasks, ongoing activities and output from each part of the process.

When there is a documented statement of what already exists, it is then possible to plan for a full, ITIL-compliant Capacity Management process.

6.5.2   Planning the process

Structure of the Capacity Management process

One of the first decisions that has to be taken is how the Capacity Management process will operate in an environment where typically, the component parts of the IT Infrastructure are widely distributed.

If the Capacity Management process is centralised in one location, does the centralised process have sufficient access and control over the components in remote locations that it has to manage? Conversely if the staff who are carrying out the Capacity Management process are co-located with the components, and so widely distributed, can sufficient control be exercised to ensure that the Capacity Management process is working effectively?

The Resource Capacity Management sub-process works best if it is platform based, i.e. the same members of staff carry out the analysis, tuning and implementation work for a particular technology resource. In general, the staff with technical knowledge to carry out the activity on one hardware platform, operating system and set of applications, do not have the necessary skills to do the work on another platform and different set of operating system and applications. So, in many organisations, Capacity Management only has responsibility for the management of these sub-processes. Capacity Management should be identifying the monitoring requirements of this sub-process, while the technical staff carry out the actual implementation.

However the Service and Business Capacity Management sub-processes are best performed by staff who can take an end-to-end view of service performance and business requirements across all the technology resources involved.

This ensures that the necessary data from all the sub-processes is available for Capacity Management to produce all reports that are required, in particular the Capacity Plan.

Monitoring

The review of the current Capacity Management capability will have identified the existing monitors to which the Capacity Management process has access. Some of the required monitors will have been supplied with the operating systems and applications that are in use, and will only need to be switched on. Other monitors and monitoring equipment will need to be purchased and installed.

Monitors are required for:

- hardware – from PCs, through file servers, up to mainframes and super-computers
- networking equipment (LANs, WANs, bridges, routers etc.)
- peripherals (bulk storage devices, printers etc.)
- software – operating system and network software, in-house developments and purchased packages.

However the monitoring of all equipment can be difficult and costly, so the monitoring should be focused on the components of the Infrastructure that support the business critical services. The potential danger of this approach is that there may be no monitoring of some component in the IT Infrastructure that nonetheless is critical to the provision of a business critical service, and that subsequently has Capacity or performance Problems.

The next decision is the data items to monitor, record and store and the intervals over which the recorded data is to be retained. The Resource Capacity Management sub-process requires data on the levels of utilisation of each of the appropriate components of the IT Infrastructure. The Service Capacity Management sub-process requires data on the throughput of applications, on-line response times etc. The Business Capacity Management sub-process requires data on the business volumes, such as number of orders processed, deliveries scheduled etc. The data needs to be collected at a variety of intervals, namely per second, per minute, per hour, per day, for measurements such as transactions per second, average utilisation over an hour etc.

All the required data items need to be identified, and the monitors checked to ensure that they can collect the data.

The CDB

The Capacity Management process needs to collect data from a variety of hardware platforms and software applications that could be widely distributed. Also many different monitoring and recording products are required, which may be incompatible with each other. So how should the CDB be designed?

In essence the Capacity Management process has the following options:

- to get all the data onto a single platform for analysis and storage
- to keep the raw data and much of the analysed data on each of the host platforms, and only transfer to a central location, a very limited amount of analysed data.
- to adopt a hybrid of these two approaches above.

The monitors provide the utilisation data for the CDB, but the other potential data is provided as follows:

- the service data from the SLAs and SLRs of the SLM process
- the business data from the business plans and strategy
- the technical data from the manufacturers' specification of the hardware and software components

- the financial data from the Financial Management process and the CMDB.

Other factors that influence the decision include:

- the Availability of suitable hardware and software for holding the data centrally
- whether a distributed Capacity Management process is being implemented.

It is probable that the final implementation results in the CDB being a conceptual database, with a number of physical storage locations. This is likely to occur because not all the various hardware and software monitors record their data in a format that is easily transferable to another platform.

Also business plans and strategies, and SLAs and SLRs are written documents containing the information that the Capacity Management process needs. These documents exist already, but not within the CDB. The necessary data could be extracted from them and then held separately in the CDB, but the problem of keeping the CDB data up-to-date then arises.

Wherever the data is held, disk space needs to be allocated for the CDB, probably in a number of locations. The size of the CDB needs to be considered in each location, together with any requirements for specific software.

It is important to maintain the integrity of the CDB. Therefore it is recommended that identified personnel have responsibility for updating the CDB and other staff have read-only access. It is vital that comprehensive operating instructions are available for all the regular monitoring activities. Recovery instructions should be available to cater for activities that fail to complete. In general, monitoring activities should be automated as much as possible.

Whatever implementation is chosen for the CDB, it is important that the CDB is covered by the Change Management process, so that Changes are considered for their impact on the CDB.

The final consideration is for a regular audit of the contents of the CDB. Such an audit should be carried out regularly, and check the contents of the CDB for completeness, i.e. that all the necessary data items are being recorded, and the length of time that information is held for each data item is appropriate.

Integration into the other planning processes

The Capacity Management process is most effective if it is linked closely with the other IT Service Management planning processes, such as Availability Management and development activities such as Application Development. This enables Capacity Management to be proactive in the work that it does, which is the key to a successful Capacity Management process. In particular the need to be an integral part of the planning processes is most apparent on the work that needs to be done to produce the Capacity Plan.

Production of the Capacity Plan

A major output from the Capacity Management process is the Capacity Plan. Its regular production needs to be planned, and depends on the following:

- the need to input to the Budgeting cycle
- the accuracy or volatility of the business plans
- the volatility of the IT Infrastructure and IT Service supported.

The Capacity Plan should be produced in a timescale that allows its recommendations to be considered as part of the budget planning cycle, because the Plan may have recommendations that require the cost of the upgrade to be included in budgets etc. Also if the business plans are shown to be inaccurate, or are being updated regularly, it will be necessary to update the Capacity Plan more regularly. Finally if there are frequent, unexpected changes in the IT Service provision or in the components in the IT Infrastructure, because new business is won or lost, the Capacity Plan may need to be updated more frequently.

All Capacity Plans should be updated at least once a year, and for organisations with very static IT Service provision and no unexpected changes in the business plans, this will be sufficient. For organisations with rapidly changing business plans and IT Service provision, the Capacity Plan needs to be updated every three months, and in extreme cases, every month.

6.5.3   Implementation of the process

In the implementation of the Capacity Management process it is necessary to draw a distinction between the activities that are carried out as part of the implementation of the process, the activities that are carried out regularly, and the activities that are carried out as necessary. In the remainder of this Section the first two activities of training staff and establishing monitoring and the CDB are initial implementation activities. The activities to be carried out regularly or as necessary, are the activities that are described in Section 6.3, and are carried out as part of the Business, Service and Resource Capacity Management sub-processes.

Train staff

The IT Services in most organisations are supported by an IT Infrastructure that consists of a large variety of hardware and software resources from many different suppliers. Probably many different operating systems and programming languages are in use, on a wide range of hardware platforms. So a wide range of technical skills are required to install, set-up and run all the necessary monitors, to analyse the information, and to make and implement tuning recommendations.

The Capacity Management process needs access to staff who have the necessary technical skills of the hardware platforms, operating systems and applications that all the sub-processes of Capacity Management require.

Establish monitoring and the CDB

The monitoring facilities need to be established on each of the hardware platforms and for each of the services. Also the CDB needs to be established, if necessary across a range of platforms. These activities should be carried out as part of the set-up of the Capacity Management process, although there is then an on-going requirement to ensure that the monitoring is occurring at all times and is at the level required. Also it is necessary to ensure that adequate security copies of the CDB are always being taken.

Business Capacity Management

When the necessary data is being produced by each of the Resource, Service and Business Capacity Management sub-processes, the Business Capacity Management sub-process can use the data to produce a series of resource and service utilisation reports and graphs for IT management and the business. Some of the reports will be linked to the achievement of the targets in the SLAs, while others will be confirmation that SLRs can be met. The main document produced by the Business Capacity Management sub-process is the Capacity Plan. All the reports and the Capacity Plan are produced on a regular basis.

In the preparation of any of the reports, modelling or application sizing may have been used to determine the future resource requirements of new services or changes to existing services or their SLA targets.

Service Capacity Management

When the necessary service monitoring has been established, the data produced needs to be analysed, and if necessary, action taken to tune the service performance. For example, the activities of monitoring and analysis may indicate that the design and implementation of a particular service needs to be tuned for improved on-line response times. Any amendments to the design of the service should be implemented under Change Management and then further monitoring undertaken. These activities are on-going from the first day that each service became operational.

The Service Capacity Management sub-process may need to consider the use of Demand Management if there are short- or long-term requirements to influence the demand for resource. This activity is carried out as necessary.

Resource Capacity Management

When the necessary resource monitoring has been established, the data produced needs to be analysed, and if necessary, action taken to tune the resources used. For example, the activities of monitoring and analysis may produce exception reports for the SLM process that indicate that the tuning of a particular resource is required. Any tuning recommendations should be implemented under Change Management and then further monitoring undertaken. These activities are on-going from the first day that each resource is installed and becomes operational.

The Resource Capacity Management sub-process considers new technology and the resilience of the IT Infrastructure as required by the Business Capacity Management sub-process.

6.6 Review of the Capacity Management process

The Capacity Management process should be reviewed for effectiveness and efficiency at regular intervals to ensure that:

- it is producing the required output at the required times for the appropriate audience
- its activities are cost effective.

Metrics

The ideal indicator for the success of the Capacity Management process is that sufficient IT Capacity exists at all times, to provide Customers with the agreed level of service. However more specific targets and metrics should be identified, of which the following are some examples, to check that:

- the utilisation of all components and services is being recorded in the CDB
- the correct amount of utilisation data is being collected in the CDB – too much data and the collection overhead becomes unacceptable and filestore is wasted, too little data and investigations into Incidents and Problems may be unsuccessful, and Capacity Plans may be inaccurate
- all recommendations for tuning actions are accompanied with predictions of their likely effect – the actions are reviewed for their success and the results documented
- the SLM process is informed of any potential or actual breaches of the targets in the SLAs

- constraints that are imposed on demand occur with the understanding of the Customers and do not seriously affect the credibility of the IT Service Provider

- all regular management reports are produced on time and all ad hoc reports are produced within the agreed timescales

- the annual Capacity Plan is produced on time and is accepted by the senior IT management

- recommendations for hardware or software upgrades that are identified in the Capacity Plan are accurate, both in terms of the financial cost and the timescale in which they are required.

Critical Success Factors

Success in Capacity Management is dependent on a number of factors:

- accurate business forecasts

- knowledge of IT strategy and plans, and that the plans are accurate

- an understanding of current and future technologies

- an ability to demonstrate cost effectiveness

- interaction with other effective Service Management processes

- an ability to plan and implement the appropriate IT Capacity to match business need.

Key Performance Indicators (KPIs)

The success of the process can be measured by producing the following KPIs in support of the CSFs:

- resource forecasts
  - timely production of forecasts of resource requirements
  - accurate forecasts of trends in resource utilisation
  - incorporation of business plans into Capacity Plan

- technology
  - ability to monitor performance and throughput of all services and components, as appropriate
  - implementation of new technology in line with business requirements (time, cost and functionality)
  - the use of old technology does not result in breached SLAs due to problems with support or performance

- cost-effectiveness a reduction in panic buying
  - no significant over-Capacity that can't be justified in business terms
  - accurate forecasts of planned expenditure

- plan and implement the appropriate IT Capacity to match business need
  - reduction in lost reduction in the Incidents due to poor performance
  - reduction in lost business due to inadequate Capacity
  - new services are implemented which match SLRs
  - recommendations made by Capacity Management are acted upon.

6.7 Interfaces with other SM processes

Capacity Management is closely related to business requirements. As such it is a vital element of the planning process and hence has close links with all aspects of Service Delivery. However Capacity

Management maintains close links with Service Support to provide support for all operational performance and Capacity issues. The major Service Management interfaces are defined below.

6.7.1   Incident Management

Incident Management keeps Capacity Management informed of Incidents related to Capacity and performance. Capacity Management supports the Incident Management process by resolving and documenting Capacity related Incidents.

Co-ordinated through Problem Management, Capacity Management provides the Incident Management with diagnostic scripts and diagnostic tools to assist with Incident Management. For example, real-time performance and Capacity monitoring tools generate automatic reports to the Service Desk. As a result Capacity Management keeps the Incident Management and Problem Management processes informed of any potential performance or Capacity Problems through automatic alerts or recording known errors.

6.7.2   Problem Management

Capacity Management provides a specialist support role to identify, diagnose and resolve Capacity related Problems. As discussed above, Capacity Management utilises and makes available, diagnostic scripts and tools to support both the Incident and Problem Management processes. Capacity Problems and known errors are documented and made available through Problem Management.

Capacity Management supports the proactive role of Problem Management through the analysis of performance and Capacity information to identify any significant trends.

6.7.3   Change Management

Capacity Management is represented on the Change Advisory Board, to assess the impact of Changes on existing Capacity and to identify additional Capacity requirements. The cumulative effect of Changes upon Capacity needs to be closely monitored by Capacity Management.

Additional Capacity requirements need to be included in the Capacity Plan and as such treated as Requests For Changes (RFCs) in their own right. Capacity Management raises RFCs for any planned upgrades, tuning activities and additional use of monitoring tools throughout the Infrastructure.

6.7.4   Release Management

Capacity Management helps determine the distribution strategy, particularly where the network is used for distribution. Factors such as network bandwidth, host and target Capacity, distribution window and number of targets need to be considered as part of the distribution strategy. Capacity Management provides the necessary planning data and technical expertise to support the strategy on an ongoing basis and for individual distribution requirements.

The Release Management checklist includes the following check:

- 'Have all the Capacity Management issues been considered and planned? For example, response times, storage requirements and LAN traffic'.

Clearly Capacity Management would provide the response to this request.

Immediately prior and post distribution, automated tools can be used to perform Capacity audits and to delay distribution and implementation if there is insufficient Capacity. Where automated tools are not used, these checks should still be performed manually to prevent Capacity related Incidents being raised.

6.7.5   Configuration Management

Conceptually the CDB forms a subset of the Configuration Management Database (CMDB). The technical, service, utilisation, financial and business data all pertain to attributes of CIs (CIs) maintained in the CMDB. Without this information on individual CIs, Capacity Management cannot function effectively. Information provided by Capacity Management is made available to other processes via the CMDB. For example, Problem Management requires access to current and historic, service utilisation data to resolve Capacity Problems. SLM requires access to current and historic performance and workload data in order to set achievable SLA targets.

6.7.6   Service Level Management

Capacity Management supports Service Level Management (SLM) to ensure that performance and Capacity targets for new or changed requirements can be achieved. Performance is dependent on a given workload, therefore both are required in an SLA with specific performance targets. Similarly there may be a requirement for Capacity Management to assist SLM in drafting and reviewing Operational Level Agreements and external contracts where Capacity or performance issues are involved.

For operational services, Capacity Management monitors and reports on performance and throughput to SLM. Where weak areas are identified, Capacity Management provides technical input to the overall Service Improvement Programme to improve service performance.

6.7.7   Financial Management for IT Services

Capacity Management is concerned with economic provision of services. Financial justification and efficiency gains are demonstrated with the assistance of Financial Management. A cost summary should be provided as part of the Capacity Plan. Procurement recommendations included in the Capacity Plan should be compared with budget forecasts and actuals before purchase.

In organisations where Customers are charged according to resource utilisation Capacity Management provides Financial Management with the usage profiles that form the basis for Charging. Capacity Management provides assistance with the definition and execution of Capacity related Charging calculations. The use of modelling to predict demand also provides revenue estimates.

6.7.8   IT Service Continuity Management

Capacity Management determines the Capacity required for all recovery options used. The minimum hardware and software configurations required are defined to provide the required performance and throughput levels following an invocation.

It is essential that the Capacity identified for recovery is maintained in line with that used in the live environment. The Capacity Plan should incorporate IT Service Continuity requirements and RFCs should be assessed for their impact on any recovery options.

6.7.9   Availability Management

Performance and Capacity Problems result in Unavailability i.e. unacceptably slow performance is effectively the same as Unavailability. Therefore Capacity and Availability Management share common goals and complement each other. Ideally Availability and Capacity Management should be aligned as there are many interdependencies. For example, implementing additional resilience requires consideration of the associated Capacity requirements. Capacity Management needs to be aware of Availability techniques deployed, such as mirroring or duplexing, in order to plan accurately for Capacity. The tools used by Availability Management and Capacity Management are often shared. Both require access to common planning, monitoring and alerting tools along with the CMDB. Both processes commonly use techniques such as Component Failure Impact Analysis (CFIA) and Fault Tree Analysis (FTA). See Chapter 8 for details of these techniques.

Annex 6A   Capacity Management – Role and responsibilities

Role

Capacity Management has overall responsibility for ensuring that there is adequate IT Capacity to meet required levels of service and for ensuring that senior IT management is correctly advised on how to match Capacity and demand, and to ensure that use of existing Capacity is optimised.

Capacity Management is also responsible for advising the SLM process about appropriate service levels or service level options.

Responsibilities

Capacity Management:

- ensures that appropriate levels of monitoring of resources and system performance are set, and that the information recorded in a CBD is kept up-to-date and used by all parts of the Capacity Management process

- produces Capacity Plans in line with the organisation's business planning cycle, identifying Capacity requirements early enough to take account of procurement lead times

- documents the need for any increase or reduction in hardware based on SLRs and cost constraints

- produces regular management reports which include current usage of resources, trends and forecasts

- sizes all proposed new systems to determine the computer and network resources required, to determine hardware utilisation, performance service levels and cost implications

- assesses new technology and its relevance to the organisation in terms of performance and cost

- assesses new hardware and software products for use by Capacity Management that might improve the efficiency and effectiveness of the process

- carries out performance testing of new systems

- reports on performance against targets contained in SLAs

- maintains a knowledge of future demand for IT Services and predicts the effects of demand on performance service levels

- determines performance service levels that are maintainable and cost justified

- recommends tuning of systems and makes recommendations to IT management on the design and use of systems to help ensure optimum use of all hardware and operating system software resources

- recommends resolutions to performance-related Incidents and Problems

- recommends to IT management when to employ Demand Management, to dampen Customer demands on systems

- carries out ad-hoc performance and Capacity studies on request from IT management

- ensures requirements for reliability and Availability are taken into account in all Capacity planning and sizing activity

- is represented on the CAB, assessing and authorising Changes

- ensures that regular and ad hoc audits are carried out on the Capacity Management process.

Annex 6B Contents of a Capacity Plan

The Capacity Plan should be published annually in line with the budgetary cycle. Ideally it should be updated quarterly. This takes extra effort, but, if it is regularly updated, the Capacity Plan is more likely to be accurate and to reflect the changing business need.

Introduction

This Section briefly explains the background to this issue of the Capacity Plan. For example:

- the organisation's current levels of Capacity
- Problems being experienced or envisaged due to over or under Capacity
- the degree to which service levels are being achieved
- what has changed since the last issue of the plan.

The introduction should also include the following Sub-sections:

Scope of the plan

Ideally, the Capacity Plan should encompass all IT resources. This Sub-section should explicitly name those elements of the IT Infrastructure that are included.

Methods used

The Capacity Plan uses information gathered by the sub-processes. This Sub-section therefore should contain details of how and when this information was obtained, for example business forecasts obtained from business plans, workload forecasts obtained from Customers, service level forecasts obtained by the use of modelling tools.

Assumptions made

It is important that any assumptions made, particularly those concerning the business drivers for IT Capacity, are highlighted early on in the plan. If they are the cornerstones upon which more detailed calculations are built, then it is vital that all concerned understand this.

Management summary

Much of the Capacity Plan, by necessity, contains technical detail that is not of interest to all readers of the plan. The management summary should highlight the main issues, options, recommendations and costs. It may be necessary to produce a separate executive summary document that contains the main points from each of the sections of the main plan.

Business scenarios

It is necessary to put the plan into the context of the current and envisaged business environment. For example, a British airline planned to move a large number of staff into its headquarters building. A ratio of 1.7 people per desktop terminal was forecast. Capacity Management was alerted and was able to calculate the extra network traffic that would result.

It is important to mention explicitly all known business forecasts so that readers can determine what is in and what is outside the scope of the plan.

Service summary

The service summary section should include the following:

Current and recent service provision

For each service that is delivered, provide a service profile. This should include throughput rates and the resulting resource utilisation, for example of memory, storage space, transfer rates, processor usage, network usage. Short-term, medium-term and long-term trends should be presented here.

Service forecasts

The business plans should provide Capacity Management with details of the new services planned, and the growth or contraction in the use of existing services. This Sub-section should report on new services and the demise of legacy systems.

Resource summary

The resource summary section should include the following:

Current and recent resource usage

This Sub-section concentrates on the resulting resource usage by the services. It reports, again, on the short-, medium- and long-term trends in resource usage, broken down by hardware platform. This information has been gathered and analysed by the sub-processes of Service Capacity Management and Resource Capacity Management and so should be readily available.

Resource forecasts

This Sub-section forecasts the likely resource usage resulting from the service forecasts. Each business scenario mentioned above should be addressed here. For example, a carpet wholesale business in the North of England could accurately predict what the peak and average processor usage would be before they decided to take over a rival business. It was proved that an upgrade would not be required. This was fed into the cost model, leading to a successful take-over.

Options for service improvement

Building on the results of the previous Section, this Section outlines the possible options for improving the effectiveness and efficiency of Service Delivery. It could contain options for merging different services on a single processor, upgrading the network to take advantage of technological advances, tuning the use of resource or service performance, rewriting legacy systems, purchasing new hardware or software etc.

Cost model

The costs associated with these options should be documented here. In addition the current and forecast cost of providing IT Services should be included. In practice Capacity Management obtains much of this information from the Financial Management process and the IT Financial Plan.

Recommendations

The final section of the plan should contain a summary of the recommendations made in the previous plan and their status, for example rejected, planned, implemented. Any new recommendations should be made here, i.e. which of the options mentioned in the plan is preferred.

The recommendations should be quantified in terms of:

- the business benefits to be expected
- the potential impact of carrying out the recommendations
- the risks involved
- the resources required
- the cost, both set up and on-going.

7 IT SERVICE CONTINUITY MANAGEMENT

7.1 Introduction

Since the IT Infrastructure Library produced its book on 'Contingency Planning', there have been significant changes in technology and the way in which technology is used within business. The dependencies between business processes and technology are now so inter-twined that Contingency Planning (or Business Continuity Management as it is now sometimes referred) incorporates both a business element (Business Continuity Planning) and a technology element (IT Service Continuity Management Planning). Their dependencies on each other determine that one is a sub-set of the other, depending on the nature of the business and the extent to which technology has pervaded the organisation. In this Chapter it is assumed that Business Continuity is the main driver and that IT Service Continuity Management (ITSCM) is a sub-set of the Business Continuity Management (BCM) process.

7.1.1 Why ITSCM?

In today's highly competitive and service oriented business environment, organisations are judged on their ability to continue to operate and provide a service at all times. ITSCM is concerned with managing an organisation's ability to continue to provide a pre-determined and agreed level of IT Services to support the minimum business requirements following an interruption to the business. This may range from an application or system failure, to a complete loss of the business premises. As such, ITSCM forms an integral part of the BCM process to ensure that IT Services and facilities can be provided.

7.1.2 Goal for ITSCM

The goal for ITSCM is to support the overall Business Continuity Management process by ensuring that the required IT technical and services facilities (including computer systems, networks, applications, telecommunications, technical support and Service Desk) can be recovered within required, and agreed, business timescales.

7.1.3 Scope of ITSCM

ITSCM focuses on the IT Services required to support the critical business processes. The impact of a loss of a business process, such as financial loss, damage to reputation or regulatory breach, are measured through a Business Impact Analysis, which determines the minimum critical requirements. The specific IT technical and service requirements are supported by ITSCM. The scope of ITSCM within an organisation is determined by the organisational structure, culture and strategic direction (both business and technology) in terms of the services provided and how these develop and change over time.

7.1.4   Basic concepts of ITSCM

As organisations become more dependent upon technology, which is now a core component of most business processes, continued Availability of IT is critical to their survival. This Availability is accomplished by introducing risk reduction measures such as resilient systems, and recovery options including back-up facilities. Successful implementation of ITSCM can only be achieved with visible senior management commitment and the support of all members of the organisation. Ongoing maintenance of the recovery capability is essential if it is to remain effective. This is achieved through:

- a rigorous Configuration Management, Change Management and review process
- education and awareness for the whole organisation
- utilising the latest technology and software supporting tools
- specific training for personnel involved in the process
- regular testing.

7.1.5   Benefits of ITSCM

ITSCM supports the BCM process and delivers the required IT supporting Infrastructure to enable the business to continue to operate following a service disruption.

> **KEY MESSAGE**
>
> **ITSCM must be an integral part of the overall business process especially when a business is highly IT dependent.**

The annual spend on ITSCM can be likened to an insurance premium and, like insurance, the optimum spend is determined by the circumstances and risks that could influence the organisation's business. The variety and frequency of events that pose a threat to businesses in today's technology age have forced organisations to regard the continuing requirement for ITSCM as part of their corporate and management philosophy and culture.

This allows an organisation to identify, assess and take responsibility for managing its risks, thus enabling it to understand better the environment in which it operates, decide which risks it wishes to counteract and act positively to protect the interests of all stakeholders (including staff, Customers, shareholders, third parties, creditors). ITSCM can complement this activity and help to deliver business benefit.

Management of risk

The IT organisation can actively manage the Infrastructure and systems to reduce the impact of component, multiple component or site failure (e.g. RAID implementation on disks, multiple processors/power supplies, mirroring or clustering of systems etc.). The consequence of not managing this and other risks effectively is likely to impact on the ability of the organisation to meet its client's expectations, potentially resulting in lost Customers, revenue and market share.

Conversely, the advantages of ITSCM include:

- **Potential lower insurance premiums:** The IT organisation can help the organisation demonstrate to underwriters or insurers that they are proactively managing down their business risks. Therefore the risk to the insurance organisation is lower and the premiums due should reflect this. Alternatively, the organisation may feel comfortable in reducing cover or self-insuring in certain areas as a result of limiting potential losses.

- **Regulatory requirements:** In some industries a recovery capability is becoming a mandatory requirement (for example, regulators stipulate that financial organisations have sufficient Continuity and security controls to meet the business requirements). Failure to demonstrate tested business and ITSCM facilities could result in heavy fines or the loss of trading licences. Within the service community, there is an obligation to provide continuous services, e.g., hospitals, emergency services and prisons.

- **Business relationship:** The requirement to work closely with the business to develop and maintain a Continuity capability fosters a much closer working relationship between IT and the business areas. This can assist in creating a better understanding of the business requirements and the capability of IT to support those requirements.

- **Positive marketing of contingency capabilities:** Being able to demonstrate effective ITSCM capabilities enables an organisation to provide high service levels to clients and Customers and thus win business.

- **Organisational credibility:** There is a responsibility on the directors of organisations to protect the shareholders' interest and those of their clients. Contingency facilities increase an organisation's credibility and reputation with Customers, business partners, stakeholders and industry peers. For example, the growth of call centres in many organisations has meant that the need to maintain Customer communications at all times is vital to the ability to retain Customer confidence and loyalty.

- **Competitive advantage:** Service organisations are increasingly being asked by business partners, Customers and stakeholders to demonstrate their contingency facilities and may not be invited to tender for business unless they can demonstrate appropriate recovery capabilities. In many cases this is a good incentive for Customers to continue a business relationship and becomes apart of the competitive advantage used to win or retain Customers.

In many industries, consumers and business Customers are requesting an ability to make enquiries, place orders, monitor progress and settle bills with much less human intervention than is currently the case. Technology allows products to be tailor-made to Customers' exact requirements and advanced just-in-time production systems allow inventories to be reduced to a minimum.

These changes make business even more dependent on technology and ITSCM than ever before. Failure of a centralised electronic order capture system or an inventory management system will stop a business in its tracks. In the digital world, 'no systems' means 'no business'. In order to address these risks, resilience, security, Business Continuity and the ITSCM components have to be designed into electronic business services from the outset in away that is rarely done today.

Examples

(1) If a mobile phone provider were to lose the messaging capability on its service, this would be unacceptable to many Customers who may transfer to another service provider either immediately or when the contract renews.

(2) Supermarkets rely on just-in-time to provide stock control and ordering. A failure at any stage in the supply chain management, such as bar code scanners, could mean that stocks of perishable items such as milk are not re-ordered This will result in no milk on the shelves within a very short period of time and a consequent loss of Customer income, confidence and loyalty.

(3) Profit for a financial institution involved in money market trading is dependent upon decisions taken based on split second Availability of pricing information delivered through the computer Infrastructure. If this information is not available, the organisation immediately loses its ability to make informed decisions and could potentially begin to lose money. Similarly, if IT services fail in a heavily automated manufacturing plant utilising just-in-time processing, the plant will almost certainly lose production time and therefore money.

(4) In the electronic commerce environment, if an organisation were to lose the Availability of its Internet site then this could lead to an immediate loss of business and Customers as they will immediately find alternative sites and organisations offering similar products and services. In addition, Customer loyalty cannot be relied on and once Customers are lost, they are unlikely to return.

7.1.6 Business Continuity Management and ITSCM

Business Continuity Management (BCM) is concerned with managing risks to ensure that at all times an organisation can continue operating to, at least, a pre-determined minimum level. The BCM process involves reducing the risk to an acceptable level and planning for the recovery of business processes should a risk materialise and a disruption to the business occur.

ITSCM must be apart of the overall BCM process and is dependent upon information derived through this process. ITSCM is focused on the Continuity of IT Services to the business. BCM is concerned with the management of Business Continuity that incorporates all services upon which the business depends, one of which is IT.

There is a need for the minimum business requirements to be determined to a level of detail and agreed between the business and the IT Service providers (internal or external) prior to the ITSCM scope being defined. These requirements may define a need to establish an immediate transfer of the service to an alternative location or a requirement to recover elements of the service over a longer period of time (e.g. a week). It is vital that these prerequisites are fully understood, defined and agreed by the business as part of the BCM process to ensure ITSCM is specifically used in the most effective and efficient manner to deliver the IT portion of these requirements.

> **KEY MESSAGE**
>
> **Business requirements drive ITSCM provision and provide what the business wants, not what the IT community think they need.**

7.1.7 Management commitment

The implementation of ITSCM mechanisms, identified through the BCM process, must be based on business requirements in order to reduce the risk from interruption or failure of critical business processes and ensure business benefit. The process is concerned with the performance and, at the most elementary level, the survival of the business and is, therefore, a top management issue. The process must be understood and visibly supported by all senior managers and directors.

> **KEY MESSAGE**
>
> **Get senior business management on board – without them effective ITSCM is impossible to achieve.**

However, management commitment does not end when the initial project has been completed. Ongoing commitment is necessary to maintain the effectiveness of the recovery capabilities and there is a requirement for a continual review, update and test process for the ITSCM plans, facilities and service provision. Providing this is achieved, ITSCM will react to changes in the business world that it is there to protect. Business Continuity and recovery must be considered as part of the culture of the organisation and indeed be part of business as usual. To help achieve this, responsibility for ITSCM should be a key objective in a business manager's job description.

Business-as-usual pressures tend to focus management time on the business itself and ITSCM typically takes a back seat. It is essential that the necessary resources are focused through a strategic directive from the highest levels of management to prevent business-as-usual pressures being used as an excuse for the non-delivery of the recovery facilities.

To this end, ITSCM becomes one of the multitude of corporate management activities performed in operational and executive roles, enabling ITSCM to be embedded, either explicitly or implicitly, within business strategy, business objectives and key performance indicators through all levels of the organisation. Similarly, as the IT strategy is generally a derivative of the business strategy, this should reflect those changes in terms of ITSCM.

Failure to include the ITSCM process as part of the corporate planning activities will result in the ITSCM mechanisms becoming inaccurate or 'out of date' and failing to meet business requirements.

7.1.8 Relationship with other IT Service disciplines

ITSCM interacts with the other IT Service disciplines such as:

- Service Level Management – understanding the obligations of IT Service Delivery
- Availability Management – delivering risk reduction measures to maintain 'business as usual'
- Configuration Management – defining the core Infrastructure

- Capacity Management – ensuring that business requirements are fully supported through appropriate IT hardware resources

- Change Management – ensuring the currency and accuracy of the Continuity Plans through established processes and regular reviews

- Service Desk/Incident Management – utilising historical data (statistics).

7.2 Scope of ITSCM

ITSCM primarily considers those IT assets and configurations that support the key business processes. However, the installation of mechanisms to deliver ITSCM may not necessarily be sufficient to keep those business processes operating after a service disruption. Should it be necessary to relocate to an alternative working location, provision will also be required for items such as office and personnel accommodation, copies of critical paper records, courier services and telephone facilities to communicate with Customers and third parties.

The ITSCM process should identify the required and agreed minimum level of business operation following a service disruption, along with a requirements definition covering systems, facilities and service requirements. The process then examines the risks and threats to these requirements and develops an IT risk reduction or mitigation programme. This programme implements mechanisms delivering the Continuity requirements necessary to provide the required optimum level of business operation. These mechanisms may include splitting a data centre over more than one location, implementing disk mirroring (or other levels of RAID as required), system replication to a stand by site, dual routing of communications links, installing secondary communications links, or provision of stand by power supply (UPS and/or generator).

> **KEY MESSAGE**
>
> **An organisation's structure, culture and strategic direction (both business and technology) are key drivers in determining the scope of ITSCM. Significant benefit can be derived from the involvement of someone, with good specific business and Infrastructure knowledge and experience, who can ensure that these are considered.**

Scope considerations include:

- the organisation's dependence on technology, its Infrastructure and any external providers of support services

- the number and location of the organisations offices and the services performed in each

- the number of critical business processes and the level of integration between them

- the level of services that need to be provided to the business to support those critical business processes

- any limitations in the provision of ITSCM mechanisms (e.g. cost of downtime)

- the organisation's attitude towards risk.

At the broadest level, the scope of ITSCM is usually defined in terms of the:

- business processes to be covered and their IT support requirements (e.g. systems, networks, communications, support staff skills, data and documentation etc.)
- risks that need to be addressed.

7.2.1 Risks 'in scope'

Organisations continually face risks, ranging from a localised service disruption in a single department to major service disruptions that affect multiple organisations and communities. As the business activities and Infrastructure of an organisation change, so do the business processes and the organisation's risk assessment profile. The risks covered by ITSCM tend to be those that could result in serious disruption to business processes, for example the loss of, or denial of access to, IT systems or networks. These risks are discussed in more detail later in this Chapter.

The likelihood of events such as these happening has been proven over the years. Talking to Building Services and IT Operations Support Management provides an insight into the frequency, types and nature of regular service disruptions. In addition, the press has provided substantial coverage of major service disruptions, from terrorist activities to natural disasters and Infrastructure Problems. Below is a brief list of high profile events that have caused significant problems to organisations over the years:

Poison Gas	Tokyo Underground System, Japan (March, 1995)
Power Loss	Auckland, New Zealand (December, 1997)
Earthquake	Los Angeles, USA (January, 1994)
	Kobe, Japan (January, 1995)
Bomb	World Trade Centre, New York, USA (February, 1993)
	Bishopsgate, London, England (April, 1993)
	Oklahoma City, Oklahoma, USA (April, 1995)
	Docklands, London, England (February, 1996)
	Manchester, England (June, 1996)
Flood	Bangladesh (July, 1996)
	Pakistan (August, 1996)
Technical Failure	London Stock Exchange (2000)
	Web site denial of service attacks e.g. Yahoo (2000)

Example

In the late 1970s a major earthquake in Romania left 1000 dead in Bucharest alone. This is a phenomenon that recurs approximately every 40 years. There were no major IT networks in Romania 20 years ago. It is almost certain that there will be a major earthquake by 2020 that will destroy all existing IT Infrastructure within the fault area. Contingency for them is not a potential luxury, it is an absolute survival essential, which affects not only existing IT Infrastructure but every significant IT change.

7.2.2   Risks 'out of scope'

ITSCM does not usually directly cover longer-term risks such as those from changes in business direction, diversification, restructuring, and so on. While these risks can have a material impact on IT Service elements and their Continuity mechanisms, management usually has some time to identify and evaluate the risk and include risk mitigation through changes or shifts in business and IT strategies, thereby becoming part of the Change Management programme.

Similarly, ITSCM does not usually cover minor technical faults (for example, non critical disk failure), unless there is a possibility that the impact could have a material impact on the business. These risks would be expected to be covered mainly through the Service Desk and the Incident Management process, or resolved through the planning associated with the disciplines of Availability Management, Problem Management; and to a lesser extent through Change Management, Configuration Management and 'day to day' operational management.

7.2.3   Roles and responsibilities

The initial implementation of ITSCM is typically progressed as a project and needs to be considered as apart of other projects, whereas, on an ongoing basis ITSCM evolves into operational responsibilities. Without the roles and responsibilities being addressed, and openly endorsed and communicated from a senior level within the organisation at an early stage in the project, it will struggle to generate the support, resourcing and 'buy-in' required for it to deliver the business requirements. This could have a number of consequences resulting in the recovery capability being delayed, running over budget, the scope being reduced or work not being completed to the required standard.

Due to the understanding required of the business and the management of risks within the project, there is a logical fit within the Security Management and Business Analysis areas of most IT organisations. Quite often these roles possess similar skills/knowledge and often have to undertake risk and impact assessments, and implement risk reduction measures as part of their usual role. For this reason it is not unusual to find an ITSCM responsibility within an Information Security function.

The roles and responsibilities of individuals within the initial project and ongoing support of the ITSCM facilities are discussed later in this Chapter.

KEY MESSAGE

Roles and responsibilities need to be endorsed and communicated from a senior level to ensure respect and commitment for the process.

7.3 The Business Continuity Lifecycle

It is not possible to develop an effective ITSCM plan in isolation, it must fully support the requirements of the business. This Section considers the four stages of the Business Continuity lifecycle with particular emphasis on the IT aspects. A full understanding of the Business Continuity process can be obtained through the OGC ITIL publications, 'An Introduction to Business Continuity Management' and 'A Guide to Business Continuity Management'.

The process is illustrated in the Figure 7.1.

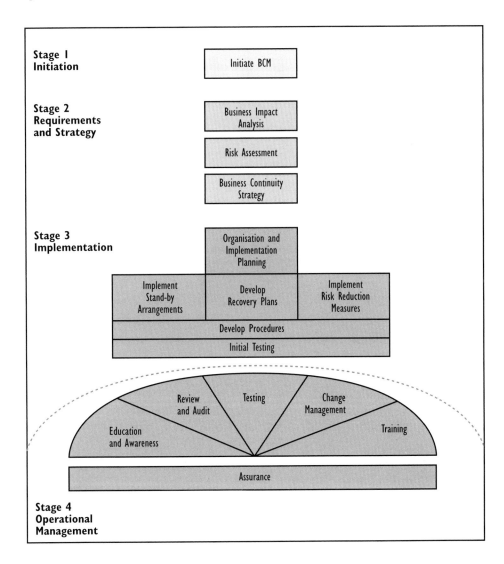

Figure 7.1 – Business Continuity Management Process Model

7.3.1   Stage 1 – Initiation

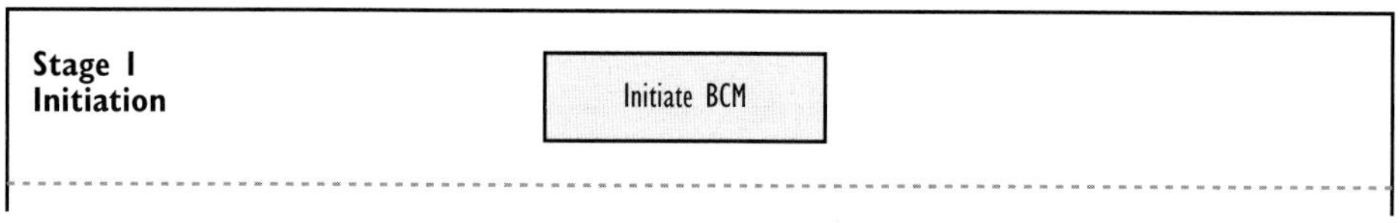

Stage 1 Initiation		Initiate BCM	

Figure 7.2 – Initiation

The activities to be considered during the initiation process (See Figure 7.2) depend on the extent to which contingency facilities have been applied within the organisation. Some parts of the business may have established individual Continuity Plans based around manual Work-arounds and IT may have developed contingency plans for systems perceived to be critical. This is good input to the process, however, effective ITSCM is dependent on supporting critical business functions and ensuring that the available budget is applied in the most appropriate way.

> **KEY MESSAGE**
>
> **The only way of implementing effective ITSCM is through the identification of critical business processes and the analysis, and co-ordination, of the required Infrastructure and IT supporting services.**

The initiation process covers the whole of the organisation and consists of the following activities:

- **Policy setting** – this should be established and communicated as soon as possible so that all members of the organisation involved in, or affected by, Business Continuity issues are aware of their responsibilities to comply with and support ITSCM. As a minimum the policy should set out management intention and objectives.

- **Specify terms of reference and scope** – this includes defining the scope and responsibilities of managers and staff in the organisation, and the method of working. It covers such tasks as undertaking a risk assessment and Business Impact Analysis and determination of the command and control structure required to support a business interruption. There is also a need to take into account such issues as outstanding audit points, regulatory or client requirements and insurance organisation stipulations, and compliance with standards such as BS 7799, the British Standard on Information Security Management (which also addresses Service Continuity requirements).

- **Allocate resources** – the establishment of an effective Business Continuity environment requires considerable resource both in terms of money and manpower. Depending on the maturity of the organisation, with respect to ITSCM, there may be a requirement to familiarise and/or train staff to accomplish the Stage 2 tasks. Alternatively, the use of experienced external consultants may assist in completing the analysis more quickly. However, it is important that the organisation can then maintain the process going forward without the need to rely totally on external support.

- **Define the project organisation and control structure** – ITSCM and BCM projects are potentially complex and need to be well organised and controlled. It is advisable to use a standard project planning methodology such as PRINCE2 complemented with a project-planning tool such as Project Manager Workbench or Microsoft Project. The appointment of an experienced project manager reporting to a steering committee and guiding the working groups is key to success. As IT is an important component of the overall process, it may be that the project is best driven from the IT area reporting through to the highest levels of management.

■ Agree project and quality plans – plans enable the project to be controlled and variances addressed. Quality plans ensure that the deliverables are achieved and to an acceptable level of quality. They also provide a mechanism for communicating project resource requirements and deliverables, thereby obtaining 'buy-in' from all necessary parties.

KEY MESSAGE

A well planned project initiation enables ITSCM work to proceed smoothly with the necessary sponsorship, 'buy-in' and awareness, with all contributing members of the organisation aware of their responsibilities and commitment.

7.3.2 Stage 2 – Requirements Analysis and Strategy Definition

Figure 7.3 – Requirements and Strategy

This stage is depicted in Figure 7.3. It provides the foundation for ITSCM and is a critical component in order to determine how well an organisation will survive a business interruption or disaster and the costs that will be incurred.

KEY MESSAGE

If the requirements analysis is incorrect or key information has been missed, this could have serious consequences on the effectiveness of ITSCM mechanisms.

This stage can effectively be split into two sections:

■ Requirements – perform Business Impact Analysis and risk assessment

■ Strategy – determine and agree risk reduction measures and recovery options to support the requirements.

Requirements

Business Impact Analysis

A key driver in determining ITSCM requirements is how much the organisation stands to lose as a result of a disaster or other service disruption and the speed of escalation of these losses. The purpose of a Business Impact Analysis (BIA) is to assess this through identifying:

■ critical business processes

■ the potential damage or loss that may be caused to the organisation as a result of a disruption to critical business processes.

The BIA also identifies:

■ the form that the damage or loss may take including lost income, additional costs, damaged reputation, loss of goodwill, loss of competitive advantage

■ how the degree of damage or loss is likely to escalate after an service disruption

■ the staffing, skills, facilities and services (including the IT Services) necessary to enable critical and essential business processes to continue operating at a minimum acceptable level

■ the time within which minimum levels of staffing, facilities and services should be recovered

■ the time within which all required business processes and supporting staff, facilities and services should be fully recovered.

The latter three items provide the drivers for the level of ITSCM mechanisms that need to be considered or deployed. Once presented with these options, the business may decide that lower levels of service or increased delays are more acceptable based upon a cost/benefit analysis.

> **Hints and tips**
>
> **Key inputs into the Business Impact Analysis include any service or application definitions for business areas or business processes.**

These definitions and their components enable the mapping of critical service, application and Infrastructure components to critical business processes, thus helping to identify the ITSCM elements that need to be provided. The business requirements are ranked and the associated ITSCM elements confirmed and prioritised in terms of risk assessment/reduction and recovery planning.

Impacts are measured against particular scenarios for each business process such as an inability to settle trades in a money market dealing process, or an inability to invoice for a period of days.

The impact analysis concentrates on the scenarios where the impact on critical business processes is likely to be greatest.

Impacts are measured against the scenarIos and typically fall into one or more of the following categories:

■ failure to achieve agreed internal service levels

■ financial loss

■ additional costs

- immediate and long-term loss of market share
- breach of law, regulations, or standards
- risk to personal safety
- political, corporate or personal embarrassment
- breach of moral responsibility
- loss of goodwill
- loss of credibility
- loss of image and reputation
- loss of operational capability, for example in a command and control environment.

This process enables a business to understand at what point the Unavailability of a service would become untenable. This in turn allows the types of ITSCM mechanisms that are most appropriate to be determined to meet these business requirements.

Example

In a money market dealing environment, loss of market data information could mean that the organisation starts to lose money immediately as trading cannot continue. In addition, Customers may go to another organisation, which would mean potential loss of core business. Loss of the settlement system does not prevent trading from taking place, but if trades already conducted cannot be settled within a specified period of time, the organisation may be in breach of regulatory rules or settlement periods and suffer fines and damaged reputation. This may actually be a more significant impact than the inability to trade because of an inability to satisfy Customer expectations.

It is also important to understand how impacts may change over time. For instance, it may be possible for a business to function without a particular process for a short period of time, for example invoicing, but over a longer period re-establishment will become critical, i.e. in order to maintain cash flow to pay bills and staff. This can be effectively represented using a graphical illustration of how business impacts vary with length of disruption as shown in Figure 7.4.

In a balanced scenario, impacts to the business will occur and become greater over time, however, not all organisations are affected in this way. In some organisations, impacts are not apparent immediately, such as a consultancy organisation where the need to issue reports can be deferred and impacts to the business do not begin to accrue for a period of time. In this case the 'contingency' line of Figure 7.4 is applicable. In other organisations, such as investment banks, a loss of service for even a short period of time will cause major impacts to accrue immediately and the 'preventative' line applies. At some point however, for any organisation, the impacts will accrue to such a level that the business can no longer operate. ITSCM ensures that contingency options are identified so that the appropriate measure can be applied at the appropriate time to keep business impacts from service disruption to a minimum level.

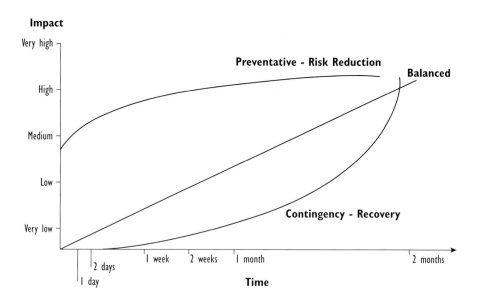

Figure 7.4 – Graphical representation of business impacts

In the majority of cases, business processes can be re-established without a full complement of staff, systems and other facilities, and still maintain an acceptable level of service to clients and Customers. The business recovery objectives should therefore be stated in terms of:

■ the time within which a pre-defined team of core staff and stated minimum facilities must be recovered

■ the timetable for recovery of remaining staff and facilities.

It may not always be possible to provide the recovery requirements to a detailed level. There is a need to balance the potential impact against the cost of recovery to ensure that the costs are acceptable. The recovery objectives do, however, provide a starting point from which different business recovery and ITSCM options can be evaluated.

> **KEY MESSAGE**
>
> **The Business Impact Analysis identifies the minimum critical requirements to support the business.**

Risk Assessment

The second driver in determining ITSCM requirements is *the likelihood that a disaster or other serious service disruption will actually occur*. This is an assessment of the level of threat and the extent to which an organisation is vulnerable to that threat. This is demonstrated in Figure 7.5.

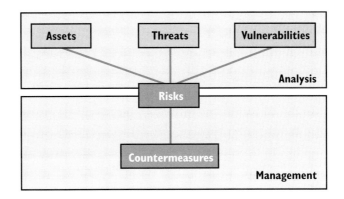

Figure 7.5 – Risk Assessment Model

See Paragraph 8.9.3 for definitions of Risk Analysis and Risk Management. The top section of Figure 7.5 refers to the Risk Analysis – if an organisation's assets are highly valued and there is a high threat to those assets and the vulnerability of those assets to those threats is high, there would be a high risk. The bottom section of Figure 7.5 shows Risk Management – where Countermeasures are applied to manage the business risks by protecting the assets.

As a minimum, the following risk assessment activities should be performed:

- Identify risks – i.e. risks to particular IT Service components (assets) that support the business process which cause an interruption to service.

- Assess threat and vulnerability levels – the threat is defined as 'how likely it is that a service disruption will occur' and the vulnerability is defined as 'whether, and to what extent, the organisation will be affected by the threat materialising'. A threat is dependent on such factors as:
  - likely motivation, capability and resources for deliberate service disruptions such as malicious damage to computer systems, commercial failure of a key technology provider, attack against a organisation's web servers and corruption of Internet sites for accidental service disruptions, the organisation's location, environment, and quality of internal systems and procedures
  - business processes are vulnerable where there are single points of failure for the delivery of IT Services (for example, a travel agent relies on information feeds for flight bookings, if the link were to fail and no backup is available, flights cannot be sold).

- Assess the levels of risk – the overall risk can then be measured. This may be done as a measurement if quantitative data has been collected, or qualitative using a subjective assessment of, for example, low, medium or high. An example of a tabular format used to express the level of risk is illustrated in Figure 7.6. Each risk can be assessed in terms of the associated threat and vulnerability. Using the table in Figure 7.6 it is possible to determine the probability of specified risks occurring (e.g. a high threat and high vulnerability implies a high probability of occurrence).

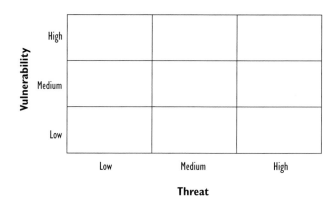

Figure 7.6 – Risk Measurement table

There are many tools and methodologies available to assist in the measurement of risks of which the preferred solution is CRAMM (see Paragraph 8.9.3).

> **Hints and tips**
>
> **ITSCM needs to consider and assess potential risks and reduction measures across the whole Infrastructure.**

Following the Risk Analysis it is possible to determine appropriate countermeasures or risk reduction measures (ITSCM mechanisms) to manage the risks, i.e. reduce the risk to an acceptable minimum level or mitigate the risk.

In the context of ITSCM there are a number of risks that need to be taken into consideration. Table 7.1 provides a checklist of some of the risks and threats to be considered by the IT Manager:

Risk	Threat
Loss of internal IT systems/networks, PABXs, ACDs, etc.	Fire
	Power failure
	Arson and vandalism
	Flood
	Aircraft impact
	Weather damage, e.g., hurricane
	Environmental disaster
	Terrorist attack
	Sabotage
	Catastrophic failure
	Electrical damage, e.g. lighting
	Accidental damage
	Poor quality software
Loss of external IT systems/networks, e.g., e-commerce servers, cryptographic systems, etc.	All of the above
	Excessive demand for services
	Denial of service attack, e.g. against an Internet firewall
	Technical failure, e.g. cryptographic systems
Loss of data	Technical failure
	Human error
	Viruses, malicious software, e.g. attack applets
Loss of network services	Damage or denial of access to network service providers' premises
	Loss of service provider's IT systems/networks
	Loss of service provider's data
	Failure of the service providers
Unavailability of key technical and support staff	Industrial action
	Denial of access to premises
	Resignation
	Sickness/Injury
	Transport difficulties
Failure of service providers, e.g. outsourced IT	Commercial failure, e.g. insolvency
	Denial of access to premises
	Unavailability of service provider's staff
	Failure to meet contractual service levels

Table 7.1 – Risks and Threats to be addressed by the IT Manager

Business Continuity Strategy

The information collated in the impact analysis and the risk assessment, and the associated ITSCM mechanisms chosen, enables an appropriate strategy for the organisation to be developed with an optimum balance of risk reduction and recovery or Continuity options. This includes consideration of the relative service recovery priorities and the changes in relative service priority for the time of day, day of the week, and monthly and annual variations.

As businesses become more dependent and driven through the use and Availability of technology (e.g. e-commerce developments), ITSCM elements become a more integral part of the overall Business Continuity Strategy. Referring back to Figure 7.4, an organisation that identifies high impacts in the short term will want to concentrate efforts on preventative risk reduction methods e.g. through full resilience and fault tolerance, while an organisation that has low short-term impacts would be better suited to comprehensive recovery options.

Risk Reduction Measures

Most organisations have to adopt a balanced approach where risk reduction and recovery are complementary and both are required. This entails reducing, as far as possible, the risks to the continued provision of the IT Service and usually achieved through Availability Management. However well planned, it is impossible to completely eliminate all risks – for example, a fire in a nearby building will probably result in damage, or at least denial of access, as a result of the implementation of a cordon. As a general rule, the invocation of a recovery capability should only be taken as a last resort. Ideally, an organisation should assess all of the risks to reduce the potential requirement to recover the business and/or IT Services.

Example

A financial institution dealing in the equities market relies on high Availability of market information and computer systems to analyse that information. Failure of the market data feeds would mean that the business process fails with an immediate financial impact to the organisation. The failure may result from a failure of the information provider (in which case competitors may suffer the same loss so the impact is lessened) so, to prevent this, the organisation takes feeds from multiple providers. Alternatively there may be a technical failure of the equipment or damage to the location where the feeds enter the building (in which case competitors are unaffected and the impacts are greater) so the organisation establishes at least two entry points and alternative equipment on immediate Availability.

Typical risk reduction measures include:

- a comprehensive backup and recovery strategy, including off-site storage

- the elimination of single points of failure such as a single power supply into a building or power supply from a single utility organisation

- outsourcing services to more than one provider

- resilient IT systems and networks constantly change-managed to ensure maximum performance in meeting the increasing business requirements

- greater security controls such as a physical access control system using smartcards

- better controls to detect local service disruptions such as fire detection systems coupled with suppression systems

- improving procedures to reduce the likelihood of errors or failures such as Change control.

Hints and tips

Outsourcing mainframe processing to a third party who provides the service remotely means that a service disruption affecting the organisation's building will not necessarily affect the Availability of the host system. Outsourcing to different third parties will have the benefit of reducing the risk of a major failure as component parts of the service will always be available. This can be likened to a bookmaker 'laying off' bets to reduce the exposure on a particular gamble. This does, of course, assume the Availability of resilient networks to maintain Continuity of service and the fact that the third party has itself an effective and tested Service Continuity Plan.

The above measures will not necessarily solve an ITSCM issue and remove the risk totally, but all or a combination of them may significantly reduce the risks associated with the way in which services are provided to the business. As with recovery options, it is important that the reduction of one risk does not increase another. The risk of Availability of systems and data may be reduced by outsourcing to an off-site third party, however, this potentially increases the risk of compromise of confidential information unless rigorous security controls are applied.

It is important that organisations check that recovery and ITSCM options selected are capable of implementation and integration at the time they are required, and that the required service recovery can be achieved.

KEY MESSAGE

An organisation's ITSCM strategy is a balance between the cost of risk reduction measures and recovery options to support the recovery of critical business processes within agreed timescales.

Recovery Options

Recovery options need to be considered for:

- People and accommodation – including alternative premises either owned, leased or through agreement with a third party; reciprocal arrangements with other organisations; and rapid procurement of alternative premises or refurbishment of existing premises. Consideration should also be given to the respective location of the proposed premises, the mobility of the staff who will be supporting the recovered business operations including IT staff and the total number of staff required to support the business process.

- IT systems and networks – these options need to be identified and agreed by the IT Manager responsible for ITSCM and include recovery of IT systems, hardware, applications, software and networks, and the data used within these systems and facilities. This relies on the Availability of effective backups to enable restoration of the service and needs to be performed in collaboration with Availability Management. This strategy should also include the implementation of Continuity mechanisms to support local disruption/interruption of IT Services supporting critical business processes, such as disk mirroring, UPS or dual power supplies, dual communication links, etc.

- Critical services such as power, telecommunications, water, couriers and post.

- Critical assets such as paper records and reference material.

There may be a need to consider different options for short-term and long-term recovery. Where business processes are highly dependent on external service providers, there is a need to consider the options to address failure of, or peak contention for, the services.

The costs and benefits of each option need to be analysed. This involves a comparative assessment of the:

- ability to meet the business recovery objectives
- likely reduction in the potential impact
- costs of establishing the option
- costs of maintaining, testing and invoking the option
- technical, organisational, cultural and administrative implications against the risk of disruption or disaster and the potential impact if no action is taken.

When undertaking the analysis there is a need to consider whether the introduction of an option will adversely affect other risks.

Hints and tips

Do not forget to check the organisation's insurance provision to determine whether adequate cover is provided.

IT Recovery Options

There are a number of options that can be considered by IT to provide contingency:

Do nothing

Few, if any, organisations can function effectively without IT Services. Even if there is a requirement for stand-alone PC processing, there is still a need for recovery to be supported.

Manual Work-arounds

IT facilities enable organisations to process information much more quickly and efficiently. Indeed the justification for much IT spend is made on the basis of a reduced headcount. In some organisations, such as the finance, banking and insurance industries, complex calculations are undertaken by applications which would be difficult to reproduce manually in a short period of time. They are dependent upon a succession of calculations by different systems with information fed between them or are dependent upon information being fed to them from external sources. However, manual Work-arounds can be an effective interim measure until the IT Service is resumed wherever they are practical and possible.

Reciprocal arrangements

Entering into an agreement with another organisation using similar technology used to be an effective contingency option when the computing workload was essentially batch processing. Today, the distributed computing environment means that there is a much greater requirement for individual processing power and high Availability, which suggests that this is not a practical solution and may not support an effective resumption of service. In addition, there are maintenance difficulties in keeping reciprocal arrangements in step and increased need for security. Benefits can exist, however, in maintaining some reciprocal arrangements, for example, in the off-site storage of backups and other critical information.

Gradual Recovery

This option (sometimes referred to as 'cold stand by') is applicable to organisations that do not need immediate restoration of business processes and can function for a period of up to 72 hours, or longer, without a re-establishment of full IT facilities. This may include the provision of empty accommodation fully equipped with power, environmental controls and local network cabling Infrastructure, telecommunications connections, and available in a disaster situation for an organisation to install its own computer equipment.

The accommodation may be provided commercially by a third party, for a fee, or may be private, (established by the organisation itself) and provided as either a fixed or portable service.

A fixed facility may be located at the premises of the third party that provides the service, or specially built at a location owned by the subscriber. There is a need to ensure that all services including telecommunications, market data feeds, etc. are established and adequate accommodation is available to house staff involved in the recovery process.

A portable facility is typically a prefabricated building provided by a third party and located when needed at a predetermined site agreed with the organisation. This may be in a car park or another location some distance from the home site, perhaps, another owned building.

The organisation calls on contracts for the supply of required computer equipment including PCs, servers, and mini computers. The organisation or the contractor (whichever has been formally pre-agreed) then configures the equipment to the organisational requirements and loads all data before a service can be provided.

Third parties rarely guarantee replacement equipment within a fixed deadline, but would normally do so under their best efforts.

When opting for a gradual recovery, consideration must be given to highly customised items of hardware or equipment that will be difficult, if not impossible, to replace if no spares are kept securely by the organisation. Other contingency measures may be needed to cope with having to use different equipment. The same difficulties apply to items supplied by organisations that have since gone out of business and alternatives need to be identified, possibly putting the Service Delivery at risk due to delays or potential Problems.

Intermediate Recovery

This option (sometimes referred to as 'warm stand by') is selected by organisations that need to recover IT facilities within a predetermined time to prevent impacts to the business process. This typically involves the re-establishment of the critical systems and services within a 24 to 72 hour period.

Most common is the use of commercial facilities, which are offered by third party recovery organisations to a number of subscribers, spreading the cost across those subscribers. Commercial facilities often include operation, system management and technical support. The cost varies depending on the facilities requested such as processors, peripherals, communications, and how quickly the services must be restored (invocation timescale).

The advantage of this service is that the Customer can have virtually instantaneous access to a site, housed in a secure building, in the event of disaster. It must be understood, however that the restoration of services at the site may take some time as delays may be encountered while the site is re-configured for the organisation that invokes the service, and the organisation's applications and data will need to be restored from backups.

There is a disadvantage in that the site is almost certainly some distance from the home site, which presents a number of logistical problems. The positions are shared (usually up to 20 to 30 times) with other organisations so there can be no guarantee of Availability if a service disruption were to affect two organisations at the same time. There is a need to ensure that a recovery organisation is not providing the same services for firms within an immediate geographical area. This is well understood by the recovery organisations, who apply good Risk Management to the sale of the positions in order to reduce the risk of multiple invocations. It is also a fairly expensive option and can be likened to insurance. What is being paid for is peace of mind. In recent years the number of recovery centres has increased considerably and, together with the falling cost of computer hardware, good deals can be negotiated for 3, 5, or 7-year contracts.

If the site is invoked, there is often a daily fee for use of the service in an emergency, although this may be offset against additional cost of working insurance. Most commercial agreements limit invocation access to a pre-determined length of time, typically between 6 to 12 weeks and therefore longer term options are also required.

It is important that any arrangements of this sort include adequate opportunity for testing at the contingency site.

Commercial recovery services can be provided in portable form where an agreed system is delivered to a Customer's site, within a certain time, typically 24 hours. The computer equipment is contained in a trailer and transported to the site by truck. The trailer is fitted out as a computer environment with the necessary services and only needs power and telecommunications links from the site to the trailer for the service to be established. Special measures may need to be taken to make the site secure.

The service provider normally charges an annual fee for such a service, and there is often a 'call-out' charge if the service is invoked. However in some circumstances, such as when there is damage to the site or when an exclusion zone is applied by the emergency services to the site, this option cannot be used.

An advantage of this approach is that the trailer can be installed close to the main site subject to the necessary parking consents having been obtained. Parking a trailer on a busy road in a city is likely to draw the unwelcome attention of the police who may insist on removal.

Organisations with alternative locations may opt for a mutual fallback arrangement where accommodation is provided through displacement of non-critical staff at the unaffected building and computer facilities provided via mobile recovery.

Immediate Recovery

This option (sometimes referred to as 'hot stand by') provides for immediate restoration of services and is usually provided as an extension to the intermediate recovery provided by a third party recovery provider. The immediate recovery is supported by the recovery of other critical business and support areas during the first 24 hours following a service disruption. Instances where immediate recovery may be required are where the impact of loss of service has an immediate impact on the organisation's ability to make money, such as a Bank's dealing room.

Where there is a need for a fast restoration of a service, it is possible to 'rent' floorspace at the recovery site and install servers or systems with application systems and communications already available and data mirrored from the operational servers. In the event of a system failure, the Customers can immediately switch to the backup facility with little or no loss of service.

In the case of building loss or denial of access an organisation can pay for a limited number of exclusive positions at a recovery centre. This is a highly expensive option and is not appropriate for the majority of organisations. However, these positions are always available and ready for immediate occupation and use.

Some organisations may identify a need for their own exclusive immediate recovery facilities provided internally. This again is an expensive option but may be justified for a certain business process where non- Availability for a short period could result in a significant impact. The facility needs to be located separately and far enough away from the home site that it will not be affected by a disaster affecting that location.

For highly critical business processes, a mirrored service can be established at an alternative location, which is kept up to date with the live service, either by data transfer at regular intervals, or by replications from the live service. Such a service could be used merely as a backup service, but it might also be used for enquiry access (such as reporting) without affecting the live processing performance. This is also useful if there are legal or legislative obligations to safeguard the completeness and integrity of all financial records. As this is essentially spare Capacity, under normal circumstances this spare Capacity can be used for development, training or testing, but could be made available immediately when a Service Continuity situation demands it.

The ultimate solution is to have a mirrored site with duplicate equipment as part of the live operation. However, these mirrored servers and sites options, should be implemented in close liaison with Availability Management.

It is important to distinguish between the previous definition of 'hot stand by' and 'immediate recovery'. Hot stand by typically referred to Availability of services within a short timescale such as 2 or 4 hours whereas immediate recovery implies the instant Availability of services. A recovery plan for an organisation will include a combination of some or all scenarios. Instant recovery for critical business processing, 4 hour recovery for additional business processes, 8 hour recovery for key support services and the other business areas being recovered as and when required.

7.3.3   Stage 3 – Implementation

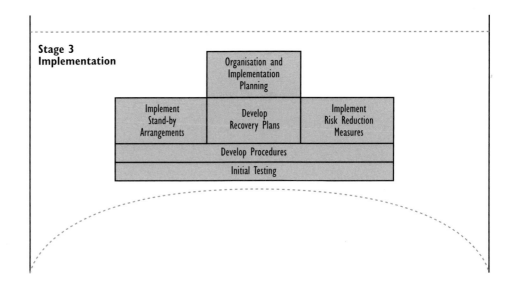

Figure 7.7 – Implementation

Once the strategy has been agreed the Business Continuity lifecycle moves into the implementation stage (see Figure 7.7), involving IT at a detailed level. The implementation stage consists of the following processes:

- establish the organisation and develop implementation plans
- implement stand-by arrangements
- implement risk reduction measures
- develop IT recovery plans
- develop procedures
- undertake initial tests.

Each of the above is considered with respect to the specific responsibilities that IT must action.

Organisation planning

The IT function is responsible for the provision of IT Services to support the business requirements identified during the Business Impact Analysis and requirements definition. However, for recovery purposes, IT in itself only forms part of the overall command, control and communications structure. The structure is based around three tiers:

- **Executive** – including senior management/executive board with overall authority and control within the organisation and responsible for crisis management and liaison with other departments, divisions, organisations, the media, regulators, emergency services etc.

- **Co-ordination** – typically one level below the Executive group and responsible for coordinating the overall recovery effort within the organisation.

- **Recovery** – a series of business and service recovery teams representing the critical business functions and the services that need to be established to support these functions. Each team is responsible for executing the plans within their own areas and for liaison with staff, Customers and third parties. Within IT the recovery teams should be grouped by IT Service and application, for example the Infrastructure team may have one or more people responsible for recovering external connections, voice services, local area networks, etc., the support teams may be split by platform, operating system or application. In addition, the recovery priorities for the service, application or its components identified during the Business Impact Analysis should be documented within the recovery plans and applied during their execution.

Implementation planning

Plan development is one of the most important parts of the implementation process and without workable plans the process will certainly fail. At the highest level there is a need for an overall co-ordination plan that includes:

- Emergency Response Plan
- Damage Assessment Plan
- Salvage Plan
- Vital Records Plan
- Crisis Management and Public Relations Plan.

These plans are used to identify and respond to a service disruption, ensure the safety of all affected staff members and visitors and determine whether there is a need to implement the business recovery process. If so, then the next level of plans are invoked which include the key support functions such as:

- Accommodation and Services Plan
- Computer Systems and Network Plan
- Telecommunication Plan
- Security Plan
- Personnel Plan
- Finance and Administration Plan.

Finally, each critical business area is responsible for the development of a plan detailing the individuals who will comprise the recovery team and a detailed task list to be undertaken on invocation of recovery arrangements. The owners of each plan must ensure that they have identified and agreed support and services from other parties upon who they have a reliance for a service or resource.

The ITSC Plan must contain all the information needed to recover the computer systems, network and telecommunications in a disaster situation once a decision to invoke has been made and then to manage the business return to normal operation once the service disruption has been resolved. There is a need to consider the various sources of information that are required in the development of the plan and these include the minimum requirements identified through the Business Impact Analysis, Service Level Agreements, security requirements, operating instructions and procedures, and external contracts. This plan will be complemented by the other plans such as the Personnel plan that will address the need for transport and accommodation of key IT recovery personnel to the recovery site, or the use of overnight accommodation for critical staff. This is especially important if the recovery site has to be used for extended periods of time (e.g. weeks).

As part of the implementation planning process, it is vitally important to review key and critical contracts required to deliver business critical services. These contracts should be reviewed to ensure that, if appropriate, they provide a BCM service, there is a defined Service Level agreed and the contracts are still valid and in-force if operations have to switch to the recovery site (either wholly or partially). If contracts do not include these details, then the service criticality should be reviewed and the risks associated with the service not being provided should be assessed.

> ### Hints and tips
>
> **Check all key and critical contracts to ensure they provide a BCM service if required, have SLAs defined for business as usual and check that BCM will still be valid if the recovery site has to be invoked.**

Implement risk reduction measures

The risk reduction measures detailed in Paragraph 7.3.2 need to be implemented. This is often achieved in conjunction with Availability Management as many of these reduce the probability of failure affecting the Availability of service. Typical risk reduction measures include such things as:

- installation of UPS and back-up power to the computer
- fault tolerant systems for critical applications where even minimal downtime is unacceptable, for example, a bank dealing system
- offsite storage and archiving
- RAID arrays and disk mirroring for LAN servers to prevent against data loss and to ensure continued Availability of data
- spare equipment / components to be used in the event of equipment or component failure, for example, a spare LAN server already configured with the standard configuration and available to replace a faulty server with minimum build and configuration time.

Some of the ITSCM measures that can be implemented to maintain the Availability of services due to a localised disruption are described in more detail in Chapter 8.

Implement stand-by arrangements

The recovery options were detailed in Paragraph 7.3.2. It is important to remember that the recovery is based around a series of stand-by arrangements including accommodation as well as systems and telecommunications. Certain actions are necessary to implement the stand-by arrangements, for example:

- negotiating for third party recovery facilities and entering into a contractual arrangement
- preparing and equipping the stand-by accommodation
- purchasing and installing stand-by computer systems
- negotiating with external service providers on their ITSC Plans and undertaking due diligence if necessary.

this. In addition, tests must have clearly defined objectives and critical success factors which will be used to determine the success or otherwise of the exercise.

7.3.4   Stage 4 – Operational Management

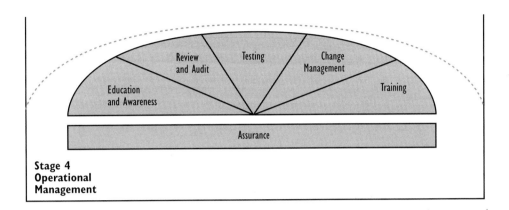

Figure 7.8 – Operational Management

Once the implementation and planning has been completed there is a need to ensure that the process is maintained as part of business as usual. This is achieved through operational management (see Figure 7.8) and includes:

- **Education and awareness** – this should cover the organisation and in particular, the IT organisation, for Service Continuity-specific items. This ensures that all staff are aware of the implications of Business Continuity and of Service Continuity and consider these as part of their normal working routine and budget.

- **Training** – IT may be involved in training the non-IT literate business recovery team members to ensure that they have the necessary level of competence to facilitate recovery.

- **Review** – regular review of all of the deliverables from the ITSCM process needs to be undertaken to ensure that they remain current. With respect to IT this is required whenever there is a major Change to the IT Infrastructure, assets or dependencies such as new systems or networks or a change in service providers, as well as when there is a change in business direction, business strategy or IT strategy. As organisations typically have rapid change, it is necessary to invest in an ongoing review programme and incorporate ITSCM into the organisational business justification processes. New requirements will be implemented in accordance with the Change control process.

- **Testing** – following the initial testing it is necessary to establish a programme of regular testing to ensure that the critical components of the strategy are tested at least annually or as directed by senior management or audit. It is important that any changes to the IT Infrastructure are included in the strategy, implemented in an appropriate fashion and tested to ensure that they function correctly within the overall provision of IT Services.

- **Change control** – following tests and reviews and in response to day to day Changes, there is a need for the ITSCM plans to be updated. ITSCM must be included as part of the Change Management process to ensure that any Changes in the Infrastructure are reflected in the contingency arrangements provided by IT or third parties. Inaccurate plans and inadequate recovery capabilities may result in the failure of ITSCM. Further guidance is provided in Chapter 8 in the Service Support book.

■ **Assurance** – the final process in the ITSCM lifecycle involves obtaining assurance that the quality of the ITSCM deliverables is acceptable to senior business management and that the operational management processes are working satisfactorily.

7.3.5   Invocation

Invocation is the ultimate test of the Business Continuity and ITSCM plans. If all the preparatory work has been successfully completed and plans developed and tested then an invocation of the Business Continuity Plans should be a straightforward process.

Invocation is a key component of the plans, which must include the invocation process and guidance. It should be remembered that the decision to invoke, especially if a third party recovery facility is to be used, should not be taken lightly. Costs will be involved and the process will involve disruption to the business. This decision is typically made by a 'crisis management team' comprising senior managers from the business and support departments (including IT) using information gathered through damage assessment and other sources.

A disruption could occur at any time of the day or night, so it is essential that guidance on the invocation process is readily available. Plans must be available both in the office and at home and key members of the crisis management team should be issued with a short aide memoire, which they must keep with them at all time detailing:

■ the locations of these plans

■ the associated key actions and decision points

■ contact details of the crisis management team.

The decision to invoke must be made quickly, as there may be a lead-time involved in establishing facilities at a recovery site. In the case of a building fire, the decision is fairly easy to make, however, in the case of power failure, where a resolution is expected within a short period, a deadline should be set by which time if the Problem has not been resolved, invocation will take place. This deadline will be established by the crisis management team working back from the critical point by which the business processes must be re-established to prevent an unacceptable impact to the organisation.

> **Hints and tips**
>
> **Whenever there is a situation where invocation may be required, put the recovery service provider on alert immediately so that facilities can be made available as quickly as possible if a decision to invoke is made.**

The decision to invoke needs to take into account a number of factors:

■ the extent of the damage and scope of the potential invocation

■ the likely length of the disruption and Unavailability of premises and/or services

■ the time of day/month/year and the potential business impact. At year end the need to invoke may be more pressing to ensure that year-end processing is completed on time

■ specific requirements of the business depending on work being undertaken at the time.

Once the crisis management team has decided to invoke business recovery facilities, there is a need to communicate this within the organisation. This is typically done through the use of call trees, a mechanism for communicating quickly and efficiently with identified recovery personnel throughout the organisation. The crisis management plan should include details of key personnel to be contacted to initiate the business and ITSCM recovery plans. Within each of these plans, contact details for essential personnel (and their deputies) should be included to enable the plans to be initiated.

Hints and tips

It is vital to ensure that the message has been passed to all essential personnel involved in the recovery process. The last person to receive the message should 'close the loop' by contacting the initiator and confirming the action to be taken.

The ITSCM plan should include details of activities that need to be undertaken including:

■ retrieval of backup tapes or use of data vaulting to retrieve data

■ retrieval of essential documentation, procedures, workstation images, etc. stored off-site

■ mobilisation of the appropriate technical personnel to go to the recovery site to commence the recovery of required systems and services

■ contacting and putting on alert telecommunications suppliers, support services, application vendors, etc. who may be required to undertake actions or provide assistance in the recovery process.

Throughout the initial recovery, it is important that all activities are recorded. These will be used following the service disruption to analyse what went well and identify areas for improvement. The plans should include blank logs that must be given to all personnel to record activities (such as telephone conversations, timings for activities, etc.) and issues experienced.

The invocation and initial recovery is likely to be a time of high activity involving long hours for many individuals. This must be recognised and managed by the recovery team leaders to ensure that breaks are provided and prevent 'burn-out'. Planning for shifts and handovers must be undertaken to ensure that the best use is made of the facilities available. The commitment of staff (especially technical staff who will typically spend in excess of 24 hours ensuring a successful recovery) must be recognised and potentially rewarded once the service disruption is over. It is also vitally important to ensure that the usual business and technology controls remain in place during invocation, recovery and return to normal to ensure that information security is maintained at the correct level and that Data Protection is preserved.

Hints and tips

It is vital to ensure that Information Security and Data Protection controls and mechanisms are maintained and enforced during the invocation, recovery and return to normal stages of Service Continuity.

Once the recovery has been completed, the business should be able to operate from the recovery site at the level determined and agreed in the Business Continuity strategy. The objective, however, will be to build up the business to normal levels and vacate the recovery site in the shortest possible time. The recovery period will depend on the original service disruption. In the case of a power failure, return to normal may be achieved fairly quickly, whereas in the case of a fire, reoccupation of the affected building may be impossible and alternative accommodation should be sought. Whatever the period, a return to normal must be carefully planned and undertaken in a controlled fashion. Typically this will be over a weekend and may include some necessary downtime in business hours. It is important that this is managed well and that all personnel involved are aware of their responsibilities to ensure a smooth transition.

7.4 Management Structure

As with most IT issues, ITSCM crosses organisational boundaries and consumes management time and financial resources, these should however, be in proportion to the risks being addressed. Sponsorship at the highest level and integration into the IT and ITSCM structure is paramount to its success. Without this level of sponsorship, ITSCM risks include:

- misalignment with the business and IT strategies, thereby failing to address the true values and risks as perceived by senior management

- lack of momentum, profile or resources to develop into a successful management and operational discipline

- lack of extensive co-operation and input required from management at all levels.

Hints and tips

Without senior management sponsorship investment in ITSCM may be wasted and fail to address the requirements of the business, resulting in the organisation failing to survive a major disruption to its business due to IT systems failure.

In order for ITSCM to be successful within an organisation, a suitably capable management structure should be implemented. The roles should be integrated into the existing suite of IT management responsibilities. The optimum management structure will:

- allow responsibilities for ongoing ITSCM to be clearly defined and allocated

- integrate into existing management structures, hierarchies and responsibilities

- avoid concentrating responsibility in an isolated centre of excellence

- allocate responsibilities to functions or individuals that have the necessary presence, credibility, skills, knowledge and expertise within the IT organisation

- ensure that the management structure to manage ITSC on an ongoing basis, closely resembles the structure that will control and facilitate Continuity or recovery should the ITSCM mechanisms have to be invoked

- ensure the ITSCM strategy and requirements are integrated with the business and IT strategies.

Hints and tips

A frequent mistake is for the IT organisation to implement recovery mechanisms for business processes that it considers to be the most critical, without proper consultation with the business, and in isolation from the overall process.

Invariably, these mechanisms will be, at best, only partially right and result in some business interruption and lead to a lack of faith in the IT organisation and the ITSCM process. Conversely, the business may assume that IT and service Infrastructures will be available and provided. Unless these mechanisms have been notified to and agreed with the IT providers, this is unlikely to be the case. If ITSCM is driven by business need and is fully integrated into the management structures of the organisation, significant benefit will be achieved in terms of awareness, education, and the effectiveness of the mechanisms implemented.

Hints and tips

Ensure that the business and the ITSCM process are fully integrated to determine the mechanisms to be implemented – otherwise there is a strong likelihood they will fail to fully meet the business requirements.

7.4.1 Management roles

A typical management structure for large organisations, that supports both ongoing management and invocation for ITSCM is shown in Figure 7.9.

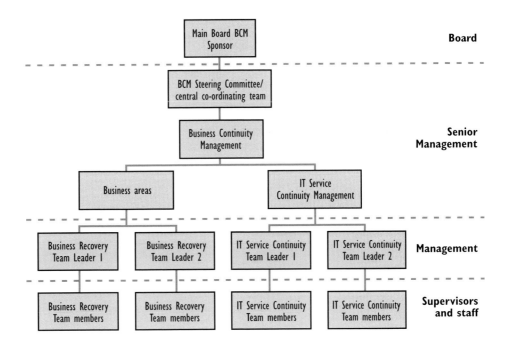

Figure 7.9 – Typical management structure for business and ITSCM

Since management sponsorship at Board level is often given to a person whose responsibilities already encompass most of the organisation (for example Facilities, Finance or IT) it is not unusual for an IT Director to have responsibility for ITSCM. Day to day responsibility for Business Continuity, often falls to a senior manager (shown in Figure 7.9 as Business Continuity Management) in an operational management role, who:

- advises the Board representative or Board on ITSCM strategy and policy, and ensures that these are in-line with the Business and IT strategies and policies

- ensures that the ITSCM strategy and mechanisms remain up-to-date and effective

- ensures that Change control, testing, auditing, awareness and training programmes are established.

In larger organisations, the Business Continuity Manager may be supported by a junior manager for day to day activities. The ITSC Manager supports the Business Continuity Manager in achieving these objectives within the IT organisation. Within small and medium organisations, there may not be the resources available to allocate individual roles as illustrated. In organisations such as these it may be necessary to allocate one or more roles to an individual. For example, the Business Continuity Manager might also be a Business Area Manager or the IT Service Continuity Manager. In the latter case, being responsible for both Business Continuity and ITSCM.

Many larger organisations establish steering committees at senior management level to co-ordinate Business Continuity activities across the organisation and support the Business Continuity Manager. The steering committee should meet regularly to:

- confirm the ITSCM strategy is still valid and that deliverables are still being maintained

- ensure that any Changes that could effect the strategy, e.g. business or IT strategy Changes, are addressed and reflect in the ITSCM strategy

- review and agree test programmes for ITSCM mechanisms

- initiate any actions necessary to address upcoming Changes or to resolve difficulties.

Senior management within the IT organisation is typically given ownership of the ITSCM deliverables that relate to their area of expertise or responsibility, e.g. the ITSCM mechanisms for external communications such as voice and data links will be owned by the External Communications IT manager. Ownership not only involves responsibility for ensuring deliverables are met, but also for ensuring that they remain up to date and fit for purpose.

Invocation of Continuity mechanisms and recovery options is usually undertaken by one or a series of ITSCM teams, focused on specific areas of the IT organisation (e.g. external communications, local area networks, servers, mainframes, etc.). During periods of operational stability, the Service Continuity teams play a vital role in the implementation, testing, maintenance and support of these Continuity or recovery and risk reduction mechanisms and associated plans.

The approach described above correlates the management structure with the ITSCM structure and allows the team, in times of operational stability, to convert easily into an IT Service command and control structure during times of Problems and crisis (e.g. hardware or network failure, or major service disruption to the operational environment). This in turn facilitates commitment, education, and awareness and allows cross-functional integration to take place with business activities.

IT may establish a working group that, typically, fills key roles in the IT recovery process and fills operational management roles to deal with the Continuity and Availability management issues. ITSCM typically chairs the working group and leads the co-ordination team during recovery.

Hints and tips

Responsibilities for ITSCM should be integrated with corresponding operational responsibilities to maximise synergy and capitalise on existing knowledge, skills and expertise in the operating environment.

7.4.2   Responsibilities

Normal Operation

Figure 7.10, outlines the typical responsibilities for ITSCM during times of normal operation. These layers of responsibility also correlate with the typical management structure for ITSCM shown in Figure 7.9 and if properly implemented allow these responsibilities to be carried out in an effective and efficient manner.

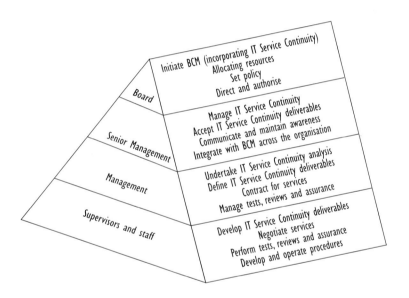

Figure 7.10 – Typical responsibilities for ITSCM during normal operation

These responsibilities should be clearly defined, communicated to the managers concerned and documented in appropriate role or job descriptions. To ensure continual management of ITSCM at an operational level (for instance Change control of the ITSCM mechanisms), best results have been achieved by incorporating specific deliverables into individual staff objectives and responsibilities into job descriptions.

Invocation Responsibilities

Following a disruption to the normal operating environment and the invocation of crisis control, management responsibilities change in line with command, control and operational roles and responsibilities outlined in the crisis control and recovery plans. These include responsibilities for taking corrective action to minimise impact and contingency or recovery facility invocation. Typical responsibilities for the various management layers during times of crisis or disruption to normal operations are shown in Figure 7.11.

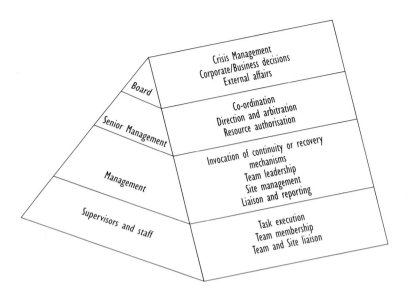

Figure 7.11 – Typical responsibilities for ITSCM during times of crisis

Hints and tips

For individuals associated with ITSCM, ensure high-level responsibilities are documented in job descriptions, deliverables are detailed in personal objectives and performance is monitored and reviewed during the appraisal process.

Specific responsibilities during the invocation include recording all actions taken – to be used in subsequent debriefs, agreeing additional costs of working, liaison with the media and regulatory bodies. It is also important to understand that there may be casualties involved, such as after a terrorist bomb explosion, which may require a need for counselling during and after the service disruption and subsequent claims on the organisation for mental and physical disability.

7.5 Generating awareness

In order to establish a successful ITSCM initiative within an organisation, it is imperative that there is awareness and commitment from the Board and senior management. The initiative has to be fully endorsed and sponsored in order to obtain the acceptance and commitment of key managers and staff, and ensure the quality of contribution that they are able to make.

Similarly, continuing success of ITSCM depends on a continuing commitment at all levels in the organisation and on people's awareness of their respective responsibilities. Management needs to continually monitor this and prioritise Business Continuity work against operational activities.

ITSCM can deliver other business benefits through the implementation of mechanisms that also improve Availability Management. However, in order to meet and support the true business requirements, ITSCM needs to be fully integrated into the corporate management activities for which awareness is vital.

7.5.1   Awareness of the need for ITSCM

An awareness of the need for ITSCM may be generated from:

- the range of risks facing an organisation and its vulnerability

- the potential business impacts that could result should any of the risks materialise

- the likelihood of each of the risks materialising

- personal responsibilities and liabilities, e.g. of directors

- external pressures, e.g. from regulators, shareholders or clients.

In London, and in particular the City, a number of high profile bombings helped focus senior executives minds on the risks from terrorism and many new business and ITSCM initiatives followed. Other major events have had a similar effect in other major cities in the world, including the bombing of the World Trade Centre in New York, the power loss in Auckland, New Zealand, earthquakes in Los Angeles and South America, and so on.

Although major events and service disruptions such as terrorism have often been the primary concern over recent years, there are many other risks that could result in serious disruption to the business and/or services on which businesses depend. Service disruptions such as computer or telecommunications failure, failure of key third parties, localised fires and floods have, collectively, caused much greater damage than high profile terrorist bombings.

Experience has demonstrated that the best way to raise awareness of the need for ITSCM is to highlight the potential risks and business impacts facing an organisation. Wherever possible, these should be stated in relation to the failure of business processes and key performance indicators for those processes, for example, Customer Service Levels, costs, turnover, profitability, market share, etc. If the business strategy and objectives are known, comparison of risks against these also provides a useful mechanism to identify key risks.

> **Hints and tips**
>
> **The best and most effective way to raise senior management awareness is to highlight the potential risks and business impacts facing an organisation in terms of business failure to meet key performance indicators or corporate objectives.**

If the potential impacts and risks are unclear or if there is some resistance to the concepts of ITSCM at senior levels, then a useful first step may be to undertake a scoping study, in order to bring the risks and impacts to senior management attention. The scoping report can then be used to raise awareness of the need for ITSCM, identify some of the high-level business benefits that could be realised, generate an initial senior management commitment and act as the starting point for more detailing project plans.

7.5.2   Initial awareness

Successful awareness cannot be achieved without obtaining 'buy-in' from key IT and business staff (e.g. IT Support staff and Operational Business Managements) early on during this process. This is especially difficult as they can often be busy and sceptical.

> **KEY MESSAGE**
>
> **The way in which the ITSCM message is communicated to those involved and the way in which the project is conducted are critical to its success.**

Initial briefing sessions for the project team, stakeholders and the business areas, are always worthwhile to raise awareness, prompt support and manage expectations. Ideally these develop into an ongoing awareness campaign along with other communication methods (a section on the staff notice board, inclusion in the organisation newsletter, etc.). Regular feedback to participants also serves to demonstrate that progress is being made as a result of their contributions.

7.5.3 Ongoing awareness

As an organisation progresses through to the final stages of the Business Continuity project, emphasis shifts from awareness of the need for ITSCM mechanisms towards the responsibilities and actions necessary to implement, test and maintain those mechanisms in an operational environment. Involvement of people from across the IT organisation and business areas will have helped to train and educate personnel and generate a good level of awareness.

The investment made by organisations in the ITSCM deliverables, both in terms of time and money, warrants that organisations protect this investment through an ongoing programme of awareness, education and training. Used correctly, the testing programme is an ideal way of educating and raising awareness for key individuals. For example technical and functional tests raise awareness and educate staff about potential Problems and issues to be faced. The test programme can also confirm the operation of ITSCM mechanisms that have been installed. The use of different staff during each test helps to educate and train deputies, in order to provide cover in case of absence of the primary staff.

> **Hints and tips**
>
> **Use a business or ITSCM testing programme to help deliver the training and education to staff.**

The following aspects of education and awareness are also required:

- ongoing programme of briefings to all staff on the need for vigilance, on emergency procedures and security guidelines and procedures
- regular desktop walkthroughs of the plans – especially following significant Change
- demonstration of stand-by facilities to staff that will use them
- use of an organisation's newsletter, notice boards, or an intranet to maintain the profile of ITSCM
- inclusion of an overview of the organisation's business and ITSCM mechanisms in the staff induction process
- regular progress reports to the Board and regular agenda items on other management and IT committees.

It is important that wherever possible senior management personnel are involved, in order to demonstrate commitment from the top and so that they can see and understand how the money has been spent. The overall aim must be to get to a stage where management considers Business and ITSCM issues in relation to, and prior to, making key business decisions. This allows a balanced assessment of the risks to be considered in the decision making process.

> **KEY MESSAGE**
>
> **The primary awareness aim is to get management to consider business and ITSCM issues in relation to and prior to making key business decisions.**

7.6 The Future of ITSCM

There are numerous challenges that face all organisations in the future – this Section outlines some of the influencing factors and highlights how they are likely to affect ITSCM.

As the corporate world develops through the use of technology and an ever increasing demand on optimisation, globalisation and an ever increasing competitive environment, the dependence upon technology in the work place and within business processes increases. This direct correlation instils the need for a co-ordinated ITSCM and Change Management programme that spans business processes and their supporting Infrastructure. This has already been discussed at various stages throughout this Chapter. However, when this need is directly referenced against ongoing initiatives within many organisations today, the need becomes even more apparent.

7.6.1 The Corporate challenge

The influence of technology in the workplace today cannot be underestimated. The rapid improvements in the cost/benefit of processing power, disk storage and global connectivity now allows organisations to achieve speeds of information processing and transfer that could not even be dreamed of previously.

This evolution has enabled organisations both to centralise and de-centralise functions to suit the particular needs of a business stream, division or office. Where technology may be centralised in a data centre in one part of the world, business activities may take place across the globe using those systems in order to provide access to local markets and resource. Conversely, technology and IT processes may be de-centralised where business activities are centralised, making use of inexpensive labour in other countries.

This new reality allows organisations to choose how they operate their business, with few limitations, and corporate management focus can now be on the most efficient method. Consequently the impact on IT Services is immense.

As businesses merge, or change their operating structure or strategy, in many cases this has a direct impact on which business processes continue to be the most critical and which elements of those business processes are more at risk. Unless organisations undertake to re-assess their Business Impact Analysis and risk assessment as part of this process, the Continuity or recovery mechanisms put in place and being maintained to support the business will not support all the elements of a critical business process (and it therefore fails) or will not support new critical business processes (therefore they run the risk of failure or disruption).

People, processes, organisation structures and information systems are focused on helping the organisation achieve its objectives. In order to do this, management essentially has to do three things:

- use its resources effectively and efficiently
- monitor and exploit new opportunities that could help it achieve or better its targets, e.g. expand into new markets, acquire new businesses or merge with other organisations, or implement improved technology
- monitor and manage risks that could stop it from achieving its targets.

The modern business environment is characterised by risk. ITSCM aids an organisation in reducing its exposure to risks. Effective and efficient management of key risks to the organisation through ITSCM is therefore essential if business objectives and targets are to be achieved and maintained. Decisions to exploit new opportunities must also balance benefit against cost and risk and incorporate potential changes to ITSCM initiatives as part of the decision making process.

ITSCM addresses risks that could cause a sudden and serious impact, such that they could *immediately threaten the Continuity of the business*. These typically include the following subset of the risks described earlier:

- loss, damage or denial of access to key Infrastructure services
- failure or non-performance of critical providers, distributors or other third parties
- loss or corruption of key information
- sabotage, extortion or commercial espionage
- deliberate infiltration or attack on critical information systems.

Where these risks affect critical business processes the consequences can be severe and include substantial financial loss, embarrassment and loss of credibility or goodwill for the organisation concerned. The consequential damage can extend much wider impacting on staff welfare, Customers, third parties, shareholders and the general public. Ultimately they obstruct organisations from achieving their objectives and targets.

Organisations that practice ITSCM effectively will have assessed the risks to Business Continuity, identified minimum acceptable levels of business and put in place tested plans to ensure that these can be maintained.

If an organisation does not manage Business Continuity effectively, the chances are that it does not even understand its minimum acceptable levels of business. Should a serious service disruption occur, there will not be a consistent corporate view of priorities and the organisation will not have the Infrastructure, plans and procedures in place to deal with the crisis. In these circumstances, survival of the business will then depend entirely on:

- how management reacts to the crisis – without tested crisis management plans, this may be chaos and panic
- the time within which key Infrastructure services can be resumed in the absence of tested stand-by arrangements – it may take weeks or months to obtain replacement computer or communications hardware if provisions have not been made in advance and recovery rehearsed
- the adequacy of insurance arrangements – these may exclude certain risks, limit the cover (e.g. to additional cost of working but not consequential loss) and place a time limit on the benefit (e.g. so that long term loss of market share is not covered).

7.6.2   Future developments

These days, such a reactive approach to dealing with risks to Business Continuity is not acceptable. Directors have a 'duty of care' to their shareholders, Customers and creditors and could find themselves personally liable if they have been negligent, whatever their professional discipline.

Over the next few years the greatest challenge facing organisations will be the move to electronic business and many organisations will need to re-invent themselves to prosper in the new digital world. ITSCM will need to react to changes in the business world that it is there to protect. These changes will make business even more dependent on technology than it is already. In order to address these risks, resilience, security and ITSCM will have to be designed into electronic business services from the outset in away that is only partly done today.

Technological development, the need to optimise efficiency and reduce overheads will force changes to other parts of the business Infrastructure. For example, the emergence of a smaller number of huge warehouse and distribution facilities from which goods can be delivered direct to the home, at the expense of the existing large network of retail outlets. Disruption to a major distribution centre could halt the business at a time when timely delivery and Customer Service Levels are a key differentiator between competitors or could result in increased costs of operations to meet Customer requirements, negating the efficiencies and cost reductions expected. Again, one would expect part of the investment in this new Infrastructure to be in building resilience and security into the Infrastructure.

Risk Management and Business Continuity Management will be fundamental to the re-design of business for the information age. Technology will be able to support this and, in the future, successful organisations will be those that can not only exploit the opportunities of new technology but can also harness it within their business to minimise risk by building fully resilient and secure systems and business processes. This will require ITSCM to be implemented as an integral part of the development process.

7.6.3   In conclusion

ITSCM is a critical tool in the armoury if today's business environment is to continue to operate in spite of the plethora of risks faced. As organisations strive for greater efficiency, so the use of technology and the consequent dependence upon it increases; thereby the requirement for ITSCM increases in order for the business to be able to sustain its operations. Failure to implement adequate ITSCM measures will impact that organisation's ability and its perception by Customers following an interruption.

The Business Continuity Infrastructure developed must be able to respond quickly and efficiently to changes in the organisation and be regularly tested to ensure that the different components of the IT environment will work together.

The commercial world today is realising its dependence upon, and requirement for, technology and the disciplines that have to run in parallel, including ITSCM. There are greater demands being placed on organisations by clients, third parties, shareholders and regulators for directors of organisations to perform better Risk Management i.e. the appropriate implementation of BS 7799, Data Protection Act and the Turnbull Report (see Chapter 11). This in turn requires ITSCM to become an integral part of corporate management.

KEY MESSAGE

The dependence upon technology and the greater demands being placed upon organisations require ITSCM to become an integral part of Corporate Management in order for business objectives and targets to be achieved and maintained.

| Annex 7A | ITSCM Manager – Role, responsibilities and key skills |

Role

To implement and maintain the ITSCM process in accordance with the overall requirements of the organisation's Business Continuity Management process and to represent the IT Services function within the Business Continuity Management process.

Responsibilities

- Develop and manage the ITSCM Plan to ensure that, at all times, the recovery objectives of the business can be achieved.

- Ensure that all IT Service areas are prepared and able to respond to an invocation of the Continuity plans.

- Maintain a comprehensive IT testing schedule.

- Undertake quality reviews of all procedures and ensure that these are incorporated into the testing schedule.

- Communicate and maintain awareness of ITSCM objectives within the business areas supported and IT Service areas.

- Undertake regular reviews, at least annually, of the Continuity plans with the business areas to ensure that they accurately reflect the business processing environment.

- Negotiate and manage contracts with providers of third party recovery services.

- Manage the IT Service delivery during times of crisis including:
  - Co-ordination with the crisis control team
  - Invocation of the appropriate recovery facilities
  - Resource management, direction and arbitration
  - Recovery site management.

Key skills

- Senior IT Management level.

- Experience in ITSC.

- Knowledge and experience of Contract Management type roles.

- Ability to translate business recovery requirements into technical requirements and specifications.

- Good IT technical knowledge to enable quality assurance of procedures to be undertaken.

- Ability to communicate at all levels within the organisation.

Annex 7B   Example Project Plan

Timescales shown are purely illustrative; emboldening and indentation shows analysis levels

Task Name	Duration Days	Task Name	Duration Days
Stage 1 – Initiation	8	Computer System	1
Define and set Policy	1	Networks	1
Define the Project organisation	1	Telecommunications	1
Define Project control structure	1	IT Security	1
Develop Project plan	1	Implement Risk Reduction Measures	1
Define quality plan	1	**Implement Standby Arrangements**	6
Identify initial costs	1	Negotiate third party recovery facilities	1
Develop Project Initiation Document (PID)	1	Enter into a contractual arrangement	1
Agree PID	1	Preparing and equipping the stand-by accommodation	1
		Purchase and install stand-by computer systems	1
Stage 2 – Requirements Analysis & Strategy Definition	13	Negotiate with external service providers on their contingency plans	1
Requirements	6	Undertaking due diligence if necessary	1
Identify critical processes	1	Develop ITSCM plans	1
Identify IT Service Support processes	1	Develop Procedures	1
Conduct impact analysis	1	**Initial Recovery Testing**	3
Extract support requirements	1	Component Testing	1
Conduct risk assessment & vulnerability analysis	3	System Testing	1
Identify risks	1	Integrated Testing	1
Assess threat and vulnerability levels	1		
Assess the levels of risk	1	**Stage 4 – Operational Management**	29
Strategy		**Education and Awareness**	2
Determine risk reduction measures	1	Establish Awareness programme	1
Determine recovery options	4	Establish Education programme	1
People and accommodation	1	**Training**	3
IT systems and networks	1	Induction training	1
Critical services	1	Management training	1
Critical assets	1	General staff training	1
Analyse costs and benefits	1	**Review/Audit**	4
Make recommendations	1	Establish review schedule	1
Agree	1	Establish review Terms of Reference	1
		Establish resource requirements	1
Stage 3 – Implementation	11	Establish feedback process	1
Organisation Planning	3	**Ongoing Testing**	4
Executive	1	Establish test schedule	1
Co-ordination	1	Establish test scope and objectives	1
Recovery	1	Establish participants	1
Implementation Planning	11	Establish corrective process	1
Emergency Response	1	**Change Control**	2
Crisis Management	1	Review overall Change Control process	1
Damage Assessment	1	Ensure ITSCM is adequately covered	1
Salvage	1	**Assurance**	2
Personnel	1	Review ITSCM deliverables with Management	1
Vital Records	1	Review ITSCM process	1
Accommodation and Services	1		

Annex 7C   IT Service Continuity Management

Generic Recovery Plan

I   DOCUMENT CONTROL

This document must be maintained to ensure that the systems, Infrastructure and facilities included, appropriately support business recovery requirements.

1.1   Document distribution

Copy	Issued to	Date	Position
I			
2			
3			
4			

1.2   Document revision

This document will be reviewed every X months.

Current Revision: *date*

Next Revision: *date*

Revision Date	Version No	Summary of Changes

1.3   Document approval

This document must be approved by the following personnel.

Name	Title	Signature

2   SUPPORTING INFORMATION

2.1   Introduction

This document details the instructions and procedures that are required to be followed to recover or continue the operation of systems, Infrastructure, services or facilities to maintain Service Continuity to the level defined or agreed with the business.

2.2   Recovery strategy

The *systems, Infrastructure, services or facilities* will be recovered to *alternative systems, Infrastructure, services or facilities*.

It will take approximately *X hours* to recover the *systems, Infrastructure, services or facilities*. The system will be recovered to the last known point of stability/data integrity, which is *point in day/timing*.

The required recovery time for this system, Infrastructure, service or facility is:

The recovery time and procedures for this *system, Infrastructure, service or facility* was last tested on:

2.3   Invocation

The following personnel are authorised to invoke this plan

> *1.*

2.4   General guidance

All requests for information from the media or other sources should be referred to the *Company procedure*.

When notifying personnel of a potential or actual disaster follow the defined operational escalation procedures, and in particular:

- be calm and avoid lengthy conversation
- advise them of the need to refer information requests to escalation point
- advise them of expectations and actions (avoid giving them details of the Incident unless absolutely necessary)
- If the call is answered by somebody else
    - ask if the contact is available elsewhere
    - if they cannot be contacted leave a message to contact you on a given number
    - do not provide details of the Incident
    - always document call time details, responses and actions.

All activities and contact/escalation should be clearly and accurately recorded. To facilitate this, actions should be in a checklist format and there should be space to record the date and time the activity was started and completed, and who carried out the activity.

2.5 Dependencies

System, Infrastructure, service, facility or interface dependencies should be documented (in priority order) so that related recovery plans or procedures that will need to be invoked in conjunction with this recovery plan can be identified and actioned. The person responsible for invocation should ensure recovery activities are co-ordinated with these other plans.

System	Document Reference	Contact

2.6 Recovery team

The following staff/functions are responsible for actioning these procedures or ensuring the procedures are actioned and recording any issues or problems encountered. Contact will be made via the normal escalation procedures.

Name	Title	Contact Details

2.7 Recovery team checklist

To facilitate the execution of key activities in a timely manner, a checklist similar to the following should be used.

Task	Target Completion	Actual Completion
Confirm invocation has taken place		
Initiate call tree and establish Recovery Team		
Identify issues and advise Crisis Management Team		
Arrange for back-up media, vital records to be shipped from off-site store to recovery site		
Establish Recovery Team rota		
Confirm progress reporting requirements		
Inform Recovery Team of reporting requirements		
Confirm liaison requirements with other Recovery Teams		
Initiate recovery actions		
Advise the estimate for system recovery and commencement testing		
Advise estimate for when system will be ready for user processing		

3   RECOVERY PROCEDURE

Enter recovery instructions/procedures here.

Content/format should be in-line with company standards for procedures. If there are none, guidance should be issued by the Manager or Team Leader for the area responsible for the *system, Infrastructure, services or facility*. The only guideline is that the instructions should be capable of being executed by an experienced professional without undue reliance on local knowledge.

Where necessary, references should be made to supporting documentation (and its location), diagrams and other information sources. This should include the document reference number (if it exists). It is the responsibility of the plan author to ensure that this information is maintained with this plan. If there is only a limited amount of supporting information, it may be easier for this to be included within the plan, providing this plan remains easy to read/follow and does not become too cumbersome.

8 AVAILABILITY MANAGEMENT

8.1 Introduction

The continued advances in IT technology design have resulted in significant improvements in the Availability and reliability of the IT Infrastructure. Fault tolerant and error correction design features in hardware and software now reduce the risk of IT component failure to enable improving levels of Availability to be delivered.

However, against this background of improving levels of Availability and reliability, the need for Availability Management is now greater than ever.

8.1.1 Why Availability Management?

The importance of the Availability of IT to the success of the business has never been more apparent. Over the years the interdependency between the business process and the IT operation has developed to the point where quite simply if the IT stops, then the business stops.

This importance in supporting the business should also be seen in the context of the trends affecting society: trends such as the global economy, 24hr economy, E-Commerce and flexible working. These are the impetus for a growing demand for the Availability of IT Services that are time and place independent.

The business response to marketplace and consumer demand is to increase their exploitation of IT to create new and innovative ways to provide their Customers with flexibility and choice in the way they wish to do business. This is evidenced by the emergence of Internet based online business-to-business and business-to-consumer services. These are now viewed as essential if a business is not only to attract new Customers but also retain their existing Customers.

In today's competitive marketplace Customer satisfaction with the service(s) provided is paramount. Customer loyalty can no longer be relied on and dissatisfaction with the Availability and reliability of service can be a key factor in Customers taking their business to a competitor.

The role of IT is now pivotal. The Availability and reliability of IT can directly influence Customer satisfaction and the reputation of the business. This is why today Availability Management is essential in ensuring IT delivers the right levels of Availability required by the business to satisfy its business objectives and deliver the quality of service demanded by their Customers.

> **KEY MESSAGE**
>
> **Effective Availability Management influences Customer satisfaction and determines the market place reputation of the business.**

8.1.2 The need for a business and User focus

Given the business dependency on IT Availability, it is essential that the deployment of Availability Management has a strong business and User emphasis. This is to ensure that the IT Infrastructure delivers the required levels of Availability to support the vital business functions key to the business operation. It also ensures that Availability improvement opportunities are focused to deliver true User benefits. This requires Availability Management to understand the business and User perspective of the IT Service provided. This should be evidenced in the key process inputs and outputs.

By having this emphasis, the deployment of Availability Management can make a positive contribution to enhancing the relationship with the business: the IT organisation being seen to recognise and respond to IT Availability opportunities and challenges with the business needs understood.

8.1.3   Goal of Availability Management

The goal of the Availability Management process is to optimise the capability of the IT Infrastructure, services and supporting organisation to deliver a cost effective and sustained level of Availability that enables the business to satisfy its business objectives.

This is achieved by determining the Availability requirements of the business and matching these to the capability of the IT Infrastructure and supporting organisation. Where there is a mismatch between the requirement and capability, Availability Management ensures the business is provided with available alternatives and associated cost options.

Availability Management should ensure the required level of Availability is provided. The measurement and monitoring of IT Availability is a key activity to ensure Availability levels are being met consistently. Availability Management should look continuously to optimise the Availability of the IT Infrastructure, services and supporting organisation, in order to provide cost effective Availability improvements that can deliver evidenced business and User benefits.

> **Hints and tips**
>
> **A suggested goal statement for Availability Management:**
>
> 'To understand the Availability requirements of the business and to plan, measure, monitor and continuously strive to improve the Availability of the IT Infrastructure, services and supporting organisation to ensure these requirements are met consistently.'

8.1.4   Objectives

The objectives of the Availability Management process are to:

- ensure IT Services are designed to deliver the levels of Availability required by the business

- provide a range of IT Availability reporting to ensure that agreed levels of Availability, reliability and maintainability are measured and monitored on an ongoing basis

- optimise the Availability of the IT Infrastructure to deliver cost effective improvements that deliver tangible benefits to the business and User

- achieve over a period of time a reduction in the frequency and duration of Incidents that impact IT Availability

- ensure shortfalls in IT Availability are recognised and appropriate corrective actions are identified and progressed

- create and maintain a forward looking Availability Plan aimed at improving the overall Availability of IT Services and Infrastructure components to ensure existing and future business Availability requirements can be satisfied.

8.1.5   Scope

Availability Management is concerned with the design, implementation, measurement and management of IT Infrastructure Availability to ensure the stated business requirements for Availability are consistently met. Availability Management:

- should be applied to all new IT Services and for existing services where Service Level Requirements (SLRs) or Service Level Agreements (SLAs) have been established

- can be applied to those IT Services deemed to be business critical regardless of whether formal SLAs exist

- should be applied to the suppliers (internal and external) that form the IT support organisation as a precursor to the creation of a formal SLA

- considers all aspects of the IT Infrastructure and supporting organisation which may impact Availability, including training, skills, policy, process effectiveness, procedures and tools

- is not responsible for Business Continuity Management and the resumption of business processing after a major disaster – this is the responsibility of IT Service Continuity Management (ITSCM) – but it does provide key inputs to ITSCM and the two have a close relationship.

8.2   Basic concepts

8.2.1   The IT Infrastructure and IT support organisation

The Availability of the IT Infrastructure components that deliver IT Services to the business and their Users are influenced by the:

- complexity of the IT Infrastructure and service design

- reliability of the IT Infrastructure components and environment

- IT support organisation's capability to maintain and support the IT Infrastructure

- levels and quality of maintenance provided by suppliers

- quality, pattern and extent of deployment of operational process and procedures.

The IT provider is accountable to the business for the delivery of the IT Service(s). The required levels of Availability for the IT Service(s) should be documented within a formal SLA.

The IT provider needs to formally agree with each Infrastructure supplier and maintainer the appropriate conditions and controls necessary for the SLA to be met.

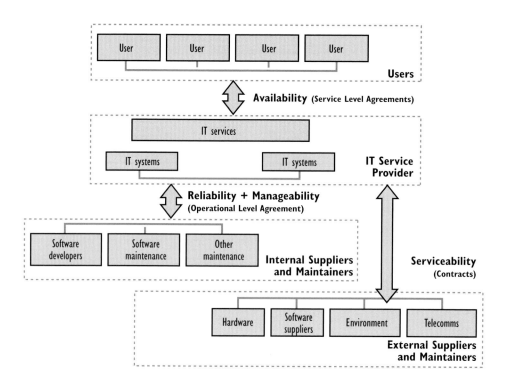

Figure 8.1 – The relationships with suppliers and maintainers of the IT Infrastructure

For internal suppliers these requirements are documented within an Operational Level Agreement (OLA). For external suppliers they must be documented within an underpinning contract. Figure 8.1 shows the relationship and where the formal agreements need to be established.

To ensure that the required level of Availability is being delivered to the business requires all formal agreements to be measured, monitored and reviewed on a regular basis.

8.2.2 Guiding principles

An effective Availability Management process can 'make a difference' and will be recognised as such by the business if the deployment of Availability Management within the IT organisation has a strong emphasis on the needs of the business and User.

To reinforce this emphasis there are three guiding principles that should underpin the Availability Management process and thinking:

Guiding Principle # 1 – 'Availability is at the core of business and User satisfaction'

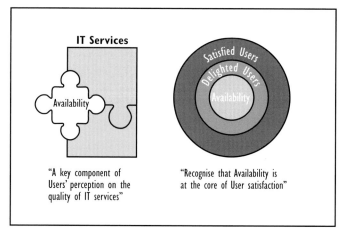

Figure 8.2 – Availability is at the core of business and User satisfaction

Figure 8.2 promotes some simple messages that make an important point. As a consumer of an IT Service, its Availability and reliability can directly influence both the perception and satisfaction of the overall IT Service provision.

A good analogy for example is to consider the purchasing of a new car. Cost, style, performance and features are all important. However, if the car breaks down frequently the buyer is unlikely ever to purchase another car from that manufacturer again.

Within the IT organisation it is unlikely that anyone would disagree with the above messages. However, with today's commercial and business pressures it is all too easy for new IT strategies and initiatives to create diversionary activities. The result is that focus on Availability drifts with the potential for the IT organisation to become so internally focused that it loses sight of the business and User(s) it serves. By embracing this principle, Availability Management ensures that Availability is recognised by all (senior management to junior staff) as the primary IT deliverable.

Guiding Principle #2 – 'Recognising that when things go wrong, it is still possible to achieve business and User satisfaction'

While emphasising the importance of Availability to the business operation and its influence on User satisfaction and business reputation, the reality is that on occasions things do go wrong. For the IT organisation this is their 'moment of truth' in the eyes of the business. How the Incident is managed and resolved plays an important role in how the business views the responsiveness and quality of the IT organisation.

To make a point it is often necessary to show the extreme. Figure 8.3 challenges the view that business and User satisfaction following IT failure scenarios is simply based on Incident duration. By comparing the duration of two Incidents and the impact on business and User satisfaction, it highlights that satisfaction levels are not simply driven by Incident duration. The key message being that in any IT failure situation the business and User will have a wider range of needs, in addition to speed of recovery, that must in total be satisfied.

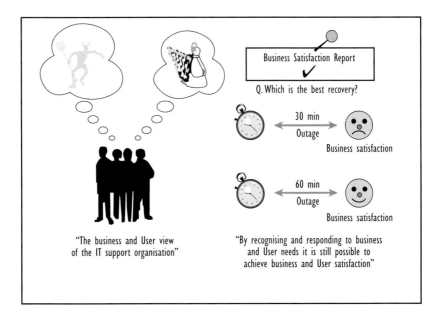

Figure B.3 – Business and User satisfaction levels following an IT failure

The Availability Management process plays a crucial role in the anticipation of IT failure and the assessment of the business and IT needs that must be satisfied. For the business, these revolve around information needs that enable the business to manage the impact of failure on their business and Customers. For IT, these revolve around the provision of processes, procedures and tools to enable the technical recovery to be completed in an optimal time.

Industry view

'The Customer doesn't always expect everything will go right all the time, the big test is what you do when things go wrong ....

Occasional service failure is unavoidable'

Source:– Sir Colin Marshall – Chairman, British Airways

Guiding Principle #3 – 'Improving Availability can only begin after understanding how the IT Services support the business'

Availability Management should not simply understand the Availability of each component. By taking a business and User perspective it is important to understand how each technology component supports the vital business functions upon which the business operation relies. Figure 8.4 illustrates that by taking a business perspective of Availability the understanding in business terms on the contribution of each component to the business operation and User is enhanced.

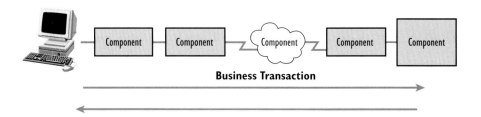

Business Transaction

Figure 8.4 – Understanding how the technology supports the business by taking an end-to-end business and User perspective.

This is fundamental if Availability Management is to optimise the IT Infrastructure and supporting organisation to deliver the levels of Availability required by the business and to drive Availability improvements that deliver true business and User benefits.

KEY MESSAGE

Availability Management needs to consider Availability from an IT Service perspective and from an IT component perspective. These are entirely different aspects. While the underlying concept is similar, the measurement, focus and impact are entirely different.

Validation

A Financial services organisation had for years continually looked to improve its Auto Teller Machine (ATM) Availability by looking at how individual component Availability could be improved. The reasoned thinking being that by improving the Availability of IT component(s) that this would improve the overall end-to-end Availability. Despite this approach, Customer satisfaction levels did not improve and subsequent benchmarking indicated competitors were achieving higher levels of Availability

A new approach was required and a project was defined to establish the underlying reasons that prevented Customers from obtaining cash from its ATMs. This required new methods of measurement and reporting which identified a wide range of causes.

The IT organisation was able to identify the range of IT component causes that prevented Customers obtaining cash and proceeded with a programme of focused improvement activities. This had two effects. Firstly, it improved the overall end-to-end Availability of the ATM service to provide improved Availability of the ATM to the Customer and secondly, resulted in the number of Customers unable to withdraw cash due to IT component non-Availability being significantly reduced.

Key observations from this exercise were:

■ the IT improvements were about 'changing the way' things are done, e.g. scheduling

■ no technology upgrades were necessary

■ measurement identified improvement opportunities that traditional measures masked

■ the IT support organisation now gained valuable insight into the end-to-end service

■ that further improvements to the end-to-end service were also achieved by business process improvements, e.g. cash replenishment procedures.

8.2.3   Terminology

To aid and provide ease of understanding, the most important terms used throughout this Chapter are explained in this Paragraph:

Availability

Availability is the ability of an IT Service or component to perform its required function at a stated instant or over a stated period of time.

Availability (or rather UnAvailability) is the key indicator of service quality perceived by the business and User. Availability is underpinned by the reliability and maintainability of the IT Infrastructure and effectiveness of the IT support organisation. In summary, Availability depends on the:

■   Availability of components

- resilience to failure
- quality of maintenance and support
- quality, pattern and extent of deployment of operational process and procedures
- security, integrity and Availability of data.

An IT Service that consistently meets its SLA Availability targets has the characteristics of low frequency of failure and rapid resumption of service after an Incident has occurred.

Reliability

The reliability of an IT Service can be qualitatively stated as freedom from operational failure. The reliability of an IT Service is determined by the:

- reliability of each component within the IT Infrastructure delivering the IT Service, i.e. the probability that a component will fail to provide its required functions
- level of resilience designed and built into the IT Infrastructure, i.e. the ability of an IT component failure to be masked to enable normal business operations to continue.

Maintainability

Maintainability relates to the ability of an IT Infrastructure component to be retained in, or restored to, an operational state. Maintainability of an IT Infrastructure component can be divided into 7 separate stages:

- the anticipation of failures
- the detection of failures
- the diagnosing of failures
- the resolving of failures
- the recovery from failures
- the restoration of the data and IT Service
- the levels of preventive maintenance applied to prevent failures occurring.

Security

The Confidentiality, Integrity and Availability (CIA) of the data associated with a service; an aspect of overall Availability.

Serviceability

Serviceability describes the contractual arrangements made with Third Party IT Service providers, e.g. Facilities Management. This is to assure the Availability, reliability and maintainability of IT Services and components under their care.

It is important to recognise that Serviceability in itself cannot be measured as a specific metric. It is the Availability, reliability and maintainability of IT Service and components under their care that must be measured.

Vital Business Function

The term Vital Business Function (VBF) is used to reflect the business critical elements of the business process supported by an IT Service. An IT Service may support a number of business functions that are less critical. For example an ATM service VBF would be the dispensing of cash. However the ability to obtain a mini statement print from an ATM may not be considered as vital. This distinction is important and should influence Availability design and associated costs.

User

The term User is used to describe the consumer of an IT Service. Thus no distinction is made or necessary between describing Availability from the internal (business Customer) or external (Customer of a business to consumer service) perspective.

IT support organisation

The term IT support organisation is used to describe the IT functions necessary to support, maintain and manage the IT Infrastructure to enable an IT Service to meet the level of Availability defined within the SLA. The IT support organisation can consist of internal and/or external suppliers.

The requirements for internal suppliers are documented within Operational Level Agreement(s), Underpinning contracts are commissioned for external suppliers.

Availability Management (the activity)

The term 'Availability Management' is used throughout each Section of this Chapter to indicate the execution of activities within the process. A process, however, requires people for its successful deployment and execution. An organisation may wish to assign this to one individual, one organisational function or have roles and responsibilities associated with the process assigned across multiple organisational areas.

8.3 The Availability Management process

The scope of Availability Management covers the design, implementation, measurement and management of IT Infrastructure Availability. This is reflected in the process description shown diagrammatically in Figure 8.5 and described in the following Paragraphs.

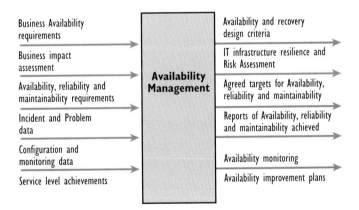

Figure 8.5 – High level Availability Management process diagram

Availability Management commences as soon as the Availability requirements for an IT Service are clear enough to be articulated. It is an ongoing process, finishing only when the IT Service is decommissioned.

8.3.1 Key inputs

The key inputs to the Availability Management process are:

- the Availability requirements of the business for a new or enhanced IT Service

- a business impact assessment for each vital business function underpinned by the IT Infrastructure

- the Availability, reliability and maintainability requirements for the IT Infrastructure components that underpin the IT Service(s)

- information on IT Service and component failure(s), usually in the form of Incident and Problem records

- a wide range of configuration and monitoring data pertaining to each IT Service and component

- service level achievements against agreed targets for each IT Service that has an agreed SLA.

8.3.2 Key outputs

The key outputs from the Availability Management process are:

- Availability and recovery design criteria for each new or enhanced IT Service

- details of the Availability techniques that will be deployed to provide additional Infrastructure resilience to prevent or minimise the impact of component failure to the IT Service

- agreed targets of Availability, reliability and maintainability for the IT Infrastructure components that underpin the IT Service(s)

- Availability reporting of Availability, reliability and maintainability to reflect the business, User and IT support organisation perspectives

- the monitoring requirements for IT components to ensure that deviations in Availability, reliability and maintainability are detected and reported

- Availability Plan for the proactive improvement of the IT Infrastructure.

8.3.3 Key activities

The key activities of the process are as follows:

- determining the Availability requirements from the business for a new or enhanced IT Service and formulating the Availability and recovery design criteria for the IT Infrastructure

- in conjunction with ITSCM determining the vital business functions and impact arising from IT component failure. Where appropriate reviewing the Availability design criteria to provide additional resilience to prevent or minimise impact to the business

- defining the targets for Availability, reliability and maintainability for the IT Infrastructure components that underpin the IT Service to enable these to be documented and agreed within SLAs, OLAs and contracts

- establishing measures and reporting of Availability, Reliability and Maintainability that reflects the business, User and IT support organisation perspectives

- monitoring and trend analysis of the Availability, Reliability and Maintainability of IT components

- reviewing IT Service and component Availability and identifying unacceptable levels

- investigating the underlying reasons for unacceptable Availability.

- producing and maintaining an Availability Plan which prioritises and plans IT Availability improvements.

8.3.4   Relationships with other IT Service Management disciplines

All IT Service Management disciplines have an influence on IT Availability. Therefore Availability Management, by implication, interfaces with all disciplines. These can be considered bi-directional with Availability Management providing inputs while also having a dependency on the outputs from the other IT Service Management disciplines.

Example 1

Service Level Management

An input from Availability Management to the Service Level Management process is an assessment of the Availability that can be delivered for a new IT Service to enable the SLA to be negotiated and agreed. An output from Service Level Management to the Availability Management process is details of the agreed SLA that enables the appropriate Availability measurement and reporting to be instigated.

Example 2

IT Service Continuity Management

An output from IT Service Continuity Management is a business impact assessment detailing the vital business functions dependent on IT Infrastructure Availability. An Input from Availability Management to IT Service Continuity Management is the Availability and recovery design criteria to maintain 'business as usual' by preventing or minimising the impact of failures by use of techniques such as Component Failure Impact Assessment (CFIA).

Example 3

IT Financial Management

An input from Availability Management to IT Financial Management is the cost of non-Availability arising from the loss of an IT Service(s) to help cost justify improvements defined within the Availability Plan. An output from IT Financial Management to Availability Management is the costs associated with proposed upgrades to the IT Infrastructure to deliver increased levels of Availability.

Example 4

Capacity Management

An input from Availability Management to Capacity Management is a completed CFIA for a new IT Service denoting where Availability techniques are to deployed to provide additional Infrastructure resilience. An output from Capacity Management to Availability Management is the Capacity Plan detailing how the Capacity requirements associated with the provision of additional Infrastructure resilience will be met.

Example 5

Change Management

An input from Availability Management to Change Management is details of the planned maintenance regime, i.e. frequency, duration and impact, for components underpinning a new IT Service. An output from Change Management to Availability Management is a schedule of planned maintenance activities for IT components detailing the times and IT Services that will be impacted.

Deficiencies in any of the IT Service Management processes may impact Availability. Techniques such as Systems Outage Analysis (SOA) may identify process improvement opportunities for the other IT Service Management processes. In this context, Availability Management can be a driver for process improvements within the overall IT Service Management framework deployed within an organisation. Please refer to Paragraph 8.9.8 for more information on SOA.

8.3.5   Benefits, Costs and Problems

Benefits of Availability Management

The principal benefit of Availability Management is that IT Services with an Availability requirement are designed, implemented and managed to consistently meet that target. The IT Availability requirement being delivered at a known and justified cost and to a predetermined level of quality and security.

Availability Management if deployed with a strong emphasis on the business and User ensures the IT organisation recognises Availability as the primary IT deliverable to generate and sustain the behaviours of continuous improvement and a service culture.

The benefits of Availability Management can be summarised as follows:

- a single point of accountability for Availability (process owner) is established within the IT organisation
- IT Services are designed to meet the IT Availability requirements determined from the business
- the levels of IT Availability provided are cost justified

- the levels of Availability required are agreed, measured and monitored to fully support Service Level Management

- shortfalls in the provision of the required levels of Availability are recognised and appropriate corrective actions identified and implemented

- a business and User perspective of IT Service Availability is taken to ensure optimal usage and performance of the IT Infrastructure is achieved to deliver maximum benefit

- the frequency and duration of IT Service failures is reduced over time

- IT support organisation mindset moves from error correction to service enhancement; from reactive to proactive attitude

- the IT support organisation is seen to 'add value' to the business.

Without an effective deployment of Availability Management the following are examples of the likely difficulties and issues that can arise:

- it is difficult to define service levels regarding Availability that are specific, measurable, achievable and comprehensible to both the business and IT support organisation

- the management and performance of internal and external suppliers is jeopardised by the lack of agreed and measured Availability targets

- it becomes difficult to assess what level of IT Service Availability is achievable and cost effective

- new IT Services are implemented without full consideration of how IT Availability will be delivered. The lack of design focus on Availability and recovery may lead to costly retrospective Changes to improve Availability

- instability of new IT Services results in lost business opportunity and damage to business reputation

- Availability issues are not recognised or owned within the IT support organisation due to a lack of clear accountability

- the consequences of failing to deliver consistent and agreed levels of Availability inevitably leads to dissatisfaction, a lack of trust and conflict between the business and the IT support organisation.

KEY MESSAGE

'Where today's problems are seen as addressed by the latest technology and tools, it is important to reflect that Availability cannot be purchased... it must be designed, implemented, measured and managed. This is Availability Management'.

Costs

The costs associated with implementing and executing Availability Management include:

- the staff costs associated with the process owner role for Availability Management which include salary, training, recruitment costs and if needed the cost of initial consultancy

- accommodation costs

- process deployment costs to define and implement the necessary process, procedures and techniques

■ support tools for monitoring and reporting.

Availability Management may identify investment opportunities to improve Availability, e.g. new IT Service Management tools. However, these costs should be considered against the Availability requirement and the business case justified or rejected as appropriate. These are not the costs of implementing Availability Management.

Possible problems

The possible problems that may inhibit the establishment and deployment of Availability Management are often of an organisational nature. Typical problems encountered are:

■ the IT organisation view Availability as a responsibility of all senior managers and therefore are reluctant to justify the costs of appointing a single individual as accountable for Availability

■ the IT organisation and supporting organisation have difficulty understanding how Availability Management can make a difference particularly where the existing disciplines of Incident Management, Problem Management and Change Management are already deployed

■ the IT organisation view current levels of Availability as good so see no compelling reason for the creation of a new role within the organisation

■ there is resistance to process ownership and the concept of an accountable individual/role who has authority over all the IT support organisation

■ the IT organisation fail to delegate the appropriate authority and empowerment to enable the process owner for Availability Management to influence all areas of the IT support organisation.

The above are clearly major inhibitors. However, assuming the IT organisation intends to establish the process and associated role, then other problems can impact implementation and ongoing activity. These can include:

■ lack of available resources with the required skills and competencies to establish Availability Management

■ lack of specific Availability Management tools to underpin and support the process

■ need to create bespoke tool and reporting solutions in the absence of appropriate in-house or marketplace offerings

■ lack of mature service management processes that provide a key input to Availability Management, i.e. Service Level Management, Configuration Management, Incident Management and Problem Management

■ Availability Management being viewed by some managers as everything or nothing.

None of the problems identified are insurmountable providing there is strong leadership and commitment from the IT organisation in creating and empowering the role and pragmatism during its implementation to focus on areas of immediate benefit and to accept support tool shortcomings.

Validation

Following period of IT systems instability the senior executive of an IT organisation requested a major IT consultancy group to perform an independent Availability review

A key emphasis placed on the review was not simply to focus on the Incidents that had occurred but to assess the capability of the IT organisation to meet the anticipated demand for increasing levels of Availability for future IT Services.

When the review concluded, two key points within the executive summary presented to the senior executive and sponsor of the review were:

■　　'There is a lack of focus on Availability within the IT support organisation'

■　　'The User view has been lost'

The major recommendation proposed to address these issues was to implement an Availability Management process and appoint the role of an Availability Manager as the process owner.

The recommendation was accepted and progressed. Two years later, the same consultancy group was asked to undertake an audit of the Availability Management process and its implementation to assess progress. The executive summary of this review concluded:

■　　'A dramatic change in attitude in the last 2 years'

■　　'Availability now recognised as the key element in providing IT Services'

■　　'Decisions now being made on the basis of value and cost of downtime'

■　　'Recognised as important to the success of the business'

■　　'Gets things done'

■　　'Greater sharing of responsibilities between IT and the business.'

It is important to reflect that the above achievements were accomplished by appointing a single individual as process owner with sole accountability for the implementation and ongoing execution of the Availability Management process.

8.4　The Cost of (Un)Availability

8.4.1　Availability

The level of Availability required by the business influences the overall cost of the IT Service provided. In general, the higher the level of Availability required by the business the higher the cost. These costs are not just the procurement of the base IT technology and services required to underpin the IT Infrastructure. Additional costs are incurred in providing the appropriate service management processes, systems management tools and high Availability solutions required to meet the more stringent Availability requirements.

When considering how the Availability requirements of the business are to be met, it is important to ensure that the level of Availability to be provided for an IT Service is at the level actually required and is affordable and cost justified by the business. Figure 8.6 indicates the products and services required to provide varying levels of Availability and the cost implications.

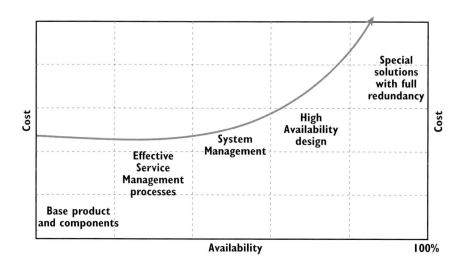

Figure 8.6 – The relationship between levels of Availability and overall cost

New IT Services

Where new IT Services are being developed it is essential that Availability Management takes an early and participating role in determining the Availability requirements. This enables Availability Management to positively influence the IT Infrastructure design to ensure that it can deliver the level of Availability required.

The importance of this participation early in the design of the IT Infrastructure cannot be underestimated. The benefits of this early involvement are:

- provides an early indication of the costs required to meet the Availability requirement
- where costs are seen as too high, enables alternative options with their associated costs and consequences to be presented to the business
- higher levels of Availability can be achieved when Availability is designed in, rather than added on
- avoids the costs and delays of late design Changes to meet the required levels of Availability
- ensures the IT Infrastructure design will deliver the required levels of Availability.

KEY MESSAGE

'Having to retrofit and re-engineer late in the design stage or once in production will incur significant additional costs and in many cases this can be more expensive than building or procuring the initial IT Service'.

Existing IT Services

Changing business needs and consumer demand may require the levels of Availability provided for an IT Service to be reviewed. Such reviews should form part of the regular service reviews with the business undertaken by Service Level Management.

Where high levels of Availability are already being delivered it may take considerable effort and incur significant cost to achieve a small incremental Availability improvement.

A key activity for Availability Management is to continually look at opportunities to optimise the Availability of the IT Infrastructure. The benefits of this approach being that enhanced levels of Availability may be achievable but with much lower costs.

The optimisation approach is a sensible first step to delivering better value for money. A number of Availability Management techniques can be applied to identify optimisation opportunities. It is recommended that the scope should not be restricted to the IT Infrastructure, but also include a review of the business process and other end-to-end business owned responsibilities.

Validation

The previous example of how a financial organisation raised ATM Availability levels without additional technology investment included a review of their business process.

The approach to identify the reasons for Customers being unable to obtain cash from their ATMS highlighted many IT component Availability root causes. However, it also identified weaknesses in business process. This led to a range of improvements that contributed significantly to improved end-to-end Availability of the ATM service to its Customers.

Areas included:

- improving cash replenishment procedures
- increased frequency of cash replenishment at high usage ATM locations
- improved 'cash out' detection and reporting
- improved ATM hardware fault detection and reporting
- improved cash demand forecasts to ensure sufficient cash available for peak demand periods.

As illustrated in Figure 8.7, there is a significant increase in costs when the business requirement is higher than the optimum level of Availability that the IT Infrastructure can deliver. These increased costs are driven by major redesign of the IT Infrastructure and the changing of requirements for the IT support organisation.

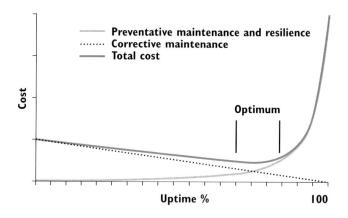

Figure 8.7 – Going beyond optimum Availability significantly impacts costs

(See Section 8.9 for guidance on how to apply a range of approaches to further optimise Availability for a given service.) Information relating to Changes in Availability requirements and the associated costs should be included in the Availability Plan. If the business has an urgent need to progress this enhanced level of Availability an exception report should be produced as the basis for an initial business case.

> **KEY MESSAGE**
>
> 'Improving levels of Availability can often be achieved by a small step change in thinking rather than a large step change in technology'.

8.4.2 UnAvailability

The overall costs of an IT Service are influenced by the levels of Availability required and the investments required in technology and services provided by the IT support organisation to meet this requirement. Availability certainly does not come for free.

However, it is important to reflect that the UnAvailability of IT also has a cost …therefore UnAvailability isn't for free either. For highly critical business systems it is necessary to consider not only the cost of providing the service but also the costs that are incurred from failure. The optimum balance to strike being the cost of the Availability solution weighed against the costs of UnAvailability.

8.4.3 How much did that failure cost?

Impact on vital business functions

The cost of an IT failure could simply be expressed as the number of business or IT transactions impacted, either as an actual figure (derived from instrumentation) or based on an estimation. When measured against the vital business functions that support the business operation this can provide an obvious indication of the consequence of failure.

The advantage of this approach is the relative ease of obtaining the impact data and the lack of any complex calculations. It also becomes a *'value'* that is understood by both the business and IT organisation. This can be the stimulus for identifying improvement opportunities and can become a key metric in monitoring the Availability of the IT Service. This approach is recommended as the basis for enhanced SLA reporting (see Section 8.7).

The major disadvantage of this approach is that it offers no obvious monetary value that would be needed to justify any significant financial investment decisions for improving Availability.

The monetary impact

Where significant financial investment decisions are required it is better to express the cost of failure arising from system, application or function loss to the business as a monetary *'value'*.

The monetary value can be calculated as a combination of the tangible costs associated with failure, but can also include a number of intangible costs. The monetary value should also reflect the cost impact to the whole organisation, i.e. the business and IT organisation.

Tangible costs

These can include:

- lost User productivity
- lost IT staff productivity
- lost revenue
- overtime payments
- wasted goods and material
- imposed fines or penalties.

These costs are often well understood by the finance area of the business and IT organisation and in relative terms are easier to obtain and aggregate than the intangible costs associated with an IT failure.

Intangible costs

These can include:

- loss of Customer goodwill (Customer dissatisfaction)
- loss of Customers
- loss of business opportunity (to sell, gain new Customers etc)
- damage to business reputation
- loss of confidence in IT Service provider
- damage to staff morale.

It is important not to simply dismiss the intangible costs (and the potential consequences) on the grounds that they are difficult to measure.

> **KEY MESSAGE**
>
> **The Internet and other electronic delivery channels are accelerating the trend that results in changes to the way business Customers now react to IT Service failure.**
>
> **In the emerging world of E-Commerce these intangible costs (business reputation, Customer dissatisfaction, loss of existing Customers and loss of business opportunity) become far more important.**

8.4.4   The benefit of understanding the cost of UnAvailability

The major benefit provided is that it provides a true financial cost on the consequences of UnAvailability and therefore provides an objective view of any 'cost versus benefit' assessment. In organisations where decision-makers invariably have to consider the 'bottom line' this provides them with information that should facilitate sensible and informed decisions.

The importance of understanding the cost of UnAvailability should be highlighted as a key performance indicator within the design and operational phases of Service Level Management.

Problems with deriving a cost of UnAvailability

There are however some problems to consider and overcome with this approach, namely:

- the wide scope of what can be factored into the cost calculation

- the difficulties of quantifying the cost impact of many of the intangible consequences

- resistance from the business to divulging cost information (concerns about how the IT organisation use information, i.e. lowered priority if cost is low or continued approaches to invest if costs are high)

- reluctance of the IT organisation to disclose and make public the service costs of each of their business Customers

- the time and effort of obtaining the cost impact data.

A pragmatic approach is recommended and the level to which an attempt is made to quantify the monetary cost of a failure is invariably influenced by the cost investment to be justified.

An example of a calculation to be used in quantifying the cost of a failure can be found in Paragraph 8.9.5.

8.5   Availability Planning

8.5.1   Determining Availability requirements

Before any service level requirement is accepted and ultimately the SLR or SLA is agreed between the business and the IT organisation it is essential that the Availability requirements of the business are analysed to assess if/how the IT Infrastructure can deliver the required levels of Availability.

This applies not only to new IT Services that are being introduced but also any requested Changes to the Availability requirements of existing IT Services.

It is important that the business is consulted early in the development lifecycle so that the business Availability needs of a new or enhanced IT Service can be costed and agreed. This is particularly important where stringent Availability requirements may require additional investment in service management processes, IT Service management tools, high Availability design and special solutions with full redundancy.

It is likely that the business need for IT Availability cannot be expressed in technical terms. Availability Management therefore provides an important role in being able to translate the business and User requirements into quantifiable Availability terms and conditions. This is an important input into the IT Infrastructure design and provides the basis for assessing the capability of the IT Infrastructure design and IT support organisation in meeting the Availability requirements of the business.

The business requirements for IT Availability should at least contain:

- a definition of the vital business functions supported by the IT Service

- a definition of IT Service downtime, i.e. the conditions under which the business consider the IT Service to be unavailable

- the business impact caused by loss of service

- quantitative Availability requirements, i.e. the extent to which the business tolerates IT Service downtime or degraded service

- the required service hours, i.e. when the service is to be provided

- an assessment of the relative importance of different working periods

- specific security requirements.

Hints and tips

The translation of User and business Availability requirements into quantifiable terms and conditions is crucial. To avoid any confusion or misunderstanding between the Business and IT the first step should be to document and agree a description or definition of the Availability terms and conditions that will be used.

What the business understands by downtime, Availability, reliability etc may differ from the IT perspective. This avoids any misunderstandings and enables subsequent design activities to commence with a clear and unambiguous understanding of what is required.

Availability Management having assessed the combined capability of the IT Infrastructure design and IT support organisation is then in a position to confirm if the Availability requirements can be met. Where shortfalls are identified, dialogue with the business is required to present the cost options that exist to enhance the proposed design to meet the Availability requirements. This enables the business to reassess if lower or higher levels of Availability are required and to understand the appropriate impact and costs associated with their decision.

Determining the Availability requirements is likely to be an iterative process particularly where there is a need to balance the business Availability requirement against the associated costs. The necessary steps are:

- determine the business impact caused by loss of service

- from the business requirements specify the Availability, reliability and maintainability requirements for the IT components controlled by the IT support organisation

- for IT Services and components provided externally, identify the serviceability requirements

- estimating the costs involved in meeting the Availability, reliability, maintainability and serviceability requirements

- determine with the business if the costs identified in meeting the Availability requirements are justified

- determine from the business the costs likely to be incurred from loss or degradation of service

- where these are seen as cost justified, define the Availability, reliability, maintainability and serviceability requirements in agreements and negotiate into contracts.

Hints and tips

If costs are seen as prohibitive, either:

Reassess the IT Infrastructure design and provide options for reducing costs and assess the consequences on Availability

Or:

Reassess the business use and reliance on the IT Service and renegotiate the Availability targets to be documented in the SLA.

The Service Level Management (SLM) function is normally responsible for communicating with the business on how their Availability requirements are to be met and ultimately negotiating the SLA for the IT Service. Availability Management therefore provides important support to the SLM function during this period.

While higher levels of Availability can often be provided by technology investment there is no justification for providing a higher level of Availability than that needed and afforded by the business. The reality is that satisfying Availability requirements is always a balance between cost and quality.

This is where Availability Management can play a key role in optimising Availability of the IT Infrastructure to meet increasing Availability demands while deferring an increase in costs. (See Paragraph 8.5.4 and Section 8.9 for additional guidance.

8.5.2 Design activity

Designing for Availability is a key activity driven by Availability Management. This ensures that the required level of Availability for an IT Service can be met.

Availability Management needs to ensure that the design activity for Availability looks at the task from two related but distinct perspectives:

DESIGNING FOR AVAILABILITY: This relates to the technical design of the IT Infrastructure and the alignment of the internal and external suppliers required to meet the Availability requirements for an IT Service.

> **KEY MESSAGE**
>
> **Designing for Availability can be considered the proactive perspective aimed at avoiding loss of IT Service Availability.**

DESIGNING FOR RECOVERY: This relates to the design points required to ensure that in the event of an IT Service failure, the service can be reinstated to enable normal business operations to resume as quickly as is possible.

> **KEY MESSAGE**
>
> **Designing for Recovery can be considered the reactive perspective aimed at minimising the business and User impact from an IT Service failure.**

Taking this two phased approach to the design activity ensures that new IT Services do not suffer unnecessary and extended recovery when the first failure situation occurs.

Additionally, the ability to recover quickly may be a crucial factor. In simple terms it may not be possible or cost justified to build a design that is highly resilient to failure(s). The ability to meet the Availability requirements within the cost parameters may rely on the ability to recover in a timely and effective manner, consistently.

8.5.3   Designing for Availability

Availability should be considered in the design process at the earliest possible stage of the development lifecycle. This avoids the potential for:

- increased development costs arising from re-work
- unplanned expenditure on IT upgrades necessary to meet the Availability requirement
- unplanned expenditure on additional systems management tools required to operationally control and manage the IT Service and supporting IT Infrastructure
- unplanned expenditure to eliminate Single Points of Failure (SPOF) within the configuration
- the inability of internal or external suppliers to meet the maintainability and serviceability requirements
- delays to the planned implementation and the potential for missed business opportunity
- incurring avoidable IT Service failures.

Figure 8.8 illustrates a high level outline of how initial Availability requirements are progressed by Availability Management to ensure these can be met by the IT Infrastructure and IT support organisation. This simple framework can be applied to new IT Services or existing IT Services where a Change of Availability requirements has required major redesign.

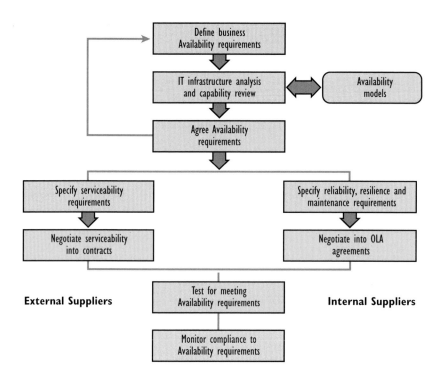

Figure 8.8 – Progressing Availability requirements for an IT Service

The role of Availability Management within the design activities is to provide:

■ the specification of the Availability requirements for hardware and software

■ the requirements for Availability measurement points (instrumentation)

■ the requirements for new/enhanced systems management

■ participation in the IT Infrastructure design

■ the specification of the reliability, maintainability and serviceability requirements for components supplied by internal and external suppliers

■ validation of the final design to meet the minimum levels of Availability required by the business for the IT Service.

The framework that Availability Management should utilise to determine the appropriateness of a given design to meet the stated Availability requirements consists of the following:

■ the minimum levels of Availability required by the business for the IT Service

■ the proposed technical design which should cover the full end-to-end configuration

■ identification of the internal and external suppliers

■ the minimum reliability, maintainability and serviceability levels for each component

■ the provision of an Availability modelling tool

■ the ability to test or simulate that new components within the design match the specified requirements.

Method of approach

IT INFRASTRUCTURE ANALYSIS – CAPABILITY REVIEW

The first stage is to understand the vulnerability to failure of the proposed IT Infrastructure design.

Single Points of Failure

A Single Point of Failure (SPOF) is any component within the IT Infrastructure that has no backup capability and can cause impact to the business and User when it fails.

It is important that no unrecognised single points of failure exist within the IT Infrastructure design. The use of Component Failure Impact Assessment (CFIA) as a technique to identify single points of failure is recommended.

Where these are identified, CFIA can be used to identify the business and User impact and help determine what alternatives can or should be considered to cater for this weakness in the design. See Paragraph 8.9.1 for additional guidance on the use of CFIA.

Risk Analysis and Management

To assess the vulnerability of failure within the configuration and capability of the IT support organisation it is recommended that the proposed IT Infrastructure, service configurations, service design and supporting organisation (internal and external suppliers) are subject to a formal Risk Analysis. CRAMM is a technique that can be used to identify justifiable countermeasures that can protect the Availability of IT Systems. (See Paragraph 8.9.3 for additional guidance on CRAMM).

Testing or Simulation

To assess if new components within the design can match the stated requirements it is important that the testing regime instigated ensures that the Availability expected can be delivered. Simulation tools to generate the expected User demand for the new IT Service should be seriously considered to ensure components continue to operate under volume and stress conditions.

Improving the design

The second stage is to re-evaluate the IT Infrastructure design if the Availability requirements cannot be met and identify cost justified design Changes.

Improvements in design to meet the Availability requirements can be achieved by reviewing the capability of the technology to be deployed in the proposed IT Infrastructure design, e.g.:

- the exploitation of fault tolerant technology to mask the impact of planned or unplanned component downtime
- duplexing or the provision of alternative IT Infrastructure components to allow one component to take over the work of another component
- improving component reliability by enhancing testing regimes
- improved Release Management and Change Management for Changes to key components
- improved software design and development

■ improved processes and procedures

■ Systems Management enhancements/exploitation.

Chapter 7 of this book provides additional guidance on this aspect of IT Infrastructure design.

Hints and tips

Consider documenting the Availability design requirements and considerations for new IT Services and make available to the areas responsible for design and implementation. Longer term seek to mandate these requirements and integrate within the appropriate governance mechanisms that cover the introduction of new IT Services.

Considerations for high Availability

Where the business operation has a high dependency on IT Availability and the cost of failure or loss of business reputation is considered not acceptable, the business may define stringent Availability requirements. These factors may be sufficient for the business to justify the additional costs required to meet these more demanding levels of Availability.

Achieving high levels of Availability begins with the procurement and/or development of good quality products and components. However, these in isolation are unlikely to deliver the sustained levels of Availability required.

To achieve a consistent and sustained level of high Availability requires investment and deployment of effective Service Management processes, systems management tools, high Availability design and ultimately special solutions with full redundancy.

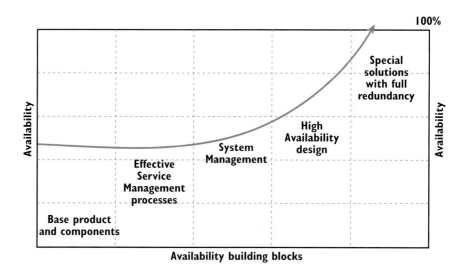

Figure 8.9 – The building blocks to meet the more stringent Availability requirements

Figure 8.9 illustrates quite simply, that to achieve higher levels of Availability requires investment in more than just the base product and components. This is a similar diagram to that presented in Figure 8.6 which emphasises how the higher the Availability demand the higher the overall costs.

The above can therefore be viewed as a framework for what needs to be considered within the overall design for Availability where stringent Availability requirements are set.

This suggested framework is described as follows:

Base product and components

The procurement or development of the base product and components should be based on their capability to meet stringent Availability and reliability requirements. These should be considered as the cornerstone of the Availability design. The additional investment required to achieve even higher levels of Availability will be wasted and Availability levels not met if these base products and components are unreliable and prone to failure.

Service Management processes

Effective Service Management processes contribute to higher levels of Availability. Processes such as Availability Management, Incident Management, Problem Management, Change Management etc play a crucial role in the overall management of the IT Service.

Systems Management

Systems Management should provide the monitoring, diagnostic and automated error recovery to enable fast detection and resolution of potential and actual IT failure.

High Availability design

The design for high Availability needs to consider the elimination of single points of failure and/or the provision of alternative components to provide minimal disruption to the business operation should an IT component failure occur.

The design also needs to eliminate or minimise the effects of planned downtime to the business operation normally required to accommodate maintenance activity, the implementation of Changes to the IT Infrastructure or business application.

Recovery criteria should define rapid recovery and IT Service reinstatement as a key objective within the designing for recovery phase of design.

Special solutions with full redundancy

To approach continuous Availability in the range of 100% requires expensive solutions that incorporate full redundancy. Redundancy is the technique of improving Availability by using duplicate components. For stringent Availability requirements to be met these need to be working autonomously in parallel. These solutions are not just restricted to the IT components, but also the IT environment, i.e. power supplies, air conditioning, telecommunications.

Helpful additional definitions when defining stringent Availability requirements.

As stated in Paragraph 8.5.1, the translation of the business and User Availability requirements into quantifiable Availability terms and conditions is crucial.

Where stringent levels of Availability are required additional definitions should be documented and agreed between the business and IT to ensure both parties understand the specific high Availability conditions.

The suggested additional definitions are:

High availability

A characteristic of the IT Service that minimises or masks the effects of IT component failure to the User.

Continuous operation

A characteristic of the IT Service that minimises or masks the effects of planned downtime to the User.

Continuous availability

A characteristic of the IT Service that minimises or masks the effects of ALL failures and planned downtime to the User.

These definitions help to define the often-used term of 'High Availability'. This provides a better structure for determining which areas of Availability design are most important to the business.

Industry view

Many suppliers commit to high Availability or continuous Availability solutions only if stringent environmental standards are used. They often only agree to such contracts after a site survey has been completed and additional, sometimes costly improvements have been made.

8.5.4   Designing for recovery

Designing for Availability is a key activity driven by Availability Management. This ensures that the stated Availability requirements for an IT Service can be met.

However, Availability Management should also ensure that within this design activity there is focus on the design elements required to ensure that when IT Services fail, the service can be reinstated to enable normal business operations to resume as quickly as is possible.

'Designing for Recovery' may at first sound negative. Clearly good Availability design is about avoiding failures and delivering where possible a Fail-Safe IT Infrastructure. However, with this focus is too much reliance placed on technology and has as much emphasis been placed on the Safe-Fail aspects of the IT Infrastructure? The reality is that failures will occur. The way the IT organisation manages failure situations can have the following positive outcomes:

- normal business operations are resumed quickly to minimise impact to the business and User

- the Availability requirements are met within the cost parameters set as a result of timely and effective recovery reducing the amount of downtime incurred by the business

- the IT organisation are seen as responsive and business focused.

KEY MESSAGE

Every failure is a 'moment of truth' – every failure is an opportunity to make or break your reputation with the business.

By providing focus on the 'designing for recovery' aspects of the overall Availability design can ensure that every failure is an opportunity to maintain and even enhance business and User satisfaction.

Designing for Recovery – needs

To provide an effective 'design for recovery' it is important to recognise that both the Business and the IT organisation have needs that must be satisfied to enable an effective recovery from IT failure.

Business needs

These are informational needs which the business requires to help them manage the impact of failure on their business and set expectation within the business, User community and their business Customers.

IT needs

These are the process, procedures and tools required to enable the technical recovery to be completed in an optimal time.

Hints and tips

Consider documenting the Recovery design requirements and considerations for new IT Services and make available to the areas responsible for design and implementation. Longer term seek to mandate these requirements and integrate within the appropriate governance mechanisms that cover the introduction of new IT Services.

Key elements in the Design for Recovery

The role of incident management and the service desk

A key aim is to avoid small Incidents becoming major by ensuring the right people are involved early enough to avoid mistakes being made and to ensure the appropriate business and technical recovery procedures are invoked at the earliest opportunity.

This is the responsibility of the Incident Management process and role of the Service Desk.

To ensure business needs are met during major IT Service failures and to ensure the most optimal recovery, the Incident Management process and Service Desk need to have defined and execute:

- stringent escalation procedures

- clearly defined roles and responsibilities for handling major Incidents

- a communications plan to support the wider informational needs associated with major Incidents.

KEY MESSAGE

The above are not the responsibilities of Availability Management. However, the effectiveness of the Incident Management process and Service Desk can strongly influence the overall recovery period. The use of Availability Management methods and techniques to further optimise IT recovery may be the stimulus for subsequent continuous improvement activities to the Incident Management process and Service Desk.

Understanding the Incident 'lifecycle'

It is important to recognise that every Incident passes through a number of stages. These are described as follows:

- Incident start

- Incident detection

- Incident diagnosis

- component repair

- component recovery

- service restoration (and verification).

This 'lifecycle' view provides an important framework in determining amongst others, systems management requirements for Incident detection, diagnostic data capture requirements and tools for diagnosis, recovery plans to aid speedy recovery and how to verify that IT Service has been restored.

Chapter 5 of the Service Support book provides information on Incident Management and the Incident 'lifecycle' from the Incident handling perspective. To aid the designing for recovery this lifecycle has been expanded to reflect an IT Availability perspective of an Incident.

Paragraph 8.9.9 provides additional guidance on, and illustrates the use of, the expanded Incident lifecycle.

Systems Management

The provision of Systems Management tools positively influences the levels of Availability that can be delivered. Implementation and exploitation should have strong focus on achieving high Availability and enhanced recovery objectives.

In the context of recovery, such tools should be exploited to provide automated failure detection, assist failure diagnosis and support automated error recovery.

Diagnostic data capture procedures

When IT components fail it is important that the required level of diagnostics are captured, to enable Problem determination to identify the root cause. For certain failures the capture of diagnostics may extend service downtime. However, the non-capture of the appropriate diagnostics creates and exposes the service to repeat service failures.

Where the time required taking diagnostics is considered excessive; a review should be instigated to identify if techniques and/or procedures can be streamlined to reduce the time required. Equally the scope of the diagnostic data available for capture can be assessed to ensure only the diagnostic data considered essential is taken.

The additional downtime required to capture diagnostics should be included in the recovery metrics documented for each IT component.

Determine backup and recovery requirements

The backup and recovery requirements for the components underpinning a new IT Service should be identified as early as possible within the development or selection cycle. These requirements should cover hardware, software and data. The outcome from this activity should be a documented set of recovery requirements that enable the development of appropriate recovery plans.

Develop and test a backup and recovery strategy and schedule

To anticipate and prepare for performing recovery such that reinstatement of service is effective and efficient requires the development and testing of appropriate recovery plans based on the documented recovery requirements.

The outcome from this activity should be clear, operable and accurate recovery plans that are available to the appropriate parties immediately the new IT Service is introduced.

Wherever possible, the operational activities within the recovery plan should be automated.

The testing of the recovery plans also delivers approximate timings for recovery. These recovery metrics can be used to support the communication of estimated recovery of service and validate or enhance the CFIA documentation.

Recovery metrics

The provision of a timely and accurate estimation of when service will be restored is the key informational need of the business. This information enables the business to make sensible decisions on how they are to manage the impact of failure on the business and on their Customers. To enable this information to be communicated to the business requires the creation and maintenance of recovery metrics for each IT component covering a variety of recovery scenarios.

Paragraph 8.9.1 provides techniques for guidance on how Component Failure Impact Analysis (CFIA) can be used to derive recovery metrics to support the communications element by providing estimated recovery timings.

Backup and recovery performance

Availability Management must continuously seek and promote faster methods of recovery for all potential Incidents. This can be achieved via a range of methods including automated failure detection, automated recovery, more stringent escalation procedures, exploitation of new and faster recovery tools and techniques.

It is recommended that this aspect of Availability measurement is included in the basic set of IT Availability measures utilised to measure and report IT Availability.

Paragraph 8.9.9 describes how to use the expanded 'Incident lifecycle' as a model for metrics creation. These metrics could be used to drive the 'review backup and recovery performance' process.

Service restoration and verification

An Incident can only be considered 'closed' once service has been restored and normal business operation has resumed. It is important that the restored IT Service is verified as working correctly as soon as service restoration is completed and before any technical staff involved in the Incident are stood down. In the majority of cases this is simply a case of getting confirmation from the User. However, the User for some services may be a Customer of the business, i.e. ATM services, Internet based services.

For these types of services it is recommended that IT Service verification procedures are developed to enable the IT support organisation to verify that a restored IT Service is now working as expected. These could simply be visual checks of transaction throughput or User simulation scripts that validate the end-to-end service.

> **Hints and tips**
>
> **There is potential for confusion in distinguishing the aspects of Incident Management appropriate to the Service Desk and those appropriate to Availability Management.**
>
> **The goal of the Incident Management process and the aims of Availability Management in designing for recovery are completely complementary, i.e. to restore normal business operation as quickly as possible and to minimise the impact to the business and User.**
>
> **The Incident Management process is used by the Service Desk to provide a structured and consistent approach to the handling, tracking and ultimate resolution of all Incidents. This is the management perspective best described by the Incident lifecycle (ITIL Service Support – Chapter 5).**
>
> **Availability Management is concerned with the methods, tools and techniques employed by the IT support organisation within each stage of the Incident Management 'lifecycle'. This is the technical perspective best described by the expanded Incident 'lifecycle' (ITIL Service Delivery).**

8.5.5   Security considerations

Availability Management is concerned with the Availability of all IT Service components, including data. Availability Management is therefore closely connected with Security Management. The importance of Availability being recognised as one third of the security 'CIA' tenet:

- Confidentiality
- Integrity
- Availability.

242

Example

An IT Service may not be available due to the erroneous deletion of data, this (security) Incident resulting in a breach of the Service Level Agreement.

The overall aim of IT security is 'balanced security in depth' with justifiable controls implemented to ensure continued IT Service within secure parameters (viz., **Confidentiality, Integrity** *and* **Availability**).

During the gathering of Availability requirements for new IT Services it is important that requirements that cover IT security are defined. These requirements need to be applied within the design phase for the supporting IT Infrastructure. The points made in the earlier Sections about designing Availability into the design at the earliest opportunity equally apply to security controls.

For many organisations the approach taken to IT security is covered by an IT security policy owned and maintained by Security Management. In the execution of security policy, Availability Management plays an important role in its operation for new IT Services.

Hints and tips

There is potential for confusion between the process owners for Security Management and Availability Management with regard to security requirements for new IT Services.

Security Management can be viewed as *accountable* for ensuring compliance to IT security policy for the implementation of new IT Services. Availability Management is *responsible* for ensuring security requirements are defined and incorporated within the overall Availability design.

Availability Management can gain guidance from the information contained within the organisation's IT security policy and associated procedures and methods. However, the following are typical security considerations that must, amongst others be addressed:

- products and services must only be available to authorised personnel
- products and services must be recoverable following failure to ensure confidentiality and integrity are not compromised and Availability of service not further compromised
- products and services must be recoverable within secure parameters, i.e. must not compromise IT security policy
- physical access to computer and network equipment should be restricted to authorised personnel only
- logical access to software should be restricted to authorised personnel only
- Operating System and Systems Management command authority should be commensurate with role and responsibility
- data must be available to authorised personnel at agreed times as specified in the SLA
- OLAs and underpinning contracts must reflect the adherence to security controls required by the IT support organisation.

Industry view

The Purpose of information security?

'Information Security protects information from a wide range of threats in order to ensure Business Continuity, minimise business damage and maximise return on investments and business opportunity'

Source: BS 7799 – The UK code of practice for Information Security.

For further reference to Information Security refer to ITIL Security Management, OGC, ISBN 011330014X.

8.5.6 Managing planned downtime

Maintenance

All IT components should be subject to a planned maintenance strategy. The frequency and levels of maintenance required varies from component to component taking into account the technologies involved, criticality and the potential business benefits that may be introduced.

Planned maintenance activities enable the IT support organisation to provide:

- preventative maintenance to avoid failures
- software or hardware upgrades to provide new functionality or additional Capacity
- business requested Changes to the business applications
- activation of new Infrastructure features for exploitation.

The requirement for planned downtime clearly influences the level of Availability that can be delivered for an IT Service, particularly those that have stringent Availability requirements.

In determining the Availability requirements for a new or enhanced IT Service the amount of downtime and the resultant loss of income required for planned maintenance may not be acceptable to the business. This is becoming a growing issue in the area of E-commerce. In these instances it is essential that continuous operation is a core design feature to enable maintenance activity to be performed without impacting the full IT Service.

Where the required service hours for IT Services are less than 24 hrs per day and/or 7 days per week, it is likely that the majority of planned maintenance can be accommodated without impacting IT Service Availability.

However, where the business needs IT Services available on a 24 hour and 7 day basis, Availability Management needs to determine the most effective approach in balancing the requirements for planned maintenance against the loss of service to the business. Unless mechanisms exist to allow continuous operation, scheduled downtime for planned maintenance is essential if high levels of Availability are to be achieved and sustained. For all IT Services there should logically be a 'low impact' period for the implementation of maintenance.

Once the requirements for managing scheduled maintenance have been defined and agreed, these should be documented as a minimum in the following:

■ SLAs

■ OLAs

■ underpinning contracts

■ Change Management schedules

■ Release Management schedules.

The areas responsible for implementing and managing Change, i.e. Service Desk, Network Management and Computer Operations, need to be made aware of the maintenance targets and any future revisions.

KEY MESSAGE

Availability Management should ensure that building in a low impact period for preventative maintenance is one of the prime design considerations for a '24 hours per day/7 days a week' IT Service.

Minimising business impact

Assessing service impact

The output from the Component Failure Impact Analysis (CFIA) indicates for a given component the impact on the User when the component is not available. The definition of IT Service downtime obtained when determining the Availability requirements establishes the level of business impact arising from the non-Availability of this component.

The CFIA also indicates if an alternative CI can continue to provide the service. Where an alternative CI is available, service impact is minimal dependent on how quickly the alternate CI is activated.

For components that have an alternative CI, the maintenance policy agreed with the internal or external supplier should be to ensure planned maintenance to these components are not scheduled concurrently.

Scheduling downtime

The most appropriate time to schedule planned downtime is clearly when the impact on the business and its Customers is least. This information should be provided initially by the business when determining the Availability requirements.

For an existing IT Service or once the new service has been established, monitoring of business and Customer transactions helps establish the hours where IT Service usage is at its lowest. This should determine the most appropriate timing window for the component(s) to be removed for planned maintenance activity.

Aggregation of maintenance activity

To accommodate the individual component requirements for planned downtime while balancing the IT Service Availability requirements of the business provides an opportunity to consider scheduling planned maintenance to multiple components concurrently.

The benefit of this approach is that the number of service disruptions required to meet the maintenance requirements is reduced.

While this approach has benefits, there are potential risks that need to be assessed, for example:

- the capability of the IT support organisation to co-ordinate the concurrent implementation of a high number of Changes

- the ability to perform effective Problem determination where the IT Service is impacted after the completion of multiple Changes

- the impact of Change dependency across multiple components where backout of a failed Change requires multiple Changes to be removed.

Service maintenance objectives

The effective management of planned downtime is an important contribution in meeting the required levels of Availability for an IT Service.

Where planned downtime is required on a cyclic basis to an IT component(s), the time that the component is unavailable to enable the planned maintenance activity to be undertaken should be defined and agreed with the internal or external supplier. This becomes a stated objective that can be formalised, measured and reported.

The Service Maintenance Objective (SMO) for a given planned maintenance activity should be the total time required for the IT component to be unavailable. The SMO should therefore be an aggregate of the following timeline events:

- the time required to prepare the component for the maintenance activity, e.g. closedown of the system software

- the time required to complete the implementation of the maintenance activity

- the time required to reinstate the component to enable IT Service to be resumed.

The benefits of defining Service Maintenance Objectives for cyclic planned maintenance activity are:

- to agree realistic implementation times for the planned maintenance activity

- to provide Change Management with advance information on Change duration

- to provide the business with advance information on the duration of service downtime

- to provide the time necessary to abort implementation and backout defective Change(s)

- to enable excess downtime to be recorded as a non-compliance with the appropriate supplier

- to provide a focus on implementation defects

- to provide a measure on quality of Change

- to provide a focus on planned downtime reduction and/or continuous operation techniques.

In addition they also provide an early warning during the maintenance activity of the time allocated to the planned outage duration being breached. This can enable an early decision to be made on whether the activity is allowed to complete with the potential to further impact service or to abort the activity and instigate the backout plan.

Planned downtime and performance against the stated SMO for each component should be recorded and used in service reporting.

Validation

An IT organisation that supported a 24 hr IT Service looked at ways that they could reduce the amount of downtime required for scheduled maintenance. A review of the scheduled outages revealed wide ranges in the amount of downtime incurred. These were due to a combination of Change quality issues impacting the implementation and operational issues with system closedown and restart procedures. Responsibilities for the successful implementation of the Changes were split between the area of the IT support organisation supplying the Change and the operational area responsible for implementing the Change.

The first step taken was to get both parties to agree on what should be a realistic time to complete the Change implementation (closedown, application of Change, restart of system).

Once agreed this was documented as a formal agreement between both parties upon which there was a shared ownership for meeting the maintenance objective.

Formal reporting and regular reviews were held. The reasons for failing to meet the target were investigated and addressed. In addition both parties explored opportunities to reduce the target time allocated. Where improvements were made and the results showed a sustained improvement a new maintenance objective was set.

This process continued year on year until the implementation time was considered optimal. In this time the duration for planned mainframe maintenance had been reduced from extremes of 3 hrs to consistently less then one hour.

8.6   Availability improvement

A key output from the Availability Management process is the creation of an Availability Plan.

The Availability Plan should be a long-term plan for the proactive improvement of IT Availability within the imposed cost constraints.

The impetus to improve Availability comes from one or more of the following:

- the inability for a new IT Service to meets its SLA on a consistent basis
- period(s) of IT Service instability resulting in unacceptable levels of Availability

- Availability measurement trends indicating a gradual deterioration in Availability

- unacceptable IT Service recovery and restoration time

- requests from the business to increase the level of Availability provided

- increasing impact on the business and its Customers from IT Service failures as a result of growth and/or increased business functionality

- a request from SLM to improve Availability as part of an overall SIP

- Availability Management monitoring and trend analysis.

8.6.1 Important considerations

Availability Management monitoring and trend analysis

Availability Management should take a proactive role in identifying and progressing cost justified Availability improvement opportunities. The ability to do this places reliance on having appropriate and meaningful Availability measurement and reporting.

To ensure Availability improvements deliver benefits to the business and Users it is important that Availability measurement and reporting reflects not just IT component Availability but Availability from a business operation and User perspective. (See Section 8.7 for additional guidance).

Determining (changed) Availability requirements

Where the business has a requirement to improve Availability the process outlined in Section 8.5 should be followed to reassess the IT Infrastructure and IT support organisation capability to meet these enhanced requirements.

An output of this activity is enhanced Availability and recovery design criteria.

The cost of improving Availability

To satisfy the business requirement for increased levels of Availability may require additional financial investment to enhance the underpinning IT Infrastructure and/or extend the services provided by the IT support organisation.

It is important that any additional investment to improve the levels of Availability delivered can be cost justified. Determining the cost of an IT failure(s) can help support any financial investment decision. Section 8.4 provides additional guidance on how to derive the cost of IT failure.

However, a key benefit of Availability Management is the opportunity to optimise the Availability of the IT Infrastructure to deliver an improved level of Availability with reduced cost. This optimisation approach is a sensible first step to deliver better value for money. A range of Availability Management methods and techniques can be applied to identify the potential for improved levels of Availability at a much lower cost.

8.6.2 Methods and techniques

There are a number of methods and techniques that can be utilised to identify Availability improvement opportunities. These are described as follows:

Component Failure Impact Assessment

Component Failure Impact Assessment (CFIA) can be used to predict and evaluate the impact on IT Service arising from component failures within the IT Infrastructure. The output from a CFIA can be used to identify where additional Infrastructure resilience should be considered to prevent or minimise the impact of component failure to the business operation and Users.

Fault Tree Analysis

Fault Tree Analysis (FTA) is a technique that can be used to determine the chain of events that causes a disruption to IT Services. FTA in conjunction with calculation methods can offer detailed models of Availability. This can be used to assess the Availability improvement that can be achieved by individual IT Infrastructure design options.

CRAMM

CRAMM can be used to identify new risks and provide appropriate countermeasures associated with any Change to the business Availability requirement and revised IT Infrastructure design. See Paragraph 8.9.3 for fuller information on CRAMM.

Systems Outage Analysis

Systems Outage Analysis (SOA) is a technique designed to provide a structured approach to identifying the underlying causes of service interruption to the User. SOA utilises a range of data sources to assess where and why shortfalls in Availability are occurring. SOA enables an holistic view to be taken to drive not just IT Infrastructure improvements but improvements to the IT support organisation process, procedures and tools.

SOA is run as an assignment and may utilise other Availability Management methods and techniques to formulate the recommendations for improvement.

The Expanded Incident 'lifecycle'

An aim of Availability Management is to ensure the duration and impact from Incidents impacting IT Service are minimised, to enable business operations to resume as quickly as is possible.

The expanded Incident 'lifecycle' enables the total IT Service downtime for any given Incident to be broken down and mapped against the major stages that all Incidents progress through (the lifecycle).

This makes it possible to identify where 'time is being lost' and provides the basis for the identification of improvements that can improve recovery and restoration times.

Continuous Improvement

Availability Management can play an important role in helping the IT support organisation recognise where they can add value by exploiting their technical skills and competencies in an Availability context. The continuous improvement technique can be used by Availability Management to harness this technical capability. This can be used with either small groups of technical staff or a wider group within a workshop environment.

Technical Observation Post

A Technical Observation Post (TOP) is a prearranged gathering of specialist technical support staff from within the IT support organisation brought together to focus on specific aspects of IT Availability. Its purpose being to monitor events, real time as they occur, with the specific aim of identifying improvement opportunities or bottlenecks which exist within the current IT Infrastructure.

For more detailed information and guidance on how these methods and techniques can be deployed please refer to Section 8.9.

8.6.3   The Availability Plan

To provide structure and aggregation of the wide range of initiatives that may need to be undertaken to improve Availability, these should be formulated within a single Availability Plan.

The Availability Plan should have aims, objectives and deliverables and should consider the wider issues of people, process, tools and techniques as well as having a technology focus. In the initial stages it may be aligned with an implementation plan for Availability Management, but the two are different and should not be confused.

As the Availability Management process matures the plan should evolve to cover the following:

- Actual levels of Availability versus agreed levels of Availability for key IT Services. Where possible Availability measurements should be business focused to report Availability as experienced by the business and User.

- Activities being progressed to address shortfalls in Availability for existing IT Services. Where investment decisions are required, options with associated costs and benefits should be included.

- Details of changing Availability requirements for existing IT Services. The plan should document the options available to meet these Changed requirements. Where investment decisions are required the associated costs of each option should be included.

- Details of the Availability requirements for forthcoming new IT Services. The plan should document the options available to meet these new requirements. Where investment decisions are required the associated costs of each option should be included.

- A forward looking schedule for the planned SOA assignments.

- Regular reviews of SOA assignments should be completed to ensure that Infrastructure Availability is being proactively improved.

- A technology futures section to provide an indication of the potential benefits and exploitation opportunities that exist for planned technology upgrades. Anticipated Availability benefits should be detailed, where possible based on business focused measures. The effort required to realise these benefits where possible should also be quantified.

During the production of the Availability Plan, it is recommenced that liaison with the following functional areas is undertaken:

- Service Level Management, concerning changing business and User requirements for existing IT Services

- IT Service Continuity Management concerning business impact and resilience improvements

- Business Relationship Management to understand major Customer concerns and/or future needs that relate to IT Availability

- Capacity Management, concerning the scenarios for upgrading (or downgrading) the software, hardware and network layers of the IT Infrastructure

- IT Financial Management concerning the cost and budget implications of the various options identified for Availability improvement

- Application Management, concerning the Availability requirements for new services

- areas responsible for IT supplier management and the managing of relationships and contracts with suppliers

■ technical support groups responsible for testing and maintenance functions, concerning the reliability and maintainability of existing services.

The Availability Plan should cover a period of one to two years with a more detailed view and information for the first six months. The plan should be reviewed regularly with minor revisions every quarter and major revisions every half year. Where the IT Infrastructure is only subject to a low level of Change this may be extended as appropriate.

It is recommended that the Availability Plan is considered complementary to the Capacity Plan and publication aligned with the Capacity and business Budgeting cycle.

If a demand is foreseen for high levels of Availability that cannot be met due to the constraints of the existing IT Infrastructure or budget, then exception reports may be required for the attention of both senior IT and business management.

Hints and tips

There is potential for confusion on the purpose of an Availability Plan versus a Service Improvement Programme.

The Availability Plan is a forward looking plan aimed at improving the overall Availability of the IT Infrastructure to ensure that existing and future levels of Availability can be provided on a timely and cost effective basis.

The Availability Plan is a key output and deliverable of the Availability Management process. It is reviewed and revised on an ongoing basis. Improvements to the IT Infrastructure may benefit many IT Services where common Infrastructure is utilised.

Service Level Management is responsible for instigating service improvements that improve the overall quality of the whole IT Service provision.

The mechanism used to achieve this is the Service Improvement Programme (SIP). This SIP should be used to co-ordinate all IT Service improvement opportunities into an overall programme of improvement activities.

The SIP has a defined start and end and its scope can include all elements of the service provided to the business. This may include Availability, but equally may not dependent on the overall service indicators and the areas of desired improvement.

Availability Management can play a key role in supporting a SIP by the appropriate use of Availability Management techniques, e.g. Systems Outage Analysis.

8.7 Availability measurement and reporting

A key output from the Availability Management process is the measurement and reporting of IT Availability. This provides the basis for:

- establishing measures of Availability and agreeing Availability targets with the business
- monitoring of the actual Availability delivered versus agreed targets
- identifying unacceptable levels of Availability that impact the business and User
- reviewing Availability with the business and User representatives
- reviewing Availability with the IT support organisation
- continuous improvement activities to optimise Availability.

Availability measures should be incorporated into SLAs, OLAs and any underpinning contracts. These should be reviewed regularly at Service Level review meetings.

Famous saying and truths about measurements:

'If you don't measure it, you can't manage it'

'If you don't measure it, you can't improve it'

'If you don't measure it, you probably don't care'

'If you can't influence it, then don't measure it'

8.7.1   IT Availability reporting

'What to measure and how to report it' inevitably depends on which activity is being supported, who the recipients are and how the information is to be utilised. It is important to recognise the differing perspectives of Availability to ensure measurement and reporting satisfies these varied needs:

- the **IT Support Organisation** perspective considers IT component Availability with regard to Availability, Reliability and Maintainability.
- the **User** perspective considers IT Service Availability as a combination of three factors, namely the frequency, the duration and the scope of impact, i.e. all Users, some Users, all business functions or certain business functions – the User also considers IT Service Availability in terms of response times. For many performance-centric applications poor response times are considered equal in impact to IT component failures.
- the **Business** perspective considers IT Service Availability in terms of its contribution or impact on the vital business functions that drive the business operation.

In order to satisfy the differing perspectives of Availability, Availability Management needs to consider the spectrum of measures needed to report the 'same' level of Availability in different ways. Measurements need to be meaningful and add value if Availability measurement and reporting are ultimately to deliver benefit to the IT and business organisations. This is influenced strongly by the combination of 'what you measure' and 'how you report it'.

KEY MESSAGE

Availability Management needs to consider Availability from an IT Service perspective and from an IT component perspective. These are entirely different aspects. While the underlying concept is similar, the measurement, focus and impact are entirely different.

8.7.2   IT Availability measures – the traditional view

The IT support organisation have for many years measured and reported on their perspective of Availability. Traditionally these measures have concentrated on component Availability and have been somewhat divorced from the business and User views.

Typically these traditional measures are based on a combination of an Availability percentage (%), time lost and the frequency of failure. Some examples of these traditional measures are as follows:

- **% Available** – The truly 'traditional' measure which represents Availability as a percentage and, as such, much more useful as a component Availability measure than a service Availability measure. It is typically used to track and report achievement against a service level target. It tends to emphasise the 'big number' such that if the service level target was 98.5% and the achievement was 98.3%, then it does not seem that bad. This can encourage a complacent behaviour within the IT support organisation.

- **% Unavailable** – The inverse of above. This representation however has the benefit of focusing on non-Availability. Based on the above example, if the target for non-Availability is 1.5% and the achievement was 1.7% then this is a much larger relative difference. This method of reporting is more likely to create awareness of the shortfall in delivering the level of Availability required.

- **Duration** – Achieved by converting the percentage unavailable into hours and minutes. This provides a more 'human' measure that people can relate to. If the weekly downtime target is 2 hrs but one week the actual was 4 hrs; this would represent a trend leading to an additional 4 days of non-Availability to the business over a full year. This type of measure and reporting is more likely to encourage focus on service improvement.

- **Frequency of failure** – Used to record the number of interruptions to the IT Service. It helps provide a good indication of reliability from an User perspective. It is best used in combination with 'duration' to take a balanced view of the level of service interruptions and the duration of time lost to the business.

- **Impact of failure** – This is the true measure of service UnAvailability. It depends upon mature Incident recording where the inability of Users to perform their business tasks is the most important piece of information captured. All other measures suffer from a potential to mask the real effects of service failure.

The business may have, for many years, accepted as a fait accompli that the IT Availability that they experience is represented in this way. However, this is no longer being viewed as acceptable and the business is keen to better represent Availability in measure(s) that demonstrate the positive and negative consequences of IT Availability on their business and Users.

8.7.3   The disadvantages of traditional IT Availability measures

The continued advances in IT technology design and service management focus are resulting in Availability improvements. These improvements are clearly evidenced by the traditional IT Availability measurements.

A positive consequence of technology advancement and IT Availability improvements is the creation of new business opportunity i.e. to offer new and enhanced services, to gain more Customers and to increase Customer value. However, with this business benefit comes an increased business dependency on IT Availability and a greater business impact when IT failure occurs.

Figure 8.10 illustrates an interesting paradox. The traditional IT Availability measures show a trend of continuous improvement with non-Availability declining. Whereas the business oriented measures used by the business show the impact from non-Availability increasing!

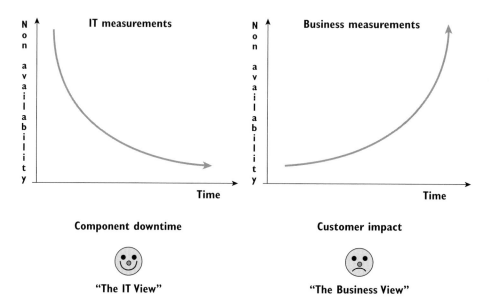

Figure 8.10 – The disadvantages of traditional IT Availability measurements

The traditional IT approach to measurement and reporting provides an indicator on IT Availability and component reliability which is important for the internal IT support organisation. However, to the business and User these measures fail to reflect Availability from their perspective and are rarely understood. This often fuels mistrust between the business and IT where despite periods of instability the '%' target has been met even though significant business disruption has occurred and Customer complaints have been received.

Furthermore, this method of measurement and reporting can often hide the benefits delivered to the business from IT improvements. The traditional IT Availability measures can simply mask real IT 'added value' to the business operation.

While the traditional IT Availability measurement and reporting methods can be considered appropriate for internal IT reporting, the disadvantages of this approach are that they:

■   fail to reflect IT Availability as experienced by the business and the User

■   can conceal service 'hot spots' whereby regular reporting shows the SLA 'met', but the business and/or User is becoming increasingly dissatisfied with the IT Service

■   do not easily support continuous improvement opportunities to drive improvements that can benefit the business and the User

■ can mask IT 'value add' where tangible benefits to the business and User have been
delivered but the method of measurement and reporting does not make this visible.

8.7.4 Measuring User Availability

Availability, when measured and reported to reflect the experience of the User, provides a more
representative view on overall IT Service quality.

The User view of Availability is influenced by three factors:

■ the frequency of downtime

■ the duration of downtime

■ the scope of impact.

Measurements and reporting of User Availability should therefore embrace these factors.

The methodology employed to reflect User Availability could consider two approaches:

■ Impact by User minutes lost. This is to base calculations on the duration of downtime
multiplied by the number of Users impacted. This can be the basis to report Availability
as lost User productivity or to calculate the Availability percentage from a User
perspective.

■ Impact by business transaction. This is to base calculations on the number of business
transactions that could not be processed during the period of downtime. This provides a
better indication of business impact reflecting differing transaction processing profiles
across the time of day, week etc. In many instances it may be the case that the User
impact correlates to a vital business function, e.g. if the User takes Customer purchase
orders and a vital business function is Customer sales. This single measure is the basis to
reflect impact to the business operation and User.

The method employed should be influenced by the nature of the business operation. A business
operation supporting data entry activity is well suited to reporting that reflects User productivity loss.
Business operations that are more Customer facing, e.g. ATM services, benefit from reporting
transaction impact.

8.7.5 Business driven measurement and reporting

The IT support organisation needs to have a keen awareness of the User experience of Availability.
However, the real benefits come from aggregating the User view into the overall business view.

A guiding principle of the Availability Management process is that '**Improving Availability can only
begin when the way technology supports the business is understood**'. Therefore Availability
Management is not just about understanding the Availability of each IT component.

From the business perspective, an IT Service can only be considered available when the business is
able to perform all vital business functions required to drive the business operation. For the IT Service
to be available it is therefore reliant on all components on which the service depends to be available,
i.e. system, key components, network, data and application.

The traditional IT approach would be to measure individually the Availability of each of these
components. However, the true measure of Availability has to be based upon the positive and negative
impacts on the vital business functions upon which the business operation is dependent.

This approach ensures that SLAs and IT Availability reporting are based on measures that are understood by both the business and IT. By measuring the vital business functions that rely upon IT, measurement and reporting becomes business driven with the impact of failure reflecting the consequences to the business.

> **Industry view**
>
> 'Effective management requires the ability to view Availability from the perspective of the business application'
>
> Source: – International Data Corporation

Establishing the VBF to measure

This clearly needs to be undertaken and agreed with the business. A simple way to establish this is to simply ask the business *'what is the major consequence on your business or Customers if there is an IT failure?'*

While for most IT Services the major consequence will be understood and obvious, it is still worth probing the business on their initial response to ensure that jointly the true consequence is established.

> **Example**
>
> ATM service
>
> Q: – what is the major consequence on your business or Customers if there is an IT failure?
>
> Is it:
>
> A1: The consequence of IT failure impacting an ATM service is that our ATM machines are unavailable.
>
> A2: The consequence of IT failure impacting an ATM service is that our Customers cannot obtain cash from our ATM machines.
>
> While both are correct, the vital business function for an ATM service is the ability to dispense cash not provide an ATM. The more meaningful and powerful metric to measure therefore is the obtaining of cash.

Benefits

The benefits of basing Availability measurement and reporting upon the vital business functions can be summarised as follows:

- provides a 'common' measure which both parties to the SLA can understand
- can visibly demonstrate to the business tangible service improvement enabling the IT organisation to show the 'added value'
- can more easily identify degrading levels of service to enable the IT support organisation to be proactive in responding without formal business escalation

■ can be used to demonstrate the business and User impact with suppliers to drive and influence positive supplier behaviour.

Problems

Some of the possible problems with trying to develop this approach are:

■ how to relate business experience to Incidents, especially if no end-to-end monitoring is available

■ an absolute measure, e.g. number of business transactions impacted, on a rapidly expanding IT Service can show a downward trend even when the overall % Availability improves

■ who owns the VBF measurements and data

■ integration and mapping of this data with IT component Availability data.

See Section 8.9 for some example approaches that can be undertaken to develop business and User driven measurement.

8.7.6   What to measure

To satisfy the differing reporting needs of the business and IT support organisation it is necessary to provide a spectrum of measures that reflect the differing perspectives of IT Service and component Availability.

The following are examples of the different elements of an IT Service that should be measured and reported:

Vital business functions

To provide measurement and reporting that demonstrate the consequences (contribution and impact) of IT Availability on the business function(s) key to the business operation, e.g. for a Tele-sales business a vital business function would be Customer order fulfilment.

Application services

To provide measurement and reporting of the application services required to run the business operation and service User input.

Data

To provide the measurement and reporting of data Availability that is essential to support the business operation. For example, many business operations are dependent on all data being updated by overnight batch processing to provide a new 'start of day' position.

Key components

To provide measurement and reporting that reflects Availability, Reliability and Maintainability of IT Infrastructure components supplied and maintained by the IT Support Organisation.

Platform

To provide measurement and reporting of the IT platform that ultimately supports the processing of the business application(s).

Reporting dimensions

To provide a balanced and meaningful view of the Availability of an IT Service or component, reporting should consider the following dimensions:

Availability

To provide measurement and reporting that reflects Availability against defined and agreed targets.

Reliability

To provide measurement and reporting that reflects the frequency of failures.

Maintainability

To provide measurement and reporting that reflects the duration of failures.

Response times

To provide measurement and reporting that reflects the performance as experienced by the User. Capacity Management may supply (reports).

8.7.7   IT Availability Metrics Model

The IT Availability Metrics Model (ITAMM) in Figure 8.11 is recommended as an aid to considering the range of measures and reporting dimensions that should be borne in mind when establishing Availability measurement and reporting.

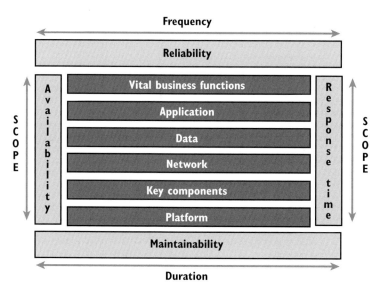

Figure 8.11 – The IT Availability Metrics Model

> **KEY MESSAGE**
>
> **Measurements need to be meaningful and add value if Availability measurement and reporting are to ultimately deliver benefit to the IT and business organisation. This is influenced strongly by the combination of 'what you measure' and 'how you report it'.**

Gaining additional value from measurement and reporting

Consider where the Availability measurement and reporting produced to support the Availability Management process can be used as input to other IT Service Management processes. Some examples are as follows:

- Capacity Management: – to highlight Availability trends that indicate Capacity or response time issues

- IT Financial Management: – to provide cost of failure information, incorporate Availability levels into profit/cost models

- Service Level Management: – to provide reporting for SLA and OLA activities

- Incident and Problem Management: – to highlight Problem blackspots impacting Availability, useful areas for increasing preventative maintenance

- Change Management: – Availability impact due to poor quality Change, % of planned maintenance activities that have overrun their agreed Service Maintenance Objectives.

8.8 Availability Management tools

Availability Management, to be effective, needs a range of tools to support the key activities of the process. The initial tool requirements to support the establishment of Availability Management can be summarised as follows:

- IT component downtime data capture and recording
- Database repositories for the collection of appropriate Availability data and information
- Report generation
- Statistical analysis
- Availability modelling
- Systems Management.

It is important when considering the requirements for tools to initially distinguish between those that are required to support the activities associated with the Availability Management process and those required to improve IT Availability, i.e. Systems Management.

However tool selection should be influenced where an integrated solution is available that meets the needs of the process while helping achieve the overall aim of improved levels of Availability.

8.8.1   IT component downtime data capture and recording

The capture and recording of data pertaining to IT component downtime (planned and unplanned) is a key requirement for the forecasting and reporting of Availability. It would be usual to find this information available from the Service Desk, Problem Management and Change Management sections of the IT support organisation.

To improve the accuracy and quality of information it is recommended that component downtime detection and data recording be automated.

8.8.2   Database repositories

Shared database repositories

A number of database repository tools are required to support other IT Infrastructure Management processes. Therefore, the implementation and deployment of Availability Management can be simplified where these database tools already exist.

The database support tools that can be utilised by Availability Management are as follows:

Configuration Management Database

The Configuration Management Database (CMDB) provides information regarding the IT Infrastructure configuration. Information from the CMDB can provide essential input to assist Availability Management with forecasting the Availability of a given IT Infrastructure, assessing single points of failure, identification of IT component owners etc.

The CMDB is also an essential source of information relating to Incidents, Problems and Changes affecting the IT Infrastructure and IT Services.

Capacity Management Database

The Capacity Management Database (CDB) provides information regarding the Capacity Management of the IT Infrastructure. Information from the CDB can provide essential input to assist Availability Management identify planned upgrades to hardware, software and network components, workload and application Capacity/performance data.

The Availability Management Database

Availability Management may wish to consider having its own database repository. The Availability Management Database (AMDB) can be utilised to record and store selected data and information required to support key activities such as report generation, statistical analysis and Availability forecasting.

The AMDB should be the main repository for the recording of IT Availability metrics based on the ITAMM model.

The AMDB can also be used to store Availability Management deliverables such as the Availability Plan and SOA assignment report and action plans.

All other information pertaining to Availability should reside within the CMDB and CDB to provide reusability of data to multiple IT Service Management processes and avoid unnecessary duplication and cost.

Hints and tips

Be pragmatic. Define the initial tool requirements and identify what is already deployed that can be used and shared to get started as quickly as possible.

Where basic tools are not already available, work with other IT Service Management disciplines to identify common requirements with the aim of selecting shared tools and minimising costs.

The AMDB should address specific reporting needs of Availability Management not provided/or accommodated by existing repositories.

8.8.3   Report generation and statistical analysis

Reporting and analysis tools are required for the manipulation of data stored in the various databases utilised by Availability Management. These tools can either be platform or PC based. This will be influenced by the database repository technologies selected and the complexity of data processing and reporting required.

Availability Management, once implemented and deployed, will be required to produce regular reports on an agreed basis, e.g. monthly Availability reports, Availability Plan, SOA status reports etc.

However the proactive nature of the role in seeking opportunities to further optimise the Availability of the IT Infrastructure and the need to respond to emerging Availability requirements requires flexibility. When defining requirements the need for interactive database query tools should be stated as an essential requirement.

For reporting purposes organisational reporting standards should be used wherever possible. If these don't exist then IT standards should be developed so that IT reports can be developed using standard tools and techniques. This means that the integration and consolidation of reports will subsequently be much easier to achieve.

8.8.4   Availability modelling

Modelling tools are required to forecast Availability and to assess the impact of Changes to the IT Infrastructure. Inputs to the modelling process include descriptive data of the component reliability, maintainability and serviceability.

A spreadsheet package to perform calculations is usually sufficient. If more detailed and accurate data is required a more complex modelling tool may need to be developed. The lack of readily available Availability modelling tools in the marketplace may require such a tool to be developed and maintained 'in-house'.

Unless there is a clearly perceived benefit from such a development and the ongoing maintenance costs, the use of existing tools and spreadsheets should be sufficient.

8.8.5   Systems Management

An output from the Availability Management process is the real time monitoring requirements for IT Services and components. To achieve the levels of Availability required and/or ensure the rapid restoration of service following an IT failure requires investment and exploitation of a systems management toolset.

Systems Management tools are an essential building block for IT Services that require a high level of Availability (see Figure 8.9) and can provide an invaluable role in reducing the amount of downtime incurred.

Availability Management requirements cover the detection and alerting of IT Service and component exceptions, automated escalation and notification of IT failures and the automated recovery and restoration of components from known IT failure situations.

8.9   Availability Management methods and techniques

The capability of the Availability Management process is positively influenced by the range and quality of methods and techniques that are available for deployment and execution within the process.

To provide the reader and prospective process owners with the benefits of established best practice within the field of Availability Management this Section documents a number of proven methods and techniques that can be applied to support key activities within the process. These are:

- Component Failure Impact Analysis (CFIA)
- Fault Tree Analysis (FTA)
- CRAMM
- Calculating Availability
- Calculating the cost of UnAvailability
- Developing basic IT Availability measurement and reporting
- Developing business and User measurement and reporting
- Systems Outage Analysis (SOA)
- The Incident 'lifecycle'
- Continuous improvement methodology
- Technical Observation Post (TOP).

The above techniques support the three key facets of Availability Management, namely the planning for Availability, the improvement of Availability and the reporting of Availability.

Table 8.1 provides guidance on which aspect of Availability Management these techniques can be utilised:–

Technique	Facet	Availability Planning	Availability Improvement	Availability Reporting
CFIA		✓	✓	✓
FTA		✓	✓	
CRAMM		✓	✓	
Calculating Availability		✓	✓	✓
Calculating the Cost of Unavailability		✓	✓	✓
Developing basic IT Availability measurement and reporting			✓	✓
Developing business and User measurement and reporting			✓	✓
SOA			✓	
The expanded Incident 'Lifecycle'		✓	✓	✓
Continuous improvement			✓	
TOP			✓	

Table 8.1 – Guidance on the use of Availability Management techniques

8.9.1   Component Failure Impact Analysis

During the 'design for Availability' activities it is necessary to predict and evaluate the impact on IT Service Availability arising from component failures within the proposed IT Infrastructure and service design.

Component Failure Impact Analysis (CFIA) is a relatively simple technique that can be used to provide this information. IBM devised CFIA in the early 1970s with its origins based on hardware design and configuration. However, it is recommended that CFIA be used in a much wider context to reflect the full scope of the IT Infrastructure, i.e. hardware, network, software, application and Users.

Additionally the technique can also be applied to identify impact and dependencies on IT support organisation skills and competencies amongst staff supporting the new IT Service.

This activity is often completed in conjunction with ITSCM.

Benefits of CFIA

The output from a CFIA provides vital information to ensure that the Availability and Recovery design criteria for the new IT Service is influenced to prevent or minimise the impact of failure to the business operation and User.

CFIA achieves this by providing and indicating:

- single points of failure that can impact IT Availability
- the impact of component failure on the business operation and Users
- component and people dependencies
- component recovery timings
- the need to identify and document recovery options
- the need to identify and implement risk reduction measures.

The above can also provide the stimulus for input to ITSCM to consider the balance between recovery options and risk reduction measures, i.e. where the potential business impact is high there is a need to concentrate on high Availability risk reduction measures, i.e. increased resilience or standby systems.

Performing a CFIA

Basic CFIA

Having determined the IT Infrastructure configuration to be assessed, the first step is to create a grid with CIs on one axis and the IT Services which have a dependency on the CI on the other. This information should be available from the CMDB. Alternatively this can be built using documented configuration charts and SLAs.

The next step is to perform the following procedure at each intersection point in the grid:

- leave a blank when a failure of the CI does not impact the service in any way
- insert an 'X' when the failure of the CI causes the IT Service to be inoperative
- insert an 'A' when there is an alternative CI to provide the service
- insert a 'B' when there is an alternative CI, but the service has to be recovered first.

Figure 8.12 contains a completed grid for the configuration shown.

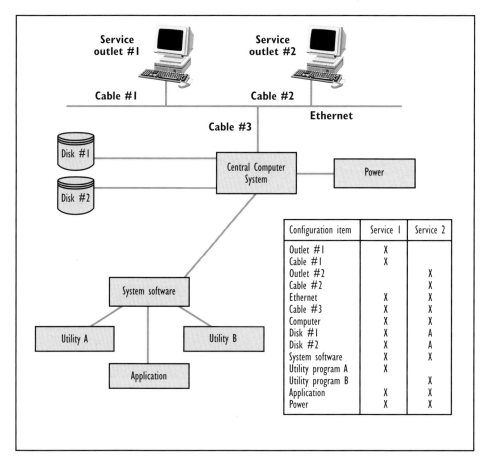

Configuration item	Service 1	Service 2
Outlet #1	X	
Cable #1	X	
Outlet #2		X
Cable #2		X
Ethernet	X	X
Cable #3	X	X
Computer	X	X
Disk #1	X	A
Disk #2	X	A
System software	X	X
Utility program A	X	
Utility program B		X
Application	X	X
Power	X	X

Figure 8.12 – Sample configuration and basic CFIA grid

Having built the grid, CIs that have a large number of Xs are critical to many services and can result in high impact should the CI fail. Equally, IT Services that have high counts of Xs are complex and are vulnerable to failure.

This basic approach to CFIA can provide valuable information in quickly identifying single points of failure, IT Services at risk from CI failure and what alternatives are available should CI fail.

It should also be used to assess the existence and validity of recovery procedures for the selected CIs.

The above example assumes common Infrastructure supporting multiple IT Services. The same approach can be used for a single IT Service by mapping the component CIs against the vital business functions and Users supported by each component, thus understanding the impact of a component failure on the business and User. This approach is illustrated in Table 8.2.

Configuration Item	VBF	End Users Impacted
Power	All	1,000
Central computer	All	1,000
Applications	All	1,000
Disk # 1	Payments	50
Disk # 2	Orders	100
Utility A	Enquiry	25

Table 8.2 – CFIA matrix reflecting association between components, VBF and User population

Advanced CFIA

The above approach can be expanded to provide more detailed information and/or to extend the coverage of the CFIA e.g. data feeds from 3rd party organisations.

Hints and tips

An online IT Service can be impacted by failures in batch processing, e.g. the IT Service is unable to be started due to dependencies on the completion of overnight database updates.

A suggested first step prior to undertaking an advanced CFIA is to identify all the software CIs that are essential to the 24hr processing cycle. These would include for example transaction processing subsystems, Network Management subsystems, Security Management subsystems, systems management subsystems such as tape management, silo management, job scheduling.

It can also include software CIs that support key IT operational processes such as Incident Management, Problem Management, Change Management and Configuration Management.

To undertake an advanced CFIA requires the CFIA matrix to be expanded to provide any additional fields required for the more detailed analysis.

Some examples of the additional fields that can be included are as follows:

■ Probability of Failure – this can be based on the Mean Time Between Failure (MTBF) information if available or on the current Availability trends. This can be expressed as a low/medium/high indicator or as a numeric representation.

- Recovery Time – this is the estimated recovery time to recover the CI. This can be based on recent recovery timings, recovery information from disaster recovery testing or a scheduled test recovery.

- Recovery procedures – this is to verify that up to date recovery procedures are available for the CI.

- Device Independence – where software CIs have duplex files to provide resilience this is to ensure that file placements have been verified as being on separate hardware disk configurations.

- Dependent IDs – this is to show any dependencies between CIs. If one CI is to fail, there may be an impact on other CIs, e.g. if the security CI was to fail, the operating system may prevent tape processing.

USING CFIA TO IMPROVE RECOVERY FROM FAILURE

A detailed CFIA provides additional information that can be used to improve recoverability. While technology design is continually improving as yet no IT CI can ever be considered fail-safe.

A detailed CFIA can provide important information to support the recovery process:

- Recovery timings – to enable IT to provide the business with accurate estimations of when service can be restored

- alternative available – to identify what alternative recovery options are available in the event of a CI failure

- Recovery procedures – confidence that valid recovery procedures exist for each CI

- dependencies – what other CIs may have a dependency, a scenario being that a failed CI may have a low impact but if not recovered quickly may cause a dependent CI to fail or stop processing causing high impact.

Example

A tape management software failure preventing tape usage may not immediately impact the User. However, the Online Transaction Processing Systems (OLTP) may need to regularly archive system logs to tape. If this cannot be achieved, after a period of time the OLTP may suspend processing directly impacting the User.

8.9.2   Fault Tree Analysis

Fault Tree Analysis (FTA) is a technique that can be used to determine the chain of events that causes a disruption of IT Services. This technique, in conjunction with calculation methods can offer detailed models of Availability.

The main advantages of FTA are:

- FTA can be used for Availability calculations
- operations can be performed on the resulting fault tree; these operations correspond with design options

■   the desired level of detail in the analysis can be chosen.

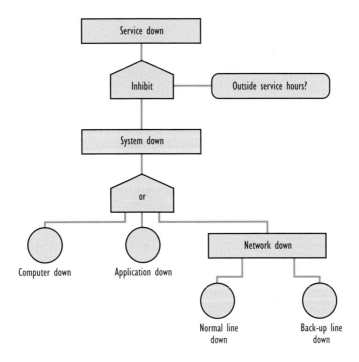

Figure 8.13 – Example Fault Tree

FTA makes a representation of a chain of events using Boolean notation. Figure 8.13 gives an example of a fault tree.

Essentially FTA distinguishes the following events:

■   **Basic events** – terminal points for the fault tree, e.g. power failure, operator error. Basic events are not investigated in greater depth. If basic events are investigated in further depth, they automatically become resulting events.

■   **Resulting events** – intermediate nodes in the fault tree resulting from a combination of events. The top most point in the fault tree is usually a failure of the IT Service.

■   **Conditional events** – events that only occur under certain conditions, e.g. failure of the air-conditioning equipment only affects the IT Service if equipment temperature exceeds the serviceable values.

■   **Trigger events** – events that trigger other events, e.g. power failure detection equipment can trigger automatic shutdown of IT Services.

These events can be combined using logic operators, i.e.:

■   **AND-gate** – the resulting event only occurs when all input events occur simultaneously

■   **OR-gate** – the resulting event occurs when one or more of the input events occurs

■   **Exclusive OR-gate** – the resulting event occurs when one and only one of the input events occurs

■   **Inhibit gate** – the resulting event only occurs when the input condition is not met.

The mathematical evaluation of a fault tree is beyond the scope of this Chapter.

8.9.3 CRAMM

The identification of risks and the provision of justified countermeasures to reduce or eliminate the threats posed by such risks can play an important role in achieving the required levels of Availability for a new or enhanced IT Service.

Risk Analysis should be undertaken during the design phase for the IT Infrastructure and service to identify:

■ Risks that may incur non-Availability for the IT components within the IT Infrastructure and service design

■ Risks that may incur confidentiality and/or integrity exposures within the IT Infrastructure and service design.

CRAMM describes a means of identifying justifiable countermeasures to protect Confidentiality, Integrity and Availability of the IT Infrastructure.

The general concepts can be represented by a simple diagram that shows Risk Analysis and Risk Management as being two related but separate activities in Figure 8.14

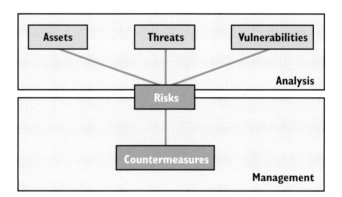

Figure 8.14 – Risk Analysis Management

Risk Analysis involves the identification and assessment of the level (measure) of the risks calculated from the assessed values of assets and the assessed levels of threats to, and vulnerabilities of, those assets.

Risk Management involves the identification, selection and adoption of countermeasures justified by the identified risks to assets in terms of their potential impact upon services if failure occurs, and the reduction of those risks to an acceptable level.

This approach when applied via a formal method ensures coverage is complete together with sufficient confidence that:

■ all possible Risks and Countermeasures have been identified

■ all Vulnerabilities have been identified and their levels accurately assessed

■ all Threats have been identified and their levels accurately assessed

■ all results are consistent across the broad spectrum of the IT Infrastructure reviewed

■ all expenditure on selected Countermeasures can be justified.

Formal Risk Analysis and Management methods are now an important element in the overall provision of IT Services.

> **Hints and tips**
>
> **CRAMM is a methodology that can be utilised by a number of IT Service Management processes.**
>
> **CRAMM is used and referenced within Chapter 7.**
>
> **'CRAMM is the UK Government's preferred Risk Analysis and Management method for identifying all the necessary technical and non-technical controls to ensure the security of both current and future information systems processing valuable or protectively marked data.' – UK Security Service.**

8.9.4 Calculating Availability

This Section describes some of the simple mathematics required to enable component and total Infrastructure Availability to be calculated. This information is needed to help formulate Availability targets for IT components and IT Services. Additionally, these output calculations can also be input to any Availability modelling tools that are available.

The examples provided in this Section are fairly straightforward with the calculations presented sufficient to provide adequate estimates of Availability. Where more detailed estimates of Availability are required it may be necessary to research more complex mathematical calculations. The statistical analysis of Incident data and the forecasting of Availability are a rich study field in many industries outside of IT, i.e. electronics, aviation.

Basic Availability calculation

To determine the basic Availability of a given IT Service or component as an Availability percentage (%) the following basic formula can be used:

$$\text{Availability} = \frac{(AST - DT)}{AST} \times 100$$

= Service or Component Availability (%)

Where:–
AST = Agreed service time
DT = Actual downtime during agreed service time

Example

A 24x7 IT Service requires a weekly 2-hour planned downtime period for application maintenance. Following the completion of the weekly maintenance an application software error occurs which results in 3 hours of unplanned downtime.

The weekly Availability for the IT Service in this reporting period is therefore based on the following:

The AST should recognise that the planned 2 hr weekly downtime is scheduled.

The DT is the 3hrs of unplanned outage following the application maintenance.

The AST value is therefore 24hrs x 7days – 2 hrs maintenance = 166 hrs/week.

The DT value is therefore the 3 hrs unplanned downtime.

The Availability calculation is:–

$$A = \frac{166 - 3}{166} \times 100 = 98.78\%$$

Total Infrastructure Availability

The Availability percentage for each IT component within the total IT Infrastructure may be different and as such it is necessary to provide a calculation that reflects the total Infrastructure Availability.

The levels of resilience provided positively influence the Availability percentage for the total Infrastructure.

Serial configuration

Figure 8.15 illustrates a basic IT Infrastructure configuration where no additional components are provided for resilience. The Availability percentage for this configuration is based on the product of all the individual component Availability percentages.

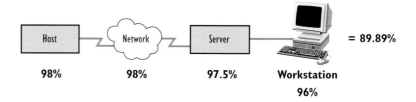

Figure 8.15 – Simple IT Infrastructure configuration

Availability as viewed from the User workstation is therefore calculated as:

■ Availability = Host * Network * Server * Workstation

- Calculation = 0.98 * 0.98 * 0.975 * 0.96 = 0.8989
- Total Infrastructure Availability = 89.89%.

Parallel configuration

Where additional components are added to provide resilience so that the backup component takes over automatically, then the Availability percentage is calculated by multiplying the UnAvailability (reciprocal of Availability) of each component.

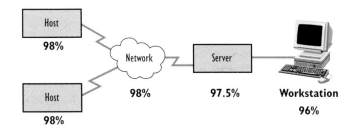

Figure 8.16 – Simple IT configuration with component resilience provided

In the configuration in Figure 8.16, the host component now has a backup component to provide greater resilience. The host component Availability percentage is now recalculated as follows:

- Availability = 1- ((1-0.98)*(1-0.98)) = 0.9996
- Host Availability = 99.96%.

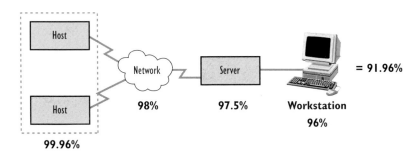

Figure 8.17 – Revised host Availability percentage to reflect additional resilience provided

With the additional resilience provided for the host component, the total Infrastructure Availability can now be calculated as shown in Figure 8.17:

- Availability = Host x Network x Server x Workstation
- Calculation = 0.9996 * 0.98 * 0.975 * 0.96 = 0.9169
- Total Infrastructure Availability = 91.69%.

Availability design implications

To deliver the required levels of Availability for an IT Service requires focusing on all components within the IT Infrastructure design that underpin the IT Service. The Availability of each individual component influences the overall Availability that can be provided by the total Infrastructure.

When viewing Availability consider the following points:

- the total Infrastructure Availability is limited by the weakest link

271

■ the total service Availability cannot exceed the Availability percentage of the least available component, unless the weakest components are used in parallel with automatic fail over

■ improving the Availability of one component may have minimal end-to-end benefit

■ one unreliable component can lead to significant damaging impact to Availability.

8.9.5 Calculating the cost of UnAvailability

To cost justify improvements to the IT Infrastructure that improve Availability, it is necessary to demonstrate how the proposed improvements deliver tangible business benefits.

Where the proposed improvements require a significant re-investment in the IT Infrastructure the benefits often need to be expressed in financial terms, i.e. the business case.

A good technique to justify IT Infrastructure improvements is to quantify the total cost to the organisation of an IT Service failure(s). These costs can then be used to support a business case for additional IT Infrastructure investment and provide an objective 'cost versus benefit' assessment.

Figure 8.18 is a sample calculation that can be used to quantify the costs associated with IT Service failure:

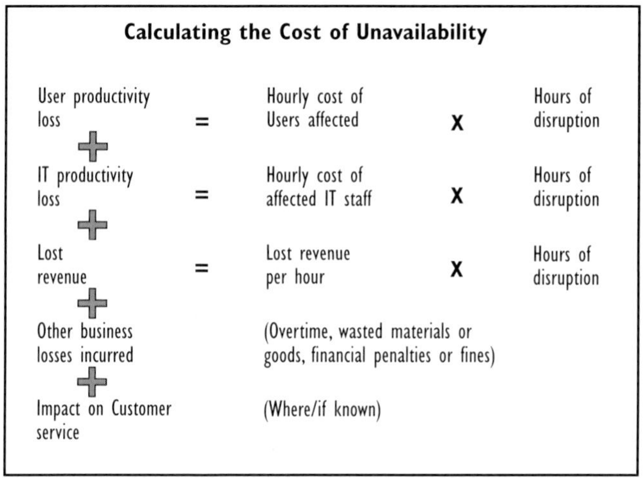

Figure 8.18 – Example calculation for the cost of an outage

Hints and tips

Consider undertaking this exercise 'once only' to deliver what the business and IT organisation agree is an indicative cost of failure for a single or range of time periods, e.g.:

The cost of one hours peak SLA outage = £xx.

The cost of a full day SLA outage = £yy.

This then enables an indicative cost to be assigned to each IT Service failure and included in the regular service reporting.

These figures should then be reviewed at least annually.

Another approach to obtain an indicative cost of a failure is to take the annual cost to the business of taking the service and simply divide by the number of service hours contracted in the SLA for a year. This gives the IT expenditure cost to the business by hour.

8.9.6 Developing basic IT Availability measurement and reporting

At the component level there are a number of metrics that should be defined, measured and reported to provide a truly holistic view on how the component meets the range of Availability criterion, e.g.:

- Availability
- reliability
- maintainability
- serviceability – in itself not a metric but reported in terms of service or component Availability, reliability and maintainability.

Within the Availability Management Chapter, a number of Sections refer to the creation of metrics that can be utilised to provide this range of component Availability reporting. A suggested framework for these metrics is described in the remainder of this Paragraph.

Basic Availability calculation

The simplest form of measurement is to report the proportion of time that a component is actually available for use by the business within the agreed service time. This is usually expressed as the Availability percentage.

This is a simple method of providing a measurement of Availability for hardware, software application and network components and requires minimal investment in measurement and reporting tools. Consequently many SLAs are constructed with Availability measures based on the Availability percentage (%).

Downtime reporting

Further basic forms of measurement can be considered to provide information concerning the Availability or non-Availability of an IT component, for example the reporting of downtime to reflect the total amount of time a dependent IT Service was unavailable. This can be represented as:

- Unscheduled – the amount of downtime incurred during service hours due to IT component failure(s)

- Planned – the amount of planned downtime incurred during service hours to apply maintenance

- Extended – the amount of excess downtime required to complete the planned maintenance activity.

Where Service Maintenance Objectives (SMO) have been agreed for a given planned maintenance activity the total downtime incurred should be recorded as follows:

- planned downtime: – the agreed SMO time

- actual downtime: – the total downtime incurred

- extended downtime: – the excess downtime (actual downtime – SMO time).

This method of recording enables a clear distinction to made between agreed planned downtime and the extended downtime incurred due to deficiencies within the implementation process.

Extended downtime reporting can be used to review Change quality issues with internal and external suppliers and be formally reported as non-compliance within OLA and service contract reporting.

Incident based reporting

Measures that reflect the overall reliability and maintainability of an IT Service and supporting components can be derived from Incident reporting. These can be represented as:

- frequency of failure – the number of occurrences of component failure that impacted the IT Service

- backup and recovery performance – the time taken to recover from a component failure (measured against the recovery metrics defined within the 'designing for recovery' and/or CFIA activity).

In addition, Incident based reporting can also enable data to be produced which provides an indication of improving or deteriorating trends:

- MTBF (Mean Time Between Failures) – the average elapsed time from the time an IT Service or supporting component is fully restored until the next occurrence of a failure to the same service or component

- MTBSI (Mean Time Between System Incidents) – the average elapsed time between the occurrence of one failure, and the next failure

- MTTR (Mean Time To Repair) – the average elapsed time from the occurrence of an Incident to resolution of the Incident.

Please refer to Paragraph 8.9.9 and Figure 8.20 for additional guidance.

8.9.7 Developing business and User measurement and reporting

The final word on the quality of the IT Service provided rests with the business. While traditional IT measures may show the '%' SLA target met, this does little to change the feeling of dissatisfaction if IT Service Problems have impacted the business operation.

In Section 8.7, it is recommended that a wide range of measures be produced to reflect Availability from a number of perspectives, the key measures being those that reflect the consequence of IT Availability on the business and User.

This business and User approach to Availability reporting provides a number of benefits:

- provides a 'common' measure which both parties to the SLA can understand
- can visibly demonstrate to the business tangible service improvements enabling the IT organisation to show the 'added value'
- can more easily identify degrading levels of service to enable the IT organisation to be pro active in responding without formal business escalation
- can be used to demonstrate the User impact with suppliers to drive and influence positive supplier behaviour.

Approaches to develop business and User driven metrics

So how can business and User driven metrics be developed to gain the above benefits? The remainder of this topic provides a number of approaches that can be undertaken.

CFIA

CFIA is used to help predict and evaluate the impact on IT Availability arising from component failures within the IT Infrastructure design. As shown in Table 8.3, the CFIA matrix used during this activity can be expanded to include fields that can map the number of Users supported by each component.

Component Description	End Users Affected
Host	1,000
OLTPl	750
OLTP2	250
Order application	800
Payments application	50
Order database	800
Payments database	50
Server XYZ	20
Workstation A	1

Table 8.3 – CFIA matrix denoting the number of Users affected by each component

Thus when a component is unavailable, the number of Users impacted is understood. This can enable Availability calculations to be based on the number of Users impacted and/or amount of lost User processing time:

- Advantages – an easy to use approach that enables impact to be readily identified at the component level.
- Disadvantages – the number of User workstations does not necessarily equate to the number of Users at any one point in time, e.g. lunch hours, staggered shift patterns or weekday vs. weekend periods. In these instances a suggestion would be to base the number of Users within the CFIA matrix upon an average for Users active within selected periods.

Instrumentation

For new IT Services the requirement for enhanced Availability reporting should be captured in the design phase. It is easier and more cost effective to provide this instrumentation within the application during design than to attempt to retrofit once the IT Service is live. Availability Management requirements should be based on the capture of information that relates to the impact on the vital business functions arising from IT component failure:

■ Advantages – requires no external measurement systems or methods and provides immediate Availability reporting for new IT Services.

■ Disadvantages – if not included in design may be resisted on the grounds of cost to retrofit. For performance-centric applications there may be resistance to add any processing overhead to each transaction.

Estimation

A valid technique is to estimate the impact of IT failure against the transaction volumes (related to the vital business functions or User activity) normally processed during the period of failure. The data to base the estimations against should be captured and maintained by Capacity Management:

■ Advantages: relatively simple and easy to produce for all IT Services using existing data sources.

■ Disadvantages – provides only the indicative impact. Requires access to up to date volume information to ensure business growth trends etc are reflected, e.g. using November data to assess the ATM Customer impact during December/Christmas peak periods is not an accurate reflection of impact.

End-user assessment

For organisations unable to justify the costs of more advanced Availability measurement techniques, the use of a daily 'User assessment' is a simple technique that provides a business and User view of IT Availability. In its basic form, this is an agreed set of criteria against which the business can assess IT Availability and service quality in support of their business operation. Each day the business User representative should be contacted for their end-of-day assessment, this could be reported as a GOOD day, ACCEPTABLE day or BAD day. This can be recorded and reported using the 'RAG' (Red, Amber, and Green) method.

This approach can be expanded to enable more specific assessment information to be gathered, e.g. the business can assess a number of categories, e.g. Availability, performance, recoverability and be extended to include other IT Service Management functions, i.e. Service Desk:

■ Advantage – low cost and effective. Provides the business view of IT Availability and service quality.

■ Disadvantages – requires business commitment. Without a framework of assessment criteria may be open to subjective opinion. May not provide sufficient detailed information to drive continuous improvement activities.

End-user simulation tools

Systems Management tools which seek to simulate User activity can be deployed to provide end-to end Availability reporting (real-time and off-line reports). These tools execute scripts to generate sample transactions and monitor and report on areas such as Availability, performance, throughput etc:

- Advantages – provide real-time exception reporting and range of off-line reports. Additionally as a by-product continually verify the end-to-end Infrastructure and provide an immediate post Change implementation health check.

- Disadvantages – the cost of procurement and need to customise scripts to reflect the organisation's application(s).

Customer complaints

The correlation of Customer complaints received against specific IT failures can provide an indication of true Customer impact and frustration:

- Advantages – low cost and reflects a true sense of Customer dissatisfaction.

- Disadvantages – not every Customer complains so not a true reflection of impact. Time lag between Incidents and complaints being received delays and dilutes Availability reporting.

Compensation claims and penalty payments

For certain businesses a consequence of IT failure may be claims for financial compensation by impacted Customers. An example being for the loss of interest due to delayed or missed payments. This is not restricted to the financial services sector, for example some motorist assistance companies pay compensation (or a penalty) for failing to meet a request for assistance within a set time period:

- Advantages – provides a good indication on the cost of failure.

- Disadvantages – not all Customers make claims or exercise penalty payment. Again time lag between the Incidents and resultant claims (often months) can delay and dilute Availability reporting.

Sample User Availability calculations

Where the number of Users impacted by an IT failure is known, this information can be used to report User Availability as:

- User impact reported as an absolute value per Incident or reporting period

- User productivity loss as a time based value per Incident or reporting period

- User Availability as an Availability percentage (%) for the reporting period.

Calculating User Availability

End-user impact (absolute)

This can be derived from the CFIA documentation to associate the User population impacted by each Incident with a component failure. An example of such reporting is shown in Table 8.4.

Incident No.	Date	Time	Duration (mins)	Incident Description	Failed Component	User Impact
1	01 October	09:25	60	Payments database full	Payments database	50
2	04 October	12:48	25	Server hang – rebooted	Server XYZ	20
3	05 October	09:56	125	Host operating system failure	Host	1,000
4	05 October	16:40	20	Fuse blown in power supply	Workstation A	1
						1,071

Table 8.4 – Example IT Service reporting to denote User impact per Incident

277

End-user impact (productivity)

To enable the reported User impact to reflect User productivity loss, requires the amount of downtime per Incident to be expressed as the total amount of End User Downtime (EUDT). This EUDT needs to reflect the number of Users affected by the Incidents.

This enables the amount of User downtime to be derived which can then optionally be used to report as man-hours or man-days lost productivity. An example of such reporting is shown in Table 8.5, where EUDT is calculated by multiplying the DT by the number of Users impacted.

Incident No.	Date	Time	Duration (mins)	Incident Description	Failed Component	User Impact	EUDT mins)
1	01 October	09:25	60	Payments database full	Payments database	50	3,000
2	04 October	12:48	25	Server hang – rebooted	Server XYZ	20	500
3	05 October	09:56	125	Host operating system failure	Host	1,000	125,000
4	05 October	16:40	20	Fuse blown in power supply	Workstation A	1	20
			230				128,520

Table 8.5 – Example IT Service reporting to denote User downtime

End-user impact (availability percentage)

To provide a User view of Availability, the basic Availability calculation described in Paragraph 8.9.4 needs to be developed. The Agreed Service Time (AST) and the Down Time values need to be replaced with End-User Processing Time (EUPT) and EUDT.

- EUPT is calculated by multiplying the AST by the total number of Users.

- EUDT is calculated by multiplying the DT by the number of Users impacted and summing all Incidents within a period as illustrated in Table 8.5. (The sum of (Actual downtime during Agreed service time x number of Users)).

End-User Availability (EUA) can therefore be calculated in a reporting period based on the following calculation:

$$\text{Availability} = \frac{(EUPT - EUDT)}{EUPT} \times 100 = \text{User Availability (\%)}$$

Example

Consider a 24-hour x 7-day service having 1,000 Users and a 2 hour planned downtime slot per week. The calculations in Paragraph 8.9.4 can now be developed using the values obtained from Table 8.5 as follows:

The weekly Agreed Service Time for the service would be:

AST = (24 x 7) – 2 = 168 – 2 = 166 hours

EUPT = AST x number of Users = 166 x 1000 = 166,000 hours or (166,000 x 60) = 9,960,000 minutes.

EUDT = (60 x 50) + (25 x 20) + (125 x 1000) + (20 x 1) = 128,520 minutes.

Therefore EUA can be calculated as follows:

$$EUA = \frac{(EUPT - EUDT)}{EUPT} \times 100 = \frac{(9960000 - 128520)}{9960000} \times 100 = 98.7\%$$

Hints and tips

The approaches outlined in this Section should enable a start to be made towards business driven measurement and reporting to complement the existing traditional IT measures. Cost and effort influence the extent to which this kind of reporting is developed. As always the key principle with measurement and reporting applies, in that the cost and effort of producing the measures and reports should not outweigh the benefits.

8.9.8 Service Outage Analysis

The detailed analysis of service interruptions can identify opportunities to enhance levels of Availability.

SOA is a technique designed to provide a structured approach to identify end-to-end Availability improvement opportunities that deliver benefits to the User. Many of the activities involved in SOA are closely aligned with those of Problem Management. In a number of organisations these activities are performed jointly by Problem and Availability Management.

The high level objectives of SOA are:

- to identify the underlying causes of service interruption to the User
- to assess the effectiveness of the IT support organisation and key processes
- to produce reports detailing the major findings and recommendations
- to initiate a programme of activities to implement the agreed recommendations
- that Availability improvements derived from SOA driven activities are measured.

The key principles of the SOA approach are that:

- the underlying reasons for service interruption can be caused by shortfalls in technology, process, procedure or behaviours (culture)
- wider ranges of data sources are used to support the analysis
- business and User input is fundamental
- a specifically mobilised cross-functional team undertakes that analysis
- SOA assignments have a recognised sponsor(s) (Ideally joint sponsorship from the IT and business).

The reasons for adopting an SOA approach are:

- traditional IT Availability reporting often only provides an IT component perspective
- business and User input provides an ultimate view of Availability and the important issues from their perspective
- it provides a structured, focused and detailed analysis of a selected IT Service or set of Infrastructure components
- it provides a mechanism to ensure the IT Infrastructure delivers optimal Availability.

The benefits from taking an SOA approach are that:

- it can enable requests for enhanced levels of Availability to be met without major cost

- it provides the business with visible commitment from the IT support organisation

- it develops in-house skills and competencies to avoid expensive consultancy assignments related to Availability improvement

- the cross-functional team approach is an enabler to 'think outside of the box' to challenge traditional thinking and provide innovative and often inexpensive solutions

- SOA delivers a programme of improvement opportunities that can make a real difference

- SOA improvement opportunities are focused on delivering benefit to the User

- it provides an independent 'health check' of IT Service Management processes and is the stimulus for process improvements.

A structured approach

To maximise both the time of individuals allocated to the SOA assignment and the quality of the delivered report a structured approach is required. This structure is illustrated in Figure 8.19 shown below. This approach is similar to many consultancy models utilised within the industry and in many ways Availability Management can be considered as providing via SOA a form of internal consultancy.

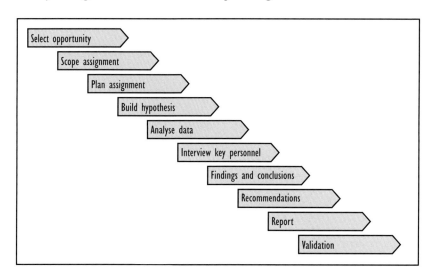

Figure 8.19 – The structured approach for a Systems Outage Analysis assignment

The above high level structure is described briefly as follows:

Select opportunity

Prior to scheduling an SOA assignment there needs to be agreement as to which IT Service or Infrastructure is to be selected. Within the Availability Plan it is recommended that 4 assignments are scheduled per year and if possible the IT Service is selected in advance as part of the proactive approach to Availability Management.

Before commencing with the SOA it is important that the assignment has a recognised sponsor from within the IT organisation and/or the business. This ensures organisational visibility to the SOA and ensures recommendations are endorsed at a senior level within the organisation.

Scope assignment

This is to state explicitly what areas are and are not covered within the assignment. This is normally documented in a Terms of Reference issued prior to the assignment.

Plan assignment

The assignment needs to be planned a number of weeks in advance of the assignment commencing. The typical areas that require advance planning are:

- the start and end dates of the assignment
- key milestones, e.g. delivery of final report
- the individuals who form the SOA team
- role and responsibilities of the individual team members
- the data sources required to provide the data for analysis
- premises and equipment, i.e. a dedicated room, whiteboards, terminals etc.
- an interview schedule for key IT and business personnel
- a visit to the business operation and the IT operation.

The SOA assignment should be looking at identifying improvement opportunities that benefit the User. It is therefore important that an end-to-end view of the data and MIS requirements is taken. A suggested list of data sources is as follows:

- Incident Management records and MIS
- Problem Management records and MIS
- Change Management records and MIS
- SLAs and Service Level reporting
- Vital Business Function measures that reflect User impact
- formal complaints to the business from their Customers
- formal complaints from the business to the IT organisation
- Customer satisfaction survey results
- process metrics.

For practical reasons the coverage period for the above should be limited to approximately 6 months. This limits the amount of data to analyse but, importantly, ensures that only current issues are being investigated.

To support the team with analysis, supporting documentation should be available to the team, e.g. operational procedures, process documentation, IT policies, configuration diagrams, Industry best practice reference material, e.g. ITIL.

Build hypotheses

This is a useful method of building likely scenarios, which can help the study team draw early conclusions within the analysis period. These hypotheses can be built from discussing the forthcoming assignment with key roles, e.g. Senior Management, Problem Management, Change Management, and Service Level Management or by using the planning session to brainstorm the list by the assembled team.

The completed hypotheses list should be documented and input to the analysis period to provide some early focus on data and MIS that match the individual hypotheses.

It should be noted that this approach also eliminates perceived issues, i.e. no data or MIS substantiates what is perceived to be a service issue.

> **Example**
>
> If an SOA was planned to review Availability for a Call Centre based IT Service; it is likely that system performance is crucial. Hypotheses to help assess if performance issues are impacting the User Availability could be based on the following:
>
> 'Performance issues are the single largest cause of "Service Unavailability" Incidents impacting Call Centre operation'
>
> 'Existing system and performance monitors do not enable "Service Unavailability" Incidents to be identified, diagnosed and resolved effectively'.

Analyse data

The number of individuals that form the SOA team dictates how to allocate specific analysis responsibilities.

During this analysis period the hypotheses list should be used to help draw some early conclusions.

Interview key personnel

It is essential that key business representatives and Users are interviewed to ensure the business and User perspective is captured. It is surprising how this dialogue can identify quick win opportunities as often what the business views as a big issue can be addressed by a simple IT solution.

The study team should also seek input from key individuals within the IT support organisation to identify additional problem areas and possible solutions which can be fed back to the study team.

The dialogue also helps capture those issues that are not easily visible from the assembled data and MIS reports.

Findings and conclusions

After analysis of the data and MIS provided, interviews and continual revision of the hypothesis list, the study team should be in a position to start documenting initial findings and conclusions.

It is recommended that the team meet immediately after the analysis period to share their individual findings and then take an aggregate view to form the draft findings and conclusions.

It is important that all findings can be evidenced by facts gathered during the analysis. During this phase of the assignment it may be necessary to validate finding(s) by additional analysis to ensure the SOA team can back up all findings with clear documented evidence.

Recommendations

After all findings and conclusions have been validated the SOA team should be in a position to formulate recommendations. In many cases the recommendations to support a particular finding are straightforward and obvious.

However, the benefit of bringing a cross functional team together for the SOA assignment is to create an environment for innovative 'think outside of the box' approaches. The SOA assignment leader should facilitate this session with the aim of identifying recommendations that are practical and sustainable once implemented.

Report

The final report should be issued to the sponsor with a management summary. Reporting styles are normally determined by the individual organisations.

It is important that the report clearly shows where Availability loss is being incurred and how the recommendations address this. If the report contains many recommendations an attempt should be made to quantify the Availability benefit of each recommendation together with the estimated effort to implement.

This enables informed choices to be made on how to take the recommendations forward and how these should be prioritised and resourced.

Validation

It is recommended that for each SOA, key measures that reflect the business and User perspectives prior to the assignment are captured and recorded as the 'before' view.

As SOA recommendations are progressed the positive impacts on Availability should be captured to provide the 'after' view for comparative purposes. Where anticipated benefits have not been delivered this should be investigated and remedial actions taken.

Hints and tips

Consider categorising the recommendations under the following headings:–

AVOIDANCE

Recommendations that if implemented will eliminate this particular cause of IT Service interruption.

MINIMISE

Recommendations that if implemented will reduce the User impact from IT Service interruption, e.g. recovery and/or restoration can be enhanced to reduce impact duration.

DETECTION

Recommendations that if implemented will provide enhanced reporting of key indicators to ensure underlying IT Service issues are detected early to enable a proactive response.

Build programme

Having invested time and effort in completing the SOA assignment it is important that the recommendations once agreed by the sponsor are then taken forward for implementation.

The best mechanism for achieving this is by incorporating the recommendations as activities to be completed within the Availability Plan or SIP.

It is recommended that these activities are also managed and tracked by Programme Management, Project Management and Change Management processes.

The SOA team

The team should consist of experienced IT practitioners selected from a range of areas within the IT organisation.

For example the SOA team could consist of individuals from the following functions:

- Availability Management (possibly process owner and SOA assignment leader)
- Computer Operations
- Network Management
- Problem Management
- Change Management
- Service Desk
- Service Level Management User
- 3rd party supplier
- a leading technical expert.

The size of the team should be influenced by the size of the IT organisation and the topic selected for the SOA. A team of at least three is the recommended minimum.

The focus of the SOA assignment determines which of the above it may be advisable to include or schedule within the assignment plan.

As scheduled events, the Availability Management process owner should have these events defined within the Availability Plan and identified resources committed in advance.

Measure SOA effectiveness

SOA should be viewed as a key element of the Availability Plan that underpins the Availability Management process. Measures should be established to monitor the effectiveness of SOA as an organisational activity and in optimising service Availability.

To measure the effectiveness of each SOA the following metrics could be used:

- number of recommendations
- number of recommendations rejected
- number of recommendations completed
- number of recommendations in progress
- number of recommendations with no progress.

The above measures provide a clear indication on how progress is being made with each completed SOA assignment. The number of recommendations rejected may reflect the quality of recommendations made. Conversely a high completion rate would indicate the 'do-ability' of the recommendations made.

8.9.9   The expanded Incident 'lifecycle'

A guiding principle of Availability Management is to recognise that it is still possible to gain Customer satisfaction even when things go wrong. One approach to help achieve this requires Availability Management to ensure that the duration of any Incident is minimised to enable normal business operations to resume as quickly as is possible.

Availability Management should work closely with Incident Management and Problem Management in the analysis of UnAvailability Incidents.

A good technique to help with the technical analysis of Incidents affecting the Availability of components and IT Services is to take an Incident 'lifecycle' view.

Every Incident passes through several major stages. The time elapsed in these stages may vary considerably. For Availability Management purposes the standard Incident 'lifecycle' as described within Incident Management has been expanded to provide additional help and guidance particularly in the area of 'designing for recovery'. Figure 8.20 illustrates the expanded Incident 'lifecycle'.

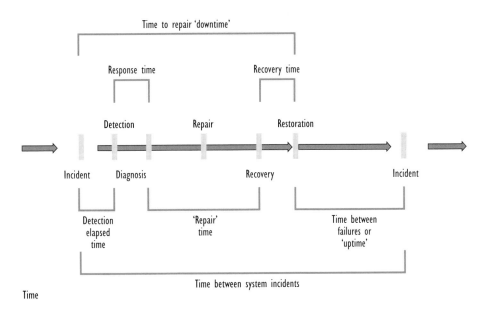

Figure 8.20 – The expanded Incident 'lifecycle'

From the above it can be seen that an Incident can be broken down into stages which can be timed and measured. These stages are described as follows:

- Incident start – the time at which the Customer recognises a loss or deviation of service or the time at which the Incident is first reported, whichever is the earliest

- Incident detection – the time at which the IT organisation is made aware of an Incident

- Incident diagnosis – the time at which diagnosis to determine the underlying cause has been completed
- Incident repair – the time at which the failure has been repaired/fixed
- Incident Recovery – the time at which component recovery has been completed
- Incident restoration – the time normal business operations resume.

Each stage, and the associated time taken, influences the total downtime perceived by the User. By taking this approach it is possible to see where time is being 'lost' for the duration of an Incident, e.g. the service was unavailable to the business for 60 minutes, yet it only took 5 minutes to apply a fix, where did the other 55 minutes go?

Using this approach identifies possible areas of inefficiency that combine to make the loss of service experienced by the business greater than it need necessarily be. These could cover areas such as poor automation (alerts, automated recovery etc.), poor diagnostic tools and scripts, unclear escalation procedures (which delay the escalation to the appropriate technical support group or supplier), or lack of comprehensive operational documentation.

Availability Management needs to work in close association with Incident and Problem Management to ensure repeat occurrences are eliminated.

It is recommended that these measures are established and captured for all Incidents. This provides Availability Management with metrics for both specific Incidents and trending information. This information can be used as input to SOA assignments, Service Improvement Programmes and regular Availability Management reporting and provide an impetus for continuous improvement activity to pursue cost effective improvements.

It can also enable targets to be set for specific stages. While accepting that each Incident may have a wide range of technical complexity, a number of stages should be expected to be consistent and reflect consistency in how the IT support organisation responds.

8.9.10 Continuous improvement

The primary purpose of the Availability Management process is to ensure that the Availability requirements agreed with the business for IT Service(s) are consistently met. It is the responsibility of Availability Management to ensure that corrective actions are being progressed to address any shortfalls in meeting the levels of Availability required and expected by the business.

Availability Management can also play a key role in further optimisation of the existing IT Infrastructure to provide improved levels of Availability at a lower cost when Availability requirements change.

The Availability Management process should wherever possible contribute activities to support an overall SIP.

To help achieve these aims Availability Management needs to be recognised as a leading influence over the IT support organisation to ensure continued focus on Availability and stability of the IT Infrastructure.

As the 'champion' for Availability in the IT organisation the function should embrace and engender the ethos of continuous improvement' within the IT support organisation.

Continuous Improvement is a key element of 'Quality Management' utilised to empower staff to drive improvements that benefit the business and User. There are a number of Quality Management methodologies available, e.g. Total Quality Management (TQM), however 'continuous improvement' can be embraced without the need for an organisation to adopt a Quality Management methodology.

A suggested technique

The 'continuous improvement' methodology can be employed as a technique by Availability Management to facilitate improvements that can be progressed by the IT support organisation to deliver Availability improvements that benefit the business and User.

Availability Management can provide the IT support organisation with a real business and User perspective on how deficiencies within the IT Infrastructure and the underpinning process and procedures impact the business operation and ultimately their Customers.

The use of business-driven metrics can demonstrate this impact in real terms and importantly also help quantify the benefits of improvement opportunities.

Availability Management can play an important role in helping the IT support organisation recognise where they can add value by exploiting their technical skills and competencies in an Availability context. The continuous improvement technique can be used by Availability Management to harness this technical capability. This can be used with either small groups of technical staff or a wider group within a workshop environment.

The basic steps of the continuous improvement methodology are described in Figure 8.21.

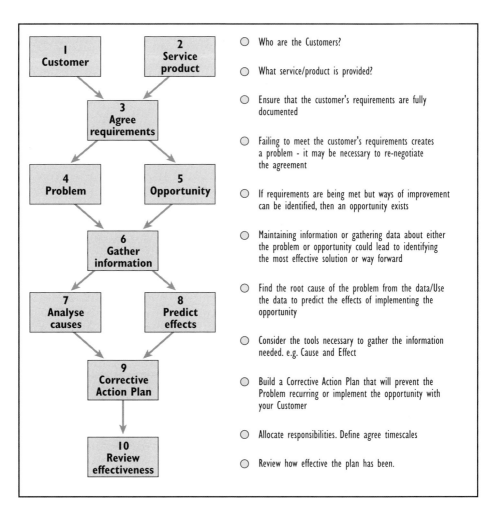

Figure 8.21 – Example of a continuous improvement methodology

The wider benefits of adopting this approach within the IT support organisation are that it:

- provides direction to best exploit skills and competencies
- creates an understanding of how the business uses the technology
- can identify 'quick win' low cost improvements
- delivers incremental Availability improvement
- provides positive feedback to staff on 'how they have made a difference'
- demonstrates to the business the added-value of the IT support organisation
- helps promote a 'service culture'.

8.9.11   Technical Observation Post

Continuous improvement is an ethos fundamental to all Service Management processes and Service Management as a whole. An alternative approach for progressing continuous improvement opportunities is the establishment of a Technical Observation Post (TOP).

The TOP is best suited for delivering pro active business and User benefits from within the real-time IT environment.

What is a TOP?

A TOP is a prearranged gathering of specialist technical support staff from within the IT support organisation brought together to focus on specific aspects of IT Availability. Its purpose being to monitor events, real-time as they occur, with the specific aim of identifying improvement opportunities or bottlenecks which exist within the current IT Infrastructure.

Why?

A wide range of systems management products and tools are available to provide real-time and retrospective analysis on specific aspects of components within the IT Infrastructure. Some are better than others. However, to acquire a global end-to-end view of the IT Infrastructure or a given IT Service using real-time monitors or historical data can often be difficult, time consuming and require significant effort.

Another consideration is the reality that the people who design and support IT systems are not the people who run and operate them. Assumptions and misunderstandings can occur between both parties which unconsciously result in inefficient operational processes, e.g. how many IT support staff actually observe and understand the overnight application processing lifecycle and the key operational events?

Bringing together specialist technical staff to observe specific activities and events within the IT Infrastructure and operational processes creates an environment to identify improvement opportunities.

Scope

The scope of a TOP can be wide ranging but must be focused with an overall objective set.

Example

A TOP is convened with an objective to 'Improve the efficiency of the overnight batch window'. The areas to focus on to identify contributory improvements to the TOP objective could include:

- batch scheduling
- batch restart and recovery procedures
- automation
- application performance
- Infrastructure performance
- operational processes and procedure.

When?

A TOP can be convened at any time where this approach is considered appropriate and its invocation would be planned and scheduled by Availability Management.

Considerations

The provision of a small area or room with terminals that enables the cross-functional team of specialist technical staff to work together is an important success factor that ensures:

- the TOP has visibility
- the TOP team remains focused
- the TOP team members are able to interact unhindered by physical or organisational barriers

Availability Management as sponsors of the TOP should play a facilitation role providing guidance and ensuring the team remains focused on the TOP objective(s). The role should also ensure that all observations and outline recommendations are captured and subsequently create an action plan that forms part of either the Availability Plan or the appropriate SIP.

Benefits

The benefits of using a TOP as an approach to continuous improvements are that it:

- is an informal structure which technical staff are comfortable with and has limited management overhead
- is cost effective
- creates an environment that can positively harness the technical capabilities of staff
- creates a cross functional team that is focused and shares a common sense of purpose
- creates an environment for the sharing of information to the benefit of all attending
- enables IT support organisation staff to observe the operational environment
- can identify areas of improvement masked by inefficient tools, processes and procedures.

Industry view

An organisation had failed to recognise the early warning signs of gradual erosion of the overnight 'batch window'.

A steady decline in overnight batch processing completion times resulted in SLAs for key services being regularly breached at start of day. The factors behind this increase in elapsed time were difficult to identify after the event, so the decision was taken to form a TOP in order to observe the batch real time.

In this particular case, the TOP ran for several consecutive nights, producing recommendations each evening for progression (wherever possible) during the following working day.

A daily report detailing both observations and recommendations was created on a daily basis. By the end of the TOP, over fifty opportunities for improvement had been identified and many implemented.

The initial 'quick win' actions taken resulted in a reduction in overnight batch elapsed times such that the workload could now be completed within the SLA.

As a result of completing all the main recommendations from the TOP exercise, the overnight batch processing elapsed time was reduced by almost 4 hours.

| Annex 8A | Availability Manager – Role, responsibilities and key skills |

Role

In today's competitive market place organisations are demanding more and more from IT to enhance their business and deliver cost effective, high levels of service to their Customers. As business needs and Customer expectations increase, the Availability and reliability of IT Services is essential in ensuring the organisation can meet its business objectives.

The objectives of Availability Management are:

- to define and deploy the Availability Management process within the organisation and be accountable for execution and compliance of the process across the IT support organisation

- to ensure IT Services are designed to deliver the required levels of Availability required by the business

- to provide a range of IT Availability reporting to ensure that agreed levels of Availability, reliability and maintainability are measured and monitored on an ongoing basis

- to optimise the Availability of the IT Infrastructure to deliver cost effective improvements that deliver tangible benefits to the business and User

- to achieve over a period of time a reduction in the frequency and duration of Incidents that impact on IT Availability

- to ensure shortfalls in IT Availability are recognised and appropriate corrective actions are identified and progressed

- to create and maintain a forward looking Availability Plan aimed at improving the overall Availability of IT Services and Infrastructure components to ensure that existing and future business Availability requirements can be met.

Responsibilities

- to be accountable for the deployment of the Availability Management process and associated methods and techniques

- to be responsible for ensuring the Availability Management process, its associated techniques and methods are regularly reviewed and audited, and that all of these are subjected to continuous improvement and remain fit for purpose

- to be responsible for determining the Availability requirements from the business for new or enhanced IT Services

- to be responsible for the creation of Availability and recovery design criteria to be applied to new or enhanced Infrastructure design

- to be responsible for ensuring the levels of IT Availability required are cost justified

- to be responsible for defining the targets of Availability required for the IT Infrastructure and its components that underpin a new or enhanced IT Service as the basis for an SLA agreement

- to be responsible for the establishment of measures and reporting that reflect business, User and IT support organisation requirements

- to be responsible for the monitoring of actual IT Availability achieved vs targets and to ensure shortfalls are addressed

- to be responsible for the production and maintenance of an Availability Plan which prioritises and plans IT Availability improvements

- to promote Availability Management awareness and understanding within the IT support organisation

- to maintain an awareness of technology advancements and IT best practice, e.g. ITIL.

Key skills

- to have practical experience of process management

- to have a good understanding of the ITIL disciplines

- to have practical experience of continuous improvement methods and techniques

- to have a good understanding of statistical and analytical principles and processes

- to possess good interpersonal skills for written, oral and face to face communications

- to possess skills in influencing and negotiation methods and techniques

- to have reasonable numeric skills

- to have a good understanding of available and emerging IT technologies

- to have the ability to understand how the IT technology supports the business

- to have a reasonable understanding of Cost Management principles.

9 SERVICE MANAGEMENT SOFTWARE TOOLS

The first question to ask on this topic is '*Do I really need software tools?*' If the answer is 'Yes' then, assess the need formally with a well-researched selection process.

According to the glossy brochures and the sales talk, Service Management tools are indispensable. However, good people, good process descriptions, and good procedures and working instructions are the basis for successful Service Management. The need for, and the sophistication of, the tools required depends on the business need for IT services and, to some extent, the size of the organisation.

In a very small organisation a simple in-house developed database system may be sufficient for logging and controlling Incidents. However, in larger organisations, a sophisticated, distributed, integrated Service Management toolset may be required, possibly linking all the processes with event-management systems. While tools can be an important asset in today's IT-dependent organisations, they are a means, not an end in themselves. When implementing Service Management processes, the starting point should always be looking at the way processes work and the need for management information. This provides the information needed to define the specifications for the tool best suited to assist the organisation.

Why the need? Here are some of the reasons:

- more sophisticated Customer demands
- a shortage of IT skills
- budget constraints
- business dependence on quality IT services
- integration of multi-vendor environments
- increasing complexity of IT infrastructure
- the emergence of international standards
- increased range and frequency of IT Changes.

Automated tools allow:

- the centralisation of key functions
- the automation of core Service Management functions
- the analysis of raw data
- the identification of trends
- the preventive measures to be implemented.

9.1 Types of tools

Software tools range from simple to complex and from inexpensive to very expensive. They generally fall into one of the two following categories:

- CMDB and Service Desk; traditional Service Desk tools without separate databases and modules for the Service Management processes

- integrated Service Management tools comprising modern client server based tools, with or without a knowledge database.

9.2 Summary of tool evaluation criteria

The following criteria should generally be used to assess software tools under consideration:

- an 80% fit to functional and technical requirements
- a meeting of ALL mandatory requirements
- little (if any) product customisation
- adherence of tool and supplier to Service Management best practice
- a sound data structure and handling
- business-driven not technology-driven
- administration and maintenance costs within budget
- acceptable levels of maintenance and release policies
- security and integrity
- availability of training and consultancy services
- good report generation.

Software tools should handle processes in conformity with the practices discussed in the IT Infrastructure Library. A set of guidance (the Appraisal and Evaluation Library) is available for the guidance of organisations wishing to select Service Support and Service Delivery tools. The prime areas to consider are:

- functional requirements support, and the level of integration with, for example, service delivery processes and tools
- data structure, data handling and integration, including the capability to support the required functionality
- integration of multi-vendor infrastructure components, and the need to absorb new components in the future – these will place particular demands on the data handling and modelling capabilities of the tool
- conformity to international open standards
- flexibility in implementation, usage and data sharing
- usability: the overall ease of use permitted by the User interface
- service levels: performance and availability
- distributed clients with a centralised shared database (e.g. client server)
- back-up, control and security provisions
- the quality of information provided by the supplier, and its validation by contact with other users.

9.2.1 Service Management tools

Few enterprises have no Service Management tools and many are considering replacing or upgrading those that are in use. The range and sophistication of tools for Service Management automation has grown rapidly in recent years.

Tools for the automation of core processes such as Incident logging and tracking have been supplemented by computer-integrated telephony, software capable of handling complex and multiple Service Level Agreements (with separate targets and business clocks), and remote support technology. Other tools include:

- interactive voice response (IVR) systems

- the Internet, internal electronic mail, voice mail

- self-help knowledge

- case-based reasoning/search systems

- network management tools (including remote support capabilities)

- system monitoring

- Configuration and Change Management systems

- release and distribution systems

- security monitoring and control, including password control, detection of violations and virus protection

- capacity planning

- IT Service Continuity Management (including automatic back-ups).

Although some of the tools are not yet commonly used, there are few areas of Service Management that cannot be helped by automation. Some areas of Service Management are too resource intensive to be performed effectively without automation. Each tool for the automation of Service Management has advantages and disadvantages but automation is still recognised as vital.

It is necessary to ensure that the combination of technology, processes and people are integrated and meet the needs of the Customers. Automation should be used to enhance Service Management, not replace it.

Automation is increasingly being treated as part of workflow management, linking each task in the life-cycle from a new service being planned through to disposal. The technology should be used to complement and enhance service delivery, not replace it.

Automation that provides support for distributed computing has revolutionised the ability of an enterprise to diagnose Problems remotely, and in many cases also to fix them remotely (and therefore faster). Remote support technology has also made it possible for an enterprise to make changes by downloading the new versions of software and to monitor the capacity of the infrastructure, identifying capacity problems before they become serious.

Automation has enabled easier IT Service Continuity Planning, with work being switched in the event of a local overload or a serious problem that has taken the service out from a specific area.

Some final considerations:

- *supplier and product credibility and viability* – installed base and degree of support; consider issues such as the financial viability of the vendor (are they likely to be around in a few years when you need them?); also consider large time-zone differences between the supplier and your organisation and language differences

- *costs, including ongoing cost to upgrade and support* – consider which is better
  - buying a standard package at reasonable initial cost, where the trade-off is that customisation may be very expensive and complex

- or a more flexible package at higher initial costs where customisation may be relatively easy and cheap

■ *adaptability* – will the tool be able to meet organisation specific requirements and constraints in the years to come.

9.3 Product training

To ensure effective use of software tools, product training is required. Therefore budget provision should be made at the planning stage of the implementation project. Furthermore, the training supplier employed should have a suitable portfolio of training programmes, covering the requirements of practitioners, supervisors and managers.

10 PLANNING FOR THE IMPLEMENTATION OF SERVICE MANAGEMENT

More and more organisations are recognising the importance of Service Management to their business. However, it is common for working practices to be based on historical or political considerations rather than the current needs of the business or best practice. It is therefore essential, before implementing any or all of the components of Service Management, to gain management commitment, to understand the working culture of the organisation, and to assess any existing processes and to compare these to the needs of the business and to best practice.

10.1 Use of Project Management concepts

To analyse the needs of the organisation and implement the desired solution requires a temporary organisation to be set up to undertake these activities. Thus this can readily be considered to be a project, or a series of projects, to implement the required Service Management processes.

One of the benefits of adopting a project approach to this activity is that it is possible to undertake the necessary investigations and have designated decision points where a decision can be made to continue with the project, change direction, or stop.

The project needs to consider the current position and where it would like to be, and to plot the path between these states. For each option identified, it can begin to articulate:

- the business benefits
- the risks, obstacles and potential problems
- the costs of the move plus longer-term running costs, including decommissioning
- the costs of continuing with the current structure.

It is then possible to begin to see how the business needs can be supported and see the associated costs. The benefits can then be balanced against costs and risks. Undertaking the investigative work could be considered to be one project that can then be followed by an implementation project.

There are two separate drivers to adoption of Service Management – the Supplier and the Customer. Each will have different drivers and each will need to ensure that these are supported by their projects.

10.2 Feasibility study

It is essential to investigate and understand the current service levels and costs by baselining all appropriate aspects of the current service before making any major changes. This enables the measurement of the impact of the improved Service Management processes on the baseline service levels and costs. (When comparison with other enterprises forms part of the baselining exercise, it is usually referred to as 'benchmarking'.)

Some advice is necessary before starting; the ITIL is not a magic wand. Do not expect miracles to happen when implementing the process framework. In the past, many organisations have tried to use process implementations as the basis for company reorganisations, or to assist with company mergers.

Too many disparate goals for the project will lead to failure and disappointment. So, the targets and objectives associated with a Service Management project should relate to the objectives of the organisation itself. The target should be to enable the delivery of quality IT services aligned to business need.

10.3 Assessing the current situation

10.3.1 Introduction

Figure 3.1 in Section 3.2 represents a model that can be used by an organisation as the framework for process improvement. The model is also a framework for benchmarking. It can be used generically for any change-related situation, strategic, tactical or operational. The current situation is compared with best practices; the result is the input for the transition plans, together with the goals related to the change process.

The transition plans describe the way that procedural changes take place and result in the actual changes. Thanks to continuous measurement, *through measurement of defined processes*, assessment of the changes compared with the goals is possible, and may result in the changing of actions, facilitating the process of continuous improvement.

10.3.2 A 'health check'

A 'health check' based on the current procedures can be used as an objective way of assessing the effectiveness of Service Management processes in an organisation. This assessment should aim to identify those aspects that are functioning well, thus determining which best practices are in current use and should be retained, and also to pinpoint problem areas and constraints. Using the recommendations from a health check better equips an organisation to define its implementation or improvement priorities.

To summarise, a health check should:

- objectively assess the effectiveness of the Service Management processes
- identify constraints and problem areas
- provide advice on how to manage the processes more effectively
- provide advice on how to re-design or improve the processes.

Non-IT-related issues that can influence the performance in delivering services such as people management and resource management can be assessed by using (self-) assessment provided by Total Quality Management methods. Be aware that in many cases it is these factors that have the major effect upon the actual performance from the Service Management processes. For further reading, see Appendix D.

Some examples of general topics that should be addressed by questions in a health check include:

- the existence of a strategic business plan
- how the plan supports IT planning
- the extent to which IT supports the needs of the business
- the alignment of IT and business growth plans.

Some examples of process topics, which should be addressed by questions in a health check, include:

- activities for each process
- the organisation of tasks and responsibilities
- communication lines between processes
- the overall control of Service Management
- an IT infrastructure description
- control over changes to the IT infrastructure
- the level of Customer satisfaction with IT services.

Some improvements will require major change to the current processes, within the organisation, and it may be a considerable time before they can be implemented. Wherever possible, some 'quick wins' should be implemented and communicated so that everyone involved can see that improvements are being achieved prior to the final implementation. Using the health check can assist in the identification of quick-win areas.

Health checks and self-assessments can also help to determine the maturity level of the organisation. This is important if the target is better IT and business alignment. Maturity of process is an important issue, but has to be modified by the knowledge of what the business requires and is prepared to pay for in terms of maturity.

10.4 General guidelines on project planning

The OGC project management method PRINCE2 (Projects IN Controlled Environments) version 2 is widely adopted internationally and is used to describe an approach to projects within the ITIL context. The guidelines below are consistent with a PRINCE2 approach.

10.4.1 Project characteristics

A project can be defined as:

a temporary organisation that is needed to achieve a predefined result at a predefined time using predefined resources.

A 'temporary organisation' means that a project has a beginning and a clear ending and is conducted alongside day-to-day activities. By doing this, the project activity can be isolated from ongoing work.

PRINCE2 concentrates on creating an appropriate management environment to achieve the stated aim of the project. To achieve this a PRINCE2 project requires the following to exist:

- a finite and defined lifespan for the project
- a set of defined and measurable business products (to achieve quality requirements)
- a set of activities to achieve the business products (i.e. the 'doing' of the project)
- a defined amount of resources
- a project organisation structure, with defined responsibilities, to manage the project.

Before starting a project, an organisation should have a vision about what the results are intended to be. By defining the means necessary to achieve the project result, it is possible to isolate these assets (people, budget, etc.) from the day-to-day activities. This increases the success rate of the project.

Before a project actually starts, management should have an overall 'feel' for the project and be able to document:

- the project definition, explaining what the project needs to achieve – this should give background information, project objectives and scope, and it should outline the desired outcome and state the constraints on the project

- the business case, describing how the project outcome will support business needs and justify its existence – including reasons for selection of the approach

- known quality expectations of the business solution

- acceptance criteria for the final outcome

- known risks

- a high-level plan identifying necessary roles and, if possible, assigning them to individuals, as well as identifying the major 'go/no go' decision points.

10.4.2 Business case for the project

The business case describes the added value of the project for the organisation: why should this project be carried out? Of course, to establish the answer, the project costs and benefits should be compared. The difficulty in doing this, however, is that while the costs are relatively easy to quantify (people, budget, etc.), this is not the case with the benefits. Some useful ideas are described in Appendix F with its example cost-benefit analysis.

Particularly with process-oriented projects, assessing and describing the revenues/savings is a hard task. This has to do with the fact that process implementation results in higher quality service provision, higher service levels and a more flexible organisation; these are not always quantifiable financial results. Sometimes investments are made (or costs incurred, depending on the point of view) without knowing clearly the benefit; it is no use telling the budget holder that chances sometimes have to be taken in order to succeed. The business case should enable the reader to understand the value of investing in Service Management process improvement.

10.4.3 Critical success factors and possible problems

Successful Service Management processes should:

- be of sound design, adapted to the culture of the organisation in question but rigorous in their expectation of discipline in the manner of their following

- provide a good understanding of the Customer's requirements, concerns and business activities, and deliver business-driven rather than technology-driven services

- enhance Customer satisfaction

- improve value for money, resource utilisation and service quality

- deliver an infrastructure for the controlled operation of ongoing services by formalised and disciplined processes

- equip staff with goals and an understanding of the Customer's needs.

Problems with Service Management processes that may be encountered include:

- excessively bureaucratic processes, with a high percentage of the total support headcount dedicated to administering Service Management

- inconsistent staff performance for the same process (often accompanied by noticeable lack of commitment to the process from the responsible staff)

- lack of understanding on what each process should deliver

- no real benefits, service-cost reductions, or quality improvements arising from the implementation of Service Management processes

- unrealistic expectations, so that service targets are rarely hit

- no discernible improvement.

Some of the major issues concerned with defining and running a successful Service Management function and the project to implement it are discussed in Appendix C.

10.4.4   Project costs

When building the business case for a project, it is essential to be clear about what the project costs are and what will be the ongoing running costs of the Service Management processes. Project costs are one-off costs, while the running costs form a commitment for the organisation that may involve long-term contracts with suppliers.

The costs of implementing IT Infrastructure Library processes clearly vary according to the scale of operations. The costs associated with the implementation and running of the processes are roughly categorised as follows:

- project management costs

- project delivery costs (consultancy fees, project team for implementation, process owner)

- equipment and software training costs (including awareness, training in specific tools, and training in business awareness)

- documentation costs

- ongoing staff and accommodation costs (for running the processes, including subsequent training needs).

The costs of failing to provide effective processes can be considerable. Some examples are provided in Appendix F.

10.4.5   Organisation

A project needs to be managed, as well as to produce something, in order to achieve the stated end result. Managing a project needs to take account of three viewpoints:

- business – will the outcome support a real business need?

- User – when using the product, will it achieve the objective the User wants?

- supplier/technical – can the product be created (particularly within any given constraints)? Can the product be supported effectively when in operation?

A project needs to balance these three views if it is to achieve a viable result that is 'fit for its business purpose' and be achievable within the other constraints of time and cost.

Typically senior managers provide direction in these areas but wish to leave the day-to-day activity of managing the project to a project manager. PRINCE2 identifies a project board to cover these three interests and provide direction and advice to the project manager without being involved in day-to-day activities.

The project board is responsible for ensuring that the project results in the desired outcome and so should ensure that quality assurance is applied to the project in an appropriate manner. This activity needs to be separated from the project manager to ensure the board gets an objective answer to the question 'Are things really going as well as we are being told?'

In a Service Management process-implementation/improvement project, the three viewpoints will be represented by:

- the business executive – represents the (Customer) interest of the organisation in which the project is being run
- the User
- the supplier.

10.4.6 Products

Many contemporary project management methods have a product approach. The advantage is that products – unlike activities – can be described even before the project starts. In this way, a certain outcome of the project can be guaranteed by setting norms for the products to be delivered.

The principle of product planning presupposes good product description and management.

For further information, look at PRINCE2 or refer to the organisation's own project management approach.

10.4.7 Planning

After having defined the results in terms of products, the project manager should work out what other products need to be produced on the way to achieving the final outcome. A clear view of the activities can be built up for those products needed in the short-term (typically three to six months) with a high-level view of what is required in the longer term.

The project manager outlines the total project and produces a detailed plan for short-term activity. At this point, resources can be assigned to the activities to build products in the short term and skills requirements for the longer term can also be assessed.

While it is widely accepted that effective project planning and management are essential to project success, many IT projects continue to be poorly planned and badly managed. Often, people won't back out once (large) investments have been made. *'We've already invested heavily in this project, we can't stop now!'* has been used more than once in most organisations. Sometimes the runaway cost is the very reason for dissatisfaction and project cancellation should have taken place much earlier. To resist the temptation of an endless pursuit of a positive outcome of the project, an experienced project manager should assign a number of 'go/ no go' decision moments to his project.

This means that before the project is started, it is accepted that it may never be finished successfully. In fact, with each 'go/ no go' decision moment the business case of the project should be re-evaluated. In PRINCE2 these decision points come at the end of 'stages' where project progress to date is assessed and the ongoing viability of the future of the business case (and so the project) is actively revisited before the next stage is started.

10.4.8 Communication plan

Managing change can only succeed with the correct use of communication. A Service Management project will involve a lot of people but, typically, the outcome will affect the working lives of many more. Implementing or improving Service Management within an organisation requires a change of mindset by IT management and IT employees as well as IT Customers and Users. Communication around this transformation is essential to its success.

In order to ensure that all parties are aware of what is going on and can play a relevant part in the project, it is advisable to clarify how the project will communicate with all interested parties. A well-planned and executed communication plan will have a direct positive contribution to the success of the project.

A good communication plan should be built on a proper conception of what communication is. Communication is more than a one-way information stream. It requires continuous attention to the signals (positive and negative) of the various parties involved. Managing communications effectively involves the following nine steps:

1. describe the communications process in the Change process from the start

2. analyse the communication structure and culture

3. identify the important target groups

4. assess the communication goals for each target group

5. formulate a communication strategy for each target group

6. choose the right communication media for each target group

7. write a communication plan

8. communicate

9. measure and redirect if necessary.

A communication plan describes how target groups, contents and media are connected in a timeframe. Much like a project plan, a communication plan shows how actions, people, means and budget are to be allocated for the communication process.

10.5 Project review and management reporting

When a project is set up it is important to consider the reporting needs. Project management should be used to ensure appropriate decisions can be made. By exercising control over a project it should be possible to show that the project:

- is producing the required results, namely the results which meet predefined quality criteria

- is being carried out to schedule and in accordance with its previously agreed resource and cost plans

- remains viable against its business case (balancing benefits against costs/risks).

To support the decision-making processes, organisations should expect a number of reports throughout the life of a project. At the very least, a project should produce:

- regular progress reports

- post-completion project evaluation (of the way the project was run)

■ post-completion project review to assess if the projected benefits have materialised.

As part of the need to evaluate the project it is essential to maintain records that enable the project to be audited. Auditing may cover compliance and efficiency as well as looking at improvements that have been achieved or that could still be attempted.

On completion of a project, management will require further, regular, reports to show how well the Service Management processes are supporting the business needs.

10.5.1 Progress reporting

Progress against plans should be assessed on a regular basis, so that problems can be identified early and can be dealt with in a timely manner. The project manager should ensure that progress reports are produced for the project board at regular, agreed intervals. The reports should include statements regarding:

■ achievements in the current period

■ achievements expected in the next period

■ actual or potential problems and suggestions for their prevention or resolution.

Progress reports should provide a clear picture of the status of the project against plan and the business case so that adequately informed decisions can be made as to whether or not to continue expending resources on the project. It is important to look at the risks, at any changes in these within the current period and, if appropriate, identify their impact on subsequent project activities.

If a problem arises between progress reports that the project manager is not authorised to sort out, then an interim report should be compiled for the project board without waiting for the next progress report to be due. Within this report, the project manager states the nature and scope of the problem that has arisen, identifies options for its resolution, and recommends a course of action.

10.5.2 Evaluation of the project

As the project draws to a close, it is important to analyse how the project was managed and to identify lessons that were learned along the way. This information can then be used to benefit the project team as well as the organisation as a whole. An End Project Report typically covers:

■ achievement of the project's objectives

■ performance against plan (estimated time and costs versus actuals)

■ effect on the original plan and business case over the time of the project

■ statistics on issues raised and changes made

■ total impact of changes approved

■ statistics on the quality of the work carried out (in relation to stated expectations)

■ lessons learned

■ a post-project review plan.

10.5.3 Post-project review

The business case will have been built from the premise that the outcome of the project will deliver benefits to the business over a period of time. Thus, delivery of benefits needs to be assessed at a point after the project products have been put into use. The post-project review is used to assess whether the expected benefits have been realised, as well as to investigate whether problems have arisen from use of the products.

Each of the benefits mentioned in the business case should be assessed to see how well, if at all, it has been achieved. Other issues to consider are whether there were additional benefits – or unexpected problems. Both of these can be used to improve future business cases.

If necessary, follow-up actions may be identified to improve the situation that then exists.

10.5.4   Auditing for compliance using quality parameters

Process quality parameters can be seen as the 'operational thermometer' of the IT organisation. Using them, it is possible to determine whether the IT organisation is effective and efficient. Quality parameters need to be quantified for individual circumstances. However, this task is made easier once the required Service Levels and internal Service requirements are determined. There are two types of quality parameters, process specific and generic.

Generic quality parameters for IT Service Management

Generic quality parameters that need to be considered include:

- Customer satisfaction
- staff satisfaction
- efficiency
- effectiveness.

Appropriate information should be collected to rate the organisation's performance relative to these parameters. The nature of the information required will vary depending on how it is decided to judge each aspect, but what information is required should be clearly thought through from the start of the project so that measurement is possible during the post-project review.

Process-specific parameters

Process-specific metrics for each process are discussed in each of the process-specific Chapters of this book.

10.5.5   Auditing for improvement using key performance indicators

Introduction to the 'Balanced Scorecard'

The 'Balanced Scorecard' is an aid to organisational performance management. It helps to focus, not only on the financial targets but also on the internal processes, Customers and learning and growth issues. The balance should be found between these four perspectives.[1]

The four perspectives are focused around the following questions:

1. Customers: what do our Customers desire?
2. internal processes: how do we generate the added value for our Customers?
3. learning and growth: how do we guarantee we will keep generating added value in the future?

---

[1] Kaplan and Norton introduced the Balanced Scorecard in the early 1980s. Contemporary measurements from the time, particularly in US companies, focused on financial targets. Because financial figures are solely concentrated on past events, Kaplan and Norton sought a means to measure and steer using future activities as well. See the appropriate entry in Chapter 11.

4.   financial: how did we do financially?

As you can see, the first three questions focus on the future, the last question reviews what has gone before. It is worthwhile discussing the Balanced Scorecard further at this point:

- The Balanced Scorecard is not complex but to implement the scorecard successfully is complex. In practice, it can take an organisation up to three years to see the benefits of a Balanced Scorecard approach.

- The Balanced Scorecard is not an exclusive IT feature. On the contrary, many organisations use scorecards in other departments – even at board level.

- When implementing the Balanced Scorecard, it pays to start very conservatively. Start with three or four goals for each perspective. To do this, an organisation has to make choices; for many, this is extremely difficult and time consuming to do.

- The most difficult part of using the Balanced Scorecard is not the implementation; it is the consolidation. Usually, consultants are employed to assist in the introduction of the Balanced Scorecard. The challenge is to keep measuring once they have gone.

- The danger is in the temptation to fall back on prior measuring techniques or not measuring at all.

The Balanced Scorecard is complementary to ITIL. It is away of measuring the effectiveness of the performance of the organisation. Some of the links include the following:

- *client perspective:* this is relevant to most processes and is particularly relevant to Service Level Management where it is documented in Service Level Agreements

- *internal processes:* these of course cover the ITIL processes

- *financial:* Financial Management covers the way costs are allocated to the Customer organisation

- *learning and growth:* refers to staffing, training and investments in software.

10.5.6 Management reporting

After implementation of an initial Service Management system, or some improvements to it, a regular system for management reporting has to be set up. The following types of management reports should be considered:

- IT management reports that are used for planning and control of services

- reports matching achieved internal service levels, with service levels as described in the Service Level Agreements

- internal process-management reports, used by the process manager to determine the process' efficiency and effectiveness and for auditing for compliance

- Service Management reports, which Service Management uses for higher-level process control.

▮▮ BIBLIOGRAPHY

Note: that the entries in this Bibliography are given throughout in alphabetical order of title within each Section.

▮▮.▮ References

Acquisition

> IS Management Guide, www.ogc.gov.uk Tel: +44(0) 1603 704567
> Published by Format
> ISBN 1-90309-1-03-9

Balanced Scorecard (The): Translating strategy into action

> Robert S. Kaplan, David P. Norton/Hardcover/Published 1996
> Harvard Business School Press
> ISBN 0-87584-651-3

Business Case Development

Brief on business cases – www.ogc.gov.uk (response to the Successful IT report)

Capability Maturity Model (The): Guidelines for Improving the Software Process

> Carnegie Mellon University, Software Engineering Institute, Addison-Wesley
> ISBN 0-201-54664-7

Code of Practice for IT Service Management (A), DISC 0005

> Extracts are reproduced with the permission of BSI under licence number PD\ 1999 0877. Complete copies of the standard can be obtained by post from BSI Customer Services, 389 Chiswick High Road, London W4 4AL.
> www.bsi.ork.uk/disc/products, Tel: 020-8996 9001

Cultures of work organisations (The)

> Trice/Beyer (1993). Prentice Hall, N.J. U.S.A.
> ISBN 0-13-191438-3

Data Protection Act

> Available from The Stationery Office, www.the-stationery-office.co.uk
> ISBN 010 543 5848

In Search of Excellence: Lessons From America's Best-Run Companies

> Thomas Peters, Robert H. Waterman, Tom Peters
> Warner Books
> ISBN 0-44-638507-7

IS Management Handbook

> OGC
> www.ogc.gov. uk/handbook

Leading change

John P. Kotter/Hardcover/1996
Harvard Business School Press
ISBN 0-875847-47-1

Managing Change

IS Management Guide, www.ogc.gov.uk Tel: +44(0) 1603 704567 Published by Format
ISBN 1-90309-1-01-2

Managing Partnerships

IS Management Guide, www.ogc.gov.uk Tel: +44(0) 1603 704567
Published by Format
ISBN 1-90309-1-06-5

Managing Performance

IS Management Guide, www.ogc.gov.uk Tel: +44(0) 1603704567
Published by Format
ISBN 1-90309-1-05-5

Managing Services

IS Management Guide, www.ogc.gov.uk Tel: +44(0) 1603704567
Published by Format
ISBN 1-90309-1-04- 7

Managing Successful Projects with PRINCE 2

OGC, www.ogc.gov.uk Tel: +44(0) 1603704567 or The Stationery Office, Tel 020-7873 9090
ISBN 0-11-330855-8

Modernising government: e-government – A strategic framework for public services in the Information Age

Published April 2000, CITU, The Cabinet Office
ISBN 0-7115-0394-X

Modernising Government White Paper

Presented to UK Parliament, March 1999
Cm4310. Price £8.50.
www.cabinet-office.gov.uk/moderngov/

Organisational transformations

Espejo/Schumann/Schwaninger/Bilello (1996). John Wiley and Sons; Chichester, England
ISBN 0-471-96182-5

PRINCE2 (reference manual)

ISBN 0-11-3306857

Process Innovation

Davenport (1993). HBS, Boston, Massachusetts U.S.A.
ISBN 0-87584-366-2

Risk Handbook

> IS Management Handbook
> from OGC website www.ogc.gov.uk

Security Management

> ITIL Publication
> OGC
> ISBN 0-11-330014-X

Service Quality

> Brown/Gummesson/Edvardsson/Gustavsson (1991). Lexington Books; N.Y., U.S.A.
> ISBN 0-669-21152-4

Structures in fives: designing effective organisations

> Minzberg (1993). Prentice Hall, N.J. U.S.A.
> ISBN 0-13-855479-X

Successful IT: Modernising Government in Action

> Cabinet Office Report, published by the Office of the e-Envoy. May 2000.
> www.citu.gov.uk/itprojectsreview.htm

Turnbull Report on Corporate Governance

> Institute of Chartered Accountants of England and Wales
> ISBN 1 841520101

11.2 Other sources

British Standards Institution

BS 7799-1:1999	Information security management. Code of practice for information security management
BS 7799-2:1999	Information security management. Specification for information security management systems
BS 15000:2000	Specification for IT Service Management
DISC PD 0005:1998	Code of practice for IT Service Management
DISC PD 0015:2000	IT Service Management. Self-assessment workbook

> Website at www.bsi-global.com

W. Edwards Deming Institute (The)

> Website at www.deming.org. 'We should work on our process, not the outcome of our processes.' W. Edwards Deming

European Foundation for Quality Management

> Website at www.efqm.org. '... the battle for Quality is one of the prerequisites for the success of your companies and for our collective success'.

Jacques Delors

> ISO 9000 Information Forum
> Website at www.iso-9000.co.uk

APPENDIX A | TERMINOLOGY

A.1 | Acronyms used in this book

AMDB	Availability Management Database
AST	Agreed Service Time
ATM	Auto Teller Machine
BCM	Business Continuity Management
BIA	Business Impact Analysis
BRM	Business Relationship Management
CAB	Change Advisory Board
CDB	Capacity Database
CFIA	Component Failure Impact Analysis
CI	Configuration Item
CIA	Confidentiality, Integrity and Availability
CMDB	Configuration Management Database
CSBC	Computer Services Business Code
CSS	Customer Satisfaction Survey
DT	Down Time
EFQM	European Foundation for Quality Management
EUA	End User Availability
EUDT	End User Down Time
EUPT	End User Processing Time
FTA	Fault Tree Analysis
ICT	Information and Communication Technology(ies)
ISP	Internet Service Provider
ITAMM	IT Availability Metrics Model
ITIL	Information Technology Infrastructure Library
ITSC	IT Service Continuity
ITSCM	IT Service Continuity Management
ItSMF	IT Service Management Forum
IVR	Interactive Voice Response

KPI	Key Performance Indicator
LAN	Local Area Network
MBNQA	Malcolm Baldrige National Quality Award
MIM	Major Incident Management
MTBF	Mean Time Between Failures
MTBSI	Mean Time Between System Incidents
MTTR	Mean Time To Repair
OGC	Office of Government Commerce
OLA	Operational Level Agreement
OLTP	On-line Transaction Processing
PAD	Package Assembly/Disassembly device
PKI	Public Key Infrastructure
PRINCE	Projects IN Controlled Environments
QA	Quality Assurance
RAG	Red-Amber-Green
RAID	Redundant Array of Inexpensive Disks
RFC	Request For Charge
ROCE	Return On Capital Employed
ROI	Return On Investment
RWO	Real World Object
SIP	Service Improvement Programme
SLA	Service Level Agreement
SLAM	SLA Monitoring
SLM	Service Level Management
SLR	Service Level Requirement
SMO	Service Maintenance Objectives
SOA	System Outage Analysis
SPOF	Single Point of Failure
TCO	Total Cost of Ownership
TOP	Technical Observation Post
TOR	Terms Of Reference
TQM	Total Quality Management

UPS	Uninterruptible Power Supply
VBF	Vital Business Function
VSI	Virtual Storage Interrupt
WAN	Wide Area Network

A.2   Glossary of ITIL terms

Absorbed overhead	Overhead which, by means of absorption rates, is included in costs of specific products or saleable services, in a given period of time. Under- or over-absorbed overhead. The difference between overhead cost incurred and overhead cost absorbed: it may be split into its two constituent parts for control purposes.
Absorption costing	A principle whereby fixed as well as variable costs are allotted to cost units and total overheads are absorbed according to activity level. The term may be applied where production costs only, or costs of all functions are so allotted.
Action lists	Defined actions, allocated to recovery teams and individuals, within a phase of a plan. These are supported by reference data.
Alert phase	The first phase of a business continuity plan in which initial emergency procedures and damage assessments are activated.
Allocated cost	A cost that can be directly identified with a business unit.
Apportioned cost	A cost that is shared by a number of business units (an indirect cost). This cost must be shared out between these units on an equitable basis.
Asset	Component of a business process. Assets can include people, accommodation, computer systems, networks, paper records, fax machines, etc.
Asynchronous/synchronous	In a communications sense, the ability to transmit each character as a self-contained unit of information, without additional timing information. This method of transmitting data is sometimes called start/stop. Synchronous working involves the use of timing information to allow transmission of data, which is normally done in blocks. Synchronous transmission is usually more efficient than the asynchronous method.
Availability	Ability of a component or service to perform its required function at a stated instant or over a stated period of time. It is usually expressed as the availability ratio, i.e. the proportion of time that the service is actually available for use by the Customers within the agreed service hours.
Balanced Scorecard	An aid to organisational performance management. It helps to focus, not only on the financial targets but also on the internal processes, Customers and learning and growth issues.
Baseline	A snapshot or a position which is recorded. Although the position may be updated later, the baseline remains unchanged and available as a reference of the original state and as a comparison against the current position (PRINCE 2).

Bridge	Equipment and techniques used to match circuits to each other ensuring minimum transmission impairment.
BS7799	The British standard for Information Security Management. This standard provides a comprehensive set of controls comprising best practices in information security.
Business function	A business unit within an organisation, e.g. a department, division, branch.
Business process	A group of business activities undertaken by an organisation in pursuit of a common goal. Typical business processes include receiving orders, marketing services, selling products, delivering services, distributing products, invoicing for services, accounting for money received. A business process usually depends upon several business functions for support, e.g. IT, personnel, accommodation. A business process rarely operates in isolation, i.e. other business processes will depend on it and it will depend on other processes.
Business recovery objective	The desired time within which business processes should be recovered, and the minimum staff, assets and services required within this time.
Business recovery plan framework	A template business recovery plan (or set of plans) produced to allow the structure and proposed contents to be agreed before the detailed business recovery plan is produced.
Business recovery plans	Documents describing the roles, responsibilities and actions necessary to resume business processes following a business disruption.
Business recovery team	A defined group of personnel with a defined role and subordinate range of actions to facilitate recovery of a business function or process.
Business unit	A segment of the business entity by which both revenues are received and expenditure are caused or controlled, such revenues and expenditure being used to evaluate segmental performance.
Capital Costs	Typically those assets of the costs applying to the physical (substantial) organisation. Traditionally this was the accommodation and machinery necessary to produce the enterprise's product. Capital Costs are the purchase or major enhancement of fixed assets, for example computer equipment (building and plant) and are often also referred to as 'one-off' costs.

Capital investment appraisal	The process of evaluating proposed investment in specific fixed assets and the benefits to be obtained from their acquisition. The techniques used in the evaluation can be summarised as non-discounting methods (i.e. simple pay-back), return on capital employed and discounted cash flow methods (i.e. yield, net present value and discounted pay-back).
Capitalisation	The process of identifying major expenditure as Capital, whether there is a substantial asset or not, to reduce the impact on the current financial year of such expenditure. The most common item for this to be applied to is software, whether developed in-house or purchased.
Category	Classification of a group of Configuration Items, Change documents or problems.
Change	The addition, modification or removal of approved, supported or baselined hardware, network, software, application, environment, system, desktop build or associated documentation.
Change Advisory Board	A group of people who can give expert advice to Change Management on the implementation of Changes. This board is likely to be made up of representatives from all areas within IT and representatives from business units.
Change authority	A group that is given the authority to approve Change, e.g. by the project board. Sometimes referred to as the Configuration Board.
Change control	The procedure to ensure that all Changes are controlled, including the submission, analysis, decision making, approval, implementation and post-implementation of the Change.
Change document	Request for Change, Change control form, Change order, Change record.
Change history	Auditable information that records, for example, what was done, when it was done, by who and why.
Change log	A log of Requests for Change raised during the project, showing information on each Change, its evaluation, what decisions have been made and its current status, e.g. Raised, Reviewed, Approved, Implemented, Closed.
Change Management	Process of controlling Changes to the infrastructure or any aspect of services, in a controlled manner, enabling approved Changes with minimum disruption.
Change record	A record containing details of which CIs are affected by an authorised Change (planned or implemented) and how.
Charging	The process of establishing charges in respect of business units, and raising the relevant invoices for recovery from customers.

Classification	Process of formally grouping Configuration Items by type e.g. software, hardware, documentation, environment, application.
	Process of formally identifying Changes by type e.g. project scope change request, validation change request, infrastructure change request.
	Process of formally identifying incidents, problems and known errors by origin, symptoms and cause.
Closure	When the Customer is satisfied that an Incident has been resolved.
Cold stand-by	See 'Gradual Recovery'.
Command, control and communications	The processes by which an organisation retains overall co-ordination of its recovery effort during invocation of business recovery plans.
Computer Aided Systems Engineering	A software tool for programmers. It provides help in the planning, analysis, design and documentation of computer software.
Configuration Baseline (see also Baseline)	Configuration of a product or system established at a specific point in time, which captures both the structure and details of the product or system, and enables that product or system to be rebuilt at a later date.
Configuration control	Activities comprising the control of Changes to Configuration Items after formally establishing its configuration documents. It includes the evaluation, co-ordination, approval or rejection of Changes. The implementation of Changes includes changes, deviations and waivers that impact on the configuration.
Configuration documentation	Documents that define requirements, system design, build, production, and verification for a configuration item.
Configuration identification	Activities that determine the product structure, the selection of Configuration Items, and the documentation of the Configuration Item's physical and functional characteristics including interfaces and subsequent Changes. It includes the allocation of identification characters or numbers to the Configuration Items and their documents. It also includes the unique numbering of configuration control forms associated with Changes and Problems.
Configuration item (CI)	Component of an infrastructure – or an item, such as a Request for Change, associated with an infrastructure – which is (or is to be) under the control of Configuration Management. CIs may vary widely in complexity, size and type – from an entire system (including all hardware, software and documentation) to a single module or a minor hardware component.

Configuration Management	The process of identifying and defining the Configuration Items in a system, recording and reporting the status of Configuration Items and Requests for Change, and verifying the completeness and correctness of configuration items.
Configuration Management Database	A database which contains all relevant details of each CI and details of the important relationships between CIs.
Configuration Management plan	A document setting out the organisation and procedures for the Configuration Management of a specific product, project, system, support group or service.
Configuration Management Tool (CM Tool)	A software product providing automatic support for Change, Configuration or version control.
Configuration Structure	A hierarchy of all the CIs that comprise a configuration.
Contingency Planning	Planning to address unwanted occurrences that may happen at a later time. Traditionally, the term has been used to refer to planning for the recovery of IT systems rather than entire business processes.
Cost	The amount of expenditure (actual or notional) incurred on, or attributable to, a specific activity or business unit.
Cost effectiveness	Ensuring that there is a proper balance between the quality of service on the one side and expenditure on the other. Any investment that increases the costs of providing IT services should always result in enhancement to service quality or quantity.
Cost Management	All the procedures, tasks and deliverables that are needed to fulfil an organisation's costing and charging requirements.
Cost unit	In the context of CSBC the cost unit is a functional cost unit which establishes standard cost per workload element of activity, based on calculated activity ratios converted to cost ratios.
Costing	The process of identifying the costs of the business and of breaking them down and relating them to the various activities of the organisation.
Countermeasure	A check or restraint on the service designed to enhance security by reducing the risk of an attack (by reducing either the threat or the vulnerability), reducing the Impact of an attack, detecting the occurrence of an attack and/or assisting in the recovery from an attack.
Crisis management	The processes by which an organisation manages the wider impact of a disaster, such as adverse media coverage.
Customer	Owner of the service; usually the Customer has responsibility for the cost of the service, either directly through charging or

	indirectly in terms of demonstrable business need. It is the Customer who will define the service requirements.
Data transfer time	The length of time taken for a block or sector of data to be read from or written to an I/O device, such as a disk or tape.
Definitive Software Library (DSL)	The library in which the definitive authorised versions of all software CIs are stored and protected. It is a physical library or storage repository where master copies of software versions are placed. This one logical storage area may in reality consist of one or more physical software libraries or filestores. They should be separate from development and test filestore areas. The DSL may also include a physical store to hold master copies of bought-in software, e.g. fire-proof safe. Only authorised software should be accepted into the DSL, strictly controlled by Change and Release Management.
	The DSL exists not directly because of the needs of the Configuration Management process, but as a common base for the Release Management and Configuration Management processes.
Delta Release	A release that includes only those CIs within the Release unit that have actually changed or are new since the last full or Delta Release. For example, if the Release unit is the program, a Delta Release contains only those modules that have changed, or are new, since the last full release of the program or the last Delta Release of the modules – see also 'Full Release'.
Dependency	The reliance, either direct or indirect, of one process or activity upon another.
Depreciation	The loss in value of an asset due to its use and/or the passage of time. The annual depreciation charge in accounts represents the amount of capital assets used up in the accounting period. It is charged in the cost accounts to ensure that the cost of capital equipment is reflected in the unit costs of the services provided using the equipment. There are various methods of calculating depreciation for the period, but the Treasury usually recommends the use of current cost asset valuation as the basis for the depreciation charge.
Differential charging	Charging business customers different rates for the same work, typically to dampen demand or to generate revenue for spare capacity. This can also be used to encourage off-peak or night time running.
Direct cost	A cost that is incurred for, and can be traced in full to a product, service, cost centre or department. This is an allocated cost. Direct costs are direct materials, direct wages and direct expenses.

Disaster recovery planning	A series of processes that focus only upon the recovery processes, principally in response to physical disasters, that are contained within BCM.
Discounted cash flow	An evaluation of the future net cash flows generated by a capital project by discounting them to their present-day value. The two methods most commonly used are:

- yield method, for which the calculation determines the internal rate of return (IRR) in the form of a percentage

- net present value (NPV) method, in which the discount rate is chosen and the answer is a sum of money.

Discounting	The offering to business customers of reduced rates for the use of off-peak resources (see also Surcharging).
Disk cache controller	Memory that is used to store blocks of data that have been read from the disk devices connected to them. If a subsequent I/O requires a record that is still resident in the cache memory, it will be picked up from there, thus saving another physical I/O.
Duplex (full and half)	Full duplex line/channel allows simultaneous transmission in both directions. Half duplex line/channel is capable of transmitting in both directions, but only in one direction at a time.
Echoing	A reflection of the transmitted signal from the receiving end, a visual method of error detection in which the signal from the originating device is looped back to that device so that it can be displayed.
Elements of cost	The constituent parts of costs according to the factors upon which expenditure is incurred viz., materials, labour and expenses.
End-User	See 'User'.
Environment	A collection of hardware, software, network communications and procedures that work together to provide a discrete type of computer service. There may be one or more environments on a physical platform e.g. test, production. An environment has unique features and characteristics that dictate how they are administered in similar, yet diverse manners.
Expert User	See 'Super User'.
External Target	One of the measures, against which a delivered IT service is compared, expressed in terms of the customer's business.
Financial year	An accounting period covering 12 consecutive months. In the public sector this financial year generally coincides with the fiscal year which runs from 1 April to 31 March.

Forward Schedule of Changes	Contains details of all the Changes approved for implementation and their proposed implementation dates. It should be agreed with the Customers and the business, Service Level Management, the Service Desk and Availability Management. Once agreed, the Service Desk should communicate to the User community at large any planned additional downtime arising from implementing the Changes, using the most effective methods available.
Full cost	The total cost of all the resources used in supplying a service i.e. the sum of the direct costs of producing the output, a proportional share of overhead costs and any selling and distribution expenses. Both cash costs and notional (non-cash) costs should be included, including the cost of capital.
	See also 'Total Cost of Ownership'
Full Release	All components of the Release unit are built, tested, distributed and implemented together – see also 'Delta Release'.
Gateway	Equipment which is used to interface networks so that a terminal on one network can communicate with services or a terminal on another.
Gradual Recovery	Previously called 'Cold stand-by', this is applicable to organisations that do not need immediate restoration of business processes and can function for a period of up to 72 hours, or longer, without a re-establishment of full IT facilities. This may include the provision of empty accommodation fully equipped with power, environmental controls and local network cabling infrastructure, telecommunications connections, and available in a disaster situation for an organisation to install its own computer equipment.
Hard charging	Descriptive of a situation where, within an organisation, actual funds are transferred from the customer to the IT organisation in payment for the delivery of IT services.
Hard fault	The situation in a virtual memory system when the required page of code or data, which a program was using, has been redeployed by the operating system for some other purpose. This means that another piece of memory must be found to accommodate the code or data, and will involve physical reading/writing of pages to the page file.
Host	A host computer comprises the central hardware and software resources of a computer complex, e.g. CPU, memory, channels, disk and magnetic tape I/O subsystems plus operating and applications software. The term is used to denote all non-network items.
Hot stand-by	See 'Immediate Recovery'.

ICT	The convergence of Information Technology, Telecommunications and Data Networking Technologies into a single technology.
Immediate Recovery	Previously called 'Hot stand-by', provides for the immediate restoration of services following any irrecoverable incident. It is important to distinguish between the previous definition of 'hot stand-by' and 'immediate recovery'. Hot stand-by typically referred to availability of services within a short timescale such as 2 or 4 hours whereas immediate recovery implies the instant availability of services.
Impact	Measure of the business criticality of an Incident, Problem or Request for Change. Often equal to the extent of a distortion of agreed or expected Service Levels.
Impact analysis	The identification of critical business processes, and the potential damage or loss that may be caused to the organisation resulting from a disruption to those processes. Business impact analysis identifies:

- the form the loss or damage will take

- how that degree of damage or loss is likely to escalate with time following an incident

- the minimum staffing, facilities and services needed to enable business processes to continue to operate at a minimum acceptable level

- the time within which they should be recovered.

The time within which full recovery of the business processes is to be achieved is also identified.

Impact scenario	Description of the type of impact on the business that could follow a business disruption. Usually related to a business process and will always refer to a period of time, e.g. customer services will be unable to operate for two days.
Incident	Any event which is not part of the standard operation of a service and which causes, or may cause, an interruption to, or a reduction in, the quality of that service.
Indirect cost	A cost incurred in the course of making a product providing a service or running a cost centre or department, but which cannot be traced directly and in full to the product, service or department, because it has been incurred for a number of cost centres or cost units. These costs are apportioned to cost centres/cost units. Indirect costs are also referred to as overheads.

Informed Customer	An individual, team or group with functional responsibility within an organisation for ensuring that spend on IS/IT is directed to best effect, i.e. that the business is receiving value for money and continues to achieve the most beneficial outcome. In order to fulfil its role the 'Informed' Customer function must gain clarity of vision in relation to the business plans and assure that suitable strategies are devised and maintained for achieving business goals.
	The 'Informed' Customer function ensures that the needs of the business are effectively translated into a business requirements specification, that IT investment is both efficiently and economically directed, and that progress towards effective business solutions is monitored. The 'Informed' Customer should play an active role in the procurement process, e.g. in relation to business case development, and also in ensuring that the services and solutions obtained are used effectively within the organisation to achieve maximum business benefits. The term is often used in relation to the outsourcing of IT/IS. Sometimes also called 'Intelligent Customer'.
Interface	Physical or functional interaction at the boundary between Configuration Items.
Intermediate Recovery	Previously called 'Warm stand-by', typically involves the re-establishment of the critical systems and services within a 24 to 72 hour period, and is used by organisations that need to recover IT facilities within a predetermined time to prevent impacts to the business process.
Internal target	One of the measures against which supporting processes for the IT service are compared. Usually expressed in technical terms relating directly to the underpinning service being measured.
Invocation (of business recovery plans)	Putting business recovery plans into operation after a business disruption.
Invocation (of stand-by arrangements)	Putting stand-by arrangements into operation as part of business recovery activities.
Invocation and recovery phase	The second phase of a business recovery plan.
ISO9001	The internationally accepted set of standards concerning quality management systems.
ITIL	The OGC IT Infrastructure Library – a set of guides on the management and provision of operational IT services.
Known Error	An Incident or Problem for which the root cause is known and for which a temporary Work-around or a permanent alternative has been identified. If a business case exists, an RFC will be raised, but, in any event, it remains a Known Error unless it is permanently fixed by a Change.

Latency	The elapsed time from the moment when a seek was completed on a disk device to the point when the required data is positioned under the read/write heads. It is normally defined by manufacturers as being half the disk rotation time.
Lifecycle	A series of states, connected by allowable transitions. The lifecycle represents an approval process for Configuration Items, Problem Reports and Change documents.
Logical I/O	A read or write request by a program. That request may, or may not, necessitate a physical I/O. For example, on a read request the required record may already be in a memory buffer and therefore a physical I/O is not necessary.
Marginal Cost	The cost of providing the service now, based upon the investment already made.
Maturity level/Milestone	The degree to which BCM activities and processes have become standard business practice within an organisation.
Metric	Measurable element of a service process or function.
Operational Costs	Those costs resulting from the day-to-day running of the IT Services section, e.g. staff costs, hardware maintenance and electricity, and relating to repeating payments whose effects can be measured within a short timeframe, usually less than the 12-month financial year.
Operational Level Agreement	An internal agreement covering the delivery of services which support the IT organisation in their delivery of services.
Opportunity cost (or true cost)	The value of a benefit sacrificed in favour of an alternative course of action. That is the cost of using resources in a particular operation expressed in terms of foregoing the benefit that could be derived from the best alternative use of those resources.
Outsourcing	The process by which functions performed by the organisation are contracted out for operation, on the organisation's behalf, by third parties.
Overheads	The total of indirect materials, wages and expenses.
Package assembly/disassembly device	A device that permits terminals, which do not have an interface suitable for direct connection to a packet switched network, to access such a network. A PAD converts data to/from packets and handles call set-up and addressing.
Page fault	A program interruption that occurs when a page that is marked 'not in real memory' is referred to by an active page.

Paging	The I/O necessary to read and write to and from the paging disks: real (not virtual) memory is needed to process data. With insufficient real memory, the operating system writes old pages to disk, and reads new pages from disk, so that the required data and instructions are in real memory.
PD0005	Alternative title for the BSI publication 'Code of Practice for IT Service Management'.
Percentage utilisation	The amount of time that a hardware device is busy over a given period of time. For example, if the CPU is busy for 1800 seconds in a one hour period, its utilisation is said to be 50%.
Phantom line error	A communications error reported by a computer system that is not detected by network monitoring equipment. It is often caused by changes to the circuits and network equipment (e.g. re-routing circuits at the physical level on a backbone network) while data communications is in progress.
Physical I/O	A read or write request from a program has necessitated a physical read or write operation on an I/O device.
Prime cost	The total cost of direct materials, direct labour and direct expenses. The term prime cost is commonly restricted to direct production costs only and so does not customarily include direct costs of marketing or research and development.
PRINCE2	The standard UK government method for project management.
Priority	Sequence in which an Incident or Problem needs to be resolved, based on impact and urgency.
Problem	Unknown underlying cause of one or more Incidents.
Process	A connected series of actions, activities, Changes etc, performed by agents with the intent of satisfying a purpose or achieving a goal.
Process Control	The process of planning and regulating, with the objective of performing the process in an effective and efficient way.
Programme	A collection of activities and projects that collectively implement a new corporate requirement or function.
Queuing time	Queuing time is incurred when the device, which a program wishes to use, is already busy. The program therefore has to wait in a queue to obtain service from that device.
RAID	Redundant Array of Inexpensive Disks – a mechanism for providing data resilience for computer systems using mirrored arrays of magnetic disks. Different levels of RAID can be applied to provide for greater resilience.

Reference data	Information that supports the plans and action lists, such as names and addresses or inventories, which is indexed within the plan.
Release	A collection of new and/or changed CIs which are tested and introduced into the live environment together.
Request for Change (RFC)	Form, or screen, used to record details of a request for a change to any CIs within an infrastructure or to procedures and items associated with the infrastructure.
Resolution	Action which will resolve an Incident. This may be a Workaround.
Resource cost	The amount of machine resource that a given task consumes. This resource is usually expressed in seconds for the CPU or the number of l/Os for a disk or tape device.
Resource profile	The total resource costs that are consumed by an individual online transaction, batch job or program. It is usually expressed in terms of CPU seconds, number of I/Os and memory usage.
Resource unit costs	Resource units may be calculated on a standard cost basis to identify the expected (standard) cost for using a particular resource. Because computer resources come in many shapes and forms, units have to be established by logical groupings. Examples are:

a) CPU time or instructions

b) disk I/Os

c) print lines

d) communication transactions.

Resources	The IT Services section needs to provide the customers with the required services. The resources are typically computer and related equipment, software, facilities or organisational (people).
Return to normal phase	The phase within a business recovery plan which re-establishes normal operations.
Risk	A measure of the exposure to which an organisation may be subjected. This is a combination of the likelihood of a business disruption occurring and the possible loss that may result from such business disruption.
Risk Analysis	The identification and assessment of the level (measure) of the risks calculated from the assessed values of assets and the assessed levels of threats to, and vulnerabilities of, those assets.

Risk Management	The identification, selection and adoption of counter measures justified by the identified risks to assets in terms of their potential impact upon services if failure occurs, and the reduction of those risks to an acceptable level.
Risk reduction measure	Measures taken to reduce the likelihood or consequences of a business disruption occurring (as opposed to planning to recover after a disruption).
Role	A set of responsibilities, activities and authorisations.
Roll in roll out (RIRO)	Used on some systems to describe swapping.
Rotational Position Sensing	A facility which is employed on most mainframes and some minicomputers. When a seek has been initiated the system can free the path from a disk drive to a controller for use by another disk drive, while it is waiting for the required data to come under the read/write heads (latency). This facility usually improves the overall performance of the I/O subsystem.
Seek time	Occurs when the disk read/write heads are not positioned on the required track. It describes the elapsed time taken to move heads to the right track.
Self-insurance	A decision to bear the losses that could result from a disruption to the business as opposed to taking insurance cover on the risk.
Service	One or more IT systems which enable a business process.
Service achievement	The actual service levels delivered by the IT organisation to a customer within a defined life-span.
Service Catalogue	Written statement of IT services, default levels and options.
Service Desk	The single point of contact within the IT organisation for users of IT services.
Service Improvement Programme	A formal project undertaken within an organisation to identify and introduce measurable improvements within a specified work area or work process.
Service Level Agreement	Written agreement between a servIce provider and the Customer(s), that documents agreed Service Levels for a Service.
Service Level Management	The process of defining, agreeing, documenting and managing the levels of customer IT service, that are required and cost justified.
Service Management	Management of Services to meet the Customer's requirements.
Service provider	Third-party organisation supplying services or products to customers.
Service quality plan	The written plan and specification of internal targets designed to guarantee the agreed service levels.

Service Request	Every Incident not being a failure in the IT Infrastructure.
Services	The deliverables of the IT Services organisation as perceived by the Customers; the services do not consist merely of making computer resources available for customers to use.
Simulation modelling	Using a program to simulate computer processing by describing in detail the path of a job or transaction. It can give extremely accurate results. Unfortunately, it demands a great deal of time and effort from the modeller. It is most beneficial in extremely large or time-critical systems where the margin for error is very small.
Soft fault	The situation in a virtual memory system when the operating system has detected that a page of code or data was due to be reused, i.e. it is on a list of 'free' pages, but it is still actually in memory. It is now rescued and put back into service.
Software Configuration Item (SCI)	As 'Configuration Item', excluding hardware and services.
Software Environment	Software used to support the application such as operating system, database management system, development tools, compilers, and application software.
Software Library	A controlled collection of SCIs designated to keep those with like status and type together and distinctly segregated, to aid in development, operation and maintenance.
Software work unit	Software work is a generic term devised to represent a common base on which all calculations for workload usage and IT resource capacity are then based. A unit of software work for I/O type equipment equals the number of bytes transferred; and for central processors it is based on the product of power and CPU-time.
Solid state devices	Memory devices that are made to appear as if they are disk devices. The advantages of such devices are that the service times are much faster than real disks since there is no seek time or latency. The main disadvantage is that they are much more expensive.
Specsheet	Specifies in detail what the customer wants (external) and what consequences this has for the service provider (internal) such as required resources and skills.

Standard cost	A pre-determined calculation of how much costs should be under specified working conditions. It is built up from an assessment of the value of cost elements and correlates technical specifications and the quantification of materials, labour and other costs to the prices and/or wages expected to apply during the period in which the standard cost is intended to be used. Its main purposes are to provide bases for control through variance accounting, for the valuation of work in progress and for fixing selling prices.
Standard costing	A technique which uses standards for costs and revenues for the purposes of control through variance analysis.
Stand-by arrangements	Arrangements to have available assets which have been identified as replacements should primary assets be unavailable following a business disruption. Typically, these include accommodation, IT systems and networks, telecommunications and sometimes people.
Storage occupancy	A defined measurement unit that is used for storage type equipment to measure usage. The unit value equals the number of bytes stored.
Super User	In some organisations it is common to use 'expert' Users (commonly known as Super or Expert Users) to deal with firstline support problems and queries. This is typically in specific application areas, or geographical locations, where there is not the requirement for full-time support staff. This valuable resource however needs to be carefully co-ordinated and utilised.
Surcharging	Surcharging is charging business users a premium rate for using resources at peak times.
Swapping	The reaction of the operating system to insufficient real memory: swapping occurs when too many tasks are perceived to be competing for limited resources. It is the physical movement of an entire task (e.g. all real memory pages of an address space may be moved at one time from main storage to auxiliary storage).
System	An integrated composite that consists of one or more of the processes, hardware, software, facilities and people, that provides a capability to satisfy a stated need or objective.
Terminal emulation	Software running on an intelligent device, typically a PC or workstation, which allows that device to function as an interactive terminal connected to a host system. Examples of such emulation software includes IBM 3270 BSC or SNA, ICL C03, or Digital VT100.
Terminal I/O	A read from, or a write to, an online device such as a VDU or remote printer.

Third-party supplier	An enterprise or group, external to the Customer's enterprise, which provides services and/or products to that Customer's enterprise.
Thrashing	A condition in a virtual storage system where an excessive proportion of CPU time is spent on moving data between main and auxiliary storage.
Total Cost Of Ownership	Calculated including depreciation, maintenance, staff costs, accommodation, and planned renewal.
Tree structures	In data structures, a series of connected nodes without cycles. One node is termed the root and is the starting point of all paths, other nodes termed leaves terminate the paths.
Underpinning contract	A contract with an external supplier covering delivery of services that support the IT organisation in their delivery of services.
Unit costs	Costs distributed over individual component usage. For example, it can be assumed that, if a box of paper with 1000 sheets costs £10, then each sheet costs 1p. Similarly if a CPU costs £1m a year and it is used to process 1,000 jobs that year, each job costs on average £1,000.
Urgency	Measure of the business criticality of an Incident or Problem based on the impact and on the business needs of the Customer.
User	The person who uses the service on a day-to-day basis.
Utility cost centre (UCC)	A cost centre for the provision of support services to other cost centres.
Variance analysis	A variance is the difference between planned, budgeted or standard cost and actual cost (or revenues). Variance analysis is an analysis of the factors that have caused the difference between the pre-determined standards and the actual results. Variances can be developed specifically related to the operations carried out in addition to those mentioned above.
Version	An identified instance of a Configuration Item within a product breakdown structure or configuration structure for the purpose of tracking and auditing change history. Also used for software Configuration Items to define a specific identification released in development for drafting, review or modification, test or production.
Version Identifier	A version number; version date; or version date and time stamp.
Virtual memory system	A system that enhances the size of hard memory by adding an auxiliary storage layer residing on the hard disk.
Virtual storage interrupt (VSI)	An ICL VME term for a page fault.

Vulnerability	A weakness of the system and its assets, which could be exploited by threats.
Warm stand-by	See 'Intermediate Recovery'.
Waterline	The lowest level of detail relevant to the customer.
Work-around	Method of avoiding an Incident or Problem, either by a temporary fix or by a technique that means the Customer is not reliant on a particular aspect of the service that is known to have a problem.
Workloads	In the context of Capacity Management Modelling, a set of forecasts which detail the estimated resource usage over an agreed planning horizon. Workloads generally represent discrete business applications and can be further sub-divided into types of work (interactive, timesharing, batch).
WORM (Device)	Optical read only disks, standing for Write Once Read Many.

APPENDIX B PROCESS THEORY AND PRACTICE

B.1 Process theory

This Appendix provides a general introduction to process theory and practice, which is the basis for the ITIL process models. We become aware of 'process' through process models that define work-flows and provide guidance on performing it. A process model enables understanding and helps to articulate the distinctive features of a process.

A Process can be defined as:

a connected series of actions, activities, changes etc, performed by agents with the intent of satisfying a purpose or achieving a goal.

Process control can similarly be defined as:

the process of planning and regulating, with the objective of performing a process in an effective and efficient way.

Processes, once defined, should be under control; once under control, they can be repeated and become manageable. Degrees of control over processes can be defined, and then metrics can be built in to manage the control process.

The output produced by a process has to conform to operational norms that are derived from business objectives. If products conform to the set norm, the process can be considered effective (because it can be repeated, measured and managed). If the activities are carried out with a minimum effort, the process can also be considered efficient.

Process-results metrics should be incorporated in regular management reports.

B.1.1 The product-oriented organisation

Process activities exist in many organisations. However, they are often carried out throughout an organisation, but without any process-oriented co-ordination. This results in problems, which have to be addressed during process implementation. Some examples include:

- processes lacking a clear purpose and focus on business results
- similar processes with inconsistent approaches
- actions or processes performed many times instead of once
- activities that are missing
- no focus on existing business-oriented results.

B.1.2 Moving towards a process-oriented organisation

Since processes and their activities run through an organisation, they should be mapped and co-ordinated by process managers. Figure B.1 shows how process activities may be assigned to people in several different organisational units. The simple box diagram indicates the apparent consecutive flow of processes in a linear sequence. Reality is better reflected in the organisational view, where the flow is clearly non-linear and where it is possible to think of delays and interactions that might take place.

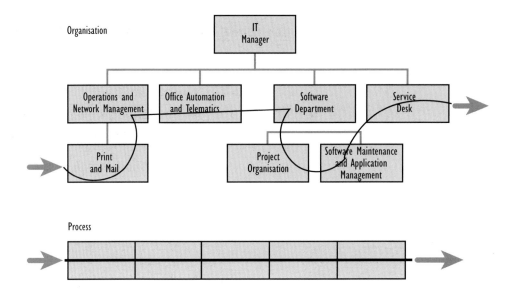

Figure B.1 – Process mapped to organisational unit

In a product-oriented organisation, the flow of activities and processes in Figure B.1 is not generally recognised at all; the focus is on the product, and management and control is often lacking. The evidence is in the lack of any useful metrics related to the production process, because the process activities are not clear or even not identified.

B.1.3   The process approach

The model shown in Figure B.2 is a generic process model. Data enters the process, is processed, data comes out, the outcome is measured and reviewed. This very basic description underpins any process description. A process is always organised around a goal. The main output of that process is the result of that goal.

Working with *defined* processes is a novelty for many organisations. By *defining* what the organisation's activities are, which inputs are necessary and which outputs will result from the process, it is possible to work in a more efficient and effective manner. Measuring and steering the activities increases this efficacy. Finally, by adding norms to the process, it is possible to add quality measures to the output.

The approach underpins the 'plan-do-check-act' cycle of any quality-management system. Plan the purpose of the process in such a way that the process action can be audited for successful achievement and, if necessary, improved.

The output produced by a process has to conform to operational norms that are derived from business objectives. If the products conform to the set norm, the process can be considered effective. If the activities are also carried out with a minimum effort, the process can also be considered efficient. Process-measurement results should be incorporated in regular management reports.

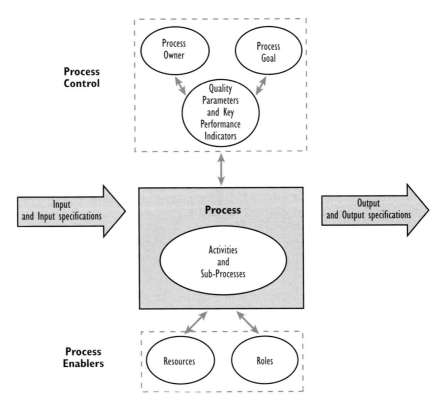

Figure B.2 – The generic process model

'Norms' define certain conditions that the results should meet. Defining norms introduces quality aspects to the process. Even before starting, it is important to think about what the outcome should look like. This enables:

■ inputs and activities to be considered beforehand because what to do is known

■ effective measurement because what to measure is known

■ assessment of whether the result fulfilled expectations because what to expect is known.

Defining objective norms is a tedious task and also often very complex since objectivity can often be subjective (to slightly misquote Woody Allen).

To discover whether or not activities are contributing optimally to the business goal of the process, measure their effectiveness on a regular basis. Measuring allows comparison between what has actually been done to what the organisation set out to do and to consider the improvement that may be needed.

APPENDIX C IMPLEMENTING SERVICE MANAGEMENT PROCESSES – ISSUES TO CONSIDER

When implementing, or improving, any aspects of Service Management processes, there are a wide range of issues to take into consideration. This Appendix looks at some of the issues that need to be taken into account when deciding to implement, or change, Service Management processes. The topics covered also look at planning the project for such an implementation.

C.1 Process implementation

A practical implementation of Service Management should include:

- earning and communicating 'quick wins' to demonstrate the benefits of Service Management
- starting with something simple and adopting a phased approach
- involving Customers, especially those that have been critical of the service
- explaining the differences that will be seen by Customers and Users
- including third-party service suppliers
- managing the changes, and explaining what is being done (and why) to everyone involved or affected – support staff are often cautious about changes, and it is particularly important that they understand the benefits in order to overcome their resistance
- educating staff and managers to become service managers.

Vital elements to consider are:

- the extent of the organisation
- the resources at your disposal, including staff numbers
- the level of maturity of staff, of the processes and of the organisation
- the impact of IT on the business
- the culture of the organisation
- continuous communication with the User population.

C.2 Applicability / scalability

The size of an organisation is an important factor when implementing ITIL processes. In a small organisation, many of the roles defined may well be the responsibility of one person.

- Generally it is not a good idea to link planning roles with reactive support roles, as the reactive element will always take priority.
- If the person responsible for setting up SLAs also has responsibility for the Incident Management process then there is a danger that the SLA element will not be done.

- The skills required of the person responsible for the Financial Management process are not the same as for IT Service Continuity Management.

- There is a tension between Incident Management and Problem Management, because of their different goals. Incident Management is responsible for minimising the effect of Incidents for Users. Problem Management's task is to find the underlying Problem and is less interested in the continuity of the Users' activities. When combining these two roles, this tension should be acknowledged.

- There is a similar tension between Problem Management and Change Management. When combining these roles, there is the danger of Changes being implemented too quickly by Problem Management. It is better to separate these functions to ensure that the proper checks and balances exist.

- Configuration Management and Release Management are roles that are quite commonly shared. Both roles have an administrative component and are concerned with maintaining an up-to-date database.

- Configuration Management and Change Management can also be easily shared, because both roles are centered on CMDB information, and no direct conflict of interest exists between the roles.

- Combining the roles of Service Level Management with Financial Management would not present any conflicting interests or issues.

C.2.1   Large and small IT units

In small IT units, one group (or individual) has responsibility for a wide variety of processes. Typically, such a person or group is much more effective in performing one role than the others. The range of personalities and skills in the group determines which of the processes is done most effectively.

Conversely, a large organisation is able to allocate individual processes to specialist groups composed of people with specialist skills who also have a personality that is a good match for the process. However, over-specialisation has its disadvantages, as specialisation may be perceived as tedious and demotivating if an individual is simply left in place without looking after their needs and aspirations.

C.3   Process implementation projects: a checklist

Most organisations planning to implement ITIL may already be following some formal practices of their own so a totally Greenfield situation will hardly ever be found. Some other methods advocate discarding your own best practices; the ITIL view is that those elements that are working for you should not be discarded unless they will not be able to fit within your vision for the future.

> IT Infrastructure Library process assessment services are commercially available, and can help you to determine the way in which processes, activities and communication lines are already in place in your organisation.
> Furthermore, they can help you to determine the maturity level of your process framework. Simple self-assessment could also be provided.

The following checklist is of a general nature, since these topics are discussed in detail in the process-specific Chapters. The checklist can function as a guideline for Service Managers controlling the overall implementation of processes.

C.3.1   Processes

- describe process ownership and management responsibilities
- provide a definitions of terms
- obtain sponsorship
- write mission
- set objectives
- provide a detailed process description – designed and described for the organisation in question
- indicate clearly where process management responsibilities lie
- indicate clearly where process execution responsibilities lie
- define data and coding requirements
- define the tools required
- define the skills and experience required
- define the management information requirement
- set out the benefits and risks
- define the metric and KPIs
- explain the audit and continuous improvement cycle
- describe the interdependencies with the other service management processes
- describe process roles and responsibilities
- list the associated procedures and work instructions.

C.3.2   Procedures

- establish the procedure framework
- implement reactive procedures
- implement proactive procedures
- implement supporting tools
- establish a managed documentation system
- establish control over procedures used.

C.3.3   Dependencies

- establish a dependency and relationship framework
- describe interdependencies with all other processes within the model, both operational and tactical
- establish process interfaces with the IT organisation – these interfaces will be crucial at the outset of process implementations, although the role of the IT organisation relative to tactical matters should diminish over time as tactical processes are put in place
- include vendor relationships

■ establish a Customer liaison function on an operational level to organise publicity campaigns.

C.3.4 People

■ implement the staff training plan and make this an ongoing activity – focus on both social and technical skills

■ assign roles within the ITIL model to people, and make this part of their function description

■ delegate tasks and authorisations as low as possible in the organisation.

C.3.5 Timing

■ control the project timescale because other stages or projects may depend on it

■ consider the timing of 'going live', including the timing and communication of the 'go live' event, as well as any special considerations for the 'go live' day and the period of days or weeks immediately after the 'going live'.

C.4 Impact on the organisation

An often-asked question in this regard is: 'Do I have to change my organisational structure?' The question often crops up because the ITIL process approach means that processes have to be managed over more than one department within traditional hierarchical company structures. Some organisations have tried the 'matrix' organisation approach, but whatever structure you choose, there will always be benefits and disadvantages connected to each approach. Consider the following examples:

C.4.1 Hierarchical structure

+ the traditional role model

+ clear lines of communication

+ clear function and task descriptions within each department

− may result in a bureaucracy if you describe procedures in too much detail

− difficult to place process roles in this model

− process approach will require a complex communication structure.

C.4.2 Matrix organisation

+ process oriented structure

+ flexible

+ clear communication model

− no (or less) clear responsibilities

− no (or less) clear leadership roles (informal leadership).

C.4.3   Self learning teams (coaching management)

+   continuous quality improvement from within

+   equality within the different teams

−   requires quality awareness

−   no control over performance

−   possible role confusion.

C.5   Benchmarking

In some circumstances, it may be possible to compare a service with that provided by other organisations. This comparison is only useful to the degree that the compared organisations are either the same or very similar. In the latter case, the differences must be understood and quantified before the comparison can provide useful information. Benchmarking is used to find out if a service is cost-effective, responsive to the Customer's needs and effective in comparison with outside. Some Customers use benchmarking to decide if they should change their service provider.

A number of organisations provide benchmarking services. These generally fall into four categories:

1.   a baseline set at a certain point in time for the same system or department (service targets are a form of benchmark)

2.   comparison to industry norms provided by external organisations

3.   direct comparisons with similar organisations

4.   comparison with other systems or departments within the same company.

Differences in benchmarks between organisations are normal. All organisations and service-provider infrastructures are unique, and most are continually changing. There are also intangible but influential factors that cannot be measured, such as growth, goodwill, image and culture.

Of the four types of benchmark listed above, the first is usual for Service Management. The second and third involve comparisons with other organisations. Comparison against industry norms provides a common frame of reference but may be misleading if the comparisons are used without an understanding of the differences that exist across a wide variety of organisations. The differences between organisations may be greater than the similarities, and comparison with a 'typical' result may not be useful as a consequence.

Direct comparison with *similar* organisations is most effective if there is a sufficiently large group of organisations with similar characteristics. It is important to understand the size and nature of the business area, including the geographical distribution and the extent to which the service is used for business, or time-critical, activities.

The culture of the Customer population also has an influence. Many support services are influenced by the extent to which Customers will or will not accept restrictions on what they may do with the technology provided. For example, it is difficult to have good security standards with Customers who will not keep their passwords secure, or who load unlicensed or untested software. Finally, comparison with other groups in the same organisation normally allows a detailed examination of the features being compared, so that it can be established whether or not the comparison is of 'like with like'.

Most benchmarks include some financial measures, such as 'cost per unit', and an assessment of cost-effectiveness is a common reason for benchmarking against other organisations. This is particularly so for organisations that have only limited historical information and that are therefore unable to use service or financial trends to measure objectively whether the service is getting better or worse. Financial benchmarking is very difficult. Establishing genuine baselines is nearly impossible, and organisational factors involved in arriving at the cost of similar processes make it hard to make true comparisons.

C.6 A sample implementation strategy

In general, the impact of current weaknesses on IT service quality should determine priorities. For example, if User services are less affected by 'real' errors than those that arise from poor implementation of Changes, Change Management must have priority. While each organisation must therefore set its own priorities, the following phased approach may be used as a starting point:

C.6.1 Phase I:

- determine the base line
- start with an assessment to determine priorities.

C.6.2 Phase 2:

- survey the services/system(s) currently used by the organisation for providing day-to-day User support and for handling Incidents, Problems and Known Errors
- review the support tools used, and the interfaces to Change Management and Configuration Management, including inventory management, and the operational use of the current system by the IT provider; identify strengths to be retained, and weaknesses to be eliminated
- identify and review the agreements in place between service providers and Customers.

C.6.3 Phase 3:

- determine and document service level requirements
- plan and implement the Service Desk using tools designed for this function that support Incident control – these tools should either support, or be capable of integration with, tools for Problem Management, Configuration Management and Change Management
- implement at least the inventory elements of Configuration Management that are required for Incident Management and Change Management.

C.6.4 Phase 4:

- extend the Incident control system to allow other domains, such as Computer Operations and Network Control staff, to log Incidents directly
- negotiate and set up SLAs.

C.6.5 Phase 5:

- develop the management reporting system.

C.6.6 Phase 6:

- implement the balance of 'reactive' Problem Management (Problem control, error control and management reporting) and Configuration Management

- realise the proactive parts of Problem Management as staff are released from reactive duties by gradually improving service quality

- establish the Release Management process.

This six-phased approach reduces the development overhead experienced at any given time for the four IT infrastructure management systems under consideration (Incident Management, Problem Management, Change Management and Configuration Management). It should, nevertheless, be noted that, although busy sites will appreciate this smoothing of the development bulge, the approach increases the overall timescale for implementation.

C.7   Process improvement

Regrettably, even a high standard of Service Management may not be adequate for rapid and major Changes. This can be an issue, for example, when two organisations merge and two sets of Service Management processes, functional groups and support technology have to be rationalised. The most common reason for normal service tuning not being adequate are when one or more of the components of Service Management are missing or deficient, so that the service has degraded and Customers are dissatisfied with its quality or cost.

Under these circumstances, management is faced with a potential or real crisis and should react by initiating a project or series of projects to address the situation. These are required to make much faster improvements to the service, costs or the processes than are possible within the scope of normal ongoing Service Management.

Projects may be directly related to the activities of Service Level Management. For example they may be part of a Service Improvement Programme (SIP) or may be focused on improving Customer and/or staff satisfaction. However, apart from this reactive reason to start a process improvement project, many proactive ones should also be considered, such as:

- providing the operational processes with a tactical planning horizon

- aiming for a higher IT maturity level

- improving alignment with, and support for, business objectives

- reducing costs or improving business profits

- implementing a planning and control system

- increasing quality awareness amongst staff

- making the 'feedback loop work'.

In all cases, management needs to have a clear view of the Service Catalogue and the internal service requirements, and also needs to have a so-called 'Helicopter View' of the IT organisation.

More guidance can be obtained from the OGC ITIL book *Planning and Control for IT Services*, which covers information flows and the development of an appropriate planning-and-control system to meet the requirements of the organisation.

APPENDIX D QUALITY

D.1 Quality management

Quality Management for IT Services is a systematic way of ensuring that all the activities necessary to design, develop and implement IT services which satisfy the requirements of the organisation and of users take place as planned and that the activities are carried out cost-effectively.

The way that an organisation plans to manage its Operations so that it delivers quality services, is specified by its Quality Management System. The Quality Management System defines the organisational structure, responsibilities, policies, procedures, processes, standards and resources required to deliver quality IT services. However, a Quality Management System will only function as intended if management and staff are committed to achieving its objectives.

This appendix gives brief details on a number of different Quality approaches – more detail on these and other approaches can be found on the Internet at www.dti.gov.uk/quality.

D.1.1 Deming

> **Quote**
>
> 'We have learned to live in a world of mistakes and defective products as if they were necessary to life. It is time to adopt a new philosophy...'
>
> (W. Edwards Deming, 1900-93)

W. Edwards Deming is best known for his management philosophy establishing quality, productivity, and competitive position. As part of this philosophy he formulated 14 points of attention for managers. Some of these points are more appropriate to Service Management than others.

For quality improvement Deming proposed the Deming Cycle or Circle. The four key stages are 'Plan, Do, Check and Act' after which a phase of consolidation prevents the 'Circle' from 'rolling down the hill' as illustrated in Figure D.1.

The cycle is underpinned by a process led approach to management where defined processes are in place, the activities measured for compliance to expected values and outputs audited to validate and improve the process.

Example

Excerpts from Deming's 14 points relevant to Service Management

- break down barriers between departments (improves communications and management)

- management must learn their responsibilities, and take on leadership (process improvement requires commitment from the top; good leaders motivate people to improve themselves and therefore the image of the organisation)

- improve constantly (a central theme for service managers is continual improvement; this is also a theme for Quality Management. A process led approach is key to achieving this target)

- institute a programme of education and self-improvement (learning and improving skills has been the focus of Service Management for many years)

- training on the job (linked to continual improvement)

- transformation is everyone's job (the emphasis being on teamwork and understanding).

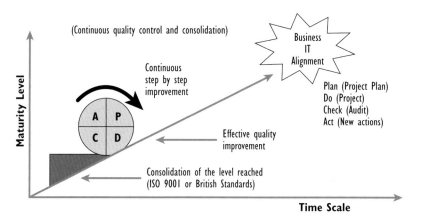

Figure D.I – The Deming Cycle

D.I.2 Juran

Joseph Juran became a recognised name in the quality field in 1951 with the publication of the Quality Control Handbook. The appeal was to the Japanese initially, and Juran was asked to give a series of lectures in 1954 on planning, organisational issues, management responsibility for Quality, and the need to set goals and targets for improvement.

Juran devised a well-known chart, 'The Juran Trilogy', shown in Figure D.2, to represent the relationship between quality planning, quality control, and quality improvement on a project-by-project basis.

A further feature of Juran's approach is the recognition of the need to guide managers; this is achieved by the establishment of a quality council within an organisation, which is responsible for establishing processes, nominating projects, assigning teams, making improvements and providing the necessary resources.

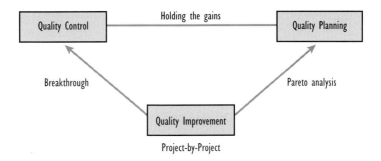

Figure D.2 – The Quality trilogy

Senior management plays a key role in serving on the quality council, approving strategic goals, allocating resources, and reviewing progress.

Juran promotes a four-phased approach to quality improvement, namely:

- Start-up – creating the necessary organisational structures and infrastructure

- Test – in which concepts are tried out in pilot programmes and results evaluated

- Scale-up – in which the basic concepts are extended based on positive feedback

- Institutionalisation – at which point quality improvements are linked to the strategic business plan.

D.1.3   Crosby

The Crosby TQM approach is very popular in the UK. However, despite its obvious success in the market, it has been subject to much criticism, primarily due to poor understanding, or a blinkered application of the approach in some organisations, using a limited definition of quality.

The approach is based on Crosby's Four Absolutes of Quality Management, namely:

- Quality is conformance to requirement

- The system for causing quality is prevention and not appraisal

- The performance standard must be zero defects and not 'that's close enough'

- The measure of quality is the price of non-conformance and not indices.

The Crosby approach is often based on familiar slogans; however, organisations may experience difficulty in translating the quality messages into sustainable methods of quality improvement. Some organisations have found it difficult to integrate their quality initiatives, having placed their quality programme outside the mainstream management process.

Anecdotal evidence suggests that these pitfalls result in difficulties being experienced in sustaining active quality campaigns over a number of years in some organisations.

Crosby lacks the engineering rigour of Juran and significantly omits to design quality into the product or process, gearing the quality system towards a prevention-only policy. Furthermore, it fails to recognise that few organisations have appropriate management measures from which they can accurately ascertain the costs of non-conformance, and in some cases even the actual process costs!

D.1.4   Six Sigma

This is commonly described as a body of knowledge required to implement a generic quantitative approach to improvement. Six Sigma is a data-driven approach to analysing the root causes of problems and solving them. It is business output driven in relation to customer specification and focuses on dramatically reducing process variation using Statistical Process Control (SPC) measures. A process that operates at Six Sigma allows only 3.40 defects per million parts of output.

The Six Sigma approach has evolved from experience in manufacturing, and is therefore not readily applied to human processes and perhaps other processes that are not immediately apparent. The approach relies on trained personnel capable of identifying processes that need improvement and who can act accordingly. It does not contain a systematic approach for identifying improvement opportunities or facilitate with prioritisation.

Six Sigma perhaps offers another path toward measurable improvement for CMM Level 3 organisations, but this alone may make it diffficult to apply in the context of Service Management compared to software engineering.

There are research reservations on applying validation and measurement to process improvement and particularly in the application of SPC to non-manufacturing engineering processes. It has been found that a Goal, Question, Metric (GQM) approach provides suitable measures, rather than a statistical method. It is still somewhat a controversial area, and even the SW-CMM at the higher levels (4-5) has come in for some academic criticism in this area. However, there are indications that Six Sigma is being applied in the service sector and, with good Service Management support tools, tracking of incidents, etc., would allow this approach to be used for process improvement.

D.2 Formal quality initiatives

D.2.1 Quality standards

International Standards Organisation ISO 9000

An important set of International Standards for Quality Assurance is the ISO 9000 range, a set of five universal standards for a Quality Assurance system that is accepted around the world. At the turn of the millennium, 90 or so countries have adopted ISO 9000 as the cornerstone of their national standards. When a product or service is purchased from a company that is registered to the appropriate ISO 9000 standard, the purchaser has important assurances that the quality of what they will receive will be as expected.

The most comprehensive of the standards is ISO 9001. It applies to industries involved in the design, development, manufacturing, installation and servicing of products or services. The standards apply uniformly to companies in any industry and of any size.

The BSI Management Overview of IT Service Management is a modern update of the original document, PD0005, which was published in 1995. The Management Overview is a management level introduction to Service Management, and in fact can be used as an introduction to ITIL. This is also now supported by a formal standard, BS 15000 (Specification for IT Service Management). ITIL is in many countries the *de facto* standard and, with the help of BSI and ISO, it is hoped that a formal international standard based on ITIL will soon be in place. The BSI Standard and Management Overview cover the established ITIL Service Support and Service Delivery processes, as well as some additional topics such as implementing the processes.

D.2.2 Total Quality Systems: EFQM

> **Quote**
>
> '... the battle for Quality is one of the prerequisites for the success of your companies and for our collective success.'
>
> (Jacques Delors, president of the European Commission, at the signing of the letter of intent in Brussels to establish EFQM on 15 September 1988.)

The EFQM Excellence Model

The European Foundation for Quality Management (EFQM) was founded in 1988 by the Presidents of 14 major European companies, with the endorsement of the European Commission. The present membership is in excess of 600 very well-respected organisations, ranging from major multinationals and important national companies to research institutes in prominent European universities.

EFQM provides an excellent model for those wishing to achieve business excellence in a programme of continual improvement.

EFQM mission statement

The mission statement is:

> **To stimulate and assist organisations throughout Europe to participate in improvement activities leading ultimately to excellence in customer satisfaction, employee satisfaction, impact on society and business results; and to support the Managers of European organisations in accelerating the process of making Total Quality Management a decisive factor for achieving global competitive advantage.**

Depiction of the EFQM Excellence Model

The EFQM Excellence Model consists of 9 criteria and 32 sub-criteria; it is illustrated in Figure D.3.

In the model there is explicit focus on the value to users of the 'Plan, Do, Check, Act' cycle to business operations (see Section D.1.1), and the need to relate everything that is done, and the measurements taken, to the goals of business policy and strategy.

Self-assessment and maturity: the EFQM maturity scale

One of the tools provided by EFQM is the self-assessment questionnaire. The self-assessment process allows the organisation to discern clearly its strengths and also any areas where improvements can be made. The questionnaire process culminates in planned improvement actions, which are then monitored for progress.

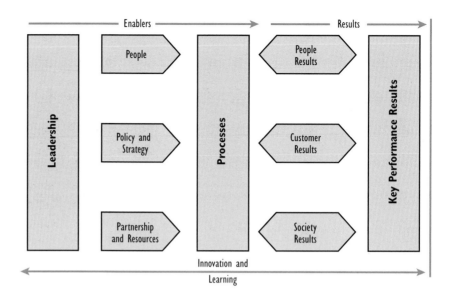

© EFQM. The EFQM Excellence Model is a registered trademark

Figure D.3 – The EFQM Excellence Model

In this assessment progress can be checked against a five-point maturity scale:

1   Product orientation

2   Process orientation (the maturity stage aimed for by the original ITIL)

3   System orientation (the maturity target for ITIL-compliant organisations in the new millennium)

4   Chain orientation

5   Total quality.

D.2.3   Quality awards

To demonstrate a successful adaptation of the EFQM model, some companies aim for the European Quality Award, a process that allows Europe to recognise its most successful organisations and promote them as role models of excellence for others to copy.

The US equivalent to this award is the Malcolm Baldridge Quality Award for Quality Management. The Malcolm Baldridge National Quality Improvement Act of 1987 established an annual US National Quality Award. The purpose of the Award was (and still is) to promote awareness of quality excellence, to recognise quality achievements of US companies, and to publicise successful quality strategies.

For the Malcolm Baldridge Award, there are three categories:

■   Manufacturing companies or sub-units

■   Service companies or sub-units

■   Small businesses.

The criteria against which firms are judged are:

1   Leadership

2   Strategic planning

3   Customer and market focus

4   Information and analysis

5   Human resource development and management

6   Process management

7   Business results.

For the European Quality Award, there are four possible categories:

- Companies
- Operational units of companies
- Public sector organisations
- Small and medium enterprises.

The criteria against which candidate organisations are measured are:

1   Leadership

2   People

3   Policy and strategy

4   Partnerships and resources

5   Processes

6   People results

7   Customer results

8   Society results

9   Key performance results.

In the EFQM Excellence Model, the first four criteria are defined as enablers. Best practice in ITIL process implementations show that placing proper emphasis on these topics increases the chances for success. The key points for the four enablers are listed below.

Leadership

- Organise a kick-off session involving everyone
- Be a role model
- Encourage and support the staff.

People management

- Create awareness
- Recruit new staff and/or hire temporary staff to prevent Service Levels being affected during implementation stages
- Develop people through training and experience
- Align human resource plans with policy and strategy
- Adopt a coaching style of management
- Align performance with salaries.

Policy and strategy

- Communicate mission, vision and values
- Align communication plans with the implementation stages.

Partnerships and resources

- Establish partnerships with subcontractors and customers
- Use financial resources in support of policy and strategy
- Utilise existing assets.

APPENDIX E COMMUNICATIONS

E.1 Introduction

Appendix D provides an overview of Quality Management in the context of IT Service Delivery. A number of approaches to quality are presented including quality systems designed around Standard specifications, Total Quality Management (TQM) philosophies for continuous improvement, and quality frameworks for base-line assessment and organisational improvement. The successful implementation of all of these approaches is dependent upon good communications across team, functional, departmental, process and organisational boundaries.

ITIL provides a framework in which to place Service Management activities in a structured context. The ITIL framework emphasises the relationships between processes, and thus can lead to improvements in communication and co-operation between the various IS/IT functions, business Customers and Users. However, the general art of communication can be easily overlooked and its significance in the development of relationships between Customers and service providers is extremely important.

Although communication is one of the most frequently discussed aspects of organisational dynamics, it is not always well understood. During review exercises of organisational, departmental, or team performance, communication is one of the most common topics mentioned that needs to be improved.

Effective communication is a basic prerequisite for the achievement of organisational goals and it plays an important role in managerial and organisational effectiveness. Indeed, studies of managerial effectiveness have shown that communication skills contribute 44% overall to a combined effectiveness measure of performance, satisfaction and commitment.

E.1.1 Background

Much of the historical studies of communications, based on organisational behaviour and structure, are directly relevant to service providers and to the successful management of IS/IT from the customer's perspective. A few of the more salient contributions to our knowledge of business communications are given below.

In the 1930s, Chester Barnard studied the then limited communication techniques. He noted that they were necessary to assert organisation purpose, but that they were also a potential problem area for many organisations. The dependency upon interpersonal skills was also recognised.

Nowadays, the available communication techniques have increased and many of these are supported by communications technologies. It is important therefore, in view of the number of options, that a planned approach is adopted that considers the available techniques in terms of their fitness for purpose, within the context of an overall communications plan, to achieve organisational goals.

---

[3] It was largely Chester Barnard in the late 1930s who developed the notion of communication as a vital factor in organisational dynamics. He ranked it with 'common purpose' and 'willingness' as one of the three primary elements of the organisation. His credibility is based on his recognition that communication techniques were deemed not only necessary to attain organisation purpose but also a potential problem area for the organisation.
'Communication techniques shapes the form and internal economy of the organisation.'
Quote from Chester I Barnard, 'The Functions of the Executive', Harvard University Press, Cambridge, Mass., 1938, p.90.
One can now recognise how 'visionary' these words from the 30s are when one considers the new communication techniques being applied, e.g. e-commerce.

Barnard also recognised seven specific communication factors, namely:

1. the channels of communication should be definitely known

2. there should be a definite formal channel of communication to every member of an organisation

3. the line of communication should be as direct and short as possible

4. the complete formal line of communication should normally be used

5. the persons serving as communication centres should be competent

6. the lines of communication should not be interrupted while the organisation is functioning

7. every communication should be authenticated.

These principles are still relevant and can be used to base-line or assess the current state of communications both internally and between the business and the service provider(s), as a precursor to a constructive programme of continual improvement.

Communication problems within organisations have also been studied e.g. in relation to managerial function in terms of command and control. A classical insight to improve communication pathways was provided by Henri Fayol[4] (1949) with his 'gangplank' concept. This provides the basis for horizontal communication systems, which today are pertinent to service management.

For effective Service Management communications there need to be dialogues both internally throughout the Customer and service provider organisational hierarchies and between corresponding levels between the business and the service provider(s). Such horizontal communications adopt Fayol's 'gangplank' concept. For example, at senior levels there needs to be effective communication concerning strategic and policy issues. At a tactical level, Service Level Management need to discuss business requirements and negotiate service targets with business managers or their representatives, e.g. 'Informed' Customer function. At the operational level, the Service Desk is an excellent example of a team where communication is extremely important, being the first point of contact for Users to report Incidents, and for maintaining contact with Users throughout the Incident life-cycle.

Internal communications within the organisational hierarchy are usually described in terms of communication 'chains'. Leavitt[5] (1951) identified other forms of communication channel that can be more readily associated with networked or process orientated organisations, e.g. 'circle', 'wheel' and 'all-channel', the latter being adopted in the more mature processes. A mature Service Desk might have 'all-channel' communications to communicate freely and use the available resources within other groups to expedite tasks.

Also in the 1950s Rogers[6] and Roethlisberger[7] published a number of books and articles (see Harvard Business Review (July-Aug. 1952) on the barriers and gateways to communication[8]). The greatest

---

[4] Henri Fayol was a pioneering management theorist who was one of the first people to attempt to give a detailed analysis of the problem of communication in organisational hierarchies. Fayol's 'gangplank' concept is described in: Henri Fayol, 'General and Industrial Management', Constance Storrs (trans.), Pitman, London. 1949, p.35.

[5] Leavitt studied decision making and communication in groups. He noted that communication within 'mature' groups tended to be dominated by what he called 'all-channel' networks, i.e. where all the members of the group communicate freely with each other. He went further in recognising the role of the leader as primarily 'chairman' or 'catalyst' rather than 'manager' or 'gate-keeper' in situations where you have more decentralised communication channels. His different structures are published in: Leavitt, H.J. (1951) 'Some effects of certain communicative patterns on group performance', Journal of Abnormal Psychology.

[6] The late Carl R. Rogers was a professor of psychology at the University of Chicago. He wrote many books. one of which 'Client-centered therapy' (Houghton Mifflin, 1951) was considered ground-breaking.

[7] The late F.J. Roethlisberger was the Wallace Brett Donham Professor of Human Relations at the Harvard Business School. He is the author of 'Man-in-Organization' (Harvard University Press, 1968) and other books and articles.

[8] Harvard Business Review is a bimonthly publication of the Graduate School of Business Administration and is published by Harvard Business School Publishing Corporation, 60 Harvard Way, Boston, MA 02163. International subscription rates p.a. are $145. Reprints of any article are $5.50, with a minimum order of $10.00.

barrier to effective communication being the tendency to evaluate, misunderstand or not really hear the message being communicated. By checking the natural tendency to make judgements, it is likely that a better understanding can be gained. As such listening with understanding is perceived as the most important gateway to communication in that a better understanding of the other person's viewpoint facilitates communication.

The importance of simply listening to Customers should not be overlooked as an essential communication technique. For example, in receiving informal feedback and in discourse about future plans etc. it is important to be receptive and demonstrate both listening and understanding of Customers through subsequent actions.

For Service Management, the classical insights presented above are still relevant today. It is imperative that communication is interwoven with both meaning and understanding. The purpose of a communication, the choice of communication method and technique need to be considered carefully. Service Management need not only ensure that relationships with Customers and Users develop, but that the internal communication channels mature so that there is effective role interaction and activity co-ordination to ensure that the services delivered meet Customer requirements at an appropriate cost. Roles and their interactions have become increasingly important in relation to communication difficulties and relationship problems. A key strength of the ITIL approach to Service Management is the definition of processes and the key roles required to fulfil those processes.

E.2   The business perspective

ITIL provides a framework on which core skills and competencies can be developed for Service Support and Service Delivery roles. However, it is also necessary to recognise the business challenge, i.e. there is a need for a framework to develop and maintain core skills and competencies necessary to manage IS/IT within the business and external service providers. The report: *Successful IT: Modernising Government in Action* (See Chapter 11), recommends the adoption of the Feeny and Willcocks framework. They specify nine 'core' capabilities, three of which are specifically relevant to the delivery of IS services, namely: contract facilitation, contract monitoring, and relationship building.

The development of competency within the business has long been associated with an 'Informed' Customer function capability. The Informed Customer function provides a communication centre and formal line of communication for:

- specifying business objectives and requirements
- directing IS/IT investment
- securing sources of supply and undertaking the necessary procurement
- ensuring that the systems and services delivered are used effectively to achieve business benefit and that the customer obtains value for money.

The Informed Customer function needs not only to understand the business vision and strategies for achievement, it must be able to effectively communicate this knowledge and understanding to service providers. It needs to ensure that IS/IT investment decisions are made on the basis of sound business cases to provide maximum business benefit, and must be clear about business objectives and priorities.

It is vital that the business direction is both known and disseminated if IS is to remain of value to the business. Service Providers need to work closely with the '*Informed*' Customer to assure that the right form of constructive relationship is created and that the customer has access to the required skills, systems and services.

As mentioned previously, for communications to be effective there needs to be a two-way process, and customers have a responsibility to communicate effectively with service providers. The onus on the '*Informed*' Customer is to define requirements clearly, package services appropriately, and agree relevant standards with service providers in order to facilitate the acquisition process, reduce risk and improve the quality of provision.

The role of the '*Informed*' Customer is evolving in terms of *The Modernising Government Agenda.*[9] Public Sector organisations need to deliver new and innovative services and are beginning to recognise that 'service' is THE organisational imperative. As the IS/IT contribution becomes more of an essential rather than optional element, and seamless integration across organisational boundaries becomes more necessary, the notion of a networked organisation, consisting of a web of relationships is becoming more of a reality. In such circumstances the '*Informed*' Customer is being transformed into an *Informed Partner* (see the IS Guide - Managing Partnerships – details in Chapter 11).

E.2.1 Communications: an essential component of any relationship

We have previously mentioned that the communication channels between servIce provider and customer are two-way. The implications of this for service providers is that they may at times need to be as proactive in requesting communications as in sending out information.

For more complex relationships, e.g. partners, there needs to be an element of strategic management in maintaining the relationships and recognising the implications for organisational governance if the relationships with partners change. To achieve partnerships that work the relationships need to be built upon mutual trust and they need to have some degree of flexibility to handle changes in the business environment.

It should be noted that communication is a personal process and this has other implications, e.g. behavioural effects, i.e. communication can influence or affect another person's behaviour and such communicative exchanges are the basis for relationships both internal and external to the organisation.

[9] The UK Government recognises that new technology offers unprecedented opportunities for modernisation throughout society, and is committed to working towards establishing the best environment for electronic commerce. The UK government has set a target that by 2005, all citizens should have access to the Internet, either in their own homes or through community access points. Information and Communications Technology learning centres in partnership with the commercial sector will be set up, along with an investment in schools and life-long learning centres to ensure that the skills in using the technology are available to all.

E.3 Importance of service provider and customer communications

Communications between the service provider and customer are important for a number of reasons, including:

- Gaining an increased understanding of the Customer's business and its needs
- Establishing and developing mutual trust in the relationship
- Providing technology briefings so that customers can gain an appreciation of where new technology can bring additional business benefits
- Managing customer expectations
- Measuring customer satisfaction
- Gaining timely insights of business initiatives that are likely to have significant impact on IT service provider(s)

The role of the '*Informed*' Customer in these communication processes has been outlined. From the service provider's perspective, ITIL can help in the distinction between back office production and front office delivery and support.

E.4 Overall benefits of improved communications

The overall benefits of improved communication are derived from:

- Business focused IS delivery, e.g. through service management being able more adequately to identify and meet customer requirements
- More efficient use of available IS/IT resources and capacity – effective communication will improve the ability of Capacity Management to produce accurate resource plans
- Better customer representation within IS, by ensuring that customer views are known and reflected in planning and service delivery
- Improved ability to actively market IT services where this is appropriate
- Customer retention and development through higher levels of customer satisfaction.

Service quality is by nature a subjective concept, which means that it is imperative to understand what the customer thinks about IS service quality, as a fundamental aspect of service management. Three related concepts contribute to this understanding, namely: customer satisfaction, service quality and customer value.

Customer satisfaction is a cognitive and affective reaction to a service encounter or to a service relationship. Satisfaction being gauged by comparing the encounter with what was expected. Hence the importance of expectation management in managing relationships.

Service providers need to be constantly aware that not only quality but price is assessed; a service may be of good quality but rated as poor value, if the price is too high. It should be noted that value is often beyond economic analysis and it is necessary to work with customers and partners to ensure that the benefits attained through the service are realised by the business.

APPENDIX F EXAMPLE COST-BENEFIT ANALYSIS FOR SERVICE MANAGEMENT PROCESSES

This Appendix is intended as an example of how to quantify the costs and benefits of implementing the processes described in the IT Infrastructure Library. It is not intended to be comprehensive. Please be sure to substitute your own organisation's specific assumptions, purposes, costs, and benefits to get an example that is more suitable to your own circumstances.

In this example, the following assumptions are made:

- all employees cost £50, an hour
- your organisation comprises 500 users
- the total number of Incidents is 5,000 per year
- the average time to fix an Incident is 10 minutes
- a working year has 200 days.

Example costs and benefits are set out below.

Process:	Purpose:	Cost/Benefit Examples:
Configuration Management	Controlling the IT infrastructure Ensuring that only authorised hardware and software is in use	Following the implementation of Configuration Management, the Service Desk has a much greater insight into the relationship between Users, CIs and Incidents. The 3 people assigned to Incident matching can be reduced to 2, resulting in a benefit of 200*8*£50 = £80,000 a year.
Incident Management	Continuity of the service levels Underpin Service Desk function	The implementation of Incident Management has resulted in a decrease in downtime per User; this is defined as the amount of time a User is on the phone to the Service Desk or cannot work because of a failure. If the downtime per User has gone down by I minute per person per day, this would save the organisation 1/60*500*200*£50 = £83,300 per year.
Problem Management	Minimise disruption of the service level	Suppose that the implementation of Problem Management decreases the amount of recurring Incidents by 500 (10% of total) per year. This means a revenue of 500* 10/60*£50 = > £4,000 per year.
Change Management	Efficient handling of Changes	Two Changes are implemented simultaneously, resulting in a major problem. The Customer support system fails, resulting in the loss of 50 Customers with an average purchasing power of £500. This has just cost your company £25,000.

Release Management	Ensuring authorised software modules are used Provide means to build Change Releases Automating release of software	Suppose that a new software module is released containing a bug. The previous version should be reinstalled, but due to poor version management, the wrong version is used, resulting in a system shutdown that lasts for 3 hours and affects two thirds of all employees. This would cost the organisation 2/3*500*£50*3 = £50,000.
Service Level Management	Agree on and control the service levels Understand business needs	Thanks to a clear set of agreements, the Service Desk is less troubled with calls that are not part of the services offered. This way the 4 Service Desk employees work 5% more efficiently, resulting in again of 4*5%*£50*8*200 = £ 16,000 a year.
Availability Management	Ensure high availability of services	Due to a physical error on a hard disk, a server supporting 100 people crashes. It takes 3 hours to have a new disk delivered and installed before starting up the system again. Costs: 100*3*£50 = £ 15,000. On a critical system, Availability Management processes would have highlighted the need for a mirror disk, which could automatically take over.
Capacity Management	Ensure the optimal use of IT	There is an overcapacity of 20%. Assuming your IT infrastructure cost you £5 million, you could gain up to £1 ml by implementing Capacity Management and frequently reassessing the necessary capacity.
IT Service Continuity Management	Ensure quick recovery after a disaster	A water pipe breaks, flooding the server room. It takes 2 days to be fully operational. The average User has missed 10 hours of work. Total costs (apart from the pumping): 500* 10*£50 = £250,000. Please note that a good contingency plan doesn't come cheap; however the recovery costs (as in this example) could be dramatic – that is, if your organisation is still in business!
Financial Management	Provide insight, control and charge the costs of a IT services	Imagine that the costs of IT services are charged to the departments that take them. A 10% reduction in the requests for new services, would directly result in a 10% reduction of IT expenditure. The insight into the real costs in IT services proves to be surprising in practice; most Users don't have a clue about the costs.

APPENDIX G SERVICE DELIVERY PROCESSES

This diagram illustrates the major interfaces and deliverables from the Service Delivery processes.

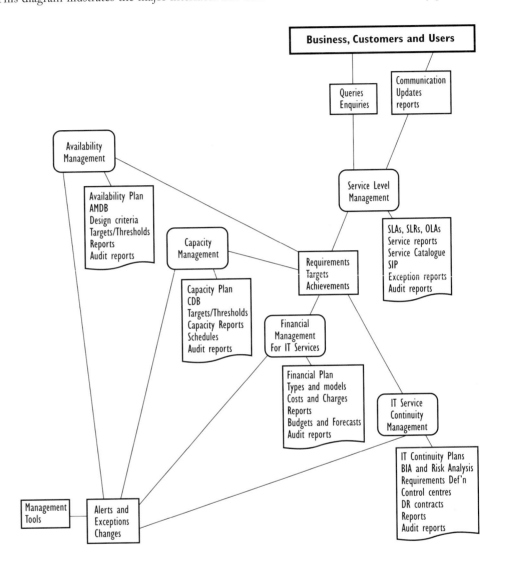

Index

availability requirements, costs of 232
availability requirements, quantification 231
of business and ITSCM integration 195
categorisation of recommendations (SOA) 283
contact procedure in recovery process 193
corporate SLA targets 38
establishment of service level requirements 37
external monitoring services 135
generation of awareness for ITSCM 199, 200
Incident Management, aspects of 242
indicative cost of failure 273
insurance provision 182
invocation of ITSCM plans 192
laws of Capacity Management 121
management sponsorship in ITSCM 194
outsourcing mainframe processing 181
percentage trap 48
pilot schemes for SLAs 37
pragmatism in Availability Management 261
recovery design requirements 239
recovery mechanism implementation 195
responsibilities for ITSCM 197
risk assessment for ITSCM 178, 180
security maintenance (ITSCM) 193
Security Management vs Availability
  Management 243
Service Level Management 44
service levels, discussions on 37
user perception and response time 40
see also examples
host computer 321

ICT Infrastructure Management
  book on 4–5
  process of 15
immediate recovery 185, 322
impact analysis/scenario 322
impact on organisation of Financial
  Management 62
implementation
  Capacity Management process 152–3
  failure in Service Management 20
  IT accounting and charging 104–8
  ITSCM 186–91
  Service Level Management 33–42
  Service Management processes 337–43

improvement model for management processes 18
improvement of availability 247–51
improvement programmes for SLM 44
inappropriate monitoring, anecdote on 39
incident based reporting 274
incident 'lifecycle'
  expanded 249, 285–6
  Service Management processes 7
  understanding 240
Incident Management
  Availability Management and 239–40, 242
  Capacity Management and 155
  process of 14
indirect costs 71, 75, 78–9, 322
information age business 203
information deficit, Capacity Management and 146–7
informed customer 323, 354, 355–6
initial awareness of ITSCM 199–200
instrumentation, metric development and 276
insurance premiums 164–5
integration into corporate management of
  ITSCM 203–4
integrity of data see Security Management
interface 323
intermediate recovery 184–5, 323
internal market 93–4
internal target 323
internal vs external money 96–7
investment appraisal 85–6
invocation
  of arrangements 323
  of ITSCM plans 192–4
IS Management Handbook (OGC) 307
ISO certification and the ITIL 2–3
ISO Standards (International Standards
  Institute) 348
ISO 9000 348
ISO 9001 323, 348
ITAMM (IT availability metrics model) 258–9
IT Infrastructure Library (ITIL)
  Applications Management, the book on 4–5
  audience target 4
  'Balanced Scorecard' and 306
  business case for management processes 17
  Business Perspective, the book on the 4–5
  customers, distinctness from users 7

Other Information Sources and Services

The IT Service Management Forum (itSMF)

How to contact us:

The IT Service Management Forum Ltd
Webbs Court
8 Holmes Road
Earley
Reading RG6 7BH
Tel: +44 (0) 118 926 0888
Fax: +44 (0) 118 926 3073
Email: service@itsmf.com
or visit our web-site at:
www.itsmf.com

The IT Service Management Forum Ltd (itSMF) is the only internationally recognised and independent body dedicated to IT Service Management. It is a not-for-profit organisation, wholly owned, and principally operated, by its membership.

The itSMF is a major influence on, and contributor to, Industry Best Practice and Standards worldwide, working in partnership with OGC (the owners of ITIL), the British Standards Institution (BSI), the Information Systems Examination Board (ISEB) and the Examination Institute of the Netherlands (EXIN).

Founded in the UK in 1991, there are now a number of chapters around the world with new ones seeking to join all the time. There are well in excess of 1000 organisations covering over 10,000 individuals represented in the membership. Organisations range from large multi-nationals such as AXA, GuinnessUDV, HP, Microsoft and Procter & Gamble in all market sectors, through central & local bodies, to independent consultants.

ITIL training and professional qualifications

For further information:

visit ISEB's web-site at:
www.bcs.org.uk

and EXIN:
www.exin.nl

There are currently two examining bodies offering equivalent qualifications: ISEB (The Information Systems Examining Board), part of the British Computer Society, and Stitching EXIN (The Netherlands Examinations Institute). Jointly with OGC and itSMF (the IT Service Management Forum), they work to ensure that a common standard is adopted for qualifications worldwide. The syllabus is based on the core elements of ITIL and complies with ISO9001 Quality Standard. Both ISEB and EXIN also accredit training organisations to deliver programmes leading to qualifications.

Best Practice:
the OGC approach with ITIL® and PRINCE®

OGC Best Practice is an approach to management challenges as well as the application of techniques and actions.

Practical, flexible and adaptable, management guidance from OGC translates the very best of the world's practices into guidance of an internationally recognised standard. Both PRINCE2 and ITIL publications can help every organisation to:

- Run projects more efficiently
- Reduce project risk
- Purchase IT more cost effectively
- Improve organisational Service Delivery.

What is ITIL and why use it?

ITIL's starting point is that organisations do not simply use IT; they depend on it. Managing IT as effectively as possible must therefore be a high priority.

ITIL consists of a unique library of guidance on providing quality IT services. It focuses tightly on the customer, cost effectiveness and building a culture that puts the emphasis on IT performance.

Used by hundreds of the world's most successful organisations, its core titles are available in print, Online Subscription and CD-ROM formats. They are:

- Service Support
- Service Delivery
- Planning to Implement Service Management
- Application Management
- ICT Infrastructure Management
- Security Management
- The Business Perspective Volume 1 and 2
- Software Asset Management

What is PRINCE2 and why use it?

Since its introduction in 1989, PRINCE has been widely adopted by both the public and private sectors and is now recognised as a de facto standard for project management – and for the management of change.

PRINCE2, the most evolved version, is driven by its experts and users to offer control, transparency, focus and ultimate success for any project you need to implement.

Publications are available in various formats: print, Online Subscription and CD-ROM. Its main titles are:

- Managing Successful Projects with PRINCE2
- People Issues and PRINCE2
- PRINCE2 Pocket Book
- Tailoring PRINCE2
- Business Benefits through Project Management

Other related titles:
- Passing the PRINCE2 Examinations
- Managing Successful Programmes
- Management of Risk – Guidance for Practitioners
- Buying Software – A best practice approach

Ordering

The full range of ITIL and PRINCE2 publications can be purchased direct via **www.get-best-practice.co.uk** or through calling TSO Customer Services on **0870 600 5522**. If you are outside of the UK please contact your local agent, for details email **sales@tso.co.uk** For information on Network Licenses for CD-ROM and Online Subscription please email **network.sales@tso.co.uk**

You are also able to subscribe to content online through this website or by calling TSO Customer Services on **0870 600 5522**. For more information on how to subscribe online please refer to our help pages on the website.

Dear customer ■ ■ ■ ■ ■ ■ ■ ■ ■ ■ ■ ■ ■ ■ ■ ■

We would like to hear from you with any comments or suggestions that you have on how we can improve our current products or develop new ones for the ITIL series. Please complete this questionnaire and we will enter you into our quarterly draw. The winner will receive a copy of Software Asset Management worth £35!

1 Personal Details

Name ....

Organisation ....

Job Title ....

Department ....

Address ....

....

Postcode ....

Telephone Number ....

Email ....

2 Nature of Organisation (tick one box only)

☐ Consultancy/Training
☐ Computing/IT/Software
☐ Industrial
☐ Central Government
☐ Local Government
☐ Academic/Further education
☐ Private Health
☐ Public Health (NHS)
☐ Finance
☐ Construction
☐ Telecommunications
☐ Utilities
☐ Other (Please specify)

....

3 How did you hear about **ITIL?**

☐ Work/Colleagues
☐ Internet/Web (please specify)

....

☐ Marketing Literature
☐ itSMF
☐ Other (please specify)

....

4 Where did you purchase this book?

☐ Web – www.tso.co.uk/bookshop
☐ Web – www.get-best-practice.co.uk
☐ Web – Other (please specify)

....

☐ Bookshop (please specify)

....

☐ Training Course
☐ Other (please specify)

....

5 How many people use **ITIL** in your company?

☐ 1-5
☐ 6-10
☐ 11-50
☐ 51-200
☐ 201+

6 How many people use your copy of this title?

☐ 0
☐ 1-5
☐ 6-10
☐ 11+

7 Overall, how do you rate this title?

☐ Excellent
☐ Very Good
☐ Good
☐ Fair
☐ Poor

8 What do you most like about the book? (tick all that apply)

☐ Ease of use
☐ Well structured
☐ Contents
☐ Index
☐ Hints and tips
☐ Other (Please specify)

....

9 Do you have any suggestions for improvement?

....

....

....

10 How do you use this book? (tick all that apply)

☐ Problem Solver
☐ Reference
☐ Tutorial
☐ Other (please specify)

....

[PTO]

11 Did you know there are 7 core titles in the **ITIL** series?

☐ No
☐ Yes

12 Do you have any other **ITIL** titles?

☐ No
☐ Yes (please specify)

....

13 Do you use the **ITIL** CDs?

☐ No
☐ Yes (please specify)

....

14 Are you aware that most of the **ITIL** series is now available as online content at **www.get-best-practice.co.uk?**

☐ Yes
☐ No

15 Do you currently subscribe to any online content found at **www.get-best-practice.co.uk?**

☐ No
☐ Yes (please specify)

....

16 Did you know that you can network your CDs and Online Subscription, to offer your project managers access to this material at their desktop?

Yes/No

☐ Please tick this box if you require further information.

17 Did you know that you are able to purchase a maintenance agreement for your CD-ROM that will allow you to receive immediately any revised versions, at no additional cost?

Yes/No

☐ Please tick this box if you require further information.

18 What business change guidance/methods does your company use?

☐ PRINCE2
☐ Managing Successful Programmes
☐ Management of Risk
☐ Successful Delivery Toolkit
☐ Business Systems Development (BSD)
☐ Other (please specify)

....

19 What is the job title of the person who makes the decision to implement **ITIL** and/or purchase IT?

....

....

20 Which three websites do you visit the most?

1 ....

2 ....

3 ....

21 Which 3 professional magazines do you read the most?

1 ....

2 ....

3 ....

22 Will you be attending any events or conferences this year related to IT, if so, which?

....

To enter your Questionnaire into our monthly draw please return this form to our Freepost Address:

Marketing – ITIL Questionnaire
TSO
Freepost ANG4748
Norwich
NR3 1YX

The ITIL series is available in a range of formats: hard copy, CD-ROM and now available as an Online Subscription. For further details and to purchase visit **www.get-best-practice.co.uk**

Any further enquiries or questions about ITIL or the Office of Government Commerce should be directed to the OGC Service Desk:

The OGC Service Desk
Rosebery Court
St Andrews Business Park
Norwich
NR7 0HS

Email: ServiceDesk@ogc.gsi.gov.uk
Telephone: 0845 000 4999

TSO will not sell, rent or pass any of your details onto interested third parties. The details you supply will be used for market research purposes only and to keep you up to date with TSO products and services which we feel maybe of interest to you. **If you would like us to use your information to keep you updated please indicate how you would like us to communicate with you:**

Telephone ☐   Email ☐   Mail ☐

For Your Tomorrow

Dearest Dad & Grandad,
Happy Father's Day.
With all our love from
Your loving family.
X X X X X X X X X X X X
18th. June 2006

Cover: International Air Monument, Plymouth

This book is dedicated to the memory
of
Margaret S. Kilgour

For Your Tomorrow

British Second World War Memorials

Derek Boorman

'When you go home
Tell them of us and say
"For your tomorrow
We gave our today"'
Kohima Epitaph

Derek Boorman
Dunnington Hall
York, England

Hardback Edition published March 1995
Paperback Edition published March 1995

Copyright: Derek Boorman © 1995

ISBN 0 9513654 1 X   Paperback
ISBN 0 9513654 2 8   Hardback

By the same author:
At the Going Down of the Sun
British First World War Memorials

Printed in 10/11 Palatino Typeface
by William Sessions Limited
The Ebor Press, York, England

CONTENTS

Except where otherwise stated, photographs
were taken by the Author

The Royal Navy Memorial, Plymouth

Introduction

WHEN THE FIRST WORLD WAR ended in November 1918 it was considered to have been the war to end all wars. In all, there had been some 10 million dead and 30 million missing or wounded, while Britain and its Empire alone had almost a million dead. It seemed inconceivable that such a calamity could ever occur again and yet, in little over 20 years, Britain was again at war with Germany.

Worldwide, this Second War was even deadlier than the First. The casualty figures are contradictory and impossible to check, but the most common estimate seems to be 55 million dead worldwide, and many more civilians died than combatants, with Russia, Poland and China suffering disproportionately. One estimate puts Polish total deaths at over 17% of its population.

Britain and its Empire lost almost half a million men under arms, and some 70,000 civilians. The peak size of Britain's armed forces in each war was in the region of five million, and although the number of deaths was smaller the Second World War left Britain economically and psychologically exhausted. The war started on 3rd September 1939 and although V.E. (Victory in Europe) Day was on 8th May 1945, V.J. (Victory over Japan) Day was not until 15th August 1945, so the struggle lasted nearly six years, or almost half as long again as had the First World War.

In the Second World War the country had to suffer indiscriminate bombing and rocket attacks, with nearly 7% of its homes destroyed and large areas in its city centres, docks and industrial quarters flattened, and for long periods, particularly when Britain stood alone after Dunkirk, there were real possibilities of invasion and shattering defeat.

Although the tactics of the Somme and Flanders were not repeated and casualty figures amongst the army did not match those of 1914-18, nevertheless deaths amongst sailors, airmen and, of course, civilians were very much higher, and memorials of the Second World War reflect this.

After 1918 every village, town, city, and church, and many schools, universities, clubs and places of work, had a memorial to commemorate those who served and died for their country. These memorials were normally erected very shortly after the war and it was a matter of pride for there to be no delay in comparison with other communities.

After 1945 there was not the same sense of urgency in the matter. It is almost as if superstition dictated that the erecting of a memorial to one war, led inevitably to the need for another within a few years. Fifty years after the war, memorials are still being commissioned, often by ex-servicemen's associations, such as the Burma Star Association, the Far East Prisoner of War Association, or veterans of Dunkirk or Normandy. Whereas there are now very few veterans of the First World War still surviving, so even the youngest Second World War veteran is now approaching three score years and ten and the desire for an appropriate local memorial may be strong.

The majority of tributes to the war dead of 1939-1945 consist of additional dates and name tablets on existing memorials built after 1918, and in considering Second World War memorials it is impossible to ignore these because it is how most of those who gave their lives are commemorated. Nevertheless this book, with information about almost 700 memorials to those who fell in World War Two, includes a high proportion unconnected with the earlier war. Many of these have no First World War element, because they are to individuals, or air-raid victims or to air force units and stations. Again, many are to our allies, forced to fight from our shores because of the occupation of most of Europe.

Only memorials in Great Britain and Northern Ireland have been considered, and the chapters of the book reflect the categories of memorial already mentioned. The memorials were visited in 1993 and 1994, and in general were well maintained although those in large cities and industrial areas are still liable on occasions to be found vandalised or neglected.

There does appear to be a growing awareness and appreciation of memorials in general. Books in recent years such as *War Memorials* by Alan Borg and *Monuments of War* by Colin McIntyre, and the excellent work of the National Inventory of War Memorials, funded by the Leverhulme Trust and managed jointly by the Imperial War Museum and the Royal Commission on the Historical Monuments of England, have obviously all contributed towards an improved situation.

The 50th anniversary of the war's end will again publicise the events to which the memorials relate, and bring increased awareness of what is owed to those who died, and of how important it is that monuments to their sacrifice be properly respected.

CHAPTER I

Memorials to Individuals

As in the First World War, those who died in action in the Second World War were normally buried where they fell and later reburied in military cemeteries on the site of the battle, or they had no known graves. There were very large numbers of naval and air force dead and, by the nature of the war which they fought, the majority had no known resting place. The large Royal Navy memorials at Portsmouth, Plymouth and Chatham, the Merchant Navy memorial at Tower Hill, London, and the Air Forces' memorial at Runnymede are evidence of this.

Very few British war dead, therefore, unless victims of air raids, were buried close to their families, and it was natural that a certain number of these families would feel the need of an individual memorial rather than the more impersonal name engraved with others on a local monument.

Most individual tributes consisted of a plaque or stained-glass window in a church, but there were also many other forms such as, for example, buildings ranging from village bus shelters to the National Sports Centre's Bisham Abbey. Again, most individual memorials were for officers, many of whom were pilots, and some were placed where the dead man's aircraft crashed.

It is convenient to include in the 'individual' category cases where more than one person might be commemorated and yet the memorial is still clearly limited. Such cases normally arise when more than one in a family has been killed and both or all are remembered. It is not even uncommon

1 *Churchill*

2 *Smuts*

2

3 *Slim*

4 *Alanbrooke*

for names from both World Wars to appear on the same family memorial.

In addition to individual memorials erected by members of the families of those who fell, many such tributes were raised to war heroes, both political and military.

Near the West Door of Westminster Abbey is the tomb of the Unknown Warrior, whose burial on 11th November, 1920, was attended by King George V, the Prince of Wales, the Duke of York, Queen Mary, many other members of the Royal Family, politicians and service chiefs. 'THEY BURIED HIM AMONG KINGS.'

The tomb is still covered with poppies at the time of the Remembrance Service each year and it is fitting that between the tomb and the Abbey's West Door, a memorial has been placed to Winston Churchill, Britain's war leader from May 1940.

The green marble stone in the floor of the Abbey was unveiled by the Queen in September 1965, a few months after his death. The wording on the stone is 'REMEMBER WINSTON CHURCHILL. IN ACCORDANCE WITH THE WISHES OF THE QUEEN AND PARLIAMENT THE DEAN AND CHAPTER PLACED THIS STONE ON THE TWENTY FIFTH ANNIVERSARY OF THE BATTLE OF BRITAIN 15 SEPTEMBER 1965'.

Another memorial to Churchill, a statue in Parliament Square, on a stone plinth and facing the Houses of Parliament, is the work of Ivor Robert-Jones, whose bronzes of Alanbrooke and Slim are in nearby Whitehall. The 12 ft. bulk of his Churchill has been said to make all other statues in the square look like matchstick men.

This certainly applies to the unflattering bronze by Epstein, of Field Marshal Smuts the South African war leader, this 1956 statue being the nearest to that of Churchill in Parliament Square.

The bronze statue of Field Marshal Viscount Slim is one of three memorials to 2nd World War leaders on Raleigh Green, Whitehall, outside the Ministry of Defence, the others being to Alanbrooke and Montgomery. The statue of Slim, in his bush hat, was unveiled by the Queen

5 *Montgomery*

in April 1990. The sculptor was Ivor Robert-Jones and the work was commissioned by the Burma Star Association. Both Slim and the sculptor, incidentally, won the Burma Star, and amongst Slim's career details on the stone plinth of the statue are the words '14TH ARMY BURMA 1943-1945'.

Another bronze by Ivor Robert-Jones is of Field Marshal Viscount Alanbrooke, who was Chief of the Imperial General Staff from 1941-1946, seeing Churchill almost daily and becoming his principal strategic adviser. In fact, carved on the steps below the plinth of the statue are the words 'MASTER OF STRATEGY'. The statue was unveiled by the Queen on 25th May 1993. The work, on a stone plinth, shows the subject turning slightly to one side with his hands behind his back.

7 *Field Marshals, St Paul's*

8 *Wingate*

6 *Alexander*

The third war-time leader with a statue on Raleigh Green, Whitehall, is Field Marshal Viscount Montgomery of Alamein, or 'MONTY' as the first word on the bronze base of his statue describes him. The bronze statue by Oscar Nemon is rough-modelled and shows Montgomery in typical pose, feet apart, hands behind his back and with the familiar beret. His career details listed include his command of the 8th Army from 1942 to 1944, and of 21st Army Group, North West Europe, in 1944 and 1945.

The memorial to Field Marshal Earl Alexander of Tunis is situated outside the Guards' Chapel in Birdcage Walk. Overall commander of the British and Allied forces in the Western Desert, and in Italy, 'Alex' was known for his diplomatic handling of both subordinates and allies. After the war he became Governor-

General of Canada. His 1985 memorial is an impressive bronze by James Butler. The subject is shown standing on uneven ground and about to raise field glasses to his eyes. The pose conveys alertness and purpose.

In the Crypt of St Paul's, a chamber, in the centre of which is the tomb of Wellington, has on the walls 10 memorials to commemorate British Field Marshals of the war. They are also intended as a tribute to the men who served under these leaders.

The Field Marshals honoured are Alexander, Slim, Montgomery, Alanbrooke, Wavell, Gort, Auchinleck, Dill, Wilson and Ironside. Each plaque has a short biography of the man in question, and the memorials were dedicated on 23rd November 1979, in the presence of the Queen.

On the Victoria Embankment near the Houses of Parliament, on the rear surface of a memorial to the Chindits, is a tribute to Major-General Orde Charles Wingate who formed, trained and led them. He was killed on active service in Burma on 24th March 1944, and his memorial has a bronze relief of the general above a quotation of Winston Churchill, 'A MAN OF GENIUS WHO MIGHT WELL HAVE BECOME A MAN OF DESTINY'.

Also on the Embankment is a statue of Lord Portal, close to that of the first Marshal of the Royal Air Force, Viscount Trenchard, a key figure of the First World War. Portal was chief of the air staff from 1940 until after the war ended, and his

9 *Portal*

10 *Dowding*

judgement was greatly respected by Churchill and by the Allies. His statue, a rough-modelled bronze by Oscar Nemon whose statue of Montgomery is in Whitehall, is on a rough hewn stone plinth and shows him looking skyward. It was unveiled in 1975 by Harold McMillan.

The bronze statue of Air Chief Marshal Lord Dowding was unveiled outside the R.A.F. Church of St Clement Danes, in the Strand, by Her Majesty the Queen Mother on 30th October 1988. The stone base of the work by Faith Winter has a metal plate with career details. Dowding was head of Fighter Command from its formation in 1936 until November 1940, and masterminded the Battle of Britain victory. He was also one of the first to realise the potential importance of radar.

Another statue by Faith Winter outside the church of St Clement Danes was unveiled, again by the Queen Mother, on 31st May 1992, amidst controversy and demonstrations by various peace groups. The 9 ft. bronze of Marshal Sir Arthur Harris has subsequently been vandalised on more than one occasion, red paint having been poured over it, and the words 'War Criminal' and 'Shame' having been painted on the stone base.

'Bomber' Harris was head of Bomber Command from February 1942 until the end of the war, and disillusioned with the results of attempted precision bombing, he was responsible for the policy of area bombing of German cities leading up to the '1,000 bombers raids', and the raid on Dresden in 1945. Whatever the views on his policies, he was held in high regard by those under him, and his memorial was built after

11 *Harris*

12 *Mountbatten*

£100,000 for its cost was raised by former members of Bomber Command.

The memorial also commemorates 'the brave crews of Bomber Command more than 55,000 of whom lost their lives in the cause of freedom. The nation owes them all an immense debt'.

The statue of Admiral of the Fleet, Earl Mountbatten of Burma is situated at the Downing Street side of Horse Guards Parade. A 1983 work by Franta Belsky, the statue is on a stone plinth surrounded by stone steps. In the middle of a grassy square, it can be seen to better advantage than can statues to other wartime leaders by the side of the traffic in Whitehall.

13 *Fraser*

On the plinth are carved the dates of his wartime and later career. 'Chief of Combined Operations 1941-1943.' 'Supreme Allied Commander South-East Asia 1943-1946.' 'Last Viceroy of India 1947.' 'Governor General of India after Independence 1947.' 'First Sea-Lord 1955-1959.' 'Chief of Defence Staff 1959-1965.'

Amongst other tributes to Mountbatten is one situated in a rose garden close to the main war memorial in Poole. A stone pillar with a plaque commemorating him is next to a further memorial to those who died in the Burma Campaign.

Also, in Hebburn Cemetery, Newcastle, close to a stone to H.M.S. 'Kelly', there is a memorial 'IN RESPECTFUL MEMORY OF LORD LOUIS MOUNTBATTEN, LATER ADMIRAL OF THE FLEET THE EARL MOUNTBATTEN OF BURMA, CAPTAIN OF H.M.S. 'KELLY', WHO WAS KILLED AT MULLACHMORE, CO. SLIGO, MONDAY 27TH AUGUST 1979'. This refers, of course to his murder by the I.R.A.

Memorials to two Admirals of the Fleet who were each First Sea Lord and Chief of Naval Staff during the war, are located in the Crypt of St Paul's. Sir Dudley Pound held the posts from 1939 to October 1943 and was then succeeded by Viscount Cunningham, who, after a successful record as a fighting admiral, became one of Churchill's chief advisors.

Another memorial to Admiral Cunningham, a bronze bust by Franta Belsky, was erected in 1967 close to the busts in Trafalgar Square of First World War admirals Jellicoe and Beatty.

In Portsmouth Dockyard, close to H.M.S. 'Victory', is a memorial to Admiral Fraser who was First Sea Lord from 1948-1951 after a distinguished war record. At various times during the war he was Commander in Chief of the Home Fleet, the Eastern Fleet, and the British Pacific Fleet. His memorial is a bronze bust on a stone plinth with a cobble stone surround, and a metal plaque on the plinth records his career.

Below the 'D' Day window in Portsmouth Cathedral are two windows commemorating Admiral Ramsey, one depicting St Nicholas and the other, St George. Above the inscription 'In memory of Admiral Sir Bertram Ramsey killed in action 1945 who commanded the seaborne forces at Dunkirk 1940 and Normandy 1944. Here are remembered also those under his command who were killed during these operations', are scenes, on one window, of soldiers being rescued from the sea by a small ship, with the Dunkirk beaches in the background, and on the other, of troops landing on the Normandy beaches with the Channel and assault craft behind them (see p. 43).

A memorial plaque to Franklin Delano Roosevelt, near the West Door of Westminster Abbey, was unveiled on 12th November, 1948, by the Prime Minister, Clement Attlee, and by Winston Churchill, at that time Leader of the Opposition. Part of the wording on the memorial with its carved eagle is 'A FAITHFUL FRIEND OF FREEDOM AND OF BRITAIN. FOUR TIMES

PRESIDENT OF THE UNITED STATES. ERECTED BY THE GOVERNMENT OF THE UNITED KINGDOM'.

Another memorial to Roosevelt is to be found in Grosvenor Square in London, the location not only of the American Embassy, but also of memorials to another American leader of the Second World War, General Eisenhower, and to the Eagle Squadrons of that war.

The statue of President Franklin Delano Roosevelt (1882-1945) was unveiled on 12th April, 1948, by Mrs Roosevelt. The bronze by Sir William Reid Dick shows the President with a cloak around his shoulders and with a walking stick in his hand. The money for this statue was raised within 24 hours of the subscription being opened. Contributions were limited to a maximum of 5/- per person and to British subscribers only, and immediately some 200,000 people contributed.

The statue of Dwight David Eisenhower, Supreme Allied Commander in Europe and later President of the United States, stands on a corner of Grosvenor Square close to the American Embassy. On a stone plinth, the bronze by Robert Dean has a shield-shaped marble surround set into the pavement, with five stars denoting rank and with a tablet giving biographical details.

A bronze statue by Angela Conner, of another allied leader, General de Gaulle, was unveiled on 23rd June, 1993, by the Queen Mother, appropriately in Carlton Gardens where he had his Free French Headquarters during the Second World War. It was pointed out that the plinth was of Hauteville stone from the Jura, so de Gaulle, characteristically, is on French soil.

The famous bandleader, Glenn Miller, who was lost on a flight on 15th December, 1944, has a memorial at the Bedford Corn Exchange which he and his band used for broadcasts and concerts during their six-month stay in Britain in 1944 before moving to the Continent. Part of the metal memorial plaque inscription reads 'TO THE EVERLASTING MEMORY OF MAJOR ALTON GLENN MILLER 1904-1944, THE "MOONLIGHT SERENADER". DIRECTOR OF THE AMERICAN BAND OF THE ALLIED EXPEDITIONARY FORCE'.

A memorial to another American, in Bottisham, near Cambridge, on the corner of a road named Thomas Christian Way, is in the form of a lychgate but with a low wall blocking the access, and pays tribute to the former commander of the 361st Fighter Group of the U.S. 8th A.F. Colonel Thomas Christian was killed in action when his Mustang was brought down as he was attacking rail targets in Northern France on 12th August 1944. Three other Mustangs of the 361st were lost on the same mission.

The road where the memorial is situated was originally part of Bottisham air base from which

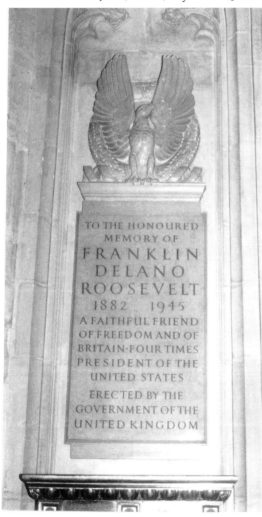

14 *Roosevelt, Westminster Abbey*

15 *Roosevelt*

16 *Eisenhower*

17 *De Gaulle*

18 *Christian Memorial, Bottisham*

the 361st operated from November 1943 until the end of September 1944. A plaque in their memory is in the Parish Church. The memorial to Christian was unveiled on 16th October 1988 by his daughter, whom he had never seen.

In the Crypt of St Paul's, near to Nelson's tomb, is a plaque to Pilot Officer William Meade Lindsley Fiske R.A.F. 'Billy' Fiske, a wealthy American stockbroker living in England, was well known in London society as an international sportsman and the husband of the former Countess of Warwick. He joined the R.A.F. on 3rd September, 1939, on the outbreak of war and died on 18th August, 1940 after action in an enemy raid on Tangmere. His plaque was unveiled on 4th July, 1941 and below it in a glass case are his R.A.F. 'wings'. It is generally believed that he was the only American to die in the Battle of Britain and his plaque has the words 'AN AMERICAN CITIZEN WHO DIED THAT ENGLAND MIGHT LIVE'.

In the boundary wall of a church at Windrush in Gloucestershire is a stone tablet with the inscription, 'TO THE MEMORY OF SGT. PILOT BRUCE HANCOCK R.A.F. V.R. WHO SACRIFICED HIS LIFE BY RAMMING AND DESTROYING AN ENEMY HEINKEL BOMBER WHILE FLYING AN UNARMED TRAINING AIRCRAFT FROM WINDRUSH LANDING GROUND DURING THE BATTLE OF BRITAIN 18TH AUGUST 1940'.

This is the same day as that on which Fiske died, and many others were to die during that period. On the road between Newchurch and St Mary, on Romney Marsh, is a memorial stone, with a post and chain surround which apparently always has fresh flowers placed on it. The stone is to Pilot Officer Arthur William Clarke aged 20, of 504 Squadron, who was killed in action near the spot on 11th September, 1940 during the Battle of Britain.

A memorial stone at the side of the A36 at Woolverton, Somerset, bears the inscription 'IN MEMORY OF KENNETH CHRISTOPHER HOLLAND-RIPLEY, SERGEANT PILOT R.A.F., KILLED IN ACTION 25TH SEPTEMBER 1940. THIS STONE MARKS THE SPOT WHERE HE FELL, HAVING DESTROYED AN ENEMY HEINKEL'.

An Australian who joined 152 squadron at Warmwell, Dorset, on 1st August, 1940, he was

19 *Crofts Memorial, Bodle Street Green*

easy to miss whilst driving. The cross was erected to his memory by the mother of Flying Officer Peter Guerin Crofts R.A.F., who died in a Battle of Britain dog-fight over the village on 28th September, 1940. According to the inscription he 'is one of the few to whom so many owe so much'.

South of Godstone Green on the east of the A22, is a memorial to an individual R.A.F. pilot. Quite difficult to find amongst trees on the edge of a field, the memorial consists of a bench seat with a metal plate, a silver cedar tree, and a small stone column near the tree, again with an inscription tablet.

The inscription on the seat reads 'BATTLE OF BRITAIN. STANLEY ALLEN FENEMORE, R.A.F., DIED HERE OCTOBER 15TH 1940' while that on the stone explains that the cedar was planted in memory of the 20-year-old sergeant-pilot. The original planting ceremony was 1944, but the stone was set up in 1992 by the pilot's sister.

In the corner of the churchyard at Great Paxton, near Huntingdon, a sundial on a brick and tile base commemorates R.A.F. Pilot Officer Philip Cardell who was killed in 1940 in the Battle of Britain, at the age of 23.

On October 8th, 1940, the little church of St Nicholas at Moreton, Dorset, suffered severe damage when a bomb fell in the churchyard close to the north wall. That wall was in ruins and none of the windows survived. As part of the re-building the windows were replaced entirely by engraved glass, the work of Laurence Whistler. One of these, the Trinity Chapel window, com-

in fact killed by the last burst of fire from the aircraft which he attacked and destroyed. The stone, in fact, is not exactly on its original site, having been moved from the middle of a field some 400 yards away.

Two miles from Bodle Street Green in Sussex is a wooden cross on a grassy roadside bank, with steps leading up to it and surrounded by a rustic timber fence. It is quite difficult to find, and very

20 *St Nicholas' Church, Moreton*

21 *Sayer Memorial, Sparham*

22 *Ketton-Cremer Memorial, Felbrigg*

24 *Nunney Memorial, Old Whittington*

memorates an un-named R.A.F. pilot shot down in the Battle of France in 1940. Below vapour trails are scenes of Salisbury Cathedral near which he was stationed, his cottage home, the English Channel and the French coast, and, on a broken propeller, the years of his marriage and two sets of initials.

This beautiful window, an anonymous gift, is an evocative and imaginative memorial and leaves the viewer wishing to know more of the identity and background of the unknown pilot.

In the church of St Michael and All Angels at Withyham in Sussex, there is a stone plaque to the memory of Flying Officer Thomas Henry Jordan Sackville, second son of the 9th Earl de la Warr. Born 13th November, 1922, he was killed in action 14th May, 1943. His memorial bears the inscription 'Radiance undimmed that grows not old'.

Alongside in the family chapel is a memorial to his father who died in 1976 and below the chapel lie the ashes of one of the best known members of the family, the poet and writer Vita Sackville-West, who died aged 70 in 1962 at Sissinghurst, the house where with her husband, Sir Harold Nicolson, she created the world famous garden.

The church of St Giles, Stoke Poges, made famous by Gray's *Elegy – Written in a Country Churchyard*, has a stained-glass window in 'memory of the men of this Church and Parish who fell in the War 1939-1945'. The names of eight men follow, including that of John Stuart Devereux. His name appears again in the Hastings Chapel of St Giles', on a stone tablet with the inscription, 'THIS CHAPEL FOUNDED AND BUILT BY EDWARD HASTINGS 2ND EARL OF HUNTINGDON A.D. 1558, WAS RESTORED BY COLONEL WALLACE C. DEVEREUX IN MEMORY OF HIS SON JOHN STUART DEVEREUX, PILOT OFFICER R.A.F. KILLED ON ACTIVE SERVICE 29.XI.1944'.

A stained-glass window in St Mary's Church, Sparham, in Norfolk, has the badge of the R.A.F., and a family crest, and is in memory

23 *Hankey Memorial, Tarrant Hinton*

25 *Pathfinder Memorial, Warboys*

of Arthur John Sayer, an R.A.F. squadron leader who was killed in action on 15th February 1944, aged 32. His body lies in a Danish churchyard. At the foot of one panel of the window are the words 'Tranquil you lie your knightly virtue proved, your memory hallowed in the land you loved'.

In St Margaret's Church next to Felbrigg Hall, Norfolk, there is a stone plaque with a coloured coat of arms at the top and a coloured badge of 113 Squadron R.A.F at the foot. This is in memory of Flying Officer Richard Thomas Wyndham Ketton-Cremer, R.A.F., V.R., who was born on 11th August, 1909 and killed in May 1941 during the Battle of Crete. The memorial is close to others of the Ketton-Cremer family.

The Church of St Mary in the Dorset village of Tarrant Hinton has a bronze portrait relief to the memory of Michael Hankey, a fighter pilot of the Fleet Air Arm who was killed protecting a Malta convoy 12th August, 1942, when he was aged 26. The rector at that time (from 1911-1946) was Basil Hankey, perhaps his father.

In the churchyard of St Luke's, Whyteleafe, Surrey, is a crucifix on which the names of the Second War dead have been added to those of the First. One of them, Sub-Lieutenant Royston Griffin, R.N.V.R., has a further memorial inside the church, in the form of a choir prayer desk. A former solo chorister, he was flying on convoy escort duty as a fighter pilot with the Fleet Air Arm in the Mediterranean, when shot down on 28th December 1941.

A memorial in St John's Church, Shotley, Northumbria, to another Fleet Air Arm pilot, Lt. Hugh John Crauford Walton-Wilson, who gave his life in H.M.S. 'Courageous' on 17th September 1939, is in the form of a stained glass window by Professor Leonard C. Evetts, who designed the thanksgiving window in Newcastle's St Nicholas' Cathedral. Far from traditional in design or colour, the window, with its central saintly figure, incorporates naval badges and a small representation of a naval vessel and is dated 1941.

A stained-glass window in the church of St Gregory the Great, Kirknewton, Northumberland, depicts St Michael and has a naval air squadron badge. This window is in memory of Lieutenant Commander D. R. B. Cosh, D.S.C., Commanding Officer of 881 Naval Air Squadron from 1943 until his death in June 1944.

An attractive 20 in. high statue of St George in Holy Trinity Church, Brathay, in Cumbria, commemorates George Michael Hough Aitchison, a Royal Artillery Air Operations pilot, who died at Anzio on 19th May 1944 (see p. 43).

The Parish Church of Old Whittington in Derbyshire, has several stained-glass windows with likenesses of the individuals commemorated. Two such windows are to men killed in the Second World War. One is to Peter Nunney, a merchant seaman killed at sea on 20th May 1941, aged 20. As well as his portrait, the window depicts a merchant vessel. The other is to a bomber pilot, whose mother's maiden name was also Nunney, David Watson-Smith, 21, killed during night bombing on Germany on 13th May 1943. The R.A.F. badge and motto are part of his memorial.

The Church of St Michael the Archangel in Mere, Wiltshire, has, as a memorial to those who gave their lives in the 1939-45 war, the clock and chimes placed in the tower in 1947. The clock dial on the tower is dedicated to the memory of Flight Lieutenant Thomas Patrick Walsh, R.A.F., who died 29th April 1945.

26 *Bennett Memorial, Guildford*

27 *Sutton Memorial, Ashdown Forest*

28 *Sedbergh School, V.C.'s*

A stone tablet on the wall of St Mary's Church, North Marston, near Aylesbury, is to the memory of Sgt. George Thomas Tattam of the R.A.F., who was killed on 3rd May 1943. 'Who stands if freedom fall, Who dies if England live', is the inscription that follows.

At the former R.A.F. airfield at East Kirkby, there is now an Aviation Heritage Centre in which there are some memorials to individuals, including one to Norman Watt, killed on 1st July, 1943. This was unveiled by his brother in October 1991.

On the edge of an industrial estate on the outskirts of Darlington, on the corner of Ellington Way and McMullen Road, stands a memorial to the heroism of the pilot after whom the latter road was named. A large rough hewn boulder carries a plaque to the memory of Pilot Officer William S. McMullen 428 Squadron Royal Canadian Air Force. On 13th January, 1945, he 'stayed at the controls of his burning Lancaster bomber KB 793 until six members of his crew had parachuted to safety and the aircraft was clear of densely populated areas of the town'. He died when the aircraft finally crashed about 600 metres from the spot where his monument stands.

In Warboys Parish Church, Cambridgeshire, a wall plaque bears the inscription 'THIS TABLET IS PLACED IN MEMORY OF FLIGHT LIEUTENANT J. L. SLOPER, D.F.C. AND BAR, R.A.F.V.R., AND IN TRIBUTE TO ALL WHO SERVED WITH 156 SQUADRON PATH-FINDER FORCE AT R.A.F. WARBOYS. 1942-45. IN GRATITUDE'.

A nearby stained-glass window depicts bombers caught in the beams of searchlights, within a laurel wreath, and has the words, 'IN MEMORY OF MEMBERS OF THE PATHFINDER FORCE 1942-1945. IF I SPREAD OUT MY WINGS TOWARDS THE MORNING YOUR HAND SHALL LEAD ME'.

The Pathfinder Force was established in August 1942 and had the responsibility for marking targets for the main bombing group. As a result of its technique Bomber Command's accuracy improved, despite the initial reservations of 'Bomber' Harris.

Another window, in Guildford Cathedral, is in memory of Air Vice-Marshal Donald Clifford Tyndall Bennett, C.B., C.B.E., D.S.O., and the Pathfinder Force 1942-1945. The Pathfinder Force badge is above the inscription.

An individual memorial in the R.A.F. museum at Hendon is a stained glass window to Stanley McGlory R.A.F. Pathfinders, aged 20 years, reported missing on 24th May 1943 after a raid on Dortmund. The window was originally erected in the Church of St Simon and St Jude in Anfield, Liverpool, and presented to the museum when the church was de-consecrated. The window shows an airman standing at the end of a path lit by a Cross, while an aircraft flies overhead. At the top of the window are the words, 'I WILL LEAD THEM IN PATHS THAT THEY HAVE NOT KNOWN I WILL MAKE DARKNESS LIGHT BEFORE THEM'. (ISIAH)

In St Mary's Parish Church, Watton, in East Yorkshire, there are two stained-glass memorials to a Pathfinder airman and his crew. One window has the framed inscription 'The East Window is to the memory of Flt.Lt. Harold Cass Ben Pexton, D.F.C., of Watton Abbey and four members of his crew, Pathfinders, 35th Squadron, Bomber Command, who failed to return from an opera-

29 *Mantle Memorial, Weymouth*

tional flight over Hamburg July 29 / 30 1943. Their ashes lie in the area of Lüneburg'. The names of the other crew members are also listed. The other window, behind the altar, has in one corner, a representation of the aircrew, and in another, R.A.F. Squadron badges. The portrait of Pexton and his crew is particularly striking (see p. 43).

On open ground in Ashdown Forest near Crowborough in Sussex, is a white cross, surrounded by a stone wall, to the memory of Sgt. P. V. R. Sutton of 142 Squadron R.A.F., who died along with five crew members when their Wellington crashed nearby on 31st July, 1941. The memorial, known locally as the 'Airman's Grave' although the crew are not buried there, was constructed at the request of Sutton's mother, and inside the wall is an attractive garden of heathers, flag stones and rockery. Against the rear wall is a plaque listing the six crew members and with the words 'TO LIVE IN THE HEARTS OF THOSE LEFT BEHIND IS NOT TO DIE'.

On an isolated hill near Beaminster in Dorset, is what is also known as 'The Airman's Grave'. This is the burial place of Lieutenant William Barnard Rhodes-Moorhouse who in 1915 won the first Victoria Cross awarded to an airman. His family lived at Parnham House, below the hill, and buried near him is his son Flight Lieutenant William Henry Rhodes-Moorhouse, D.F.C., of 601 Squadron, killed in the Battle of Britain 6th September, 1940, aged 26.

Rhodes-Moorhouse may have been the first airman to win the V.C., but many others have fol-lowed. Outside St. Mary's church at Bexwell, near Downham Market, there is a memorial plaque in a glass case on a stand. The inscription reads 'R.A.F. DOWNHAM MARKET. FROM THIS AIRFIELD DURING THE SECOND WORLD WAR MANY MEN OF THE R.A.F. FLEW ON MISSIONS FROM WHICH SOME DID NOT RETURN. THIS MEMORIAL IS DEDICATED TO THOSE MEN AND IN PARTICULAR TO TWO MEN, BOTH OF WHOM WERE AWARDED POSTHUMOUSLY THE V.C.'

The two men mentioned are Acting Squadron Leader Ian Willoughby Bazalgette, V.C., D.F.C., 635 Squadron and Flight Sergeant Arthur Louis Aaron, V.C., D.F.M., 218 Squadron. Bazalgette died on the night of 4th August 1944 after leading a Pathfinder Squadron, and Aaron died on the night of 12th August 1943 after an attack on Turin. The details of the exploits for which each man was awarded the V.C. are recorded on metal tablets. Unfortunately, the stand of the memorial is beginning to deteriorate, placing it at risk.

At Ryhope in Durham the war memorial on the village green carries a metal plaque at a lower level to the memory of Pilot Officer Cyril Joe Barton, V.C., R.A.F.V.R., of 578 Squadron, who died on 31st March, 1944, crash-landing his crippled Halifax in avoiding Ryhope. The plaque says that he 'displayed unsurpassed courage and devotion to his duty, then sacrificed his life to save others and was posthumously awarded the Victoria Cross'.

On the terrace above the cloisters at Sedbergh School, a hexagonal stone seat commemorates three V.C.'s of the Second World War, two of whom apparently died in the same action. Flying Officer Kenneth Campbell of the R.A.F. died at Brest on 6th April, 1941, while 2nd Lieutenant George Ward Gunn and Major General John Charles Campbell, both of the Royal Horse Artillery, died at Sidi Resegh on 21st November, 1941.

In a museum at Nothe Fort, Weymouth, there are memorials to two V.C.'s of the Second World War. The decoration awarded posthumously after the war to Lt. Commander G. B. Roope may well be unique in that it was first recommended by a German Admiral, through the International Red Cross. It was later confirmed by the sole surviving officer of Roope's ship, when released at the end of the war from a P.O.W. camp.

Roope's destroyer, H.M.S. 'Glowworm,' was engaged in a hopeless action with a German heavy cruiser 'Admiral Hipper' in the North Sea on 8th April, 1940 when, having fired all her torpedoes and badly hit, she closed on the enemy and with her remaining guns firing, rammed her. 'Glowworm' then sank, and although the German vessel hove to for nearly an hour picking up survivors, only 31 of the crew of 149 were saved, Roope being among those lost. A wall plaque and a display of information about the action, commemorate the V.C. and his crew.

The other V.C. commemorated at Nothe Fort is of equal interest. Of all the V.C.'s won by the navy in the Second World War, only one, it is said, was awarded for an act of gallantry in the United Kingdom itself.

On the 4th July, 1940, after Dunkirk, the armed merchant cruiser 'Foylebank' was in Portland Harbour when some 20 Stuka dive bombers attacked. During the action 23 year old Leading Seaman Jack Mantle, although wounded several times and with his left leg shattered, continued to fire his 20mm pompom gun until dying at his post. He was posthumously awarded the V.C., presented to his parents by King George VI in June 1941, and a plaque and exhibition at Nothe Fort, are dedicated to him and to the others lost in the action. Also in his memory, a sun lounge for patients was built in Portland Hospital.

Beside the Burslem, Stoke on Trent, war memorial, a fine stone monument with a soldier figure of the First World War, a brick cairn has been erected with a bronze plaque to the memory of Lance Sergeant J. D. Baskeyfield, 2nd Battalion South Staffordshire Regiment, a native of Burslem who was killed at Arnhem on 20th September 1944, aged 21, and was posthumously awarded the Victoria Cross.

Inside the entrance to Elmwood School, Croydon, is a small brass plaque in memory of former pupil Lt. George Arthur Knowland, V.C.,

who died, aged 22, on 31st January, 1945, the day that he won his V.C. while serving with the Royal Norfolk Regiment but attached to the Commandos in Burma.

On a hill above the village of Oldstead in North Yorkshire, on Forestry Commission land, sculptor John Bunting has rebuilt old farm buildings as a memorial chapel. Oldstead lies between the White Horse at Kilburn and Ampleforth College and the memorial is dedicated to three Old Boys of the College, Michael Allmand, killed 1944 and posthumously awarded the V.C., Hugh Dormer, D.S.O., killed in 1944, and Michael Fenwick killed in 1941.

Within the chapel three inscriptions are carried, on white marble in one case and on Hoptonwood stone in the others. Impressive external features are ornately carved doors below the sculpted head and shoulders of a man reaching up towards a dove with a sprig of olive in its beak. Higher still above the door are a stone Madonna and child in a niche. On the two front corners of the building, stone angels carry scrolls with the words in Latin 'Glory to God on High' and 'Peace on earth to those who seek it'.

The chapel is in a remote beautiful spot with extensive views and serves as a magnificent tribute, and it is all the more sad to hear that the angel figures have been stolen and that the doors have also been removed, although in this case subsequently recovered.

Not far from Oldstead, Fountains Hall in Yorkshire has one of the most impressive of all memorials to individuals. Inside the Hall, above the entrance staircase, the memorial is to Elizabeth Vyner, W.R.N.S., who died on active service on June 3rd, 1942 aged 18, and to her brother Charles de Grey Vyner, sub-lieutenant in the R.N.V.R., who was reported missing off Rangoon on May 2nd, 1945 aged 19.

30 *Baskeyfield Memorial, Burslem*

31 *Oldstead*

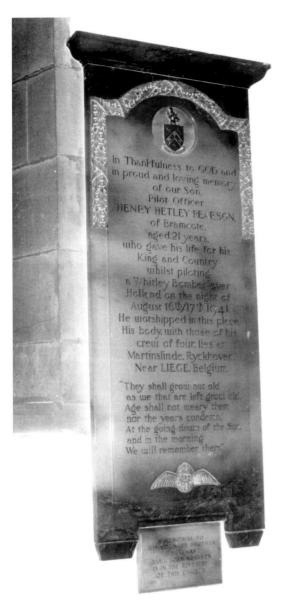

The memorial features a stained glass window surrounding a stone cross bearing two wreaths. To the left of the window stands the stone figure of a Wren and to the right the figure of an airman. Each figure is looking upwards towards the cross. On the glass are the words 'WHEN YOU GO HOME TELL THEM OF US AND SAY, FOR YOUR TOMORROW WE GAVE OUR TODAY', and in stone between the two figures are the words 'FROM THIS THEIR HOME THEY WENT FORTH TO WAR' (see p. 44).

The memorial was designed by John, Lord Mottistone and Paul Paget, and executed by sculptor Cecil Thomas and stained-glass artist Hugh Easton. It was unveiled on 9th April, 1953 by H.M. Queen Elizabeth the Queen Mother, a friend of the Vyner family.

The Church of St Leonard at Wollaton near Nottingham, has one of the most beautiful of marble plaques as a memorial to a young 2nd World War pilot. Pilot Officer Henry Hetley Pearson aged 21 died on the night of 16th/17th August 1941, and along with the crew of his Whitley bomber he is buried near Liege in Belgium. The memorial was erected by his parents and an additional tablet below it reads, 'A MEMORIAL TO HIS YOUNGER BROTHER LIEUTENANT BASIL JOHN PEARSON IS IN THE REVESTRY OF THIS CHURCH'.

St Peter's Church at Down Ampney in Gloucestershire, has a stone tablet in memory of two brothers, sons of a Royal Artillery colonel, who both died in the Second World War. Donald Macleay, himself a lieutenant in the artillery, died in the Middle East, 26th September, 1941, aged 20, and his younger brother, Robert, an Indian Army lieutenant, died on 28 February 1944, aged 21.

The porch of St Laurence Church, Frodsham, was renovated in 1946 in memory of two men whose names are engraved there on a stone tablet. Flying Officer Alan Otho Glover, of 607

32 *Pearson Memorial, Wollaton*

33 *Bisham Abbey*

34 *Swanwick Memorials, Old Whittington*

35 *Deck Memorial, Westleton*

Squadron, was killed on 29th October 1939, and Sub. Lieutenant Alexander John Glover, R.N.V.R. Dover Patrol, was killed whilst helping the army evacuate Dunkirk on 29th May 1940.

In the Chapel of Sedbergh School are several individual memorials including a pulpit given in memory of Lt. David Allardice (at Sedbergh 1927-31) killed in Egypt in November 1942, and pews given in memory of Flying Officer Philip Allardice (at Sedburgh 1931-35) killed at Malta March 1942.

The National Sports Centre at Bisham Abbey near Marlow, is a war memorial to two brothers, Berkeley and Guy Paget, sons of Leo and Elizabeth Paget, and grandsons and heirs of Sir Henry Vansittart-Neale, K.C.B., of Bisham Abbey. Berkeley was killed at El Alamein in October 1942, at the age of 23 as a lieutenant in the K.R.R.C. Guy, also a lieutenant in the K.R.R.C., was killed in Italy in October 1944, again aged 23.

In 1946 Mrs Elizabeth Paget and her sister, Miss Phyllis Vansittart-Neale handed Bisham Abbey over to the Central Council of Physical Recreation for a nominal rent, as a memorial. It was eventually purchased in 1962 and since 1972 has been administered by the Sports Council. A plaque in the Great Hall gives the background to what is described as 'a living war memorial'.

In nearby Bisham Church a bronze plaque in memory of Berkeley and Guy Paget is decorated with badges of the King's Royal Rifle Corps. A memorial to their grandfather, mother and aunt is nearby. The boys' names appear also on a beautiful marble memorial with carved figures, commemorating the dead of the parish in both wars. The Pagets are two of seven names on a separate tablet for 1939-45.

On a family memorial just inside the entrance gates to the grounds of Tewkesbury Abbey, the deaths of two brothers, who died on

36 *Ritchie Memorial, Medmenham*

successive days in the Second World War, are recorded. James Cartland, a captain in the Lincolnshire Regiment was killed, aged 27, on 29th May 1940, and on the following day his brother Ronald, a major in the Worcestershire Yeomanry, was killed aged 33.

Their father's name is also engraved on the stone base of the memorial crucifix. He died in action in France as a major in the Worcestershire Regiment, on 27th May 1918. His two sons were later to die almost within hours of the anniversary of his death. His widow lived until 1976 at

37 *Baldock Memorial, Slip End*

which time she was almost 100 years of age and had been a widow for 58 years.

In the Church of St Michael at Bramcote, near Nottingham, is a poignant marble memorial to a father and son killed respectively in 1914 and 1941. Under the badge of the Royal Artillery are the words 'TO THE GLORY OF GOD AND IN MEMORY OF MY HUSBAND AND BEST FRIEND HARRY BROCKLESBY BARTRAM CAPTAIN ROYAL HORSE ARTILLERY'. He landed in France with the British Expeditionary Force on 17th August, 1914, and the guns of his battery were the first British guns to be fired in the campaign. He died on the 16th September.

His son, Harry Bob Brocklesby, was born on 25th September, 1914, just over a week after his father's death, and he died in the defence of Hong Kong on Christmas Day 1941. He also was a Royal Artillery captain. Finally on the memorial is recorded the death in 1962 of his mother, a widow for 48 years.

Close to the village war memorial of Old Whittington in Derbyshire are individual memorials to two members of the same family. The attractive well maintained Memorial Hall is in memory of R. K. Swanwick, a lieutenant in the 1st Gloucesters, who was killed 14th September, 1914, at the Battle of the Aisne. Nearby is a bus shelter of stone and tile construction, in memory of Captain Roy Norton Swanwick of the 15th/19th King's Royal Hussars, killed in Germany, 1st March, 1945. The shelter, unfortunately, is less well maintained than the hall. Repairs to the roof are necessary and there is a good deal of graffiti in the interior.

The Church at Dowdeswell in Gloucestershire has a family stained-glass window, one part of which has a memorial to George Reginald Beale-Browne, R.A.F., who as a night fighter was killed in 1941, and another part of which honours Thomas Richard Beale-Browne who died at sea as a result of enemy action in 1918.

A further window with R.A.F. insignia was presented by the R.A.F. which had a chaplain training school near the church at Dowdeswell Court (now a nursing home).

In St Mary's Church, Great Chesterton, Oxfordshire, alongside the parish memorial to the dead of both world wars, is a stone plaque to three brothers who died in the Second World War. John Charles Lancelot Ruck Keene was an R.A.F. pilot officer, Francis Ruck Keene, D.S.C., was a naval lieutenant, and Charles Frederick Ruck Keene was a naval sub-lieutenant.

In St Peter's Church, Westleton, Suffolk, there is a stained-glass window in memory of three R.A.F.V.R. brothers who died in the Second World War. James Frederick Deck, a pilot officer, was killed in November 1941, his brother Harold, a flying officer, was killed in July 1942, and Charles, a flight lieutenant, died in April 1945. The window features an R.A.F. badge and the two saints, St Felix, who converted much of East Anglia, and St George.

38 *Pilcher Memorial, Lynch*

A double memorial window in the R.A.F. Museum at Hendon depicts St George and an airman in flying kit. Under St George are the words 'To the Glory of God and in Loving memory of four brothers killed in the Second World War', and under the airman are the names of the four, all in the R.A.F. John Bools died in 1941, Charles Bools in 1942, Martin Bools in 1943 and Geoffrey Bools in 1945. The window was removed from the David Thomas United Reform Church, Bristol, in 1983, when the church was made redundant, and presented to the museum by the sister of the four men.

St Martin's Church in Ashton-upon-Mersey has a stained-glass window in memory of an individual. Designed by F. Willford and unveiled by

39 *Parry-Jones Memorial, Osmington*

the dead man's parents on 8th May 1949, the window has a central crucifixion, flanked by two kneeling angels, under one of which is the inscription, 'IN MEMORY OF SERGEANT HERBERT CASH ROYAL ENGINEERS, KILLED IN ITALY 7TH OCTOBER 1944 AGED 26 YEARS', AND UNDER THE OTHER OF WHICH IS 'BE THOU FAITHFUL UNTO DEATH AND I WILL GIVE THEE A CROWN OF LIFE'.

Another stained-glass window, very modern both in design and colouring, in St Paul's Church in the Northumberland village of North Sunderland, commemorates William Cecil Mackenzie 'who gave his life in war' in August 1944. It is also in memory of his father who died just before the war.

Again, in the Chapel at the Guards' Barracks at Caterham is a stained-glass window to Guardsman Trevor Evans of the Welsh Guards, later a 2nd lieutenant in the Green Howards, who was killed in action in Burma, 2nd April, 1945, when aged 19. Depicted in glass are the badge of the Welsh Guards, St Michael and a Knight's Vigil.

The 12th-century Church of St Michael and All Saints at Berwick in Sussex, lost many of its windows during wartime bombing and it was decided to replace them largely by plain glass for brightness and with wall paintings. Duncan Grant and Vanessa Bell, sister of Virginia Woolf, were both well known for their 'Bloomsbury Group' connections. Grant was asked to paint the Church murals and undertook the work jointly with Vanessa Bell and her children Quentin and Angelica.

One of the paintings by Duncan Grant serves as a memorial to Douglas Hemming, killed at Caen in 1944. Over the Chancel arch is the figure of Christ in Glory. To the right are the figures of

40 *Alnwick Memorial*

the Bishop of Chichester and the Rector of Berwick, and to the left are the kneeling figures of a sailor, an airman and a soldier, the last being a likeness of Douglas Hemming (see p. 44).

The Church of St Peter and St Paul in Medmenham, near Henley, has an interesting relief profile inside a green marble frame, as a memorial to James Makepeace Thackeray Ritchie who was killed at Hazelbrouck in 1940, in an action guarding the Dunkirk Beaches.

St Andrew's Church, Slip End, near Luton, has a wooden lectern with a carved eagle, and an inscription dedicating it to the memory of Ronald Edwards, a lieutenant in the Bedfordshire and Hertfordshire Regiment, who was killed in Sicily on 20th July 1943.

In the same church, rails on either side of the aisle are a memorial to Edward Baldock, a corporal in the Loyal Regiment, and previously in the Bedfordshire and Hertfordshire Regiment. He was killed at the Anzio beach-head on 9th February 1944 and his framed photograph and biography are in a side chapel. He is described as a chorister and server in the church, 'a keen sportsman, a magnificent soldier, a fine example to the lads under his command'. These last words were written by a captain under whom he served.

The organ blower in St Ebba's Church, Beadnall, Northumberland, was given in his memory by the parents of Gerald Kenneth Kinnear, a captain in the 2nd Punjab Regiment of the Indian Army, who was killed in action in Burma on 24th January 1945. A brass plaque beside the organ completes the memorial.

In the Chapel of Ease at Lynch in Somerset, a wooden plaque near the altar rail commemorates John Allan Pilcher who was born at Lynch in 1920. An officer cadet in the Grenadier Guards, he was killed 'by enemy action at the Royal Military College Sandhurst' on 29th January

1941. Decorating the plaque are a cross and the Grenadiers' badge, a crossed sword and bayonet, and a crossed épée and sporting gun.

A stone built bus shelter with a thatched roof, in the Dorset village of Osmington, is the memorial to David Parry-Jones, a lieutenant in the 1st Battalion Rifle Brigade. He was killed in action in France on 3rd August, 1944 and the shelter, with

41 *Knebworth Memorial, Old Knebworth*

19

42 *Elvedon Memorial*

a plaque to the right of the entrance, was erected by his parents.

A marble tablet in St Andrew's Church, South Stoke, Oxfordshire, pays tribute to David Gordon Dill, Croix de Guerre, Lieutenant 60th Rifles and 2nd S.A.S., who was killed as a P.O.W. in Germany on 25th November 1944, aged 20. The German officer responsible was later hanged as a war criminal. The tablet has the S.A.S. badge and motto 'WHO DARES WINS'.

By coincidence, in the same church, another tablet is to the memory of Thomas George Pither, of the Oxford and Bucks Light Infantry, who was a prisoner of war for five years and was shot trying to escape on his 26th birthday, 4th March 1945, two months before the end of the war.

In the Parish Church of St Thomas a Becket in Ramsey, near Peterborough, is a memorial chapel to the De Ramsey family. Two stained-glass windows are memorials to members of the family who fell in the First World War, and memorial medals and letters from the King, on the death of each of them, hang on the wall between the windows. Under one window is a plaque with the inscription, 'THIS CHAPEL IS THE GIFT OF LADY DE RAMSEY IN THANKSGIVING TO ALMIGHTY GOD FOR THE SAFE RETURN OF HER HUSBAND LORD DE RAMSEY FROM A JAPANESE PRISONER OF WAR CAMP 1945. 8TH AUGUST 1956'.

A group of brick built memorial cottages in Potter's Row, Alnwick, is separated from the road by a pleasant garden with lawns, cherry trees and seats. A stone plaque on a wall in the garden is inscribed 'THESE COTTAGES ARE DEDICATED TO THE MEMORY OF HENRY GEORGE ALAN THE NINTH DUKE OF NORTHUMBERLAND, THIRD BATTALION GRENADIER GUARDS, KILLED IN ACTION

43 *Wyndham Memorial, Petworth*

IN FLANDERS 21ST MAY 1940 AGED 27 YEARS, AND THE SONS OF ALNWICK WHO LOST THEIR LIVES IN THE SECOND WORLD WAR 1939-1945'.

The main Alnwick War Memorial has three bronze figures of servicemen with reversed arms, and is situated at a road junction on the edge of the town centre. The names of the Second World War dead have been added to those of 1914-18 on the memorial's bronze plaques. In a small park behind the memorial is a column in tribute to an earlier Duke of Northumberland, within 100 yards or so, sadly, of the engraved name of the 9th Duke.

On a wall of St Mary's Church, Old Knebworth, Hertfordshire, opposite the carved names of the men of the parish who died in both wars, is a memorial to Alexander Edward John, Viscount Knebworth, M.B.E., a major in the Queen's Bays, who was killed in action at El Alamein on 4th July 1942. The memorial has a gilt sword and coat of arms of the Queen's Bays.

A window by Hugh Easton, who designed the Battle of Britain Memorial Window in Westminster Abbey, in the Church at Elvedon depicts St George and the dragon and has the inscription, 'PRAISE GOD AND REMEMBER ARTHUR VISCOUNT ELVEDON WHO GAVE HIS LIFE IN THE WAR OF 1939-1945'. The name of Viscount Elvedon also appears with two others on the 1939-45 parish memorial in the church, an ornately carved stone tablet with the words, 'In the sight of the unwise they seem to die but they are in peace' (see p. 44).

In the precincts of the Guards' Chapel is a seat in memory of William, Marquess of Hartington, killed in action while serving with the 5th Battalion of the Coldstream Guards in Belgium in September 1944. The seat was given by his brother and sisters.

On a wall in Milton Abbey, Dorset, amongst many plaques to the memory of members of the Hambro family, is one to Major Robert Alexander Hambro who died on 8th August, 1943, while serving with the 8th Army in North Africa. He was buried in Tripoli cemetery. Another Hambro is recorded as having died in the First World War, and yet another in the Boer War.

A Doric temple, possibly designed by Capability Brown, in the grounds of Petworth in Sussex, contains a memorial to Henry Scawen Wyndham, son of Colonel the Hon. Edward Wyndham, D.S.O. A lieutenant in the 9th Lancers, he was killed at El Alamein on 28th October, 1942, and the fact that his memorial is in the grounds of his family home, is due to the Chichester diocesan authority refusing permission for a commemorative window in the parish church.

The memorial within the pillared temple is in the form of an inscribed stone urn under the badge of the 9th Lancers, military flags, and with a quotation from a Victorian work *Jackanapes*. 'There be things the good of which and the use of which are beyond all calculations of worldly goods or earthly uses; things such as Love and Honour and the Soul of Man, which cannot be bought with price and do not die with death'.

The Church authorities have unwittingly contributed to one of the most touching of memorials, in the most beautiful of settings.

Two cherry trees in the churchyard of St James', Gerrards Cross, were planted in memory of Charles W. Heycock, 9th Lancers, who was killed in North Africa on 30th May 1942, and of Richard Grimsdale, R.N.V.R., killed 1945.

All Saints' Church at Calver, in Derbyshire, has a stained-glass window above the altar. Depicting a crucifixion, the window was erected by the parents of James Newton Middleton, 27 years old, missing at sea through enemy action 7th January, 1943.

A stone plaque in All Saints' Church, High Wycombe, is to the memory of Edward Coverley Kennedy, father of Ludovic Kennedy, the writer and broadcaster. He was captain of the armed merchant cruiser 'Rawalpindi' which was sunk between Iceland and the Faroes when, armed only with four 6 in. guns, it encountered the German battlecruiser 'Scharnhorst'.

The plaque records that Kennedy 'fought his ship against overwhelming odds, going down in her with colours flying 23rd November 1939'. He had served in the Royal Navy from 1892-1923 and was then Conservative Party agent in the Wycombe division from 1930 to 1939, before rejoining the Royal Navy on the outbreak of war in 1939, at the age of 60.

One of the heroes of the Battle of the Atlantic was Captain F. J. Walker, or Johnny Walker, the most successful of the anti-submarine commanders. As his group set off from Liverpool for action the sound of 'A Hunting We Will Go' could be heard without fail from his sloop H.M.S. 'Starling'. In his memory a bronze bust of Walker, by sculptor Allen Curran, was unveiled in Liverpool Cathedral and then placed in the Western Approaches Centre (see p. 44).

44 *Kennedy Memorial, High Wycombe*

On York railway station, on the wall of the main passenger waiting room, is a round memorial plaque to a former railwayman, William Milner. The 'Baedecker' raids were so called because this series of raids beginning in April 1942 was aimed at historic towns selected from the Baedecker Guide Book. During that on York on 29th April, 1942, the railway station was hit and William Milner lost his life at the height of the raid when he entered a blazing building in attempting to reach first-aid supplies urgently needed for badly injured casualties. When his body was recovered he was still clutching a box of first-aid equipment. He was posthumously awarded the King's Commendation for Gallantry. The plaque has a likeness of the man who died, together with scenes of the raid and the damaged station.

45 *Milner Memorial, York*

CHAPTER II

Schools and Universities

MANY MEMORIALS of the first World War were altered or augmented so that they became memorials to both World Wars. The larger and more ambitious the original work the more tempting it was, perhaps, to adapt it in this way, but also the easier it was to give the changes the appearance of something separate.

Of all the memorials in schools and universities after the Great War, one of the finest was that of Oundle. The Chapel of Oundle School was built in 1922-23 to the design of A. C. Blomfield and dedicated to the members of the school who gave their lives in the First World War.

A magnificent building surrounded by lawns, the chapel has at the east end an ambulatory in which now there are memorial books and inscribed tablets to the dead of both wars, together with a series of stained-glass windows by Hugh Easton depicting the Seven Ages of Man. Easton was the designer responsible for the Battle of Britain window in Westminster Abbey, and his Oundle windows were dedicated by the Bishop of Peterborough on 17th June 1950. The Books of Remembrance, one for each war, have photographs and biographies of each of the men who died, the entries being in alphabetical order.

There are also individual memorials within the ambulatory, including one to three members of the Shepley family 'who within the space of

47 *Oundle School Books of Remembrance*

one year gave their lives for their country 1939-1940'. Their names and the words 'Here on this painted glass when life has been subdued your love shall live and be renewed' are at the foot of

46 *Oundle School Chapel*

one of Easton's windows – 'AND THEN THE LOVER' (see p. 61).

The War Memorial Cloisters at Sedbergh School, Yorkshire, were dedicated, after the First World War, on 6th July, 1924, and the four tablets with the names of the fallen were unveiled by Lt. General Sir Charles Harington. To those have been added four more stone tablets to the dead of 1939-45. The 1914-18 ones are in the centre section of the cloisters, while two additional and matching tablets have been erected at each wing for the later war.

48   Sedbergh School

50   St Aloysius College

On the outside wall of the dining hall at Christ's Hospital School, Horsham, are the stone tablets and statues of boys in army uniform and in the distinctive uniform of the School, which make up the magnificent memorial to the dead of the First World War.

At each end of the 1914-18 memorial a similar stone tablet has been erected, without the decoration of additional statues, 'To the memory of

Old Blues who gave their lives in the war 1939-1945'. Over 200 names appear on the two additions, and as with the original names, those for the second war have against each the dates of the individual's school career. Under both the new and the old sections of the memorial are stone seats in blocks of three.

A memorial to the dead of St Aloysius College, Highgate, is in the form of a stone tabernacle tucked into the wall at the roadside by the

49   Christ's Hospital School

51 *King Edward VI School, Bury St Edmunds*

College. The crucifixion of Christ, and the three Marys are depicted, and to each side is a stone tablet with the names of the Aloysians who fell, the tablet to the left having 1914-18 names and the other to the right having those for 1939-45. The memorial itself is in good condition, but the name tablets are rather dirty and discoloured.

Name tablets are popular as a form of memorial, and in the cathedral of Bury St Edmunds an attractive stone plaque with a red and gold coat of arms and with a gold cross, commemorates the scholars of King Edward VI School who gave their lives in the Second World War. A similar plaque nearby is to the dead of 1914-18.

The plaque of English oak, with carved inscription, in the hall of Dorking County Grammar School, is one of several in the area, both in schools and churches, by the same craftsman, a Mr Ashley. The School's name has now changed but the carved badge on the memorial has the initials of the original name, alongside the dates 1939-1945 and a list of 22 Old Boys who gave their lives.

When the Edwardian building which housed Farnworth Grammar School was closed in the early 1980's, it soon became a target for vandals. As a result, marble plaques with the names of the dead of both wars, and also a stained-glass window from the school, were removed for safe keeping in Farnworth Town Hall. The 1939-45 memorial has now been placed at the top of the stairs leading to the former council chamber. In its present position, behind and rather too close to a stone balustrade, it is rather difficult to view clearly, but at least it has been preserved and is being appropriately respected.

A plaque of Hoptonwood stone, erected in an archway leading into King Alfred's School, Wantage, was unveiled on 10th July 1949 as a memorial to the Old Boys who died in 1939-45. The tablet has the school badge and a cross, and the names of 17 Old Alfredians, and was unveiled by Mrs Likeman, mother of one of those named. A few years later, in May 1955, a further memorial was dedicated in the form of a sports pavilion.

52 *King Alfred's School, Wantage*

Another sports pavilion, at Pocklington School, has, inside its main room, two memorial boards, one to the dead of the First War and one to the dead of the Second. Each has over 50 names on it.

A plaque between them reads 'IN PROUD MEMORY OF THE BOYS OF POCKLINGTON SCHOOL WHO GAVE THEIR LIVES IN THE TWO GREAT WARS THIS PAVILION WAS PRESENTED BY OLD POCKLINGTONIANS AND FRIENDS OF THE SCHOOL 1ST OCTOBER 1955.

YOU THAT LIVE ON MID ENGLISH PASTURES GREEN REMEMBER US AND THINK WHAT MIGHT HAVE BEEN'.

The attractive brick and tile pavilion with its angled wings, verandah and central clock, was officially opened by Sir Percy Simner, a distinguished Old Boy.

In a sports pavilion on the playing fields of Eton there is a memorial to the 263 Eton Ramblers who gave their lives in the two world wars. After the First World War the Ramblers presented to the School, as a memorial to 139 Ramblers who fell, a pavilion which became known as the Beehive. This was burned down in 1950 and the copper name tablets destroyed. These names, together with those who died in the 1939-45 war were carved on oak panels which were hung in their present position in 1958.

A wooden board in the pavilion of the Old Whitgiftian Football and Cricket Club in Croydon, lists 54 members who died in the

25

53 *Memorial Pavilion Opening, Pocklington School (Photograph – Hull Daily Mail)*

Second World War. There are two similar boards with the names of the First World War.

At Whitgift School itself, a stone memorial, set into a terrace wall in front of the school, commemorates the Second World War dead and faces the memorial cross of the 1914-18 war. On the stone are carved the dates 1939-1945, a map of the world in two hemispheres, and the words 'BY SEA, LAND, AIR', and 'TO OUR GLORIOUS DEAD'. The memorial was unveiled on 29th May 1949 by Old Whitgiftian Major General W. S. Tope, and dedicated by the Bishop of Croydon.

A library would certainly seem to be an appropriate memorial in a school or university and a plaque outside the library at King Edward VI School, Morpeth, has the inscription 'AS A MEMORIAL TO THOSE OLD BOYS OF THE SCHOOL WHO FELL IN THE WORLD WAR 1939-1945, THIS LIBRARY WAS FURNISHED AND RENOVATED FROM FUNDS SUBSCRIBED BY THE RELATIONS OF THE FALLEN, BY PAST AND PRESENT PUPILS AND BY FRIENDS OF THE SCHOOL'.

54 *Whitgift School, Croydon*

The Library was dedicated in 1952 by the Bishop of Durham but has since moved to new premises, along with the commemorative plaque. In the grounds of the School stands a stone cross which has also been re-sited, and which is to both wars, additions having been made to include the dates and names for the Second World War. Interestingly, and presumably due to the fact that the cross has been moved, reference is made to a name plate on the 'East' side of the base, while in fact, it is now on the west.

The Herbert Strutt Primary School in Belper has a panelled Memorial Library to commemorate the 1939-45 war dead associated with the School. Their names are inscribed on part of the panelling in what was once a grammar school library, the room now having the distinctive look of a primary school, with colourful displays and examples of children's art.

There is a stained-glass window in the church at Langton Matravers, Dorset, to the Old Boys of Durnforth School who fell in the 1939-45 War. Under the word 'FAITH' is the figure of St Leonard and under 'COURAGE' is that of St George. There is also a framed Roll of Honour. Below the window are the words 'The snare is broken and we are delivered'. A matching window to the Durnforth Old Boys of 1914-18 has the figures of David and St Michael.

A different style of window at Sandle Manor School at Fordingbridge, provides a most unusual and beautiful war memorial. On one side of a school hall are four windows engraved with the scenes of The Four Seasons, the name of the work by Tracey Sheppard, a fellow of the Guild of Glass Engravers. The windows are to commemorate 42 Old Boys who died in the two world wars, and the Autumn window has the names of

55 *Durnforth School, Langton Matravers*

the individuals, each engraved on a separate falling leaf. The Winter window has the lines 'At the going down of the sun and in the morning we will remember them', and also featured in the four windows are the previous and present school buildings, and New Forest scenes such as a badger and ponies.

Park School, Barnstable, has a wooden memorial listing the dead of both wars but also has a Book of Remembrance with photographs and biographies of those killed in the 1939-45 war. This beautifully presented book has two full pages to each name, the photograph facing the text. For example, the photograph of Sergeant Christopher Irwin, R.A.F., showing him in flying helmet and flying suit, faces the words: 'At school 1931-36. Volunteered for the R.A.F. 1940. Trained at Torquay and in Canada and Scotland. Joined Wellington Bomber Squadron as navigator. On air operations over Germany from Sep. 1941 to Jan 1942. He did not return from a raid over Germany on 28th Jan. 1942. Aged 21 years'.

Brandeston Hall, near Ipswich, part of Framlington College, was given by Old Boys as a memorial after the Second World War. Unveiled by Princess Alice on 2nd July 1949, a plaque inscription in Latin translates 'REMEMBER, BOYS, FOR ALL TIME THE 234 FORMER SONS OF YOUR SCHOOL WHO DIED GLORIOUSLY FOR THEIR

56 and 57 *Sandle Manor School, Fordingbridge (Photographs - Robert Pendreigh)*

27

58   *Park School, Barnstable*

59   *Brandeston Hall*

60   *Heath Grammar School, Halifax*

COUNTRY IN TWO GREAT WARS. THIS HOUSE IS THEIR MEMORIAL. THEIR SWORDS ARE IN YOUR KEEPING'.

In 1949, in the grounds of Reigate Grammar School, a Memorial Garden was dedicated by the Bishop of Southwark to the memory of the Old Boys who died in the 1939-45 war. The main entrance to the garden is from a narrow road alongside the school, up four stone steps and through wrought-iron gates in a high brick archway. The gates are decorated with the dates of the war, and with school insignia, and the garden within is surrounded by walls of brick and stone. On a section of brick wall opposite the gates is a stone tablet with the names of 76 Old Boys.

At the former Heath Grammar School building in Halifax (now the Heath Training and Development Centre) the World War II memorial consists of large double wrought-iron gates supported by two heavy stone pillars on each of which is a metal plaque. On the left hand pillar are the words 'THESE GATES WERE DEDICATED ON FOUNDER'S DAY 1949 TO THE MEMORY OF THE OLD BOYS OF THIS SCHOOL WHO DIED FOR THEIR COUNTRY 1939-1945'. On the right hand plaque are listed the names of 40 dead. The gates are painted black and gold and carry the school crest and motto.

Another establishment which has changed in character, the Conway Centre at Llanfairpwll, North Wales, is now used for occasional educational purposes only, but until comparatively

recently was the home of the naval Conway School.

In a war memorial side chapel, a wooden board has the names of those who fell in the 1939-1945 World War, and a carved female figure on a boat and holding a wreath above the motto 'QUIT YE LIKE MEN, BE STRONG'. Also on display are framed lists of awards in both wars to Old Boys of the School, and framed citations including one concerning Lt. I. E. Fraser, V.C., D.S.C., R.N.R., at Conway 1936-38, who was awarded his V.C. for a successful attack on a Japanese cruiser at Singapore in midget submarine XE-3, on 31st July 1945. A later memorial is to Lt. Commander Skinner, captain of the 'Amethyst', who died in action on the Yangtse river.

A further use of a side chapel as a war memorial is in Keble College Chapel, Oxford, where the 51 names of those who died in the Second World War are engraved in stone under the 16th-century painting *The Dead Christ Mourned by His Mother* by William Key. Also engraved are the words 'MEMENTOTE FRATRES. MEMENTO DOMINE'. Another painting in the side chapel is an 1853 version of Holman Hunt's *Light of the World*.

Elsewhere in Oxford, high up on a wall in a quadrangle of Lincoln College, a sundial erected by the Junior Common Room is in memory of the fallen of 1939-1945. Under the face of the sundial are Binyon's words 'AT THE GOING DOWN OF THE SUN AND IN THE MORNING WE WILL REMEMBER THEM'.

61   *Keble College, Oxford*

28

62 *Lincoln College, Oxford*

64 *Wye College*

Under the archway of Founder's Tower, in St John's Quadrangle of Magdalen College, Oxford, a stone plaque, with the badge of the R.A.F., has the inscription, 'DURING THE SECOND WORLD WAR THE HEADQUARTERS STAFF, NO. 43 GROUP, ROYAL AIR FORCE WERE ACCOMMODATED IN THIS COLLEGE. THEY LEAVE THIS TABLET IN GRATITUDE FOR THE GOOD FELLOWSHIP THEY ENJOYED AND FOR THE PRIVILEGE OF BEING ALLOWED TO WORSHIP IN THE COLLEGE CHAPEL 1ST FEBRUARY 1941 TO 30TH APRIL 1945'.

In the circular entrance hall to Rhodes House, Oxford, engraved in the stone walls just below the dome of the roof, are the names of the Rhodes scholars who died in both wars. The names are divided by nationality and the 1939-1945 names, on either side of a bronze bust

of Rhodes, are under the headings of South Africa, Australia, New Zealand, Canada, Newfoundland, Jamaica, Bermuda, Rhodesia, U.S.A., and, notably, Germany. The two largest groups are South Africa and Germany, each with eight of the total of 41 names.

Sixty-two former students of Wye College in Kent who lost their lives in the 1939-45 war are commemorated on a Caen stone tablet in the cloisters beside the Chapel. The memorial, sponsored by the Agricola Club of the College, was unveiled on 29th June, 1948, by Sir John Russell whose son's name appears on the stone. Other names include Henry, 6th Duke of Wellington, George, 10th Earl of Coventry, and R. T. W. Ketton-Cremer whose individual memorial is in Felbrigg, Norfolk.

63 *Rhodes House, Oxford*

CHAPTER III

Churches, Clubs and Places of Work

MEMORIALS ERECTED IN SCHOOLS, churches, sports clubs, working men's clubs, factories, offices, police stations and so on, normally commemorate those whose names already appear on the main memorial in the respective village, town or city. One name can therefore be inscribed on several memorials and be remembered and honoured in several different contexts.

Second World War memorials in churches are often in thanks for the preservation of the buildings themselves, in a conflict where few parts of the country were safe from air attack. In small communities the main local memorial was often in the church or churchyard, but in larger towns a memorial in a church would be used purely to honour those of its members who had fallen. It is not immediately clear, from the wording or numbers of dead, what is the true purpose of some church memorials. Sometimes only the absence of another war memorial in the area will help to clarify the situation.

One instance where the relationship of a memorial to the church is only too clear is at the Parish Church of St Mary in Torquay which was the scene, in 1943, of an incident tragic even by the standards of wartime.

Above the door in the stone surround of the entrance, there are today two inscriptions. One reads: '30TH MAY 1943. THE ENEMY RAZED THIS CHURCH KILLING 26 CHILDREN AND TEACHERS, R.I.P. ST LUKE VI-VV 27-28' and the other '25TH MARCH 1952. TO THE GLORY OF GOD. ALD. E. G. ELY J.P. MAYOR OF TORQUAY SET THIS STONE AND BEGAN RESTORATION'.

Inside the Church is a chapel with a plaque reading 'THIS CHAPEL OF THE HOLY INNOCENTS IS CONSECRATED TO THE GLORY OF GOD AND SET APART IN HONOUR OF THE TEACHERS AND CHILDREN OF ST MARYCHURCH WHO WERE KILLED WHEN THE CHURCH WAS DESTROYED BY ENEMY ACTION AT 2.50 P.M. ON ROGATION SUNDAY 30TH MAY 1943'. There follows the quotation from St Luke commencing 'LOVE YOUR ENEMIES'.

The re-built church was consecrated on 9th December, 1956.

On 6th November 1944 All Saints' Church at Bawdeswell, Norfolk, was destroyed by fire when an R.A.F. Mosquito crashed into it. Rebuild-ing started in March 1953, the foundation stone was laid on 21st July and the completed church was dedicated by the Bishop of Norwich on 27th September, 1955.

A wooden cross which stood on top of the bell turret survived the fire and now stands outside the church at a corner of the building. Inside, a brass plaque commemorates the two airmen who died when their aircraft hit the church. The base for the plaque is formed from parts of the aircraft.

St Paul's Church in Yelverton, Devon, has a beautiful stained-glass window above the altar, with figures of St Nicholas, St Paul, St Christopher and St George. An inscription reads, 'TO THE GLORY OF GOD AND IN THANKSGIVING FOR THE PRESERVATION OF OUR CHURCH AND LOVED ONES DURING THE SECOND GREAT WAR 1939-1945'.

This is certainly no platitude, for on 28th May, 1944, an aircraft struck the tower during Sunday morning service and although the pilot inevitably died, none of the congregation was killed and the damage to the church was surprisingly small.

A stained-glass window above the altar in the Chapel of the Ascension in Newcastle's St Nicholas' Cathedral, incorporates the words 'THANKS BE TO GOD FOR THE PRESERVATION OF THIS CATHEDRAL IN TIME OF WAR 1939-1945'. The window was designed by Professor Leonard C. Evetts and installed in 1962. The altar frontal was by the same designer.

The word 'preservation' is frequently used. In the grounds of Lullingstone Castle, Kent, St Botolph's Church contains a litany or prayer desk on the front of which are the words 'IN THANKS-GIVING FOR THE PRESERVATION OF THIS HOUSE OF GOD AND IN UNFADING MEMORY OF . . .' followed by five names and the dates of both wars. The memorial was dedicated in January 1948.

A stained-glass window in All Saints' Church, Maidenhead, was installed after the Second World War and, under a depiction of the Visitation to Mary of the angel Gabriel, has the inscription, 'FOR THE SAFETY OF THIS CHURCH 1939-1945 THANKS BE TO GOD'. In front of this window is a beautiful hanging Pyx for the Sacrament, a gift 'in thanksgiving for the

65 *All Saints' Church, Maidenhead*

66 *St Augustine's Church, Bolton*

preservation of the church and houses of this Parish in the years 1939-1945'. The Pyx was consecrated on Mothering Sunday 16th March 1947 by the Bishop of Reading.

Stained-glass windows have been used as memorials in churches over the centuries, and the form was again popular after the Second World War.

The Church of St Lawrence in Mansfield, has a memorial window dedicated on 26th March, 1949, by the Lord Bishop of Southwell. The three panels of the window have St Martin, St Nicholas and St Michael as soldier, sailor and flier, and are flanked by two brass plaques with the dates 1939-1945 and the names of 31 men commemorated.

Another window, in St Peter's Church, Westleton, Suffolk, has the inscription 'To the glory of God and as a Thanksgiving for Victory this Stained Glass window was placed here by the Vicar and Parishioners 1945', under a figure of Jesus and the WORDS 'I AM THE LIGHT OF THE WORLD' (see p. 61).

A fine memorial window in the United Reform Church in Malmesbury depicts Christ blessing a kneeling St George. Among the four names commemorated are Arthur and William Woodward, apparently two of seven brothers who served in the 1939-45 war, and Leslie Woodman whose father Edgar was killed in the First World War (see p. 61).

The Brighton and Hove New Synagogue, has a Holocaust Window as a tribute to those who died. The colours of the three windows behind the Ark, combined with those of the Ark doors, make a strikingly beautiful memorial (see p.61).

In the Christ the King Chapel, in the Church of St Augustine of Canterbury, Tonge Moor, Bolton, is a beautiful triptych by Douglas Purnell. To each side of the central panel depicting Christ, is a dark panel edged in gold with gold lettering, and recording the names of 57 dead of 1914-18, and 14 of 1939-45. On the gold bottom edge of each side panel are additional names, three in all, but it is not clear in which war they died.

Kneeling rails to either side of the altar in the church of St Mary of Bethany, Woking, form the Second World War Memorial. The names of 10 individuals are engraved on plaques attached to the front of the rails.

In the Church of St John, Hedge End, Southampton, a brass plaque near the altar rail records that six candlesticks were dedicated in memory of the men who gave their lives in the 1939-45 war. (Seven in number.)

A sanctuary lamp in St Edmund's Church, Downham Market, has beside it a wooden plaque explaining that it was a gift of the Parochial Church Council in memory of those of the Parish who gave their lives in 1939-45.

In St Giles' Cathedral, Edinburgh, a stone tablet has been placed 'TO THE GLORY OF GOD AND IN HALLOWED MEMORY OF THE MEMBERS OF THE CONGREGATION WHO DIED ON SERVICE DURING WORLD WAR 1939-1945'.

A bronze memorial of unusual design, in Ely Cathedral, is to the memory of former choristers who died in the Second World War. Set into a wall, with an irregular cross and with the names of those honoured in roughly written lettering, the memorial has the inscription 'THEY SING A NEW SONG BEFORE THE THRONE'. Along-side is the contrasting and more conventional stone plaque

67 *Ely Cathedral*

for the First World War, with coats of arms and a chorister in relief.

Another memorial to choristers can be found in St Paul's Church, North Sunderland, Northumberland. A simple brass plaque, at the end of the choir stall, names four men, 'CHOIR-BOYS WHO GAVE THEIR LIVES 1939-45'.

On the wooden panelling in Westminster Abbey's St George's Chapel (The Warriors' Chapel), there are the names of nine 'Servants of the Abbey who fell in the War 1939-1945' and also a similar tribute to 12 dead of the earlier war.

68 *Westminster Abbey Servants' Memorial*

The Parish Church of St Mary and All Saints, Chesterfield, has in the St Peter's Chapel, a beautiful reredos featuring St Peter and St Andrew, which is, in fact, a war memorial. A wall plaque nearby records that the reredos was dedicated in thanksgiving for the lives of two men, one a lieutenant in the South Wales Borderers killed in Italy in January 1944, and the other a corporal of the

69 *St Mary and All Saints' Church, Chesterfield*

Royal Welch Fusiliers killed in Normandy in July 1944. 'Both of them were faithful servers at the altar here.'

Inside Chelmsford Cathedral is a stone plaque 'TO THE MEMORY OF MEMBERS OF CHANGE RINGERS WHO FELL IN THE GREAT WAR 1914-1918' and 'ALSO IN MEMORY OF THOSE WHO FELL IN WORLD WAR II 1939-1945'. The original stone was dedicated in 1920 and an addition for the Second World War was dedicated in 1966. A gilt bell is prominent in the stone above the inscriptions.

Ten bells in Lichfield Cathedral were re-cast in 1947, as a war memorial, by the Freemasons of Staffordshire. The bells were originally cast in the 17th century.

Two other bells, this time in Holy Trinity Church in Cookham, were dedicated on 22nd June 1946 to the memory of two men who died in the First World War and one who died in the Second. The other church bells are 17th and 18th century.

St James' Church, Gerrards Cross, has a colourful illuminated Roll of Honour, within a decorated wood frame, in memory of the 26 members of the Church who gave their lives in the 1939-45 War. The Roll features the Swan of Buckinghamshire, and the emblems of the three services of the armed forces.

In Tilehouse Street Baptist Church, Hitchen, there is a plaque in memory of 82 men and women who served with the forces in the 1939-45 War and to eight who gave their lives. The names of the eight are listed and the inscription continues, 'TO THEIR DEATHLESS MEMORY AND IN THANKFUL-NESS FOR THE RETURN OF THE OTHERS THE CHURCH HAS ERECTED A "TILEHOUSE STREET" MEMORIAL WING OF THE REBUILT HOSPITAL IN SIANFU, THE ANCIENT CAPITAL OF CHINA'. The connection with China is, apparently, that William Samuel Upchurch was a missionary in China and his father was a leader in the Tilehouse Street Church. The hospital wing was completed in 1948 at a cost of £2,780.

The alabaster font in St Mary's Church, Sale, has, as a Second World War memorial, an octag-onal oak font cover with a brass plaque and an inscription commemorating 'the members of this parish who fought and fell'.

In the same Church is a prayer desk in memory of five members of St Mary's Young Mens' Christian and Amateur Football Club who died in the War.

Another football club memorial can be found in Bridlington. The original First World War memorial in a garden near the centre of the town has impressive sculptures depicting the war on land and sea and has appropriate additions for 1939-45. Nearby in the same garden is a sundial placed by the Bridlington Trinity United Amateur Football Club in memory of their colleagues who gave their lives in the Second War. The plaque attached to the base of the sundial has six names listed, together with the date of 1949.

Many other memorials are related to sports clubs. The Tynedale Rugby Football Club at Corbridge has a plaque in the clubhouse hallway, with the words 'TYNEDALE RUGBY FOOTBALL CLUB. IN MEMORY OF THOSE WHO FELL IN WORLD WAR II IN WHOSE HONOUR BROAD CLOSE WAS PRESENTED TO THE CLUB BY MEMBERS AND FRIENDS'. There are 27 names of those who gave their lives.

The memorial grounds are immaculately kept and a credit to the Club. The clubhouse and stand appear comparatively new and there are half a dozen pitches. It is not difficult to under-stand the club's progress in playing terms, in recent years.

In front of the clubhouse and behind one set of posts at the ground of Northampton Rugby Football Club, a stone memorial to the dead of World War I has an addition to commemorate the fallen of 1939-45. The base has these words 'THEY PLAYED THE GAME', the badge of the Club and 12 names from the First World War, amongst them E. R. Mobbs in whose honour the Mobbs Memorial Match is played each year between Northampton and the Barbarians. On top of the base is a rugby ball resting on a laurel wreath, and against the foot is a sloping stone with the dates 1939-45 and eight further names.

After the Second World War the efforts of a war memorial committee chaired by a Mr John Harrison, led to the construction of terracing and seating on an embankment at Bradshaw Cricket Club, Heywood, as an unusual and also useful memorial.

70 *Trinity United Memorial, Bridlington*

71 *Northampton R.F.C. Memorial*

72 *Bradshaw Cricket Club*

The sum of £2,000 appealed for proved, unfortunately, less than quotations received, but work still proceeded and culminated in the dedication of the new terraces on 21st July, 1951, at a cricket match between Bradshaw and Heaton. Framed photographs taken that day and hanging in the clubroom show a large crowd present at the ceremony and at the match. A wreath was laid at a cross on the terraces by the Club Chairman, and the Club Captain read out the names of the fallen.

An attractive stone memorial on the opposite side of the ground commemorates the dead of the First World War, and has reliefs in the stone of a crossed sword and rifle on one side, and crossed bats with ball and stumps on the other. Part of the inscription reads 'THIS CRICKET GROUND IS FOREVER DEDICATED TO THEIR HEROIC MEMORY'.

St John's Church, Shotley, in Northumbria, has a plaque commemorating two members of the village cricket team who gave their lives in the 1939-45 war, Lt. John Charles Frater, D.S.C., Fleet Air Arm, and Sergeant Henry Douglas Mackenzie, R.A.F.

Perhaps at the other end of the scale in cricketing terms, in the Long Room at the Oval, a plaque, with the badge of the Surrey County Cricket Club, commemorates the members, players and staff who gave their lives in the 1939-1945 War.

In the entrance hall of the All England Lawn Tennis and Croquet Club's premises at

73 *All England Club, Wimbledon*

Wimbledon, a wooden board, with the Club's badge of crossed racquets in the familiar Wimbledon colours of purple and green, lists those members who gave their lives in the two World Wars. Ten names of the First World War are followed by four of the Second including 'AIR COMMODORE H.R.H. THE DUKE OF KENT, K.G., ROYAL AIR FORCE, (PRESIDENT OF THE CLUB)', and 'K. C. GANDAR DOWER, WAR CORRESPONDENT'. The Duke of Kent, King George VI's younger brother and a serving R.A.F. officer, died on 25th August 1942 when his plane crashed in the North of Scotland.

In the churchyard in the Kent village of Newnham is an unusual memorial to a cycling club. The stone wall plaque with an angel relief was originally 'erected by the De Laune Cycling Club in memory of their members who fell in the Great War'. To the five names at that time have been added nine names and the dates of the Second War. Nine deaths from a cycling club seems to suggest either a very high proportion killed or a very large club indeed.

The World War Two section was unveiled on 16th November, 1947, by Captain de Laune whose family once owned Sharsted Court near the village. The Club itself was founded in 1889.

In the Ennerdale Valley in the Lake District there is an unusual memorial in the form of a footbridge, at one end of which is a bronze plaque mounted upon a rock. The bridge over the River Liza was erected by the Cumberland County Council in 1959 and the plaque records that 'THE FELL AND ROCK CLIMBING CLUB OF THE ENGLISH LAKE DISTRICT BORE A SHARE OF THE COST IN MEMORY OF THOSE OF ITS MEMBERS WHO FELL IN THE WORLD WAR OF 1939-1945'.

74 *De Laune Cycling Club, Newnham*

A substantial, two-storey scout hall at Billing Lane, Northampton has a plaque in the entrance hall with the inscription, 'THIS HALL WAS ERECTED TO THE EVERLASTING MEMORY OF THOSE SCOUTS WHO WERE CALLED HOME DURING WORLD WAR II 1939-1945', and the scout badge.

Freemasons' Hall in Great Queen Street, London, was built in memory of those freemasons who lost their lives in World War I., The building was estimated to cost £1 million, but actually cost considerably more. It was dedicated on 19th July 1933 and within it, on the first floor, are a wonderful memorial window and the most beautiful of decorated caskets holding the Roll of Honour. Within the same area a more modest glass case contains a temporary book with the names of the Second World War dead.

In the Reading Hall of the Law Society building in Chancery Lane, is a 'memorial to 1,016 solicitors and 716 articled clerks who, in the Two World Wars, 'laid down their lives for their country and in defence of the rule of law which they held sacred' (see p. 62).

The main feature of the memorial is a beautiful bronze statue by Gilbert Bayes of Pallas Athene, goddess of wisdom, counsel, and war, and protectress of cities. She stands on a marble plinth, with flowing robes, wearing a helmet and carrying a spear. Beneath the figure is a Book of Remembrance in a glass case, again on a marble plinth. The book contains a short biography of each of those recorded. Illuminated and framed panels on each side of the memorial further record the names of the fallen, and a relief fund for the families of the dead or wounded was also provided.

The striking Jacob Epstein stone statue of a figure carrying a limp victim of the war, is the Trades Union Congress memorial to its members who died in both wars. The 1958 work is erected in a completely enclosed courtyard of the T.U.C. Headquarters and backed by a massive wall of dark green mosaic. Apparently the original background of black marble had to be replaced when it started to crack (see p. 62).

A number of Second World War memorials at work places record victims of air raids on those premises.

A 1951 wooden board in the foyer of new premises of Boulton & Paul Ltd., Norwich, records both the names of employees who died whilst serving with the forces during the 1939-45 war, and also the names of those who were killed in two separate air raids on the company's Riverside Works. The first, on 9th July 1940, led to 10 deaths and the second, on 1st August 1940, to nine. At the foot of the board are the lines 'READ THROUGH OUR NAMES AND THINK OF US NOW DEAD, WHO STOOD HERE ONCE LIKE YOU AND ALSO READ, THE NAMES OF MEN WHO IN ANOTHER WAR, DIED AS WE DIED, AND SEE THERE BE NO MORE' by John Buxton.

On the wall of the Boots' printing works in Nottingham, near the entrance door, is a stone tablet recording that the building was completed on December 1st, 1952 to replace buildings destroyed by enemy action on the night of 8th May, 1941. The names of four Boots' employees who lost their lives that night, are listed.

On 18th September, 1942, 20 men and women were killed in an air raid on Philip and Son's Noss Shipyard at Dartmouth. By the side of the river at Sandquay, Dartmouth, near the marina entrance, is an English six-pounder naval cannon, circa 1750, mounted on a replica carriage built by Philip and Son in 1988, as a memorial to those killed. A granite block nearby carries an explanatory inscription.

75 *Sandquay, Dartmouth*

Another memorial related to the 'Blitz' is that to the fire fighters who gave their lives during the 1939-45 war. This was unveiled, appropriately enough, close to St Paul's Cathedral, by the Queen Mother on 4th May, 1991.

Called 'Heroes with grimy faces' by Churchill, some one thousand firemen and women are commemorated on this national monument, their names appearing on bronze tablets on the base. One tablet, with reliefs of women in uniform, lists the names of 23 women who died. The main feature of the memorial is a dramatic group of three firemen by sculptor John W. Mills. Two of the figures are directing a hosepipe while the third, looking to the rear, points to the fire and gestures for further help.

In the floor of St Paul's Cathedral is a large inlaid stone plaque with the words, 'REMEMBER MEN AND WOMEN OF SAINT PAUL'S WATCH WHO BY THE GRACE OF GOD SAVED THIS CATHEDRAL FROM DESTRUCTION IN WAR 1939-1945'.

76 *Fire Fighters Memorial, St Paul's*

A wooden table in Portsmouth Cathedral is inscribed 'IN RECOGNITION OF THE FIRE WATCHERS OF THE ROYAL NAVY WHO PRESERVED THIS CATHEDRAL FROM ASSAULTS OF THE ENEMY IN 1941-45, ESPECIALLY OF THEIR LEADER CHIEF PETTY OFFICER RICHARD EDWARD COMBEN, WHO LOST HIS LIFE ON THIS DUTY THE 8TH APRIL 1941. PRESENTED BY FRIENDS OF THE CATHEDRAL 1946'.

A stone tablet in the wall of the cathedral commemorates eight members of the Portsmouth Division of the British Red Cross who lost their lives by enemy action in 1940.

77 *Detail, Fire Fighters Memorial*

Another Red Cross memorial, in St John's Church, Cardiff, is a brass plate in memory of the members of the local division who died in both wars.

In an attractive garden, planted with shrubs and flower beds, in the grounds of Northumbria Police Headquarters at Ponteland, a granite block, with a memorial plaque, commemorates the members of the force who died in the 1939-1945 war. The plaque has the badge of the Northumberland County Constabulary and the names of eight men who gave their lives. As with other police memorials, a high proportion listed, were of senior ranks in the services.

78 *Northumbria Police Memorial*

In the Central Police Station at Blackpool, a wall clock in a carved wooden surround commemorates three men of the force who were killed in World War II. Two of them were R.A.F. flying officers and the other was a lieutenant in the East Yorkshire Regiment. The clock hangs alongside a wooden plaque in memory of eight police officers who died in 1914-18, one of them a V.C.

A bronze plaque in the entrance hall of Preston's Police Station honours the memory of three officers who gave their lives in the 1939-45 war. One was an R.A.F. pilot officer and another a lieutenant in the Loyal Regiment.

The brass plaque in the Central Police Station at Halifax commemorates three men who died in the second war, one of them as a prisoner of war in Germany. Part of the wording of the tribute is, 'COMMEMORATES MEN STEADFAST IN DUTY, AMIABLE IN LEISURE AND FORTHRIGHT IN SACRIFICE'. The memorial was moved in 1986 from the former station and unfortunately during the move the First World War memorial was apparently stolen.

On the staircase of the Central Police Station, Nottingham, are marble plaques to the dead of World War One and World War Two. Each memorial has nine names.

The main entrance hall of the East Sussex Constabulary's Malling House, near Lewes, has a long-case clock and a carved oak chair as war memorials of the 1939-45 period. The clock is in memory of former police constable Denis Peel, a 2nd lieutenant in the Royal Sussex Regiment, who died at Anzio on 29th February, 1944. The chair, with its leather cushion and heavily carved back, was presented by the members of the East Sussex Constabulary in honour and memory of their comrades who died.

The Accountant General's Office was relocated from London to Chesterfield in the early

79 *Accountant General Memorial, Chesterfield*

1960's and the war memorial was also moved at that time. A Roll of Honour lists over 70 men who died in the 1914-18 war and on each side of the board are 36 photographs of the individuals. Under the main board have been added the names and photographs of the 11 Second World War dead. It is not usual for individual photographs to be part of British war memorials but the use of them when handled tastefully, certainly adds to the poignancy and sense of loss.

In the Chapel of May Day Hospital in Thornton Heath a stained glass-window commemorates three of 'OUR FELLOW OFFICERS WHO FELL IN THE WORLD WAR 1939-1945'. At one time, in the now abandoned Chapel at Queen's Hospital, Thornton Heath, there was another memorial in the shape of a silver alms dish that survived the February 1942 massacre by the Japanese of 300 patients and staff in the Alexandra Hospital, Singapore. The dish was later recovered from a prison camp and brought back to this country, only, it seems, to have gone astray in the hospitals of Thornton Heath. It was apparently not transferred from Queen's to May Day Hospital and its whereabouts are now unknown.

The Knaphill Garden Centre (once Slocock's Nursery) near Woking has a memorial tablet on each side of the entrance door to the office. There is one for each of the two world wars and the later one is in memory of seven listed men 'WHO WENT FROM THIS NURSERY AND GAVE THEIR LIVES IN THE SECOND GREAT WORLD WAR 1939-1945'. The other plaque lists 18 names for 1914-18.

80 *Knaphill Memorial, Woking*

A memorial to the employees of quite a different size of company can be found in the Church of Our Lady and St Nicholas in Liverpool. Within the Church are four marble plaques with the names of the seagoing and shore staff of Cunard who lost their lives in the Second World War. Originally in the Cunard offices, the plaques were re-dedicated in the Church on 24th July 1990, the 150th anniversary of the company.

The Rolls Royce factory at Derby made the Merlin engines for the wartime Spitfire and Lancaster aircraft, and it is fitting that its entrance hall is the site of one of the finest Second World War memorials (see p. 62).

This is a stained-glass window in the centre of which stands the figure of a young R.A.F. fighter pilot in flying kit. He is standing on a propeller hub and looking down on the roofs of the factory which produced the engines necessary for his survival and victory. Between him and a huge bright sun in the background, is an eagle with wings outstretched. Incorporated in the window are the words 'THIS WINDOW COMMEMORATES THE PILOTS OF THE ROYAL AIR FORCE WHO, IN THE BATTLE OF BRITAIN, TURNED THE WORK OF OUR HANDS INTO THE SALVATION OF OUR COUNTRY'.

The window was unveiled by Marshal of the Royal Air Force Lord Tedder on January 11th, 1949, and dedicated by the Lord Bishop of Derby. The designer was Hugh Easton.

The bronze plaque in the entrance hall to offices at the Goodyear factory in Wolverhampton is to the memory of 40 employees of the Company who laid down their lives in the Second World War. Their names are engraved on the plaque, which was unveiled by Lord Trenchard on 31st May 1948.

Rowntree Park in York was given to the city after the First World War, as a memorial to the employees of Rowntree and Co Ltd., who had given their lives. Hope was expressed that victory at that time would lead to 'an enduring peace'. A further memorial in the form of splendid new gates to the park, was erected after the Second World War, unfortunately not very many years later.

At the entrance to a small park near Jedburgh Abbey there is a metal memorial plaque on a stone gate pillar, with the inscription 'THESE GATES WERE ERECTED IN 1947 TO THE MEMORY OF THE EMPLOYEES OF NORTH BRITISH RAYON LIMITED WHO GAVE THEIR LIVES IN THE SECOND WORLD WAR'. The names and regiments of 11 men follow. The gates in fact are no longer there, although the pillars remain.

A roadside memorial in Tillicoultry, near Alloa, has the stone figure of a mourning angel, her head lowered over a garlanded sword, in the centre of a semi-circular wall. Below the figure are inscribed in the stone the words '1939-1945. TO THE MEN OF DEVONDALE MILLS WHO GAVE THEIR LIVES FOR THEIR COUNTRY'. Eight names follow, along with their regiments or services. Devondale Mill is now a furniture centre, but the memorial

81 *Devondale Mills Memorial, Tillicoultry*

82 *Lea Mills Memorial, Matlock*

is certainly still well maintained and is flanked by attractive wrought-iron gates.

A stone tablet on the exterior wall of the John Smedley Limited premises at Lea Mills near Matlock, shows the names of nine men who died in the Second War. It gives the name, rank, regiment, place and date of death of each man, an amount of information not common on memorials. At the foot of the tablet is the inscription 'IT IS BETTER FOR US TO PERISH IN BATTLE THAN TO LOOK UPON THE OUTRAGE OF OUR NATION AND OUR ALTARS. AS THE WILL OF GOD IS IN HEAVEN EVEN SO LET HIM DO'.

In a park at East Tilbury, Essex, a marble arch with a bronze urn and flame has been erected to the memory of the employees of the British Bata Shoe Company Limited, who gave their lives in the 1939-45 war. The memorial is opposite the company's factory but is beginning to look rather neglected with broken and missing paving stones, and some graffiti.

At the Passenger Landing Stage at Tilbury Dock a 1939-45 memorial takes the form of a stained-glass window by Christopher Webb, and a Book of Remembrance. The window, with the inscription 'TO THE MEMORY OF THOSE MEMBERS OF THE STAFF OF THE PORT OF LONDON AUTHOR-ITY WHO LOST THEIR LIVES IN THE WAR 1939-1945', features a winged figure of Victory, the P.L.A. arms, and scenes of servicemen, and civil defence units and civilians during air-raids on the Port. The window was moved to its present position from the Trinity Square Head Office where it was originally unveiled by Field Marshal Viscount Alanbrooke, and dedicated by the Bishop of London in 1952. It commemorates 125 members of staff.

At the Western Docks railway station in Dover stands a wonderful memorial dedicated originally in 1922 by the Bishop of Dover. Three large bronze figures of Victory between a Sailor and a Soldier stand on a heavy stone base on which a stone plaque commemorates, in gold letters, men of both wars. To the recording of 'THE 556 MEN OF THE SOUTH EASTERN AND CHATHAM RAILWAY WHO FOUGHT AND DIED FOR THEIR COUNTRY IN THE GREAT WAR 1914-1918' have been added the words 'AND TO THE 626 MEN OF THE SOUTHERN RAILWAY WHO GAVE THEIR LIVES IN THE 1939-1945 WAR'.

83 *BATA Memorial, East Tilbury*

84 *Western Docks, Dover*

Originally known as Dover Marine the station was closed in September 1994, a victim of the Channel Tunnel. During the First World War 3,000 ambulance ships brought back nearly 1¼ million wounded who were moved via ambulance trains from the station to hospitals throughout Britain, and in 1940, after Dunkirk, the platforms were thronged by exhausted troops saved from the beaches by the fleet of little ships.

In a small Devon church an intriguing memorial pays tribute to a group who carried out their duties in an environment quite different from that of a West Country village.

The Brooke family of Sheepstor in Devon provided the famous 'White Rajahs of Sarawak' for a century from 1841 until the defeat of the Japanese in 1945. The then Rajah, feeling that his resources were unequal to the task of restoring the country after the devastation of its occupation, ceded Sarawak to Great Britain. After 18 years as a Crown Colony, in 1963 it joined the Federation of Malaysia.

85 *Sarawak Memorial, Sheepstor*

In the lovely Church of Sheepstor, a stained-glass window and a stone tablet reflect the family's unusual background. The window, with figures of St Stephen and St Leonard, has the inscription, 'TO THE MEMORY OF ALL THOSE WHO GAVE THEIR LIVES FOR SARAWAK DURING THE WAR 1941-1945'. The tablet reads 'TO THE OFFICERS OF THE SARAWAK CIVIL SERVICE WHO GAVE THEIR LIVES FOR SARAWAK DURING THE WAR 1941-1945'. Twenty six names follow.

Two further memorials relate to incidents as a result of which employees of the companies concerned were awarded the George Cross, the civilian equivalent of the Victoria Cross, or the George Medal.

On display in the Soham Village College is a glass case containing three medals, and a brass plaque formerly at the site of the local station. The medals are the George Cross, the London and North Eastern Railway Medal, and the Order of Industrial Heroism. The plaque has the emblem of the L.N.E.R. and the words, 'THIS TABLET COMMEMORATES THE HEROIC ACTION OF FIREMAN J. W. NIGHTALL G.C. WHO LOST HIS LIFE, AND DRIVER B. GIMBERT G.C. WHO WAS BADLY INJURED WHILST DETACHING A BLAZING WAGON FROM AN AMMUNITION TRAIN AT THIS STATION AT 1.43 A.M. ON JUNE 2ND 1944. THE STATION WAS TOTALLY DESTROYED AND CONSIDERABLE DAMAGE DONE BY THE EXPLOSION. THE DEVOTION TO DUTY OF THOSE BRAVE MEN SAVED THE TOWN OF SOHAM FROM GRAVE DESTRUCTION. SIGNALMAN F. BRIDGES WAS KILLED WHILST ON DUTY AND GUARD H. CLARKE SUFFERED FROM SHOCK. "BE STRONG AND QUIT YOURSELVES LIKE MEN"'.

The memorial was dedicated at the site of the destroyed station on 1st June 1947 by the Bishop of Ely. A crater 66 ft in diameter and 15 ft deep had been left after the explosion but the 5,000 population had been saved. Gimbert died in 1979, just before two trains were named after himself and Nightall. In 1984 a new sheltered housing scheme for the elderly was named after signalman Bridges.

On the night of 28th/29th November 1940, during an air-raid on Liverpool, a parachute mine penetrated a huge gasholder at Garston Gasworks but did not explode. It was not known if the mine had a delayed action device or if it was merely a 'dud', and so some 6,000 people were evacuated from the vicinity while an attempt to defuse it was made.

For their work that night Lt. Commander Newgass, of the Naval Bomb Disposal Unit, was awarded the George Cross, George Kermode and Ernest Saxon were awarded George Medals, and a number of other gas company employees and emergency service staff received decorations or commendations for their courage and disregard for personal safety. At St Michael's Church, Garston, on Sunday the 25th November 1990, a plaque was unveiled to commemorate the 50th anniversary of the defusing and removal of the mine, the three principal heroes being named in the inscription.

As a postscript, it appears that the mine bore the name 'Essen', and after the necessary replacement of parts the R.A.F. later dropped the bomb on the city from which it had come.

86 *Soham Memorial*

CHAPTER IV

Military Memorials

IGNORING THE STRICT DERIVATION of the word 'military', and including in this category naval and air force memorials, and also those of Britain's allies, we find the memorials of the Second World War to be quite different in character from those of the First.

Britain became the front line of the action in a way that was not the case between 1914 and 1918. An occasional Zeppelin had dropped its bombs and an occasional German warship had dared to shell our coastline in the First World War, but in the Second, the Battle of Britain was fought over our countryside and our airfields, first in defence and then in attack, became vital.

Similarly, the Second Front, perhaps the equivalent of the 'Great Push' in 1916 terms, was launched on 'D' Day from the South Coast, not from a trench line across Picardy It was our countryside which was full of troops and vehicles and our allies were based in Britain not in France, and were here for a considerable time, not just passing through.

The memorials of the war reflect this. While there were, for obvious reasons, almost no air force memorials of the First World War, after 1945 they were erected on most airfields, and many others were erected on the sites of air-raids or aircraft crashes. Again, after 1918 there were very few memorials in this country to the allies of Britain and the Commonwealth, whereas there are many to our allies of the Second World War. The majority of these are American, and indeed American air force memorials, but there are also many to Polish, French, Czech and Norwegian troops, for example.

Another feature of the memorials of the Second World War is the large number erected to a particular campaign. There are many, for example, placed by the Burma Star Association or Far East Prisoner of War Association, and many others by Dunkirk and Normandy veterans, and so on.

As with other types of memorial, many military memorials of the First World War were amended after 1945 to encompass the later war. The regimental badges cut into the chalk downs 800 ft. above the Wiltshire countryside at Fovant, date back in part to 1916 but some were cut after the Second World War, and they are all now considered to commemorate the sacrifices made in both wars.

87 *Fovant Badges*

C1   *Admiral Ramsey Memorial, Portsmouth*

C2   *Admiral Ramsey Memorial, Portsmouth*

C3   *Aitchison Memorial, Brathay*

C4   *Pexton Memorial, Watton*

C5 *Vyner Memorial, Fountains Hall*

C6 *Hemming Memorial, Berwick, Sussex*

C7 *Viscount Elvedon Memorial, Elvedon*

C8 *Walker Memorial, Liverpool*

88   *York and Lancaster Memorial, Sheffield*

Pilkington Jackson commemorates the Second World War dead of the Royal Scots Fusiliers. On the stone plinth of the 1960 work the inscription records that the statue was raised by the comrades of the fusiliers who gave their lives.

On a stone wall behind the statue a further inscription reads 'TO COMMEMORATE THE SERVICES IN MANY PARTS OF THE WORLD IN PEACE AND WAR OF THE ROYAL SCOTS FUSILIERS. RAISED IN 1678 THE REGIMENT SERVED UNTIL 1959 WHEN IT JOINED PARTNERSHIP WITH THE HIGHLAND LIGHT INFANTRY TO CONTINUE ITS SERVICE AS THE ROYAL HIGHLAND FUSILIERS'.

The first badge was cut by the London Rifle Brigade and 19 more followed. During the 1939-45 war it was official policy to allow the badges to become overgrown so that enemy aircraft might not be assisted by the landmarks, and only nine of the pre-war badges now remain, to which have been added those of the Royal Corps of Signals, the Wiltshire Regiment, and the Royal Wiltshire Yeomanry.

Maintaining the badges is obviously a difficult task, some being as large as a football field, and the Fovant Badges Society exists to ensure that they do not disappear. Some are better maintained than others, the Signals badge and the Australian one are being well preserved, the latter having official funding from the Australian authorities.

The wonderful memorial in Weston Park, Sheffield to the York and Lancaster Regiment has the bronze figures of Victory, an officer, and a private soldier, and is a striking tribute to the 8,814 dead of 1914-18. An inscription added later reads 'ALSO OF 1222 MEMBERS OF THE REGIMENT WHO FELL IN THE WAR 1939-1945'. The numbers illustrate dramatically the comparative infantry casualty figures in the two wars.

Bronze statues were not as common a form of memorial after the Second World War as after the First, unfortunately, but there are nevertheless some fine examples.

In a sunken garden close to the sea at Ayr a strong, realistic, bronze soldier figure by

89   *Royal Scots Fusiliers Memorial, Ayr*

90 *Black Watch Memorial, Dundee*

91 *Commando Memorial, Spean Bridge*

The Black Watch memorial at Powrie Brae, Dundee, was unveiled by the Queen Mother in 1959 but alterations to the Dundee–Forfar road led to its being re-located in the mid 1980's. The memorial, a bronze kilted figure by Scott Sutherland, whose work is on the Commando memorial at Spean Bridge, commemorates the men of the 4th and 5th (Dundee and Angus) Battalions of the Black Watch who fell in the Second World War. The figure, about 100 yards east of the Forfar road, is at the top of a flight of stone steps and on a stone plinth surrounded by paving stones and a low wall. It looks across the valley to the Law, the hill on which stands Dundee's War Memorial.

Queen Elizabeth the Queen Mother unveiled a monument to the 1,700 Commandos who died in the 1939-1945 war, on a hillside site at Spean Bridge, Invernesshire, on 27th September 1952. The memorial, three 9 ft. tall bronze figures by Scott Sutherland on a stone block plinth, was erected on the hillside overlooking Ben Nevis because the countryside around was the training ground for the Commandos during the war.

During the ceremony, Lord Lovat, the wartime Commando leader, made an address to the large crowd which included many former Commandos, and a lone piper played the lament *The Flowers o' the Forest* at the foot of the statues. A recent plaque commemorates the granting of the freedom of Lochaber to the Commando Association on 13th November 1993.

The Roll of Honour of the Combined Operations Command, or Commandos, is preserved in St George's Chapel, Westminster Abbey. It contains, in book form, the names of the Commandos who died in World War II.

St George's Chapel is known as the Warriors' Chapel, and the Padre's Flag, which originally covered the coffin of the Unknown Warrior, now hangs there. Also there is a stone tablet for each war's dead of the Royal Army Medical Corps. An additional stone under the original, commemorates 437 officers and 2,026 other ranks who died in 1939-45. The 1914-18 figures recorded are 743 officers and 6,130 other ranks.

Elsewhere in Westminster Abbey, on a wall in the cloisters, on 21st May 1948, Winston Churchill unveiled a monument to firstly, the Submarine Service of the Royal Navy, secondly, the Commandos, and thirdly, the Airborne Forces and Special Air Service.

The memorial was designed by Gilbert Ledward and depicts three bronze fighting men, one from each service. Under the submariner the inscription ends 'The last enemy that shall be destroyed is death'. Under the commando are the words 'They performed whatsoever the King commanded', and under the airborne soldier, 'They were mighty men of valour'. Separating the three figures are tablets with the dates '1939' and '1945'.

In St Paul's Cathedral a further memorial is in memory of the men of the Parachute Regiment

92 *Submarine Service Memorial*

93 *Commando Memorial*

and Airborne Forces who have died since the formation of Airborne Forces in 1940. Badges on the plaque include the Parachute Regiment and the S.A.S.

The S.A.S. Memorial at Hereford has the names of those of the regiment who have died on active service inscribed on the surface of a clock tower, leading to the S.A.S. expression 'beating the clock', or avoiding having a name on the memorial by surviving.

Also inscribed are the words, 'We are the Pilgrims, Master, we shall go Always a little further, it may be Beyond that last blue mountain, barred with snow, Across that angry or that glimmering sea'.

At Tatton Park in Cheshire, on the edge of a small wooded hill overlooking the parkland, a rough stone memorial has the carved dates 1940-1945, a Pegasus, and a metal plaque inscribed, 'THROUGHOUT MOST OF THE SECOND WORLD WAR TATTON PARK WAS THE DROPPING ZONE FOR NO. 1 PARACHUTE TRAINING SCHOOL, RINGWAY. THIS STONE IS SET IN HONOUR OF THOSE THOUSANDS, FROM MANY LANDS, WHO DESCENDED HERE IN THE COURSE OF TRAINING, GIVEN OR RECEIVED, FOR PARACHUTE SERVICE WITH THE ALLIED FORCES IN EVERY THEATRE OF WAR'.

On a wall in the car park of historic Hardwick Hall in Derbyshire, is a metal plaque to the airborne forces who trained in the grounds of the Hall and who used Hardwick as a depot and school from 1941 onwards. A Pegasus in relief with rider, is a feature of the plaque which was unveiled on 16th May 1987.

In St John the Baptist's Church, at Knutsford, beautiful oak panelling on either side of the altar is inscribed with the names of the fallen of both wars. Next to a right-hand panel with 1939-45 names, a white marble tablet commemorates the men of 2 (Parachute) Commando, 11 Special Air

94 *Airborne Forces Memorial*

95 *Tatton Park*

Service Battalion, 1 Parachute Battalion and 1 Battalion, the Parachute Regiment, who trained in the area. The white marble has red lettering and gold parachute unit badges.

At the entrance to Longhills Hall, Branston, Lincolnshire, in a small area of garden, stands a stone pillar surmounted by a glass case in which is a brass plaque and the badges of the R.A.S.C. and the 1st Airborne Division. The plaque reads 'IN PROUD AND EVERLASTING MEMORY OF ALL THE MEN OF THE 250 LIGHT COY. R.A.S.C. STATIONED AT LONGHILLS HALL AND LINCOLN WHO GAVE THEIR LIVES AT THE BATTLE OF ARNHEM SEPTEMBER 1944. WE WILL REMEMBER THEM'.

Villagers in Paulton, Somerset, on Sunday, 17th September, 1944, watching hundreds of aircraft flying overhead towing gliders towards Operation Market Garden and Arnhem, were horrified to see one glider break loose and crash in flames on Double Hills field. On 23rd September, 1979, a memorial was unveiled in that field by Major General Roy Urquhart who commanded the 1st Airborne division at Arnhem.

The stone memorial is in a commanding position with extensive views and has a tablet listing the names of those killed. Assumed to be the first casualties of the largest airborne operation of the war, two glider pilots and 21 Royal Engineers died when their Airspeed Horsa glider crashed having taken off from R.A.F. Keevil in Wiltshire, towed by a Stirling bomber of 299 Squadron. All 23 men were buried at Weston Super Mare.

A memorial to the Second World War dead was invariably added to each Regimental Chapel soon after 1945. The Regimental Chapel of the Durham Light Infantry in Durham Cathedral has in a prominent position a lectern holding the Books of Remembrance for both World War II and World War I. The books are on opposite sides of the lectern and protected by glass covers. Above

96 *Hardwick Hall*

each book, at the top of the lectern, are the dates of the appropriate war and pages of each book are turned daily so that on each day the names of those who died on that date are shown. The names commemorated in the World War II book number 3,011, while those for the first war number 12,606.

In the Cathedral grounds, outside the Cloisters, a Memorial Garden to those of the Regiment who gave up their lives in the 1939 -45 war was dedicated by the Lord Bishop of Durham on 9th July, 1950. It is designed to have something in bloom throughout the year and is maintained by the Dean and Chapter gardeners. Teak seats are provided so that visitors may sit and meditate.

In the South Transept of Lichfield Cathedral, St Michael's Chapel contains Books of Remembrance of the Staffordshire Regiment. A beautiful wooden lectern, surmounted by a gilt Warrior Saint, has glass cases holding 1939-45 books for the North Staffordshire Regiment, the South Staffordshire Regiment and the Staffordshire Yeomanry. A First World War Roll of Honour nearby, in a magnificent carved wooden case, has illuminated pages of outstanding quality.

In Exeter Cathedral the Devonshire Regimental Chapel has a stained glass window in memory of the men of the regiment who gave their lives in the 1939-45 war. Amongst the features in the window are St Michael and St George,

97　*Durham Light Infantry Memorial*

and the battle honours Malta, Sicily, Italy, Burma, Normandy, Belgium, Holland and Germany. At the apex of the window is the badge of the regiment and below it the arms of the Duke of Beaufort, who founded the regiment in 1685, and of the see of Exeter. The window was designed and executed by Reginald Bell.

In the Chapel of the Welch Regiment in Llandaff Cathedral near Cardiff, the battle honours of the regiment are inscribed in red lettering on stone tablets. Those for the Second World War include North Africa, Sicily, Italy, North West Europe and Burma.

A Chapel in Gloucester Cathedral has two matching glass fronted cases with the Rolls of Honour of the Gloucestershire Regiment for 1914-1918 and 1939-1945, a window to the 8,100 men who died in the First World War, and a memorial to the 'Glorious Gloucesters' of the Korean war.

In the Hastings Chapel of St Giles' Church, Stoke Poges, there are badges of the 4th Prince of Wales Own Gurkha Rifles together with Books of Remembrance, and in the Memorial Garden of Stoke Poges, there is an area surrounded by hedges and stone walls and with a gate and a metal plaque, each bearing the badge of the 4th Gurkhas, the plaque also being inscribed with the history and battle honours of the regiment, including 'Imphal' and 'Chindits'.

The Chapel of the Royal Norfolk Regiment in Norwich Cathedral has an attractively carved and decorated glass case on a wooden stand holding the Books of Remembrance for both wars. The books are almost upright, as on a lectern, and there is one on each side of the stand. A bronze plaque in the Chapel records the names of those of the 2nd Battalion of the regiment who died in the Battle of Kohima in April 1944.

Another plaque in the Cathedral commemorates the dead of the Norfolk Yeomanry, with the names of those who fell in the First World War being on brass tablets to each side, and the Second World War names being inscribed in a Book of Remembrance in a glass case below.

Inside Chelmsford Cathedral a stone tablet commemorates the men of the Essex Yeomanry who gave their lives during the 1939-1945 war and also 'IN THANKFUL REMEMBRANCE OF THOSE WHO SERVED IN THE REGIMENT AND RETURNED SAFELY'. Battle honours listed include North Africa, Burma, Italy and North-West Europe.

On the south-eastern wall of Guildford Cathedral is a stone monument containing a Book of Remembrance in a glass case. Above it is the inscription in the stone 'TO THE GLORY OF GOD AND IN PROUD MEMORY OF THE MEMBERS OF THE SURREY YEOMANRY WHO GAVE THEIR LIVES FOR KING AND COUNTRY DURING 1914-1918 AND 1939-1945'. At the top of the memorial is the badge of the regiment, its colours of red, blue and gold being accentuated by the lightness of the stone's hue.

In the T.A. Centre at Mitcham Road Barracks, Croydon, a large wooden board has nearly 400 names on brass panels under the badge of the City of London Yeomanry and the inscription 'PLACED HERE BY THEIR COMRADES IN MEMORY OF THOSE SHARPSHOOTERS WHO FELL IN THE SECOND WORLD WAR 1939/45'. At the bottom of the board a further panel lists the unit's battle honours, from North Africa to Italy and from Caen to the Rhine.

98 *Surrey Yeomanry Memorial, Guildford*

99 *North Irish Horse Memorial, Belfast*
(Photograph – Allen Markley, Anderson McMeekin
Photography Ltd)

Battle honours appear similarly at the foot of a memorial window to the North Irish Horse, in the entrance hall of Belfast City Hall.

A stone tablet in a walled recess in the village of Charlton, near Chichester, is a memorial to the men of the Sussex Yeomanry who fell in both wars. In a well landscaped and maintained area, the memorial was erected after the Second World War on the site of the old village pump which was, apparently, stolen.

In the Church of St Mary the Blessed Virgin at Addington in Surrey, a stained-glass window has the inscription 'TO THE GLORY OF GOD AND AS A MEMORIAL OF THEIR SERVICE TO KING AND COUNTRY BY MEMBERS OF THE 59TH SURREY (ADDINGTON) BATTALION HOME GUARD THIS WINDOW IS ERECTED 1952'. At the top of the window are the words 'EVERYONE HAD HIS SWORD BY HIS SIDE AND SO BUILDED', and the figures on the window illustrate this quotation from Nehemiah, referring to the rebuilding of Jerusalem in 6th century B.C.

To the Bolton Artillery Cenotaph, in Nelson Square, was added on 18th September, 1954, a bronze 1939-45 panel giving the names of those of the Bolton Artillery, 53rd and 111th Field Regiments R.A., who served and gave their lives in the Second War. The Bolton Artillery had had a long history of connection with the town, and in fact its centenary was celebrated four years later in 1960.

In St Giles' Cathedral, Edinburgh, there are 1939-45 memorials to the men of the 94th (City of Edinburgh) H.A.A. Regiment of the Royal Artillery, to the ex-cadets of the City of Edinburgh Wing of the Air Training Corps, and to the chaplains of the Church of Scotland. The Chaplain's memorial has a list of 22 men who fell in the war, and under a representation of St Andrew on the metal plaque are the words, 'ARE YE ABLE . . . ? WE ARE ABLE'.

Inside St Thomas' Church, Newcastle, is a stained-glass window in memory of four officers of 43 Royal Tank Regiment, and another four officers of 49 R.T.R. Each panel of the window carries the dates 1939-1945.

In Hexham Abbey grounds, ancient walls form a triangular garden of grass and stone paths, with flower beds and seats. This garden has been dedicated to those of the 4th and 8th battalions of the Royal Northumberland Fusiliers who gave their lives in the 1939-45 war, as a metal plaque on one wall signifies.

A large 1939-45 memorial, just inside the main entrance gate of Brookwood Military Cemetery at Working, commemorates over 3,500 men and women of the Commonwealth and Empire 'to whom the fortune of war denied a known and honourable grave'. An open 16-bay rotunda of Portland stone with name panels of

100 *Addington Home Guard Memorial*

101 *Chaplains Memorial, Edinburgh*

green slate, this impressive monument was dedicated on 25th October 1958 in the presence of the Queen. Amongst those named on the panels is Violette Reine Elizabeth Szabo, G.C., Croix de Guerre, who died at the hands of the Gestapo in 1945 and who was the subject of the film *Carve Her Name With Pride*.

Another memorial in Brookwood, close to the Memorial to the Missing, commemorates over 600 'soldiers, sailors and airmen of the forces of the British Commonwealth who died in Russia during two World Wars'. The monument, in the shape of a cross, is of stone with slate name tablets, and was erected in 1983.

102 *Memorial to the Missing, Brookwood*

In a side chapel of Salisbury Cathedral, a heavily carved bookcase, decorated with gilt figures of angels and St George, is a memorial to the men of the diocese who fell in the 1914-18 war. The bookcase contains several Books of Remembrance, among them 1939-45 memorials for the Glider Pilot Regiment and for the 43rd (Wessex) Division.

Another memorial to the division, a stone monument on Castle Hill, Mere, overlooking the town, has a bronze plaque 'TO THE MEMORY OF ALL RANKS OF THE 43RD WESSEX DIVISION WHO LAID DOWN THEIR LIVES FOR THE CAUSE OF FREEDOM 1939-1945. THIS MEMORIAL IS A REPLICA OF THAT ERECTED ON HILL 112 NEAR CAEN, THE SITE OF THE FIRST MAJOR BATTLE IN WHICH THE DIVISION TOOK PART JULY 10TH TO JULY 24TH 1944'.

Above the plaque is the bronze Griffin badge of the division which included battalions of the Dorset Regiment, the Somerset Light Infantry, the Duke of Cornwall's Light Infantry, the Wiltshire Regiment, the Worcestershire Regiment and the Hampshire Regiment. The Mere memorial was unveiled in 1949 by General Sir Ivor Thomas, who commanded the division.

Bodmin Moor was the training ground for the 43rd (Wessex) Division before 'D' Day, and a bronze plaque on a rock on the comparatively remote Rough Tor has the inscription under a Griffin emblem 'ROUGH TOR ON WHICH THIS MEMORIAL IS PLACED HAS BEEN GIVEN TO THE NATION IN MEMORY OF THOSE WHO LOST THEIR LIVES WHILE SERVING IN THE 43RD (WESSEX) DIVISION IN THE NORTH-WEST EUROPEAN CAMPAIGN 1944/45'.

103 *Wessex Memorial, Mere*

104 *Wessex Memorial, Bodmin Moor*

There are many other memorials related to 'D' Day. St Mary's Priory Church in Bridlington has a carved wooden Roll of Honour to the men of 'C' Squadron 23rd Hussars who trained for 'D' Day on the cliffs at Bridlington.

At Upper Chine School, Shanklin, on the Isle of Wight, on a boundary wall, there is a stone plaque to the men of 46 Royal Marine Commando who laid down their lives in Normandy, Holland and Germany. Before the Normandy landings the unit's headquarters were in the buildings of the School.

In the wall outside the Duke of Cornwall's Light Infantry depot building in Bodmin, and behind the Regiment's memorial to the dead of the Two World Wars, is a plaque in honour of the 3,533 men of the 29th Division, U.S. Army, who were killed between 'D' Day on 6th June, 1944, and 'V.E.' Day on 8th May, 1945. Units of the division were stationed at Bodmin before the attack on Omaha Beach.

The inscription adds 'THE FRIENDLINESS OF THE BRITISH PEOPLE WAS DEEPLY APPRECIATED BY THE AMERICAN SOLDIERS' and the plaque was erected in 1988 by the Maryland National Guard Military Historical Society.

Similarly, in the church at Fleet, Dorset, there is a United States flag and a plaque 'IN MEMORY OF U.S. TROOPS STATIONED AT FLEET 1944'.

An obelisk at Slapton Sands, Devon, was presented by the United States Army authorities to the people of the area who left their land and homes to provide a battle practice area prior to the 'D' Day assault in June 1944.

105 *U.S. Memorial, Slapton Sands*

A memorial at nearby Torcross commemorates the deaths of several hundred men (estimated as high as 600) in Operation Tiger held on the night of 28th April, 1944 as a practice run for the Normandy landings at Utah Beach. The operation, involving men of the U.S. Army's 1st Engineer Special Brigade, 4th Infantry Division and the U.S. Navy's 11th Amphibious Force, became a disaster when an attack by seven German E. Boats led to two landing craft being sunk and others badly damaged. The memorial, however, states: 'THE LESSONS LEARNED IN THIS TRAGEDY ADDED SIGNIFICANTLY TO THE SUCCESS OF THE ALLIES IN THE D.DAY LANDINGS ON NORMANDY'.

At Warsash on the mouth of the Hamble, there are two memorials connected with the landings on 'D' Day, both unveiled by Lady Mountbatten. The first, unveiled on 28th May, 1980, is a metal plaque on the wall of 'The Rising Sun' public house to 3,000 commandos of the 1st Special Service Brigade and 4th Special Service Brigade who embarked on the evening of 5th June, 1944 from 'The Rising Sun' pier in 36 landing craft of the 1st L.C.I.(s) Squadron. Amongst them was a battalion of French marine commandos. In the landing craft was Brigadier Lord Lovat and his piper, and the skirl of the pipes set the troops in the waiting transports cheering, the sound echoing across the Solent.

The second memorial, unveiled on 5th June, 1984, 40 years after the embarkation, is on the waterfront. Of unusual design, with three stone slabs surmounting a pyramid-like base of smaller stones, it carries the inscription 'COMBINED OPER-

ATIONS. BRITISH AND ALLIED NAVAL AND COMMANDO UNITS SAILED FROM THE HAMBLE RIVER ON THE NIGHT OF 5TH JUNE 1944 FOR THE'D' DAY LANDINGS ON THE NORMANDY BEACHES. 40TH ANNIVERSARY COMMEMORATION', and the larger words 'FOR OUR FREEDOM'.

A memorial at Saltash Passage, on the Devon side of the Tamar, is also of unusual design, with a series of irregular columns of granite into which is set a large metal plaque. The inscription reads, 'THIS TABLET MARKS THE DEPARTURE FROM THIS PLACE OF UNITS OF THE V AND VII CORPS OF THE UNITED STATES ARMY ON THE 6TH JUNE, 1944, FOR THE D.DAY LANDINGS IN FRANCE'. The memorial

106 *Combined Operations Memorial, Warsash*

in a garden with shrubs and seats by the water-side, was designed by John Gray and unveiled on 14th May, 1958, by John Hay Whitney, the U.S. Ambassador.

From 6th June, 1944 ('D' Day), to 7th May, 1945, 418,585 American troops and 144,093 vehicles left Portland Harbour for France. This information is provided on a stone memorial in Victoria Gardens, Portland, unveiled by American Ambassador John Winant on 22nd August, 1945. He also re-named the adjoining road 'Victory Road'.

In the main hall of the Civic Centre at Southampton, are two metal plaques given by the U.S. Authorities to the city at the end of the war. One is from the Navy Department, thanking the citizens of Southampton for their hospitality and co-operation from 1943-1945. The other is from the U.S. Army's 14th Major Port, recording that from 'D' Day, 6th June, 1944, to the end of the war, over 2,250,000 troops, 250,000 vehicles and millions of tons of supplies of the U.S. Army were shipped through the port of Southampton. The U.S. port authorities used part of the Civic Centre as its headquarters during that period.

A stone plaque on a wall near the Pier Head in Liverpool erected in 1944 by the U.S. 15th Port Authority was to commemorate the cooperation between British and Americans during the time that American troops and cargoes were moving through the port.

The Mayflower memorial in Southampton, commemorates the setting sail of the Pilgrim Fathers in 1620. An additional plaque added to the memorial is to the U.S. troops, over two million in number, who sailed with the allies from

107 *U.S. Memorial, Saltash*

Southampton between 'D' Day and the end of the war 'to liberate the continent of Europe from aggression in order that the freedom for which the Pilgrim Fathers strove should not be lost'.

A memorial to 'D' Day was unveiled on Southsea Front by Field Marshal Montgomery and dedicated by the Bishop of Portsmouth, on 6th June, 1948, the fourth anniversary of the invasion. British, American and French troops formed a guard of honour at the ceremony which was attended by representatives from Arromanches, the scene of British landings.

108 *'D' Day Memorial, Southsea*

The memorial, in a garden near South Parade Pier from which many troops had embarked, is in the form of a concrete block similar to those used to obstruct the coast against possible invasion in 1940. Inscriptions on the block compare the desperate situation of 1940 with the invasion of 1944.

After the ceremony two memorial windows were unveiled at Christ Church, Portsdown, in a service similar to the Knights' Vigil service held there on 4th July, 1944, and attended by the headquarters staff of the 2nd Army on the eve of 'D' Day. The windows, unveiled by Sir Miles Dempsey and dedicated by the Bishop of Portsmouth, depict the warrior saints, St Michael and St George. Above is a 2nd Army shield, below are battle scenes of landing craft and tanks, and around are badges of the divisions and arms involved. A framed illustration and description of the various badges is on the wall near the windows.

On the village green at Droxford, Hampshire, a commemorative seat carries a metal plaque with the inscription 'THE RT. HON. WINSTON S. CHURCHILL, C.H., M.P., HIS WAR CABINET AND ALLIED CHIEFS MADE THEIR HEADQUARTERS AT DROXFORD STATION FROM 2ND JUNE TO 4TH JUNE 1944 ON THE EVE OF THE INVASION OF EUROPE'.

The 'D' Day Museum at Southsea was opened on 3rd June, 1984, by H.M. Queen Elizabeth the Queen Mother. The centre piece of the museum is the Overlord Embroidery, commissioned by Lord Dulverton in 1968 and completed four years later. Designed by Sandra Lawrence and embroidered at the Royal School of Needlework, the work was inspired by the Bayeux Tapestry (see p. 62).

The Overlord Embroidery has 34 panels compared with the 32 of the Bayeux. The first few panels are taken up with the early years of the war, the Battle of Britain, the Blitz and so on. The planning and preparation for 'D' Day follow and panels 12 and 13 show the allied armada setting out. The seaborne and airborne landings follow and the latter scenes include the allied break-out and the destruction of the German army.

The embroidery had no permanent home for some years but is now in a purpose-built and appropriate setting.

Portsmouth Cathedral has several memorials to the Second World War. One window commemorating those who served on 'D' Day and in Normandy, was unveiled by H.M. Queen Elizabeth the Queen Mother on 3rd June, 1984, and dedicated by the Archbishop of Canterbury. It features badges of the three services and the 2nd British Army, the 21st Army Group and the 1st American Army. There are also coats of arms representing 12 allied countries, and the badge of the 'D' Day and Normandy Fellowship, whose members were responsible for the erection of the window.

Other memorials to those who fought in the landings, or in the subsequent Normandy campaign, are to be found at Christ Church, Swansea, in St Mary's Church, Nottingham, and in Hamilton Square Gardens, Birkenhead.

On a hillside site in the New Forest, north of Emery Down, is a wooden cross set in concrete, surrounded by a rustic wooden fence with two flag-poles, and with maple trees behind. A metal plaque at the foot of the cross explains that the cross was erected on 14th April, 1944, and services were held there until 'D' Day by men of the 3rd Canadian Division R.C.A.S.C.

109 *New Forest*

110 *Canadian Memorial, Newhaven*

During the period before 'D' Day many thousands of allied troops were stationed in the New Forest awaiting the expected invasion.

Amongst trees on the edge of Crowborough Golf Course in Sussex is a rough stone pillar with a metal plaque, in memory of nine Canadian soldiers who were killed near the spot by a flying bomb on July 5th, 1944. Part of the inscription is worded 'THIS STONE RECORDS OUR GRATITUDE TO THEM AND THEIR CANADIAN COMRADES FOR ALL THEY DID FOR THE CAUSE OF FREEDOM'.

A large granite block in a roadside garden at Newhaven has the inscription in gold lettering 'TO THE MEMORY OF THE MEMBERS OF THE CORPS OF THE ROYAL CANADIAN ENGINEERS WHO LOST THEIR LIVES IN THE RAID ON DIEPPE, FRANCE, 19 AUGUST, 1942. NEWHAVEN WAS AN EMBARKATION POINT'. Nearby is a maple tree planted on 16th August, 1992, by Prince Philip, Duke of Edinburgh, to commemorate the 50th Anniversary of the raid.

The Dieppe raid involving some 6,000 men, mostly Canadian and British, was a disaster, with about 3,600 casualties and with none of the installations marked as targets being reached. The lessons learned by the operation were, however, invaluable in the later planning of 'D' Day.

In the Royal Marine depot at Poole there is an interesting memorial to the men who took part in Operation Frankton in December 1942 – the 'Cockleshell Heroes'.

Ten Royal Marines set off in special canoes called Cockles to attack German shipping in Bordeaux Harbour with limpet mines. Only two returned, and the memorial names them,

111 *Operation Frankton Memorial, Poole (Photograph – L/A Seaward, Royal Marines)*

A/Major H. G. Hasler, O.B.E., R.M., and Marine W. E. Sparks, and their canoe 'Catfish'. Also named are those who did not return, and their cockles 'Crayfish', 'Conger', 'Cuttlefish' and 'Coalfish'.

The memorial has a carving of a cockle with its two man crew, and also a quotation of Earl Mountbatten, 'Of the many brave and dashing raids carried out by the men of Combined Operations Command, none was more courageous or imaginative than Operation Frankton'.

In 1993, Bill Sparks, the last survivor of the raid, attended the unveiling at the Imperial War Museum of a painting by Jack Russell the England cricketer, depicting the action. A year earlier, on 6th July 1992, he had unveiled a plaque commemorating the 10 marines, at the entrance to Lumps Fort rose garden, Southsea. The site was used as a training base for the unit, known as the Royal Marine Boom Detachment, formed 6th July, 1942, exactly 50 years before the ceremony.

Not far from Lumps Fort, on the wall of a rose garden in front of the Royal Marines' Museum, Eastney, is a stone tablet listing the names of the eight officers and marines killed in Fort Cumberland on 26th August, 1940 during the Battle of Britain. The memorial was originally at the entrance to the now unoccupied fort.

The Royal Marines' Museum is the site of the famous Falklands War memorial 'The Yomper'. This 18 ft. bronze statue, at the entrance gates to the museum grounds, was unveiled in 1992 by Lady Thatcher.

Many memorials, of course, are to little-known incidents or aspects of the war.

A stained-glass memorial window in the Chapel of Goodrich Castle, Herefordshire, was unveiled on 7th June 1992 in memory of those who died in radar development flights.

The unveiling marked the 50th anniversary of the worst tragedy when a Halifax bomber, carrying a prototype of a ground mapping bombing aid, crashed in flames near Goodrich. All on board were killed, including the electronics genius Alan Blumlein and five other leading scientists.

Fortunately, their work was continued after their deaths, making possible effective strategic air power, while the ASW Mk. III Radar had, within a year, effectively won the Battle of the Atlantic against the German U-Boat fleet.

A slate memorial tablet unveiled at Brougham Hall, near Penrith, in July 1992, commemorates one of the least well-known, and perhaps one of the most bizarre, operations of the war.

Fifty years before the unveiling, Brougham Hall, and nearby Lowther Castle and Greystoke Castle, were used for top secret work on the deliberately mis-named Canal Defence Light, or C.D.L. This involved fitting tanks with 13-million candle-power strobe lights with which to blind the enemy temporarily. During the war, 1,850

112   *Goodrich Castle*

tanks were converted and some 6,000 men involved in the research and training, the first batch, the 11th Royal Tank Regiment, arriving at Lowther in June 1941. The huge sum for the time of £20 million was spent on development but the device never lived up to expectations, although it was used alongside conventional tanks in the crossing of the Rhine at Remagen in March 1945.

The tablet on a wall in the grounds of Brougham Hall, is to the memory of the men of the 1st and 35th Tank Brigades of the 79th Armoured Division who served at Brougham between July 1942 and June 1944, and to their R.E.M.E. support unit who left in 1945.

A most unusual memorial in Worthing's Beach House Park, commemorates the part played by birds during the war. Apparently British pigeon breeders supplied the allied forces with about 213,000 birds for active service as carrier pigeons, and in 1949 a birdbath, drinking pool and memorial stone were constructed in a shrubbery at the southern end of the park. The inscription there reads 'IN MEMORY OF WARRIOR BIRDS WHO GAVE THEIR LIVES ON ACTIVE SERVICE 1939-45 AND FOR THE USE AND PLEASURE OF LIVING BIRDS'. Another stone nearby records that Nancy Price, an actress and author with local connections, and members of the People Theatre, London, had presented the memorial.

113 *Warrior Birds Memorial, Worthing*

On the 5th September 1992, a memorial was unveiled at the disused Skitten airfield near Wick, by Anderson Murray, president of the local British Legion and ex-airman.

The prime task of Skitten during the 1939-1945 war was the protection of the Royal Naval base at Scapa Flow, and the main plaque on the 7 ft. high granite monument pays a general tribute to all who flew from the airfield and did not return.

A further tablet, however, is to commemorate 'Operation Freshman', an unsuccessful attempt to destroy the German heavy water plant at Vermork, west of Oslo. On 19th November 1942, two Horsa gliders towed by Halifax bombers set off from R.A.F. Skitten. Only the crew of one Halifax bomber survived. One bomber flew into a mountain killing the crew, the glider crew and the commandos on board. The other glider broke its tow rope and crash-landed. It was not known until after the war that after a brief battle the survivors, including glider crew, were interrogated by the Gestapo and then executed. The second Halifax just managed to return to base on the last of its fuel. Altogether more than 40 men died on the raid which succeeded only in alerting the Germans to the danger of an attack on Vermork.

Nevertheless, despite a reinforced German garrison, the plant was eventually successfully sabotaged by Norwegian Resistance and Commandos. Amongst those present at the Skitten memorial unveiling were Resistance Veterans.

After the invasion of Norway by the Germans in 1940, a special operations force was formed, named Kompani Linge, after its commander Captain Martin Linge. This group was based in the Cairngorms whilst training for raids on enemy-occupied Norway. On 19th September 1973, a memorial stone and plaque were unveiled at Glenmore near Aviemore in memory of this group of Norwegian patriots and of the 57 men of the Kompani who gave their lives.

The most famous mission of this group was the raid recreated in the film *Heroes of Telemark*. This resulted in damage to the Germans' heavy water plant at Vermork and the sinking in a Norwegian fjord of a vessel to prevent its cargo, a hundredweight of heavy water, from being transported back to Germany. As a result of these operations German scientists were effectively obliged to abandon their attempts to develop an atomic weapon.

114 *Unveiling of the Skitten Memorial, Wick   (Photograph – J. McDonald)*

115 *Norwegian Memorial, Glenmore*

On an outside wall at St Paul's Church, just off Knightsbridge, there is an attractive memorial to the members of the Women's Transport Service (First Aid Nursing Yeomanry or F.A.N.Y.) who died in the war. The list of names includes six women who were awarded the Croix de Guerre and two who were awarded the George Cross. The latter two, Noor Inayat-Khan and Violette Szabo (who was awarded both the George Cross and the Croix de Guerre), won their awards for their highly dangerous work with the Resistance in occupied France, and both died in concentration camps at the hands of the Gestapo.

116 *Women's Transport Service Memorial*

A third woman awarded the George Cross for such work was Odette Sansom (later Odette Churchill) who was also captured and tortured, but survived.

The memorial is a stone plaque with the blue and red badge of the Service, above brick steps and a low brick wall planted with flowers. In the photograph of the memorial the left hand poppy wreath to be seen was from 'Odette'.

During morning service on Sunday 18th June 1944, a V.1. 'Flying Bomb' crashed through the roof of the Guards' Chapel, Wellington Barracks, Westminster, destroying most of the building apart from the Apse. One hundred and twenty-one people were killed and as many were injured, and a stone tablet and a Book of Remembrance in the rebuilt Chapel commemorate those who died.

On 28th May 1956 the Household Brigade War Memorial Cloister was dedicated in the presence of the Queen, and the new Chapel was dedicated on 26th November 1963, in the presence of the Duke of Edinburgh. Built into the foundations are the remains of some 2,000 memorials damaged beyond repair on the 18th June 1944. The names on those old memorials are now on the walls of the rebuilt Chapel.

The Book of Remembrance is at the entrance to the Memorial Cloister which stretches towards Birdcage Walk. Within the Cloisters are niches each with the Roll of Honour of an individual regiment, Grenadier Guards, Scots Guards, Welsh Guards, Irish Guards, Coldstream Guards, Life Guards and Royal Horse Guards.

There are several World War II Memorials on Victoria Embankment. Not far from the Houses of Parliament, that to the Chindits was unveiled on 16th October 1990 by the Duke of Edinburgh. The Chindits, more properly called the 77th Indian Brigade, were a special force formed, trained and led by Major General Orde Charles Wingate. During 1943 and 1944 the Chindits car-

117 *Chindits Memorial*

ried out operations behind enemy lines in Burma, destroying installations and cutting railways and generally disrupting Japanese activity. Drawn from a large number of countries and military units they demonstrated that allied troops could match the enemy in jungle warfare. Several V.C.'s were awarded to men of their group but losses were high, about one third of those participating in the first raid, for example.

The Chindits were named after the mythical beast which was the guardian of Burmese temples and the memorial on the Embankment depicts this creature in bronze on a tall stone base. Carved in the stone are a list of units involved in the group, a list of V.C.'s, and the motto 'THE BOLDEST MEASURES ARE THE SAFEST'. The memorial's architect was David Price and the sculptor Frank Foster.

The Burma Star Association was formed in February 1951 and its first patron was Earl Mountbatten of Burma. Its motto was taken from the words left as an epitaph on a memorial at Kohima by the British and Indian defenders, 'WHEN YOU GO HOME, TELL THEM OF US AND SAY, FOR YOUR TOMORROW WE GAVE OUR TODAY'.

Kohima and Imphal, key positions on the border between Burma and India, were surrounded by the Japanese early in April 1944 and the resulting battles led eventually to the withdrawal of the Japanese forces and to the successful defence of India. At the hill station of Kohima, fighting had taken place on a series of terraces on one of which was a small clubhouse and tennis court belonging to the local District Commissioner. At one time only the width of the court had separated the defenders from the attacking Japanese 51st Division. The tennis court now has lines marked out permanently in white concrete, and at one side is the memorial cross with the engraved epitaph, the origin of which goes back 2,500 years, to when the Greek poet Simonides wrote of the defence of the pass of Thermopylae, against a huge invading Persian army, by a mere 300 Spartans.

The memorial archways in the garden of York Minster were once part of the medieval palace of the archbishops, and were restored in 1987 as a memorial to the 2nd Division. H.M. Queen Elizabeth the Queen Mother unveiled the memorial on the 24th June, 1987 and bronze plaques at the foot of the archways give the division's battle honours since it was raised in Portugal on the 18th June, 1809. In the centre arch the plaque reads 'KOHIMA 1944' and on the railings above it is a large bronze wreath which frames a stone pillar standing a short distance to the rear and carrying the epitaph.

St George's Church at Arreton on the Isle of Wight, has a three-panel stained-glass window in honour of those who died or served in the Burma Campaign. Amongst the many features in this most impressive work by Alan Younger, are the Burma Star against a medal ribbon; badges of the three services and S.E.A.C.; the Kohima epitaph surrounded by the figures of a British soldier, an Indian soldier, a Guardsman and a nurse; and two scenes of the action in the campaign. The

118   *Memorial Archways, York Minster*

C9 *Shepley Memorial, Oundle*

C11 *United Reform Church, Malmesbury*

C10 *St Peter's Church, Westleton*

C12 *Brighton and Hove Synagogue*

C13   *Law Society Memorial*

C14   *T.U.C. Memorial*

C15   *Rolls Royce Memorial*

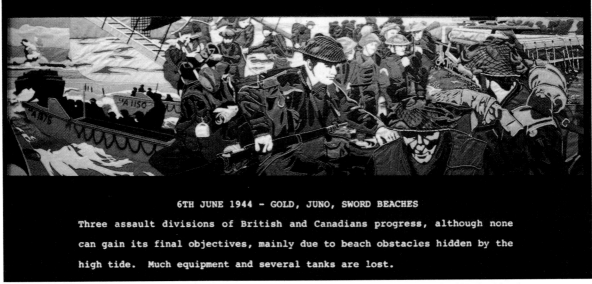

6TH JUNE 1944 - GOLD, JUNO, SWORD BEACHES

Three assault divisions of British and Canadians progress, although none can gain its final objectives, mainly due to beach obstacles hidden by the high tide. Much equipment and several tanks are lost.

C16   *Panel 24, Overlord Embroidery (Photograph by permission of the Trustees of The Overlord Embroidery)*

119 *St George's Church, Arreton*

121 *Portsmouth Cathedral*

120 *St George's Church, Arreton*

window was unveiled on 12th May, 1992 by Lady Mountbatten. Below the window in a glass case is a Roll of Honour (see p. 95).

Another memorial window, in Portsmouth Cathedral, has been presented by the Portsmouth and District Branch of the Burma Star Association and features the Burma Star and ribbon, the dates 1941-1945, and the Kohima epitaph.

Amongst the service emblems in the stained glass of Guildford Cathedral, is a Burma Star 'in memory of those who died and served in the 1941-45 Burma Campaign'.

In St John's Church, Cardiff, a stained-glass window given by the Cardiff branch of the Burma Star Association also commemorates those who lost their lives in the Burma Campaign 1941-45. The window is decorated with a Burma Star and ribbon, badges of the services, a cross, the words of the Kohima epitaph, and a screen of bamboo through which a distant mountain can be glimpsed.

The Canterbury and District branch of the Burma Star Association have erected on a beautiful site in Westgate Gardens, Canterbury, a most unusual memorial. A pillar and wall of flint and brick, which themselves are very attractive, set off the main feature of the work, a carving in stone of a British soldier in jungle uniform with, in the background, the face of a Japanese soldier, and British and Japanese graves marked by a rifle and a sword. There are also badges of the Royal Navy,

122 *St John's Church, Cardiff*

of rough hewn-stones, with flanking stone walls, planted attractively with flowers, the memorial has the usual Burma Star and the Kohima epitaph, and in addition the Deal and Dover veterans have placed inside the column a casket containing a parchment roll with all the members' names and units, and a Burma Star and Pacific Star decoration.

Within Trinity Gardens, Margate, and close to the main Margate memorial, is another Burma memorial. A pillar of rough-hewn stones, with low flanking walls, has upon it the Burma Star Association badge and two plaques carrying the Kohima epitaph and also information about the memorials. It was dedicated by the Lord Bishop of Dover on the 6th October, 1991 in the presence of Countess Mountbatten of Burma.

Also within the gardens, which are laid out as a garden of rest connected with the war memorials, are trees and seats dedicated to individuals.

In the grounds of St. Thomas' Church in Newcastle, there is an impressive Burma Campaign memorial unveiled on 18th August, 1981. A stone plinth on a paved base carries a bronze relief, featuring the words of the Kohima epitaph, the Burma Star and the head of a soldier wearing a bush hat. On the stone are carved the words 'IN HONOURED MEMORY OF ALL THOSE FROM THE NORTH EAST WHO GAVE THEIR LIVES IN THE BURMA CAMPAIGN 1941-1945'.

In Holy Trinity Church, Hull, a marble plaque has been donated by the Hull Branch of the Burma Star Association to the memory of all who served in the Burma Campaign 1941-45.

Not far from the Visitors' Centre on Cannock Chase, the local branch of the Burma Star Association have planted a copse of trees and erected a rough-stone memorial and a plaque in

Merchant Navy, R.A.F. and 14th Army, and a bronze plaque of explanation completes the memorial. The sculptor is Charles Foad, who himself served in Burma with the Royal Artillery.

The Burma Memorial opposite Deal Castle was dedicated on 9th September, 1984. A column

123 *Westgate Gardens, Canterbury*

124 *Unveiling Ceremony at St Thomas' Church, Newcastle (Photograph – Les Pringle)*

memory of those who fought and died in the Burma campaign.

A Garden of Remembrance at St Richard's Church, Pound Hill, Crawley, was constructed by Burma Star Association members, and features a rose garden, a sundial and wooden bench seats.

In a small park in Market Street, Bromsgrove, a memorial was unveiled on 16th May 1982 by Air Vice-Marshal Sir Bernard Chacksfield, National Chairman of the Burma Star Association. The memorial was built and dedicated by the local branch of the association to

those who died and also those who served in the 1941-45 Burma Campaign.

The monument is a brick column with slate tablets, on a round brick base and surrounded by a low brick wall and metal railings. Gold lettering is used for the inscriptions on the slate, including the Kohima epitaph and the badge of the Burma Star Association. Several plaques are set into the paving around the column, amongst them being one donated by the Birmingham branch of the Far East Prisoner of War Association, and one in memory of the East and

125 *Bromsgrove Memorial*

126 *Danson Park, Bexley Heath*

127 *St Peter and St Paul, Wisbech*

West African Forces who died in Burma. The memorial itself and the grass and area around it are beautifully maintained and the site chosen is a prominent one.

The Far East Prisoner of War Association unveiled a memorial on 21st November 1985 in Danson Park, Bexley Heath. The memorial is in the form of 20 oak trees with an explanatory bronze plaque on a plinth of York stone. The inscription on the plaque reads 'THESE OAK TREES ARE DEDICATED TO THE MEMORY OF ALL THOSE WHO DIED FIGHTING AGAINST JAPAN AND OF OUR COMRADES WHO DIED AS A RESULT OF THEIR CAPTIVITY IN THE JAPANESE PRISON CAMPS'. The plaque before unveiling was covered by a Union Jack which had been hidden in a Japanese prison camp and had the signatures of 124 prisoners on it.

Two widows planted trees, Mrs Edwards and Mrs Wordley. Frank Wordley died in 1945, and his daughter whom he never saw, Carol, born on Christmas Day 1941, was present at the ceremony.

The 2nd Battalion Cambridgeshire Regiment suffered heavy losses in the fighting leading up to the fall of Singapore, and a memorial in the Church of St Peter and St Paul, Wisbech, has the inscription '15TH FEBRUARY 1942 – 15TH AUGUST 1945. TO THE MEMORY OF THE MEN OF THIS AREA WHO WERE KILLED IN ACTION OR DIED IN CAPTIVITY IN THE FAR EAST'. The memorial is a tablet of black slate surrounded by a frame of white marble carved to resemble bamboo. The two dates are those of the fall of Singapore to the

Japanese, and of V.J. Day, the end of the war. The unveiling, on 20th October 1985, was performed by the Lord Lieutenant of Cambridgeshire and the dedication by the Bishop of Ely.

Sunderland Museum contains an interesting memorial of the Second World War in honour of the officers and men of the 125th Anti-Tank Regiment, a Territorial Army Unit from the Sunderland area. The memorial, presented by Colonel Sir Robert Chapman in 1951, is in the form of a silver model of the two-pounder anti-tank gun used by the regiment during the war, on a green granite base on which are four plaques recording the names of the 197 men of the regiment who were killed in action or died as Japanese prisoners of war between 1942 and 1945.

128 *125th Anti-Tank Regiment Memorial, Sunderland*

129 *Bassingbourn Barracks*

St Mary's Church, Swansea, was destroyed by enemy bombing on 21st February 1941, but on 28th May 1959 the Queen Mother unveiled a stone to commemorate the rebuilding. In a chapel of the church there is a most unusual war memorial, in the form of a Union Jack which was made in a Far-East P.O.W. camp and used in the burial of British troops. The white of the flag was made from prisoners' loin cloths, the blue was taken from mosquito nets used exclusively by the Japanese, and the red came from the linings of Indonesian straw hats. At the end of the war the flag was used in a march past when the salute was taken by Captain S. Armstrong, who later became President of the South-West Wales Far East Prisoner of War Club, and presented the flag to the Church.

In front of the headquarters building at Bassingbourn Barracks, Cambridgeshire, a wooden lychgate was erected in September 1972. This gate was originally built by British prisoners of war held by the Japanese at Changi, Singapore, and erected as an entrance to the cemetery where they buried nearly 600 of their comrades. The gate was moved when the bodies were re-interred after the war.

A large proportion of those imprisoned at Changi were from the 18th Division which had strong East Anglian connections, and so a new site for the gateway was sought in that area. The lychgate, made by members of the 18th Division in December 1942 has carved rose, leek, shamrock and thistle emblems in the interior.

An unusual memorial in the Parish Church of St John the Baptist, Halifax, consists of a cross of bamboo on a base with bamboo surround. A bronze plaque leaning against the foot of the cross reads 'IN REMEMBRANCE OF ALL THOSE WHO DIED IN THE BATTLE AGAINST JAPAN OR AS A RESULT OF CAPTIVITY IN JAPANESE PRISONER OF WAR CAMPS'. A simple but effective tribute, it was unveiled on 10th November 1985, having been presented to the local Far East P.O.W. Association by the British Legion. It is situated in the church next to the Duke of Wellington's Regiment memorial dedicated after World War I.

Outside in the grounds near the church is the main Halifax war memorial, moved recently from a position where it had become rather neglected and at risk. It now looks more appropriately respected and cared for, and those responsible should be congratulated.

An interesting feature of the Far East Prisoner of War memorial in St Martin-in-the-Fields Church in London, is the glass case containing two pieces of teak sleeper and a piece of metal rail which were part of the notorious Burma Railway built at the cost of so many lives, with prisoner of war labour.

A metal plaque above the cabinet honours the memory of those who died as P.O.W.'s or civilian internees in Japanese hands from 1941 to 1945, and of those who died subsequently as a result of their treatment.

A stone-clad clock tower in a small circular garden on Marine Parade, Great Yarmouth, was erected by the local branch of the Far East Prisoner of War Association and dedicated to those who died as a result of their captivity. Bronze reliefs on the tower have maps of the Far East.

A commemorative chair in St Giles' Cathedral, Edinburgh, was presented by the Scottish Far East Prisoner of War Association and dedicated on 13th February 1972, to those who died in captivity between 1941 and 1945. The work, designed and made by the Edinburgh College of Art, is embroidered with the emblem of a thistle and crossed swords (a claymore and a samurai sword).

130 *Marine Parade, Great Yarmouth*

A black slate plaque with gold lettering was dedicated on 1st October 1986, in the north transept of York Minster, by the Far East Prisoner of War Association, to their comrades who 'DIED IN PRISON CAMPS OR LATER AS A RESULT OF CAPTIVITY'. It is situated next to the Astronomical Clock which is a memorial to Fallen Airmen of the 1939-45 war.

In St Peter Mancroft Church, Norwich, a slate plaque with the coloured badge of the Far East Prisoner of War Association was dedicated at 3.30 p.m. 15th February 1987, the time and date of the surrender of Singapore 45 years earlier in 1942, to 'THE MANY COMRADES WHO DID NOT RETURN OR WHOSE LIVES WERE SHORTENED BY THE CONDITIONS OF THEIR CAPTIVITY'.

131 *St Margaret's Church, King's Lynn*

St Margaret's Church in King's Lynn has an unusual memorial in the form of a pulpit cross depicting a Warrior Christ with crown and loincloth, an ancient design going back to the 8th century and Celtic in origin. The cross was the gift of the local branch of the Far East Prisoner of War Association on the 20th anniversary of their release and commemorates their fellow prisoners who died in 1941-1945, or later as a result of their captivity.

The cross was dedicated on 15th August 1965 by the Bishop of Birmingham, J. L. Wilson, who was himself a prisoner, having been Bishop of Singapore at its fall.

In Morriston Hospital, Swansea, a large oak bookcase in the library building has the inscription 'TO THE GLORIOUS MEMORY OF THOSE WHO GAVE THEIR LIVES AS PRISONERS OF WAR IN THE FAR EAST 1942-1945'. The bookcase was given by Mr Harold Leigh, together with a £1,000 donation to purchase medical books on tropical diseases.

A framed relief of the Last Supper in St Peter's Church, Nottingham was placed there by the Nottingham and District Far East Prisoner of War Association, in memory of their comrades who died in Japanese prisoner of war camps between 1941 and 1945. A plaque to this effect is below the Last Supper together with a stone tablet and the words 'Our soul is escaped even as a bird out of the snare of the fowler : the snare is broken and we are delivered. Our help standeth in the name of the Lord : who hath made heaven and earth'.

In Hamilton Square Gardens, Birkenhead, a plaque with the Burma Star and the Kohima epitaph was presented by the local branch of the Burma Star Association in remembrance of those who died in that campaign and subsequently.

132 *St Peter's Church, Nottingham*

Nearby, a polished block of marble pays tribute to the men of Merseyside and Wirral who fell at Dunkirk, May – June 1940; a marble tablet, placed by the Wirral and Chester branch of the Normandy Veterans' Association, is in memory of comrades who gave their lives in the campaign from 6th June to 20th August 1944 – 'THE LIBERATORS'; and finally, another marble plaque placed by the Wirral Branch of the 8th Army Veterans' Association commemorates their fallen comrades of 1941-45.

In St Mary's Church, Nottingham, is a brass plaque to those who died and fought in the Burma Campaign, unveiled on V.J. Day (15th August) 1986, and a stone tablet to those who fought in the Normandy landings and the campaign that followed, erected on 16th July, 1989.

In the grounds of Christ Church, the Garrison Church of Swansea, there are three similar memorial stones. One has been placed by the Burma Star Association, with the words of the Kohima epitaph, another by the Normandy Veterans' Association in memory of those who took part in the liberation of Western Europe from 6th June 1944 to 8th May 1945, and a third by the Dunkirk Veterans' Association to all who took part in the 1940 evacuation.

The Dunkirk Veterans' Association of East Kent erected a memorial on the seafront at Dover on 16th August, 1975, the 35th anniversary of the Battle of Dunkirk. The memorial is a bronze panel

on a large piece of stone flanked by walls of smaller stones. The panel shows a soldier carrying a comrade over his shoulder, while in the background can be seen boats, one of which is sinking, and a large plume of smoke.

Under the bronze, a metal plaque notes that during the period May 10th to 1st June, 1940, 202,306 British Commonwealth and allied troops were evacuated to Dover alone, and goes on 'THE REMOVAL NOT ONLY PAYS TRIBUTE TO THE BRAVERY AND DISCIPLINE OF THE SERVICEMEN, BUT TO THE COURAGE OF THE CREWS OF THE ARMADA OF LITTLE SHIPS WHICH ASSISTED, AND THE PEOPLE OF THE PORT OF DOVER WHO RECEIVED THEM'.

Nearby on the seafront promenade, mounted on stone, is a section of armoured plating dismantled from one of the German long range guns near Calais. On it are recorded 84 rounds which were only a small part of the 2,226 shells fired from the batteries at the harbour and town of Dover from 1940 to 1944. The plating and the memorial were erected in 1954 by the Dover Harbour Board.

Part of the inscription on the main war memorial at Margate refers to the safe landing there of 46,000 members of the armed forces from Dunkirk in 1940.

Not part of, but very close to the main Bridlington memorial, is another commemorating the 50th anniversary of Dunkirk and placed by the Dunkirk Veterans' Association.

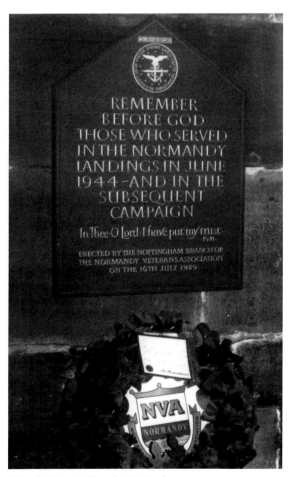

133 *St Mary's Church, Nottingham*

134 *Dunkirk Memorial, Dover*

Within the gardens of Croydon Parish Church, a tree has been planted in remembrance of the evacuation from Dunkirk in 1940. The tree was presented by the local branch of the Dunkirk Veterans' Association and a stone and plaque record the details.

In York Minster, beneath an 18th-century statue of Christ carrying the Cross, is a Dunkirk memorial unveiled on 6th May 1979 by the Lord Lieutenant of North Yorkshire, the Marquis of Normanby. Within a glass case has been placed a Book of Remembrance, a bronze medallion depicting Dunkirk, and more unusually, a casket presented by the York and District branch of the Dunkirk Veterans' Association and containing sand from the very beaches from which the evacuation took place in May and June 1940.

In Gloucester Cathedral there is a similar memorial of the Dunkirk Veterans' Association, in the form of a brass plaque and a casket containing earth from the graves in France of men of the Gloucestershire Regiment who died at the time of the 1940 evacuation.

Although British casualties amongst combatants were generally much lower in the Second World War than in the First, naval casualties were very much higher.

After the First World War three identical monuments, designed by Sir Robert Lorimer, were erected to the Royal Navy at the manning ports of Plymouth, Portsmouth and Chatham. Each memorial is an obelisk with a buttress at each of the four corners and with bronze panels,

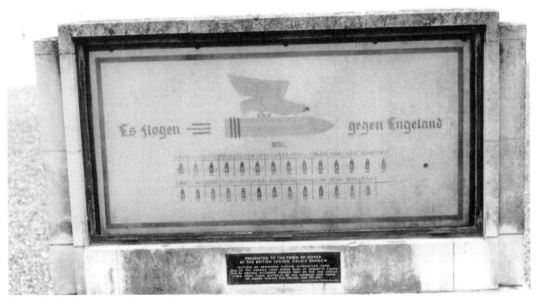

135 *German Armoured Plating, Dover*

bearing the names of the dead who belong to the port in question, on the base and buttresses.

These memorials were much enlarged after the Second War to accommodate the names of those lost between 1939 and 1945. At Plymouth a long stone wall at a lower level and with steps at each end, runs along one side of the original memorial and on this are placed the new bronze panels. At intervals there are fine stone figures of naval personnel, and the whole addition blends perfectly with the original. The architect for the extensions was Sir Edward Maufe and the sculptor Sir Charles Wheeler.

The Plymouth memorial is on the famous Hoe, between the Armada Memorial and the Drake statue, and a plaque provides the information that of the 23,182 men and women whose names are on the memorial, 7,256 died during the First World War and 15,926 died during the Second, a reflection of the greater emphasis on naval activity in this latter period.

At Southsea Common, overlooking the Solent, the Portsmouth Naval War Memorial, similar to that at Plymouth, also has an extension to record the names of those who died at sea in the Second World War. A wall to the landward side of the original obelisk, and at a lower level, is inset with 58 bronze name panels. At each end broad steps lead up through a Register Pavilion to the obelisk and the Esplanade. Again there are fine stone statues by Sir Charles Wheeler at intervals along the wall.

The monument to the Merchant Navy dead is in Trinity Gardens, close to the Tower of London. A colonnade was built after the First World War, and to this was added in 1955 a sunken garden designed by Sir Edward Maufe and with statues by Sir Charles Wheeler, the same two men who were responsible for the additions to the Royal Navy's memorials.

Between two staircases leading down into the garden is a wall flanked by two stone columns in front of each of which is a fine stone statue of

136   *Royal Navy Memorial, Plymouth*

137   *Royal Navy Memorial, Portsmouth*

138　*Royal Navy Memorial, Portsmouth*

139　*Merchant Navy Memorial*

a seaman. On the wall is engraved '1939-1945. THE TWENTY-FOUR THOUSAND OF THE MERCHANT NAVY AND FISHING FLEETS WHOSE NAMES ARE HONOURED ON THE WALLS OF THIS GARDEN GAVE THEIR LIVES FOR THEIR COUNTRY AND HAVE NO GRAVE BUT THE SEA'. Bronze plaques on the insides of the walls surrounding the garden list the names of those lost under the names of their ships. Similar plaques on the First World War colonnade list the dead of that war, 12,000 in number, or half that in the later war.

The garden itself has, at frequent intervals, seats and statuary, and although the noise of traffic is ever present, it still has an appropriately tranquil atmosphere.

The Battle of the Atlantic effectively started a few hours after the declaration of war in 1939,

and during its course resulted in the loss of some 2,500 merchant ships and some 30,000 British merchant seamen. But by the end of the war nearly 30,000 of the 40,000 U-Boat crew-men had died and the attempt to starve Britain out of the war had failed.

The turning point is accepted as being in May 1943. In the first 20 days of March 1943, 97 merchant vessels were sunk for the loss of only 16 U-Boats, but in May only 50 ships were lost against a toll of 41 U-Boats. Improved tactics, more effective code-breaking, and airborne radar developments were major factors, but for a time the losses of ships and essential supplies had seemed critical, and Churchill was quoted as saying 'The only thing that ever really frightened me during the war was the U-Boat peril'.

140   *Operations Room, Liverpool*

In May 1993, as part of the programme for the 50th anniversary of the Battle, a maritime chapel was dedicated in the Church of Our Lady and St Nicholas in Liverpool. On the wall of the chapel a bronze sculpture of Our Lady of the Quay looks down from the prow of a ship. The work is by Liverpool artist Arthur Dooley.

The Western Approaches Command Centre was transferred from Plymouth to Liverpool early in 1941 and established beneath a thick layer of steel reinforced concrete in the basement of Derby House, Rumford Street. This became known as the Citadel and it was from here that the destruction of the Bismark was directed in May 1941, and that the Battle of the Atlantic was successfully fought.

In the 50th anniversary year of the Battle these rooms were restored as a permanent memorial, the main feature being the operations room with its massive wall map some 60 ft. long and 18 ft. high. The only casualty in the bunker during the war was a young servicewoman, Patricia Lane, who fainted and fell to her death from a gantry while posting information on the control map. One report suggested that she had just recognised the name of her husband's ship amongst those sunk.

In the grounds of the Liverpool Parish Church of our Lady and St Nicholas two memorials stand to commemorate the men who served in the Arctic Convoys, taking desperately needed supplies to Russia from either the British mainland or from Iceland. The terrible weather conditions and the fact that the convoys were almost constantly within range of enemy ships and aircraft made these journeys much more risky than any others. One particularly ill-fated convoy, PQ17, in July 1942, lost all but 12 of its 36 ships. The ships which did arrive delivered 896 vehicles, 164 tanks, 87 aircraft and 57,000 tons of general supplies, but lost were some 3,350 vehicles, 430 tanks, 210 aircraft and 96,000 tons of other cargo.

It is fair to say that these efforts and risks were not sufficiently recognised, and it is ironic that although President Gorbachov bestowed the Russian Commemorative Medal on British veterans in 1986, the British Government has never awarded an Arctic Convoy medal, and has only recently allowed the Russian medal to be worn.

The memorials in Liverpool are of marble and placed on either side of a tall flagpole. One, with the badge of the Arctic Campaign Memorial Trust, is to the memory of those who died between 1941 and 1945, and the other, with the badge of the North Russia Club, is in thanksgiving for those who returned.

The Merchant Seamen's Memorial at Pier Head, Liverpool, has a central round column on which is inscribed, 'THESE OFFICERS AND MEN OF THE MERCHANT NAVY DIED WHILE SERVING WITH THE ROYAL NAVY AND HAVE NO GRAVE BUT THE SEA. 1939-1945'.

The Portland stone column is surmounted by a beacon and stands on a raised platform, at the head of a flight of steps, and surrounded by railings and a stone wall. On the wall are bronze

141   *Arctic Convoys Memorial, Liverpool*

142 *Merchant Seamen's Memorial, Liverpool*

panels with the names of some 1,400 dead, and a pair of stone globes, one terrestrial and one celestial. The vessels of the men lost are also recorded on the panels.

In Falkner Square, Toxteth, Liverpool, a bronze plaque was unveiled on 27th May 1993 with the inscription 'THIS PLAQUE IS DEDICATED TO ALL BLACK MERCHANT SEAMEN WHO SERVED DURING THE 1939-45 WAR. THEY HELD THEIR COURSE. RESPECT DUE'. The memorial was unveiled jointly by the President of the British Shipping Organisation and by an ex-merchant seaman who served in the war.

At Mill Dam, South Shields, a statue was unveiled on 19th September, 1990, by Countess Mountbatten of Burma 'in memory of the thousands of merchant seamen who sailed from this port and lost their lives in World War II'. The bronze statue, on a heavy stone base, is of a grim-faced seaman at the wheel of his vessel, the slope of the deck indicating heavy seas. This is a magnificent work, conveying tension and determination alike.

The memorial has a metal post and chain surround and on a plaque on the stone is a quotation from John Masefield, the Poet Laureate,
'Unrecognised, you put us in your debt,
Unthanked, you enter or escape the grave,
Whether your land remember or forget,
You served the land, or died to try to save'.

A Merchant Navy memorial in St Nicholas' Cathedral, Newcastle, is in the form of Remembrance Books in a glass fronted bookcase, on a wooden pillar, and with a wooden sloping book rest on three sides.

The pillar has on it the carving of a merchant vessel and on the centre rest are the words 'ROLL OF HONOUR OF THE MERCHANT NAVY AND FISH-

143 *Merchant Seamen's Memorial, South Shields*

ING FLEETS 1939-1945'. The badge of the Merchant Navy is carved on the bookcase head.

Near the entrance to St Nicholas' Cathedral is a stone plaque with the inscription 'IN MEMORY OF THE OFFICERS AND MEN OF THE TYNE DIVISION ROYAL NAVAL VOLUNTEER RESERVE WHO GAVE THEIR LIVES IN THE SECOND WORLD WAR'. The badge of the R.N.V.R. above the inscription, has the dates of the war on either side of it.

The Church of Holyrood, Southampton, erected in 1320, was damaged by enemy action on 30th November, 1940, only the tower and the shell remaining. Known for centuries as the Church of the Sailors, the ruins have been preserved as a memorial to those who served in the Merchant Navy and lost their lives at sea.

144   *Holyrood Church, Southampton*

The area has been planted with shrubs and provided with seats to form a memorial garden, and a large anchor has been placed in the corner where a metal tablet gives the history of the Church. Other plaques commemorate the crew of the Titanic, and the merchant sailors involved in the Falklands Campaign 1982.

Of the 14 Victoria Crosses awarded to British submariners in both world wars, four went to men who manned X-craft, four-man miniature submarines. Along with those who manned Chariots (or 'human torpedoes') these men carried out operations of high risk which could not be accomplished by other means.

On 22nd September, 1943, a successful attack on the 42,000 ton German battleship 'Tirpitz' in a Norwegian fjord, resulted in her never putting to sea operationally again, and led to Lt. Donald Cameron, of X-6, and Lt. Godfrey Place, of X-7, receiving V.C.'s.

Lt. Ian Fraser and Leading Seaman Magennis of XE-3 received similar awards after crippling a Japanese cruiser at Singapore, and other successful operations included attacks on Bergen, the cutting of Japanese seabed telephone cables, and the marking of 'D' Day beaches for incoming landing craft.

AT H.M.S. *Dolphin* at Gosport there is a submarine museum, a miniature submarine and a related memorial stone. On the stone is a quotation from Matthew Arnold including the words, 'Above us the waves'.

In a chapel in Gloucester Cathedral a stained-glass window was dedicated on 24th May 1986, in memory of the 723 men lost when H.M.S. *Gloucester* was sunk off Crete on 22nd May 1941. The window was unveiled by the captain of the current H.M.S. *Gloucester* and the ceremony was attended by 17 survivors of 1941.

Hebburn Cemetery, Newcastle, has a series of memorials connected with H.M.S. *Kelly*, the destroyer captained by Lord Louis Mountbatten. One is in memory of the 27 men killed in action with German E-Boats in the North Sea on 9th May, 1940. Twenty of these men are buried at Hebburn, and the names and ranks of 16 of them are recorded on a memorial stone, the remaining four being unidentified.

145   *Miniature Submarine Memorial, Gosport*

146 *H.M.S. 'Gloucester' Memorial*

A further stone is to the nine officers and 121 men who lost their lives when the *Kelly* was sunk on 23rd May 1941 during the Battle of Crete, and nearby is a memorial to Mountbatten himself.

Amongst several plaques in St Paul's Church, Castleton, a Royal Naval Chapel, is one in memory of 1,418 officers and men lost in H.M.S. *Hood* on 24th May, 1941. She was sunk by the *Bismark* in the prolonged action which eventually led to the sinking of the German battleship. It is possible that a shell penetrated the magazine of the *Hood*, and only three of her complement were saved.

H.M.S. *Stevenstone* was a Hunt class destroyer of the 1st Destroyer flotilla. The Hunt class vessels were named after hunts and, the Stevenstone country being near Barnstable, the destroyer was adopted by the town. Unfortunately, she was mined off the Walcheren Islands on 30th November, 1944, and a memorial tablet in Barnstable Guildhall commemorates the destroyer and 14 crew members who lost their lives. There is an engraving of the vessel on the tablet and alongside is the *Stevenstone's* emblem

and a white ensign. The memorial was designed by Jim Cook who served on the destroyer, and unveiled on 3rd September, 1988, by Canon Norman Crowe, formerly the ship's engineering officer.

St Mary le Strand, the church of the Women's Royal Naval Service, the 'Wren's', has two memorials to war time disasters in which many Wrens died. The first is a brass plate on which is inscribed 'IN PROUD MEMORY OF THE 21 WRENS AND A SISTER, Q.A.R.N.N.S., WHO LOST THEIR LIVES EN ROUTE TO SERVICE IN GIBRALTAR. THEY WERE ABOARD S.S. *AQUILA* WHEN SHE WAS TORPEDOED ON 19TH AUGUST 1941. THIS MEMORIAL IS GIVEN BY SOME OF THEIR SHIPMATES ON THE 50TH ANNIVERSARY OF THE SINKING'. The names of the 22 dead are also inscribed.

The second is a memorial candleholder dedicated 50 years and a day after the sinking of the troopship S.S. *Khedive Ishmael* on 12th February 1944. A total of nearly 1,300 were lost when the vessel, bound for Colombo from Mombasa, was sunk by a Japanese torpedo and of the 86 Wrens and Army nurses on board only nine survived. In all only 260 survivors from the ship were picked up after she sank in an estimated 36 seconds.

Elsewhere in the church is a Book of Remembrance to all the Wrens who died in the service of their country.

148 *H.M.S. 'Hood' Memorial, Castleton*

147 *H.M.S. 'Kelly' Memorial, Hebburn*

149 *Minelaying Memorial, Loch Alsh*

A memorial in the form of a mine, was unveiled on 24th April, 1982, on the edge of Loch Alsh and outside the Kyle of Lochalsh Hotel. This unusual but appropriate memorial is a tribute to the officers and men of H.M.S. *Trelawney* and ships of the 1st Minelaying Squadron who were based at Kyle of Lochalsh during World War II.

Although a large number of air force memorials are related to individual stations or airfields, there are also many of wider significance.

Close to the Armada and Royal Navy memorials on Plymouth Hoe, the Royal Air Force International Air Monument was unveiled on 3rd September, 1989, by Air Marshal Sir John Curtiss. The ceremony marked the culmination of nine years of work by Jim Davis, an ex air gunner, of Plymouth. He had the vision and energy to instigate the project and to bring it to fruition, and was rewarded with the city's Award for Service to the Community.

The unveiling took place before a crowd of some 20,000 people and representatives of 17 countries, and in the subsequent fly past were a Spitfire and Hurricane of the R.A.F. Battle of Britain Memorial Flight.

The main feature of the 18 ft. high memorial is the bronze figure by Pamela Taylor of the 'Unknown Airman' in flying kit, on a column of polished Cornish granite. Panels of black polished marble on the column carry, in gold lettering, tributes to those commemorated, and information about the part played by the air force in the Second World War. The top panel has the wording, under a gilt eagle, 'ROYAL AIR FORCE COMMONWEALTH AND ALLIED AIR FORCES 1939-

Fifty years after the mystery disappearance of two submarines off the West Coast of Scotland in 1943, a memorial was unveiled at Dunoon by the Submarine Old Comrades' Association, as a tribute to over 70 men who were lost. H.M.S. *Vandal* went down in the Arran Trench and H.M.S. *Untamed* was lost off Campbeltown, only one man from each crew surviving, having missed the sailings through ill health.

150 *Unveiling of the International Air Monument, Plymouth (Photograph – Devon Commercial Photos)*

151 *Air Forces Memorial, Runnymede*

1945'. On the bottom plaque is the epitaph 'THEY FLEW BY DAY AND NIGHT AND GAVE THEIR LIVES TO KEEP FOREVER BRIGHT THAT PRECIOUS LIGHT FREEDOM'.

Elsewhere are tributes to the R.A.F. leaders Bennett, Dowding, Harris, Portal, Slessor and Tedder, and to Arnold, Eaker, and Spaatz of the U.S. Air Force. Also honoured are 107,000 members of the R.A.F., 84,000 members of the U.S.A.F. and 42,000 members of the Soviet Air Force. Of the R.A.F. losses it is recorded that Bomber Command lost 58,378, Coastal Command 13,225, Fighter Command 7,436, S.E.A.C. 6,182 and the Middle East 13,225. Churchill's famous words are also engraved 'NEVER IN THE FIELD OF HUMAN CONFLICT HAS SO MUCH BEEN OWED BY SO MANY TO SO FEW'.

At the beginning of the 18th century Alexander Pope wrote, prophetically, 'On Cooper's Hill eternal wreaths shall grow, while lasts the mountain, or while Thames shall flow'.

On 17th October 1953 the Queen unveiled the Air Forces Memorial on Cooper's Hill, Runnymede, to the memory of over 20,000 airmen who were lost in Second World War operations from bases in the United Kingdom, and North and Western Europe, and who have no known graves. The largest group of those commemorated were from the Royal Air Force, with over 15,000 lost. All parts of the Commonwealth were represented, as were many countries whose airmen flew from Britain after their own lands had been occupied. During the war over 116,000 men and women of Britain and the Commonwealth's Air Forces gave their lives, and almost a third have no known graves. As well as those at Runnymede, other names are similarly recorded throughout the world.

The memorial of Portland stone and with Westmorland green slate roof, is situated in grounds of some six acres planted with trees, magnolias, azalias and rhodedendrons, and looks out over the water meadows where Magna Carta, enshrining man's basic freedoms, was sealed in 1215.

152 *Air Forces Memorial, Runnymede*

The design, by Sir Edward Maufe, is a cloister with curved wings, surmounted by a tower containing a vaulted shrine, and with a triple arched entrance. In front of the shrine is a Stone of Remembrance and above it are three stone figures by Vernon Hill representing Justice, Victory and Courage. An Astral Crown of blue and gold surmounts the tower. The names of the dead are recorded on the walls of the cloister with narrow windows lighting the stone, giving the impression of partially opened books. Arms of the Commonwealth decorate the cloister ceilings.

The site, the grounds, and the buildings themselves combine to make this one of the most impressive of all war memorials (see p. 95).

The Church of St Clement Danes in the Strand was almost completely destroyed by enemy action in 1941, only the steeple and walls remaining. After the war it was restored and re-dedicated as the central church of the R.A.F. Inside is a series of R.A.F. Books of Remembrance, each within a glass case with a cupola surmounted by an eagle stretching its wings, and on the panelling of a wall, in gold lettering, are inscribed the names of those of the R.F.C., R.N.A.S, and R.A.F. who have gained the Victoria Cross. The figure of a mounted Pegasus, by sculptor John Leslie Course, is a tribute to the glider pilots of the Second World War.

153   *Victoria Cross Panel, St. Clement Danes*

Elsewhere in the church are Books of Remembrance for the United States airmen who died in the war and an organ which was the gift of the U.S. Air Force. In the area of the floor inlaid with squadron badges, a large Polish eagle emblem surrounded by smaller squadron badges, forms the memorial to the Polish Air Force 1939-1945.

The Air Transport Auxiliary was a unit created principally to fly planes from aircraft factories to the squadrons awaiting them. One of its pilots was Amy Johnson, the air-woman famous for her 10,000 mile solo flight from Britain to Australia. She died when the aircraft which she was ferrying crashed into the Thames Estuary. It is believed that she lost her way and ran out of fuel. In St Paul's Cathedral there is a wall plaque commemorating the 173 men and women of the Air Transport Auxiliary, representing many nations, who lost their lives in the war. Below the plaque is a glass case containing a Book of Remembrance.

An Astronomical Clock in the north transept of York Minster commemorates the men of the Royal Air Forces of the Commonwealth and their allies who gave their lives in the Second World War while operating from bases in the North East of England. On the West face of the clock the edge of a large convex disc represents the horizon as seen by an airman flying over York towards the south. A Roll of Honour, in a case in front of the clock, contains the names of some 18,000 airmen, most of them in the R.A.F., but 3,537 belonging to the Royal Canadian Air Force and others from Australia, New Zealand, South Africa, Belgium, Holland, France, Norway, Czechoslovakia and Poland.

The memorial is situated in the Minster next to a screen which records the names of the women of Britain and the Commonwealth who gave their lives in the First World War.

In the grounds of the air museum at Elvington is a memorial garden, the centre-piece of which is the remains of a propeller unit mounted on a base of brick and tile. On the base is a plaque with the words 'IN EVERLASTING HOMAGE TO THE COURAGE OF THOSE WHO HAVE FOUND THEIR WINGED VICTORY THROUGH THE SKIES OF YORKSHIRE'.

154   *R.A.F. Memorial, York Minster*

155 *Elvington Memorial Garden*

Heslington Hall, York, now part of York University, was from 1941 to 1945 headquarters of 4 Group Bomber Command, and a metal plaque on the staircase above the main hall records this.

A four-panelled stained-glass window in Ely Cathedral commemorates the members of four R.A.F. Groups, 2, 3, 8 and 100, of Bomber Command, who served in the Ely district during the 1939-45 war. The figures of St George and St Michael, and airmen in uniform, are depicted on this window, together with scenes of aircraft in action and over the Cathedral, and badges of the four Group headquarters.

Under the window are Books of Remembrance for each Group, enclosed in a beautiful wooden case on a stone support. On the case are, once again, the four Group badges and the badge of Bomber Command. Above the memorial hang the colours of several R.A.F. squadrons.

In the east end of the north aisle of Southwell Minster is the Airmen's Chapel. The altar was made in the workshop at R.A.F. Norton near Sheffield, in memory of those from Norton who gave their lives in the Great War. It was made of pieces of aircraft destroyed in the war and given to the Minster in 1919. The communion kneeler was given by R.A.F. Newton in 1984 and the carpet was given by the stage and radio stars Elsie and Doris Waters. A triptych by Hamish Mayle above the altar, depicts the death of Peace and then its resurrection. An R.A.F. flag hangs beside a Polish one, and below the Polish flag is a memorial to Katyn.

The Church of St Michael and All Angels, at the Royal Air Force College at Cranwell, was built in 1962. Incorporated within it is the Memorial Chapel, rebuilt almost exactly as it was originally

A wall to the rear carries emblems of maple leaf and Yorkshire rose and memorial tablets to No. 6 (R.C.A.F.) Group Bomber Command and No. 4 Group Bomber Command R.A.F., which included squadrons of the R.A.F., Royal Australian Air Force, R.C.A.F., and French Air Force. Also within the garden are a large number of memorials to individuals and to specific squadrons, many in the form of seats and standard roses.

156 *Cranwell College Church*

in College Hall, where it was dedicated on 22nd June, 1952 by the Lord Bishop of Lincoln, the Right Reverend Maurice Harland, D.D., D.F.C.

The panelling of the chapel was provided by Hawker-Siddeley and every commissioned officer was asked to donate five shillings towards the cost of the English oak pews. Amongst many other gifts is the beautiful memorial cabinet and Roll of Honour presented by Air Chief Marshal Sir Arthur Longmore, in memory of his son. The names on the finely illuminated Roll are in alphabetical order, with the dates of their Cranwell graduation.

On a large rough-hewn grey-green stone in a garden close to the main Folkestone war memorial is a bronze plaque depicting aircraft engaged in a battle above the Channel and the high cliffs of the area. In the background are shown some bi-planes and the plaque has the badges of both the R.A.F. and the Royal Flying Corps, together with the dates 1939-1945 and 1914-1918. Also there are the motto 'PER ARDUA AD ASTRA' and the inscription 'TO COMMEMORATE THE AIRMEN AND WOMEN WHO SERVED IN TWO WORLD WARS IN DEFENCE OF AN IDEAL'.

157   R.A.F. Memorial, Folkestone

In the churchyard of the Parish Church of Walton-on-the-Naze, an unusual memorial was erected in 1970 by the local R.A.F. Association on the 50th anniversary of the formation of the R.A.F. The memorial is in the form of a stone column and R.A.F. badge, round which stand the propeller blades of a Halifax bomber of 432 Squadron, Royal Canadian Air Force, which crashed in the Naze on the night of 5th / 6th March 1945. The aircraft was returning from an opera-

tional mission and none of its crew survived. The blades were recovered in 1973 and the memorial commemorates the aircrew and also those local men and women who served in the R.A.F.

At the A650 roadside in Tingley, Yorkshire, on a nicely kept site with cherry trees and flowers is a memorial unveiled on 12th November, 1989, to a Halifax bomber crew of 51 Squadron R.A.F. who were killed when their aircraft crashed on 14th November 1944. The simple stone memorial carries the names of the seven dead.

The aircraft had been on 49 operational flights before the crash and the memorial was unveiled by two men who flew 21 bombing missions in her. The memorial was erected by Walter Townend who managed to trace relations of four of the crew. He was 13 years old at the time of the crash and the memory of it remained with him.

On one of a row of houses built for disabled ex-servicemen in Cresswell Street, Barnsley, there is a plaque to two R.C.A.F. airmen who died when their Whitley bomber crashed nearby on 6th January, 1942, the pilot staying with the aircraft to avoid the densely populated areas of the

158   Halifax Memorial, Walton-on-the-Naze

vicinity. The rest of the crew bailed out and survived. The plaque was unveiled on 5th January, 1986.

By the roadside in the village of Pennal in Mid Wales, a stone memorial, in the wall next to the Parish Room, carries a plaque in memory of the six men who died when their R.A.F. Wellington bomber crashed nearby on 17th August 1941. It is interesting to see the geographical spread of the home towns of the six men – Bristol, Kew, Hull, Newcastle, Limerick in Ireland, and Ontario in Canada.

At R.A.F. Stoke Holy Cross radio station, near Norwich, a memorial was unveiled 50 years after the crew of a Blenheim bomber and a civilian meteorologist were killed on a test flight on 18th June 1942. The aircraft crashed after it hit a 360 ft. high radio mast and the memorial is a metal plaque, attached to the former base of the mast, listing the men who died and the details of the accident.

On the wall of the Visitors' Building at the American Military Cemetery at Madingley, Cambridge, there is a memorial plaque listing an aircrew of 577 Squadron, 392 Bomber Group, and with the inscription 'TO THESE GALLANT AMERICAN AIRMEN WHO, ON AUGUST 12 1944, SACRIFICED THEIR LIVES TO PREVENT THEIR AIR-CRAFT FROM CRASHING ON OUR HOMES. THE RESIDENTS OF CHESHUNT AND WALTHAM CROSS, IN THE COUNTY OF HERTFORDSHIRE, DEDICATE THIS PLAQUE IN GRATEFUL MEMORY'.

A bronze tablet on a block of flats in Heigham Street, Norwich, was originally elsewhere in Heigham Street and was moved in 1972 due to the redevelopment of the area. The memorial is a tribute to the crew of a B-24 of 753 Squadron, 458th Bombardment Group U.S. 8th A.A.F., who died nearby on 24th November 1944. 'THE PILOT OF THE BOMBER AS HIS LAST ACT AVOIDED CRASH-ING ON THIS AND SURROUNDING COTTAGES THUS PREVENTING THE POSSIBLE LOSS OF CIVILIAN LIVES.' The nine names of the pilot and his crew follow.

A wooden cross on a stone base near the roadside at Dunnington Lodge, York, is to the memory of three members of the family living in the farmhouse and four members of the crew of a German JU 88 which crashed there on the night of 4th March, 1945. Believed to be the last Luftwaffe aircraft lost on a night sortie over Britain, the JU 88 had previously shot down two Halifax aircraft attempting to land at R.A.F. Lisset after operations over Germany, and then, turning towards R.A.F. Elvington at low level, it hit a tree and crashed into the farmhouse. On 19th June, 1993, at the dedication of the cross, wreaths were laid both by a Luftwaffe veteran and by an R.A.F. one.

This type of chivalry was often conspicuously absent in wartime.

On 24th March 1944, 76 allied officers and N.C.O.'s escaped from Stalag Luft 111 in East Germany. Only three successfully reached Britain and of the 73 who were re-captured, 50 were killed on Hitler's direct orders. A framed tribute to these 50 hangs in the R.A.F. Museum at Hendon. They were from 12 countries, 23 being from Britain, and the memorial lists their names and has national flags and emblems. It was designed and fashioned by Michael McHale in conjunction with the R.A.F. Ex-Prisoners of War Association, and at the top of the frame is an eagle and a crucifix.

The Fleet Air Arm Memorial Church in Yeovilton, Somerset, has an engraved memorial stone laid into the stone-flagged floor. The stone lists Pacific Fleet Air Arm pilots and crew from 849 TBR Squadron (Avengers) – H.M.S. *Victorious*; 1833 Fighter Squadron (Corsairs) – H.M.S. *Illustrious*; and 1839 Fighter Squadron (Hellcats) – H.M.S. *Indomitable*, nine men in all.

The inscription goes on 'Their aircraft were shot down during attacks on oil refineries at Palembang, Sumatra in January 1945. They were imprisoned at Changi Gaol, Singapore, and executed by their Japanese captors at the war's end in August 1945. NONE OF US SHOULD FORGET'.

As might be expected, some of the more significant memorials are related to the Battle of Britain.

On 9th July, 1993, Queen Elizabeth the Queen Mother unveiled a memorial to those who flew in the Battle of Britain, at a site on top of the white cliffs at Capel-le-Ferne, near Dover. The stone statue of a pilot, seated on a base bearing the crests of almost 70 squadrons involved in the battle, was covered by a Second World War parachute which was lifted off by R.A.F. officers, watched by the 92 year old Queen Mother. Blustering wind and rain prevent an air display of Spitfire, Hurricane and Blenheim aircraft but did not prevent 130 veterans of the 1940 battle, and several thousand others, from attending the ceremony.

The statue of the young fighter pilot looking out to sea forms the centre-piece of an arena some 100 yards across and featuring the three blades of a propeller cut into the ground, with the statue and base as its hub (see p. 95).

The inspiration for the memorial came from the chairman of the Battle of Britain Memorial Trust, Wing Commander Geoffrey Page, D.S.O., D.F.C. and bar, who was a 20-year-old pilot in the summer of 1940. He was badly injured during the battle and severe burns to his hands and face resulted in two years in hospital, but he returned to fly again until his wartime career was terminated after further injuries resulting from crash-landing his Spitfire at Arnhem.

A unit at Queen Victoria Hospital, East Grinstead, headed by Sir Archibald McIndoe, specialised in the first modern plastic surgery, and the wartime patients of McIndoe became known as the Guinea-Pig Club.

Information about the Battle of Britain is provided on boards in the car park of the memorial at Capel-le-Ferne, and a brass plaque on a flag-pole there has the inscription, 'THIS FLAGPOLE

WAS DISMANTLED AT THE TIME OF THE CLOSURE OF R.A.F. BIGGIN HILL IN KENT IN OCTOBER 1992. IT STANDS AS A SENTINEL TO THIS MEMORIAL AND SERVES FOREVER AS A PERPETUAL LINK WITH ALL FIGHTER STATIONS FROM WHICH R.A.F. SQUADRONS FLEW IN THE BATTLE OF BRITAIN'.

A Royal Air Force Chapel has been created in Westminster Abbey from part of the Henry VII Chapel. The main feature is a beautiful stained-glass window designed by Hugh Easton and unveiled by George VI on 10th July, 1947. This is the Battle of Britain Window and is dedicated to those who died in that crucial period of 1940.

The window comprises 48 panels in four rows of 12. The top row consists of winged seraphims, and in part of the second and third rows are representations of the Incarnation and the Resurrection, the Pieta, and the Crucifixion, each with an onlooking and kneeling airman. Most of the remaining panels have badges of the 68 squadrons which took part in the battle, together with those of the R.A.F. and the Fleet Air Arm, the Royal Arms and the flags of the countries from which the pilots came. At the very foot of the window are the words from Shakespeare's *Henry V* – 'We few, we happy few, we band of brothers' (see p. 95).

In the stonework of the chapel below the window and behind the altar are the names of six R.A.F. leaders during the war, DOUGLAS, DOWDING, HARRIS, NEWHALL, PORTAL and TEDDER.

Battle of Britain Commemorative Lace Panels were made in Nottingham after the war by Dobson-Browne Limited. A limited number of the 15 ft x 5 ft. 6 in. panels were made and records of their present whereabouts are not complete. Canada, New Zealand, Australia and South Africa each had panels, R.A.F. Hendon and Nottingham each have two, Southwell Minster has one, R.A.F. Bentley Priory has one, Southampton, Croydon, Beckenham, Sheerness, and Apeldoorn in Holland each have one and there is one at Dowding's birthplace, Moffat.

There is one on display at the R.A.F. Museum at Hendon, and amongst the scenes and objects depicted are St Paul's, the damaged House of Commons, Buckingham Palace, The Old Bailey, the City Temple in Holborn in ruins, Bow Church, the ruined St Clement Danes, the walls of the Guildhall, a country cottage, a mansion, Spitfires, Hurricanes, Defiants, M.E's, Stukas and Dorniers in combat, a fighter pilot standing by his aircraft, an airman bailing-out, firemen at work, an A.A. gun and searchlight in action, and a variety of Commonwealth badges and emblems.

The edging of the panel comprises ripening ears of corn representing the season during which the Battle of Britain took place, and at the foot are Churchill's words 'Never was so much owed by so many to so few'.

R.A.F. Biggin Hill is now closed, but St George's Chapel of Remembrance remains as a reminder of perhaps the most famous station of the Battle of Britain.

Biggin Hill squadrons provided cover for the Dunkirk invasion in May 1940, and, from August to the end of the year, seven squadrons from the airfield were involved in the Battle of Britain, accounting for the destruction of some 600 enemy aircraft. Throughout the war, 1,400 enemy were destroyed by the 50 or so squadrons of the sector.

The foundation stone for the Chapel was laid by Air Chief Marshal Lord Dowding, and the building was dedicated on 10th November 1951 by the Bishop of Rochester. This beautiful Chapel has so many impressive features, that no short description can possibly do it justice.

The reredos panels have inscribed on them the names of the 453 pilots of the 52 squadrons of the Biggin Hill sector, plus two Station Commanders, who lost their lives in the war. The names are recorded by squadron and the badge of each squadron appears on the panel. Above the reredos are the battle honours of 'DUNKIRK',

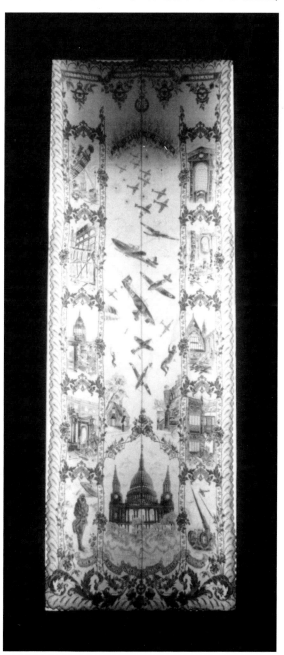

159 *Battle of Britain Lace Panel*

83

'BATTLE OF BRITAIN', 'DIEPPE', 'PAS DE CALAIS', 'NORMANDY', 'ARNHEM', 'RUHR' and 'RHINE'.

The altar frontal is embroidered with the emblems of the British Isles and the Allied Countries, and a quotation from Psalm 63, 'In the shadow of thy wings will I rejoice'. The font was presented by the Marshal of the Royal Air Force, Lord Tedder, in 1957, on behalf of the Royal Air Force Association. A Roll of Honour and a Book of Remembrance provide the names of those from Biggin Hill who died in the Battle of Britain, and those who died during the war.

The windows are the most striking aspect of the whole building. Those in the body of the Chapel were made in the studio of Hugh Easton who designed the Battle of Britain memorial window in Westminster Abbey, and were donated variously by companies, or R.A.F. formations, or to commemorate individuals. Alike in basic design, one, for example, has the inscription 'And some there be who have no memorial', and was given anonymously. Another is to two brothers, Flying Officer Ivo Cuthbert, killed in May 1940, and Major Sidney John Cuthbert, of the Scots Guards, killed in July 1944. Others were given by Rolls Royce, Hawker, and by Lloyds.

In St George's Room the west window depicts St George, and was installed in 1981 to commemorate the 40th Anniversary of the Battle of Britain. In the top part of this window are the badges of the seven squadrons serving at Biggin Hill during the battle. Another four windows in St George's Room were installed in 1985 to commemorate the ground services of the R.A.F., 'Ground Control', 'Rescue Services', 'Aircraft Servicing', and 'Parachute Packing'. In the corner of the 'Ground Control' window are shown three Military Medals, awarded to three W.A.A.F. members for bravery during two 1940 attacks on the airfield. All the windows in St George's Room were designed by Goddard and Gibbs (see p. 96).

There are also, within the Chapel, plaques commemorating Polish and Canadian airmen, a plaque of Delft tiles given in gratitude for the hospitality shown to Dutch airmen, and a low cupboard on a stand, in memory of 100 Norwegian pilots who died whilst serving with R.A.F. Fighter Command. On the doors of the cupboard are the badges of 331 and 332 Squadrons. Finally a wooden bench seat was presented in 1962 in memory of the American pilots who gave their lives whilst serving with Fighter Command.

Outside the Spitfire and Hurricane Memorial Buildings at Manston airfield near Ramsgate is a memorial to mark the 50th Anniversary of the Battle of Britain, and to honour those who fought and died in it, and also, more unusually, to 'all the people of Thanet who endured the conflict'.

The words are engraved on the polished face of an irregular shaped piece of dark granite mounted on a brick base. Also on the granite face is an interesting metal relief showing the City of London under attack with searchlights, barrage balloons and aircraft, and with a *Daily Herald*

160   *Battle of Britain Memorial, Manston*

front page carrying the words 'The Battle of Britain'. The buildings behind are themselves memorials, and the Hurricane Gallery was officially opened on 7th October, 1988, by Dame Vera Lynn.

161   *Croydon Airport Memorial*

162 *Unveiling Ceremony at Hawkinge (Photograph – 'Dover Express')*

At St Luke's Church, Whyteleafe, Surrey, under a commemorative plaque to the Battle of Britain, with the dates 'AUG. TO OCT. 1940', is a Book of Remembrance, in a glass case, recording all the names of the R.A.F. pilots engaged in the battle, many of them serving at nearby R.A.F. Kenley, where Nos. 64, 66, 253, 501, 615 and 616 Squadrons operated at various times during the battle.

Croydon Airport was London's first international airport, but returned to being a front line fighter station in the Battle of Britain.

A 23 ft. high granite-faced obelisk, surmounted by a bronze eagle, stands alongside Purley Way, Croydon, as a tribute to the fighter pilots who flew from the airfield and died and also to all others connected with the station during the war who lost their lives. The memorial, designed by ex-pilot Alan Savage, who was also largely responsible for fund-raising, was unveiled on 27th October 1991 by Air Marshal Sir William Wratten, before a crowd of some 2,000 people.

Badges of R.A.F. Fighter Command and 72, 85, 111, 92, 145, 401, 501, 605 and 607 Squadrons are displayed on the surface of the obelisk and there are tributes to many service and civilian units and organisations, for example, the Royal Artillery, Honourable Artillery Company, Home Guard, W.A.A.F., A. T. S., Royal Observer Corps, Medical Staff, Police and so on. Also inscribed are Churchill's words 'Never in the field of human conflict was so much owed by so many to so few'. The memorial is floodlit at night throughout the year and the area round it has been planted with thousands of spring bulbs and other flowers.

On 29th April, 1978 a memorial was unveiled, in front of the former gymnasium, to all who served at R.A.F. Hawkinge, Kent. A photograph taken at that time shows Marshal of the

163 *Bradwell Bay Memorial*

Royal Air Force, Sir William F. Dickson, together with Roy Humphreys who was responsible for erecting the memorial, a granite block with a bronze tablet.

Part of the wording on the tablet refers to providing 'a memorial to all who served at or flew from this green swathe never to return'. Unfortunately the memorial on Aerodrome Road is now surrounded by little that is green, as a village by-pass, a housing estate and other buildings encroach.

On the site of the old airfield a dramatic memorial, featuring a scale model of a Mosquito aircraft nose down into the ground, commemorates the men who flew from R.A.F. Bradwell Bay from 1942 to 1945. Within sight of the power station which now dominates the estuary, the memorial is on a paved stone base flanked by rose beds and with tablets recording the dead. A central tablet has the inscription 'ERECTED IN MEMORY OF THE 121 MEMBERS OF THE ALLIED AIR FORCES WHO IN ANSWER TO THE CALL OF DUTY LEFT THIS AIRFIELD TO FLY INTO THE BLUE FOREVER'.

R.A.F. Warmwell, four miles east of Dorchester, was a fighter station which played an important part in the defence of the South Coast during the war. A memorial dedicated to the men and women of the R.A.F. and the U.S. Air Force who died whilst serving there, has been erected on the edge of a recreation ground in Airfield Close, part of a modern housing estate built on the site of the old airfield. The simple stone memorial has a brick path leading up to it and attractive wrought iron gates decorated by the outline of aircraft.

In Harbour Parade, Ramsgate, the Royal Oak public house has upon its outside wall a metal plaque commemorating 27 Air Sea Rescue of the Royal Air Force H.Q. Dover, who were stationed at Ramsgate from 1942 to 1945 and based at the pub. The plaque has a relief of a rescue vessel and the words 'THE SEA SHALL NOT HAVE THEM' and also records the fact that over 13,000 British, allied and enemy aircrew were rescued by their actions.

St Peter's Church, Little Rissington, Gloucestershire, has a window to the memory of those who lost their lives from 1938 onwards whilst serving at R.A.F. Little Rissington. During

165 *Air Sea Rescue Memorial, Ramsgate*

the war, No. 6 Service Flying Training School was based there. The window was dedicated 18th December, 1983 by the Lord Bishop of Gloucester.

A metal plaque on a simple memorial by a disused runway at Down Ampney in Gloucestershire, commemorates the wartime history of the airfield. From Down Ampney, in 1944-45, 'Dakotas of 48 and 271 Squadrons of R.A.F. Transport Command, carried the 1st and 6th Airborne Division, units of the Air Despatch Regiment, and Horsa gliders to Normandy, Arnhem and on the crossing the Rhine operations'.

At the side of the road at Tarrant Rushton, Dorset, where the aerodrome once was, a large piece of rough-hewn stone has plaques honouring those who served there from 1943 onwards, including 298 and 644 Squadrons R.A.F. and 'C' Squadron Glider Pilot Regiment. A picture of an aircraft towing a glider is engraved on one of the plaques. The memorial was unveiled 6th June, 1982.

A stone plaque in St Andrew's Church, Little Snoring, Norfolk, records that the church was

164 *Warmwell Memorial*

86

166 *Tarrant Rushton Memorial*

used for worship by the R.A.F. in 1944-45. Rather more surprising is the presence in the church of boards listing the victories claimed and honours won by the airmen flying from Little Snoring. The two victory boards give each date, squadron, crew, place and claim – for example 'Lille area. ME110. destroyed. 8/5/44'. The two honours boards again list the date, squadron, name and award.

Llandaff Cathedral near Cardiff has plaques in memory of 614 County of Glamorgan Squadron, and more generally to the British and allied airmen killed in action during the war. This latter memorial was dedicated on 7th October 1989 by the Dean of Llandaff, and bears the name of the Aircrew Association of South Glamorgan.

St Peter's Church at Tempsford, in Bedfordshire, has a stone plaque under the First World War stained-glass memorial window. This plaque is 'IN THANKSGIVING FOR ALL WHO OPERATED FROM R.A.F. TEMPSFORD AIRFIELD 1941-1945, FOR THE RESISTANCE WORKERS WHO WERE FLOWN TO ENEMY OCCUPIED EUROPE, AND IN REMEMBRANCE OF THOSE WHO GAVE THEIR LIVES FOR FREEDOM'. Badges of 138 and 161 R.A.F.

Squadrons hang on the wall near the memorial together with an aerial photograph of the airfield and other momentoes.

Derwent Dam in Derbyshire, because it closely resembles the Ruhr dams, was used by 617 Squadron R.A.F., the 'Dambusters', for low level practice and bomb aiming techniques before the famous attacks in May 1943 from R.A.F. Scampton.

A memorial stone in the West Tower of the Derwent Dam mentions its use at that time, and pays tribute to the men of the Squadron. At the head of the stone is the squadron badge and its motto 'APRES MOI LE DELUGE', at the foot are the words 'THEY PAID FOR OUR FREEDOM'. A metal plaque in the wall of the tower above the stone has the inscription 'THIS PLAQUE UNVEILED ON 16TH MAY 1988 COMMEMORATES THE NIGHT OF 16TH-17TH MAY 1943, WHEN 19 LANCASTERS OF 617 SQD. R.A.F. ATTACKED THE RUHR DAMS AT LOW LEVEL. ALSO REMEMBERED HERE ARE THE 204 617 SQD. AIRCREW WHO LAID DOWN THEIR LIVES BETWEEN 1943-1945'.

In carrying out the attacks using the bouncing bombs specially designed by Barnes Wallis, the Squadron led by Wing Commander Guy Gibson lost eight of 19 aircraft and although the Möhne and Eder dams were breached, real damage to the German war effort was not significant or lasting. The psychological importance of the raid was never in doubt, however. Gibson, at 24 already the holder of a D.S.O. and two D.F.C.'s. was awarded the V.C. but died the following year on a Mosquito sortie. The extremely high percentage loss of aircraft in the attack did not encourage similar raids. Max Hastings, author of *Bomber Command* quotes Sir Arthur Harris as saying, many years later, 'Any operation deserving of the Victoria Cross, by its nature, is unfit to be repeated at regular intervals'.

167 *'Dambusters' Memorial – Derwent Dam*

168 *'Dambusters' Memorial – Woodhall Spa*

A watercolour hanging in Bamford Parish Church of a Lancaster flying low over Derwent Dam was presented by 617 Squadron when it disbanded in 1982. It marks the fact that the church was used as a turning point by aircrew practising for the raid on the Ruhr dams in 1943.

In Royal Square Gardens, Woodhall Spa, has been erected the imaginative memorial to 617 Squadron R.A.F., the 'Dambusters', who were based at Woodhall after originally being at Scampton.

The York-stone memorial, some 10 ft. high, represents a dam, and in the centre a grey-green section, sloping outwards, represents the torrent of released water. On this section is the squadron badge, again depicting a shattered dam, and the motto 'Apres moi, le deluge'. Also here are the squadron battle honours, starting with 'The Dams 1943'. To each side of this section are three green-slate panels with the the names of 204 aircrew who lost their lives in the war. Above are the words 'THEY DIED FOR YOUR FREEDOM'.

This beautiful memorial was dedicated on 17th May, 1987 and stands in a well-kept, pretty garden with a backing screen of trees. The architect was K. Stevens, A.R.I.B.A.

The memorial stone to 57 and 630 Squadrons R.A.F. at East Kirkby, Lincolnshire, stands on the site of the former guardroom of the airfield from which the two squadrons operated from August 1943 to April 1945, with the loss of over 1,000 aircrew. The memorial, with a low metal surround incorporating the shape of a bomber and the numbers of the squadrons, was dedicated in October 1979.

The roadside memorial stone to 101 Squadron R.A.F. was unveiled in July 1978 on the village green of Ludford Magna, Lincolnshire. In 1943 the squadron was chosen to carry special equipment to jam German direction aids for their fighters, and because of this 101 flew on every major raid from autumn 1943 to April 1945. In less than two years the squadron lost over 500 men, and there is a roll of honour in the village

169 *East Kirkby Memorial*

170 *Bardney Memorial*

church. The memorial carries the words 'TO SERVE WAS THEIR HIGHEST AIM'.

From December 1942 to April 1945, 100 Squadron R.A.F. operated from Waltham, near Grimsby, with Lancaster bombers. Their first raid was on Nuremburg early in 1943 and their last on the S.S. barracks at Berchtesgarten on 25th April 1945. A stone memorial to the squadron, which lost 116 aircraft, was unveiled in November 1978, by the side of the A16 which cuts through the old airfield. On the memorial are the squadron badge and the motto 'Do not attack the hornets' nest'. Also there is a plaque to the Royal Observer Corps Bravo 3 Post Fulston.

Wing Commander J. Bennett, D.F.C., the first Commanding Officer of 550 Squadron R.A.F., appropriately unveiled a stone pillar in Lancaster Approach in August 1982 as a memorial to those who served at R.A.F. North Killingholme from January 1944 to October 1945. The airfield has now been swallowed up by an industrial estate. On the pillar is the squadron badge and a translation of its Latin motto, 'Through Fire We Conquer'.

The memorial to 166 Squadron R.A.F., made of Yorkshire stone, stands in a well-kept garden with hardwood seats and a conifer screen in the Lincolnshire village of Kirmington. Unveiled in September 1988 the memorial carries a bronze plaque referring to the 921 who gave their lives while serving at R.A.F. Kirmington from 1943 to 1945, and also thanking the villagers for their wartime comradeship. A Book of Remembrance in the church records the names of the dead.

A Garden of Remembrance to the 1,000 aircrew who lost their lives on flying missions from R.A.F. Elsham Wolds from 1941 to 1945, was dedicated in August 1981. The garden is constructed in front of the Anglian Water Authorities buildings which were sited on the end of the former main runway, and features a granite column with the badges of 103 and 576 Squadrons, the squadron numbers cut into the grass, and a propeller recovered from a crashed Lancaster bomber.

An original Lancaster propeller mounted on a low wall on the village green of Bardney in Lincolnshire, commemorates the dead of 9 Squadron R.A.F. The squadron flew during the war from Honington and Waddington and finally from Bardney, from 1943 to 1945.

At the unveiling ceremony in October 1980 were former members of the Norwegian Resistance, and stone from Norway makes up part of the memorial wall. Attacks carried out on the German battleship 'Tirpitz' as it hid in Tromso fjord were among the most dangerous raids attempted by Bomber Command.

An unusual feature of the memorial at Wickenby airfield, some six miles from Lincoln, is a three-foot-high bronze figure representing Icarus. The figure is on an eight foot tall stone column with a flintstone surround and below Icarus are the words 'ROYAL AIR FORCE WICKENBY, NO. 1 GROUP BOMBER COMMAND 1942-1945. IN MEMORY OF ONE THOUSAND AND EIGHTY MEN OF 12 & 626 SQUADRONS WHO GAVE THEIR LIVES ON OPERATIONS FROM THIS AIRFIELD IN THE OFFENSIVE AGAINST GERMANY AND THE LIBERATION OF OCCUPIED EUROPE'. On the sides of the column are the squadron badges, that of 12 Squadron having a fox mask and the motto 'LEADS THE FIELD'.

171 *Wickenby Memorial (Photograph – Rena Boorman)*

One of the wreaths at the memorial, when viewed in summer 1993, carried a card reading 'WARREN GEORGE. Sergeant Air Gunner 12 Squadron R.A.F. Shot down over Rotterdam. 30.3.1943. Memories never fade, old friend, Bill (Mac) Conroy'.

The memorial, designed and sculpted by Margarita Wood was dedicated on 6th September, 1981.

In a small roadside garden in the Yorkshire village of Burn, a granite memorial, flanked by two metal seats, commemorates those who served in 578 Squadron R.A.F. Burn from 1944 to 1945, and not far away in the grounds of Selby Abbey is another granite memorial to 51 Squadron R.A.F. who served at Dishforth, Chivenor and Snaith during the war.

On 19th August, 1990 a memorial was unveiled at Alamein Barracks, Driffield in Yorkshire, to the memory of those who died almost exactly 50 years before, on the 15th August, 1940, in an air raid on what was then an R.A.F. station. There were 14 dead, mainly of the R.A.F. or East Yorkshire Regiment but also including A.C.W. M. Hudson, who, it is suggested, was the first W.A.A.F. to be killed on active service in the war. The names of the dead are on a metal plaque attached to the stone memorial. Amongst those who attended the unveiling were representatives of 77 and 102 Squadrons and of the East Yorkshire Regiment.

At the entrance to Elvington Airfield is a memorial to 77 Squadron who operated from the airfield from 1942-44. Originally formed in 1916 for the defence of Edinburgh the squadron has as its badge a thistle and the motto (in Latin) 'To be, rather than seem'. The memorial consists of a bronze eagle and thistles on a marble column in front of a curved stone wall. On the wall two plaques give the squadron history and include the quotation from Psalm 139, 'THOUGH I TAKE THE WINGS OF DARKNESS AND REMAIN IN THE UTTERMOST PARTS OF THE SKY – THY RIGHT HAND SHALL HOLD ME'.

A pair of stained-glass windows in the Church of St Gregory the Great in Kirknewton, Northumberland, commemorates both nearby R.A.F. Milfield and an individual airman. The left-hand panel, depicting St George, has an R.A.F. badge and the words 'THIS WINDOW IS ERECTED BY OFFICERS, N.C.O.'S, AIRMEN AND AIRWOMEN, R.A.F. MILFIELD TO KEEP ALIVE THE MEMORY OF THE MEN WHO DIED FOR THEIR COUNTRY WHILE FLYING FROM MILFIELD R.A.F. STATION'. The right-hand panel is to Lieutenant Commander D. R. B. Cosh.

On a grassy area backed by young trees at the side of the A167 at Dalton-on-Tees in North Yorkshire, stands a memorial to those who served in the R.A.F. and R.C.A.F. at Croft Airfield between 1941 and 1945. It consists of a stone base supporting the sculptured figure of an airman, in flying kit with a parachute at his feet, shielding his eyes from the sun as he looks up to the sky.

172 *Croft Memorial*

The memorial, by sculptor Helen Granger Young, was unveiled on the 26th September, 1987 by Brigadier General 'Bill' Newson of the R.C.A.F. and dedicated by the Dean of York, the Very Reverend John Southgate.

Information displayed in a showcase nearby gives the opening date for operations at Croft as October 1941 for R.A.F. Squadron 78 who later took part in a 1,000 bomber raid in May 1942 flying Halifax aircraft. The last operation was on April 25th, 1945 and amongst other squadrons to use Croft were 431 R.C.A.F ('Iroquois') which flew 2,573 sorties and lost 72 aircraft and 490 aircrew, and 434 R.C.A.F. ('Bluenose') which flew 2,595 sorties with losses of 74 aircraft and 493 aircrew.

Four squadrons of the Royal Canadian Air Force, 420 'Snowy Owl', 431 'Iroquois', 434 'Bluenose', and 425 'Aloutte', are commemorated by a granite memorial on the North Yorkshire village green of Tholthorpe, and also by a mile long avenue of oaks and maples between the village and the old airfield which was the scene of their wartime operations. Part of the inscription on a metal plaque on the granite base reads, 'DEDICATED BY THE PEOPLE OF THOLTHORPE AND THE SURVIVING VETERANS. JUNE 7 1986'.

At the roadside in the pretty North Yorkshire village of Sutton on Forest is the site of the former village pound, where once stray animals were kept in a walled enclosure and from where they could be recovered on payment of a fee. On this site on the 2nd June, 1990 a memorial, in the form of a sundial surmounting a grey-green stone base, and erected by families and former colleagues, was dedicated 'to all who served at EASTMOOR in World War II, many of whom gave their lives, and in gratitude to the people of Yorkshire who welcomed them'. On the sides of the memorial are the badges of the 432, 429 and 415 Squadrons of the Royal Canadian Air Force. The sundial is surrounded by a pretty garden with newly planted trees and with a wooden bench to one side.

A memorial cairn in front of the village hall at Linton-on-Ouse in North Yorkshire commemorates the dead of the Royal Canadian Air Force Squadrons who operated from June 1943 to May 1945 from the nearby airfield. Part of the inscription on the cairn reads 'This memorial cairn has been erected that we and generations to come might pause and reflect upon the dedication and sacrifice of those who died in the cause of freedom and human dignity while serving with 408 (Goose) Squadron and 426 (Thunderbird) Squadron'.

The memorial was erected jointly by former Squadron members and by the people of the village, and maple leaves and Yorkshire roses are carved into the front of the base. Over 200 veterans travelled to the dedication ceremony on 4th May, 1990 when the unveiling was performed by the Lord Lieutenant of Yorkshire, Sir Marcus Worsley.

On Pocklington airfield, now used principally by the Wolds Gliding Club, stands a grey marble column surmounted by an urn of the same material, with a low post and chain surround, paving stones and flowers. On a bronze plaque attached to the column are two squadron badges and the words 'THE HOME OF NO. 102 (CEYLON) SQUADRON R.A.F. AND NO. 405 (VANCOUVER) SQUADRON R.C.A.F., NO. 4 GROUP BOMBER COMMAND DURING WORLD WAR II, FROM WHERE SO MANY GAVE THEIR LIVES IN THE CAUSE OF FREEDOM'. The memorial was raised by old comrades who served in the squadrons.

A simple stone, outside the Alfold Barn Inn, south of Guildford, has a plaque commemorating the wartime operations from Dunsfold

174 *Waddington Memorial*

Aerodrome of 400, 414 and 430 Squadrons of the Royal Canadian Air Force; 98, 180, 231, 667 Squadrons and 83 Group Support Unit of the R.A.F.; and 320 Squadron of the Royal Netherland Naval Air Service. Badges of the three air forces complete the inscription.

In the Lincolnshire village of Waddington is an unusual memorial in the form of a clock with black dials and gold numerals and hands, mounted on a tall post, similar in design to a lamp post. Nearby is triangular brick wall on which is a metal plaque and the inscription 'LEST WE FORGET. THIS CLOCK IS A MEMORIAL TO THOSE MEMBERS OF 463 AND 467 ROYAL AUSTRALIAN AIR FORCE SQUADRONS WHO GAVE THEIR LIVES WHILE SERVING WITH NO. 5 GROUP R.A.F. BOMBER COMMAND DURING THE 1939-1945 WAR. 10TH MAY 1987'.

On a corner garden plot, at the end of the road to R.A.F. Binbrook a memorial to 460 Squadron, Royal Australian Air Force, was unveiled in September 1973, the Squadron's wartime commander Air Commodore Sir Hugh Edwards, V.C., participating in the ceremony. The memorial stone pays tribute 'TO THOSE WHO SERVED. BREIGHTON (YORKS) BINBROOK (LINCS). FROM 15TH NOVEMBER 1941 TO 2ND OCTOBER 1945'. Over 6,000 sorties were flown from which nearly 1,000 men did not return, and a Roll of Honour can be seen in St Mary's Church.

173 *Pocklington Memorial*

175 *Watton Memorial*

At the former headquarter building of R.A.F. Watton, in Norfolk, is a memorial to the men of the R.A.F. and Commonwealth Air Forces who lost their lives serving at Watton. The memorial is in the form of a propeller recovered from a Blenheim bomber shot down over Denmark on 13th August 1940 while operating out of Watton.

A nearby polished marble memorial is dedicated to those who served in the 25th Bomb Group of the U.S. 8th A.A.F. at Watton in 1944 and 1945.

A memorial dedicated on 16th June 1991 to those who served at R.A.F. Martlesham Heath, Suffolk, matches in design the memorial erected in June 1946 to commemorate the 72 dead of the 356 Fighter Group U.S. 8th A.A.F. who flew from Martlesham from October 1943 to November 1945. One of the R.A.F. squadrons which used the airfield before the 356th F.G. was Eagle Squadron 71 which was there during part of 1941 and in 1942 up to May when it transferred to Debden and eventually became part of the U.S. 8th A.A.F.

Both memorials are of Weldon stone and stand together on what was the parade ground in the centre of the old base, which is now developed as an industrial estate. The R.A.F. memor-

176 *Kings Cliffe Memorial*

ial was erected due to the work of a group of local businessmen and enthusiasts, and the unveiling ceremony featured a fly-past by the Battle of Britain flight. The American memorial is said to be the first erected in Europe to commemorate Second World War American dead.

The memorial to those who served at Kings Cliffe airfield near Wansford in Northamptonshire is notable for its very unusual design. One half, a pillar representing the fuselage of an aircraft, together with one wing, carries badges of the 8th U.S. A.A.F. and the 20th Fighter Group, while the other similar half has the insignia of the R.A.F. A connecting panel between the two parts commemorates the American, British, Belgian and Commonwealth airmen who used the airfield at different periods of the war. The memorial was unveiled in 1983 by the Duke of Gloucester.

As a reminder that Americans fought for the allied cause before Pearl Harbour on 7th December 1941, there is the Eagle Squadrons' memorial facing the statue of Roosevelt in Grosvenor Square. The memorial, a bronze eagle with outstretched wings, on a stone obelisk, was unveiled in 1986 by the Prime Minister Margaret Thatcher. Present was Charles F. Sweeny, founder of the squadrons in 1940.

Sweeny, a godson of the wife of William Randolph Hearst, the American newspaper magnate, was already a well-known social figure before the war, and in 1940 remained in this country despite the warning by Joseph Kennedy,

J.F.K.'s father and American Ambassador in London 'This country is finished. It will be overrun by the Germans in a matter of weeks. You and your children must get out'. (Ironically, his eldest son, Joseph Kennedy Junior, died over Suffolk when his aircraft blew up on 13th August 1944, and his son-in-law, the Marquess of Hartington, also died on active service.)

Instead Sweeny formed No. 71, the first of three R.A.F. Eagle Squadrons, with volunteer American pilots on 19th September, 1940, at Church Fenton, Yorkshire. The formation followed of No. 121 Squadron on 14th May, 1941, and of No. 133 Squadron on 1st August, 1941.

The motto of each squadron appears on the memorial. That of 71 Squadron is 'FIRST FROM THE EYRIES', 121 is 'FOR LIBERTY' and 133 is 'LET US TO THE BATTLE'. Also inscribed are the words 'THIS MEMORIAL IS TO THE MEMORY OF THE 244 AMERICAN AND 16 BRITISH FIGHTER PILOTS AND OTHER PERSONNEL WHO SERVED IN THE THREE R.A.F. EAGLE SQUADRONS PRIOR TO THE PARTICIPATION OF THE UNITED STATES IN THE SECOND WORLD WAR'.

In September 1942, all three squadrons were quietly transferred at Debden, Essex, from the R.A.F. to the U.S. 8th Air Force where they were renumbered 334, 335 and 336. Debden became known as 'The Eagles' Nest'.

Grosvenor Chapel in South Audley Street, not far from Grosvenor Square, was much used by American servicemen as a place of worship during the war years, and a stone plaque on the front outside wall commemorates the fact.

178   *Grosvenor Chapel*

A memorial stone in the R.A.F. Museum at Hendon is in memory of the 350,000 Americans who served in Great Britain as members of the 8th Air Force from 1942 to 1945. More than 26,000 of them died in action.

The stone was originally erected in Liverpool in May 1984, but was relocated due to the development of the original site. Inscribed on the stone are the names of Medal of Honour recipients, the badge of the 8th, and likenesses of a B-17 Flying Fortress, a Liberator, a Thunderbolt, a Lightning and a Mustang.

A small chapel behind the High Altar of St Paul's Cathedral is now the American Memorial

177   *Eagle Squadrons Memorial*

179 *U.S. Memorial, Hendon*

Chapel. It was created as a British tribute to the 28,000 Americans based in Britain who lost their lives in the Second World War. The Chapel was dedicated on 26th November, 1958, in the presence of the Queen and Vice President Richard Nixon, and contains a 500 page illuminated Roll of Honour, and stained-glass windows depicting a soldier's service, sacrifice and resurrection. Borders carry emblems of the States of America (see p. 113).

On a five-sided base of stone and brick, and surrounded by low metal railings, a memorial in Bushey Park in south-west London has an inscription 'THIS TABLET MARKS THE SITE OF THE EUROPEAN HEADQUARTERS OF THE UNITED STATES ARMY AIR FORCES JULY 1942–DECEMBER 1944 AND IS DEDICATED BY THE ROYAL AIR FORCE TO THEIR COMRADES-IN-ARMS. IT IS THROUGH FRATERNITY THAT LIBERTY IS SAVED – VICTOR HUGO'.

The monument is several hundred yards from the gates of the park and some way from the paths and roadways and so can easily be overlooked.

In the entrance hall of Wycombe Abbey School, High Wycombe, a wooden plaque records the fact that the school served as headquarters of the U.S. 8th Bomber Command from April 1942 until January 1944 and then as headquarters of the 8th Army Air Force until October 1945. The inscription goes on 'IN THESE BUILDINGS WERE CONCEIVED, PLANNED AND DIRECTED THE NIGHTLY AIR ASSAULTS ON GERMANY WHICH, WITH THOSE OF THE ROYAL AIR FORCE, PAVED THE WAY FOR ALLIED VICTORY IN EUROPE'.

Elvedon Hall in Suffolk was the headquarters during the war of Third Air Division, U.S. 8th A.A.F. A stained-glass window in the Elvedon Church of St Andrew and St Patrick is in memory of the members of the Division who died between 1942-1945. Designed by Hugh Easton the window depicts a kneeling airman being blessed by an angel with outstretched blue wings. In the background are American aircraft and an English country scene (see p. 113).

Outside the Council Chamber in Cambridge Guildhall is a Stars and Stripes on a base and with a plaque explaining that the flag was presented to the mayor of the city in September 1945 by the senior U.S. officer in Cambridge, Col. Colston, on behalf of his government and in memory of the U.S. forces' association with Cambridge during the war. In the Mayor's parlour, there is a plaque presented to the Borough of Cambridge on 2nd August 1945, by the U.S. 8th A.A.F. on the occasion of their receiving the Freedom of the Borough and in appreciation of the friendship extended to the 8th from 1942 to 1945.

180 *Bushey Park Memorial*

C17 *St George's Church, Arreton*

C18 *Air Forces Memorial, Runnymede*

C19 *Battle of Britain Memorial, Capel-le-Ferne*

C20 *Battle of Britain Window, Westminster Abbey*
   (Photograph – Jarrold Publishing)

GROUND CONTROL

GIVEN BY
11 GROUP

RESCUE SERVICES

GIVEN BY
KENT WING
OF THE
AIR TRAINING
CORPS

AIRCRAFT SERVICING

GIVEN BY THE
RAF
ASSOCIATION
AND THE
HALTON
APPRENTICES
ASSOCIATION

PARACHUTE PACKING

GIVEN BY
MEMBERS OF
THE PUBLIC

To either side of the entrance porch to Chelmsford Cathedral are stained-glass windows, one with coats of arms of the United States and the U.S. Air Force, and the other with coats of arms of the United Kingdom and Essex. Each has the inscription, 'TO THE GLORY OF GOD AND IN GRATITUDE FOR TASKS AND FRIENDSHIP SHARED BY THE PEOPLE OF ESSEX AND THE UNITED STATES AIR FORCE BETWEEN 1942 AND 1945 THIS PORCH WAS ENRICHED AND BEAUTIFIED BY ESSEX FRIENDS OF THE AMERICAN PEOPLE IN 1953'.

181 *Chelmsford Cathedral Window*

The 2nd Air Division (U.S.A.A.F.) Memorial room, at Norwich Central Library, housed the Roll of Honour of this 8th A.F. division, and thousands of books, the frontplates of many of which recorded the names of men who had died. There were memorabilia and information about the individual airfields and units, paintings, photographs, flags, and even the Purple Heart award of one pilot, Robert Couch, who died in action on 22nd April 1944, and whose family presented the medal to the library.

Unfortunately, the library in Bethel Street was severely damaged in a huge fire in August 1994 and the U.S. Air Force Memorial Room was destroyed, as were many of the printed records of Norfolk's history and over 300,000 books. The funds for the Memorial were originally raised by donations from all ranks of the division, and the 2nd Air Division Association has already started to plan a replacement. Duplicates of many of the records fortunately exist and can serve as the basis for a new collection, although many items were of course irreplaceable.

Three miles from Saffron Walden, Debden airfield was the home of 4th Fighter Group, the names of whose dead are on the Memorial Apse in the town. During the war Debden became known as the 'Eagles' Nest' when the R.A.F. Eagle Squadrons, 71st, 121st and 133rd manned by American volunteers, became the 4th Fighter Group of the U.S. 8th A.A.F. The airfield now is a British army establishment, but a bronze plaque on a granite base near the guardroom gives the war-time history of the station.

From September 1942 until the last mission on 25th April 1945 the 4th F.G. achieved 'the most victories over enemy aircraft in the entire U.S. Army Air Force – 1016 enemy aircraft destroyed'. During that time 241 aircraft went missing in action. In March 1945 a Mustang returned to Debden with two pilots on board, one having

182 *Memorial Room, Norwich Library*

landed north of Berlin to pick up another who had been forced down. This was despite an earlier ban by 8th A.F. headquarters on such rescue attempts.

The memorial is dedicated, 'IN REMEM-BRANCE OF OUR COMRADES WHO WERE NOT TO SEE THE WAR'S END, AND OF ANGLO-AMERICAN ENDEAVOURS TO A COMMON CAUSE'.

In Saffron Walden, the Anglo-American Memorial Playing Fields were purchased after the Second World War to commemorate the airmen and women based in and around the town, who gave their lives in the war. In addition, a memorial apse has a stone tablet with the inscription, 'IN HONOURED MEMORY OF THE OFFI-CERS AND MEN OF THE 65TH FIGHTER WING OF THE UNITED STATES ARMY AIR FORCE AND THE MEN AND WOMEN OF THE BOROUGH OF SAFFRON WALDEN WHO GAVE THEIR LIVES IN THE DEFENCE OF FREEDOM 1939-1945'.

Above the apse are the words, 'ANGLO-AMERICAN MEMORIAL 1939-1945' in large letters, and stone tablets on the walls have the names of the fallen from 4th Fighter Group, 479th Fighter Group, and from Saffron Walden. The apse is in a beautiful garden surrounded by a beech hedge and with lawns and rose beds.

At Goodwood airfield, on a site close to the control tower, is a memorial of stone, and with gold lettering on a dark plaque. The inscription is worded 'TO THE MEMBERS OF THE 31ST FIGHTER GROUP WHO FROM THIS AERODROME, ON 26 JULY 1942, JOINED THEIR BRITISH COMRADES IN COMBAT AS THE FIRST UNITED STATES FIGHTER GROUP IN THE EUROPEAN THEATER'. Decorative work on the plaque includes the badge of the 8th Air Force.

On the site of the old airfield at Steeple Morden a large roadside monument of Portland stone, with a centrepiece of a Mustang propeller,

183 *Anglo-American Memorial, Saffron Walden*

was dedicated on 12th May 1981 in memory of 355th Fighter Group U.S. 8th A.A.F.

The stone is decorated with squadron badges and with outlines of a P-51 Mustang and a P-47 Thunderbolt, and on the steps in front of it is a granite block inscribed '355TH FIGHTER GROUP, A.A.F. STATION 122. STEEPLE MORDEN. JULY 1943–JULY 1945'. The granite block was from a blitzed London church. Further inscriptions on the main memorial show that 1,500 enemy air-craft were damaged or destroyed by the group, and that over 2,000 American airmen served at the base.

184 *Steeple Morden Memorial*

98

One incident in the group's history is worth recording. In August 1944 a squadron leader of the group force-landed in a field near Paris, and another pilot deliberately landed near him. While other Mustangs circled to keep off German troops, the first pilot sat on his rescuer's lap to take off and return safely to base. In a later similar rescue attempt the second pilot's plane bogged down and both men were captured. 8th A. F. headquarters later banned such rescue attempts, but the Debden incident in March 1945 shows that the ban was not always observed.

On a boundary wall near the 355th's memorial, there is a plaque to the R.A.F. units who served at Steeple Morden from 1940 to 1943.

The vestry doors of St Mary's Church, Raydon, Suffolk, were dedicated in memory of the men of 353rd Fighter Group U.S. 8th A.A.F. based at the nearby airfield for the final year of the war. Also in the church are a Processional Cross and a Roll of Honour to commemorate the Group.

On 9th September, 1984, a roadside memorial was unveiled to commemorate the American airmen stationed at Goxhill in Lincolnshire, U.S.A.F. Base No. 345 from June 1942 to February 1945, while it was used as a fighter training base. The main feature on the memorial is a twisted propeller blade from a Lockheed Lightning which crashed nearby on 26th May, 1944, killing the pilot, 2nd Lt. Ferrara. He was originally buried in the American Services Cemetery at Madingley near Cambridge but after the war his body was re-buried in his home town in America.

Another propeller from a P.38 Lightning aircraft, mounted on a concrete base, in the village of Berinsfield, Oxfordshire, is the memorial of one of the more unusual units of the U.S. 8th A.A.F.

A tablet on the base reads, 'IN MEMORY OF THOSE WHO SERVED 7TH PHOTO GROUP. THE EYES OF 8TH U.S.A.A.F. MOUNT FARM. 5693 MISSIONS 1943-1945. DEDICATED 25TH MAY 1985'.

The unit initially used Lightnings and then went on to use Spitfires and Mustangs. It is claimed that more than 3 million reconnaissance photographs were taken by the group.

On a corner site, at the entrance to the former airfield of Spanhoe near Corby, a stone obelisk commemorates the men of the 315th Troop carrier Group of the U.S. Army Air Force. The group's C-47 Dakotas transported allied troops and supplies to Normandy, Arnhem and the Rhine crossing. The memorial was unveiled in 1983.

An attractive memorial in the churchyard of the now redundant Church of All Saints at Conington, Cambridgeshire, is a tribute to the American airmen of 457th Bombardment Group (Heavy), who flew from nearby Glatton Airfield in 1944-1945. In B-17 Flying Fortresses, the group flew 237 missions and lost 83 aircraft on those missions. Before returning to the U.S.A. in June 1945, it took part in 'Operation Exodus' to repatriate prisoners of war from Europe.

The memorial has the stone bust of an airman on a stone column which is decorated with the badge of the U.S. 8th Air Force, a B-17, and the words 'FAIT ACCOMPLI' in a laurel wreath. In the quiet churchyard surrounded by agricultural land it is difficult to imagine that the traffic on the A1 is a mile or so away.

186 *Glatton Memorial*

185 *Goxhill Memorial*

187 *Deenethorpe Memorial*

A triangular-shaped dark marble memorial on the site of the old main runway of Polebrook airfield, near Oundle, commemorates the 351st Bombardment Group (H) of the U.S. 8th Army Air Force. The group flew 311 missions from the airfield in B-17 Flying Fortresses from 1943 to 1945, and lost 175 aircraft and their crews. One of the unit's officers was the film actor, Clark Gable. Other film actors who served in Britain included James Stewart, the operations officer of 453rd Group at a time that Walter Matthau was also in the 453rd as a staff sergeant.

In the Church of All Saints, in Polebrook village, there is a Book of Remembrance and memorabilia of the 351st.

On the road between Oundle and Corby and in sight of the old control tower of Deenethorpe airfield, is a granite memorial to the 401st Bombardment Group (H) of the U.S. 8th A.A.F. The memorial's inscriptions include the provocative 'THE BEST DAMNED OUTFIT IN THE U.S.A.A.F.', but there is some basis for the claim, because the group had the best bombing accuracy record and the second lowest loss ratio among the B-17 groups in the 8th Air Force. Based at Deenethorpe from October 1943 to June 1945, the group flew 254 missions in B-17s and lost 94 aircraft. The memorial which was dedicated in September 1989, features a bronze B-17.

In the Church of St Mary the Virgin at Weldon, not far from Deenethorpe airfield, there is a stained-glass window presented by the 401st at the end of the war. The central panel of three depicts a bomber formation in flight, a crown, a cross and a dove, and the words 'DUTY WITHOUT HATE. IN MEMORIAM OUR COMRADES OF THE 401ST BOMBARDMENT GROUP'. The left-hand panel has the Union Flag and that of the U.S.

188 *St Mary the Virgin Church, Weldon*

flanking a handshake, and the right-hand panel has the badge of the U.S. 8th A.A.F. and the words '401ST BOMBER GROUP 1943-1945. TO WELDON PARISH CHURCH'.

Some 30 years after the gift of the window, in 1976, a Treble Bell was placed in the church tower in memory of comrades who failed to survive.

A granite memorial to the 384th Bombardment Group (H) of the U.S. 8th Army Air Force stands at the end of the former main runway of the Grafton Underwood airfield near Kettering. The group flew 314 missions in B-17s from the airfield between 22nd June 1943 and 25th April, 1945, losing 159 aircraft in action and 1,579 personnel. Other units used the airfield before the arrival of the 384th and in fact an inscription on the back of the memorial claims that the first and last bombs dropped by the 8th Air Force were from aircraft flying from Grafton Underwood. The first raid was on the 17th August 1942. The

189   *St James' Church, Grafton Underwood*

190   *St Andrew's Church, Great Cransley*

memorial was dedicated on the 5th October 1985 and, on the airfield site behind, two memorial avenues of trees have been planted to follow the lines of two runways.

A further memorial to the 384th is in the form of a stained-glass window in the church of St James the Apostle in Grafton Underwood. The window depicts a B-17 Flying Fortress and the words 'COMING HOME', and has the inscription 'THIS WINDOW IS DEDICATED BEFORE GOD IN REMEMBRANCE OF THOSE WHO GAVE THEIR LIVES FOR FREEDOM DURING WORLD WAR II WHILE SERVING AT GRAFTON UNDERWOOD 1942-1945 ESPECIALLY THOSE MEMBERS OF THE 384TH BOMB GROUP (H) OF THE UNITED STATES 8TH AIR FORCE'. The window was dedicated on 21st May, 1983, in the presence of Princess Alice of Gloucester.

St Andrew's Church at Great Cransley near Kettering, has a particularly interesting stained-glass window gifted to the church by the 384th who were stationed at Grafton Underwood. The central panel of St George is surrounded by scenes from American history, from John Cabot and the Pilgrim Fathers up the 1941 Atlantic meeting of Churchill and Roosevelt. The central lower panel, under St George, is of a British and an American soldier shaking hands, with the caption 'THE HAND OF FRIENDSHIP'.

Chelveston airfield, near Higham Ferrers, Northamptonshire, was the home from 1942 to 1945, of the 305th Bombardment Group (H) (known as the 'Can Do' group) of the U.S. 8th Army Air Force. At nearby Caldecott-cum-Chelveston the tower of the church of St John the Baptist was restored with the help of the Memorial Association of the 305th and a slate

tablet on the outside wall of the tower provides details of the group.

Part of the inscription reads 'THIS PLAQUE WAS DEDICATED ON THE 24TH SEPTEMBER 1980 IN MEMORY OF MORE THAN 769 MEN KILLED AND ALSO THOSE WOUNDED DURING THE 480 MISSIONS FLOWN BY THE GROUP'.

The airfield site of Harrington in Northamptonshire is marked by a memorial to the 801st/492nd Bombardment Group (H), the 'Carpetbaggers', of the 8th U.S. A.A.F. The stone has the dates 1944 and 1945 and depicts a Liberator bomber at low altitude with local cottages in the background.

Part of the inscription reads, 'CARPET-BAGGERS FLEW CLANDESTINE NIGHT MISSIONS FROM THIS SECRET AIRFIELD DURING WORLD WAR II IN BLACK B-24 LIBERATOR BOMBERS, DROPPING MUNITIONS AND SUPPLIES TO UNDERGROUND RESISTANCE FIGHTERS IN NAZI OCCUPIED EUROPE. THEY PARACHUTED AND LANDED O.S.S. AGENTS INTO BELGIUM, DENMARK, FRANCE, THE NETHERLANDS, NORWAY AND GERMANY TO CARRY OUT ESPIONAGE ACTIVITIES AGAINST ENEMY FORCES'.

191   *St John's Church, Caldecott-cum-Chelveston*

192 *Seething Memorial*

The 467th Bombardment Group (H) of the 8th U.S. A.A.F. has two memorials in the village of Rackheath, Norfolk. One is of polished stone on an industrial estate on the site of the old airfield. This memorial was unveiled on 29th July 1990 by the 80-year old Colonel A. J. Shower who commanded the group from October 1943 to June 1945. On the stone are a map of the airfield runways and a likeness of a B-24 Liberator.

The Rackheath village sign also incorporates a Liberator in its design, and two seats and a 1983 memorial tablet beside the sign serve as a second tribute to those men of the unit who were lost in 212 missions from Rackheath between April 1944 and April 1945.

Wrought-iron gates at the nearby church have a tablet with the inscription 'A GIFT TO THE PEOPLE OF RACKHEATH WITH GRATITUDE BY THIS B-24 CREW OF THE 467TH BOMBARDMENT GROUP'. The names of pilot James G. Coffey and those of his crew follow.

There are three memorials to the 448th Bombardment Group (H), 8th U.S.A.A.F. who served at Seething airfield, Norfolk, during the war. One is of polished marble, just inside the gate of the churchyard of the beautiful Parish Church with its round tower and thatched roof. This memorial was dedicated on 6th June 1984, the 40th anniversary of 'D' Day, and on the same day another stone was dedicated, on the airfield next to the clubhouse of the Waveney Flying Group by whom the field is still used. The third memorial, a plaque on a red brick wall, is close to the control tower which is now a museum, and was unveiled on 29th July 1990.

The group operated from Seething from December 1943 to April 1945. It flew 262 missions, dropped 15,286 tons of bombs, and lost 146 B-24 Liberators and 350 air-crew. The museum contains a Roll of Honour and memorabilia such as photographs, letters, diaries and aircraft parts.

Wooden gates to St Mary's Church, Flixton, Suffolk, were presented in 1945 by the 446th Bombardment Group (H) who operated from 1943 to 1945, from the nearby airfield. The present gates are not the original ones but were also presented by the members of the group, in 1987, when a Roll of Honour was placed in the Church.

Near the guardroom of what is now the British army establishment at Bassingbourn, Cambridgeshire, stands a memorial to the 91st Bombardment Group (H) of the U.S. 8th A.A.F. The group had the highest losses of all 8th A.F. groups, with 197 Flying Fortresses lost in action. One B-17 which was not lost was the famous 'Memphis Belle', the first Fortress whose crew completed its quota of 25 missions. A B-17 propeller on a stone base forms the memorial of the group which flew 340 missions from 7th November 1942 to 25th April 1945.

In the centre of a public park in Royston, a memorial to the men of the 91st Bombardment Group U.S. 8th A.A.F. who were stationed at nearby Bassingbourn from 1942 to 1945, was dedicated in July 1989. A marble pillar with a bronze plaque stands in the centre of a beautiful square of bedding plants with a paved surround, and appears to have taken the place of a memorial fountain originally erected in 1963.

Just off the A604 at Ridgewell in Essex, a black marble memorial to the members of the 381st Bomb Group (H) U.S. 8th A.A.F. stands near hangers of the old airfield. The group flew 297 missions from Ridgewell between June 1943 and April 1945.

A Rose Garden was created in the Abbey grounds of Bury St Edmunds after the war as a memorial to the Americans stationed in the area. The garden is enclosed by high hedges and has within it a marble column with a bronze plaque and a dedication to the men of the 94th Bombardment Group who were at nearby

193 *U.S. Memorial, Bury St Edmunds*

194 *Mendlesham Memorial*

Rougham airfield from 1943 to 1945. A more unusual memorial in the garden is a seat presented to the city by the U.S. Air Force and made out of the wing of a B-17 Flying Fortress.

Royalties from a book by a former American airman stationed at Lavenham during the war, *Suffolk Summer* by J. T. Appleby, go towards the upkeep of the garden and it is certainly a very well maintained, beautiful and peaceful area.

In the Market Place of the beautiful Suffolk town of Lavenham, a bronze plaque on a brick and flint wall is a memorial to the men of the 487th Bomb Group (H) of the U.S. 8th A.A.F. who died 'THAT THE IDEALS OF DEMOCRACY MIGHT LIVE'.

In the Swan Hotel there is a large collection of memorabilia of the war, with photographs, badges and the signatures (now behind glass) on the wall, of former airmen.

The memorial to the 34th Bombardment Group (H) of the U.S. 8th A.A.F. is by the side of the Norwich-Ipswich road at Mendlesham, Suffolk. A large bronze plaque on a brick supporting wall has a relief of a pilot leaning out of the window of his aircraft and handing down an olive branch. Behind the memorial are three flagpoles, and a gravel approach is flanked with rose bushes. The 34th were based at Mendlesham airfield from April 1944 to June 1945.

A shelter, in the shape of a lychgate, was dedicated in 1984, in the village of Eye in Suffolk, by the veterans of the 490th Bombardment Group (H) of the U.S. 8th A.A.F. A plaque outside the shelter refers to the friendship and cooperation of the people of the area where the 490th were based from April 1944 until August 1945.

On a small green opposite the Parish Church in Horham, Suffolk, a marble memorial, in the shape of a B-17 tail unit, carries a bronze plaque in memory of the men of the 95th Bombardment Group U.S. 8th A.A.F. who served at Horham airfield from June 1943, flying 320 missions and losing 157 planes in action, one of them the last 8th A.A.F. aircraft lost in action, on 7th May 1945, the day before V.E. Day. The memorial is on a base with a plan of the airfield runways, and was dedicated on 19th September 1981.

After the American, perhaps the next largest group of allied memorials is that commemorating the Polish dead.

On the corner of a busy Hillingdon road junction, not far from the old Northolt runways, from which many of them flew, is a memorial to fallen Polish airmen. A tall white stone column, surmounted by an eagle, lists the squadron numbers and the battle honours of the Polish Air Force during the period 1940 to 1945. Ten fighter squadrons and four bomber squadrons are named and the battle honours range from the Battle of Britain and the Western Desert to North-Western Europe and Germany.

The site of the memorial is well landscaped with a lily pond and flower beds. Railings to the front and trees and shrubs to the rear protect the area, and floodlights are positioned around the column.

Below the Polish flag in Southwell Minster's Airmen's Chapel is a memorial, by the former Minster architect Ronald Sims, to the 14,500 Polish prisoners of war massacred in 1940 in the

195 *Horham Memorial*

196 *Polish Memorial, Hillingdon*

Katyn Forest, and in other places in Russia. The Katyn mass grave of over 4,000 Polish officers murdered by the Russians after Russia and Germany invaded Poland in 1939, was found by the Germans in April 1943. The Russians predictably alleged that the Nazis were responsible for the massacre.

197 *Katyn Memorial, Southwell*

The memorial of grey-green slate is decorated by an eagle and a lion and has a crown of thorns round the word KATYN.

In Kensington Cemetery, Gunnersbury Park, London, a black obelisk has the inscription 'KATYN 1940' under a Polish eagle in a circle of barbed wire. On the square stepped base tribute is paid to the 14,500 Polish prisoners of war who disappeared in 1940, and those who were later identified in the mass grave at Katyn near Smolensk. The area of the obelisk is beautifully landscaped with trees, shrubs and flower beds.

A plaque on a wall in St Paul's Cathedral, decorated with a Polish eagle, is to Polish airmen, both those who reached Britain in 1939-40, and those who despite difficulties, followed later.

On the 31st January, 1942, in a blizzard, an R.A.F. Wellington with a six-man Polish crew crashed on Buckden Pike, high above Yorkshire's Wharfedale.

There was only one survivor, the rear gunner Josef Fusniak, and he had a broken leg. Fearing death from his injury and from exposure he saw the tracks of a fox in the snow and calculating that they would lead to the nearest source of food, he dragged himself agonisingly along the track. It did, indeed, lead to a farm and to safety, and years later, in 1973, he returned to Buckden Pike to erect a cross, in the stone base of which is embedded a bronze fox mask and on which is fixed a piece of the aircraft wreckage.

A plaque on the memorial has the inscription, 'THANKSGIVING TO GOD, THE PARKER FAMILY AND LOCAL PEOPLE, AND IN MEMORY OF FIVE POLISH R.A.F. AIRMEN WHO DIED HERE ON 31.1.42. BURIED IN NEWARK. THE SURVIVOR.'

In Tinwell Church, near Stamford, a framed illuminated scroll commemorates 'Thirty Four

198 *Katyn Memorial, Gunnersbury Park*

Brave Men who fell near This Place July 8th 1944.' The names of 26 Polish paratroopers and eight American airmen who died, are inscribed, together with the Polish and American Eagles, all within a border of oak leaves and acorns.

Over 500 members of the Polish community in Scotland attended the unveiling, in Perth, in November 1991, of a memorial to the Polish soldiers who died in the Second World War. The unveiling in Wellshill Cemetery was carried out by the Polish Ambassador. The memorial, three large blocks of stone placed one on top of another, has a crest of the traditional Polish eagle, an inscription in English and, on the bottom block, an inscription in Polish.

A large bronze memorial at Brookwood Military Cemetery, Woking, is 'IN MEMORY OF THE POLISH SOLDIERS WHO DIED IN THE SECOND WORLD WAR', and another, a stone memorial with a heavy bronze shield depicting a lion, commemorates the servicemen of Czechoslovakia.

On the same wall of the cloisters at Westminster Abbey as the Special Services memorial, is a bronze tablet, unveiled on 28th October, 1993, the 75th anniversary of the founding of the Czechoslovak Republic, to the memory of all members of the Czech army and air force 'who came as allies to this country and died in its defence and for the liberation of Europe 1940-1945'.

In Jepson Gardens, Leamington, a fountain of presumably unique design has a centrepiece of a stone parachute over which the water flows,

199 *Polish Memorial, Buckden Pike*
(Photograph – Mark Boon)

200 *Polish Memorial, Perth*

201 *Polish Memorial, Brookwood*

202 *Czech Memorial, Brookwood*

203 *Czech Memorial, Leamington*

and is directed down the grooves, so that when it eventually falls it appears to be the cords of the parachute.

On a brass plaque behind the fountain, is the inscription 'IN TRIBUTE TO ALL CZECHOSLOVAK SOLDIERS, AIRMEN AND PATRIOTS WHO FELL IN WORLD WAR II. FROM ROYAL LEAMINGTON SPA IN 1941, VOLUNTEERS FROM FREE CZECHOSLOVAK FORCES STATIONED IN THE TOWN WERE PARACHUTED INTO THEIR HOMELAND TO RID IT OF THE TYRANT "PROTECTOR", S.S. GENERAL HEYDRICH. TWO OF THEM – JAN KUBIŠ AND JOSEF GABČIK– ACCOMPLISHED THEIR MISSION IN MAY 1942. THEY AND THEIR COMPANIONS LAID DOWN THEIR LIVES FOR FREEDOM'.

The names of all the men involved, seven in number, are engraved round the edge of the parachute. Heydrich, in fact, died of wounds on the 4th June 1942 after the assassination attempt on 27th May. As a reprisal the Germans killed more than 1,000 people, the village of Lidice being completely obliterated. In a rose garden near to the parachute memorial in Leamington, a small brass plaque reads 'LIDICE SHALL LIVE. GARDEN OF REMEMBRANCE. 25TH ANNIVERSARY 1967'.

On the outskirts of the village of Elvington is an unusually designed memorial to the Free French airmen who were stationed at the nearby airfield in 1944-45. The two R.A.F. Squadrons 346 (Guyenne) and 347 (Tunisie) flew Halifax bombers as part of No. 4 Group. The outline of an aircraft cut clean through the main section of the memorial has under it the words 'GROUPES LOURDS'. To the side is an explanatory bronze plaque.

The small medieval church at Scawton in North Yorkshire, not far from Rievaulx Abbey, has in the porch, a metal plaque recording the names of five French airmen who died nearby when their Halifax bomber crashed on returning from an operation on 15th March, 1945. At the head of the plaque is the Cross of Lorraine, and against the respective names are the titles of pilot, navigator, air bomber, wireless operator, and air gunner, although no ranks are given.

On the outskirts of Greenock, on a hill overlooking the Clyde, is a memorial to the sailors of

204 *Free French Memorial, Elvington*

205 *Free French Memorial, Greenock*

the Free French Navy who sailed from Greenock from 1940 to 1945 and gave their lives in the Battle of the Atlantic. The memorial is a huge Cross of Lorraine and anchor combined, on a heavy stone base and with a stone pillar and wrought-iron surround. The wrought iron between the pillars is in the shape of anchors and crosses alternately. The monument, high above the town and the river, is floodlit at night.

A stone cross in Brookwood Cemetery, Woking, has engraved on the base the names of 21 French sailors lost when their vessel was sunk in the Clyde on 30th April 1940.

A metal plaque on a wall at the Pier Head, Liverpool, is in memory of the 831 seamen of the Belgian merchant navy who died at sea during the Second World War. The flags of Belgium and the U.K. are at the top of the plaque.

A 9 ft. high memorial of Norwegian granite at R.A.F. Leuchars in Fife, was unveiled on 7th June 1957 to commemorate 'THE BROTHERHOOD IN ARMS BETWEEN BRITISH AND NORWEGIAN AIRMEN WHO FOUGHT FROM THESE NORTHERN SHORES IN WORLD WAR II' and to honour those who died. No. 333 (Norwegian) Squadron operated from Leuchars from May 1943 to September

206 *Norwegian Memorial, Leuchars*

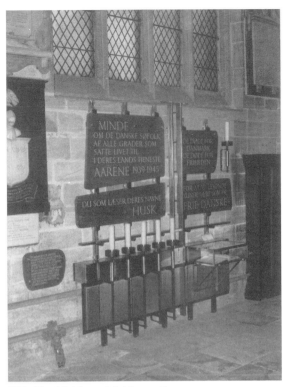

207 *Danish Memorial, Newcastle*

1944 and 1477 (Norwegian) Flight and a detachment of 330 (Norwegian) Squadron also flew from the airfield.

On 9th April 1940, when German troops occupied Denmark, all Danish ships at sea were ordered to go to Britain, and Newcastle-upon-Tyne became the home of Danish seamen. About 4,000 of them sailed out of Newcastle and 1,406 of them eventually gave their lives for Denmark.

On 13th May 1982, a Danish memorial was unveiled in St Nicholas' Cathedral, Newcastle, designed by the Cathedral Architect Ronald G. Sims and paid for by the Danish Shipowners' Association. The striking and imaginative memorial is made of green Westmorland slate and steel, and there is a Remembrance Book in a glass case. Above the memorial is a Danish flag originally outside their wartime headquarters.

Alongside the memorial, a translation of the Danish inscription reads 'IN MEMORY OF DANISH SEAMEN OF ALL RANKS WHO GAVE THEIR LIVES IN THE SERVICE OF THEIR COUNTRY IN THE YEARS 1939-1945. WHEN YOU READ THEIR NAMES REMEMBER THAT THEY DIED FOR DENMARK. THEY DIED FOR FREEDOM SO THAT WE LIKE THEM MIGHT LIVE AS FREE DANES'.

A Delft tile in the R.A.F. Museum at Hendon was presented by Dr W. Scholten, Netherlands Minister of Defence, in May 1980, to commemorate the aid give by the R.A.F. to the starving population of what was still occupied Netherlands between 29th April and 8th May 1945 when 3,156 Lancaster sorties and 145 Mosquito sorties dropped 6,684 tons of food. The operation was called 'Manna' while the Americans called their flights 'Chowhound'. As they flew, airmen often saw messages of thanks cut into the tulip fields.

Another memorial in the R.A.F. Museum at Hendon was set in place by the Bomber Command Association 'in memory of the extraordinary bravery shown by the Resistance in returning more than 2,500 members of Bomber Command safely to their squadrons after being shot down over enemy territory'. The memorial is a bronze relief showing a wounded pilot being supported by two members of the Resistance, one male, one female with, in the background, a parachute, searchlight beams, and aircraft. The bronze by Elizabeth Lucas Harrison, was unveiled on 12th July 1986 by la Comtesse de Jongh, leader of the Comête Escape Line.

208 *Resistance Memorial, Hendon*

CHAPTER V

Villages

IN THE MANY VILLAGES where crosses had been erected after the First World War as war memorials, this popular form of monument at village level could not normally be considered as a separate tribute to the dead of 1939-1945. Either the existing cross had the names of the fallen of the Second World War added to those of the First, or a different type of memorial was chosen.

The centre of village life was the church, the green and the village 'hall, and of these the church was most commonly the site of the new memorial. Stained-glass windows, plaques, church furniture, lychgates and church bells were all common examples of separate memorials. Outside the church, new village halls, or 'Memorial Halls', and playing fields were widely chosen, and other utilitarian options such as bus shelters, gardens and clocks were not uncommon.

Although the numbers of dead were not as great as those for the Great War, nevertheless most villages, however small, were affected. Upper Slaughter is one of the few 'Thankful Villages', or villages where all the men who served in both wars returned home safely. In the village hall there are plaques listing the men who fought for their country but, of course, no mention of any who died. Apparently in the Second World War an incendiary bomb fell on the village, but again there were no casualties.

In the church of Abbotsbury, Dorset, there is an unusual stone tablet with the inscription 'WE RECORD WITH HEARTY THANKS TO ALMIGHTY GOD THAT DURING THE COURSE OF THE SECOND WORLD WAR 1939-1945 NO PARISHIONERS OF ABBOTSBURY WHETHER SERVING IN HIS MAJESTY'S FORCES OR REMAINING AT HOME LOST THEIR LIVES BY ENEMY ACTION'. A First World War Roll of Honour and a cross in the churchyard show that the village was not as fortunate at that time, as 13 names are recorded as having died.

All Saints' Church at Siddington, near Macclesfield, has a stained-glass window in memory of three men who gave their lives in the 1939-1945 war, and also 'IN THANKFULNESS TO ALMIGHTY GOD FOR OUR MEN AND WOMEN, WHO SERVED AND RETURNED SAFELY TO THEIR HOMES, AND FOR THE PRESERVATION OF THIS VILLAGE, THIS WINDOW IS GIVEN BY THE PARISHIONERS'.

Incorporated in the window are the regimental badges of the three men who died.

St Luke's Church at Whyteleafe in Surrey, lays claim to being the first church in England to be damaged by enemy action. On 13th August 1940, during an air raid on Kenley airfield, a bomb blew out all the glass on the north side of the church. The fragments of old stained glass were carefully collected and now form a special window in the church.

The Church of St Philip and St James, Upnor in Kent, has a World War II memorial window which was unveiled on 16th November 1947 by the actress Dame Sybil Thorndike, who spent her childhood in nearby Rochester and whose nanny came from Upnor. The window commemorating seven men of the parish shows St George triumphant over the slain dragon, and the Saint is apparently a likeness of Dame Sybil playing St

209 *All Saints' Church, Siddington*

210 *St Ebba's Church, Beadnell*

Joan. In her tribute to the dead, the actress recited 'Fear no more the heat o' the day' from Shakespeare's *Cymbeline* (see p. 113).

Another stained-glass memorial window in Christ Church, Charnock Richard, Lancashire, incorporates the dates of both the 1914-1918 and the 1939-1945 wars. Below the window, however, is a brass plaque with the dates of the Second War only, and with the names of five who gave their lives.

St Ebba's Church at Beadnell, Northumberland, has a stained-glass window depicting St Ebba, St Oswald and a number of other Northern Saints, as a memorial to the men of the village who died in the Second World War. At the foot of the window the dates 1939-1945 are incorporated in the design, along with six service badges, and on a stone sill nine names of the fallen are inscribed.

The Memorial Chapel in All Saints' Church, Rothbury, Northumberland, was dedicated, on Easter Day 1947, to the dead of both World Wars. Its windows were designed by L. C. Evetts and are decorated with regimental badges. Several are tributes to individual members of the parish and carry either Royal Navy or R.A.F. emblems. Another was erected by Royal Northumberland Fusiliers who were prisoners of war in the Far East, in memory of their comrades who died in Japanese camps. The Chapel generally is furnished with gifts from either the families or regimental comrades of the men commemorated.

A stained-glass window featuring the badges of the three services, in the Church of St Mary the Virgin in Ponteland, Northumberland, is in memory of the men of the parish who fell in the 1939-45 war, and whose names are inscribed in stone below the window.

Sixteen men of Cookham Dean are commemorated in a stained-glass window in the Church of St John the Baptist. The names of the men who gave their lives in the 1939-45 war appear under the figures of St George and St Michael in a double panelled window by William Ackman, dedicated in November 1947.

A beautiful stained-glass window in Lochend Church in Beeswing, Galloway, was unveiled in September 1948, and the occasion was made even more poignant by the fact that one of the three men commemorated was the former minister of the parish, the Reverend Henry Smith, and that his widow unveiled the memorial.

The Reverend Smith died as a Chaplain of the Forces, the other two men being Lieut. Andrew Christian McCulloch of the Royal Navy and James Ferguson Hood of the Liverpool City Police, killed in an air raid. The names of all three appear on shields at the foot of three of the four panels of the window. Also depicted in the window are Christ and the children, and David and Abigail, with the inscriptions 'BLESSED ARE THE PURE IN HEART', and 'PEACEMAKERS'. There are also the words 'TO THE GLORY OF GOD AND IN LOVING REMEMBRANCE OF THOSE WHO GAVE THEIR LIVES IN THE SECOND WORLD WAR 1939-1945' (see p. 113).

Finally, the Church of St Peter and St Paul, Chaldon, Surrey, has a stained-glass window in memory of the men of the parish who died in the 1939-45 war. Below the figures of St Michael and St George are the names of 16 men who gave their lives, more than double the number on a First World War plaque nearby.

One of the Second World War names is that of a V.C., John Harman. In a glass case below the window is a Book of Remembrance in which are recorded in illuminated script the name, rank and short biography of each man. For example, on a page decorated with the badge of the Royal Marines, is the description 'BRIAN GRANVILLE WHITE. Captain and adjutant 45th Royal Marine Commando landed Normandy D. Day 6th June 1944. The 45th R.M. Commando held the extreme left flank of the Allied Forces on the advance across the Dives Valley. Capt. White lost his life, leading his troop on an attack on a German strong point on Sunday the 20th August, 1944.

He was aged 28 and his home was at Hill Top, Chaldon. He married Theo Hallam Swift in this church on the 29th July 1942 and left her with a baby daughter – Jennifer Robin Granville White. He lies in the British Cemetery at Ranville, Normandy'.

An unusual feature of the church is the 12th-century biblical mural, white-washed over, probably in the 17th century, and restored in Victorian times.

To many First World War memorials the names of the dead of the later war were added. On the Shetland island of Whalsay, with a population after the 1939-45 war of some 800 people, the existing memorial was unable to take the names of the 22 men who died. A new memorial stone was erected against the wall behind the cross for World War I, and an examination of the 22 names shows that all but two were seamen, explaining the very high numbers of dead for the size of the population, and highlighting the greater risk to life for seamen in the second war.

St Mary's Church, Sellindge, Kent, has as a First World War memorial, a bronze wall plaque on green marble. Over the central relief figure of Christ administering to a fallen soldier on the battlefield are the words 'EVEN THERE ALSO SHALL THY RIGHT HAND LEAD ME'.

Stone wall plaques have been placed below the original memorial to commemorate the dead of the Second War, eight in number compared with 18 of 1914-18.

The red-granite memorial stone in the outside wall of Torpichen Kirk, near Bathgate, to the 50 or so dead of World War I, was matched when a stone of similar material was unveiled on Remembrance Sunday, 9th November, 1980. The latter stone carries the names of 12 who fell in the 1939-45 War, two of whom were women. Both memorials give the regiments of those killed, the two women being shown as W.R.A.F. and A.T.S. respectively. The memorials are to either side of the main door into the 17th-century Kirk and under each is maintained a poppy wreath.

A very simple tablet, listing the names of those who fell in the 1939-45 War, on the wall of St Wilfred's Church, Davenham, Cheshire, is in sharp contrast to the elaborate and beautiful work of art that is the First World War memorial, designed by Sir Robert Lorimer, in the same church. The celebrated Scottish architect incorporated in his work a decorated marble tablet with a colourful plaque of St George and the dragon, and wonderful wooden carvings, including figures representing Courage, Gentleness, Charity and Justice.

A plaque to one side of the entrance gates to Droxford Church, Hampshire, lists the names of 10 men who died in the 1939-45 War, and another attached to the memorial to both wars in Tupton churchyard, near Chesterfield, commemorates 11 parishioners killed in an air raid on the 15th March 1941.

In the churchyard of Holy Trinity Church, Ashford-in-the-Water, a cross commemorating those who fell in 1914-18 is close to a stone tablet on the wall of the church with the names of the three men who died in the 1939-45 War. Amongst them was William John Robert Cavendish, Marquess of Hartington, of the Coldstream Guards.

In St Martin's Church, Lowthorpe, East Yorkshire, a wall plaque commemorates four men who died in the Second World War and gives their ranks, regiments and dates and places of their deaths. One, Lance Sergeant Edgar Watson of the Coldstream Guards died in London on 18th June 1944, the day that the Guards' Chapel was

211 *Whalsay Memorial (Photograph – Susan Timmins)*

212 *St Mary's Church, Sellindge*

hit by a flying bomb during the morning service, with the loss of 121 lives.

A cast-iron plaque depicting a destroyer, in the Parish Church of Ettington near Stratford-on-Avon, was presented by the ship's company of H.M.S. *Verity* to the people of Stratford Rural District and then to the Parish of Ettington 'IN

213 *Torpichen Kirk*

RECOGNITION OF OUTSTANDING CONTRIBUTIONS TO H.M.S. *Verity* 1939-45'.

The Parish Church of St Mary in Rothley, Leicestershire, has a beautiful reredos with depictions of St Michael and St George and the names, originally of the dead of the First World War, but now also with the dates 1939-1945 and 20 names from that period. The inscription also records that a new organ was installed in 1921 in memory of the fallen. Apparently at that time there was no electricity in the village and so the organ was driven by water. An examination of the list of fatalities in the 1914-18 War shows that half of them were in the Leicestershire Regiment, while the largest proportion by far in the Second World War served in the R.A.F. (see p. 113).

St Martin's Church in Stoney Middleton, Derbyshire, has a most unusual octagonal nave, built in the 18th century. The war memorial for 1939-45 takes the form of a stone reredos erected by the congregation in 1947. On the reredos is carved 'REMEMBER THE FALLEN OF THIS VILLAGE' AND 'THANKS BE TO GOD FOR DELIVERANCE'. In the churchyard a cross to the dead of the 1st World War has the added names of those commemorated by the reredos.

St Barnabus Church in Pleasley Hill, Nottinghamshire, has wrought-iron gates with the inscription 'TO THE FALLEN 1939-1945' but, more importantly, it also has a fine reredos and panelling dedicated as a memorial on 12th April, 1949, to those who gave their lives in the war.

Woods from all parts of the world were used in the work. The reredos has a Lamb of God in burr ash with a halo of satin wood. The staff of the Cross is of ebony and the white flag of fiddle-

C27 *American Memorial Chapel, St Paul's*
(Photograph – Unichrome (Bath) Ltd)

C28 *U.S. Memorial, Elvedon*

C29 *St Philip and St James' Church, Upnor*

C30 *Lochend Church, Beeswing*

C31 *St Mary's Church, Rothley*

C32 *St Peter's Church, Wootton*

C33 *Dunbar Parish Church*

C34 *The Cenotaph after Remembrance Day 1993*

C35 *Field of Remembrance 1993*

C36 *Madingley Memorial Chapel*

back sycamore. The chalice is hare wood and the background is of walnut. One section of the panelling has the painted arms of York and Southwell together with the inscription about the dedication of the memorials, and another has the painted figures of St Barnabus, St Peter and St Paul, and the list of the 16 men who died in the War.

In the Parish Church of Packington, in Leicestershire, a wooden screen lists the men and women who served in the armed forces during 1939-45. Decorated with coloured insignia of the three services, the screen lists eight women separately. On another memorial, a marble wall plaque, the names of six of the parishioners who gave their lives during the war, are recorded.

Dore Abbey, in the Herefordshire village of Abbey Dore, has a wooden memorial in the interior to commemorate 19 men and eight women of the Second World War. The proportion of females seems very high, three of them being A.T.S., 2 W.R.A.F., 2 V.A.D., and 1 N.A.A.F.I.

Doors of the memorial open to reveal the inscribed names and a shelf below holds a flower arrangement. A matching memorial for 1914-18 lists over 50 names.

In St Andrew's Church, Beesands, Devon, a tiny church on the edge of the sea, a stone font with a carved wooden lid is the memorial to seven people killed in an air raid on the village on 26th July, 1942.

A stone plaque on the wall behind the font gives the names and ages of the dead, the youngest being one year old. Another, aged 19, Phyllis Emma Waugh, was apparently a W.A.A.F., tragically on leave at that time.

St Winifred's Church, Holbeck, in Nottinghamshire, is a private church, built by the Duke of Portland for the people of the Holbeck estate. Inside it, the memorial to both wars is a bronze eagle lectern on a stone pillar base. The names of the dead of 1914-18 are on the front of the pillar and those of 1939-45 are on the side. Flanked by flowers in an immaculate and beautiful church, this is a very impressive memorial.

St John's Church in Norley, Cheshire, has brass sanctuary rails and gates placed as a memorial to four men who gave their lives in the Second World War. They were dedicated on 8th October 1949 by the Bishop of Chester.

A hanging cross constructed of a large variety of materials, including oak, pine, bronze, aluminium and gold leaf, was dedicated in November 1992 at St Mary and All Saints' Church, Bingham, Nottinghamshire. Eleven men from the area were commemorated by the cross which was dedicated by the Bishop of Southwell.

The British Legion branch secretary said that attempts were being made to contact any living survivors of the men who died in the Second World War, and agreed that there had been a long delay since the war itself.

214 St Winifred's Church, Holbeck

The church of Cummertrees village in Dumfriesshire has a lychgate, which is a tribute to those who died in both wars, and which was in fact built after the 1939-45 war. The original memorial to the dead of World War I is a stone wall plaque in a sandstone frame on the outside of the church. A similar granite plaque, again framed in sandstone, lists the six dead of 1939-45.

The parish church at Aldborough in East Yorkshire has a lychgate on the left of which a stone tablet has the inscription 'A.D. 1952. ERECTED IN MEMORY OF THOSE WHO LAID DOWN THEIR LIVES IN THE SECOND WORLD WAR 1939-45'. A similar tablet on the other side of the gate lists seven names.

In the churchyard of St Lawrence, Affpuddle, Dorset, there is a shrine of brick and wood which from a distance resembles a lychgate. The timber above the entrance is heavily carved with vine leaves and fruit and the dates 1939 and 1945, and on tablets to each side are the names of the seven men commemorated. On the back wall of the interior a crucified Christ stands above a stone carved 'THY SIN – MY PAIN'.

A beautifully illuminated plaque in St Peter's Church, Wootton, Oxfordshire, has the inscription 'THIS TABLET AND THE CHURCH CLOCK WERE ERECTED IN GRATEFUL MEMORY OF THE MEN FROM THIS PARISH WHO GAVE THEIR LIVES IN THE WORLD WAR 1939-1945'. The names of 11 men follow. The clock is in the bell tower of the church, the hands and Roman numerals of the face being painted gold(see p. 114).

215 *St Lawrence Church, Affpuddle*

Also, inside the church, is an R.A.F. ensign laid up on the 13th May 1945 in memory of the 10,000 or so men who trained at the Bomber Command Battle School at nearby Youlbury Camp between 1942 and 1945.

The unusual 13th-century church of St Augustine, Brookland, on Romney Marsh, with its detached wooden belfry, has a clock on an outer turret wall as the village Second World War memorial. Inside the church may be seen the mechanism of the clock which was added to the turret in 1955. An inscription on a tablet reads 'This clock was erected by public subscription to commemorate the part played by the people of Brookland in the Second World War'. Elsewhere are listed the dead of both wars.

As a memorial to those of New Hartley, Northumberland, who gave their lives in the Second World War, a clock column was erected outside St Michael and All Angels Church. Unfortunately, this no longer reflects well on the community. The clock no longer works and two of its faces are missing. The stone column is now defaced with graffiti and the names of those commemorated are in some cases barely legible.

216 *St Peter's Church, Wootton*

217 *St Augustine's Church, Brookland*

A stone tablet in the church at Winterbourne St Martin in Dorset, records that five bells in the church tower were given by parishioners in memory of five men who gave their lives in the 1939-45 War.

At St Giles the Abbott Church, Farnborough, near Bromley, a tenor bell was dedicated on 1st May 1990, in memory of those killed in active service in the 1939-45 War. An inscription on a stone tablet reads 'THAT ALL WHO HEAR THIS BELL MAY REMEMBER THE HIGH COST OF FREEDOM'. The names of 32 men follow.

The war memorial at Woodhouse Eaves in Leicestershire is on a hillside between the main road through the village and the Parish Church. On top of the rocky slope is a stone cross, below which a stone wall carries name tablets for both wars. The names for the Second World War have been added, together with the dates 1939-1945. Below the wall is a pretty rock garden with steps and a hand rail leading down to the road.

A beautiful 1921 work by sculptor John Cassidy near the doorway of St Oswald's Church, Lower Peover, Cheshire, has a sandstone figure of Christ on the Cross, with two reliefs in sandstone of a soldier and a sailor kneeling at his feet. Below that, bronze panels depicting war scenes flank the 19 names of the 1914-1918 dead. A further single name has been added for the 1939-1945 period.

In a recess cut into the rock below Bamburgh Castle stands a stone calvary, on the base of which the dates of both World Wars are engraved. Set into the rock around the cross are bronze plaques with the names of the Bamburgh men who died, two plaques being for 1914-1919 (as it is styled) and one for 1939-1945.

Another calvary on the outskirts of the Gloucestershire village of Salperton is enclosed in a dry stone wall with wrought-iron gates and also serves as the memorial to the dead of both wars.

The cross carved into the hillside at Shoreham in Kent was originally a First World War memorial. Covered during the 1939-45 war to avoid its use as an identification feature for enemy aircraft, it has subsequently been considered as a memorial to the dead of both wars.

A stone memorial by the edge of a stream in the village has the carved inscription 'REMEMBER AS YOU LOOK AT THE CROSS ON THE HILL THOSE WHO GAVE THEIR LIVES FOR THEIR COUNTRY'. On the front are the dates 1914-1919 and the names of the dead of that war, and on the sides are the dates 1939-1945 and the names for that period. Amongst the eight names on one side are three MCaughen's and five Puxty's, victims of German bombers on their flight path to and from London.

A brick and stone column and cross by the roadside in Chipperfield, Hertfordshire, looks out across the cricket ground to the church and could hardly be in a more prominent position in the village. The memorial is a First World War one with additions for 1939-45, and on the base has the words, 'SONS OF THIS PLACE, LET THIS OF YOU BE SAID, THAT YOU WHO LIVE ARE WORTHY OF YOUR DEAD'.

An unusual wooden cross is the war memorial of the village of Swithland in Leicestershire. It stands on a stone base which is at the top of a flight of stone steps in a pretty roadside garden. A plaque on the front of the base has been altered by the addition of an 's' to the words 'Great War', of the dates 1939-1945, and of the name of the only

218   *Woodhouse Eaves Memorial*

person from the village who died in action during those war years. Behind the cross is the attractive, well maintained Swithland Memorial Hall with its pleasant verandah.

Pool village hall in Yorkshire, opened by the Countess of Harewood in 1958, has a stone plaque on the exterior inscribed 'THOSE WHO SERVED 1939-1945' and on the inside a wooden plaque listing the names of nine of the village who gave their lives. The plaque was made by the firm of the famous 'Mousie' Thompson, and his signature of a mouse is carved into the top of the frame.

The 1939-45 war memorial in Froxfield, Wiltshire, is the War Memorial Hall which overlooks the village green. Erected in 1949 it was originally intended to be a temporary building but has never been replaced. The footings were of rubble from the runway of wartime Ramsbury airfield when it was broken up.

Wistaston, near Crewe, has a Memorial Hall to the memory of 16 men who gave their lives in the 1939-45 War, and a metal plaque above the entrance to the hall records their names. Another Memorial Hall in Ash, Somerset, was built in 1960, and has a commemorative plaque inside.

219 *Bamburgh Memorial*

To the First World War plaque on the front of the Memorial Hall in the village of Stilton, has been added another with the dates and names of the 1939-45 War.

On the wall of the old village hall in Catton, near Norwich, is a stone tablet with a most unusual inscription summarising the whole of the village's war-time contribution. A wonderful historical record would be available to us if every community had been so meticulous. The inscription reads 'DURING THE WORLD WAR 1939-1945 FROM THIS PARISH THERE SERVED, H.M. FORCES – ARMY 45, R.A.F. 19, R. NAVY 4, OF WHOM 10 GAVE THEIR LIVES. WOMEN'S SERVICES 12, HOME GUARD 34, CIVIL DEFENCE 18, W.V.S. AND CANTEEN WORK-ERS 33.

THE ENEMY DROPPED ON US 16 H.E. AND 14 H.E.1. BOMBS AND OVER A 1,000 INCENDIARIES.

ON JAN. 22ND AND FEB. 13TH 1945 TWO AMER-ICAN BOMBERS CRASHED IN CHURCH STREET CLOSE TO THIS TABLET WITH A LOSS OF TWENTY VALUABLE LIVES.

WE SAVED £6,762 AND SUBSCRIBED TO WAR CHARITIES £1,486.

INTO ALL PARTS OF THE WORLD WENT FORTH OUR CHILDREN'.

220 *Shoreham Cross*

221 *Swithland Memorial*

In the village hall of Linton, Yorkshire, on the wall above the fireplace is the 2nd World War memorial. An oak over-mantle contains the photographs of the seven men commemorated, each photograph behind oak doors above which is the appropriate regimental badge.

The centre photograph is of Major John Geoffrey Appleyard, D.S.O., M.C. and bar, of the R.A.S.C., Commandos and the Special Air Service Regiment, who was presumed killed in action in Sicily on 13th July, 1943. By coincidence an adjoining photograph is of Captain Graham Hayes, M.C., of the Border Regiment, also of the Special Service Commandos and also killed on 13th July, 1943. Flight Sergeants Leslie and Sydney Hilder were killed within a few months of each other in 1944/45.

The village hall at Cutthorpe in Derbyshire now contains the village war memorial moved some years ago from the local school. A large wooden frame, like an overmantle, contains a picture of 'Hope' and the names of the men commemorated, 15 from the First World War and five from the second. Above are the words 'THAT UNSELFISHNESS AND DUTY CHEERFULLY DONE MAY BE A LASTING EXAMPLE'.

In St Peter's Church, Scremerston, near Berwick, photographs of the men of the village who died in the 1939-45 war are mounted within a large wooden frame, the name and regiment of each man being inscribed under his portrait. A similar but larger frame exists for World War I, but both, unfortunately, are rather hidden away in the vestry of the church and not accessible to the public.

A 1939-1945 war memorial, in the form of a bus shelter, stands on the green beside the village sign of Hargrave in Suffolk. It was unveiled in 1949 but badly damaged in the 1960's by a lorry collision, and subsequently rebuilt. Constructed of brick with a tile roof, it has a wooden plaque inside with the names of four men of the village who gave their lives in the War.

A similarly well constructed brick bus shelter in the village of Escrick near York was also erected to the memory of those who served.

As recently as September 1990 a memorial to the dead of both wars was erected on a corner garden site in the village of Cronton, near Widnes. A white marble obelisk, on a marble base and in a heather garden, is surrounded by black and gold metal railings and then by an area of brick paving. The names of eight men from the First World War and six from the Second are recorded.

A granite column in the main street of Somersham, Cambridgeshire, is 'in grateful memory of the men of the parish who paid the supreme sacrifice 1939-1945'. Thirteen names appear on the column and the lines from Binyon's poem *For the Fallen* are on the base.

222 *Froxfield Memorial*

120

223   *Linton Memorial*

By the roadside at Rowland Castle, a village near Havant, is a stone column backed by a semi-circular brick and flint wall, and with the inscription 'HERE ON 22 MAY 1944 HIS MAJESTY KING GEORGE VI REVIEWED AND BADE GOD SPEED TO HIS TROOPS ABOUT TO EMBARK FOR THE INVASION AND LIBERATION OF EUROPE. DEO GRATIAS'. The memorial is now on the edge of a modern housing estate called King's Meadows.

A brick column with a slate roof, faced with flint and with stone tablets, forms the war memorial of the Buckinghamshire village of Little Kingshill. Originally unveiled in 1920, the

column now has a second tablet, below the first, to add the names of the five dead of 1939-45 to the 11 of the Great War.

A stone memorial outside the Miners' Social Centre in Lynemouth, Northumberland, is in memory of those from Lynemouth, Ellington and Cresswell who gave their lives in the 1939-1945 War. The names of 19 men and women are listed.

Near Glenridding, at the head of Ullswater, is a roadside memorial stone and garden to the Potterdale dead of both wars. The large piece of local granite has two plaques, one for each war, and with a rockery on three sides, looks out over the water of the lake.

A riverside memorial cairn at Nether Poppleton, York, has a plaque with the name of one man who died in the Second World War, added to the plaque with 11 names of 1914-18.

Dissatisfied with their 1920 war memorial, the British Legion branch of Littleport, near Ely, started anew and after a great deal of work and fund raising dedicated a new memorial, to both

224   *Cutthorpe Memorial*

225   *St Peter's Church, Scremerston*

121

226 *Cronton Memorial*

227 *Somersham Memorial*

World Wars, on 24th September, 1989. The new stone memorial, on a brick base and with a black and gold plaque with names of the fallen of both wars, is perfectly situated on an attractive green, with a background of mature trees.

Ottershaw Memorial Fields have been given in memory of the fallen of 1939-1945, and two plaques, within the grounds, record the fact. The first is in a low brick base near the entrance, and explains that the area is maintained by the local authority for the benefit of the people of the village near Woking. Certainly the playing fields, and the gardens at the entrance, are both beautifully kept, the latter with flower beds, lawns and shrubs.

The second plaque, on the outside wall of the pavilion, is inscribed 'THIS FIELD AND PAVILION CLOCK HAVE BEEN PROVIDED IN MEMORY OF THE PEOPLE OF OTTERSHAW WHO GAVE THEIR LIVES IN THE SERVICE OF THEIR COUNTRY 1939-1945. WE WILL REMEMBER THEM'.

In the village of Halsall, in Lancashire, the Memorial Playing Field has wrought-iron gates, with poppy emblems in red in the centre of each gate. To the side of each gate a stone tablet in the brick wall is inscribed with the dates of the 1939-1945 war and with the names of the 10 men of the parish who gave their lives. In the centre of the village a stone cross has plaques for both the First and Second World Wars.

On a road running alongside the playing field in the village of Great Hampden, near Aylesbury are two identical brick and tile memorials with stone tablets. The inscription on one

228 *Rowland Castle Memorial*

IN REMEMBRANCE OF THE MEN OF LITTLE KINGSHILL
WHO GAVE THEIR LIVES FOR ENGLAND IN THE GREAT WAR 1914-1918.

Sᵗ F. ADAMS. M.M.   OXFORD & BUCKS L.I.
Sᵗ R. ADAMS.   GLOUCESTERSHIRE REGT.
Tᵖʳ J. BATCHELOR.   BUCKS YEOMANRY.
Pᵗᵉ C. HAWES.   HAMPSHIRE REGT.
Sᵗ E. HILL.   OXFORD & BUCKS L.I.
Pᵗᵉ P. LANGSTON.   OXFORD & BUCKS L.I. (BUCKS BATT.)
Cᵖˡ C. LONG.   THE QUEEN'S REGT.
Pᵗᵉ J. MANLEY.   MIDDLESEX REGT.
Cᵖˡ H. A. SPRAKE.   ROYAL GARRISON ARTILLERY.
Pᵗᵉ H. H. WARE.   ROYAL MARINES.
Pᵗᵉ W. WARE.   OXFORD & BUCKS L.I. (BUCKS BATT.)

AND IN THE WORLD WAR 1939-1945

Gᵈʳ F. C. BEDFORD.   ROYAL ARTILLERY.
L/Bᵈʳ F. LEAH.   ROYAL ARTILLERY.
Cᵃᵖᵗ P. E. RANDALL.   HIGHLAND L.I.
L/Cᵖˡ C. THOMPSON.   F.M.S.V. FORCE.
L/Cᵐᵈʳ M. WILLMOTT. D.S.O. ROYAL NAVY.

229 *Little Kingshill Memorial*

explains that the road was constructed as a memorial to those villagers killed in the First World War, and the other records that the playing field was prepared as a tribute to the dead of 1939-45.

The names of the fallen of both wars are on a Roll of Honour in the parish church of St Mary Magdalene, the burial place of John Hampden, the Civil War Parliamentarian.

Behind the stone cross in memory of the dead of the First World War, a stone bench bears the names of the seven men from Rainow, Cheshire, who gave their lives in the 1939-1945 War. Both memorials are in a pretty roadside garden on a hill outside Rainow, with a stone boundary wall and a steep bank covered with rhododendrons.

A lamp post would seem to be an unusual form of war memorial, but in the village of Enmore Green, near Shaftesbury, a plaque attached to a lamp post at a T-junction, shows it to be the memorial to the 19 men who fell in the 1914-18 War. An additional plaque for the Second War lists a further three men, a father and two sons, A. G. Weir, Wing Commander R.A.F., A. N. C. Weir, D.F.C., Flying Officer R.A.F. V. R., and A. J. R. Weir, M.C., Major Scots Guards.

230 *Littleport Memorial*

On 23rd August, 1944, a U.S. Air Force B-24 Liberator bomber took off from Warton airfield and, in a thunderstorm, almost immediately crashed, on to the village school at Freckleton, Lancashire. The tragic result was the death not only of the crew of the B-24, but of 38 infant schoolchildren, two teachers and seven other civilians.

In the churchyard of Holy Trinity Church, which is next to the site of the demolished school, the village dead are commemorated by a granite cross with adjoining granite wings on which are listed the names of those killed. The cross stands at the head of a communal grave.

Not far from the church, in a garden at the entrance to extensive playing fields, is a block of stone with a metal plaque inscribed with U.S. and British insignia, and with the words, 'THIS PLAYGROUND PRESENTED TO THE CHILDREN OF FRECKLETON BY THEIR AMERICAN NEIGHBOURS OF BASE AIR DEPOT NO. 2. U.S.A.A.F. IN RECOGNITION AND REMEMBRANCE OF THEIR COMMON LOSS IN THE DISASTER OF AUGUST 23RD 1944'.

Inside the church is a clock given by an individual in memory of his son-in-law and two grand-daughters, and there is also a desk made of timber from a roof beam of the old school. On this desk is a commemorative book of the disaster showing the funeral on 26th August, 1944, when American airmen carried the coffins, and flowers were sent from all over the country.

A Staffordshire village was the scene of an accident which resulted in an even greater loss of life. On the morning of 27th November 1944, the largest explosion caused by conventional weapons in both World Wars occurred near Hanbury, when 4,000 tons of high explosive bombs stored 90 ft. below ground in old gypsum mines, blew up.

The blast was heard in London and recorded in Geneva as an earthquake, a crater nearly 400 ft. deep and covering an area of 12 acres was created, and remains to this day, debris was scattered up to 11 miles away, and a total of 70 people lost their lives, with 18 bodies never being recovered. One farm completely disappeared, with all its buildings, wagons, horses, cattle and six people.

The 21 M.U. R.A.F. Fauld disaster is commemorated by a memorial, at the edge of the crater, dedicated on 25th November 1990. The memorial is of white granite and carries a metal plaque with the 70 names of those killed. The church at Hanbury has a framed illuminated scroll with the names of those of the village who died on active service in 1939-45 and also those who died in the explosion.

231 *Ottershaw Memorial Fields*

232 *Rainow Memorial*

Several Italian prisoners of war lost their lives, and in the church there is also an Italianate painted crucifix presented by Mrs Lanzoni of Milan who attended the dedication of the memorial at the crater and whose uncle died in the explosion.

Elsewhere, there is a more uplifting story involving Italian prisoners. On a wooden frame surrounding a ceramic panel depicting a Madonna and Child, in St Aldhelm's Roman Catholic Church in Malmesbury, is a plaque decorated with the British and Italian flags. The wording on it is 'ITALIAN SOLDIERS, 2ND WORLD WAR PRISONERS, ARE GRATEFUL AND THANKFUL FOR HOW NATIVE ENGLISH PEOPLE TREATED THEM',

This was presented by former P.O.W. Franco Montanari.

233 *Hanbury Memorial*

234 *St Aldhelm's Church, Malmesbury*

125

CHAPTER VI

Small Towns

THE SCALE OF THE First World War memorials in most towns and cities made them frequently easy to adapt so that they became memorials to both World Wars. Even small towns, in many cases, erected very large monuments and it is interesting to see how these were used as the basis for a tribute to the dead of 1939-1945. Sometimes there were substantial additions so that there were, in

235 *Rawtenstall Memorial*

236 *Heywood Memorial*

fact, two separate memorials, although at first sight this was not always apparent, while on many occasions the alterations consisted purely of the addition of new dates and new name tablets.

The First World War memorial in Rawtenstall was unveiled in 1929, its main feature being a wonderful bronze frieze by L. F. Roslyn, who was responsible for many memorials at the time, including several in the Bradford area. The frieze has figures not only of service-men but also of women and children, fishermen and labourers.

Under the frieze on one side of the memorial is a bronze plaque, 'TO THE MEMORY OF ALL WHO GAVE THEIR LIVES IN THE SERVICE OF THEIR COUNTRY DURING THE SECOND WORLD WAR 1939-45. ALL WHO SERVED ON SEA, LAND OR IN THE AIR AND ALL WHO WORKED AND SERVED AT HOME'.

In a rose garden in the centre of Heywood, the First World War memorial has a 1925 bronze statue of Peace, by W. Marsden, fronting a marble

237 *Hawick Memorial*

238 *Leamington Spa Memorial*

the memorial and unveiled at a ceremony on 18th July, 1954.

The war memorials of both Kelso and Jedburgh are impressively situated next to the respective Abbeys of the towns. Erected to commemorate the dead of the First World War, the stone cross at Kelso and the stone pillar in the centre of a flight of stairs at Jedburgh, have both been amended to include the dates and names of the fallen of the Second World War.

The Hawick war memorial, erected after the First World War, is in a beautiful garden, with extensive flower beds, next to the museum, and has been extremely successful in Royal British Legion Scotland's 'Best Kept War Memorial' competitions. A stone obelisk fronted by a winged bronze figure, the memorial had been amended by the addition of the dates '1939-1945' to the stonework. The names of the fallen are on a Roll of Honour in the museum.

The 1921 bronze statue, by Albert Toft, of a bare-headed soldier with reversed rifle, stands in Euston Place, Leamington Spa, as the town's main war memorial. To the lower sections of the base have been added the dates 1939-1945 and the names of those who died during those years. The World War Two additions were dedicated in November 1951.

In the early 1960s the First World War memorial, in the form of a cenotaph, in East Dereham, Norfolk, was altered to include the dates and names of the dead of the Second World War. The unveiling of the amended memorial by the Lord Lieutenant of Norfolk, and the re-dedication by the Vicar of Dereham, were duly carried out. A photograph taken that day clearly shows that a bronze plaque above the name plates refers to 'Two World Wars' and gives the dates of 1914-1918 and 1939-1945.

Unfortunately, a recent visit shows this plaque to be missing and the original inscription in the stone refers only to 'The Great War 1914-

pillar. The memorial has been amended to include the dates 1939-1945, and has had the names of the fallen of that war added to those of 1914-1918.

The World War One memorial of Conisborough, Yorkshire, is the stone figure of a soldier on a stone column, standing in a beautiful park in the shadow of Conisborough Castle. Additional panels with the names of the dead of the Second War were added to pillars in front of

239 *Re-dedication of the East Dereham Memorial (Photograph – Robert Newell)*

128

240 *Royston Memorial*

18'. It is to be hoped that the absence of the plaque is only temporary.

The beautiful war memorial, erected after the First World War, in a recess in the wall of the public park in Royston, has as its central feature a bronze soldier of 1914-18, standing in front of a group of marble figures of his military predecessors. The group stands within an archway inscribed with the dates of the Great War, and the names of the dead of that War are on large tablets to each side.

241 *St Peter's Church, Brackley*

242 *Thornton Cleveleys Memorial*

The memorial has been amended after the Second World War by the engraving of the 1939-1945 dates, and the names of the fallen, on the plinth on which the bronze figure stands. There would not have been room on the plinth for the names of the 1914-18 dead, since there were four times the number of those who fell in the later war.

The original Word War I memorial in the grounds of St Mark's Church, Siddal, near Halifax, was unveiled in 1923. An interesting stone memorial with a good relief on the front surface, it has the addition of a metal plaque 'to the memory of those of Siddal who made the supreme sacrifice in World War II'.

The centre panel of a triptych in St Peter's Church in Brackley has a crucifix, the dates 1939 and 1945 and 15 names of those who fell in the Second World War. On the side panels are nearly 70 names from World War I. The east window of the church is dedicated to the latter.

243 *Chesham Memorial*

244 *Tillicoultry Memorial*

A street memorial in Bennett Street, Buxton, was re-dedicated in 1966 when 12 World War Two names were added to the incredibly high figure of 93, from this one street alone, killed in the 1914-18 war. The bronze plaque with wooden surround is maintained by the occupier of the corner house on which it hangs.

One of the most effective Second World War additions to a First World War memorial is at Thornton Cleveleys in Lancashire. The original memorial is a bronze statue by Albert Toft of a bare-headed soldier with rifle reversed, on a stone plinth on which are listed the names of the fallen. This stands in a circular bed of flowers and lawn in the centre of an attractive garden. To this central plot have been added three huge open books of stone, on the pages of which are inscribed the names of the 1939-45 dead. The books are placed opposite the front and sides of the statue, and the distinct impression is of a memorial which was constructed entirely at one time.

245 *Ferndown Memorial*

246 *Westhoughton Memorial*

In a Garden of Remembrance near the centre of Beverley surrounded by beautiful trees, the First World War memorial consists of a heavy base supporting four large sculptured figures and a tall obelisk, all in stone.

The dates of 1939-1945 have been added to the inscription on the base but in addition a Stone of Remembrance has been sited to the rear of the original memorial with the words 'REMEMBER THOSE WHO FELL IN DEFENCE OF THEIR KING AND COUNTRY 1939-1945' carved on the face. On the top are bronze plaques with the names of the fallen, and behind are a yew hedge and flower borders.

Two stone columns, with metal plaques bearing the names of the Second World War dead, flank the original 1921 war memorial with the stone figure of a 1914-18 soldier on a stone pedestal, in the centre of Chesham. The three parts of the complete memorial are linked by flower beds and paving stones and have a lawn and a low hedge to the rear.

The men of Tillicoultry, near Alloa, who died in the Second World War are commemorated by individual headstones placed in alphabetical order, in a Garden of Remembrance. The stones form an arc at one side of the First World War memorial, a stone mourning female figure on a tall granite plinth. Behind the headstones the inscription 'WORLD WAR 1939-1945' is carved into a stone pillar in the boundary railings. On the headstones the regiments of the fallen are recorded in addition to their names, the Argyll & Sutherland Highlanders being predominant.

The Ferndown memorials to both World Wars are outside the Royal British Legion building. On a roadside site with attractive landscaping a stone memorial carries the words of Binyon's poem *For the Fallen*, below a red poppy motif. Immediately behind is a flag pole, and on the building to the rear is a stone tablet with the names of the dead of both wars.

The introduction of a wall behind the original memorial is quite common.

On 7th November 1948, a stone wall surround, with the dates and names of the Second World War, was dedicated as an addition to

247 *Weston Super Mare Memorial*

248 *Wisbech Memorial*

Westhoughton's existing First War memorial, a granite cross on a prominent site at a road junction.

Forty years later, however, the names carved on the stone of the wall had begun to disappear. The stone proved to be too soft and the effects of erosion, traffic fumes and vandalism had left the Second World War names unreadable. The cost of a bronze plaque as replacement proved too

expensive but at the end of 1991 work was started to repair the damage, with the use of harder stone, and the memorial is now in excellent condition with a hard stone tablet carrying the names of over 100 men who gave their lives in 1939-1945.

In a lovely park setting in Weston Super Mare the Second World War memorial has been erected some 30 yards behind that for the 1914-18 War. The original memorial is a stone column supporting a bronze angel of peace, and with bronze plaques recording the names of those commemorated. The later memorial is a stone wall with a higher central section on which are five bronze panels with the names of the services dead, and with two lower side sections having a total of four panels with about 120 civilian names.

A beautiful Garden of Remembrance in the centre of Amersham has a fountain surrounded by flower beds, lawns and herbaceous borders. At the end furthest from the gates and the road, a First World War Memorial Cross stands in a paved square, to the rear of which a brick wall has been built, with a metal tablet inscribed with the names of those who gave their lives in the 1939-1945 War.

A curved dry-stone wall behind the cross to the First World War dead of Millom in Cumbria, carries metal tablets recording the names of those who fell in 1939-1945. Both memorials are in a well-maintained garden at a road junction in the town.

To the Celtic Cross which commemorates the First World War dead of Wisbech, a wall has been added with the names of those who fell in 1939-45. The wall, higher in the centre to accommodate the names, curves behind the cross and separates it from the beautiful garden at the rear.

Bognor's First World War Memorial, situated in front of the main entrance to the Town Hall, has had the additional dates, 1939 and 1945, added to it, and to each side, walls have been built on which are large tablets with the names of the

249 *Gerrards Cross Memorial*

250 *Lyme Regis Memorial*

war dead. These additions were dedicated in 1984.

A quite different form of memorial, the Gerrards Cross Community Association is based at the Memorial Centre on East Common and was founded in 1947 in memory of those who died in the Second World War.

The Association is a charitable trust, and part of its responsibility is the memorial in the grounds, now to the dead of both wars, although originally a stable block conversion by Sir Edwin Lutyens to those who gave their lives in 1914-1918. Thirty names of the Second World War and 20 of the First are now engraved on a stone tablet, below the heraldic Swan of Buckinghamshire

within a laurel wreath, and behind the four pillars of the converted building.

In Dukinfield Park, near Stalybridge, the dedication took place in July 1963, of an unusual form of memorial to the Second World War. At the ceremony, it was acknowledged by the Mayor of Dukinfield in his speech that a boating pond was not everyone's idea of a memorial. He added 'Very soon this area will ring to the sound of happy children's voices and I feel sure our fallen comrades would agree that it is an admirable choice for a memorial'.

It is unlikely that they would do so now. The boating pond has fallen into disrepair and been filled in and converted to flower beds, and the

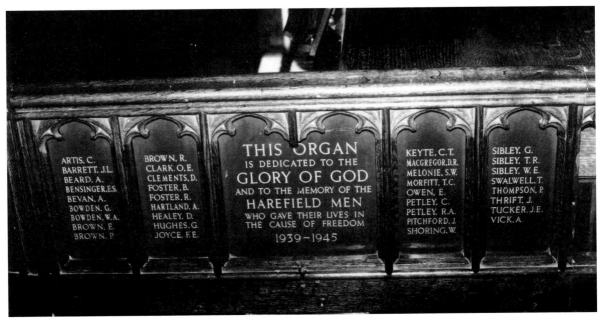

251 *St Mary's Church, Harefield*

134

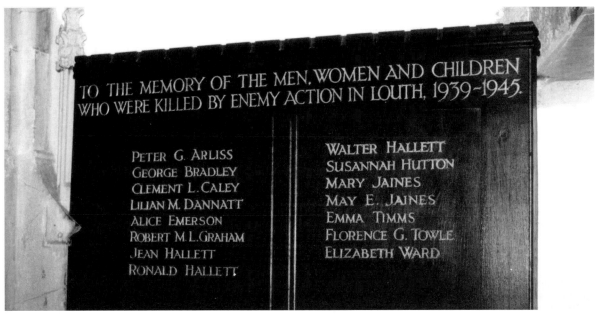

TO THE MEMORY OF THE MEN, WOMEN AND CHILDREN
WHO WERE KILLED BY ENEMY ACTION IN LOUTH, 1939–1945.

PETER G. ARLISS	WALTER HALLETT
GEORGE BRADLEY	SUSANNAH HUTTON
CLEMENT L. CALEY	MARY JAINES
LILIAN M. DANNATT	MAY E. JAINES
ALICE EMERSON	EMMA TIMMS
ROBERT M. L. GRAHAM	FLORENCE G. TOWLE
JEAN HALLETT	ELIZABETH WARD
RONALD HALLETT	

252   *St James' Church, Louth*

253   *Penryn Memorial*

original memorial column has been replaced by a small commemorative stone which is far from conspicuous.

A clock was presented by the local Royal British Legion branch in memory of those who gave their lives in 1939-45, and unveiled in November 1979 in Peacehaven's Meridian Centre, named after the Greenwich Prime Meridian which passes near the building.

The memorial dedicated in October 1992 in George Square Gardens, Lyme Regis, was very much a personal triumph for the local Royal British Legion president Cecil Quick. He led the campaign for the memorial which was built on a voluntary basis by him and other enthusiasts.

The memorial itself is an impressive one, with a large anchor, believed to be from a vessel which went down in 1848, in front of a stone-screen wall, and on a stone base. On the wall are badges representing the Army, the Navy and the Air Force, and the words 'Lest We Forget'. The garden is beautifully kept with attractive flower beds, shrubs and trees.

A modern oak desk in Dunbar Parish Church contains two Books of Remembrance bound in red leather. An inscription in the front of one reads 'THIS MEMORIAL BOOK AND LECTERN ARE DEDI- CATED TO THE MEMORY OF ALL LOTHIANS WHO LOST THEIR LIVES IN THE SOUTH AFRICAN WAR, THE FIRST WORLD WAR AND THE SECOND WORLD

254 *Torquay Memorial*

The windows are striking in both design and colour. One was donated by the Dunbar and District branch of the Royal British Legion, Scotland, in memory of the servicemen of Dunbar who lost their lives in the Two World Wars. The other is in memory of all who served in the Lothians and Border Horse Yeomanry, and also the Royal Tank Regiment and the Royal Armoured Corps. Badges of the R.T.R. and R.A.C. appear at the foot of the window (see p. 114).

Outside the gates of the church is a sandstone memorial overlooking the sea, and again to the memory of those members of the Lothians and Border Horse Yeomanry who fell in both World Wars.

Another church memorial, to the 1939-45 dead of Gowerton, South Wales, was unveiled in St John's Church by Mr John Gray, Britain's Ambassador to Lebanon, on 4th November 1986. Mr Gray's father, Myrddin Gray, died over France while on a bombing raid as an R.A.F. flight sergeant, and his name appears with 15 others on the marble tablet.

When the war memorial committee raised the money for the tablet they were shocked to find, at a very late stage, that V.A.T. would be charged. Their shock would be shared by most people, it is reasonable to assume.

In St Mary's Church, Harefield, an organ screen has the inscription, 'THIS ORGAN IS DEDICATED TO THE GLORY OF GOD AND TO THE MEMORY OF THE HAREFIELD MEN WHO GAVE THEIR LIVES IN THE CAUSE OF FREEDOM 1939-1945'. The organ has, in fact, been changed since the dedication, but the screen remains as a prominent tribute to the 35 men whose names appear on it.

In St James' Church, Louth, is a wooden board 'TO THE MEMORY OF THE MEN WOMEN AND CHILDREN WHO WERE KILLED BY ENEMY ACTION IN LOUTH 1939-1945'. Fifteen names are listed, seven from one family killed by a single bomb on the night of 7th September, 1941. Margaret Ottoway of Louth has little memory of the night

WAR AND REPLACES THE ORIGINAL ROLL OF HONOUR AND LECTERN BOTH OF WHICH WERE LOST IN THE FIRE WHICH DESTROYED THE CHURCH ON THE NIGHT OF 3RD JANUARY 1987'.

This inscription explains the very modern interior of the church today, only the old shell having survived. Two stained-glass memorial windows, therefore, are 1991 works by Shona McInnes, who won a £5,000 competition fee to undertake the commission.

255 *Hungerford Memorial*

136

256   *Victoria Gardens, Leamington*

that the bomb fell on her family home and, as a little girl, she lost her mother, her sister, her grandmother, an uncle, an aunt and two cousins.

A large rough upright stone in a pretty Penryn garden, marks the site of houses destroyed, with the loss of 18 lives, during an air raid on 13th May, 1941. The stone is in the centre of a circular grass mound and to one side of the circle is a flagpole and an explanatory plaque.

In the entrance hall of Torquay Town Hall is the 1939-1945 Roll of Honour, a beautifully illustrated book with a page to each of those commemorated, apparently in alphabetical order. When viewed, the pages visible were both for people killed in air-raids, one a retired man who died when his Torquay home was destroyed on 22nd April, 1941, and the other a W.A.A.F. who lost her life in the Guards' Chapel when it was hit on 18th June, 1944.

The Roll is in an impressive oak stand decorated by the City's coat of arms, and by golden lions supporting flaming torches. The memorial was unveiled by the Mayor and dedicated by the Lord Bishop of Exeter on 1st December 1949.

The memorial chapel in Selby Abbey has a Book of Remembrance in a beautiful wooden-mounted glass case. On the back are the dates '1939' and '1945' and above is a framed crucifixion scene.

In the Church of St Peter and St Paul, Lavenham, Suffolk, is a memorial book containing biographies of the men of the parish who died. The first page has the words, '1939-1945. This Book of Remembrance has been compiled that something more than their mere names may be known of the Lavenham men who gave their lives in the 2nd World War. Signed by M. Fountain Page   Rector of Lavenham   1947.'

257   *Pocklington Memorial*

258 *Ilkley Memorial*

This wording is almost identical to that written by an earlier rector in 1922, in a similar book for the Great War. Both books in the church are now copies of the originals placed for safe keeping in the Record Office of Bury St Edmunds.

Ashington Memorial Cricket Ground has a bronze plaque on the pavilion wall with the inscription 'TO THE IMMORTAL MEMORY OF THE MEN AND WOMEN OF ASHINGTON WHO GAVE THEIR LIVES FOR THEIR COUNTRY IN THE SECOND WORLD WAR 1939-1945, THIS GROUND IS DEDICATED. PRESENTED BY WILLIAM ARTHUR HENRY SEVENTH DUKE OF PORTLAND K.G.'. On the perimeter of the well-maintained and attractive ground, trees were planted to represent individuals killed.

The bronze name tablets which used to be on the pavilion wall have been moved to a new memorial outside the town's library. The names for both wars are now in the base of an aggressively abstract work which seems strangely at odds with the atmosphere of the cricket ground.

The Second World War memorial at Saffron Waldon is a combined effort between the town and the U.S. Air Force Units who were stationed near the town. It includes a playing field, attractive gardens and a memorial apse with the names of both American and British dead.

The 28 men of Hungerford who died serving their country in the Second World War are commemorated by an Avenue of Remembrance and a 12-acre sports ground, which were dedicated on

259 *Romsey Memorial*

260 *Memorial Hospital, Tywyn*

August Bank Holiday Monday in 1949. £6,000 was raised for the ambitious project. Wrought-iron entrance gates between brick-stone pillars lead to an avenue of 28 trees, one for each of the dead. At the head of this avenue, just as it opens out into the playing fields, is a massive three-and-a-half ton block of stone on which is a bronze dedication plaque.

Nine trees in the shape of a cross were planted in 1946 over-looking a lake in Princes' Avenue, Llandrindod Wells, to commemorate fund raising for the Red Cross Agricultural Fund during the 1939-45 war. Part of the inscription on a metal plate nearby reads, 'Now with our freedom saved from tyrant's yoke, We plant these trees, Remember why they stand'.

Inside each of the two main entrances to Victoria Gardens, Leamington, is a large boulder with a bronze plaque. On the plaques is the inscription 'THIS AVENUE OF TREES WAS PLANTED IN MEMORY OF THOSE MEN AND WOMEN OF LEAMINGTON SPA WHO FELL IN THE WORLD WAR 1939-1945'. The avenue of trees is basically in good condition although it appears that a few trees have been replaced by less mature ones.

Two adjoining Gardens of Remembrance in Felling near Newcastle, are similarly dedicated to the dead of World War II. The first, on a corner roadside site, was presented by the Felling W.V.S. The second and more elaborate garden with boundaries of railings and low walls in which are planted flowers, lies immediately behind the

261 *Tywyn Memorial*

262 *Memorial Hospital, Knutsford*

W.V.S. garden, and was subscribed by the Felling Welcome Home and Memorial Fund and opened on 2nd June 1953. Each garden contains an explanatory metal plate, on a low stone wall in the first case, and on a sloping stone base in the second.

In the centre of Bakewell, facing the roundabout on which is situated the memorial cross of World War One, is a memorial garden to the dead of 1939-45. The main feature of the well laid-out garden is a tall flag pole on a stone plinth with bronze name plates and the inscription 'IN PROUD AND EVER-LIVING MEMORY OF THE MEN OF THIS TOWN WHO FELL IN THE WORLD WAR 1939-1945'.

Pocklington has a Second World war memorial garden close to the town centre. Semi-circular in shape it has at the rear a brick wall, high in the centre, to accommodate a large stone tablet on which are listed 18 names of those 'who gave their lives in the service of their country' and also to those 'who were killed in this town by the enemy'. At the front of the well laid-out and well tended garden is a low brick wall with low wrought-iron gates painted black and decorated with red poppies.

Extensive and attractive riverside gardens are Ilkley's memorial to the dead of the Second World War. A flight of stone steps leads from the roadway down to the lower levels of the garden

263 *Memorial Hospital, Burnham on Sea*

264 *Tamworth Memorial*

and at the top of the steps wrought-iron gates are supported by stone pillars on one of which is '1939' and on the other of which is '1945'. At the foot of the steps and at the start of the garden a stone boulder supports a bronze plaque and the words 'THESE GROUNDS WERE PROVIDED BY PUBLIC SUBSCRIPTION IN MEMORY OF THE ILKLEY RESIDENTS WHO MADE THE SUPREME SACRIFICE IN THE SECOND WORLD WAR 1939-1945'.

On a hill in Frodsham, Cheshire, overlooking the Mersey, a memorial has large entrance gates painted black and gold, with the dates of both wars and with the words 'BELLUM' and 'PAX' within metal wreaths. A notice reads 'MEMORIAL FIELD WILDFLOWER MEADOW'.

An unusual feature of the War Memorial Park in Romsey is a Japanese 150mm field gun captured by the 14th Army in Burma in 1945, and presented to the town by Lord Mountbatten, formerly Supreme Allied Commander in South East Asia, on the occasion of his becoming the first freeman of the borough on 29th June, 1946.

The gun is on a raised area with steps leading up to it and with a stone surround planted with flowers. It faces a stone memorial originally unveiled in 1921 and now bearing the names of the dead of both wars. The park was first opened to the public in 1920.

Memorial gates and a garden beside the river commemorate the Malmesbury men who gave their lives in the Second World War. The names of some 20 dead are on plaques in the stone pillars of the gates. The garden which cost about £1,000 was chosen ahead of the alternative suggestion of a new hospital wing when the latter was estimated to cost £12,000.

The First World War Memorial of Tywyn, Gwynedd, is the War Memorial Cottage Hospital which is still very much used and well main-

tained, unlike many hospitals built after 1918 as tributes to the fallen. The stone monument at the hospital gates is unusual in that it has the hospital visiting days and hours inscribed on the stone as well as the dates of the war and so on. Presumably the original visiting hours are no longer exactly accurate.

The dates '1939-1945' have now also been inscribed, and in addition there is another new monument, in a memorial park in the town, for the dead of both wars. The park is well landscaped and well kept, and the monument is on a mound in the middle, surrounded by a low stone wall and with flagpoles and seats. The memorial is for several villages of the area and the names of the fallen are listed by village. One unusual error in the inscriptions, is on the 1914-18 list for Pennal, where a Capt. Lascelles has his decorations, V.C., M.C. included in his initials, rather than after his name.

The Knutsford and District War Memorial Cottage Hospital is a beautiful building and seems still to be in good condition, but sadly, like so many similar buildings, it is now closed. It seems difficult to justify such a waste of resources, even apart from the fact that a war memorial should not be so blatantly disregarded. Originally it was a World War One memorial, but a marble plaque at the front of the building dedicates it also to the memory of those who died on active service in 1939-1945.

The Burnham on Sea War Memorial Hospital was opened in 1922 and is still flourishing today, with a very active League of Friends who are continuing to raise funds for improving or updating the facilities. In a garden in front of the hospital a bronze plaque set in stone records the names of the First World War dead and below it has been added, on a separate base, a tablet for 1939-45.

Tamworth's First World War Memorial was a room in the local hospital in which bronze name plaques were displayed. With the uncertainty of the hospital's future and with a general desire for an open air memorial, representatives of the local British Legion, the Borough Council and the Parish Church were all involved in the decision which led to the dedication of a new memorial in July 1991, on a site next to St Editha's Church.

The memorial is intended to honour all Tamworth's war dead and others who have died in the service of the community, and is officially termed a 'Service Memorial'. The design is unusual and apparently caused some controversy. The stone of a broad cross carries slate tablets with the words, 'IN MEMORY OF THOSE WHO DIED THAT WE MIGHT LIVE'. Behind the cross is a crown of thorns which is also symbolic of barbed wire. Although far from traditional, the monument is striking and effective.

The War Memorial at Penmaenmawr in North Wales, is built into the front of the 'Young Men's Institute' on the main road. In front of the plaques with the names of the First World War dead, an additional tablet was added for those of 1939-45. Unfortunately, three names were omitted from the new list, and as there was no room for additional names, within the last few years a supplementary granite and bronze memorial has been added, in memory of the two R.A.F. flight sergeants and one submariner who were overlooked.

265   *Penmaenmawr Memorial*

CHAPTER VII

Large Towns and Cities

266 *Paisley Memorial*

267 *Norwich Memorial*

ONCE AGAIN, MANY MEMORIALS in large towns and cities were altered after 1945, so that the dates and names of the fallen of the Second World War were added to those of 1914-18. One group exclusively World War II, however, were the many memorials related to air-raids. Naturally, the larger conurbations attracted the majority of enemy air attacks, and Greater London had the added burden, later in the War, of the V-1 and V-2 campaigns.

The Paisley War Memorial unveiled in the town centre in 1924 to commemorate the 1,953 dead of the First World War, is one of the most impressive. This perhaps is not surprising since the architect, Sir Robert Lorimer, and the sculptress, Alice Meredith-Williams, were each chosen to play a leading part in the development of the Scottish National War Memorial at Edinburgh Castle.

The main feature of the Paisley memorial is a large bronze group of four soldiers of the First World War around the mounted figure of a medieval knight. The soldiers look tired and wet, their heads are down and their collars up, and two are wearing waterproof capes. The knight and the horse, on the other hand, seem alert and ready for battle and the pennant streaming back from the lance bears the cross of St Andrew. It seems that tradition and history and love of country is what is urging on the tired infantrymen.

The group is on a tall stone pillar with coats of arms and surrounded by a stone wall. With the inscription referring to the 1914-18 war is a similar one for the 1939-45 period, one difference in style being the reference to the 'MEN AND WOMEN OF THIS BURGH' who gave their lives, compared with the 'MEN OF PAISLEY' originally commemorated.

A bronze plaque on the plinth lists the battle honours of the Second World War, including the

Battle of Britain and Normandy for example, and a further plaque on the surrounding wall is to the memory of 92 personnel of Paisley First Aid Post No. 5 West, who died on 6th May 1941, in the course of their duty.

After the First World War an ex-serviceman was chosen by lot to unveil the Norwich War Memorial, and the same system was used in 1947, after alterations had been made to the original Lutyens memorial of a Cenotaph and a Stone of Remembrance.

Ex-corporal Percy Stubbs of the Royal Engineers was chosen to unveil the amended memorial with the new dates 1939-1945, in a ceremony attended by Lord Tedder, Marshal of the Royal Air Force, and to which Bertie Withers, who had unveiled the original memorial, was invited.

The First World War Memorial in Warrington has had additional bronze tablets added to the wall behind the central stone obelisk. These tablets carry the names of those who fell in the Second War, and have a separate list for civilians. On a corner pillar in the wall another bronze tablet has been placed, by the local branch of the Burma Star Association 'to honour those who laid down their lives in the war in the Far East 1941-45'.

The memorial erected in Worthing after the First World War took the form of a stone base supporting a fine bronze figure of a soldier with his arm aloft in victory. The base was inscribed with the names of the fallen and after the Second War the lower section of the base had the words 'ALSO IN MEMORY OF THOSE WHO FELL IN THE WAR 1939-1945' added, along with the further names of that period.

At one time Worthing Council put flower boxes against the memorial in an effort to beautify the area, but since these obscured the lower sections carrying the 1939-45 names, there were

268 *Worthing Memorial*

many complaints and the boxes were sensibly removed.

The massive stone First World War Memorial in Hamilton Square Gardens, Birkenhead, has had the dates of 1939-1945 added, but there is no room for additional bronze name tablets and so the names of the Second World War dead are recorded in a Book of Remembrance kept in the Town Hall, and available for inspection.

Near the main memorial in the gardens are several smaller memorials of the 1939-45 War.

The First World War Memorial Clock Tower in Golders Green has at one side a Stone of Remembrance with the inscription 'THEIR NAME LIVETH FOR EVERMORE', and a bronze plaque with the names of the fallen. To this has been added a large open stone book in memory of the men and women of Golders Green, Hampstead Garden Suburb and Childs Hill who gave their lives in 1939-45.

Southport's 'Project 91' had as its aim the updating of the town's war memorial to include the names of the dead of World War II and later. Launched in March 1991, with the support of councillors and ex-servicemen, the project had a target of £20,000 to cover the cost of the additions and an existing Roll of Honour was used as a reference basis for the work, although newspaper publicity was used to ensure that lists were accurate and complete.

269 *Birkenhead Memorial*

145

270 *Burnley Memorial, Townley Hall*

As a result of 'Project 91' the original 1923 memorial, a central obelisk between two colonnades, with gardens and reflective pools, was amended to accommodate additional stone tablets with the names of the later dead, the work being completed in 1992.

The original Burnley memorial was erected after the First World War in the gardens of Townley Hall, certainly some distance from the city centre, but nevertheless a beautiful and appropriate setting. The 1926 memorial has a large central block of stone out of which are carved figures of three servicemen, and to each side of which is a bronze mourning female figure. To the 1914-18 inscription has been added 'THE MONUMENT STANDS ALSO IN HONOUR OF THOSE WHO DIED FOR OUR FREEDOM 1939-1945'.

Although Burnley has one of the most impressive war memorials, in Townley Hall Garden, nevertheless many ex-servicemen felt that there was a requirement for another in the city centre. After the Town Council had opposed moving the original memorial, the Burnley and District Association of Ex-Servicemen raised the

271 *Burnley Memorial*

272 *Peterborough Memorial*

273 *Gateshead Memorial*

necessary finance, and on 30th October, 1966, a new memorial stone was unveiled and dedicated in the place of their choice.

The Peterborough War Memorial in Bridge Street is to the fallen of both wars. On one side is engraved Binyon's verse *For the Fallen*, and on the other the Kohima epitaph commencing 'When you go home . . .'.

The Memorial, an 8 ft. cube of Weldon stone, was unveiled on 2nd November, 1986, amid considerable controversy over both the siting and design. The controversy has not diminished since. Only £4,000 of the £30,000 cost had been raised at the time of the unveiling, and since then the condition of the memorial has deteriorated alarmingly quickly, to the extent that a further considerable sum, approaching £10,000, has been suggested as necessary for conservation. In the meantime, the original memorials, at the Memorial Wing of the local hospital, lie neglected.

The Gateshead War Memorial stands at a prominent road junction and is an impressive well-maintained tribute to the fallen. On the stone wall behind it, the words have been added, 'IN MEMORY OF THE PEOPLE OF GATESHEAD WHO DIED IN THE SECOND WORLD WAR'.

In a nearby garden and opposite the Art Gallery, another curved stone wall has an inscription again to 'ALL WHO MADE THE SUPREME SACRIFICE IN THE WORLD WAR 1939-1945'. This latter wall, and the paving in front of it, are unfortunately less well-maintained than is the principal memorial nearby.

The First World War Memorial in Oldham was erected on Church Terrace outside St Mary's Church. With an exceptional group of bronze soldier figures by Albert Toft, it was unveiled shortly after the war by General Sir Ian Hamilton.

In the heavy stone base of the memorial has been constructed a glass fronted chamber hold-

274 *Oldham Memorial*

ing a Book of Remembrance for the fallen of the Second World War, the pages being turned mechanically. Both the Book and the turning mechanism were donated in the early 1950's by Ferranti, a major employer in the town at that time. This treatment of the names is quite differ-ent to that of the First World War names which are recorded on bronze plaques on the walls of the churchyard behind the monument, and is a more thoughtful addition to an earlier memorial than the usual mere changes in inscription.

275 *Margate Memorial, with Burma Memorial in background*

Trinity Gardens, Margate is the site of the First World War Cross raised in 1922. Behind it on a low curved stone wall have been erected stone tablets listing the dead of the Second World War. The slightly higher central stone has the inscription 'IN MEMORY OF THOSE OF THIS TOWN WHO LOST THEIR LIVES DURING THE 1939-1945 WAR AND AS AN EXPRESSION OF GRATITUDE FOR DELIVERANCE FROM MANY DANGERS FROM THE LAND, SEA AND AIR. ALSO TO COMMEMORATE THE SAFE LANDING AT MARGATE OF OVER 46,000 MEMBERS OF THE ARMED FORCES FROM DUNKIRK IN 1940. THESE TABLETS WERE ERECTED BY THE MAYOR ALDERMEN AND BURGESSES OF THE BOR-OUGH OF MARGATE. A.D. 1951'.

The Great Yarmouth Memorial for the Second World War was dedicated by the Bishop of Norwich on 12th November 1949. An open stone enclosure, with bronze tablets with the names of the dead, the memorial is to 'THE MEN, WOMEN AND CHILDREN OF THIS BOROUGH WHO LOST THEIR LIVES AS THE RESULT OF ENEMY ACTION AT HOME AND ABROAD IN THE WORLD WAR'.

This monument faces the obelisk which was dedicated by the Bishop of Norwich, in January 1922, to the dead of the First World War. Both memorials are enclosed in the same style of rail-ings, both are decorated by bronze swords on stone crosses, and both have beautiful flower

276 *Great Yarmouth Memorial*

149

277 *Kingston Cemetery, Portsmouth, with Polish Memorial in background*

beds alongside. The whole area is perfectly maintained.

Two brothers-in-law from the area shared a strange distinction. Both Fred Naisbitt and Jack Parramint had their names on the list of the 1939-45 fallen, although both survived the war. The mistakes apparently arose because they were each reported missing, one in Crete and the other in Italy. Although Mr Parramint's name is still on the memorial, Mr Naisbitt's appears to have been removed.

Dunkirk veteran George Howell recently requested that his name be removed from the lists of those who fell in the Second World War and are named on the bronze plaques forming part of Gloucester's memorial to both wars.

Mistakes of this kind are not uncommon but it seems to have taken a very long time for this one to have been rectified. In some cases, of course, there has been no request for a mistake to be corrected and so it is perpetuated. The more normal error is for the name of the man who was killed, to be omitted from a memorial and, once again, it is sometimes many years before an attempt is made, often by relatives, to correct the omission.

The memorial to the dead of 1914-18, erected in a large Memorial Garden in Ashton-Under-Lyne, had, amongst the names recorded on bronze plaques, those of Peter and William Mannion, both Grenadier Guardsmen.

When further names were added to commemorate those who fell in the Second World War, the name of Bill Mannion, the nephew of Peter and William and himself a Grenadier Guardsman, was unfortunately omitted. Bill died in 1940 near Dunkirk and it was 43 years, despite

the efforts of his family, before his name was finally added to his home town's memorial and then only after the intervention of the *Manchester Evening News*.

Sergeant-navigator Stanley Brownhill was killed at the age of 21, in December 1942, when his Halifax bomber crashed on its return from a raid on Germany. His name, however, was not amongst those inscribed on the Altrincham War Memorial near St Margaret's Church. It was, in fact, 50 years before pressure from his family led to the name being added.

Stretford Town Hall, Manchester, has two beautifully bound and illuminated Books of Remembrance, one for each war, in an impressive

278 *Hull Memorial*

279 *Gunnersbury Park Memorial*

display cabinet. The pages are turned daily, and included are the names of civilians who were killed, along with their dates of death.

A stone memorial in Stretford Cemetery, Manchester, has the carved inscription 'THIS GARDEN IS DEDICATED TO THE MEMORY OF THE RESIDENTS OF STRETFORD, ALSO SEVENTEEN UNIDENTIFIED PERSONS WHO LOST THEIR LIVES THROUGH ENEMY ACTION IN DECEMBER 1940 AND WERE INTERRED HERE'.

Other Books of Remembrance for 1939-45 are to be found on a display table in Portsmouth Cathedral. One of the books is for civilian casualties.

280 *Croydon Memorial*

In Kingston Cemetery, Portsmouth, a stone memorial is inscribed '1939-1945. ERECTED TO THE MEMORY OF THOSE MEN WOMEN AND CHILDREN, BOTH KNOWN AND UNKNOWN, WHO DIED AS A RESULT OF ENEMY BOMBING ON THIS CITY, AND WHOSE LAST RESTING PLACE IS NEAR THIS SPOT'. There are four bronze tablets under the inscription, with lists of more than 130 dead, many of them merely recorded as 'unidentified'.

Near this memorial is an unfinished monument of brick and stone cladding which was to have been a memorial to the long-established Polish community in Portsmouth, and also to those Poles who died fighting for the Allies in 1939-45. It was never completed through lack of funds and is now in an extremely dangerous condition.

Hull's industry and docks made it a prime target for German bomber raids during the war. From the first civilian fatalities in August, 1940, when a bomb blast killed six and injured 10, some 1,200 civilians died in the city's air-raids, over 3,000 were injured, 152,000 made homeless and 86,000 houses destroyed and damaged.

In the city's Northern Cemetery an impressive memorial to the citizens killed in air-raids, stands on a semi-circular site with beautiful flower beds to either side, a bronze torch at each flank, the City coat of arms in front and a beech hedge backing the whole. Also in the cemetery is a communal grave, again attractively landscaped with extensive flower beds and a plaque reading 'In this area lie the remains of 327 persons killed in enemy air raids upon this city 1939-45'.

In Abney Park Cemetery, Stoke Newington, a stone memorial commemorates all who lost their lives in the borough through enemy action during the 1939-45 War. The surface of the memorial is covered with names, their addresses and dates of death, and although there are half a dozen or so other incidents the longest list by far is for Coronation Avenue on 13th October 1940. Nearly 100 names are listed but apparently the death toll was much higher than that. It is claimed as the second highest toll of the Blitz, resulting from a single 1,000 kg. bomb hitting an air raid shelter and bursting a water main so that many of the victims were drowned. Censorship covered up the true extent of the loss, but the King and Queen visited the site and decorated two of the rescuers.

The memorial itself is in a fairly poor condition, dirty and overgrown, but so is most of this cemetery, and subsidence appears to be an added problem.

A short distance from the Katyn Memorial in Gunnersbury Park, a circular garden with low boundary walls, in which flowers are growing, contains a war memorial in the form of a sundial. Round the edge of the sundial are carved Binyon's words commencing 'AT THE GOING DOWN OF THE SUN . . .' and a plaque at the base is inscribed 'THIS GARDEN IS DEDICATED TO THE MEMORY OF 51 AIR RAID VICTIMS WHOSE BURIAL

281 'Croydon Courageous'

IN THIS CEMETERY WAS UNDERTAKEN BY THE BOR-
OUGH COUNCIL, AND ALL OTHER KENSINGTON
CITIZENS WHO WERE KILLED BY ENEMY AIR
ATTACKS IN THE 1939-1945 WAR'.

A Portland-stone cenotaph with the borough
coat of arms in Croydon Cemetery, is to the
memory of the men, women and children who
lost their lives in Croydon during the Second
World War as a result of enemy action.

In 1956 the churchyard of Croydon Parish
Church was laid out as a Garden of Remembrance
and a memorial to all from Croydon who lost their
lives in the 1939-45 War.

282 Southwark Memorial

A 1946 painting by Norman Partridge hangs
in Thornton Heath Library as a tribute to the for-
titude of the people of Croydon during the war
years. Entitled 'CROYDON COURAGEOUS', it
depicts the aftermath of an air-raid, with people
being rescued from damaged buildings.
Amongst the many figures in the painting most
arms and services are represented, from sailors to
W.A.A.F and from firemen to land girls.

A stone memorial in Southern Cemetery
Nottingham was erected 'to the memory of 49
employees of the Nottingham Co-operative
Society Limited who lost their lives through
enemy action May 9th 1941 whilst discharging
their duties'. This inscription on one side of the
column is slightly at odds with a metal plaque on
the other, referring to 48 dead. This plaque was
transferred to the cemetery memorial from the
original site at Window Lane. The newer inscription is in fact correct, as the original plaque counts
a married couple, Mr and Mrs C. P. Judd, as one
casualty only.

In an industrial park in Warrington, on the
edge of a lake in a beautifully landscaped area, a
large rough-hewn boulder carries a bronze
plaque with the inscription, 'ON THE 14TH SEP-
TEMBER 1940, A SUMMER GALA WAS HELD ON THIS
SITE, THEN KNOWN AS ARPLEY MEADOWS. MORE
THAN 2,500 PEOPLE WERE PRESENT. AT 5.03 P.M. A
LONE GERMAN BOMBER PASSED OVERHEAD, TWO
BOMBS WERE RELEASED. SIXTEEN MEN, WOMEN
AND CHILDREN LOST THEIR LIVES. MANY MORE
WERE SERIOUSLY INJURED. THIS STONE WAS
ERECTED IN THEIR MEMORY 5.03 P.M. SUNDAY 29TH
SEPTEMBER 1991'.

The memorial was unveiled by Jack Lawson
who was blinded in the raid. His wife and one
daughter were also blinded and another 18
month-old daughter was killed. One report suggests that the gala was being held to raise money

283 *Coventry Cathedral*

to buy Spitfires. It was also assumed that the German bomber was attacking the nearby British Aluminium rolling mills, but that the bombs fell short.

A memorial plaque on a stone on Devonshire Green, Sheffield, has the wording 'This open space is dedicated to the memory of those Citizens of Sheffield who died on the nights of 12th 13th and 15th of December 1940 during aerial bombardment of the City in the Second World War 1939-45. This stand of five trees was planted by The Lord Mayor of Sheffield (Councillor W. Owen, J.P.) on the 14th December, 1980 to commemorate the 40th Anniversary of the Raids'. Unfortunately, the area around the memorial is very untidy and the plinth is even used as a surface on which to stick posters.

To one side of the entrance to Southwark Town Hall an attractive stone and brick memorial, set into the wall of the building, sits back behind a garden of lawn, crazy paving and flower beds. The stone centre panel carries the inscription 'IN MEMORY OF 925 INHABITANTS OF SOUTH- WARK WHO LOST THEIR LIVES IN THE ENEMY ATTACKS ON LONDON 1939-1945. THE FOLLOWING MEMBERS OF THE CIVIL DEFENCE SERVICES GAVE THEIR LIVES IN THE SERVICE OF THE COMMUNITY'. Below this is a tomb-shaped stone engraved with over 60 names of civil defence personnel. To the sides of the centre panel are stone tablets in memory of 1,014 inhabitants of Camberwell, and 709 of Bermondsey, who also died.

The Cathedral Church of St Michael in Coventry, one of the most beautiful perpendicu-

284 *Coventry Cathedral*

285 *Exeter Memorial*

lar Gothic churches in England, was destroyed on the night of 14th November, 1940, by the incendiary bombs of a German air raid. The shell, and the 14th-century west tower and spire survived to be incorporated, after the war, by Sir Basil Spence in his new Coventry Cathedral. Inside the ruined building a cross of damaged timbers, on an altar, has engraved in the wall behind it the words 'FATHER FORGIVE'.

Nearby, is a plaque unveiled by the Queen Mother as part of a service of Remembrance and Reconciliation on 14th November, 1990, 50 years after the raid. It has the words '. . . nation shall not lift sword against nation – neither shall they learn war any more'.

Not far from Trinity Gardens, Margate, at the entrance to what is now a car park, is a plaque reading, 'ON THIS SITE STOOD HOLY TRINITY CHURCH, CONSECRATED IN 1829, DESTROYED BY ENEMY ACTION 1ST JUNE, 1943'.

Charles Church in Plymouth was built in 1641 and was named in honour of King Charles I. It was completely gutted by enemy air action on the night of 21st March, 1941, and partially restored in 1957 as a memorial to the citizens of Plymouth who died in air raids in the 1939-45 war. Plaques inside the ruined church explain the history and commemorate the 50th anniversary of the raid.

Plymouth Guildhall, built in 1874, was destroyed in an air raid in 1941. It was rebuilt and

286 *Bethnal Green Memorial*

officially opened in September 1959 by Field Marshal Montgomery. In the new building a series of stained-glass windows depicts the city's history. One of these shows 'ENEMY AIR ATTACK 1941' and another 'THE REBUILDING OF THE CITY COMMENCED 1947'.

An octagonal monument in Efford Cemetery, Plymouth, has a series of metal plaques on one of which is engraved 'THIS MEMORIAL WAS ERECTED TO THE SACRED MEMORY OF THE 1,174 CIVILIANS WHO LOST THEIR LIVES BY ENEMY AIR ATTACKS ON THE CITY OF PLYMOUTH DURING THE SECOND WORLD WAR 1939-45 OF WHOM 397 ARE INTERRED IN THE NEARBY COMMUNAL GRAVE AND WHOSE NAMES ARE INSCRIBED ON THIS MEMORIAL'.

The Exeter Phoenix fountain, sited in the centre of Exeter in a shopping precinct, is a memorial to those killed in air-raids on the city in 1942. The construction is circular and the water jets of the fountain are backed by a raised semi-circular wall on which are scenes of the air-raid with the cathedral standing amidst the damage and destruction of the city. A list of contributors towards the cost of the memorial is given, and the sculptor is named as Roger Dean. An inscription reads, 'THE EXETER FOUNTAIN, BUILT BY THE CITIZENS OF EXETER IN 1992, IN MEMORY OF THOSE WHO LOST THEIR LIVES IN 1942'.

The ruins of St Catherine's Almshouses in Catherine Street, and the Vicar's Choral in South Street, both in the city centre of Exeter, and both damaged in the air-raids of 1942, have been left as memorials and garden areas created around them.

Above the stairs of Bethnal Green Underground Station is a memorial plaque which thousands pass every week without noticing. It commemorates the worst civilian disaster of the Second World War, when 173 people (27 men, 84 women and 62 children) were killed in the space of some 15 seconds on 3rd March 1943, and yet no bomb fell.

In response to an air-raid warning people were running into the shelter of the underground station when a woman tripped and fell, in the blackout, on the staircase. Others behind her collapsed on top of her and a domino effect resulted, with the victims being crushed or suffocated.

The German 'V' Weapon Campaign started in June 1944. Named after the German for 'reprisal weapon' the first V-1 flying bomb fell on London on the night of 12th/13th June 1944. It destroyed a railway bridge and killed six people in Grove Road, Bethnal Green. Today, a plaque placed by English Heritage on the present bridge commemorates the incident.

Over 9,000 V-1's or 'Doodlebugs' were launched against Britain, with some 5,000 reaching their target. Of these 2,419 fell on London and 1,444 fell on Kent. The more sophisticated V-2 rockets followed, the first of 1,115 which landed on Britain, falling on 8th September 1944. It has been estimated that nearly 8,000 people were killed by these 'secret weapons' between June 1944 and the end of the war.

In Orpington late on 27th March 1945, a V-rocket caused, it is believed, the last casualty of the home front in the war. Just before that another V-2 falling on Hughes Mansions, Vallance Road, Bethnal Green, killed 134 and seriously injured 49. A memorial to what is believed to be the last V-2 attack on London, and to those who died, has been erected on the site of the destroyed buildings.

287 *Memorial Homes, Bournemouth*

IN LOVING MEMORY OF
THE MEN OF CYPRUS STREET
WHO MADE THE GREAT SACRIFICE 1914-1918

J. AMOS	J. GODWIN
E. A. COMBAR	J. H. HODGES
A. BOARDMAN	C. J. HARRIS
A. H. COLE	T. HAMBLIN
W. H. DILON	C. LIBKA
T. A. DOYLE	F. LIBKA
C. DOWSETT	W. NASH
T. DOWSETT	C. T. PARKER
W. FARMER	T. W. SIMPSON
T. FENNINGS	W. J. THORNE
W. J. GARDNER	W. H. WATHEWS
A. GADD	W. WATHEWS
J. GRAY	C. POWIS

ERECTED BY THE DUKE OF WELLINGTONS
DISCHARGED AND DEMOBILISED SOLDIERS AND SAILORS
BENEVOLENT CLUB

1939 - 1945
A. LYONS. W. WAREN
J. FLETCHER. A. PARKER

THEY ARE MARCHING
WITH THEIR COMRADES
SOMEWHERE ON THE
ROAD AHEAD

288 *Cyprus Street Memorial*

An entirely different form of memorial is to be found in Bournemouth's War Memorial Homes, provided for disabled ex-servicemen and women, and built on six acres of land on the north side of Castle Lane, given generously for the purpose by the Misses Cooper-Dean. Public subscription paid for the building of the houses which were completed in 1948, a foundation stone having been laid on October 28th, 1946, by Lord Mountbatten. The houses were extensively renovated in the 1980's and certainly now appear to be well maintained. Of red brick and tile they are on a service road well back from the main traffic and with extensive areas of grass and trees.

Elsewhere in Bournemouth, in the Memorial Gardens, close to the town's war memorial to both World Wars, a tree has been planted to commemorate Victory in Europe Day, May 8th, 1945.

In the entrance doorway to the Guildhall in Cambridge there is a beautifully decorated Roll of Honour in memory of those of the Borough who gave their lives, both in the forces and as civilians.

In Sunderland Museum there is a plaque issued to the city by the Ministry of Aircraft Production in 1940. The inscription reads 'IN THE HOUR OF PERIL PEOPLE OF SUNDERLAND EARNED THE GRATITUDE OF THE BRITISH NATIONS SUSTAINING THE VALOUR OF THE ROYAL AIR FORCE AND FORTIFYING THE CAUSE OF FREEDOM BY THE GIFT OF FOUR SPITFIRE AIRCRAFT'.

In the beautifully kept Cyprus Street in Bethnal Green, on the wall of one of the houses with attractive shuttered windows, is a marble tablet, erected by the Duke of Wellington's Discharged and Demobilised Soldiers and Sailors Benevolent Club, and in memory of 26 men of Cyprus Street who died in the First World War. Under this is a shield shaped marble plaque for the 1939-45 war with four names and the words 'THEY ARE MARCHING WITH THEIR COMRADES SOMEWHERE ON THE ROAD AHEAD'. Flower containers surround the shield and a poppy wreath hangs on the wall below.

Another street memorial, in Hendon, the Fuller Street Roll of Honour, is also to the dead of both Wars and has been increased in size to accommodate two additional names for the period 1939-45. The original memorial, a stone tablet in a wooden frame on the outside wall of one of the houses, lists 11 men who died in the First World War.

CHAPTER VIII

National Memorials

THE CENOTAPH IN LONDON'S WHITEHALL was unveiled by King George V on Armistice Day, 11th November, 1920, as our national War Memorial, and now commemorates British dead of both World Wars and subsequent wars.

Three quarters of a century after its unveiling, the monument of Portland stone, designed by Sir Edwin Lutyens is still the centrepiece of the annual Remembrance Day ceremony when wreaths are laid by the Queen, Prince Philip, the Prince of Wales, the Duke of Kent and other members of the Royal Family (see p. 114).

There are other memorials of a national nature, although some are fairly limited in their aims.

The national memorials of Scotland, Wales and Northern Ireland, respectively in Edinburgh Castle, Alexandra Gardens, Cardiff and Waring Street, Belfast, all commemorate the dead of both Wars.

Inside the Scottish National War Memorial with its wonderful stone carvings and bronze reliefs, and its beautiful stained glass, each of the bays containing memorials of the Scottish Regiments and other services and units in which Scots fought and died, has the addition of a Book of Remembrance with the names of the dead of

289   *Scottish National War Memorial*

290   *Hall of Friendship, Belfast (Photograph – Allen Markley, Anderson McMeekin Photography Ltd)*

291 *U.S. Memorial, Belfast (Photograph – Allen Markley, Anderson McMeekin Photography Ltd)*

the Second World War, to lie alongside the similar book for the First War.

A bronze plaque on the wall of the Hall of Honour has the inscription, 'OPENED IN 1927 BY H.R.H. THE PRINCE OF WALES AS A MEMORIAL TO THOSE FROM SCOTLAND WHO DIED IN THE GREAT WAR, THIS IS NOW A SHRINE TO THE MEMORY OF THE FALLEN IN TWO WORLD WARS AND SINCE 1945'.

The Northern Ireland War Memorial, although to the dead of both wars, was not in fact dedicated until well after the Second World War. A four-storey building in Waring Street, Belfast,

it was opened on 28th October 1963 by the Queen Mother. Behind its colonnade of dark-blue slate there is a Hall of Friendship to celebrate the relationship between the people of Northern Ireland and the United States forces who lived and trained in Ulster before the allied invasion of Europe.

The walls of the Hall are finished in light-coloured Cliffdale marble from Missouri, shipped over the Atlantic specially for the memorial. Two friezes of hammered copper are set into the marble walls, one showing the efforts of the peoples of Ulster during the war with scenes of

292 *Memorial Hall, Belfast (Photograph – Allen Markley, Anderson McMeekin Photography Ltd)*

ship-building, heavy industry and rebuilding after the air raids, while the other shows American forces moving through Ulster from west to east on their way towards the fighting in Europe.

293 *British Empire Memorial, Westminster Abbey*

Elsewhere in Belfast, outside the City Hall, a short stone column commemorates the arrival in the city of U.S.A.A.F. units on 26th January 1942.

Beyond the Hall of Friendship in the War Memorial Building is the Memorial Hall. Two Books of Remembrance bound in red leather and containing the names of over 20,000 men and women of Northern Ireland who died in the two World Wars, rest inside a bronze casket on a block of rough-hewn Ulster granite.

On the opposite side of the hall is a large stained-glass window featuring two columns of fire on which are superimposed the badges of the various Services and above which are the dates of the two Wars, and a field of crosses. In the centre the words 'WE WILL REMEMBER THEM' are inscribed below a laurel wreath and dove of peace.

The upper floors of the building are occupied by the British Legion, ex-servicemen's organisations, and so on.

The Field of Remembrance which is created in the grounds of Westminster Abbey each year around the time of Remembrance Day, has crosses and poppies placed by thousands of regiments, organisations, and individuals.

Our photograph shows a huge poppy wreath with the words 'FIELD OF REMEMBRANCE' and lines from Binyon's poem *For the Fallen*, and an enormous cross of poppies 'placed in personal remembrance' by the Queen Mother in November 1993 (see p. 114).

In the Abbey itself, there is a memorial in St George's Chapel to 'THE DEAD OF THE BRITISH EMPIRE WHO FELL IN THE TWO WARS 1914 AND 1939'. This tablet, with coats of arms of the United Kingdom, Canada, South Africa, New Zealand, Newfoundland, Australia and India, was originally unveiled in 1926 to the million dead of the

294 *Civilian Memorial, Westminster Abbey*

Great War, but has since been altered to incorporate the Second War.

Near the West Door of the Abbey and below the Roosevelt memorial, is a wooden glass-fronted case containing seven Books of Remembrance with the names of the Civilian War Dead of 1939-45.

On 3rd June 1994 the Canada memorial was unveiled by the Queen in Green Park, close to Buckingham Palace, to commemorate the 1,000,000 Canadians who came to Britain to fight in the Two World Wars, and the 110,000 who died. The ceremony was attended by Prime Ministers John Major and Jean Chrétien and by several members of the Royal Family.

The memorial is of unusual design, and is in the form of a shallow marble pyramid with bronze maple leaves on the sloping sides. A compass rose has been built into the centre of the cobbled way leading up to the memorial.

295 *Canada Memorial, Green Park*

296 *Madingley Memorial*

The American Military Cemetery and Memorial at Madingley, near Cambridge, was dedicated on 16th July 1956, in 30 acres of land donated by Cambridge University. At the base of a 72 ft. high flagpole near the Visitors' Building is an inscription from the poem *In Flanders Fields* by John McCrae, 'TO YOU FROM FALLING HANDS WE THROW THE TORCH – BE YOURS TO HOLD IT HIGH'.

From the flagpole to the Memorial building the Wall of the Missing stretches, 472 ft. long, of Portland stone, and with the names of 5,125 who died but had no known graves. Amongst these names is that of Major Alton Glenn Miller, the leader of the American Forces band. At intervals along the wall are four stone statues of a soldier, a sailor, an airman and a coast guard.

297 *Madingley Memorial*

298 *Madingley Memorial*

A reflecting pool, bordered by rose beds, stretches the whole length of the wall, to the entrance doors of the Memorial building. The main doors are of teak, decorated with bronze models of military and naval equipment. The building is divided into a museum and a chapel.

Down one side of the museum chamber is a mural map of the Atlantic and Europe, 'The Mastery of the Atlantic – The Great Assault', showing sea routes and land and sea assault lines. The other side of the chamber has windows with replicas of the seals of the States of the Union and, above the doors, there are replicas of the seals of the War and Navy Departments.

An elaborate mosaic in the ceiling and behind the altar of the chapel, features angels, ghostly aircraft, crosses and the words, 'HE RESTORETH MY SOUL, HE MAKETH ME TO LIE DOWN IN GREEN PASTURES'. The altar rails bear the words 'FAITH' and 'HOPE' (see p. 114).

On the outside of the building there is a map, on the stone wall, of the British Isles and the sites

299 *Madingley Memorial*

lent by the people of Britain to the United States during the War. The scale is 30 miles to one foot.

The main elevation of the Memorial has five pylons each inscribed with a year from 1941 to 1945. This looks out onto the cemetery in which 3,812 American war dead are buried.

An unusual memorial unveiled on 4th May 1969 in Gladstone Park, North London, is to the memory of all prisoners of war and victims of concentration camps. In a landscaped area surrounded by metal railings are five bronze figures, four sitting, one standing, all in attitudes of terror and despair. The figures by sculptor Fred Korms are all at different terraced levels and behind them is a plain white right-angled triangular wall. Despite the fact that the gate in the railings is kept locked, nevertheless the white wall has been defaced by general graffiti, and of all things, a swastika.

The Holocaust Memorial Garden at the Dell in Hyde Park, has at its centre, a large piece of irregular-shaped stone with the inscription 'FOR THESE I WEEP. STREAMS OF TEARS FLOW FROM MY EYES, BECAUSE OF THE DESTRUCTION OF MY PEOPLE (LAMENTATIONS)'. The stone is in a grove of silver birch trees, on a site given by the government in 1983, for a memorial to the estimated 6,000,000 victims of the Holocaust, of whom 1,500,000 were children.

This monument above all others, in a war in which the deaths of non-combatants far exceeded those of the armed forces, and both sexes and all ages were treated indiscriminately, should offer some consolation to the families of those commemorated by the many memorials of the Second World War, and should provide the certainty that they died in the most just of all causes.

300 *Prisoners' Memorial, Gladstone Park*

301 *Holocaust Memorial, Hyde Park*

Acknowledgements

I wish especially to thank my wife Rena for all her encouragement and assistance whilst this book was being researched and written, and in particular for her work on proof-reading. I should also like to thank Barbara Jones for the many hours spent deciphering and typing the almost illegible original manuscript.

Catherine Moriarty, the Co-ordinator of the National Inventory of War Memorials has been particularly helpful and I wish to thank her for her time and patience.

Finally, I should like to acknowledge the following sources of information and to thank all those who provided background material. My choice of air force memorials to visit was greatly influenced by George Fox's book *8th Air Force Remembered*, and many newspapers were kind enough to publish appeals for information on my behalf.

Ashton Weekly Newspapers

Backham, F. J.
Banting, D. R.
Barber, J.
Blair, E. M.
Blaker, A. J. D.
Body, R. S.
Bolton Evening News
Bolton Public Library
Boon, M.
Boorman, T. R.
Borg, A. – *War Memorials*
Bournemouth Evening Echo
Brighton Evening Argus
Brooks, S.
Brown, D.
Burge, Lt. Col. M. H.
Burma Star Association
Burnley Central Library
Butcher, J.

Cartwright, C.
Chapman, J.
Chesterfield Family History Society
Clark, A.
Clarke, J.
Coats, E. H.
Cobb, A. and D.
Coles, T.
Cook, J.
Counsell, M.
Country Life
Cox, Dr. R.

Croydon Advertiser Group
Croydon Central Library

Daily Telegraph
D-Day Museum
Derbyshire, J.
Devon County Council
Downs, J. P.
Dunkirk Veterans Association
Dyer, B. F.

Eastern Daily Press
East Lancashire Newspapers Limited
Eaton, A. E.
Ennals, M. S.
Exeter Central Library

Fairbanks, D. E.
Far East P.O.W. Association
Flack, J. J.
Fovant Badges Society
Foweraker, L.
Fox, George H. – *8th Air Force Remembered*

Gaskin, C. J.
Gavin, M.
Gordon-Heath, Dr. S.
Grantham Journal
Gray, J. R.
Grimsby Evening Telegraph

Halstead, S. A.
Harris, D.
Harrison, J. M.
Heather, C. B.
Hindle, G. C.
Holloway, K.
Hope, L. E.
Hornshaw, T. R.
Howes Percival
Hull Daily Mail
Humphreys, R.

Ibbetson, P.
Iceton, S.
Imperial War Museum
Irving, D.
Isle of Wight County Press

James, R. T.

Kinsey, G.

Lawrence, J.
Lawson, C.

Lawson, K.
Leicester Mercury
Le Messurier, C.
Lord, S. R.

McCombie, G.
Macdonald, B.
McDowell, W.
McIntyre, C. – *Monuments of War*
Maclean, R.
Makin, E.
Makinson, W. R.
Manchester Evening News
Marsh, E. A.
Martin, G. W.
Mees, G. C.
Mein, I. R. W.
Millwood, M. J.
Milner, B.
Mincher, B.
Monk, M.
Morris, E. J.
Morriston Hospital
Murray, A.

Newbury Weekly News Group
Norfolk and Suffolk Aviation Museum
Northern Echo
Northumberland Local History Societies
    Association
North Wales Weekly News
Norwich Central Library

Ottaway, M.
Oundle School
Overlord Embroidery Trustees

Panton, H.
Parker, R.
Pease, C. R.
Peterborough Evening Telegraph
Pocklington School
Portsmouth City Council

Radford, D. E.
Ratter, C.

Reporter Group of Newspapers
Rolls Royce
Royal Air Force College, Cranwell
Royal British Legion
Royal Marines, Poole
Rubins, A.
Rutherford, P. M.

Salisbury Journal
Salt, D.
Salthouse, E.
Sandle Manor School
Savage, E. and A.
Sheppard, T.
Sherwood, C.
Sismey, R.
Smith, J.
Sneap, B. P.
Southport Visiter
South Wales Argus
South West Counties Newspapers
Stanbridge, D.
Stott, W. T.
Sussex Yeomanry Association

Taylor, D. N.
Taylor, J.
Taylor, M. C.
Tamworth Herald
Terry, C.
Thompson, D. C. & Co.
Tilney, R. D.
Times Newspapers Limited
Timmins, S.
Towlard, A.
Townend, W.
Tyler, J. W. L.

Western Morning News
Westrop, F. J.
Whitehead, A. P.
Willis, C. L.
Wills, K. M.
Wishart, M.

Yorkshire Evening Press

Index

Bold figures indicate references to photographs

Bold figures indicate references to photographs

169

Bold figures indicate references to photographs

Bold figures indicate references to photographs